For Phil

12/84

# THE COLLECTED PLAYS OF PETER SHAFFER

# THE COLLECTED PLAYS OF PETER SHAFFER

Harmony Books / New York

Published by Harmony Books, a division of Crown Publishers, Inc., One Park Avenue, New York, New York 10016.

HARMONY BOOKS and colophon are trademarks of Crown Publishers, Inc.

Manufactured in the United States of America

Library of Congress Cataloging in Publication Data

Shaffer, Peter, 1926–
The collected plays of Peter Shaffer.

Contents: Five finger exercise—The private ear—The public eye—[etc.]
I Title.
PR6037.H23A6 1982 822'.914 82-11793
ISBN: 0-517-546809

10 9 8 7 6 5 4 3 2 1

First Edition

# CONTENTS

## ABOUT THE AUTHOR

PETER SHAFFER was born in Liverpool and educated at St. Paul's School and Trinity College, Cambridge. He had several jobs before earning fame as a playwright; among them: working in the acquisition department of the New York Public Library and for a London music-publishing firm.

In 1958 came his first big success in the theater—*Five Finger Exercise.* The play, which ran for nearly two years at the Comedy Theatre in London, was presented in New York and was also filmed. Other Shaffer successes are *The Private Ear/The Public Eye, White Liars, Black Comedy,* and *The Royal Hunt of the Sun,* which was proclaimed by the critics as a masterpiece. In 1970 *Shrivings*, directed by Peter Hall and starring Sir John Gielgud and Patrick Magee, had a successful run at the Lyric Theatre in London. Peter Shaffer has had four of his plays presented at the National Theatre. The third, *Equus,* proved a triumph both in London and New York, where it was awarded the Antoinette Perry Award for the Best Play, 1975; and the fourth, *Amadeus,* won the *Evening Standard* Drama Award for best play of 1979, the London Theatre Critics Award, and the Antoinette Perry Award for Best Play, 1981.

Peter Shaffer lives in New York, a city for which he feels a strong and undiminishable passion.

# PREFACE

I believe that many playwrights compose their first plays in order to be pitied in public. Chekov certainly did. Almost all of his early plays end with the suicide of a sensitive and misunderstood man. It is only in *Uncle Vanya,* when the sensitive man turns his pistol on a tedious old professor instead—and misses!—that a mature dramatist is born. Not to compare myself in any way with this giant of art, it does seem to me, contemplating the plays printed here, that my work for the theater charts a reasonably direct course away from self-pity. This is not, of course, automatic evidence of their maturity, but it is surely a step in the right direction.

My first play to reach the stage—there had been some for television and radio—was *Five Finger Exercise.* Unquestionably it expressed a great deal of my own family tensions and also a desperate need to stop feeling invisible. The need was rapidly fulfilled. A successful play is a highly visible object: The author takes his concerns and actually lights them up for all to see. When *Five Finger Exercise* won the *Evening Standard* Drama Award in London and the Drama Critics Award in New York, it turned me into that suspect phenomenon an Overnight Success, and also raised all manner of expectations concerning me which I felt seriously unqualified to fulfill. Such an experience removes some of the thornier of one's self-doubts—and replaces them firmly with new ones.

The play was produced at the Comedy Theatre, London, in 1958, and at the Music Box Theatre, New York, the following year. To my extreme delight, it was directed by John Gielgud, who had been my idol since the age of twelve, when I saw him play Richard II. (Nobody in the world was then—or is now—able to speak Shakespeare with half the intelligence, truth, and sheer beauty that he can command. In my view, he is the greatest English-speaking classical actor of the twentieth century.) Our producer was the famous firm of H. M. Tennent, presided over by two distinguished and utterly charming gentlemen, Hugh Beaumont and John Perry. For many years, their organization presented the kind of immaculately produced theater which was once known in England as West-End, and which—despite some palpable limitation in intellectual curiosity—provided the public with infinitely more theatrical pleasure than do most of the shrill, self-advertising entrepreneurs of today. Under the aegis of Tennent, audiences saw, along with the most skillful boulevard work, the great comedies of Sheridan and

Shaw, Giraudoux and Anouilh, and they were taught to assume, as a matter of excellent course, a presentation of literate theater in every way superior to the styleless infantilism which all too frequently passes as today's sincerity.

My first play, therefore, appeared under generous guidance, and for that I remain extremely grateful. I was quite old, as these things go, to be making my debut, but I had spent my earlier life being cowed, and this accounted for my tardy appearance as a dramatist. I mean by this that as an adolescent I had bought the lie, assiduously circulated by the world I was born into, that business is reality and art pretence. In fact, as one discovers through the years, exactly the opposite is true. A frustrated fellow in my twenties, I went on believing that what I enjoyed doing—writing—was frivolous, and what bored me completely—commerce—was serious. The theater was much too seductive a place to be a proper habitation, and the only true space for real work had to be an office. I do not blame my parents for this pathetic puritanism; far too much craven behavior is blamed by children on their parents. The truth is that I have always experienced difficulties in following the immediate promptings of my spirit. I regret this deeply, although I have some cause to be thankful for it as well. Repression, properly used, can be a beneficial force.

I hope that this fact is evident in *Five Finger Exercise.* I have not seen the play in many years—it is still quite often done by repertory companies in England—and perhaps to some sophisticated tastes today it might seem a little tame. In its defense I can say that the repression I speak of—a reticence in the play which somewhat reflected my own at the time—injects a kind of fear into its rage which I do not find inappropriate even now. In addition, one must never forget that the sophistication which critics must possess to do their work—if their work has to be done at all, which I very much doubt—does not remotely reflect a universal feeling. Most people are behind what critics call "the times." In many a small town and in many a scarcely sufferable family, the same pains are endured today by youngsters, and the same rebellions attempted, as in this play. Tensions like these do not alter very much over the years.

On balance, I feel I did crafted work in my first piece. It said what I wanted it to say, and it possessed a shape which made it play easily and finally accumulated its power. This quality of *shape* is very important to me. I have always entertained the profoundest respect for art, meaning "arte-fact," and for the suffix "wright" in the word *playwright.* I hope that all the plays in this book are wrought properly and that they proclaim this fact sufficiently to give audiences a deep satisfaction in their form and their finish. I also hope that these qualities are not too assertively evident—because if a play irritates by seeming to be too well made, this surely means that it has not been well made enough: that the smoothness of the joinery is sealing the work off from the viewer.

My next piece consisted of a double bill, *The Private Ear/The Public Eye.*

Each of the plays had three characters and was concerned with aspects of love. In the first of them, I was undeniably persisting in my hopes of being pitied in public; the misunderstood and maladroit Bob was close to my heart. Perhaps in the second also, I was attempting to elicit sympathy for other incarnations of self: one man who thought of himself as prematurely middle-aged and another who always made three where two were company. This attempt was probably inevitable. Playwrights, after all, have to match actors in being encyclopedias of human experience: They have to dig inside themselves and discover what in them also belongs to their neighbors. I suspect that my initial sense of being invisible in the world and of having been too careful with my youth paralleled similar feelings in many of my audiences. Their patent pleasure in this double bill certainly seemed to confirm this.

*The Private Ear/The Public Eye* was presented at the Globe Theatre, London, in May 1962 and at the recently and wantonly destroyed Morosco Theater, New York, in the following year. The plays were again produced by H. M. Tennent and directed with great verve and imagination by Peter Wood. The London performance was a tremendous success, and the plays ran for a long time. The mime at the end of the first one was received with breathless amusement; the detective in the second was enjoyed as an original creation. Both featured the young Maggie Smith and really established her as the finest comedienne of her generation. Cristoforou was played by the coruscating Kenneth Williams, and I would stand at the back of the theater night after night just to experience the hysterical accuracy with which he would explode every line of his closing scene—an object lesson in comic timing. Alas, the New York performance, which enshrined an exquisite piece of acting by Brian Bedford as Bob—the same marvelous actor who played Clive so memorably in *Five Finger Exercise*—was curtailed almost at the start by the assassination of President Kennedy some seven weeks after the play opened. The prevailing mood of the city was scarcely conducive to comedy, and though the *New York Times* hailed *The Public Eye* as soaring like an unfettered bird, the grim mood of the time soon shot it down to earth, along with its romantic companion.

At this point, the National Theatre of Great Britain was established under the directorship of Laurence Olivier, and thereafter virtually all my playwrighting was done in the service of this illustrious institution.

I think it was the largeness of resource at the command of a subsidized company—a largeness which no commercial management could begin to rival—which led me to abandon the West End of London and join the monumental enterprise being developed at the Old Vic Theatre across the River Thames. This excellent nineteenth-century building possessed the most beautiful auditorium in London, and in the ten years before Sir Denis Lasdun built his pile of twentieth-century concrete to keep the National Theatre in the brutalist style to which it should never have become accustomed, it showed the most exciting and various repertory in Europe.

Largeness of resource was, in fact, precisely what I was looking for. Because John Gielgud as Richard II was my archetypal image, I became a playwright finally to be a part of the grandiloquent and showy world of imaginative reality. It took me some time to acknowledge this to myself. The times, after all, scarcely favored such an ambition. The mid-1950s did not constitute a time when one could admit, with much chance of being sympathetically heard, a purpose to write about gods and grand aspirations, orators and ecstatics. It was a surging time for England, but the cry tended to be for social realism.

Certainly my association with Peter Brook, with whom I collaborated on the film script for *Lord of the Flies,* helped to strengthen my defenses. Brook was the most innovative and brilliantly articulate man I had ever met. He had already produced his grandly ritualistic *Titus Andronicus,* and he was embarked on his experiments with the Theatre of Cruelty. His relentless chameleonism impressed me almost as much as his profound aestheticism. But it was actually the more austere, though no less intense, figure of John Dexter who turned my yearnings into reality. Even before I had produced *Five Finger Exercise* on the stage, I had composed the draft of a play about the conquest of Peru, suggested by a perfect parabola of action contained in Prescott's third expedition in Ecuador and concluding with the death of the Inca Atahuallpa. My head had long been invaded by visions of this gold-encrusted, blood-splashed story, but it took a hardheaded and hard-driven man from Derbyshire to make them real.

When I first showed *The Royal Hunt of the Sun* to H. M. Tennent, the firm clearly regarded it as unproduceable and me as an eccentric for having written it. People did not climb the Andes Mountains in Tennent productions. They did, however, in Mr. Dexter's. My play, in fact, was precisely what this extraordinary man had been looking for. He found it in a pile of neglected scripts at the National Theatre office and immediately offered to direct it—and we advanced together through the spring of 1964 into the by-then nearly abandoned kingdom of epic theater. The result made a special kind of theatrical history.

*The Royal Hunt of the Sun* was produced by the National Theatre at the Chichester Festival of 1964 and transferred at the end of the year to the Old Vic. New York saw the show the following year, housed in the Anta Theater and presented by no less than seven producers who shared the burden of its extensive demands. It boasted a superb musical score by Marc Wilkinson—perhaps the best score for a play to be written since Grieg embellished *Peer Gynt*—played live on an exotic variety of gourds, pipes, and rattles by an army of masked young men wrapped in ponchos and seated around the perimeter of the stage.

The setting by Michael Annals was unforgettably distinguished. It consisted of a metal disc hung high above the bare boards, incised with swords to form a Christian cross. At the moment the action of the play moved to Peru, this disc slowly opened outward to cries of "Inca!" and turned into a gigantic petaled sun containing in turn Atahuallpa's court, his prison, and his treasure house, and which was finally ripped apart by the looting Spaniards to hang spoiled and blackened as a dreadful symbol of his ruined empire. People who saw this extraordinary production still talk feelingly of their memories—of the stylized massacre at the end of Act One, when a vast cloth of scarlet vomited from the throat of the sun to lie over the stage like a sinister lake of blood; of the ritual feeding of the Inca to the sound of tiny bells; of the roping of the Inca; of his execution and awaited resurrection, with a stage full of golden funerary masks in the darkness of predawn turning anguished triangular eyes toward an audience which seemed to share their desperate expectation that he would rise again. Many people asked the same question about this final scene: "How does one get the masks to change expression?" Of course, they did nothing of the kind. The audience itself was simply investing those masks with its one hope and despair. It was, in fact, exercising the least used of its many muscles, the imaginative.

I do not think that I ever enjoyed doing anything so much as *The Royal Hunt of the Sun*—and the wonderful thing was that hordes of people shared my intoxication. I still recall the extra chairs being carried into the large Chichester Theatre and placed right across the dividing aisle of the auditorium to appease the crowds waiting outside. In the sunburst of the play's success, which certainly owed as much to the authority and passion of Dexter as to my own dream of what theater should be like, I felt my last inhibitions dissolve. I knew then that it was my task in life to make elaborate pieces of theater—to create things seen to be done, like justice, yet also to invoke the substance of things unseen, like faith. The theater is the only ultimately indispensable public art; it is badly diluted by the literalism of cinema. It is both a shared and a private act, like sex; and like sex (and unlike the cinema), it can never be precisely reproduced. It is done before your very eyes, for your very eyes, by your very eyes. That is why stage actors possess a sacerdotal quality which film actors never have: They are partially created by audiences whom they simultaneously partially create. Not for them is the imperviousness of cinematic performers, who give out the same emotions at six, eight, and ten o'clock entirely unqualifiable by our coughs or giggles or our yawns.

The next year and in the same festival house, I again worked with John Dexter. I had long wanted to try my hand at a farce and indeed had long cherished an idea as the basis for one. Farce to me has always seemed to be closely allied to melodrama. Feydeau, the greatest master of the genre, is after all an expert melodramatist. "Open that door," his situations declare with absolute authority, "and your marriage is at an end! Look behind that screen and you are ruined!" Years before, at the Palace Theatre in London I had watched the Peking Opera perform the most hair-raising extract from a Chinese play in which a warrior and a bandit fight savagely in the dark with very sharp swords. The dark was represented by an intense white light. We could see the duelists as they feinted and slashed at each other, but, in convention, they could see nothing at all. The result was five minutes of the purest imaginable theater. An English audience was caught precisely between laughter and terror and became literally hysterical. Over the ensuing years I had often wondered whether this wonderful Chinese notion of reversing light and dark could be used in an English comedy.

One day in the early spring of 1965, with *The Royal Hunt* happily established in the repertory of the National Theatre, I was asked by its masterly dramaturge Kenneth Tynan if I had a one-act play for the company to accompany Strindberg's *Miss Julie,* which Maggie Smith and Albert Finney were proposing to act during the coming season at Chichester. Without much conviction, but with the sort of energy which Tynan always elicited from me, I described my idea of a party given in a London flat, played in Chinese darkness—full light—because of a total power failure in the building. We would watch the guests behave in a situation of increasing chaos, but they would of course remain throughou' quite unable to see one another. Ever one to appreciate a theatrical idea, Tynan dragged me off instantly to see Laurence Olivier, the director of the National. In vain did I protest that there really was no play, merely a convention, and that anyway I had to travel immediately to New York to write a film script. Olivier simply looked through me with his own Chinese and unseeing eyes, said, "It's all going to be thrilling!" and left the room.

In the event, it *was* all thrilling, almost too much so. The stories of rehearsing *Black Comedy* are legion and hilarious. One day I shall set them down fully. Suffice it here to quote Tynan on the whole experience: "This was farce rehearsed in farce conditions." Due to difficulties of scheduling at Chichester, we were offered very little rehearsal time and had to open without even one public preview before the assembled critics of England, on the very same stage where the year before we had been able to present the Inca piece after ten weeks of preparation. Despite this handicap, Dexter directed the play with blazing precision, and it was acted with unmatchable brio by Smith and Finney, by Derek Jacobi as an incomparable Brindsley, and by Graham Crowden as a savagely lunatic Colonel Melkett.

In composing *Black Comedy,* I encountered one serious problem. The reversal of light and dark was not in itself a sufficiently sustaining idea to keep the play going for the required length. In actuality, someone would, of course, produce a candle and end the situation. What was needed was a reason for one of the people to *keep* the others in the dark. From this necessity arose the actual plot: the idea that the host had borrowed all the furniture in the room from an antique-collecting neighbor without telling him and that on the unexpected appearance of this dangerous neighbor the poor host had to return every scrap of it—chairs, tables, lamps, even a sofa—in the dark and unaided, before he could restore the light which would otherwise expose him as a thief. The gods really blessed me with this solution. The resultant sequence of furniture moving created some seven minutes of continuous laughter. Indeed the first night turned into a veritable detonation of human glee. A stern-looking middle-aged man sitting directly in front of me suddenly fell out of his seat into the aisle during this section of the play and began calling out to the actors in a voice weak from laughing, "Oh stop it! Please, stop it!" I cannot remember a more pleasing thing ever happening to me inside a theater.

Like all the plays in this volume, with the exception of *Shrivings, Black Comedy* was produced in New York a year after its English appearance. The theater was the Barrymore, and the cast included Geraldine Page, Lynn Redgrave, and Michael Crawford. One unenvisaged fact about this production was that the title—a perfect one for England—proved far less satisfactory in America. Some people thought that I had written a propaganda play about blacks. I suppose I should have called it *Light Comedy,* an equally good title, and one far more appropriate for New York.

To precede the farce, I wrote a companion piece, *White Lies.* Geraldine Page was characteristically sensitive in this play about a fortune-teller sitting alone on a rotting English pier in a rotten English summer. But I am afraid that I did not manage to get it quite right. The dramatic pulse was too low, and the work came out a little mechanically. A rewritten version entitled *The White Liars* was subsequently done in England, very cleverly directed by Peter Wood, with Ian McKellen as the pop singer. This was better, though it was marred by an offstage tape representing the voice of Sophie's Greek lover. Only in a third version *(White Liars),* directed at London's Shaw Theatre by Paul Giovanni, did I feel the play finally work for me. It is this satisfactory version which is printed here. One day I should like to see a film of this tale. I suspect that its sea-misted atmosphere of illusion would suit the screen very well.

Rewriting work has become a frequent habit with me over the years. I note this fact with slight gloom as a fact of obsessive life. I do not claim that there is an automatic relationship between the excellence of a work and the amount of time spent composing it. *The Private Ear* was largely sketched out complete on an hour's train journey from Lewes to London, and *Black Comedy* took really less than a month; yet both of these are actually more natural plays than the later threnody set on Grinmouth pier or the dialectical battle fought at the commune of Shrivings—both of which occupied me for far longer times. *Shrivings,* in fact, was rewritten in its entirety after its production in London; it has yet to be seen in America at all. I invested more sheer effort into this play than any other. It is really covered with the fingermarks of struggle. The earlier version appeared at the Lyric Theatre, Shaftesbury Avenue in 1970, under the title *The Battle of Shrivings.* It was directed by Peter Hall—my first collaboration with this superb director—produced by H. M. Tennent—my last collaboration with the management which launched me—and acted by my idol John Gielgud. Neither the critics nor the public took to the play at all, and it was withdrawn after a bare two months.

I was deeply depressed by the failure of this piece and by the derisory quality of the notices which greeted it. The work had meant a great deal to me, so much so that I have included in this volume my original preface to the first printed edition, which describes in some detail the mental state I was in when I wrote the play. However, after the pain of dismissal finally abated, I came to acknowledge a certain justness in the verdict—though none at all in the palpable pleasure with which it had been delivered. It seemed to me, on reflection, that there was a danger in my work of theme dictating event, and that a strong impulse to compose rhetorical dialectic was beginning to freeze my characters into theoretical attitudes.

All the more powerfully, therefore, did I feel the shock of excitement when I first heard from a friend the bare and certainly inaccurate details of a dreadful story and an appalling crime. I recall to this minute that quickening inside, which is the harbinger of authentic creative activity. The world of *Shrivings* was deliberately cold, though its second act is still deeply exciting to me, and I think it works admirably both on the levels of action and of argument. The world of *Equus* was hot.

The tale told to me by my friend James Mossman of the BBC (now, alas, dead) was not remotely the one I told the audience. In the version which he briefly referred to as we drove through a bleak English landscape composed of stables, the boy was the son of very repressive and religious eccentrics; he had been seduced by a girl on the floor of the stable; he had blinded the animals in a panic to erase the memory of his sin and to prevent them from bearing witness to it before his parents. This climax, allegedly told to Mossman by a magistrate, I found absolutely impossible to write. There was no way in which a boy's first satisfactory sexual encounter could lead on stage to such horrific violence—unless it had not been satisfactory at all. Unless, that is, the presence of the horses had directly prevented that satisfaction. And why would that be—unless the horses themselves were the focus of some deep attachment which consummation with the girl would betray? This disturbing thought vitalized the story for me and took hold of my mind. I set about writing a play of obsession, possibly unshareable in its nature by very many people and probably shocking to them as well. The immense surprise which awaited me was that such a private piece could achieve so public a success, evoking an enormous and passionate response from audiences all over the world. I think I had not sufficiently realized when I began *Equus* how deeply the leveling and limiting of the human psyche by the cult of a narrowly defined Normality is a common preoccupation of our time.

Once again, John Dexter directed, and he was of indispensable help. In my first version, Doctor Dysart was a somewhat shadowy figure, too much the simple questioner. Dexter persuaded me to etch the character with deeper lines of professional self-doubt. This gave the play an even more disturbing dimension. He also pointed out that at the very heart of my treatment of this terrible story lay a rejection of environment as a too exclusive explanation for psychic disturbance, and that this point was badly obscured if the boy's parents appeared as blatantly weird. Dysart's perception is that Equus finally arises unprovoked by family tensions, even though they are partially instrumental in forming him. I immediately redrew Mr. and Mrs. Strang to more unassertive proportions, and their very averageness then threw the passion of their son into the highest relief.

The preparation of *Equus* was a deeply involving and exciting time for me. During the entire period of its creation I sat in the rehearsal room at the top of the Old Vic Theatre, hearing the sound of traffic rising from a warm Waterloo Road and watching the stylization of the story gradually acquire confidence. First came the masks: striated horse-heads in light silver wire, through which the actors' own snorting and glaring faces could be seen. These created a double image in one shape, effortlessly fulfilling the central idea of the play. Next, after a period when the *essence* of horse was still eluding us, came hooves—metal *cothurni,* relentlessly scraping and stamping on the wooden floor. More than anything else, this dangerous sound scared up for audiences the presence of Alan's sweaty and minatory god.

Throughout this time of rehearsal, I felt a good and sustaining tension but, curiously, no anxiety. The power of the play seemed to be constantly inside me, telling me where to go with it. I think the director would agree that it largely told him also. The excellence of Dexter's achievement lay in controlling that power—avoiding from beginning to end the slightest sense of absurdity, which can easily arise when actors perform as animals—and allowing giant specters to appear on stage. *Equus* was his barest production and yet his most unnerving. It contained, toward its close, the most explicit and prolonged scene of nudity the British theater had so far witnessed; yet because it was entirely suitable and appropriate, this scene caused no affront at all. Its intention was clinical and antierotic—the erotic climax of the play occurs of course at the end of the first act—and the juxtaposition of bare flesh with the sharp metal hooves of careening horses greatly increased the horror of the catastrophe. Also, it was indisputable that the final image of an unconscious boy thrown on a wooden bench naked under a blanket, immeasurably lost power if he was clothed. The image of a human sacrifice, which was intended although only lightly stressed, vanished entirely with the assumption of a sweater and jeans.

Critically, *Equus* was very well received in London, and even more so in New York, where it was presented by the kind and distinguished producer Kermit Bloomgarden. In fact, I was totally unprepared for the play's almost hysterical reception on Broadway. Alan was acted by Peter Firth with exactly the kind of visceral bravado which excites American audiences, and Dysart by Anthony Hopkins, who paralleled him in intensity. (England had seen Alec McCowen give a devastating demonstration of a doctor slowly losing control.) Of course, I had reckoned completely without the American addiction to psychiatry. In London, you would be surprised to find more than, say, four people in any row of theater seats who are in full-time psychoanalysis. In New York, you would be hard pressed to find four who are not. Unquestionably the implied criticism of analysis at the heart of *Equus*—the portrait of a doctor crucified on doubts about the validity of his profession—directly echoed suspicions already present in the minds of audiences. Night after night I heard the unmistakable sound of their long-suppressed resentment of analysts, and in the furious denunciation of the play by some doctors I also heard quite clearly the fear of priests whose congregation is rapidly abandoning the temple. When the English were outraged by the play, it was because it showed cruelty to horses; when Americans were outraged, it was because it showed cruelty to psychiatrists. But the outrage of the latter was palpably tinged with glee.

Either way, rage was heavily overbalanced by welcome. Londoners admired the play and gave it a long run; New Yorkers adored the play and it played to them for more than a thousand performances. For the only time in my life I was accorded a standing ovation—on the first night at the Plymouth Theatre—an event no playwright is likely to forget. Approval of this kind, poured from an American bottle down a European throat, is an exilir of youth. I experienced the undeniable euphoria of feeling psychically younger at fifty than I had at thirty. Strangely, this optimism has persisted with me for years. It sustained me all through the long period of time I spent working on *Amadeus,* and it buoys me up now as I write this preface.

*Amadeus* is currently playing in almost every capital city in Europe, as well as at the Broadhurst Theatre in New York. This fact is exceedingly hard for me to believe, because in 1977 when I started a play concerning Mozart and Salieri in a tiny workroom on Riverside Drive, it seemed almost impossible to write. I spent virtually a whole year attempting a different opening scene every week. It was an exceedingly hard task to find the center of the work—to reduce a mass of historical material to anything remotely coherent and yet dramatic—and at times I really believed I would never achieve it. Even when finally I began to rehearse the play in London with Peter Hall—indisputably the greatest Mozart director in the world—the work was still too elaborate, and it had to be slimmed down immediately after the first reading, with the active cooperation of Paul Scofield, who was the first Salieri and a marvel to work with. Despite this highly successful effort, after a year's triumphant run in London to sold-out houses in the huge Olivier Theatre, I sat down and rewrote a great deal of the piece for its American presentation. My reasons for this were various and compelling.

One of the faults which I believe existed in the London version was simply that Salieri had too little to do with Mozart's ruin. In the second act he was too often reduced to prowling hungrily around the outside of the composer's apartment, watching his decline without sufficiently contributing to it. Dramatically speaking, Salieri seemed to me to be too much the observer of the calamities he should have been causing. Now, in this new American version, he stands where he properly belongs—at the wicked center of the action.

This new, more active Salieri offers himself as a substitute father upon Leopold Mozart's death. He establishes a much closer human contact with Wolfgang. And he finally induces the trusting composer to betray the rituals of the Freemasons in *The Magic Flute.* I, of course, took certain obvious liberties with this part of the story. I have no reason whatever to believe that the Masons actually repudiated Mozart, or that Baron van Swieten announced that he should never speak to him again. Nevertheless, Masonic displeasure over *The Magic Flute* constitutes one of the most persistent rumors attached to the Mozartian legend; and the worthy Baron actually did pay for a third-class funeral for the genius he patronized when he could easily have afforded much better, which does suggest some deep offense which Mozart had given him. Indeed, one totally absurd story, which never quite dies out, actually implicates the Masons in Mozart's early death.

The great gain in dramatic terms was that I could now show the (factually true) visit of Salieri and his mistress to a performance of *The Magic Flute.* I must confess to a fondness for this new scene. It is rowdy and vigorous; it contains devices of mime which are pleasingly theatrical; it dramatizes the moment—previously only hinted at—when Salieri perceives Mozart to be himself the Flute of God; and it enables me to transform the huge accusing silhouette of Leopold-as-Commendatore seen on the backdrop into the forgiving silhouette of Leopold-as-Sarastro, his hands extended to the world in a vast embrace of love. This transformation immensely clarifies the mental journey which Mozart made from *Don Giovanni* to *The Magic Flute.*

The main change in *Amadeus,* however, was concerned with the treatment of the Masked Figure who appeared to Mozart to commission a Requiem Mass and whom Mozart in the frenzy of his sick imagination came to regard as the Messenger of Death. In London this figure was actually Salieri's grim manservant Greybig, a religious fanatic dispatched by his murderous master to drive Mozart toward madness. My dissatisfaction with this theatrical idea lay mainly in my awareness that Salieri could not possibly guess that Mozart would react to the appearance of the Figure in the demented way we know he did. This was to read history backward. And anyway, such tactics did not consort at all with the character of my oblique and indirect villain. My unease ended with the total removal of Greybig from the play, since he had no real function other than to be this dreadful Messenger.

Much of the rewriting occurred in Washington, after we had actually opened the play, prior to bringing it to New York. There was a very tense period for me, when I experimented with a series of different confrontation scenes between Salieri and Mozart, at one point dispensing with a masked figure altogether. Ian McKellen and Tim Curry—the actors chiefly concerned—were heroic in assisting. Their patience and dedication finally enabled me to discover what I wanted to happen in this climactic passage. As a result, the play now boasts a much better scene on a human level than the one we played in London. I finally replaced the mask on Salieri's face, but by this time he was not a crudely melodramatic figure—a spooky, improbable Messenger of Death—but a more poetic and dangerous apparition, a Messenger from God stepping out of Mozart's confessed dreams. This scene was also composed with the active and generous encouragement of Peter Hall, who displayed throughout this time of trial a most supportive calm, and who staged the final result with superb assurance.

*Amadeus* opened in New York on December 17, 1980, produced by the Shubert Organization, with the administrative assistance of Elizabeth McCann and Nelle Nugent. The public flocked to see it, as they had to see *Equus,* and like its predecessor, it was festooned with the Tony and other awards. Yet by far the best accolade it received was that quick and immediate love which is the unique gift of New Yorkers to bestow. If I mention this gift once more, it is because as long as I live I shall remain untellably grateful for the unstinting enthusiasm with which Americans have received my work. It is true to say that over the years they have actually extended to me as excited a reception as to any native-born playwright. It remains my central desire to continue pleasing them to the same rapturous extent for the rest of my working life.

These pages seem to me to resemble those Japanese toy shells which, dropped into a tumbler of water, release a string of colored flowers. My water is the atmosphere of a theater. The more the reader can supply that for himself, the more he will see the plays released from their shells of paper and expand into their full life and colors.

The theater is where they belong, where I belong, where we all belong. These pages represent my offerings so far to it—and therefore to you. Conjure them up.

PETER SHAFFER

*July 1982*

# FIVE FINGER EXERCISE

*For*
*Harry and Jean*

*Five Finger Exercise* was first produced at the Comedy Theatre, London, on July 16, 1958, with the following cast:

| | |
|---|---|
| STANLEY HARRINGTON | Roland Culver |
| LOUISE | Adrianne Allen |
| CLIVE | Brian Bedford |
| PAMELA | Juliet Mills |
| WALTER LANGER | Michael Bryant |

Directed by John Gielgud

The New York production opened at the Music Box Theater on December 2, 1959. The cast was the same with the exception of Jessica Tandy, who played Louise.

*The action of this play takes place in the Harringtons' weekend cottage in Suffolk. The time is the present.*

*A multiple set enables us to see a fair amount of this little house: the living room, the hall, the landing, and the schoolroom where* PAMELA *has her lessons.*

*The living room occupies all of the stage on the ground floor. It is well furnished, and almost aggressively expresses* MRS. HARRINGTON'*s personality. We are shown by it that she is a person of taste; but also that she does not often let well alone. There is more here of the town, and of the expensive town, than is really acceptable in the country—the furnishings are sufficiently modish and chic to make her husband feel, and look, perpetually out of place. To the left (all directions are taken from the viewpoint of the audience), there is a sofa or banquette, and a coffee table. A comfortable armchair bridges the gap between the social center of the room, and its eating center. This last is to the right, and slightly more upstage: it is occupied, of course, by a dining table, and chairs to match. The right wall contains the French window, down right, through which comes all the light the room receives—autumn light from an old garden. A door at the back leads into the kitchen. Up center, against the back wall, stands a sideboard bearing bottles, glasses, a vase of flowers, etc. In the left wall which comes down at right angles to the audience before changing direction to form a scrim behind the sofa, is the door into—*

*The hall. This can be seen (when lit) through the scrim wall behind the sofa. It is quite small and contains the usual paraphernalia of cottage halls: hats and coats on pegs;* PAMELA'*s riding cap and crop; a sporting print, and perhaps a barometer. The front door opens into it, left, and the staircase of the cottage leads out of it, right, on to—*

*The landing. This occupies a fairly small but important central area above the living room.* WALTER'*s bedroom door opens on to it, right: the door must be recessed and not too prominent; for most of the evening it can even be screened by a curtain. On the left of this, a corridor leads off to two bedrooms (*CLIVE'*s and his parents') and the bathroom—all of which are invisible. On the extreme left a further short flight of steps leads up to—*

*The schoolroom, which is directly above the sofa area of the living room. This is very much* PAMELA'S *room: it is littered with her possessions, her books and old toys and clothes. In the center is a round table where her studies are done, and two chairs. Its right wall contains the door to her bedroom. Its left wall has the window, gaily framed in frilly curtains, a hanging lamp, and a gas fire. The room is brightly colored, and reflects the liveliness of its chief occupant.*

*The whole stage shows a compact dwelling, disposed with feminine care.*

## ACT ONE

### SCENE 1

*A bright Saturday morning in early September.*

CLIVE *is sitting at the breakfast table. He is a boy of nineteen, quick, nervous, taut, and likable: there is something about him oddly and disturbingly young for his age, the nakedness of someone in whom intellectual development has outstripped the emotional.* LOUISE, *his mother, comes in with a plate of eggs and bacon for him. She is a smart woman in her forties dressed stylishly, even ostentatiously, for a country weekend. Her whole manner bespeaks a constant preoccupation with style, though without apparent insincerity or affectation. She is very good-looking, with attractive features, which are reflected—though with greater instability—in her son.*

LOUISE [*Looking out of the French window*]: Your father's going back to nature.

CLIVE: How far?

LOUISE: Wait till you see. He's got one of his open-air fits. This morning we're going shooting with that dreary stockbroker from the Gables—Whatsisname.

CLIVE: Benton.

LOUISE: Yes. Well, to honor Mr. Benton he's gone and got himself one of those vulgar American hunting jackets made out of a car rug. Can you imagine anything more ridiculous?

CLIVE [*Eating*]: He probably saw it in one of those American mags that Chuck left here last weekend. . . . Apart from the jacket, how is he?

LOUISE: He's all right. Came down on the six-thirty. What time did *you* get in?

CLIVE: Midnight.

LOUISE: Of course he wanted to know where you were.

CLIVE: And did you tell him?

LOUISE: I didn't know. I supposed you were still in London.

CLIVE [*Resentfully*]: I was out. O-U-T.

LOUISE: Yes, dear.

CLIVE: Just plain out.

LOUISE: Alll right, dear. [*She makes for the kitchen.*] Could you manage another egg if I did one quickly? The pan's still hot.

CLIVE: No, thanks.

[LOUISE *goes out.* STANLEY *comes in from the garden. He is dressed in a brightly colored hunting jacket. He is a forceful man in middle age, well built and self-possessed, though there is something deeply insecure about his assertiveness.* CLIVE'S *nervousness increases with his appearance.*]

CLIVE: Good morning.

STANLEY: Morning. [*He takes his place at the table.*]

CLIVE: Very becoming.

STANLEY [*Vaguely*]: What?

CLIVE: I said "Very becoming."

STANLEY [*Pleased*]: Oh . . .

[LOUISE *returns with the toast.*]

Where's Pam?

LOUISE: Walter's taken her for a walk before they start their lessons. They've had their breakfast; I'll get you yours. [*To* CLIVE.] Are you sure you don't want anything more, dear?

CLIVE: Quite sure, thank you.

LOUISE [*Fondly*]: Well, you're having a very good breakfast for a change. I shan't press you.

[LOUISE *goes out.*]

CLIVE [*Nervously*]: I think Pam likes to get the French over with early. Still, it's a bit desperate, starting the day with irregular verbs.

STANLEY [*Brusquely*]: You know who we are? We're millionaires.

CLIVE: What?

STANLEY: Now we've got a tutor we must be. We don't send our girl to anything so common as a school. You like the idea, I suppose?

CLIVE [*Eager to agree*]: As a matter of fact, I think it's ridiculous. I mean, well, unnecessary.

STANLEY: Your mother thinks different. Apparently the best people have tutors, and since we're going to be the best people whether we like it or not, we must have a tutor too. Herr Walter Langer, if you please.

Ten quid a week and a whole term's fees to the school we didn't send her to. Did you know that?

CLIVE: No.

[LOUISE *comes in with the porridge for her husband.*]

STANLEY: Oh yes. Still, I can afford it. What's money, after all? We had a town place so we simply had to have a country place, with a fancy decorator to do it up for us. And now we've got a country place we've simply got to have a tutor.

LOUISE: Are you starting on that again? Well, please remember it's Walter's first weekend down here, and I want everyone to be nice to him. So just keep your ideas to yourself, would you mind? We don't want to hear them.

STANLEY: We? Clive agrees with me.

LOUISE: Oh? Do you, Clive?

CLIVE [*Quietly*]: Isn't it a little early for this sort of conversation?

STANLEY: You just said you thought a tutor was ridiculous.

CLIVE: Well, not that exactly . . . I mean . . .

[*He lowers his eyes and proceeds to examine his breakfast with interest.*]

LOUISE: Get on with your breakfast, dear.

[*She sits down at the other end of the table and pours the coffee.* STANLEY *regards his son balefully. A slight pause.*]

STANLEY: You were in late last night.

CLIVE [*Avoiding his eye*]: Yes, I—I got involved.

STANLEY: Involved?

CLIVE: Well, I had some work to do in London.

STANLEY: Work?

CLIVE: Well, not exactly work—sort of criticism really. I promised to review something. It's going to be printed.

STANLEY: In a paper?

CLIVE: Sort of paper.

STANLEY [*Sarcastic*]: Oh, *The Times,* I suppose?

CLIVE [*Unhappily*]: Well, it's more of a magazine, actually. It's not very—well, famous.

STANLEY: What's it called?

CLIVE: *New Endeavor.*

STANLEY: New what?

CLIVE [*Low*]: *Endeavor.*

STANLEY: Hm. . . . Well, why did they ask you?

CLIVE: It was more me did the asking. You see, the usual man's ill, so I asked this friend of mine—who's a friend of the editor's— if I could do it, and he said yes. So I did. Anyway, it was two free seats.

STANLEY: What for?

CLIVE: A play.

STANLEY [*Aloofly*]: Was it any good?

CLIVE: Yes. . . . It was splendid, as a matter of fact.

LOUISE: What was it, dear?

CLIVE: *Elektra*.

STANLEY: What's that?

LOUISE [*With exaggerated surprise*]: You can't mean it!

STANLEY: Mean what?

LOUISE: You just can't mean it. Really, Stanley, there are times when I have to remind myself about you—actually remind myself.

STANLEY [*Quietly*]: Suppose you tell me, then. Educate me.

LOUISE [*Loftily*]: Clive, dear, tell your father, will you?

[CLIVE *sits eating.*]

STANLEY [*To him*]: Well, go on.

CLIVE [*Low*]: It's Greek.

STANLEY: Oh, one of those.

LOUISE [*Brightly, putting her husband in his place*]: Who was in it, dear? Laurence Olivier? I always think he's best for the Greek things, don't you? . . . I'll never forget that wonderful night when they put out his eyes—you know the one; you and I went when you father was in Leeds that time. I could hear that scream for weeks and weeks afterward, everywhere I went. There was something so *farouche* about it. You know the word, dear: *farouche?* Like animals in the jungle.

STANLEY [*To* CLIVE]: And that's meant to be cultured?

CLIVE: What?

STANLEY: People having their eyes put out.

CLIVE: I don't know what "cultured" means. I always thought it had something to do with those pearls they sell in Oxford Street.

LOUISE: Nonsense, you know very well what your father means. It's not people's eyes, Stanley: it's the *poetry*. Of course I don't expect *you* to understand.

STANLEY [*To* CLIVE]: And this is what you want to study at Cambridge when you get up there next month?

CLIVE: Well, more or less.

STANLEY: May I ask why?

CLIVE: Well, because . . . well, poetry's its own reward, actually. Like virtue. All art is, I should think.

STANLEY: And this is the most useful thing you can find to do with your time?

CLIVE: It's not a question of useful.

STANLEY: Isn't it?

CLIVE: Not really.

STANLEY [*Staring at him gravely*]: You don't seem to realize the world you're living in, my boy. When you finish at this university which your mother insists you're to go to, you'll have to earn your living. I won't always be here to pay for everything, you know.

CLIVE [*With a spurt of anger*]: Look, I'm not exactly five years old.

STANLEY [*Extinguishing it*]: Then it's time you acted your age. All this culture stuff's very fine for those who can afford it; for the nobs and snobs we're always hearing about from that end of the table—[*indicating* LOUISE]—but it's not going to earn you the price of a sausage outside this front door. I mayn't be much in the way of education, but I know this: if you can't stand on your own two feet you don't amount to anything. And not one of that pansy set of spongers you're going round with will ever help you do that. And you know why? Because they've got no principles. No principles worth a damn.

CLIVE: You know nothing about my friends.

STANLEY: *I know.* I've seen them. Arty-tarty boys. They think it's clever going round Chelsea and places like that giggling and drinking and talking dirty, wearing Bohemian clothes. Tight trousers. Who gave them the right to look down on other people, that's what I want to know, just because they don't know about the—[*affected voice*]—*operah* and the *ballay* and the *dramah?*

LOUISE: And who gave you the right to talk about Bohemian clothes? What are you supposed to be, a lumberjack?

STANLEY [*Ignoring her*]: Who did you go with last night? Well? Who's this friend of the editor?

CLIVE [*Subdued*]: Chuck.

STANLEY: Oh yes. Your American pal. The one who stayed here last weekend—sings in cafés and wants to stay in school till he's thirty, living on grants. Such a dignified way to go on.

LOUISE [*Sharply*]: I should have thought it was a sign of maturity to want to become more educated. Unfortunately, my dear, we weren't all born orphans; we didn't all go to grammar schools, or work up a furniture factory on our own by sheer willpower. We can never hope to live down these shortcomings, of course, but don't you think you might learn to tolerate them? We just didn't have the advantage of your healthy upbringing in the tough world outside.

[*The effect of this speech is momentarily to crush* STANLEY *into silence.*]

Jou-jou, come and help me clear away, dear. I'm going to get Walter to give me a music lesson later on.

STANLEY [*Disbelieving*]: Music lesson?

LOUISE: Yes. And don't get yourself shot by mistake. Though there can't be many birds that color.

STANLEY: What time's lunch?

LOUISE: Oh, oneish. It depends. After my lesson I'm going to take Walter down to the bay. I'm going to show him some plants I've found. Did you know he was a botanist as well? And such charm! Well, of course, it's exactly what I've said all along. It takes a Continental to show us just how ignorant we really are. Jou-jou, *la porte!*

[CLIVE *opens the kitchen door for her and she goes through it with a loaded tray.*]

STANLEY [*To* CLIVE]: I'll see you later. That is, unless you want to come shooting with me. No, of course you wouldn't. Well, just see you get out into the air. I didn't take this cottage so you could lounge about indoors all day. You know, Clive, I just don't understand you at all. Not at all.

[*He goes out into the hall and through the front door, banging it behind him.* LOUISE *returns.*]

CLIVE [*With dull rage*]: Breakfast as usual.

LOUISE [*Clearing*]: Never mind. It was just one of his moods.

CLIVE: Yes. . . .

LOUISE: Oh, Jou-jou, I want you to be very happy down here, darling. Really happy, not just pretending. After all, it's why I made Daddy buy this place—to get away from the house and London and all the squabbling. To come into the country and relax in our own little retreat. . . . So you've just got to be happy. You can't let me down. Can you?

CLIVE: *Votre Majesté.* My Empress!

LOUISE [*Permitting her hand to be kissed*]: *Levez!*

CLIVE: The Empress Louise, ill fated, tragic, dark-eyed queen from beyond the seas! What is your wish, madame? I am yours to command.

LOUISE: I've told you already, my little Cossack. *Sois content.* Be happy.

CLIVE: *Bien.* On my honor as a guardsman, and on my beautiful hat of genuine black sheepskin, I promise to you six big laughs a day, and twelve little giggles.

LOUISE: Darling. My darling Jou-jou!

CLIVE: *Maman!*

[*They embrace very fondly.*]

LOUISE: Now that's a promise, you know. To be happy. Then I can be happy too. Because I can tell when you're not, you know: and that makes me miserable also. So remember: no complexes.

CLIVE: No complexes, *Majesté.*

[*He bows again. She kisses his forehead.*]

LOUISE: Come on. I'll wash and you dry. They won't take five minutes.

CLIVE: It'll take at least twenty. I can't think why you don't get a maid in.

LOUISE: Oh Jou-jou, not that again! For one thing, it's three miles to the village and no bus service, so who do you think we're going to get out here? [*Warmly.*] And anyway, my dear, this is meant to be a *retreat.* For just us. Housework's all in the fun. Everyone does it these days. . . .

[*She gives him a warm smile and leads him into the kitchen. As the scene ends,* PAMELA *comes noisily through the front door and races upstairs into the schoolroom. She is followed closely by her tutor,* WALTER LANGER, *carrying a bunch of wild flowers.*]

PAMELA [*As she runs*]: If I'm there first, no French today!

WALTER: Oh no, you do not get out of it that way! . . . [*Arriving in the schoolroom.*] Come on. We're ten minutes late already. Now we do the French. [*He puts down the flowers.*]

PAMELA: Oh it's too cold to think in French, Walter.

WALTER [*Not to be put off*]: Very well. I light the gas fire. Where are the matches?

PAMELA: On the windowsill.

[*Walter fetches them and lights the gas fire.* PAMELA *sits resignedly at the table. She is a happy girl of fourteen, as volatile as her brother, but wholly without his melancholy—or the seriousness that touches* WALTER. *The tutor is now seen to be a German youth of twenty-two, secret, warm, precise yet not priggish, and happily at ease with his young pupil.*]

WALTER: *Parler.* To talk. Future tense. Think hard.

PAMELA: *Je parlerai . . . ?*

WALTER: Good.

PAMELA: *Je parlerai, tu parleras, il parlera, nous—nous parlerons?*

[WALTER *nods, putting on the spectacles he wears for reading.*]

*Vous parlerez, ils parleront.*

WALTER: Good, that's the first time you have it right!

PAMELA: Oh, phooey to French. I hate it. Really.

WALTER: Why?

PAMELA: Because the French are a decadent nation. Personally I think we all ought to study Russian and American.

WALTER: But American is the same as English.

PAMELA: Of course it's not. When they say "dame" they mean young girl, and when we say "dame" we mean old girl. But when we call someone "old girl" we really mean what they call a dame. So you see.

WALTER: No.

PAMELA: Well, of course, I know all about Americans from Mary. You've still to meet her. She's my only friend here.

WALTER: Where does she live?

PAMELA: Over the stables in Craven Lane. You'll just fall when you see her.

WALTER: How? In love?

PAMELA: Of course. Mummy says she's common, but that's just because she wears shocking-pink socks and says "Drop dead" all the time. I know her mother drinks and has lovers and things. But, her husband's dead so you really can't blame her, can you? Just like Clive says: There-but-for-the-Grace-of-God Department.

WALTER: And she knows all about America because she says "Drop dead"?

PAMELA [*Loftily*]: Of course not. How can you be so brutish? For one thing, she's got an American boyfriend in the Air Force.

WALTER: How old is she?

PAMELA [*Airily*]: Sixteen. But that's all right; they like them young. I don't think they actually . . . well, you know. . . . Sometimes she gets decked up in her black jeans and goes off to some sexy club in Ipswich under a Polish restaurant. But her mother doesn't like her going round the streets looking like that, so she has to sneak off when no one's looking.

WALTER: Like witches.

PAMELA: Witches?

WALTER: Going to their Sabbath.

PAMELA: What's that?

WALTER: When they used to worship the Devil. They used to dress up and sneak off just like that. It was the same thing like the Teddy boys. You make yourself very excited, then people give you a bad name and start being afraid of you. That's when you really do start worshiping the Devil.

PAMELA: Oh, phooey.

WALTER [*More gravely*]: Not phooey.

PAMELA: You talk as if you'd seen him.

WALTER: The Devil? I have.

PAMELA: Where?

WALTER: Where he lives.

PAMELA: Where's that?

WALTER: Where I was born.

PAMELA: And what was he doing?

WALTER: Sitting down.

PAMELA: Where?

WALTER: Behind people's eyes. . . . [*Seeing her confusion.*] Well, isn't that a good place to sit?

PAMELA: Do you miss it?

WALTER: What?

PAMELA: Your home.

WALTER: It's not my home.

PAMELA: Still, there must be things you miss. Birthdays or Christmases or something.

WALTER: Christmas, yes. In our little town it was better. It's called Muhlbach. The stars are more clear there.

PAMELA: Just the stars?

WALTER [*With a small spurt of excitement*]: No, ice too. Ice grows all down the river, and at night you go skating all alone, all alone for miles in the black, and it's terribly cold and fast—and suddenly you see torches coming toward you, and voices come, and there's a crowd of happy people with nuts and fruit and hot rum, kissing you a good New Year.

PAMELA: Oh, wonderful!

WALTER [*With reservation*]: Yes, for that . . .

PAMELA: Let's go! Just for Christmas, you and me. You can teach me enough German in twelve weeks so I can understand everyone—Oh, I'm sorry. I forgot. You don't teach German.

WALTER: No.

PAMELA: Walter, I never asked before—but why not? I mean you'd make more money doing that than anything else.

[WALTER *shakes his head slowly "No."*]

You're really a very strange young man.

WALTER: Am I?

PAMELA [*Kindly*]: I suppose part of it's living in a foreign country all the time.

WALTER: It's not foreign. Not for always, anyway. I've been here five years, and soon now I get my citizenship.

PAMELA: Then you'll be English?

[WALTER *nods "Yes."*]

Then you'll like Christmas here too, because this'll be home and you'll spend it with us here in the country. Don't you have any family at all?

[WALTER *shakes his head.*]

No one?

WALTER: No.

PAMELA: But that's the wrong answer. When I say "Have you got no family?" you must say "Yes, of course I have a family, and a very fine one too." Now repeat after me: "My family lives at 22 Elton Square, London, and The Retreat, Lower Orford, Suffolk."

WALTER: My family lives at 22 Elton Square, London, and The Retreat, Lower Orford, Suffolk.

PAMELA: Good. Ten out of ten. Now you look much happier. . . . You should wear a high collar. And one of those floppy ties. Then you'd look like Metternich or someone. And wear your hair very sleek and romantic.

[*She smooths his hair.*]

Like this. . . .

WALTER [*Dodging*]: Hey!

PAMELA: No, it's terribly becoming. . . . Count Walter Langer, Knight of the Holy Golden Soupladle! [*She ruffles his hair.*]

WALTER: Pamela, no!

[*He ducks away from the table. She chases him. He grabs the flowers and runs down the stairs on to the landing.*]

Stop it! You're not to—

PAMELA: Pompous, pompous, pompous!

WALTER: Now you stop it or I'll be very cross.

PAMELA: Augustus Pompous!

WALTER: And very sick!

PAMELA: Phooey!

WALTER: I will. You don't believe me . . . ?

LOUISE [*Calling "off" from kitchen*]: Walter!

WALTER: There's your mother. I go now. What's that in French—"I go"?

PAMELA: *Je allez?*

WALTER: No, I've told you one million times. *Je vais.* Now you go back and do some history.

PAMELA: Oh, all right. [*She goes back to the schoolroom.*] Hey!

WALTER: Yes?

PAMELA: See you anon, Mastodon.

WALTER: Quarter to four, Dinosaur!

[*He goes downstairs to the living room.* PAMELA *applies herself to the history book, sitting at the table and making notes. Entering the living room.*]

Good morning.

CLIVE: Hello.

WALTER: Mrs. Harrington was calling me.

CLIVE: She's in the music room through there.

WALTER: You have a music room in the cottage?

CLIVE: Only an outside one. When we took this place it used to be the scullery, but Mother wasn't daunted by that. She picked up an upright for two pound ten and knocked down a wall to get it in. It's lucky it's at the back because His Godship doesn't care for music.

WALTER: Oh, I'm afraid I was playing my gramophone last night—I'm sorry.

CLIVE [*Wryly*]: He'll soon tell you if he minds. . . . Tell me, how d'you like being tutor to my demon sister?

WALTER: Oh, she's delightful. When your mother first met me and invited me to live with you, I—I didn't know what I should find. My last job was . . . not so easy.

CLIVE: You lived with a family too?

WALTER: No. I had a flat in Paddington. More of a basement, really.

CLIVE: I can imagine.

WALTER: This is . . . my first family.

CLIVE: Yes?

WALTER: Yes.

CLIVE [*Lightly*]: Well, let me give you a warning. This isn't a family. It's a tribe of wild cannibals. Between us we eat everyone we can.

[WALTER *smiles.*]

You think I'm joking?

WALTER: I think you are very lucky to have a family.

CLIVE: And I think you're lucky to be without one.

[*He sees a faint distress in* WALTER.]

I'm sorry. I'm making tasteless jokes. Actually, we're very choosy in our victims. We only eat other members of the family.

WALTER [*Catching the mood*]: Then I must watch out. Your sister thinks I'm almost a member already.

CLIVE: Pam? You know, I don't like the way she's growing up at all. She wants to *include* people all the time: she doesn't appear to want to exclude or demolish anybody.

WALTER: Perhaps that's because she takes after her mother. . . . [*Confused.*] Excuse me.

CLIVE: That's quite all right. A girl who took after Stanley would be almost unthinkable.

[LOUISE *comes in from the kitchen, with an album of music.*]

LOUISE: Walter, my dear, I do hope I didn't disturb your lesson. I'm simply longing to hear you try my little piano.

WALTER: Mrs. Harrington—I play so badly.

LOUISE: Nonsense! You have such beautiful hands. [*She takes one of his hands.*] I remember once shaking hands with Paderewski. Of course it was many years ago, and I was only a girl, but I've never forgotten it. He had hands almost exactly like yours, my dear boy. Much older of course—but the same bone formation, the same delicacy. . . . This was my mother's album.

WALTER [*Putting on his spectacles to examine it*]: It's charming.

LOUISE: What are you going to play for me? Something Viennese, of course.

WALTER: What would you like? Beethoven? Brahms?

LOUISE: Wonderful! And you can explain to me all about it. I mean where it was written and who for. I always think it so much increases one's enjoyment if you know about things like that. Take the *Moonlight*, for example. Now what was the true story about that?

CLIVE: Well, it wasn't really moonlight at all, Mother. Moonlight was the name of the brothel where Beethoven actually was when he started writing it.

LOUISE: Jou-jou!

CLIVE: He got one of the girls to crouch on all fours so he could use her back for a table. It's in one of the biographies, I forget which.

LOUISE [*To* WALTER]: He's being very naughty, isn't he? Really, Jou-jou!

WALTER [*Picking up the flowers and presenting them to her*]: Mrs. Harrington, I found these in the lane. They are quite rare, you know. I thought you might be interested.

LOUISE [*Very pleased*]: Oh, thank you, Walter. I'm most touched. Aren't they beautiful, Jou-jou? [CLIVE *shrugs.*] You know, I must give you a name. Walter is much too formal. Wait. Of course! [*Taking the idea from his spectacles.*] Clive's Jou-jou, so you can be Hibou. Perfect. Hibou, the owl. [*To* CLIVE.] He looks rather like an owl, doesn't he?

CLIVE: Why not Pou? That's better still—Louise.

LOUISE: Oh, he's impossible this morning. Your father's right: a walk in the fresh air would do you a lot of good.

[PAMELA *snaps her book shut and comes bounding out of the schoolroom and down the stairs.*]

PAMELA [*Running downstairs*]: Mother! Mother!

LOUISE: Good heavens, what a noise that girl makes! [*To* WALTER.] I'm afraid you're going to have to teach her some etiquette as well.

[PAMELA *comes bursting into the living room.*]

PAMELA: Mother!

LOUISE: Quietly, dear. Quietly.

PAMELA [*Breathless*]: Sorry. Mother, will you test me on my history?

LOUISE: Ask Clive, will you, dear? I'm busy now. Walter's going to play for me.

PAMELA: Are you, Walter? How nice . . .

LOUISE [*To* WALTER]: Come along, my dear. We haven't got too much time.

[LOUISE *goes out with* WALTER *into the kitchen.* PAMELA *studies her brother, then knocks on the door.*]

PAMELA [*In a coy exaggerated voice*]: General . . . General Harrington.

CLIVE [*Old soldier's voice*]: Eh? What's that?

[*The following dialogue is conducted in these voices.*]

PAMELA: May I come in?

CLIVE: Well, if it's not little Daphne! Spike me cannon! How very kind of you to call. Come in, me dear. Don't be afraid.

PAMELA: Thank you. [*She minces into the room.*]

CLIVE: And how are you, eh? Eh?

PAMELA: Fine, thank you. And how's the—[*whispers*]—you-know-what?

CLIVE [*Normal voice*]: Do I?

PAMELA [*Normal voice*]: Gout.

CLIVE: Ah. [*General's voice.*] Oh, it comes and goes, y'know. Comes and goes.

PAMELA [*Daphne's voice again, gushing*]: I think it's wonderful of you to take it so well. I'm sure I'd be complaining all the time. I'm a real silly-billy about pain.

CLIVE: Nonsense, me dear. Lord, though, how yer remind me of yer dear mother. Hair just like hers. Yellow as a cornflower, I always used to say.

PAMELA [*Normal voice*]: There's something wrong about that.

CLIVE [*Normal voice*]: Is there? What?

PAMELA: Cornflowers are blue.

CLIVE: Well, your mother certainly didn't have blue hair.

PAMELA [*Archly*]: That's all you know. . . . Anyway, you've got to test my history.

CLIVE [*Beckoning*]: Your ribbon.

[*Automatically she goes to him for it to be tied. He sits on the couch; she kneels beside him. The sound of piano music from the music room.*]

PAMELA [*Listening*]: He's the best, isn't he?

CLIVE: Just about.

PAMELA: Oh, you can tell. I knew just as soon as he came in the door.

[*They listen for a moment.*]

CLIVE: How d'you get on together?

PAMELA: Oh, we simply adore each other.

CLIVE: Is he going to teach you anything?

PAMELA: Everything, my dear. Just wait and see, I'll be the most erudine girl for my age in London.

CLIVE: Dite.

PAMELA: What?

CLIVE: Eru*dite.* Well, supposing we make a start.

[PAMELA *hands over her list.* CLIVE *studies it earnestly for a moment.*]

Which was the most uncertain dynasty in Europe?

PAMELA: I haven't the faintest.

CLIVE [*As if reading*]: The Perhapsburgs.

PAMELA: Who?

CLIVE: The Perhapsburgs.

PAMELA: Now, Clive, really—

CLIVE [*Enthusiastically*]: I don't know much about them yet, but I'm working on it. I'll have them fixed by the end of the week. So far there's just Thomas the Tentative—a successor of Doubting Thomas, of course—and Vladimir—the Vague.

PAMELA: That's marvelous! How about a woman?

CLIVE: By all means.

PAMELA: Dorothea.

CLIVE: Nice.

PAMELA: Dorothea the—the Downright.

CLIVE: But that's just the opposite. There's nothing Perhaps about her.

PAMELA: Well, she could be the black sheep of the family.

CLIVE: We'll see. . . . Now. [*He consults the list.*] Pay attention. Who was known as the Crying Cavalier?

PAMELA [*Protesting*]: No, Clive, seriously—I've really got to—

CLIVE: Answer me. Who?

PAMELA: I don't know.

CLIVE: Who was the Unknown Civilian?

PAMELA: I don't know.

CLIVE: Who was the Curable Romantic?

PAMELA: I don't know. I don't know . . . !

[*She throws herself at* CLIVE. *The music stops.*]

CLIVE: Really, you are the most impossibly ignorant child. . . . [*Struggling with her happily.*] I'm never going to teach you anything!

PAMELA [*Springing away from* CLIVE]: Tell me a story!

CLIVE: Sweet or sour?

PAMELA: Sour.

CLIVE: All right. Once upon a time there was a little girl who lived all by herself in a prison.

PAMELA: Why? What had she done?

CLIVE: Nothing: that's the whole point. They took away all her clothes and made her wear blankets instead.

[WALTER *enters from the kitchen.*]

WALTER: Mrs. Harrington was asking for her handbag.

PAMELA: Here it is. [*Takes handbag from armchair and hands it to* WALTER.] Stay with us. Clive's telling me a story.

WALTER: A story? About history?

PAMELA: About a prison.

CLIVE [*Showing off to* WALTER]: Yes, it's going to be brilliant! All Gothic darkness and calamities. It's called the "Black Hole of East Suffolk." [*Mock grave.*] Sit down and I'll unfold.

WALTER: No, not now. Your mother is waiting. Excuse me. [*He goes back into the kitchen.*]

[CLIVE *stares after* WALTER. *His gaiety leaves him.*]

PAMELA: What's wrong?

CLIVE: Nothing.

PAMELA: What about the little girl in prison?

CLIVE: It wasn't a girl. It was a boy. A little German boy with blond hair, who played the piano rather well. He walked straight into the prison of his own free will and shut the door behind him.

[CLIVE *walks out through the front door. The piano resumes offstage.*]

CURTAIN

## SCENE 2

*A Saturday night two months later.*

*The family has finished dinner and is drinking coffee. At least* STANLEY *and* LOUISE *are:* CLIVE, *sitting by his mother, is drinking whisky. His suitcase stands by the door.*

LOUISE [*To* CLIVE]: Don't you want any coffee?

CLIVE: No thanks.

LOUISE: What are you drinking?

CLIVE: Whisky.

LOUISE: Really, I do think you might have caught an earlier train from Cambridge. I cooked a special dinner for you, all your favorite things.

CLIVE: I'm sorry, Mother. But don't worry, I had a perfectly good sandwich from British Railways.

LOUISE: Well, that's not enough for you.

[*The sound of piano practicing comes from the music room: a simple piece of Bach being repeated with many mistakes and stumbles.* WALTER *comes in from the kitchen and is about to go on up to his room.*]

STANLEY [*Referring to piano practicing*]: How much longer is that going on, may I ask?

LOUISE: For another half-hour, I hope. [*To* WALTER.] How's she getting on, dear?

WALTER: Oh, very well, Mrs. Harrington. [*To* STANLEY.] It is only six weeks, you know, sir.

LOUISE: Yes, it's amazing, isn't it? Oh, Walter, would you mind taking Clive's suitcase upstairs as you go?

WALTER: Certainly, Mrs. Harrington. [*Exit.*]

LOUISE: Thank you so much. [*To* CLIVE.] I don't know why you can't put your own things away.

STANLEY [*To* CLIVE]: And that's what you call great music? Is that right? Great music?

CLIVE [*Nervously, with an attempt at humor*]: Let's say it's a little distorted at the moment.

STANLEY: Distorted? It's driving me mad.

CLIVE: I suppose we can't expect her to be an expert in two months. Run Before You Can Walk Department.

LOUISE: Your father imagines that everything can be done without hard work. Everything except making money out of the furniture business. [*To* STANLEY.] Really, you are absurd. How do you think Paderewski sounded when he was practicing? What is that piece she's learning, dear? Mozart? . . . Jou-jou, I'm talking to you.

CLIVE [*Low*]: Bach.

LOUISE: You could play too if you wanted to. You've got the hands for it.

[LOUISE *goes out to kitchen.* CLIVE *smiles faintly. There is a pause. A passage is repeated on the piano several times. Then an irritated bang on the keys and the noise stops.*]

STANLEY [*Carefully to* CLIVE]: Do you remember when you came to the factory to fetch your allowance the day you went up to Cambridge?

CLIVE: Yes. . . .

STANLEY: Did you have a talk to my manager while you were waiting?

CLIVE: Did I, yes . . . I suppose I did.

STANLEY: Yes. Is it true you told him you thought the furniture we make was—what was it?—"shoddy and vulgar"? [*Pause.*] Well?

CLIVE: I think I said it—it lacked . . .

STANLEY: What?

CLIVE: Well, that it didn't use materials as well as it might. Wood, for example. [*He smiles hopefully.*]

STANLEY: And the design was shoddy and vulgar?

CLIVE: Well—well, yes, I suppose I gave that impression. Not all of it, of course—just some things. . . .

STANLEY: What things?

CLIVE [*Plucking up a little courage*]: Well, those terrible oak cupboards, for example. I think you call it the Jacobean line. And those three-piece suites in mauve moquette. Things like that . . .

STANLEY [*Impassive as ever*]: Mr. Clark said you called them "grotesque."

[CLIVE *lowers his eyes.*]

Is that right—grotesque?

CLIVE [*Mumbling*]: I think they are, rather.

STANLEY: And I suppose you think that's clever. That's being educated, I suppose; to go up to my manager in my own factory and tell him you think the stuff I'm turning out is shoddy and vulgar . . . is it?

[LOUISE *has come back from the kitchen in time to hear this.*]

LOUISE: Just because *you've* got no taste, it doesn't mean we all have to follow suit.

[STANLEY *gives her a look which silences her, then turns again to his son.* CLIVE *continues to sit rigidly.*]

STANLEY: Now you listen to me. You get this through your head once and for all: I'm in business to make money. I give people what they want. I mean ordinary people. Maybe they haven't got such wonderful taste as you and your mother; perhaps they don't read such good books—what is it?—*Houses and Gardens?*—but they know what they want. If they didn't want it, they wouldn't buy it, and I'd be out of business. Before you start sneering again, my boy, just remember something—you've always had enough to eat.

[*The explosive opening of the Brahms* Third Symphony *is heard from* WALTER'*s room.*]

[*Looking up, dangerously.*] One stops, the other starts. I'm going out.

[STANLEY *stands up.*]

LOUISE: Where to—Mr. Benton?

STANLEY: And if I am at least I can get some peace there.

LOUISE: Ssh.

STANLEY: Don't you ssh me!

LOUISE: This is the first weekend we've all been here together since Clive went up to Cambridge. I think the least you can do is stay home, his first evening back. Why must you be so disagreeable? [*She goes into the hall calling "Walter, Walter!"*]

WALTER: Did you call, Mrs. Harrington?

LOUISE: Do you think you could play your gramophone another time, dear? Mr. Harrington has got a slight headache.

WALTER: Of course, Mrs. Harrington.

[*He goes into his room. Music stops, and he reappears.*]

I'm so sorry. So very sorry.

LOUISE: That's quite all right, dear. Thank you very much. I hate to disturb your concentration.

WALTER: Oh, please.

LOUISE: Come down when you want to. I've got some delicious petits fours, and I'll make you some fresh coffee.

WALTER: Thank you, Mrs. Harrington. [*He goes into his room and shuts the door.*]

LOUISE: Now try and be a bit more agreeable will you? Jou-jou, it's washing-up time, are you going to help me?

CLIVE: Can't we leave it for once?

LOUISE: It's all right. I can manage perfectly well without you. [*She goes into the kitchen. There is a silence.*]

CLIVE: I'm sorry I said that about the furniture, Father. I suppose it was tactless of me.

STANLEY: Never mind. [*Pause.*] How are you doing at Cambridge? What about the other boys, do you get on with them?

CLIVE [*Softly*]: It's not exactly like school, you know. You rather pick your own friends.

STANLEY: Yes, I suppose you do. Well, what do they do there? I mean apart from lessons.

CLIVE: Anything you like. There are all sorts of clubs and societies.

STANLEY: Do you belong to any?

CLIVE: Well, I joined a dramatic society as a matter of fact.

STANLEY: You mean for acting?

CLIVE: It's quite professional, you know. They have their own theater—and get reviews in *The Times*.

STANLEY: Don't any of them play any games?

CLIVE: Yes, but—well, the cricket and rugger are sort of professional standard. I thought of taking up fencing, it's not as odd as it sounds. It's meant to be very good for coordination—

STANLEY: What's that?

CLIVE: Muscles I think.

STANLEY: Clive, as you know, your mother and I didn't see eye to eye over sending you to university. But that's past history now. The point is, what use are you going to make of it?

CLIVE: That's rather as it turns out, I should have thought. I mean, you can't judge things in advance, can you?

STANLEY: Ah now, that's just what I mean. Clive, if you don't know where you're going, you might as well pack up.

CLIVE: Why?

STANLEY: It's quite simple, I should have thought.

CLIVE: It isn't. It just isn't like that. I mean, if I knew where I was going I wouldn't have to go there, would I? I'd be there already.

STANLEY: What kind of silly quibble is that?

CLIVE: It's not a quibble. Look, education—being educated—you just can't talk about it in that way. It's something quite different—like setting off on an expedition into the jungle. Gradually most of the things you know disappear. The old birds fly out of the sky and new ones fly in you've never seen before. And everything surprises you too. Trees you expected to be just a few feet high grow right up over you—like the nave of Wells Cathedral. [*Suddenly embarrassed.*] Anyway, if you had seen all this before, you wouldn't have to go looking. I think education is simply the process of being taken by surprise, don't you see?

STANLEY: Be that as it may.

CLIVE: You don't see.

STANLEY: Clive, I'm not talking about education. By all means, take advantage of your lessons. Look my boy, let's not pretend. Everyone doesn't get to Cambridge: you know it and I know it. You're in a privileged position and you must make the most of it. What you do now will influence the rest of your life. You know that, don't you?

CLIVE: I suppose it will.

STANLEY: Of course it will. Take your friends, for example. What kind of friends do you have?

CLIVE: Do you want a list?

STANLEY: Now don't start getting on any high horse. I'm simply saying this. People still judge a man by the company he keeps. You go around with a lot of drifters and arty boys, and you'll be judged as one of them. I don't say you do, and you're old enough to decide for yourself anyway. Right?

[CLIVE *nods.*]

Number two is this. Now's the time for you to be making contacts with the right people. I mean people who will be valuable to you later on. I don't mean the smart people, or the fancy la-de-da people your mother's always on about. I mean the people who really matter. The people who have influence. Get in with them now, and you won't go far wrong. I never had your advantages. The contacts I made I had to work up myself. So I know what I'm talking about. Do you understand?

CLIVE: Yes.

STANLEY: You've got a good brain and I'll see to it you've got enough money. There's no harm in having a few quid in your pocket, you know.

[LOUISE *enters.*]

Don't ever be so stupid as to look down on money. It's the one thing that counts in the end.

LOUISE: Money! Is tht all you ever think about?

STANLEY: You don't have any difficulty spending it, I notice. [*To* CLIVE.] Now let's see, how long have you been at Cambridge? Is this your half-term holiday?

LOUISE: Half-term! You talk about it as if it were a grammar school, instead of our leading university. Really, Stanley, I don't know how one can even begin to talk to you.

[STANLEY *stands up, furious, but trying to control himself.*]

STANLEY [*To* CLIVE]: Do you want to walk with me over to Benton's?

[LOUISE *turns and stares at him in annoyance.*]

CLIVE: I—I've got some reading to do actually.

STANLEY: We can stop in at the Lion for a quick one.

CLIVE: No. I don't think so, really.

STANLEY: Very well.

CLIVE: It's important, or I would.

[STANLEY *nods and goes out of the front door.* LOUISE *looks after him, then goes to her son.*]

LOUISE: Are you going to be intense?

CLIVE: No.

LOUISE: Oh, Jou-jou! *Mon petit* Cossack. *Embrasse-moi. . . . Non? . . .* It's your Empress.

CLIVE: Your Majesty.

LOUISE: Every family has its rows, you know. Come on, help me get the coffee—just the two of us.

CLIVE: In a moment, Mother.

LOUISE: All right, dear. But there's no need to take everything as if it were one of your Greek tragedies. [LOUISE *goes out into the kitchen.*]

[CLIVE *pours himself a drink.*]

[WALTER *comes out of his room down the stairs, knocks on the door and enters from the hall.*]

WALTER: May I come in? I'm so sorry about the noise; if I had known I would not have played the machine.

CLIVE: Yes, it's a pity. Music always affects him that way. The better the music the stronger the headache. Do you want a drink?

WALTER: No, thank you.

CLIVE: Was that the new record?

WALTER [*Eagerly*]: Yes. It's what's called "high fidelity." You know—more bright and clear.

CLIVE: It sounds like the motto of a matrimonial agency. "High Fidelity Guaranteed."

WALTER: Splendid! It's nice to have you back, Clive. How are you finding Cambridge?

CLIVE: It's all right, I suppose.

WALTER: Is that all? Just all right?

CLIVE [*Suddenly alive*]: No, it's wonderful! Like going to a new country. I suppose one of the thrills of travel is hearing people speak a foreign language. But the marvelous thing about this is, well, hearing them speak my own for the first time.

WALTER: I know.

CLIVE: Pam speaks a few words of it, of course, but it isn't quite enough. Where is she, by the way? Did she go for a walk?

WALTER: I think so, yes. It's a beautiful night.

CLIVE: Oh yes. A night for walks. Pam tripping along so gaily. Father marching along so . . . rightly. And I should be by his side. Or, better still, a pace or two behind. "Clive, to heel, sir. Heel!" Let me introduce myself: "Spaniel Harrington." What's the matter?

WALTER: Nothing.

CLIVE [*Mocking*]: Fathers should not be talked about like that . . . is that it?

WALTER: I think if you forgive me . . .

CLIVE: Well?

WALTER: You have a duty to your father.

CLIVE: Duty? What a very German thing to say. . . . Oh, that's terrible of me, isn't it? Forgive me, I'm not quite sober.

WALTER: I did not mean duty like that. I meant that it seems to me . . . clever children have a duty—to protect their parents who are not so clever.

CLIVE: Protect?

WALTER: I do not put it very well perhaps.

CLIVE: Walter, I want to . . .

[LOUISE *enters from kitchen with a tray of coffee.*]

LOUISE: Hibou! I'm so sorry about the gramophone.

WALTER [*Recovering*]: Oh, it's me to be sorry. . . . How is Mr. Harrington?

LOUISE: It's nothing serious, my dear. He's gone out to clear his head. Well now, we seem to have the house to ourselves. What are we going to do? I know! Walter shall recite some beautiful poetry for us in German.

CLIVE: You don't understand German.

LOUISE: It's not the meaning, it's the sound that counts, dear. And I'm sure this boy will speak it adorably. Most people make it sound like a soda siphon, but when you speak it I'm sure I'll feel exactly what the poet wanted to say—even more than if I actually knew the language and to cope with all those millers' daughters and woodcutters, and people. It's difficult to explain—but you know what I mean.

CLIVE: I don't. I'm going out.

LOUISE: Where?

CLIVE: To the pub.

LOUISE: You can't be serious.

CLIVE: Too vulgar?

LOUISE: Don't be silly, Clive. No, it's just so . . . uncivil, dear. There's plenty of drink in the house if you really need it, though I think you've had quite enough already.

CLIVE [*Gravely*]: You're right, I have. [*To* WALTER.] Excuse me. I'm sure you recite beautifully. [*He makes for the French window.*]

LOUISE [*With a resurgency of desperation*]: But your father asked you if you wanted to go to the pub and you said no.

CLIVE: True.

[*He goes out.* WALTER *stands stiffly, very uncomfortable.*]

LOUISE: Poor boy. I'm afraid he gets very upset down here. He's essentially a town person really, like me. And I get it from my mother. Being French, of course.

[*She wanders to the sofa, turning off the lamp, so that only the standard and a table lamp remain on, creating a warmer atmosphere.*]

Like all Parisians she detested the country. She used to say "Fields are for cows, drawing rooms are for ladies." Of course it sounds better in French. [*She sits on the sofa.*] What's the matter? Are you upset too? Oh, Hibou . . .

WALTER: It is nothing.

LOUISE [*Semihumorously*]: It is something. . . . Has Clive been teasing you? He can be very naughty.

WALTER: I think he is not very happy.

LOUISE: He gets that from me, too.

WALTER [*Sitting: impulsively*]: Mrs. Harrington—is there any help I can give? Anything at all?

LOUISE: I'm not a very happy person either, you know. . . . Well, you can see for yourself. [*Brightly.*] Whatever you do, my dear boy, marry a girl who's your equal. If you can find one. I'm sure it'll be hard! You see when I married I was a very young girl. Believe it or not, I had hardly met anybody outside Bournemouth. My parents didn't consider it proper for me to run about on my own. And when I met Stanley they did everything in their power to arrange a marriage. You see, they weren't exactly very dependable people. My mother was an aristocratic little lady from France who'd never learned to do a thing for herself all her life. My father was equally irresponsible: far too imaginative to make a good solicitor. And when he actually inherited a little money, he lost it all in speculation. "Spec-u-lation." Do you understand, dear?

WALTER: Oh, yes.

LOUISE: Your vocabulary's really amazing. Would you like a cigarette?

WALTER: Thank you, yes. [*He takes it awkwardly.*]

LOUISE: There. Where was I? Oh yes, my parents. Well, they acted in my best interests: I'm sure that's how they saw it. They wanted me to have all the comforts they couldn't give me themselves. . . . [*She warms her hands by the fire.*] Father kept saying it was a—what was the word?—a solid match. That's it. Stan the Solid: that's what I used to call him—as a joke, of course. And really a bit of admiration too, because my family was—well, so *liquid*, if you like. Just the opposite, anyway. No one ever worked consistently or made out budgets. So you see, the man had his fascination. Naturally, father had reservations about the marriage. I mean socially the thing was far from ideal—as I'm sure you realize. His people had always been professional men. Marrying me into the furniture business—[*with a faint smile*]—well, it was rather like going into trade in the old days. Still, I was rather attracted to Stanley. I won't deny it. He had a sort of rugged charm. He was born with nothing, of course, practically an orphan as well. His mother died in childbirth and his father was in the merchant navy. I gather he had a frightful time as a boy—but I will say this: it never showed in his manners. He was always terribly polite. Obviously I was interested in all sorts of things like art and music and poetry which he'd never had time for. But when you're young, things like that don't seem to matter. It's only later—when the first excitement's gone—you start looking a little closer. . . . [*With desperate seriousness; all trace of lightness suddenly going.*] Walter, these last few years have been intolerable. There are times when I listen to you playing; when I go almost mad with sheer pleasure. And yet year after year I've had to kill that side of myself, smother it, stamp it out. . . . Heaven knows, I've tried to be interested in his bridge and his golf club, and his terrible friends. I just can't do it. . . . [*Intimately.*] You know, don't you? You of all people must know.

[WALTER *looks down in embarrassment.*]

I'm sorry. I didn't mean to talk like this. I'm embarrassing you.

WALTER: No.

LOUISE [*Lightly*]: I'm being vulgar, aren't I?

WALTER: You could never be.

LOUISE: Dear Hibou . . . you understand—you understand why I'm still here. The children. At least I could see that *they* weren't stifled too. . . .

[*As he still sits with his head lowered.*]

Do you condemn me?

WALTER: How could I condemn—in your house?

LOUISE [*Wryly*]: I think we can leave hospitality to one side.

WALTER [*Pursuing his own thought*]: In the house you have given me also to live in, so I can sit here by a fire and talk, as if always I had had the right.

LOUISE [*Sympathetically*]: Walter . . .

WALTER: Where I worked before I taught the children for two or three hours, and then was paid by their mothers, and back always to my small room—[*a faint smile*]—with my cooking, which is not so good. You will never know how much I owe to you.

LOUISE: My dear boy. . . . Tell me about your family. Your people in Germany.

[WALTER *stiffens perceptibly into withdrawal.*]

WALTER: There is nothing to tell.

LOUISE: There must be something.

WALTER: I was an orphan. Like Mr. Harrington. My parents died when I was too young to remember them. I was brought up by my uncle and his wife.

LOUISE: Were they good to you?

WALTER [*Noncommittal*]: Very good, yes.

LOUISE: And—that's all you want to say?

WALTER: There is nothing else.

LOUISE: Don't think I'm being inquisitive. . . . It's only that you've come to mean so much to us all in such a very short time. You know that.

WALTER: I do not deserve it.

LOUISE [*Warmly*]: You deserve far more. Far, far more. I knew as soon as I saw you at that terrible cocktail party in Knightsbridge, standing all by yourself in the corner pretending to study the pictures. Do you remember—before even I spoke to you I knew you were something quite exceptional. I remember thinking: such delicate hands . . . and that fair hair—[*touching it*]—it's the hair of a poet. He'll have a soft voice that stammers a little from nervousness, and a lovely Viennese accent. . . .

WALTER [*Stiffly*]: I am not Viennese, you know. I am German.

LOUISE: Well, it's not so very different. . . .

WALTER [*Dogged*]: I am German. This is not so poetic . . . even the name . . . I hate.

LOUISE [*A little intimidated by the darkness in him*]: But Hibou, there's good and bad in all countries—surely?

WALTER [*Gently*]: You are too good to understand what I mean. I know how they seem to you, the Germans: so kind and quaint. Like you yourself said: millers' daughters and woodcutters. . . . But they can be monsters.

LOUISE [*Prepared to mock him*]: Really now—

WALTER: Yes! . . .

[*He gets up sharply and moves away. He is plainly distressed.* LOUISE *looks at him curiously.*]

LOUISE: You know, even in England, we're not all angels.

WALTER: Yes, angels to me! Because this to me is Paradise.

LOUISE: How charming you are.

WALTER [*With increasing heat*]: No, I am sincere. Here in England most people *want* to do what's good. Where I was born this is not true. They want only power. . . . They are a people that is enraged by equality. It needs always to be ashamed, to breathe in shame—like oxygen—to go on living. Because deeper than everything else they want to be hated. From this they can believe they are giants, even in chains. . . . [*Recovering.*] I'm sorry. It's difficult to talk about.

LOUISE: Anything one feels deeply about is hard to speak of, my dear.

WALTER: One thing I know: I will never go back. Soon I'll be a British subject.

LOUISE: You really want to stay here.

WALTER: If you had seen what I have, you would know why I call it Paradise.

LOUISE: I can see for myself how you've suffered. It's in your face. . . . [*Extending her hand to him.*] Walter. . . .

[*He approaches her slowly, takes her hand, and sits down beside her again. He is still plainly upset.* LOUISE *speaks very calmly.*]

You mustn't torment yourself like this. It's not good for you. You're among friends now. People who want to help you. People who love you. . . . Doesn't that make a difference?

[*Impulsively he bends and kisses her hands.*]

WALTER: You are so good! So good, good. . . .

[*Suddenly she takes his head in her hands and holds it close to her.*]

LOUISE [*Tenderly*]: Oh, my dear . . . you make me feel ashamed.

[CLIVE *comes abruptly in through the French window. He stares at them fascinated.*]

It's been so long since anyone has said things like this to me.

[CLIVE *bangs a chair hard against the table.*]

Jou-jou!

[*She rises and tries to recover her composure.*]

Have you had a nice walk? Did you see Pam?

[CLIVE *remains where he is, still staring at his mother.*]

You know, it's absurdly late for her to be walking alone. Are you sure you didn't see her? She's probably gone over to that dreadful friend of hers, Mary whatever-her-name-is. I think it's high time she found another friend, don't you?

[*As* CLIVE *goes on staring, her last remnant of poise deserts her.*]

Perhaps she's upstairs after all. She may have come in by the front door. I'll just go up and see. . . .

[*She leaves the room and goes quickly upstairs to her own room. All the while the two boys have stayed quite still,* WALTER *on the sofa,* CLIVE *by the door. Now* CLIVE *goes slowly over to* WALTER *and fingers his disheveled hair. He is evidently fairly drunk, but alcohol does not impair his speech. Rather it gives it energy and turns of speed. Now he is more disturbed than he himself is aware.*]

WALTER: Clive, what is the matter? Why are you looking at me like that?

CLIVE: Hair is being worn disheveled this year. The Medusa style. What would have happened if Medusa had looked in a mirror? Are monsters immune against their own fatal charms? . . . Observe, please, the subtle and dialectical nature of my mind. It's the French in me, you understand. An inheritance from my very French, very aristocratic ancestors. Perhaps you've been hearing about them. In reality, I regret to say, they weren't as aristocratic as all that. My great-grandpa, despite any impression to the contrary, did not actually grant humble petitions from his bedside: merely industrial patents from a run-down little office near the Louvre. The salary was so small that the family would have died of starvation if Hélène, my grandmother, hadn't met an English solicitor—on a cycling tour of the Loire—married him, and exchanged Brunoy for Bournemouth. Let us therefore not gasp too excitedly at the loftiness of Mother's family tree. Unbeknown to Father, it has, as you see, roots of clay. Still, they *are* French roots. I even have them in me. For example—my mother's name for me—Jou-jou. Toy. More accurately in this case, ornament.

[WALTER *remains silent. As he talks on, with increasing bitterness,* CLIVE *wanders aimlessly round the room.*]

Being French, you know, Mother imagines she's real ormolu in a sitting room of plaster gilt. She suffers from what I might call a plaster-gilt complex, if you see what I mean. To her the whole world is irredeemably plebeian—especially Father. The rift you may detect between them is the difference between the salon and the saloon. At least that's what she'd have you believe. . . . I won't deny that she's only really at home in the salon, but then where else can you be so continuously dishonest?

WALTER [*Stung into speech*]: Please—

CLIVE: Yes?

WALTER: I do not wish to hear this. It's not right.

CLIVE: Ah—you do not wish! The young *charming* tutor does not wish. . . . So delicate, so Old World! A tutor and his employer by the fireside. Paris calling to Vienna. The waltz plays on the deserted boulevard: Europe crumbles. Oh, the *charm* of it! . . . Do let's salvage what we can. If we can't have a château in Brittany, then we *can* have a country place in Suffolk, which is almost as desolate but rather more convenient. If we can't install scholars in our library, because we haven't got a library, since nobody reads in our house, why, then, the least we can do is get in a dear gentle tutor for the girl. Someone with tone, of course; nothing grubby from the Polytechnic. . . . You see, we're specialists in delicacy.

WALTER: I do not understand you.

CLIVE: What, our delicacy?

WALTER: Why you talk like this.

CLIVE: Because I'm not really so damned delicate after all. Because actually, if you want to know, I'm getting less bloody delicate all the time.

WALTER [*Rising*]: I do not think I can listen to any more.

CLIVE: Where are you going?

WALTER: If you had come from Europe, if you had been taken in, as I was—alone—

CLIVE: Taken in! Taken in is right!

WALTER: Excuse me.

CLIVE [*Going after him*]: Or no—taken up! Like a fashion. Or an ornament; a piece of Dresden, a dear little Dresden owl.

[*He pushes him down into the armchair and leans over him, staring intensely into his face. A long pause.* CLIVE *becomes aware of his position and draws back a little.*]

And believe me, love, sooner or later, like any other valuable possession, you will be used. I know this family, let me tell you. If you can't help one of us score a point over the others—you've no claim on our notice. Oh, my dear fellow—

[*The front door slams.* PAMELA *comes in and runs upstairs.*]

LOUISE [*Calling*]: Pam, is that you?

[*She appears on the landing.* CLIVE *opens the door and stands in an attitude of listening, stockstill.* WALTER *watches him uncertainly.*]

PAMELA [*Breathlessly*]: Yes. It's all me!

LOUISE: It's rather late, dear. I wish you'd take your walks earlier.

PAMELA [*Taking off her coat*]: I'm sorry.

LOUISE: Where did you go?

PAMELA: Over to Mary's. You know, she is the absolute best. She tells the funniest stories in the world. D'you know what happened? Last week Ted—that's her brother—took his daughter to the ballet. She's just eight, and it was a sort of extra birthday present. Well, she watched all these girls going up on their toes—[*illustrates*]—and dancing about—and you know what she said at the end? "Daddy, why don't they just get taller girls?" [LOUISE *is unamused.*] Don't you think that's funny?

LOUISE: Yes, dear, very funny. [*She kisses her daughter.*] Good night, dear.

PAMELA: Good night, mother.

[*She goes into the schoolroom and then into her own room, closing the door.* LOUISE *looks after her for a moment, then returns to her room.* CLIVE *closes the door again.*]

CLIVE [*Keeping still and quiet: to himself*]: She's the only one who's free, with her private star of Grace. . . . It's a marvelous dispensation: to escape one's inheritance. [*To* WALTER.] I don't mean you. . . . Walter, you're one of the best people who ever came into our house. You think I don't know how lonely you were before you came here. You're wrong. I can smell your loneliness. . . . You see, I've only one real talent; being able to see what's true, and just what isn't. And that's an awful thing to have. [*With sudden animation.*] Come away with me.

WALTER [*Startled*]: What? Come away?

CLIVE: Look—in four weeks my term ends. We could go somewhere; to the West Country, if you like. Wells Cathedral is the most astonishing thing in England. It's like walking down the throat of a whale: a skeleton whale, with the vertebrae showing. No one will be there at Christmas. Cheddar Gorge without a single charabanc! That's a bus, you know. . . .

WALTER: Yes, I know!

CLIVE: Please say yes. . . . You'd love it.

WALTER [*With a shy smile*]: I'm sorry. Christmas is a family time. For so long I have missed it. This year I wish very much to pass it here.

CLIVE [*Insistently*]: Well, afterwards. I could wait.

WALTER [*Awkwardly: his whole stance awkward*]: I'm afraid it's not possible. My lessons, you see. I have been paid already to the end of January.

CLIVE: So what? Everyone takes Christmas off.

WALTER: I do not think I can go away just now.

CLIVE: Because you've been paid?

WALTER: No. . . .

CLIVE: Then why?

WALTER: I—I have an obligation.

CLIVE: To my mother?

WALTER: Yes. An obligation.

CLIVE: Is that what you call it—obligation? Well, doff my plumed hat! Gallant Walter Langer. . . . The Cavalier Tutor to his Mistress! Or do I mean the Cavalier Teuton? . . . Don't look so startled. Proper cavaliers have only figurative mistresses.

[*He turns away, swept into frantic remorse. As before, he holds himself very stiffly.*]

This is quite beyond anything, isn't it? [*With the quietness of desperation.*] If you came away with me, it would be for my sake—not yours. I need a friend so badly.

WALTER [*As stiff himself*]: You are unhappy. I am sorry.

CLIVE [*The bitterness returning*]: Is that all you can say? "I'm sorry." "I regret." Such an awkward position I put you in, don't I? The poor little immigrant, careful not to offend. So very sensitive. [*With sudden fury.*] When in hell are you going to stop trading on your helplessness—offering yourself all day to be petted and stroked? Yes, just like I do! Okay, you're a pet. You've got an irresistible accent. You make me sick.

WALTER: Excuse me.

[*He makes for the door.* CLIVE *seeks to detain him, clumsily.*]

CLIVE: Walter, Walter, I didn't—please—

[WALTER *leaves the room and goes up to his own.* CLIVE *stands looking at the closed door.*]

[*Dully.*] Please!

[*Slowly he turns away from it and goes eventually to the bottle of whisky.* WALTER *reaches the landing.* PAMELA *comes out of her room in her nightdress, on her way to the bathroom.*]

PAMELA: Hello? Oh, it's you.

WALTER: Yes.

PAMELA: Is there anything wrong?

WALTER: No.

PAMELA: You look as if they were going to cut off your head in the morning.

WALTER [*Smiling, with effort*]: Do I? . . . You were walking?

PAMELA: Yes. Mary and I discovered a new place in the woods, with a huge stream you can dam up. I don't suppose it's anything compared with your river, the one you could skate on.

WALTER: You show it to me tomorrow.

PAMELA: Yes. [*Pulling out her nightdress.*] Are you shocked because I'm in my this?

WALTER: Yes. Very.

PAMELA: Then you'd better leave, sir. I'm on my way to the bathroom and I've no wish to cause you embarrassment.

[*He bows. She curtsies.*]

Good night.

WALTER: Good night.

[*He goes into his own room and shuts the door. She looks after him for a second and blows him a kiss before passing on to her bath.*
*Downstairs* CLIVE *is pouring out another drink.* STANLEY *comes in through the front door, takes off his overcoat, hangs it up in the hall and comes into the living room.* CLIVE *puts down the glass guiltily.*]

STANLEY: What are you doing?

CLIVE: Stealing your drink.

STANLEY: You don't have to steal from me, Clive. You're old enough to take a drink if you want one. Where's your mother?

CLIVE: I don't know—upstairs. . . .

STANLEY [*Expansively*]: You ought to have come with me to Benton's. We went over to the club. Jolly nice crowd there. The sort of fellows *you* ought to be mixing with. There was a chap there in publishing. You'd have been interested. . . . [*Pause.*] Clive, I've told you before, in this world you want to get in with the people who matter. But you've got to make an effort, my boy. Make yourself a bit popular. You see? And you're not going to do that sitting here drinking by yourself. Are you?

CLIVE [*Low*]: No, I suppose not.

STANLEY: What d'you want to do it for anyway?

CLIVE [*Shrugging*]: I don't know.

STANLEY: Well, it's damn silly and it's not normal. If you want to drink—drink with others. Everyone likes a drink. You come over to the club with me, you'll soon find that out. I'll make you a member. You'll get in with them in a jiffy if you'll only try.

CLIVE: Yes. [*Pause.*] Well . . . I think I'll go to bed now.

STANLEY [*As* CLIVE *makes for the door*]: Just a minute. What's the matter? Aren't they good enough for you? Is that it?

CLIVE [*Gently*]: No, of course it isn't.

STANLEY: Then what?

CLIVE [*Gaining courage*]: Well, all this stuff—right people, wrong people—people who matter. It's all so meaningless.

STANLEY: It's not a bit meaningless.

CLIVE: Well, all right, they matter! But what can I say to them if they don't matter to *me?* Look, you just can't talk about people in that way. It's unreal—idiotic. As far as I'm concerned one of the few people who really matters to me in Cambridge is an Indian.

STANLEY: Well, there's nothing wrong in that. What's his father? A rajah or something?

CLIVE: His father runs a cake shop in Bombay.

STANLEY: Well, what sort of boy is he? What's he like?

CLIVE: He's completely still. . . . I don't mean he doesn't move. I mean that deep down inside him there's a sort of happy stillness, that makes all our family rows and raised voices here seem like a kind of—blasphemy almost. That's why he matters—because he loves living so much. Because he understands birds and makes shadow puppets out of cardboard, and loves Ella Fitzgerald, and Vivaldi, and Lewis Carroll; and because he plays chess like a devil and makes the best prawn curry in the world. And this is him. Well, parts of him. Bits of him.

STANLEY [*Bewildered and impatient*]: Well, of course I'm glad you've got some nice friends.

CLIVE [*Sharp*]: Don't do that.

STANLEY: What?

CLIVE: Patronize. It's just too much.

STANLEY: I'm not patronizing you, Clive.

CLIVE: Oh yes, you are. That's precisely what you're doing.

STANLEY: That's very unfair.

CLIVE [*Working himself into a deep rage*]: Precisely. Precisely! "I'm very glad you have some nice chums, Clive. I did too at your age." . . . These aren't my little play pals, Father. They're important people. Important to me.

STANLEY: Did I say they weren't?

[PAMELA *returns from the bath. She listens for a brief moment in the schoolroom to her brother's raised voice, then goes on into her room.*]

CLIVE [*Frantic*]: Important! It is important they should be alive. Every person they meet should be altered by them, or at least remember them with terrific—terrific excitement. That's an important person. Can't you understand?

STANLEY [*Crushingly*]: No, Clive. I'm afraid I don't. I don't understand you at all.

[*A slight pause.* CLIVE *subsides. When he speaks again it is to renew the attack in a colder and more accusing voice.*]

CLIVE: You're proud of it too.

STANLEY [*Getting angry*]: What now?

CLIVE: That you don't understand me at all. Almost as if it defined you. "I'm the Man Who Doesn't Understand!" [*Furiously.*] Has it ever occurred to you that *I* don't understand *you?* No. Of course not! Because you're the one who does the understanding around here—or, rather, fails to. What work did you ever put in to be able to understand anybody?

STANLEY: I think you'd better go to bed.

[*For a moment* CLIVE *seems ready to obey. Then*]:

CLIVE: I'll go to bed when I'm good and ready! . . . D'you think it falls into your lap—some sort of a grace that enters you when you become a father?

STANLEY: You're drunk.

CLIVE: Yes, you think you can treat me like a child! But *you* don't even know the right way to treat a child. Because a child is private and important and *itself*. Not an extension of you, any more than I am.

[*He falls quiet, dead quiet—as if explaining something very difficult. His speech slows and his face betrays an almost obsessed sincerity as he sits.*]

I am myself. Myself. Myself. You think of me only as what I might become. What I might make of myself. But I am myself now—with every breath I take, every blink of the eyelash. The taste of a chestnut or a strawberry on my tongue is me. The smell of my skin is me. The trees and sofas that I see with my own eyes are me. And you should want to become me and see them as I see them. But we can never exchange. Feelings don't *unite* us, don't you see? They keep us apart. And words don't help because they're unreal. We live away in our skins from minute to minute, feeling everything quite differently, and any one minute's just as true about us as any other. Yes, I'm drunk. You make me drunk.

[*Pause.*]

STANLEY: I do?

CLIVE [*Losing heart*]: You and everything. . . .

STANLEY: What are you talking about?

CLIVE: Nothing. It doesn't matter. Everything stays as it is.

STANLEY: Well—

CLIVE [*With a final spurt of energy*]: I'm talking about *care*. Taking care. Care of people you want to know. Not just doing your best for them, and hoping the best for them. I mean you've got to care for them *as they are*, from blink to blink. . . . Don't you see? The—the renewing of your cells every day makes you a sacred object, or it should do, in the eyes of people who care for you. It's far more important than whether you speculate in fish or furniture. Because what you do in the world and so on isn't important at all, not in the slightest, compared with what you look like and sound like and feel like as the minutes go by. That's why a question like "What are you going to be?" is quite unreal. Do you see?

[*A long pause.*]

STANLEY: Well, that's given me something to think about, old boy. Why don't we go on with it in the morning? What?

[CLIVE *does not reply.* STANLEY *goes to the door.*]

Good night, then. . . . I said good night, Clive.

[*Still* CLIVE *takes no notice.* STANLEY *shrugs and leaves the room, turning out the lights, so that only the glow of the fire and one lamp remain. He goes slowly upstairs.*

*For a moment* CLIVE *remains where he is, in a trance of private depression. Then slowly he rises and crosses to the sofa. On the coffee table are* WALTER'S *spectacles in their case. He picks them up and takes them out. He begins to cry, terribly, almost silently. Up on the landing* STANLEY *hesitates, conscious of his failure. He shakes his head and returns on impulse downstairs.*]

Don't forget to turn off the fire. . . .

[CLIVE *makes an effort to control himself and fails.* STANLEY *goes to him.*]

STANLEY: What is it, boy? What's the matter?

[CLIVE *shakes his head "No."*]

What? Come on, now. Out with it. What's the matter—can't you tell me? That's a silly attitude to take, isn't it? After all, I'm your father. It's what I'm here for.

[CLIVE *shies away from the thought of contact as* STANLEY *makes to touch his arm.*]

Here! There's something really wrong, isn't there?

CLIVE [*Whispering*]: No.

STANLEY: Something's happened.

CLIVE: No. . . .

STANLEY: When?

[CLIVE *goes on shaking his head.*]

While I was out? That's it, isn't it? While I was out.

CLIVE: No!

STANLEY: What was it? Did your mother say something? [*He sees the spectacles.*] Was it something to do with Walter? Yes!

[*He snatches the spectacles as* CLIVE *breaks free from him and moves sharply away.*]

That's it, isn't it? Well, what? What happened with Walter?

CLIVE [*Frightened*]: I don't know. I don't know.

STANLEY [*Relentlessly*]: What happened with Walter? Answer me!

[CLIVE *bolts away to the door, then suddenly he changes his mind, closes it, comes back into the room and faces his father.*]

CLIVE [*Very quiet*]: It was Mother.

STANLEY: What?

CLIVE: There on the sofa. I saw them. I came in and there they were. The light was turned down. They were kissing. *Kissing!* She was half undressed, and he was kissing her, on the mouth. On the breasts. Kissing . . .

[STANLEY *hits him. He falls on the sofa.*]

[*Hard.*] And before that, I think the light had been turned off.

[STANLEY *stares at him, stunned. Nervelessly he drops the spectacles into the armchair.*]

Department of Just Deserts?

CURTAIN

## ACT TWO

### SCENE 1

*The following morning. Sunday. A bright, cold day.*

WALTER *and* PAMELA *are sitting at the breakfast table. The girl, in her dressing gown, is reading one of the better Sunday papers.*

PAMELA: Walter, what does "salacious"mean?

WALTER: What word?

PAMELA: Salacious—it's in this article.

WALTER: Show me. [*Takes paper.*] Where are my glasses? [*He sees them in the armchair where* STANLEY *dropped them the night before.*] Ah. Now. Salacious. . . . Yes. It means "wise."

PAMELA: Does it? I suppose I should have guessed. You ought to teach English.

WALTER: I wouldn't dare.

PAMELA: Oh, phooey. I'm sure you'd be miles better than the man at my last school. Anyway, he was a Dutchman. [*Taking back the paper.*] Mother says this is the only Sunday paper she'll have in the house. I think it's mean of her. Everyone else has the popular ones with pictures of rapes. . . .

[LOUISE *comes in with a tray from the kitchen.* WALTER *immediately stands.*]

LOUISE: Did you enjoy the kippers?

WALTER: Yes, they were splendid, thank you.

LOUISE: Do sit down, my dear.

[*He does so.*]

PAMELA: Mother, why can't we have Sunday papers with sexy pictures in?

LOUISE [*Loading the tray with used plates*]: Because they're vulgar, and give you a distorted view of life.

PAMELA: I don't mind.

LOUISE: Well, I do. Where's Clive?

PAMELA: Not down yet.

LOUISE: Really, you children are the limit. I just don't see why you can't all have your breakfast together. It's late enough, heaven knows. [*Lifting the tray.*] Pamela, you'd better hurry up and finish dressing if you're going riding.

[*She goes back to the kitchen,* WALTER *holding open the door for her.*]

PAMELA: Have you ever gone riding?

WALTER [*Coming back to the table and sitting*]: No.

PAMELA: It's the best, absolutely. What games did you play in Germany?

WALTER: I—I used to walk.

PAMELA: You mean on hiking parties, all dressed up in those leather shorts?

WALTER: No. By myself. I liked it better.

PAMELA [*Impulsively*]: Are you happy here? Are you really, really happy?

WALTER: Of course.

PAMELA: Who do you like best?

WALTER: You.

PAMELA: No, seriously.

WALTER: I like you all. You and your mother . . .

PAMELA: And Clive?

WALTER: Of course and Clive. I like him very much. I'm only sorry he is so unhappy.

PAMELA: Is he very unhappy?

WALTER: I think so, yes.

PAMELA: That's because he was spoiled when he was young.

WALTER: Spoiled?

PAMELA: You know—to spoil someone. Like damage.

WALTER: Oh, damage: yes! . . .

PAMELA [*Down right; drinking her coffee*]: I'm sure he ought to get married.

WALTER: Oh, he's so young!

PAMELA: For some people it's the best thing. You must help him find a girl.

WALTER: Has he not had friendships with girls before?

PAMELA [*In her "affected" voice*]: Not even acquaintanceships, my dear. [*Normal.*] Except one: a girl called Peggy-Ann who worked in the tobacconist's when we were in the Isle of Wight. She used to wear leopard-skin trousers and great sort of brass bells in her ears. Clive said they used to go down on the beach and neck, but I bet he was just bragging. So you see, you've got to help him. I'm sure you know hundreds of girls.

WALTER [*Amused*]: Oh yes. What kind would you suggest?

PAMELA: Someone who'll pay him lots of attention. At home, everyone keeps on at him but no one really takes any notice of him. [*Brightly.*] Clive spends his whole time not being listened to.

WALTER: His mother listens, doesn't she?

PAMELA: Not really listens, no. . . . Well, of course you can't expect her to. No mother ever really listens to her children. It's not done.

WALTER: You seem to know a lot about it.

PAMELA: Yes, I do. Poor Clive. You know, they really only use him to help them when they're rowing. [*Directly.*] Can you understand why they row?

WALTER: I think everyone has quarrels.

PAMELA: Yes, but this is different. With Mother and Daddy the row is never really *about*—well, what they're quarreling about. I mean . . . behind what they say you can feel—well, that Mother did this in the past, and Daddy did that. I don't mean anything *particular*. . . . [*She stops, confused.*] Oh dear . . . I think marriage is a very difficult subject, don't you?

WALTER [*Humorously; he is a little uncomfortable*]: You don't take your exam in it till you're a little older.

PAMELA [*Pursuing her own thought*]: I mean, who begins things? Do you see?

WALTER: Please, Pamela—

PAMELA: I know Mother's frightful to him about culture, and uses music and things to keep him out—which is terrible. But isn't that just because *he* made *her* keep out of things when they were first married? You know he wouldn't even let her go to concerts and theaters although she was dying to, and once he threw a picture she'd bought into the dustbin; one of those modern things, all squiggles and blobs. [*Gestures*] . . . But then, mightn't *that* just have been because being brought up by himself he was afriad of making a fool of himself. Oh, poor Daddy . . . poor Mother, too. [*To him, brightly.*] You know, I shouldn't wonder if parents don't turn out to be my hobby when I grow up.

[STANLEY *appears on the landing and descends the stairs.*]

WALTER [*Warmly*]: You have a wonderful mother, you know.

PAMELA: Yes, I suppose so.

WALTER: Only suppose?

PAMELA: People who make you feel stupid are always called wonderful.

[STANLEY *comes into the living room. He looks tired and strained.*]

Good morning, Daddy.

STANLEY [*Kissing her*]: Morning, dear.

[*He stares at* WALTER *with a curious unwilling stare.* WALTER *rises rather awkwardly.*]

WALTER: Good morning, sir.

PAMELA: What's wrong? Aren't you feeling well?

[*He looks at her fixedly, almost unseeingly; then sits slowly down at the table.* LOUISE *comes in from the kitchen, wearing an apron.*]

LOUISE: Stanley . . . ? [*Entering.*] You might let me know when you come down. Walter, dear, will you come and get Mr. Harrington's cereal for me?

WALTER [*Eager to help*]: Of course, Mrs. Harrington.

[*She goes into the kitchen again.*]

I hope your headache is better this morning, sir.

[*He exits to kitchen.* STANLEY *nods, apparently unable to speak.*]

PAMELA: You aren't wearing your lovely coat.

STANLEY: No. I'm not going shooting today, darling, it's Sunday.

PAMELA: Well, come riding with me, then.

STANLEY [*Wrapped in himself*]: No. . . . Not today. I . . . just want to take things quiet.

PAMELA [*Mischievously*]: You're getting old.

[*He looks at her searchingly.*]

STANLEY: Why don't you ever learn to tie that ribbon? Come here.

[*She inclines her head. He fixes the ribbon.*]

Has Clive come down yet?

PAMELA: No, the lazy pig. You were talking to him late last night, weren't you? I could hear you from upstairs. Well, really, it seemed more like Clive was talking to you.

[WALTER *reappears, smiling, with porridge, a napkin over his arm.*]

WALTER [*Placing it smartly before* STANLEY *and acting the waiter for* PAMELA *behind his back*]: Mrs. Harrington asks would you prefer eggs or kippers?

STANLEY [*Quietly*]: Nothing.

PAMELA: Daddy, you must have something.

STANLEY: Don't fuss, Pam, please. [*Curtly, to* WALTER.] Nothing.

WALTER [*With a half-bow*]: Yes, sir.

[*He goes back to the kitchen, deflated, his smile gone.*]

PAMELA: He'd make a wonderful waiter, wouldn't he? How did you like

Clive talking to you man to man? [*Brightly.*] He must have been drunk.

STANLEY: Why do you say that?

PAMELA: Because if he wasn't, he never would have. Not properly, anyway. He'd be too nervous.

[*He looks at her sharply.*]

That's because you like him to answer questions all the time, and he hates to.

STANLEY: Why?

PAMELA: I don't know. I suppose he's just not the answering type. D'you know he even has a dream about you?

STANLEY: Clive?

PAMELA: Yes. He gets it quite often, so he must think an awful lot about you. You ought to be flattered, though it's not exactly what I'd call a flattering dream. . . . [*Recounting it carefully, with increasing drama.*] Apparently, he's always in bed lying down under thick blankets. Near him is a window and he can see into a big garden all covered in snow. It's freezing so hard he can hear twigs snapping on the trees. Then suddenly you appear, coming slowly over the snow toward him—crunch . . . crunch . . . crunch. You disappear inside the house and he can hear you coming upstairs—crunch . . . crunch . . . and along the passage to his bedroom. Then the door slowly opens and you come in, and cross the room to see if he's asleep. So while you stand there he pretends to be asleep as asleep can be, except that sometimes he starts shivering, which spoils the effect. Then you start taking off the blankets one by one. Clive says there must be about ten blankets on the bed, and with each one you take off he gets colder and colder. Usually he wakes up with all his bedclothes on the floor. Isn't that the silliest dream you ever heard . . . ? I told him the next time he heard you coming upstairs he was to wait till you came up to the bed, then sit bolt upright and shout "Go to hell!"

[STANLEY *has listened to this impassively but with the greatest attention. He still sits involved in his own silent conflict as* LOUISE *returns from the kitchen.*]

LOUISE [*To* PAMELA]: Pamela! Are you still here? You're going to be very late for your ride. And I've told you before, unpunctuality is just bad breeding.

[WALTER *enters.*]

PAMELA [*To* WALTER]: I've decided you'd make the most wonderful waiter. . . .

LOUISE [*Shocked*]: Pamela! What a thing to say.

PAMELA: Well, he would. Can't you just see him bowing to old ladies with Pekineses?

LOUISE: Stop it, Pamela. That's very rude. A waiter! Can't you think of anything else for Walter to be? I only hope one day you'll have a tiny part of his education [*To* WALTER.] and a few of his manners. [*To* PAMELA.] Now hurry up and get dressed.

[WALTER *goes out and upstairs into the schoolroom to get a book.*]

Your picnic's all ready.

PAMELA: Daddy, can I borrow your red jacket? Please say yes.

STANLEY [*Quiet*]: Of course—it'll be a bit big, though, won't it?

PAMELA: Nonsense—I shall wear it as a cape. Of course I won't look half so good in it as you do.

STANLEY: Enjoy the ride.

PAMELA [*Intimately*]: You bet.

LOUISE: And tell Clive from me, if he's not down right away he won't get any breakfast.

[PAMELA *goes out and upstairs, getting her riding cap and crop from the hall as she passes.*]

Stanley, what are you sitting there for? I hear you didn't want any cooked breakfast. And you haven't even touched your cereal. That's absurd. You must have something to eat. [*He stares now at her.*] What's the matter? Did you have too much to drink last night or something?

[*He rises and goes to the French window.*]

Stanley . . .

[*Abruptly he goes into the garden.* LOUISE *stares after him in astonishment. She sits down at the table.*]

[PAMELA *emerges on the landing.*]

PAMELA: Walter?

WALTER [*Coming from the schoolroom and joining her on the landing*]: Hello?

PAMELA: I wasn't really rude just now, was I?

WALTER: No, of course not. As a matter of fact, I was a waiter once, for a short time in Berlin. But they threw me out.

PAMELA: Why?

WALTER: No dignity. That's what they said.

PAMELA: How ridiculous. You're the most dignified man I ever met. [*Running off to* CLIVE'S *door and banging on it.*] Clive! Wake up, wake up, whoever you are! Into your slippers, go down for your kippers . . . ! Wake up, wake up—

[*She returns, carrying the hunting jacket; after a pause,* CLIVE *follows, wearing sports coat and slacks. He is tousled and with a slight hangover. He bows, Oriental fashion.*]

CLIVE: Good morning.

PAMELA [*Bowing also; in the act at once*]: Salaams. A thousand welcomes, O handsome slave boy, mine eyes rejoice in the sight of you! Dance for me, my little pomegranate! Madden me with desire!

CLIVE: Drop dead! [*To* WALTER.] Good morning. [*To* PAMELA.] Get him to do it.

WALTER: Excuse me. I think I work a little . . .

[*He dives into his room and slams the door.*]

CLIVE: Where is everybody?

PAMELA: Downstairs. You'd better go down.

[CLIVE *groans.*]

You look a bit green. Do you want a fizzy?

CLIVE: No, thanks.

PAMELA: Well, salaams.

CLIVE: Salaams.

[*She runs off into her room.* CLIVE *goes slowly downstairs, where* LOUISE *still sits at the table. He is clearly reluctant to go.*]

LOUISE: You slept late. Perhaps you had a little too much to drink last night, too.

[*He does not reply.*]

There's kippers or eggs.

CLIVE: No, thank you. Is there any coffee?

LOUISE: Now what is this? First your father and now you.

CLIVE: Where is he?

LOUISE: Outside.

CLIVE [*Perplexed*]: Where?

LOUISE: In the garden. Well—isn't he?

CLIVE [*Looking out*]: Yes. He's sitting down under the apple tree.

LOUISE: *Sitting?* In this weather? Without an overcoat? He'll catch his death. Tell him to come in at once.

CLIVE: Perhaps he prefers it outside.

LOUISE: Don't be ridiculous, Clive. The man must be mad, sitting out there on a freezing morning like this. [*Advancing to the French window.*] What on earth he thinks he's doing, I can't imagine.

CLIVE [*Sharply*]: Leave him alone!

LOUISE [*Amazed*]: Are you talking to me?

CLIVE [*Firmly; almost surprised at himself*]: Leave him alone.

LOUISE: Are you sure you're feeling all right?

CLIVE: I—I'm sorry.

LOUISE: So you should be. That was very, very ill bred.

CLIVE [*Whispering*]: Not really done?

LOUISE: Clive, I don't understand you this morning. I really don't.

[*He smiles, delighted, to himself.*]

CLIVE [*French accent*]: *Votre Majesté* should not worry 'erself about eet. It makes, as the Eenglish say, no nevaire mind. My Empress!

[*He extends his hand in salutation. His mother, made uncertain by the mockery in his manner, warily allows her own to be taken and kissed. At the same moment the warm slow movement of the Brahms* Symphony *is heard from* WALTER'S *room. Suddenly she draws him to her—he allows himself to be drawn—and embraces him. A brief instant of great intimacy recurs, as it happened in the first scene.*]

LOUISE: Jou-jou . . . !

CLIVE: *Maman* . . . !

LOUISE: *Mon petit* Cossack. *Mon petit, petit* . . . Silly boy.

[*She holds him tenderly, in the position of subservience he took up before his Empress, only now very close to her. His back is to the audience, and from his inclined posture she can fondle his head.*]

D'you think I'm so stupid I don't know what's wrong? D'you think I can't see for myself . . . ? We're a little bit jealous, aren't we?

[*He moves sharply, but she continues to hold him.*]

As if you didn't always come first. You know that. Don't you?

[*He nods, stiff now with reluctance.*]

Then it's so ridiculous, isn't it, to be jealous? And of whom? A poor lonely boy with no people of his own to care for him, all by himself in a foreign country. Really, Jou-jou, you ought to be ashamed. Let's say no more about it. I want you always to be happy—remember?

[*He nods again.*]

There. [*She releases him.*] Now, let me cook you some breakfast. You could eat an egg, couldn't you?

CLIVE [*Low*]: I suppose so.

LOUISE: Good. Come on then. You finish your coffee while I get started. [*She looks at him tenderly and kisses him on the forehead.*] Silly . . .

[*She goes out into the kitchen.*]

CLIVE [*With a sort of bitter disgust; to himself*]: On waves of sympathy. On waves . . . !

[*He rises, turns to clear the table—then glances through the window and bolts quickly for the kitchen door.*

STANLEY *comes in from the garden. He stands irresolute, as if searching for something he cannot find, his eyes blank, his whole manner distracted. The Brahms* Symphony *plays on. Unseen,* CLIVE *watches him through the kitchen door. Then, suddenly, he leaves the room and the house, banging the front door behind him.*

*The door of* PAMELA'S *bedroom opens after a moment, and she comes into the schoolroom, dressed in riding clothes, the hunting jacket on her arm. She goes out of the schoolroom and starts downstairs with her picnic box and thermos. She misses her footing and falls in an undignified heap on the landing.*]

PAMELA: Damn! Damn! Damn!

[*Music stops.* WALTER *comes rushing out, startled by the great crash. At the same time,* LOUISE *appears at the kitchen door.*]

LOUISE [*Calling up*]: Pamela! Are you all right? What on earth's that noise?

WALTER: What's the matter, Pamela? I help you . . .

[*He helps her solicitously to her feet.*]

Are you hurt?

PAMELA [*Indignant at being found like this*]: Of course not!

WALTER: What happened?

PAMELA: I tripped and fell. I knew I would.

LOUISE [*Running upstairs*]: Pamela!

PAMELA: I'm all right—don't fuss, Mother. Anyone would think I was dying. [*Feeling her head.*] Ow!

WALTER: See? You bumped your head.

PAMELA [*Witheringly*]: When you fall down, you must bump something. It's usual.

WALTER: I look.

PAMELA: No!

[LOUISE *arrives on the landing.*]

LOUISE: My darling, are you all right . . . ?

PAMELA [*Cool*]: Perfectly, thank you.

WALTER [*Concerned*]: She fell. I think you should look on her head.

PAMELA: Fuss, fuss, fuss.

LOUISE [*With a faint touch of hauteur*]: Thank you, Walter. You can leave her to me, now.

WALTER: Yes, Mrs. Harrington. Of course.

[*He gives his half-bow and goes back into his own room.*]

LOUISE [*Examining her daughter's head now*]: Let me see. . . . Go on upstairs. Does it hurt? [*She takes her daughter into the schoolroom.*]

PAMELA: No, it doesn't.

LOUISE: You say that as if you wanted it to. What on earth were you doing?

PAMELA [*Exasperated*]: Nothing. I just fell. And that stupid Walter has to come in and pick me up as if I was a chandelier or something. Holding me that way.

LOUISE [*Carefully*]: What way, darling?

PAMELA: Well, trying to carry me, as if I was a baby.

LOUISE: But he was only trying to help, wasn't he?

PAMELA [*Angrily*]: I think he's just plain soppy.

LOUISE: Because he was worried about you?

PAMELA: Oh, Mother, for heaven's sake! You don't understand anything. . . . It's just so *undignified,* can't you see? It shows no *respect* for you. I mean, if you're two years old it's all right to pick you off floors that way, and even then it's an invasion of your privacy. If children of two could speak, d'you know what they'd say? "Why can't you keep your filthy hands to yourself?"

LOUISE: I think you'd better be off on your ride before you get into any more trouble.

PAMELA: Oh, it's one of those mornings. I bet you anything the horse breaks its leg.

[*They leave the schoolroom. The* Symphony *starts again in* WALTER'*s room.*]

PAMELA: Do you think he heard?

LOUISE: Well, you weren't exactly whispering, were you?

[*They go downstairs. While the stage is empty, the record sticks. The passage is repeated several times, then the needle is moved on.*]

PAMELA [*Coming into the living room*]: I think I'm the most impossible person I know. . . . But then I suppose wonderful people always make you feel like that. Sort of ashamed all the time.

LOUISE: He makes you feel ashamed?

PAMELA: Not exactly ashamed but, well, like in those advertisements for washing powder. I always feel like the grubby shirt next to the dazzling white one. He's so fresh! Fresh and beautiful. . . . [*Brightly.*] Don't you think he's beautiful?

LOUISE [*Confused*]: I hadn't thought.

PAMELA: It's just what he is. He should wear a frock coat and have consumption.

LOUISE: What nonsense.

PAMELA: Why? There *are* people like that.

LOUISE [*With sudden irritation*]: Well, Walter certainly isn't one of them. He's obviously quite a happy, normal young man. There's simply no reason for you to weave any romantic ideas about him being tragic or different in any way.

PAMELA [*Grandly*]: I'm afraid it's obvious you don't know him very well.

[*But* LOUISE *is unamused. Instead, she is making an effort at self-control.*]

LOUISE: If you're going, you'd better go. And I think you'd better put on a jersey.

PAMELA: Oh, phooey.

LOUISE: Darling, it's cold out.

PAMELA: It isn't really.

LOUISE: Pam, it's very cold. Now do be sensible.

PAMELA: Mother, I can't put on any more—I'd just die.

LOUISE [*Snapping*]: Do as I say! Put on your jersey!

[*She leaves the room abruptly and goes up into the schoolroom.* PAMELA *looks after her in surprise.*]

PAMELA [*Puzzled*]: 'Bye.

CLIVE [*In kitchen, off*]: Pam, is that you?

PAMELA: I'm just off.

[CLIVE *comes in, carrying a plate of eggs.*]

CLIVE: Have a good time.

PAMELA: You should come with me.

CLIVE: I know. It does you good to get in the air.

PAMELA [*In a wildly affected, cheerful voice*]: Well then, bye-bye, darling. You're sure there's nothing I can get you from the village? A barrel of beer? Harris tweed?

CLIVE [*Matching her accent*]: No, thanks, old girl. Just bring back the usual papers, will you? The *Hunting Gazette* and the *Shooting Gazette.*

PAMELA: Righty-ho!

CLIVE: And the *Fishing Gazette.* And some wax for the old mustache.

PAMELA: Certainly, dear.

CLIVE: I say, Pamela—you are a brick!

PAMELA [*Blowing him a kiss*]: Cheeribye, darling.

[*She shimmies out through the French window.* CLIVE *starts eating his breakfast.* LOUISE *begins to collect the clothes which* PAMELA *has spread around the room at one time or another.* WALTER *emerges from his room. He sees* LOUISE *at work through the door, is about to go up, then thinks better of it and, instead, comes downstairs.* LOUISE *finally goes into* PAMELA*'s bedroom.*]

CLIVE: Hello.

WALTER: Hello.

CLIVE: Do you know that a judge trying a copyright case in this country once asked learned counsel: "What exactly *are* Brahms . . . ?"

[WALTER *smiles in appreciation.*]

CLIVE: What's the matter with your gramophone?

WALTER: Oh, I know; it keeps sticking. It's the table, I'm afraid, which is not quite level.

CLIVE: Oh, really? It must be one of Father's. Well, how are you? Clearly unwell, I should say. Only the sick and corrupt would spend a bright Sunday morning listening to music. You must know that in all decent

English homes this time is reserved for sport. Staying indoors is the absolute proof of decadence.

WALTER: Yes. This is familiar to me. At home—I mean where I was born—to sit reading was an offense too.

CLIVE: You had to be out playing games?

WALTER: Games. But in small uniforms.

CLIVE [*Scenting difficulty*]: I suppose every kid wants to be a soldier.

WALTER: Oh, yes. [*Pause.*] But in England they are not told it is a good thing to be.

CLIVE: Did your uncle believe it was?

[WALTER *does not reply.*]

[*Cheerfully.*] Well, parents and guardians are desperately unreliable. It's what I've been telling you for weeks.

WALTER [*Turning, smiling*]: Maybe we expect too much of them. After all, they are only us, a little older.

CLIVE: Older and more depended on.

WALTER: Exactly.

CLIVE: So not a bit like us. Absolute Power Department.

WALTER [*Mischievously*]: Do you think *you're* going to make a very good father?

CLIVE: I don't see why not. I was a complete success as a baby. I was so demanding, I gave my parents the idea they were indispensable.

WALTER [*Amused*]: You must have been a terrible boy.

CLIVE: Oh, desperately average, I think. Stamp collection and all.

WALTER: I wish I had known you then.

CLIVE: What on earth for?

WALTER: It would have been nice when I was a child.

CLIVE [*Speculatively*]: Sometimes you make me wonder if you ever were.

[WALTER *lowers his eyes.* CLIVE *goes on in a rush.*]

Well, you're such an *excluded* person. It's the thing about you.

WALTER: Not now.

[CLIVE *stares at him for a moment, then speaks almost brusquely.*]

CLIVE: Have you always wanted to be a teacher?

WALTER: Oh yes. Since I was fifteen.

CLIVE: I think that's splendid. I wish *I* had something positive I wanted to be.

WALTER: Haven't you

CLIVE [*Gaily*]: No. I only know what I *don't* want to be. But there really isn't anything I could give a life to. The trouble is if you don't spend your life yourself, other people spend it for you. . . . As I see it, unless I suddenly feel a call from above, I'm going to wind up unemployable.

WALTER: I don't think so. life attracts you too much. Clive, I'm sorry I ran out on you last night.

CLIVE [*Stiffly*]: Let's forget it.

WALTER: It was kind of you to suggest a holiday together.

[CLIVE *looks away.*]

I know you're not happy here. . . . I would be honored if you could talk to me. If there are things you want to say—like last night I felt there were things. Living alone is an education, you know. If you think I would be offended—

CLIVE [*Sharply*]: I think we'll forget it! [*Pause.*] [*Indifferently.*] Walter, don't take me wrong—but are you sure you did the best thing when you left Germany?

WALTER: You think I should go back?

CLIVE: I think you ought to try.

WALTER [*In amazement*]: You talk as if you wanted me to go away.

CLIVE [*Very quiet*]: Yes.

WALTER: Why . . . ?

[CLIVE *does not reply.*]

Last night you did not want it.

CLIVE [*With sudden desperate anger*]: Last night . . . ! I want it now. I want you to go. [*Modifying his tone with effort.*] For your sake. Only for your sake, believe me. . . . You've got a crush on our family that's almost obscene. Can't you see how lucky you are to be on your own? Just because you never had a family you think they're the most wonderful things in the world.

WALTER: Just because . . . !

CLIVE: Why have you got to depend all the time? It's so damned weak!

WALTER: Clive—

CLIVE: Well, it is!

WALTER: You know nothing!

CLIVE: I can see.

WALTER: What? My parents? My father—can you see him, in his Nazi uniform?

CLIVE: But—you told me they died.

WALTER: No. They are alive. [*Pause.*] Back in Muhlbach. Alive. There was no uncle.

CLIVE [*Slow*]: Your father was a Nazi?

WALTER: Oh, yes. He was a great man in the town. People were afraid of him, and so was I. . . . When war broke out, he went off to fight and we did not see him for almost six years. When he came back, he was still a Nazi. Now, everyone else was saying, "We never liked them.

We never supported them." But not him! "I've always supported them," he said. "Hitler was the best man our country has seen since Bismarck. Even now we are defeated, we are the bravest country in Europe. Sooner or later we will win, because we have to win. . . ." Every night he used to make me recite the old slogans against Jews and Catholics and the Liberals. When I forgot, he would hit me—so many mistakes, so many hits.

CLIVE: But your mother?

WALTER: Oh, she worshiped him. Even after we found out.

CLIVE: What?

WALTER: That during the war he—worked . . . at Auschwitz concentration camp. . . . One of the most efficient officers. Once he told me how many . . . [*He stops in distress. His voice dead with loathing.*] I could have killed him. Killed him till he was dead. And she worshiped him—my mother. She used to smile at him, stare at him—as if he owned her. And when he hit me, she would just—just look away, you know, as if what he was doing was difficult, yes—but unavoidable, like training a puppy. That was my mother.

CLIVE [*Speaking quietly after a moment*]: And so you left?

[WALTER *nods.*]

I'm sorry.

WALTER [*Recovering*]: So you see, I do know what it is to have a family. And what I look for . . . [*In a strange tone.*] A house where now and then good spirits can sit on the roof.

CLIVE: And you think you've found it here? Do you?

[WALTER *does not answer.*]

You're fooling yourself every minute.

WALTER [*Gravely*]: Don't you think I should find that out for myself?

CLIVE: Oh, for God's sake! If that horrible story was meant to change my mind, it didn't.

WALTER: I did not tell it for that.

CLIVE: Then go. Just get the hell away from here.

WALTER: Clive—my friend—

CLIVE: For my sake—*I* want it.

WALTER: But why?

CLIVE: Because . . . because I can't bear to watch.

WALTER: I don't understand you.

CLIVE: Well, then, just because. [*He turns away.*]

[LOUISE *comes out of* PAMELA*'s bedroom, goes through the schoolroom and on to the landing.*]

[*In private pain.*] Because. Because—

LOUISE [*Calling downstairs*]: Walter . . . ?

[WALTER *looks at* CLIVE *inquiringly, unwilling to court interruption.*]

CLIVE: Go on. Answer her. It's your duty, isn't it?

WALTER [*Low, appealing*]: Clive . . .

CLIVE [*Turning on him ferociously*]: Answer her!

[*As* WALTER *stands irresolutely,* CLIVE *turns again and goes out abruptly, half running, through the French window.* LOUISE *descends the stairs.*]

LOUISE [*Calling*]: Walter!

WALTER [*Faintly, looking after* CLIVE]: I'm in here, Mrs. Harrington.

LOUISE [*Coming into the living room*]: Ah, there you are. My dear boy, all alone . . . ? [*Going to sofa.*] Come and talk to me, it's not good for you to be on your own too much.

WALTER: I was not alone. Clive was here. He's just gone out.

LOUISE: Out? Where?

WALTER: I don't know. . . . Mrs. Harrington, I am worried for him.

LOUISE [*Smiling*]: Poor Hibou, you worry about everybody, don't you? But you mustn't about Clive, really. It's just a tiny case of old-fashioned jealousy, that's all. Well, it's only to be expected, isn't it? We've always been so wonderfully close, he and I.

WALTER [*Courteously*]: Of course.

LOUISE: It's nothing serious. One day he'll understand about women. At the moment, of course, he thinks there must be room in my heart for only one boy. So silly. . . . [*Warmly.*] I don't believe you can ration friendship, do you?

WALTER [*Admiringly*]: With someone like you it is not possible.

LOUISE: Nor with you, my dear. You know, last night held the most beautiful moments I've known for many years. I felt—well, that you and I could have a really warm friendship. Even with the difference . . . I mean in—in our ages.

WALTER: Between friends there are no ages, I think.

LOUISE [*Tenderly*]: I like to think that, too.

WALTER: Oh, it's true. Like in a family—you never think how old people are, because you keep growing together.

LOUISE: Yes. Dear little owl. . . . What's the matter . . . ? Are you embarrassed?

[*He shakes his head "No."*]

It's the last thing you must ever be with me.

[WALTER *smiles.*]

What are you thinking? Come on: tell me.

WALTER: Some things grow more when they are not talked about.

LOUISE: Try, anyway. I want you to.

WALTER [*Looking away from her*]: It is only that you have made me wonder—

LOUISE [*Prompting eagerly*]: Tell me.

WALTER [*Lowering his voice still more*]: Mrs. Harrington, forgive me for asking this, but do you think it's possible for someone to find a new mother?

[LOUISE *sits very still. The expression of eagerness fades, and its remnant hardens on her face. She stares at him.*]

Have I offended you?

LOUISE [*Smiles, without joy*]: Of course not. I am . . . very touched.

WALTER [*Moved*]: Thank you. [*Eagerly.*] That is why I feel I can talk to you about Clive, for example. I am most worried for him. He is not happy now. And I do not think it is jealousy. It is something else—more deep in him—trying to explode. Like the beginning of an earthquake or so.

[LOUISE *rises.*]

LOUISE [*With increasing coolness*]: Really, my dear, don't you think you're being a little overdramatic?

WALTER [*Dogged*]: No. I mean exactly this. It is hard to explain.

LOUISE [*Wryly*]: I appreciate your attempt. . . . But really, I'm sure I know my children a little better than you.

WALTER [*Persisting*]: Of course. But just in this case—with Clive—I feel something which frightens me—I don't know why—

LOUISE [*Her temper breaking*]: Oh, for heaven's sake!

[WALTER *recoils.*]

[*Recovering quickly.*] I mean . . . after all, as you admit yourself, you *are* only a newcomer to the family, remember. [*Sweetly.*] Now why don't you go and play me some of your nice music?

[WALTER *looks confused and lowers his eyes before her strained smile. He goes into the kitchen.* LOUISE *is left alone.*]

CURTAIN

## SCENE 2

*The same night, after supper.*

*The living room is empty. Up in the schoolroom,* WALTER *is hearing* PAMELA *in her irregular verbs. They are sitting in their usual position at the table.*

PAMELA: *Je meurs, tu meurs, il meurt, nous meurons*—

WALTER: No.

PAMELA: It must be.

WALTER: *Mou—*

PAMELA: *Mourons*. Oh, phooey. . . . You know, this is the perfect way to end today. It's been a stinker, hasn't it?

WALTER: Has it? I thought you had a good ride this morning.

PAMELA: Oh, that. . . . I mean the atmosphere since I got back. What Mother calls the *aura*. And Clive not coming in for lunch or dinner. D'you think he's run away?

WALTER: I think we do more French.

PAMELA: Mother was livid tonight when he didn't turn up. That's funny too. I'd have thought Daddy would have been the one to explode, but he didn't say a word. . . . Do you think Clive's lost his memory or something?

WALTER: What is the future of *mourir?*

PAMELA: Perhaps he's been kidnapped. Just think of Daddy paying ransom. I wonder if he would.

WALTER: I think Clive can take care of himself. Now, *please*, Pamela—

PAMELA: Oh, I'm sick of French! It's Sunday, and that's supposed to be a day of rest.

WALTER: Yesterday you said you felt Jewish and Saturday was your day of rest.

PAMELA: That was Saturday—not Sunday. Today I'm going to have a hot bath and go straight to bed and read. Mary gave me a most important scientific book last week and I just haven't had a moment to glance at it.

WALTER [*Suspiciously*]: What kind of science?

PAMELA: Actually it's a kind of story.

WALTER [*Resigned*]: Ah-ha.

PAMELA: But completely scientific. It tells what would happen if the earth got invaded by Venus. The people are just sweeties. They're all ten foot high and covered with blue jelly.

WALTER: Very educational.

[LOUISE *comes out of her bedroom. She looks strained and anxious.*]

LOUISE: Pamela—

PAMELA: There you are. You can't even have a scientific discussion any more without being interrupted by the world of triviality.

[LOUISE *comes into the schoolroom.* WALTER *rises.*]

LOUISE [*To her daughter*]: How's the bruise, darling? I've turned on your bath.

PAMELA: Has Clive come back yet?

LOUISE [*Wearily, but with a vestige of deep anger*]: No. Not yet. . . . [*Softening.*] Now get into your bath and don't dawdle, will you?

[*She goes to the door. Having virtually ignored* WALTER, *who has stood uncomfortably by the table, she just notices him on the way out.*]

Good night, Walter.

WALTER: Good night, Mrs. Harrington.

[LOUISE *goes downstairs.*]

PAMELA [*Whispering*]: She looks as if she needs a fizzy.

WALTER: Ssh! Tch. Tch.

PAMELA: Well, she does. Mother always goes like that when she's lost an argument. It's meant to mean she's been misunderstood.

WALTER: She is worried about Clive.

PAMELA: Phooey! Anyone would think he was still a baby, the way she goes on. [*Wickedly.*] I hope he stays out all night. Wouldn't it be wonderful if he was giving babies to all the schoolgirls in Ipswich . . . ? [*She goes into her room, where she calls in her affected voice.*] Well, I'd better go and have my bath, dear boy. Oh, Lord, Sunday night. Breakfast at half-past seven for that rotten train. I think Mondays stink. . . .

[*She returns with her nightdress and dressing gown.*]

Is there any religion with its day of rest on Mondays?

WALTER: Yes. The religion of Lazy Girls.

PAMELA: Oh, you are brutish!

[*She goes off for her bath. Presently the front door opens.* STANLEY *comes in and walks into the living room, taking off his overcoat.*]

LOUISE [*Hearing the noise of his entry*]: Clive? Oh, it's you. . . .

STANLEY [*Coming in*]: Isn't he back?

LOUISE: No.

STANLEY: Well, no one's seen him in the village. He hasn't been in any of the pubs.

LOUISE [*Bitterly*]: The pubs. Always the pubs.

STANLEY: Well, where else would he be likely to go? You know what the trouble is? Your son's turning into a drunkard.

LOUISE: The way you've been behaving lately's enough to make anyone drink. No one would think he's your son. You treat him abominably.

STANLEY: Do I?

LOUISE: You haven't the faintest idea how to deal with sensitive people. If I was Clive, I'd have run away from home long ago.

STANLEY [*Bitterly*]: If it weren't for the saving grace of his mother. His sensitive mother.

LOUISE: At least I understand him. I make an effort. Just because you can't see beyond the end of your selfish, commonplace nose—

STANLEY [*Savage*]: Shut up!

LOUISE: Charming.

STANLEY [*His pain also becoming rage*]: And what have you done for him that's so wonderful, may I ask? I'll tell you. Turned him into a sniveling little neurotic. A mother's boy. That's what!

LOUISE [*Trying to recover poise*]: That's not true.

STANLEY: And I'll tell you something else. He's going peculiar. Yes: loony, if you want to know. He talked to me last night and I didn't understand one word he said.

LOUISE [*Loftily*]: That doesn't surprise me.

STANLEY: It was like listening to a lunatic.

LOUISE: And that's my fault, too? Just because I take an interest in our son, which you've never bothered to do in all these years, I'm driving him insane.

STANLEY [*With wild demand in his tone*]: And when I tried to take an interest, what happened? When I offered to teach him things—

LOUISE: What things?

STANLEY: Golf—swimming—I don't know, I can't remember. Who was it said, "Clive's too delicate"? "Clive can't waste his time on silly games. He's got his reading to do. . . ."

LOUISE: So it was wrong of me to encourage his reading?

STANLEY: He was my son as much as yours!

LOUISE: Yes, and what did you want to do for him? Push him straight into your third-rate furniture business for the rest of his life. Well, that's not good enough for *me*, Stanley.

STANLEY [*Cutting through this*]: Well, he was my son, wasn't he?

LOUISE: He still *is*, my dear.

STANLEY [*Hard*]: No. Not any more. You've seen to that.

[LOUISE *looks away from him sharply.*]

LOUISE [*Collected*]: That's the nastiest thing you've ever said to me.

STANLEY: I didn't mean it.

LOUISE: Yes, you did.

STANLEY [*Wearily*]: I don't know what I mean any more. . . . It's all so bloody mixed up.

LOUISE: Must you swear?

STANLEY: *I* don't know. . . .

LOUISE: I can't stand much more. I just can't.

STANLEY [*Dead*]: What?

LOUISE: It's no good, Stanley. My life was never meant to be like this—limited this way. . . . I know I'm unpredictable sometimes. I say things I don't mean. But don't you see I'm just so frustrated I don't know what I'm doing half the time? I'm sorry, but it's the only word, Stanley. There are times I feel I'm being absolutely choked to death—suffocated under piles of English blankets. Yes, my dear: I'm not English and won't ever be, no matter how hard I try. Can't you ever understand that you married someone who's really a Parisian at heart? A Frenchwoman, my dear man, with all that means—faults too, of course—frivolity and being irresponsible. If I've disappointed you, it's because I've never really become *acclimatée*—you know, acclimatized—that's all. I've never been able to take your world of shops and business seriously. Can't you understand?

[*He makes a futile gesture.*]

STANLEY [*Flat*]: What do you want me to do, Louise? Louise, I'm asking you. D'you want a divorce . . . ? Well?

LOUISE: Oh, it's all so vulgar.

STANLEY [*Tired*]: I'm a vulgar man.

LOUISE: Do *you?* What do *you* want?

STANLEY [*Plainly*]: I'm too old to start again.

LOUISE: That's a nice way of putting it.

STANLEY: Oh, for heaven's sake, *nice*. . . . And there's Pam. It wouldn't do her any good.

LOUISE: I notice you don't mention Clive.

STANLEY: Clive's no longer a child. Although it probably upsets you to think of it, he's almost twenty years old.

LOUISE: I think it's you who haven't gathered that.

STANLEY: Don't start—just don't start.

LOUISE: I didn't begin it.

STANLEY [*Getting up, frantic*]: Louise . . . ! [*After a moment, in an altered voice—not looking at her.*] Do you think if we went away it would help? Just the two of us, alone together? We could go back to Monte.

[PAMELA *comes from the bathroom in her dressing gown, and goes downstairs.*]

LOUISE: You know I can't stand the place.

STANLEY [*Controlling himself*]: Well, anywhere. . . .

[PAMELA *enters.*]

LOUISE: Clive? Oh, it's you, Pam.

PAMELA: Yes, Mother. Isn't Clive back yet?

LOUISE: Don't worry, darling. He'll be in soon. Now sleep well, and don't read too late.

PAMELA: Good night. Good night, Daddy. [*She kisses him and goes out and upstairs to the schoolroom.*]

STANLEY: It's worth a try, isn't it, Louise?

LOUISE: Yes, Stanley. It's worth a try.

PAMELA [*In the schoolroom*]: Good night.

WALTER [*In the schoolroom*]: Sleep tight.

PAMELA: Mind the bugs don't bite.

[PAMELA *goes into her room and shuts the door.* LOUISE *pauses for a moment. When she speaks her tone is light, almost winning and subservient, wholly without a sense of calculation.*]

LOUISE: Stanley, I want to ask you to do something for me—something rather difficult.

STANLEY: What's that?

LOUISE: It's to do with Pamela. I feel it's something you can manage better than I can.

STANLEY: Pam?

LOUISE: Actually, it's about Walter. I'm afraid he's having rather a bad effect on her. She's just at that stage, you know—impressionable, romantic—long walks in the moonlight. Well, I'm afraid she's got a bit of a crush. Nothing serious, of course—she'll soon get over it. But—well, it's her first and, naturally, she's rather unhappy. She threw quite a little scene this morning, as a matter of fact. . . . The boy, of course, is a Continental, and can't resist angling for admiration all the time. So he flatters her, I suppose, and pays her compliments. In the normal way I'd encourage it: it would help to give her a little poise. But in this case she seems to be taking it all just a little too seriously.

STANLEY: You want me to talk to her?

LOUISE: No. Something rather more drastic I'm afraid. I think we must let Walter go. In the most tactful way, of course. Actually I think the sooner the better.

STANLEY: I see.

LOUISE: I think he's up in the schoolroom now—shall I ask him to come down? I'll make myself scarce. And you will be tactful, won't you?

[CLIVE *blunders in through the front door. He is drunk but—as on the previous evening—perfectly coherent.*]

Clive!

CLIVE: Good evening, all.

STANLEY: Would you mind telling me where you've been? Did you hear me? You've been out since twelve.

CLIVE: Like the tide. But we're back, you see.

STANLEY: Answer me!

CLIVE: Why the hell do we always have to ask expected questions?

STANLEY: Now listen, my boy, you've been drink—

LOUISE [*Quietly*]: Why don't you go upstairs, dear, and do what I asked you to?

STANLEY [*To* LOUISE]: Very well. I'll leave you to look after your sensitive son.

[*He goes out of the room and up the stairs. At the top, he knocks at* WALTER'*s door, receives no answer, and, less resolutely, approaches the schoolroom.*]

LOUISE [*Bitterly*]: Your father and I have been worried to death.

CLIVE [*Insolently*]: Do I detect a new note in the air? Your father and I? How splendid. The birth of a new moral being. Your-father-and-I. . . . When did you last see your-father-and-I? Or is it just a new alliance . . . ? All the same, I congratulate you. I always thought you two ought to get married.

LOUISE: You're drunk and disgusting. I'll get you something to eat and you can go up to bed.

CLIVE [*Coldly*]: Your-father-and-I will now get your supper.

[LOUISE *goes into the kitchen. The brightness of the room troubles* CLIVE. *He shuffles clumsily across and turns off the lights so that only the glow from the fire remains as he sinks wearily into the armchair and covers his eyes.*

STANLEY *enters the schoolroom.*]

STANLEY: Are you busy?

WALTER [*Standing up; as always, made nervous by his appearance*]: Of course not, Mr. Harrington. I was just reading—is Clive back yet?

STANLEY: He just came in—drunk. Do you drink? I don't remember seeing you.

WALTER: Not very much, no.

STANLEY: Sensible. [*Pause*] My son drinks. A lot. Doesn't he? [WALTER *says nothing.*] Why does he drink? Can you see any good reason for it?

WALTER: I do not think people drink for good reasons.

STANLEY: Sit down.

[WALTER *sits wearily.* STANLEY *sits also, facing him at the table.*]

You don't think much of me, do you?

WALTER: Mr. Harrington—

STANLEY: Why? Because I'm not educated. Is that it?

WALTER: Of course not.

STANLEY: Then why? Because the children say things?

WALTER: Mr. Harrington, please, I—

STANLEY: And what do they know? People say parents are selfish. They've got nothing on children. Do children ever think about anything but themselves? *Their* troubles . . . ? As if nobody ever had 'em before. Well . . . ? You ought to know. You teach 'em.

WALTER [*Softly*]: I think children are not so able to help themselves with their troubles.

STANLEY [*Not really listening*]: I tell you, children are the most selfish things in the world. . . . So he drinks. Did you know it was my fault? I drive him to it. So I hear.

[WALTER *says nothing.*]

Well . . . ? Have you lost your tongue?

WALTER [*Very low*]: No.

STANLEY: I'll tell you why he drinks. So he can get over being with me. Have you noticed how this family of mine never get together in this house? Are you afraid of me?

WALTER [*Straight*]: No.

STANLEY: Well, that's a wonder. My son is. That's something else I hear. What do you think?

WALTER: I think . . . yes.

STANLEY [*Blankly*]: Do you?

WALTER [*With difficulty*]: I think he feels you do not love him, but still are expecting him to love you.

STANLEY: Rubbish.

WALTER [*Retreating at once*]: I'm sorry. You did ask me.

STANLEY: He's my *son*. How can he think that?

WALTER: He does not wish to be alone with you because always he feels you are—well—judging him. When you look at him, he sees you are thinking—"How useless he is."

STANLEY: And when he looks at me—what's *he* thinking? Ah, that's a different story, isn't it? [*Bitterly.*] "How common."

WALTER: Oh, no—

STANLEY: Don't tell me. Common! I've seen it too often.

WALTER [*Overbearing him urgently*]: No! You are wrong about him. You see, in front of you he must always justify his life. His Greek, maybe, or because he loves an opera. When a boy must apologize for ears and eyes, it is very bad.

STANLEY: Apologize? When have I asked him to apologize?

WALTER: That's not what I mean.

STANLEY: Then why use such ridiculous words? I can see now where he gets them from.

WALTER [*Gravely*]: Your son has got nothing from me. I wish he had. Sir, your son needs help. Will he get it?

STANLEY: He can always come to me. He knows that.

WALTER [*Raising his voice slightly*]: And will he come? *Does* he come?

STANLEY [*Gathering dignity about him*]: As a matter of fact, we had a very frank talk last night. You didn't know that, did you? What are you thinking?

WALTER: You know, you are very like your son, Mr. Harrington.

STANLEY [*Sarcastic*]: Oh, yes. In education, I suppose.

WALTER: I say too much always. . . .

[STANLEY *shrugs. Suddenly he begins to talk more or less to himself.*]

STANLEY: What's it matter? . . . You start a family, work and plan. Suddenly you turn round and there's nothing there. Probably never was. What's a family, anyway? Just—just kids with your blood in 'em. There's no reason why they should like you. . . . You go on expecting it, of course, but it's silly really. Like expecting 'em to know what they meant to you when they were babies. They're not supposed to know, perhaps. It's not natural, really, when you come to think of it. You can't expect anybody to know what they mean to somebody else—it's not the way of things. [*He stops, confused. When he resumes, his voice is even softer.*] There's just nothing. Bloody nothing.

[*Unseen by him,* WALTER *gestures toward him in a futile attempt at communication. He goes on staring into space, not heeding the tutor at all.*]

You get a wife and family and you work for them. And all the time you think, It'll be better next year. Next year it'll be all right. The children going to prep school, leaving it. Short trousers, long trousers. Perhaps he'll make the rugger fifteen or the cricket team or something—anything—and then his first girl friend and taking her home—or perhaps just keeping her to himself till he's sure. . . . [*Frankly.*] But nothing. . . . Nothing . . . and now he hates me.

WALTER: No. . . .

STANLEY [*Focusing again*]: D'you think I don't know? How sensitive do you have to be for that? Tell me—because I don't know too much about that sort of thing. [*His bitterness rises once more.*] I'm always too busy making money. [*Violently.*] Go on, tell me. Sensitive people have deep feelings, don't they? They suffer a lot!

WALTER: Please, Mr. Harrington—

STANLEY [*Violently*]: I don't want to hear!

WALTER: Excuse me, sir.

[*Pause.*

*Moved and bewildered,* WALTER *rises and then leaves the room. On the landing he hesitates for a moment then, on an impulse, goes downstairs.* STANLEY *is left staring into space. He rises and moves aimlessly to the window. He stares out of it unseeingly, then sits slowly in the chair vacated by* WALTER, *so that we see only his back.*

WALTER *reaches the living room, where* CLIVE *has been lying inert in the armchair, in a strange awkward position suggesting acute depression.*]

WALTER: Clive? What's the matter? Why are you sitting in the dark?

I've been talking to your father. He thinks you hate him.

[CLIVE *does not appear to hear.*]

Clive, listen to me. . . . The Kings of Egypt were gods. Everything they did was right, everything they said was true, and when they died, they grew faces of gold. You must try to forgive your parents for being average and wrong when you worshiped them once. Why are you so afraid? Is it—because you have no girl friend? Oh, you are so silly. Silly. Do you think sex will change you? Put you into a different world, where everything will mean more to you? I thought so, too, once. I thought it would change me into a man so my father could never touch me again. I didn't know exactly what it would be like, but I thought it would burn me and bring me terrible pain. But afterward, I'd be strong and very wise. . . . There was a girl in Muhlbach. She worked in her mother's grocery shop. One night I had a few drinks and, just for a joke, I broke into her bedroom through the window. I stayed with her all night. And I entered heaven. I really did. Between her arms was the only place in the world that mattered. When daylight came, I felt I had changed forever. A little later I got up. I looked round, but the room was exactly the same. This was incomprehensible. It should have been so huge now—filled with air. But it seemed very small and stuffy, and outside it was raining. I remember I hated the soap for lying there in the dish just as it had done the night before. I watched her putting on her clothes. I thought, "We're tied together now by an invisible thread."And then she said, "It's nine o'clock: I must be off"—and went downstairs to open the shop. Then, I looked into the mirror: at least my eyes would be different. [*Ironically.*] They were a little red, yes—but I was exactly the same—still a boy. Rain was still here. And all the problems of yesterday were still waiting.

[*He pauses and puts his hand on* CLIVE*'s arm.*]

Sex by itself is nothing, believe me. Just like breathing—only important when it goes wrong. And, Clive, this only happens if you're afraid of it. What are you thinking . . . ? Please talk to me.

CLIVE [*Very low*]: Walter . . .

WALTER: Yes?

CLIVE [*Low, his head buried*]: What's wrong with me?

WALTER: There's nothing wrong with you. Nothing.

CLIVE: Don't fool me. I know.

WALTER: There's nothing wrong but in your mind. What you think about.

CLIVE [*Despairing*]: What is it? What have they done to me?

WALTER: Clive—your parents love you. Everything they have done has been from love. I am sure of this.

CLIVE: Then God save me from love.

WALTER: He will not. . . . You have more in you than any man I've ever met.

CLIVE [*Breaking free*]: Stop it. . . .

WALTER: Clive, my dear friend, let me help you.

CLIVE: Cut that out!

WALTER: What?

CLIVE: Pity. D'you think I'd have let him take the guts out of me, if his attempts to love me weren't so rotten to watch?

WALTER [*Gently*]: I don't pity you, Clive. And you mustn't pity yourself. You can end this and you must. You must leave here. You—not me. At the moment you are—[*gestures*]—on your family. I don't know the word. Like a butterfly on a pin.

CLIVE [*With distaste*]: Impaled.

WALTER: Yes. And you must get off the pin. At the end of term in Cambridge, don't come back here. Go anywhere else you like. Join your American friend singing. Go into a factory. Anything. The important thing is this—as soon as you are out of here, people will start telling you who you are. [*Tenderly.*] Maybe you will not like it, but that's nonsense, you must always like the truth.

[CLIVE *shakes his head "No."*]

You think you can't do this, but you must. Oh, is this so difficult? . . . I could tell you what *I* want.

CLIVE: Go on.

WALTER: To live in England. To be happy teaching. One day to marry. To have children, and many English friends. . . . And now you. What do *you* want?

[*Pause.*]

CLIVE [*Faintly*]: Something—I'm not sure. [*Intimately.*] Yes—I think I want . . . to achieve something that only I could do. I want to fall in love with just one person. To know what it is to bless and be blessed. And to serve a great cause with devotion. [*Appealing.*] I want to be *involved.*

WALTER: Then break the glass! Get out of the coffin! Jump up and begin yourself. Make up your own time without one minute when you don't care who you are.

[STANLEY *rises from the table in the schoolroom and leaves the room. He goes downstairs.*]

Trust everything, not because it's wise, but because not to trust will kill you. Trust me, for instance. I'll see you often. But you must go away from here. Say yes—you will go.

[STANLEY *enters the room, unheard.*]

CLIVE [*Nodding*]: Yes. I'll go.

WALTER: The next vacation.

CLIVE: The next vacation.

WALTER: Good!

CLIVE: Isn't it silly? We seem to spend all the time ordering each other out of the house!

WALTER: A very friendly way to spend the time.

[*The main light snaps on.* STANLEY *stands in the doorway.*]

STANLEY: Clive—don't you think it's time you went to bed?

CLIVE: I suppose so.

WALTER [*Gently to* CLIVE]: You're sure you are all right now?

CLIVE: Yes, I'm all right.

[CLIVE *goes out, upstairs, and into his room.* WALTER *gives his half-bow and makes as if to follow, but is stopped by* STANLEY.]

STANLEY [*Raging*]: Just who the hell do you think you are?

WALTER: I'm sorry?

STANLEY: The world owes you a living: that's it.

WALTER: Mr. Harrington—

STANLEY [*Brutally*]: Don't "Mr. Harrington" me, with your smarmy voice and bowing from the waist. You had the gall to patronize me just now—tell me what's wrong with my home. . . .

WALTER: You forget—you asked me for my opinion.

STANLEY: Oh, yes. And what else did I ask you to do? Turn my son into a sissy?

WALTER: Your son is a fine, intelligent boy.

STANLEY: He's a mess, that's what he is. And it's your fault.

WALTER: My fault—?

STANLEY [*Blindly*]: Yes, yours. *Yours.* You, the arty boys. It's you who've taken him. . . . [*Hurling the names as if they were insults.*] Shakespeare! Beethoven! . . . All the time, till I can't touch him. . . . What gave you the right to steal my boy?

WALTER [*With pity*]: You will believe what you please.

STANLEY: I'm not blind, you know—and I'm not deaf. I heard you telling him just now—"Get out of this house," you said.

WALTER: Yes, I did.

STANLEY: How dare you say a thing like that? What right have you—in my house, working for me—to say a thing like that?

WALTER: My friendship for your son.

STANLEY: Oh, of course! And your friendship with my daughter Pamela, too, what about that?

WALTER: Pamela?

STANLEY [*Crisply, with satisfaction*]: Your employer, Mrs. Harrington, has asked me to dismiss you because she thinks you are having a bad effect upon our daughter.

[*Slight pause.*]

WALTER [*Incredulous*]: Mrs. Harrington said this?

STANLEY: Yes.

WALTER: But it's not true. Not true at all. . . .

STANLEY [*Carefully*]: No. I don't think it is.

[*Slight pause.* WALTER *looks in utter distress and bewilderment at* STANLEY.]

WALTER: Then—why . . . ?

STANLEY: Could it be because you've been trying to make love to my wife?

[WALTER *reacts sharply to protest.* STANLEY *goes on in the same quiet tone.*]

You filthy German bastard.

[*The boy winces as if he has been slapped.*]

Once a German, always a German. Take what you want and the hell with everyone else.

[WALTER *stands rigid, with face averted.* STANLEY *moves round him as if he were a statue.*]

You're a fool, too. Did you really think my wife would ever risk anything for you? Oh, I know it's very cultured to look down on money, but that's a very different thing from giving it up. Well, now you've had your chips, and she's sent me to give them to you.

[*A long pause.*

*When* WALTER *speaks, it is very quietly, from the depth of his humiliation.*]

WALTER: You really believe . . . ? It's not possible. . . .

STANLEY: Oh, yes—it's quite possible. I've got a perfect witness, "unimpeachable," as we say in England.

[WALTER *looks at him.*]

Can't you guess . . . ? No . . . ? [*Hard.*] Your pal. Your good pal.

WALTER [*Whispering*]: Clive?

STANLEY: Of course Clive. Who else?

WALTER [*In disbelief*]: No!

STANLEY: He told me he saw you both—in this room, last night.

WALTER: No—oh no—but—

STANLEY: Do you know what we do with people like you in England? Chuck 'em out. [*Lowering his voice.*] I'm going to fix it so you never get your naturalization papers. I'm going to write to the immigration people. I'll write tonight, and tell them all about you. I'll say—let's see—'Much though I hate to complain about people behind their backs, I feel it my duty in this case to warn you about this young German's standard of morality. While under my roof, he attempted to force his attentions on my young daughter, who is only fourteen." Try and get your papers after that. They'll send you back to the place where you belong! . . .

[LOUISE *enters from kitchen.* WALTER *faces away from them.*]

LOUISE: Stanley, I thought you were upstairs—Walter! What's the matter?

STANLEY: I did what you asked me.

LOUISE: Yes, but *how* did you do it? I can just imagine.

[*She puts down the tray and goes to* WALTER.]

Was he very brutal, *mon cher?* Oh . . . poor little Hibou—

[WALTER *does not look at her.*]

But you know yourself it's for the best, don't you? It's so silly, being . . . upset. . . .

[*Suddenly, unexpectedly,* WALTER *falls on his knees and grasps her hand in an imploring, desperate, filial gesture.*]

WALTER: Don't . . . I beg of you. . . .

[STANLEY *moves sharply away from them.*]

LOUISE [*Trying to free herself*]: Walter, please. . . .

WALTER: No. . . .

LOUISE: Really, Walter . . . ! Get up at once.

WALTER: Please . . . don't. . . .

LOUISE: Do you hear me?

STANLEY [*Who has turned round*]: Too sensitive for you, my dear?

LOUISE [*Stung by his mockery*]: Walter! Will you stop making an exhibition of yourself? You're being embarrassing and ridiculous.

[*He stiffens. She moderates her tone.*]

Now, please get up, and stop making an exhibition of yourself.

[*He does so, slowly relinquishing her hand and looking away from her.*]

I'm sorry, but I'm afraid you deserved to be spoken to like that. I'm really very disappointed in you. . . . Both our children have been considerably disturbed by your presence in our house. And of course I could never allow that. They have always come first with me. I'm sure you understand.

[*No reply.*]

Now, as regards finances, we will make it as easy for you as possible. You could manage a month's wages, I think, Stanley?

STANLEY: Oh . . . yes.

LOUISE: There you are. A month's wage. I call that quite generous, don't you?

WALTER [*In a remote, disinterested voice*]: Yes.

LOUISE: Good. [*Seeing his distress*] Oh, don't look so stricken, Hibou. It makes it so much more difficult for everybody.

[*A pause.* WALTER *leaves the room.*]

[*Calling after him.*] Well, of all the embarrassing, hysterical scenes . . . ! [*Rounding on* STANLEY.] You seem to have handled it brilliantly.

[*As* WALTER *reaches the landing,* CLIVE *appears.*]

CLIVE: Walter—

WALTER: No!

[WALTER *shakes him off and rushes into his room, slamming the door.* CLIVE *enters from hall.*]

CLIVE: What's the matter with Walter?

LOUISE: He's a little upset. There's some supper here for you—you'd better eat it.

CLIVE: Why is he upset? What's been going on down here?

LOUISE: I think it's better if we don't talk about it.

CLIVE: Do you want to talk about it, Father?

[STANLEY *is standing at the window curtain. He is trembling.*] Father—I'm asking you a question. Do you hear me?

LOUISE: Don't be so impertinent, Clive, speaking to your father like that.

CLIVE: Ah—your father and I—the new alliance. What have you both done to Walter—both of you? I'm only asking a simple question.

[*A pause.* STANLEY *turns then, with difficulty. He speaks.*]

STANLEY: If you really want to know, I told him what you said last night about him and your mother.

LOUISE: Me?

STANLEY: Yes, my dear. You and your daughter's tutor—a pretty picture.

LOUISE [*Shaken*]: What did he tell you? Clive, what did you say?

STANLEY: Never mind—I didn't believe it.

LOUISE: I want to know what Clive said to you.

STANLEY: What's it matter—it never matters what he says.

CLIVE: So you didn't believe me?

STANLEY: Did you really think I would?

CLIVE: Then why did you talk to Walter just now as if you did? Why was he so upset? Well?

[*But* STANLEY *is past reply, past justification, or even the attitude of parenthood. He opens his mouth to speak, stares at them both in mute pain, then goes out without a word, and upstairs to his room.* CLIVE *stares after him.*]

CLIVE: Well, Mother?

LOUISE: Jou-jou! Jou-jou, you didn't suggest . . . but this is horrible. . . . You couldn't have said such things about me, surely?

CLIVE: Yes—I said them.

LOUISE: But why?

CLIVE: I don't know.

LOUISE: Jou-jou!

CLIVE: I don't know. I do something terrible that I'll remember all my life, that'll make me sick whenever I think of it—and I don't know why.

LOUISE: You're ill—you must be.

CLIVE: Oh no! It only means *I* can damage people, too—that's all. I can dish it out—just like everyone else.

LOUISE: But it's not true. It's not true, what you said.

CLIVE: True? I told the lie, yes. But what I felt *under* the lie—about you and Walter—was that so untrue? No, don't answer, because whatever you said just wouldn't be real. You've forgotten what it is to be honest about true feelings. True! The only true thing I know is what's happened to him—my father!

LOUISE: You're ill.

CLIVE: Yes—and you're so worried about me. Department of Flattering Unction.

LOUISE: Clive—you frighten me. Why are you being so terrible? What have I done?

CLIVE: Don't you know? Can't you *see* what you've done? There isn't a Stanley Harrington any more. We've broken him in bits between us.

LOUISE: I don't know what you're talking about. I really don't.

CLIVE: No—you don't. . . . Poor man.

LOUISE: Clive—you hate me.

CLIVE: I hate. Isn't that enough? [*Pause.*] Is the war in this house never going to end?

LOUISE: War?

CLIVE: The war you both declared when you married. The culture war with me as ammunition. "Let's show him how small he is"—"Let's show her where she gets off." *And always through me!* . . . He wasn't always a bully—I'm sure of that. You made him into one.

LOUISE: I'll not go on with this conversation another moment. It's obscene. Your father's upset. Simply upset, that's all.

CLIVE: But why is he upset?

LOUISE: About something I asked him to do.

CLIVE: It was something to do with Walter, wasn't it? What have you done to Walter?

LOUISE: If you must know—he's been dismissed.

CLIVE: Mother—no!

LOUISE: I assure you there were excellent reasons.

CLIVE: But you can't dismiss him. You *can't*. Not even you— [*In sudden despair.*] He can't go away from here!

[*She looks at him curiously.*]

LOUISE [*Calmly*]: If you want to know, I did it for Pam. I'm afraid his influence over her was getting rather stronger than I cared for.

[*A slight pause. She sits.*]

CLIVE [*Also calm*]: I see.

[*The slow third movement of Mahler's* Fourth Symphony *is heard from* WALTER'*s room.*]

LOUISE: Well, evidently the boy himself is not so shattered by the news as you are. . . . Don't you think you'd better eat your supper?

CLIVE [*Matter-of-fact*]: What was it? Jealousy? Shame, when you saw them so innocent together? Or just the sheer vulgarity of competing with one's own daughter?

LOUISE: How dare you!

CLIVE: Dearest Mother, who are you trying to fool? I know your rules. Don't give sympathy to a man if others are giving it, too—he'll never see how unique you are. Besides, doing what everyone else does is just too vulgar. Like going to Monte, or falling in love.

[LOUISE *bursts into tears.*]

[*Anguished.*] Mother!

[*She sobs helplessly for a moment.*]

[*With a wild, hopeless grief.*] Oh, it goes on and on. No meeting. . . . Never. . . . Why can't we be important to each other? Why can't we ever come back into the room and be new to each other? Why doesn't a night's sleep lying all those dark hours with ourselves forgotten and then coming alive again, why doesn't it ever change us? Give us new things to see—new things to say too: not just "Eat your eggs," or "You were in late"—the old dreariness. [*Desperately, to his mother.*] I want to *know* you. But you wonderful—changed into yourself. . . . Don't you understand? So that you can change me.

[*She sits unmoving, no longer crying, giving no indication of having heard. Her son kneels to her and embraces her with desperate tenderness.*]

[*Tenderly.*] *Maman . . . Maman, chérie . . .*

[*For a moment she endures it, then, with a gesture of repulsion, she shakes him off.*]

LOUISE: Don't—!

CLIVE [*Falling back*]: *Maman. . . .*

LOUISE [*Rounding on him*]: D'you think you're the only one can ask terrible questions? Supposing I ask a few. Supposing I ask them . . . ! You ought to be glad Walter's going, but you're not. Why not? Why aren't you glad? You want him to stay, don't you? You want him to stay very much. Why?

CLIVE [*In panic*]: *Maman!*

LOUISE [*Pitiless*]: Why . . . ? You said filthy things to your father about me. Filth and lies. Why? Can you think of an answer? . . . Why, Clive? Why about me and Walter? Why? Why . . . ? Why?

CLIVE [*In a scream*]: You're *killing* . . . !

[*She stops, her arm stretched out in a sudden gesture of true maternal protectiveness.* CLIVE *has both his hands before his face, as if to ward off a blow. In the silence, they both become aware of a strange sound: the record playing in* WALTER'*s room has stuck. The same phrase is being played again and again. The needle is not moved on. The pause is held.* CLIVE *lowers his hands. A dawning alarm expresses itself on* LOUISE'*s face.*

STANLEY *comes from his room and appears on the landing, drawn by the noise. He goes to* WALTER'*s room and knocks. There is no reply. He turns the handle, but has to push the door hard to get it open.* WALTER'*s jacket is stuffed under it. He disappears for a second, then comes out coughing.*]

STANLEY: Louise!

LOUISE: Stanley?

[*She runs upstairs.* CLIVE *still stays where he is.*]

STANLEY [*Returning to the room*]: Get the doctor.

[LOUISE *arrives on the landing. The record is switched off.*]

LOUISE: What is it? What's happened?

STANLEY [*From the bedroom*]: It's Walter . . . get a doctor. . . . Quick!

[LOUISE *runs downstairs again, coughing from the gas.* CLIVE *has moved slowly out of the room and starts going upstairs as his mother comes down them and starts to telephone.*]

LOUISE: Hello . . . hello . . . 342, please.

[STANLEY *reemerges, dragging the unconscious boy out of the room. He lays him on the landing.*]

STANLEY [*Over the body, rapidly and urgently*]: Dear God, let him live. Dear God, let him live . . . please—dear God. I'll never . . .

[CLIVE *appears on the landing. He kneels next to his father.*]

Oh, God, please!

CLIVE: Walter!

[WALTER *stirs.*]

STANLEY: He's all right. He's all right.

WALTER: *Schon gut. Mir fehlt nichts.*

STANLEY [*Joyfully*]: Boy! . . . Boy . . .

[*Woken by the noise,* PAMELA *comes from her room into the schoolroom. Sleepily she turns on the light.* CLIVE *moves quickly to prevent her seeing the scene on the landing.*]

PAMELA: What is it? What's the matter?

CLIVE: Nothing. It's all right. It's all right. Walter fell down and hurt himself. Just like you did. Now go back to bed. . . . [*Kindly.*] Go on.

[*She allows herself to be pushed gently back into her bedroom.* CLIVE *closes the door.*]

CLIVE [*In a whisper*]: The courage. For all of us. Oh, God—give it.

CURTAIN

# THE PRIVATE EAR

A PLAY IN ONE ACT

*For*
*Peter Wood*
*with love*

*The Private Ear* was first presented with *The Public Eye* at the Globe Theatre, London W1, on May 10, 1962, by H. M. Tennent, Ltd. It was directed by Peter Wood; decor was by Richard Negri and lighting by Joe Davis. The cast was as follows:

| | |
|---|---|
| TED | Douglas Livingstone |
| BOB | Terry Scully |
| DOREEN | Maggie Smith |

The New York production, also directed by Peter Wood, opened at the Morosco Theatre on October 9, 1963, with *The Public Eye*. The cast was as follows:

| | |
|---|---|
| TED | Barry Foster |
| BOB | Brian Bedford |
| DOREEN | Geraldine McEwan |

---

SCENE: BOB'S *sitting room in Belsize Park, London. A summer evening, about seven o'clock.*

*It is a fairly shabby attic room: the room of a young and rather disorganized bachelor. There is a window at the back looking out over a grimy London roofscape. Besides the bed, over which hangs a large print of Botticelli's* "Birth of Venus," *there is a frayed armchair, a chest of drawers, a couple of chairs, and a stool. The room is dominated by the twin speakers of a stereophonic gramophone, attached to the sloping roof on both sides of the window.*

*The machine itself is downstage to the left (audience view) and nearby are shelves of* BOB'S *records. Over to the right is the kitchen: through its sliding door can be glimpsed another window opening onto the same flushed sky. The main door to the landing and stairs is downstage, right.*

*When the curtain rises music is playing: Bach on the gramophone. The door bursts open and* BOB *dashes in, toweling his head. He is an awkward young man in his late teens, or early twenties, and his whole manner exudes an evident lack of confidence—in himself and in life. Throughout this first scene he displays the greatest agitation and indecision in his preparations. There is an iron plugged into the electric light. He switches it on—then runs to his chest of drawers, unwraps, and applies a new deodorant stick. It is evident he has never used one before. He runs to the cupboard for his trousers and then back to the iron to press them—but the iron is still cold. Impatiently the boy sits down to wait.*

*Another sort of music is heard approaching.* TED *comes in carrying a blaring little transistor and a carrier bag full of shopping, including a bottle of wine.* TED *is about twenty-five, cocky and extroverted, fitted out gaily by Shaftesbury Avenue to match his own inner confidence and self-approval.*

TED: Christ! D'you know what time it is?

BOB: What?

TED [*Switching off gramophone and then his own radio*]: Seven twenty-two. What the hell have you been up to while I've been doing your shopping?

Dreaming, I suppose, as usual.

BOB: I haven't.

TED: You're marvelous! The most important night of your life, and you can't even get yourself dressed. All you can do is listen to bloody music.

BOB: I wasn't listening. It was just on.

TED: I bet. And what are you doing now?

BOB: Pressing my pants. But it won't get hot.

TED: If she's on time you've got eight minutes. . . . I bought you some flowers. They'll provide that chic touch you're just a tiny bit in need of up here. [*Getting the vase*] Did you have a bath?

BOB: Yes.

TED: Did you use that stick I gave you?

BOB: Yes.

TED: Did you?

BOB: Oh, for heaven's sake!

TED: Did you?

BOB: Yes.

TED: I'll do that. You get your shirt on. [*Takes the iron from him and uses it quickly and expertly.*] What are you wearing over that?

BOB: I thought my blazer.

TED: It's a bit schooly, but she'll probably like that. Makes you look boyish. You'll bring out the protective in her. What tie?

BOB [*Producing a tie*]: I thought this.

TED: Oh yes, gorgeous. What is it? The Sheffield Young Men's Prayer Club?

BOB: Don't be daft. What's wrong with it?

TED: You really don't know, do you? Look: that sort of striped tie, that's meant to suggest a club or an old school. Well, it marks you, see? "I'm really a fifteen pound a week office worker," it says. "Every day I say, 'Come on five-thirty,' and every week I say, 'Come on Friday night.' That's me and I'm contented with my lot." That's what that tie says to me.

BOB: Well, you must have very good hearing, that's what I say.

TED: Where's that green shantung one I gave you last Christmas?

BOB: I lost it.

TED: Typical.

BOB: It isn't. I never lose anything.

TED: I think your subconscious would make you lose anything that was chic.

BOB: That's idiotic. And so's that word.

TED: What? Chic?

BOB: Yes. What's it supposed to mean?

TED: It's French for "with it."

BOB: With it?

TED: Yes. With it, which is what you're not, and high time you were. You can't stay in the provinces all your life, you know. Come on! You've got six minutes. . . . You're not going to let me down tonight, are you?

BOB: What do you mean?

TED: You know what you're going to do this evening? I mean, you know what I'm expecting you to do, don't you?

BOB: Look, Ted, it's not that way at all.

TED: No?

BOB: No, not at all.

TED: Well then, I'm wasting my time here, aren't I? With all due respect, mate, there are rival attractions to playing chef to you, you know. Do you know where I could be tonight? This very night?

BOB: Where?

TED: With her! [*He produces a photograph.*] Look.

BOB: Goodness!

TED: How about them for a pair of bubbles? And that hair—you can't keep your hands off it. It's what they call raven.

BOB: Raven?

TED: Raven black. It's got tints of blue in it.

BOB: Where did you meet this one?

TED: In the Sombrero, last night, dancing herself giddy with some gorilla. I sort of detached her. She wanted a date right away, for tonight, but I said, "Sorry, doll, no can do. I'm engaged for one night only, at great expense, as chef to my mate Tchaik, who is entertaining a bird of his own. *Très* special occasion." So be grateful. Greater love hath no man than to pass up a bird like this for his mate. Look at the way she holds herself. That's what they used to call "carriage." You don't see too much of that nowadays. Most of the girls I meet think they've got it, ignorant little nits. That is the genuine article, that is. Carriage. [*He sets the photo on the table.*] Miss Carriage.

BOB: What's her name?

TED: You won't believe me if I tell you. Lavinia.

BOB: Lavinia?

TED: Honest. How's that for a sniff of class? The rest of it isn't so good. Beamish. Lavinia Beamish.

BOB: She's beautiful.

TED: Do you think so?

BOB: Yes.

TED: She's going to go off fairly quickish. In three years she'll be all lumpy, like old porridge.

BOB: I don't know how you do it. I don't, honest.

TED: Just don't promise them anything, that's all. Make no promises, they can't hang anything on you, can they?

BOB: I wouldn't know.

TED: Well, you're going to, after tonight.

BOB [*Exasperated*]: Ted! Please . . .

TED: Here, I heard a good one the other day. The National Gallery just paid ten thousand pounds for a picture of a woman with five breasts. D'you know what it's called?

BOB: What?

TED: Sanctity.

BOB [*Not understanding*]: Sanctity.

TED: *Un, deux, trois, quatre, cinq*. . . . What do you call this, laying a table?

BOB: What's wrong with it?

TED: So we're all left-handed?

BOB: Oh, Lord. [*He hurries to relay the table. In his haste he upsets the vase. He stares at the mess.*]

TED: You've got the pit-a-pats, haven't you? Well, get a cloth.

[BOB *scurries to get it.*]

You've wet my Lavinia. We'll have to dry you out, love.

[*He crosses and puts the photograph in the corner of Bob's mirror.*]

Now look, Tchaik: if you get in a state, the evening will be a fiasco. So sit there and calm down.

BOB [*Biting his nails*]: I am calm.

TED [*Producing nail clippers*]: Don't ruin your appetite. After all, this is just a girl, isn't it? Even if you say she looks like a Greek goddess, she's still only flesh and blood.

BOB: What time do you make it?

TED: Seven-thirty, just gone.

BOB: Do you think she's not coming?

TED: Of course she's coming. It's a free dinner, isn't it? I hope you've put clean sheets on this bed.

BOB: Oh, Ted, I wish you'd stop talking like that.

TED: Look: let's get things a bit clear. You go to hundreds of concerts.

This is the first time you've picked up a bird and invited her home for lamb chops and vino, isn't it?

BOB: I didn't pick her up. She was sitting next to me and dropped her program.

TED: On purpose.

BOB: Don't be silly. She's not that sort.

TED: Everyone's that sort.

BOB: Well, she isn't. I just know.

TED: Well, what's wrong if she did? She wanted to get to know you. It's just possible, you know, that someone might want to get to know you.

BOB [*Uncomfortably*]: Don't be daft.

TED [*Softer*]: You might try believing that, Tchaik.

[*A tiny pause. Ted sits too.*]

BOB: In any case, I didn't pick her up. That's a ridiculous expression, anyway. Sort of suggests weightlifting.

TED: What did you do, then?

BOB: Well, I asked her if she liked music. It was a daft question really, because she wouldn't have been at a concert otherwise, would she? It turned out that she was on her own, so I asked her to have a coffee with me after. I could hardly believe it when she said yes.

TED: Why not? Even goddesses get thirsty.

BOB: We went to an expresso bar in South Ken.

TED: And held hands over two flat whites?

BOB: Not exactly. As a matter of fact, I couldn't think of anything to say to her. We just sat there for a little while and then left.

TED: So that's why you asked me here tonight? To help out with the talk?

BOB: Well, you know what to say to women. You've had the practice.

TED: There's no practice needed. Just keep it going, that's all. Bright and not too dirty. The main thing is to edge it subtly toward where you want it to go. You know. In your case you'll be able to start off with music—"What a nice concert that was. I do like Bach so much, don't you?" Then if she's got any sense at all she'll say, "Oh yes, he does things to me!" and you'll say, "What kind of things?"—and you're off to the races. I'll give you a tip that usually works a treat. After a couple of hours, if she asks for a cigarette, don't give it to her; light it in your mouth and then hand it to her. It's very intimate.

BOB: I don't smoke.

TED: Well, you'll have to work out your own style, of course.

BOB: What's it matter? She's not coming anyway.

TED: [*Sarcastic*]: Of course not.

BOB: I mean it. Look at the time. It's nearly quarter to eight. [*He stands up nervously.*] She's thought better of it, I bet you.

TED: Oh, don't be silly. Most girls think it's chic to be a little late. They think it makes them more desirable. It's only a trick.

BOB: No, that's not her. She doesn't play tricks. That's why all that stuff is so silly—all this plotting: I say this, and she says that. I think things should just happen between people.

TED: Oh yes. And how many times have they just happened with you?

BOB: Well, that depends on what you want to happen.

TED: You know bloody well what you want to happen.

BOB [*Urgently*]: I don't. I don't. This isn't the sort of girl you can make plots about. It would be all wrong. Because she's sort of inaccessible. Pure—but not cold. Very warm.

TED: And you know all this after ten minutes' silence in a coffee bar?

BOB: You can know things like that without talking. She's not a talker—she's a listener. That can be more profound, you know. And she's got a look about her—not how people are, but how they ought to be. Do you know when I said about a goddess, do you know who I was thinking of? [*Indicating the print above the bed.*] Her.

TED: Venus?

BOB: She's got exactly the same neck—long and gentle. That's a sign.

TED: What the hell for?

BOB: Spiritual beauty. Like Venus. That's what that picture really represents. The birth of beauty in the human soul. My Botticelli book says so. Listen.

[*He picks up a Fontana pocket book and reads.*]

"Venus, that is to say Humanity, is a nymph of excellent comeliness, born of heaven. Her soul and mind are Love and Charity. Her eyes, Dignity. Her hands, Liberality. Her feet, Modesty." All signs, you see. "Venus is the Mother of Grace, of Beauty, and of Faith."

TED: And this bird of yours is the mother of all that?

BOB: No, of course not. Stop trying to make me into a fool. What I mean is, that look of hers is ideal beauty, Ted. It means she's got grace inside her. Really beautiful people are beautiful inside them. Do you see?

TED: You mean like after taking Andrews Liver Salts?

BOB: Yes, that's exactly what I mean.

TED: Oh, Tchaik, now seriously, come off it. That's all a lot of balls, and you know it. There's a lot of dim, greedy little nitty girls about who are as pretty as pictures.

BOB: I don't mean pretty. I mean . . . well, what you called carriage, for instance. What your Lavinia's got. It's not just something you learn, the way to walk and that. It's something inside you. I mean real carriage, the way you see some girls walk, sort of pulling the air around them like clothes—you can't practice that. You've got first to love the world. Then it comes out.

[*Tiny pause.*]

TED: You poor nut.

BOB: What d'you mean?

TED: Nut. Nut.

BOB: Why?

TED: Oh dear, for you.

[*The door bell rings.*]

BOB: God! There she is.

[*He dashes about on a last-second tidying of the flat.* TED *watches, amused.* BOB *grabs his blazer.*]

TED: Now listen. Last swallow of coffee and I'm away. Leave you to it. Nine-thirty you'll see me. Nine-thirty-one you won't. Work to do at home? Get it? Now—where is the bottle of Dubonnet?

[BOB *says nothing.*]

It's the one thing I left you to do.

BOB: I know. I forgot.

TED: You nit! Now you've nothing to give her for a cocktail.

[*The bell rings again.*]

BOB: What am I going to do?

TED: Well, there's nothing you can do, is there? Just don't mention it, that's all. Say nothing about it. She comes from the outer suburbs. She probably won't expect anything. Wine at dinner will impress her enough.

BOB: Oh, hell.

TED: Why don't you leave her standing there? She'll go away in five minutes.

[BOB *dashes out.* TED *gives the room a final lookover, elaborately combs his hair in the mirror, and then strolls into the kitchen. Steps are heard running upstairs.* TED *quickly shuts the kitchen door as* BOB *returns with* DOREEN, *a pretty girl of about twenty, wearing an imitation ocelot coat. It is at once obvious that she is as nervous as he is and has no real pleasure in being there. Her reactions are anxious and tight, and these, of course, do nothing to reassure* BOB.]

DOREEN: I'm not too early?

BOB: No. Just right. It's just half-past seven. You're very punctual.

DOREEN: "Unpunctuality's the thief of time," as my dad says.

BOB: To coin a phrase.

DOREEN: Pardon?

BOB: Can I take your coat?

DOREEN: Thank you.

[*She slips it off. Under it she is wearing a sweater and skirt.*]

BOB [*Taking the coat*]: That's pretty.

DOREEN: D'you like it?

BOB: I do, yes. Is it real? I mean real leopard.

DOREEN: It's ocelot.

BOB [*Hanging it up*]: Oh! [*Imitating* TED.] Very chic.

DOREEN: Pardon?

BOB: Won't you sit down?

[*They advance into the room.*]

DOREEN: Thanks. Is this all yours? Or do you share?

BOB: No, I live alone.

DOREEN [*Looking at the table*]: But you've got three places.

BOB: Actually, there's a friend here at the moment. He's helping with the dinner. We work in the same office.

DOREEN: Can I do anything?

BOB: No, it's all done. Really. All you can do is sit down and relax. [*With an attempt at "style" he gestures at the armchair.*]

DOREEN: Thanks. [DOREEN *sits in it. A tiny pause.*]

BOB: Do you smoke?

DOREEN: I do a bit, yes.

BOB: Good! Tipped or plain? [*He picks up a cigarette box and opens it with a flourish.*]

DOREEN: Well! There's luxury for you, isn't it—both kinds! Tipped, thank you.

BOB: Allow me. [*He picks up a lighter with his other hand and tries to snap it alight. It doesn't work. He puts down the box and fumbles with it, to no avail.*]

DOREEN: It's all right. I've got a match. [*Fetching matches from her handbag, and proffering the light.*]

[*He sits. Another tiny pause.*]

BOB: So, how have you been?

DOREEN: Fine. You?

BOB: Yes, can't complain. Er . . . you're a typist, aren't you?

DOREEN: Stenographer. The place that trained me said, "Never call yourself a typist: it's lowering."

BOB: Oh. What kind of things do you—well, stenog, I suppose?

DOREEN: The usual letters.

BOB: Yours of the tenth?

DOREEN: Pardon?

BOB: "Dear Sir, reply to yours of the tenth." Things like that?

DOREEN: Oh, I see. Yes, that's right.

BOB: Do you mind it?

DOREEN: What?

BOB: Doing the same thing, day in, day out.

DOREEN: Well, there's not much choice, is there?

BOB: I suppose not.

DOREEN: You've got to earn your living, haven't you? Like my dad says, "It doesn't grow on trees."

BOB: No. Wouldn't they look odd if it did?

DOREEN: Pardon?

BOB: The trees.

DOREEN: Oh. Yes. [*She looks at him nervously.*]

BOB [*Plunging on*]: Like when people say unpunctuality's the thief of time—like your dad says. I always used to try and imagine unpunctuality in a mask—you know—with a sack labeled "swag." That's what comes of having a literal mind. I remember I had awful trouble at school one day with that poem which says, "The child is father of the man." I simply couldn't see it. I mean, how could a child be a father? I couldn't get beyond that. I don't think imagination's a thing you can cultivate though, do you? I mean, you're either born with it or you're not.

DOREEN: Oh yes, you're born with it.

BOB: Or you're not.

DOREEN: No.

BOB: There ought to be a sign so parents can tell. There probably is, if we knew how to read it. I mean, all babies are born with blue eyes, but no one ever says there's a difference in the blue. And I bet there is. I bet if you looked really hard at six babies the first day they were born you'd see six different blues. Milky blue—sharp blue, you know, like cornflower color—even petrol blue. And they each mean something different about character. Of course, after the first day, they all fade and become the same. . . . It's a thought, anyway.

DOREEN: Oh yes!

BOB: Daft one. [*Desperately*] Would you like a drink?

DOREEN: Well, I wouldn't say no.

BOB: Good. [*Unhappily*] What would you like?

DOREEN: Whatever you suggest. I'm not fussy.

BOB: Dubonnet?

DOREEN: That'd be lovely.

[*A brief pause. Then he rises quickly. He starts emptying an old whisky bottle on the dresser, containing an old collection of coins.*]

BOB: Well, if you'll excuse me.

DOREEN: What are you doing?

BOB: I won't be a moment.

DOREEN: Can I help?

BOB: I won't be a second.

DOREEN: Where are you going?

BOB: Just around the corner. To the pub. It's only a step away.

DOREEN: Haven't you got any in?

BOB: No. I—[*Inventing it*]—I don't drink.

DOREEN: You don't?

BOB: That's all right. I mean, I want to.

DOREEN: That's silly.

BOB: Why?

DOREEN: Because I don't drink either.

BOB: You're only just saying that.

DOREEN: No, honest, I don't.

BOB: Ever?

DOREEN: Well, only on special occasions, at Christmas and that. But I don't want one now. I only said it to be sociable.

BOB: You're sure?

DOREEN: Positive.

BOB: Well, that's all right then.

[*Enter* TED *with two glasses of wine on tray, playing the waiter.*]

TED: Cocktails, madame?

DOREEN [*Delighted*]: Ohh!

BOB: Ted, this is my friend, the one I told you about. Miss Marchant: Ted Veasey.

TED: Pleased to meet you.

DOREEN: How d'you do?

TED: All the better for seeing you, thank you. You know, most people never answer that question—how do you do? That's because those who ask it don't really want to know. How do *you* do?

DOREEN [*Beginning to giggle*]: Oh: very nicely, thank you.

TED: That's all right, then. Do I have to call you miss?

DOREEN: Well, it is a bit formal, isn't it? Why don't you call me Doreen?

TED: Thanks, I will. If it's not too presumptuous. You see, I'm only the butler around here.

[*Offers her a drink.*]

Doreen? A little chilled vino *avant le diner?*

DOREEN [*Hesitating to take one*]: Well . . .

BOB: I'm afraid she doesn't drink.

TED: No?

DOREEN: Well, only on special occasions.

TED: Well, tonight's an occasion, isn't it? Of course it is. A real proper [*French*] "occasion"! Come on. Do you good.

DOREEN: Well . . . just to be sociable.

TED: That's it.

[*Offering drink to* BOB.]

Tchaik?

BOB: Not for me. You know I don't.

TED: Come on, it's a special occasion.

DOREEN: Come on, I'm having one.

BOB: I don't think I will, not on an empty stomach.

TED: [*Drinks*]: Well, waste not, want not, I say! The servants you get these days! [*To Doreen.*] Well, I'll see you—in two shakes of a lamb's tail. Or should I say chop? [*He ducks back into the kitchen.*]

DOREEN: He's funny.

BOB: Yes, he is. He's marvelous to have in the office. Always cheerful.

DOREEN: Aren't you?

BOB: Not always, no.

DOREEN: What office do you work for?

BOB: Import-export. I'm just a glorified office boy really. At least that's what Ted keeps on telling me, and I suppose he's right.

DOREEN: Why, is he above you?

BOB: In a way he is, yes.

DOREEN: What way?

BOB: Well, he's just been promoted to look after a small department of his own. It means quite a bit of responsibility. He's going to go a long way, I think. I mean he's interested and keen—you know.

DOREEN: Aren't you?

BOB: Well, not so much as he is. He knows all about economics. Tariffs and all that. I'm afraid it's all rather beyond me.

DOREEN: I like people who want to get on. Who've got drive. That's something I respect. My dad's got drive.

BOB: What does he do?

DOREEN: Well, he's retired now. He used to be a foreman in a factory.

BOB: Where?

DOREEN: Edmonton.

BOB: Oh.

DOREEN: He says, if you haven't got drive, you might as well be dead.

BOB: He's probably right. [*Pause.*] Is that drink all right?

DOREEN: Yes, it's lovely.

BOB: Good.

DOREEN: Cheerio.

BOB: Cheerio.

[*Enviously he watches her drink.*]

DOREEN: This is a nice room.

BOB: D'you like it?

DOREEN: It must be nice, living high up.

BOB: It is. And they're very tolerant here.

DOREEN: Tolerant?

BOB: I mean, they don't interfere with your private weaknesses—you know.

DOREEN: Pardon?

BOB: I mean your habits. I'm afraid I've got rather a weakness and some people would get a bit irritable about it, but not here. They let me play Behemoth all night long. [*Indicating the stereophonic machine.*] This is him, of course. Behemoth means a great monster, you know. It's in the Bible.

DOREEN: What is it then, a gramophone?

BOB: Stereo.

DOREEN: It looks lovely.

BOB [*A new note of warmth and pride in his voice*]: You should hear him. Do you know anything about these animals?

DOREEN: I'm afraid not, no.

BOB: Well, I shan't bother you with technical names then. But I can tell you this is really the best machine a chap of my means could possibly afford, anywhere in the world. Of course, if you want to spend thousands, it'd be different. [*With an uncontrollable burst of true enthusiasm, the boy is off on his hobbyhorse.*] Behemoth's a real marvel, I can tell you! Most big sets you can't play properly below a certain level. You can't hear them properly, unless they blast you out of your seat. That's because they've got bad speakers. [*Indicating.*] These things. Most speakers have only got between five and seven percent efficiency. These have fifteen to twenty. Wharfedale speakers. They're the best! . . . I'm sorry: I promised not to give you technical names. It's the music that counts, anyway, isn't it? [*With great warmth.*] I'm glad you like music. I can't tell you how glad I am to know that. You know, last week I'd been watching you for ages before you dropped that program. I was watching you through the Bach: and you were so wrapped up in listening, so concentrating, there were wrinkles all over your face!

[*She looks at him, startled and displeased. He falters.*]

Well, I mean, they were very becoming. . . . I love to see lines on people's faces. I mean, that's their life, isn't it? It's what's happened to them. Most girls you see have got so much powder and muck on, you can't tell anything's happening to them. You know, they're like eggs, their skins. Eggshells, I mean. . . . You're different.

DOREEN: You mean I've got inner beauty.

BOB: Do I?

DOREEN: That's what a man told me once. Inner beauty. It was his way of saying he was off me.

BOB: That's not what I mean at all. [*Desperately.*] You know the really wonderful thing about this machine? You can turn it up as loud as you like, and all you hear is the faintest hum. [*He switches it on.*] Listen, I'm going to turn it right up. [*He turns the volume control as far as it will go. A pause. They listen.*] See?

DOREEN [*Blankly*]: Wonderful.

BOB [*Happily*]: You must have been listening to music for an awfully long time to like Bach. Most people come to him only after a bit. When I first started, it was all the *Symphony Pathétique* and *Swan Lake.* You know.

DOREEN [*Who has heard of this*]: Oh—yes!

BOB: That's why Ted calls me Tchaik: it's short for Tchaikovsky. I was mad about his music once. I thought Bach was boring, like exercises. Then one day I was shaving—isn't it daft how things happen?—I always play records when I'm shaving, or in the bath—and I'd put on one of *Brandenburg*s, you know, the *Fourth* with two flutes, and suddenly—just suddenly—I heard what made it marvelous. It wasn't about love or victory, or those romantic things that change all the time. It was about things that *don't* change. D'you see what I mean?

[*She gives him a quick, tight smile, but says nothing.*]

Anyway, would you like to hear one? I've got all six.

DOREEN: Lovely . . .

BOB: Good. Well, if you wouldn't mind moving here, you'd enjoy it better. You'd be midway between the two speakers at just the right distance. Let me help you.

[*She gets up and he pushes her chair into the proper position.*]

That's it. [*He motions her to sit.*] Now . . . behold! [*He throws open a cupboard which is crammed full of records.*]

DOREEN [*Impressed*]: Help! Are all those yours?

BOB: Every one!

DOREEN: But you must spend all your pay on records!

BOB: Well, you've got to spend it on something, haven't you? Which *Brandenburg* would you like? Or maybe you'd prefer the *Goldbergs*? or the *Musical Offering*?

DOREEN [*Who has never heard of any of these*]: You choose.

BOB: No, it's your pleasure, madame!

DOREEN: Well, to be frank, I don't know that much about it. That old stuff isn't really me.

BOB: You mean you prefer modern?

DOREEN [*Seeing a gleam of hope*]: That's right. Modern.

BOB: What d'you like? Stravinsky? Shostakovich?

DOREEN: Well, I don't quite mean that.

BOB: You mean something more tuneful?

DOREEN: Yes.

BOB: Britten! Like me. I think Britten's the greatest composer in the world! I mean, he writes tunes, and makes wonderful sounds you can understand, not just plink-plonk. I hate all that twelve-tone stuff, don't you? It's sort of not—human. I know what I'll play you! [*Grabbing an album.*] *Peter Grimes*! Decca's done the most marvelous recording of it ever! D'you know it?

DOREEN: I can't say I do.

BOB: It's the greatest thing you ever heard! It's all about this lonely fisherman who lives by himself, and the village hates him because he's different, and has dreams and visions about what life should be. He dreams about this girl, Ellen—someone to share his life, you know, only he's not very good at expressing himself. In the end the village turns against him and accuses him of killing his apprentice. There's a sort of manhunt at night—people calling and shouting, hurrying in with lanterns, making up a posse—you know: it's terrifying!

It's like a rising sea, getting wilder and wilder, up and up and up till it suddenly bursts over the town! [*Taking the record out of its sleeve and putting it on the turntable.*] I think it's the most marvelous thing I ever heard. Listen!

[*He puts on the record at the moment in Act 3 of* Peter Grimes *when the lynch chorus begins its dangerous song of hate:* "Him who despises us we'll destroy!" BOB *listens to it, entranced, beating time to its hurtling rhythms and mouthing the words, which he clearly knows.* DOREEN *watches him with something much less like involvement: she obviously detests the music.* BOB *has put it on very loudly: it becomes quite deafening as it boils up into the great shouts of "Peter Grimes!" punctuated by silence.*]

[*Explaining in a hushed voice.*] That's his name, "Peter Grimes." They all just stand there and call it. Sssh! . . .

[*The chorus yells "Grimes!" Silence.*]

[*Sings.*] "Peter Grimes!"

[TED *comes in from the kitchen carrying a tray of soup: on his head is a chef's hat made from a grocery bag.*]

TED [*Facetiously*]: Did someone call me?

[DOREEN *laughs.*]

[*Going over to the table and distributing the soup.*] Turn it down, for God's sake, or you'll have the neighbors in. Come on, dinner up. [*To* DOREEN.] Madame!

DOREEN [*Rising*]: Ooh, lovely.

[BOB, *his face set, stops the gramophone.*]

TED: Hey, Tchaik, stop fussing with that damn thing, and come and be host. It's your party, isn't it? *Potage à la Heinz! Champignon!* Note that g-n sound, that's pronouncing it proper. Followed by lamb à la Ted Veasey.

[BOB *approaches the table, and with a sudden spurt of aggressiveness, suddenly holds out his glass.*]

TED: Well! What d'you know! He's going to have some after all!

DOREEN: Good for you!

TED [*Pouring him wine*]: Here you are, then. The first drop on the long road to ruin!

DOREEN: Cheers!

BOB: Cheers!

TED: That's better! You know, how you stand that stuff I'll never know. Opera! How so-called intelligent people can listen to it I just can't imagine. I mean, who ever heard of people singing what they've got to say?

[*Singing to the Toreador Song in* Carmen.]

"Will you kindly pass the bread?" "Have a bowl of soup?" "*Champignon*!"—

"I must go and turn off the gas!" Well, for heaven's sake! If that's not a bloody silly way to go on, excuse language, I don't know what is. I wish someone would explain it to me, honest. I mean, I'm probably just dead ignorant.

BOB [*Speaking very quietly*]: You are.

[TED *looks at him in surprise.* BOB *has never said anything like this before.*]

Dead ignorant.

[*A brief pause.* DOREEN *looks anxiously from one to the other.*]

TED [*Smiling*]: Come on. Drink up before it gets cold.

[*All three lift their spoons. They freeze. The lights go down.* BOB *alone is visible sitting in a spot.*]

THE NEXT PIECES OF DIALOGUE ARE ON TAPE.

DOREEN: Ooh, lovely soup! Is it mushroom?

TED: Of course not, it's toadstool.

DOREEN [*Giggling*]: Ooh.

TED: My own creation, mademoiselle, especially for you. It's an old French recipe—only I left out the garlic.

DOREEN: Why?

TED: Well, you never know how the evening might end.

DOREEN [*Laughing*]: Oh!

[*The dialogue becomes a high-pitched gabble as the tape is deliberately speeded up.* BOB *puts down his spoon and drinks off an entire glass of wine, quickly. He picks up his spoon again, and freezes.*]

Ooh, lovely! Chops!

TED: Do you like 'em?

DOREEN: They're my favorite, actually, chops! They always were, ever since I was small. I always used to like the way there was a meaty bit right in the middle of the fatty bit.

[*Again the conversation moves into a high-pitched gabble.* BOB *empties the bottle of wine into his glass and drinks it, then freezes again.*]

DOREEN: Ooh lovely! . . . What is it?

TED: Passion fruit.

DOREEN: What?

TED: That's its name—passion fruit.

DOREEN [*Coyly*]: I don't think I ought to have any.

TED: Go on. One mouthful and you become a hopeless slave of desire.

DOREEN: I think you're pulling my leg.

TED: I wouldn't mind trying.

DOREEN: Pardon?

TED: What time is it then? What time is it then? What time is it then? . . .

*[Echo.]*

What time is it then?

END OF TAPE.

BOB: Nine o'clock.

*[They lower their spoons and resume the scene as the lights come up.* BOB *sits perfectly still, half in a world of his own.]*

TED: Some more vino, then?

DOREEN: I don't mind if I do.

TED *[Picking up the bottle]*: Well, what d'you know? There isn't any. Tchaik's taken it all!

DOREEN: He hasn't. I thought he didn't drink.

TED: Not on an empty stomach. You certainly make up for it on a full one. You want to watch it, mate. Alcohol isn't really a stimulant at all, you know. It's a depressant. It depresses you. That's something most people don't know.

DOREEN: My dad says, "Drink is the curse of the working classes."

TED: Does he?

DOREEN: Yes. Mind you, he can't drink himself because of his ulcer. He suffers from it terribly. Well, of course, he's a natural worrier. Worries about everything.

TED: Does he worry about you?

DOREEN *[Primly]*: He's got nothing to worry about in that department, thank you.

TED: No?

DOREEN: No. I mean politics. Things like that. The way the world's going. I think his ulcer started the day he was appointed branch secretary of the union.

TED: Well, that's enough to worry anybody. He's a union man, then?

DOREEN *[Proudly]*: All his life.

TED: Well, good luck to him.

DOREEN *[Indignant]*: What do you mean?

TED: I'm a Young Conservative myself.

DOREEN *[Suddenly hostile]*: I thought so.

TED: I don't care who knows it. Bloody unions. If you ask me, they're doing their best to ruin the country. Wherever you look you come back to the same thing, the unions. Always at the bottom of everything, the unions, demanding, demanding, demanding all the time. They make me bloody sick.

DOREEN: Well, I don't agree with you there.

TED: No?

DOREEN: No, I don't. My dad can remember the time when he had to fight to get twopence halfpenny a week.

TED: Your dad?

DOREEN: Yes, my dad!

TED: And how old a gentleman would he be, may one ask?

DOREEN: Well, he's getting on now.

TED: How old?

DOREEN [*Defeated*]: Sixty-one.

TED: Well, there you are, then. That's all in the past. It's all so old-fashioned, the bosses against the workers. I can tell you one thing, if the unions are going to run this country I'm moving out. Because the rate they're going, they're going to bankrupt it completely and utterly inside ten years.

BOB [*Dreamily*]: There's a notice in the pub next door that says, "Work is the curse of the drinking classes."

[*A pause.*]

DOREEN: Pardon?

BOB: It's a joke.

TED [*To* DOREEN]: Come on, luv, give us a hand.

[*Singing again to* Carmen.]

"That really was a very lovely meal. I'll collect the mats . . ."

DOREEN [*Singing*]: "The knives and forks and spoons."

[TED *takes tray to the kitchen, whistling.*]

TED: Well, at least make the coffee, Tchaik—I'm worn out.

[BOB *rises, unsteadily. He moves to the kitchen.*]

You'd better put your head under the tap.

[BOB *goes into kitchen and* TED *shuts the door on him.*]

How d'you like old Tchaik?

DOREEN: He's nice.

TED: Certainly is. And a very good son to his old mother, let me tell you.

DOREEN: Which is more than you are, I bet.

TED: Me? I look after Number One.

DOREEN: I'm sure.

TED: Well, the way I look at it, I'm enough to look after. I haven't got time to take on anyone else. Anyway, Tchaik's lucky; his old lady lives in Sheffield. Anyone can be a good son to someone living in Sheffield. He goes up there, has a couple of days, high tea, tripe and onions, quick kiss, and he's away. Now me, my people live practically on the doorstep. Wimbledon. Well, that's different, isn't it? "Why can't you live at home?" they say. Home! . . . You're a very lucky girl, you know.

DOREEN: Me?

TED: To have a sensible old dad like yours. You should meet mine—Mr. Alcohol, 1934. That's when he decided draft beer was the secret of life. Well, not decided exactly. He hasn't decided anything since he married Mum. And he was pushed into that by me. She's not much better, mind.

DOREEN: Your mum?

TED: I was a middle-aged slave, or Seven Years in a Bingo Hall. That's when she bothers to go out at all. Mostly she stays in with "Twenty Questions" and a half-bottle of gin. Am I shocking you?

DOREEN: No, not at all. I think it's all very sad.

TED: Do you?

DOREEN: Yes.

TED: I bet there's a lot of fun in you once you loosen up.

DOREEN: Pardon?

TED: What do you think of me?

DOREEN: Well, if you're like most boys, your mind's on just one thing.

TED: Well, I'm not like most boys, I'm me. And my mind's on a lot of things. What's your mind on most of the time? That's when you're not looking after your old dad or going to concerts. What's with that, anyway—I don't get it. You're not the concerty type.

DOREEN: You know it all, don't you?

TED: Well, are you?

DOREEN: No, as a matter of fact, I was given the ticket by a girl friend. She couldn't go and it seemed silly to waste it. [*Indicating the kitchen.*] Now he thinks I'm a music lover, and know about Bach and everything. Actually it was ever so boring.

[TED *laughs loudly.*]

I realized I shouldn't have said "Yes" to him for tonight as soon as he asked me.

TED: What made you?

DOREEN: Well, I don't know. I don't get out that much. And he was ever so nice and courteous.

TED: I bet.

DOREEN: A blooming sight more better mannered than what you are!

TED: Well who's denying it? Tchaik's always had manners. He's one of nature's gentlemen.

DOREEN: You're wicked, you know.

TED: I mean it. He's a good boy. He wouldn't hurt a fly—and that's not because he's a fly himself either. Because he isn't. He's got feelings inside him I wouldn't know anything about—and you neither.

DOREEN: Thanks.

TED: I mean it. Real deep feelings. They're no use to him, of course. They're in his way. If you ask me, you're better off without all that dreamy bit.

DOREEN: What d'you mean?

TED: Dreams. Ideas about perfect women. He's got one about you.

DOREEN: He hasn't.

TED: He has. Why d'you think you're here? How many girls do you think he's ever asked here?

DOREEN: I dunno.

TED: None. [*Spelling it.*] N-o-n-e.

DOREEN: Well, what's he want with me, then?

TED: Nothing. You're a vision. You've got a long neck like Venus coming out of the sea.

DOREEN: Who's she?

TED: He thinks you're the dead spit of *her*.

[*He points to the print from the wall and shows it to her.*]

DOREEN: Oh, I haven't a long neck like that! . . .

TED: I know you haven't. Yours is the standard size, but he won't leave it at that. He's got to *stretch* it a bit. A long neck's a sign of a generous nature!

DOREEN: He's a bit nutty, isn't he?

TED: Not really.

DOREEN: I think he is. When he was talking about that record, his eyes were all glary.

TED: Oh, that's nothing. Just the old Celtic Twilight in him.

DOREEN: Twilight?

TED: Just a phrase. [*He rehangs the picture.*]

DOREEN: You don't half have a way of putting things. You've got a gift for words, haven't you?

TED: Always had. Words, language. It's why I took up French in the evenings.

DOREEN [*Admiringly*]: I like that.

TED: Do you? Most people would say it was pretentious. Then most people don't count. They've got no drive—no ambition—nothing. I could never be serious about a girl like that.

DOREEN: I don't think you could be serious about anyone.

TED: That's where you're wrong. That's where you are completely and utterly wrong. You don't know me. Not at all.

[*He produces his transistor radio. Faint pop music fills the room.*]

You dance?

DOREEN: Sometimes. When I feel like it.

[*He begins to dance, moving his body at her. Noiselessly* BOB *slides open the kitchen door and starts to carry in the tray of coffee. What he hears stops him.*]

TED: You ever been to the Sombrero?

DOREEN: I can't say I have.

TED: You'd like that. It's quite classy. You might just appreciate it.

DOREEN: Really?

[*She watches him dance for a moment.*]

TED: I'll take you there, if you like.

DOREEN: When?

TED: You name it.

DOREEN: I'm not sure I'd care to, thank you.

TED: 'Course you would. It's a decent place, honest. Would I go there otherwise? What about next Friday?

DOREEN: No, next Friday I'm busy.

TED: Friday after, then?

[*He stops dancing.*]

Well?

DOREEN [*Suddenly capitulating*]: All right.

TED: Good. You'd better give me your phone number, then.

DOREEN: No, I'll meet you there.

TED: I can't have you going there on your own. I'll have to pick you up. That's if you don't live in Norwood, or some lousy place like that.

DOREEN: Putney.

TED: You're lucky. That's just inside my cruising area. [*Serious.*] You're all right, you know. You've got it.

DOREEN: Got what?

TED: Oh, that certain something. It used to be called "carriage." People nowadays call it class, but it's not quite the same thing.

[*Suddenly* BOB *comes boldly in with the tray of coffee cups and a pot and sets it down on the sideboard.*]

[*Seeing him: with false breeziness*] Well—I'm away! I'll just have my coffee, and allez. Love you and leave you.

DOREEN [*Disappointed*]: Oh! Why?

TED [*Executive voice*]: Duty calls. All that work I took home from the office, clamoring for my attention!

DOREEN: Go on!

TED: Well, that's my story, and I'm stuck with it. No sugar?

BOB: Sorry.

[*He goes back into the kitchen.*]

TED: Cigarette?

DOREEN: No, thank you.

TED [*Offering her the pack*]: Go on.

DOREEN: No, really.

TED [*Sotto voce*]: Telephone.

DOREEN: What?

TED [*Through clenched teeth*]: Number!

DOREEN [*Understanding*]: Oh. You got a pencil?

[BOB *returns.* TED *walks away casually.* DOREEN *is very flustered.*]

It's lovely coffee. It tastes really Continental. Like it was perking away for hours in one of those machines. Italian . . .

[*An embarrassed pause.* DOREEN *looks helplessly across at* TED *and becomes aware that he has slipped a pencil into her bag.*]

Can I have the little girl's room?

BOB: It's out on the landing. I'll show you.

DOREEN [*Grabbing her handbag*]: It's all right. I can find it.

[DOREEN *runs out of the room.* BOB *closes the door. The boys look at one another in silence.*]

TED [*Nervously*]: What are you playing at? I've been knocking myself out keeping things going here. What the hell were you doing in the kitchen all that time?

BOB [*Bluntly*]: Listening to you.

TED: Well . . . you heard me giving her the chat, then. You know how she feels about you. She thinks you're the most courteous man she's ever met. And so you are, mate. Just don't overdo it, that's all. This is a girl, not a goddess. Just you give her a shove off her pedestal. You'll find she won't exactly resent it.

BOB: Any more advice?

TED: Are you all right?

BOB: That's like "How do you do," isn't it? No answer expected.

TED: Now look, don't start those pit-a-pats going again. This is the critical moment. If you louse this up, I'm going to be very upset.

BOB: Are you?

TED: Well, of course. I've gone to no little trouble to set this up for you. Flowers—vino—cooking the dinner—the old sexy dance afterward to get her in the proper receptive mood. And all for you.

BOB: For me.

TED: Of course. That's why you asked me here, isn't it? To give you the benefit of my *savoir-faire.*

BOB [*Suddenly exploding*]: *Savoir-faire!* D'you know something? You're so ignorant it's pathetic.

TED: Ignorant? That's twice in one night. If I'm so ignorant I'd better take myself off.

BOB [*Opening the door*]: Why don't you?

TED: Ignorant! That's lovely, that is! Well, I'll know better next time, won't I? I'll know better than to ever help anyone again.

BOB: You don't know what help is. You do your best as you see it, but what if that's nothing, what you see? You'll have lived in vain.

[TED *slams the door violently.*]

TED: Don't you lecture me, boy. It's not me who doesn't help. It's you, who doesn't want it. Maybe that's your whole bit, Tchaik. You *want* it all to be a bloody total disaster. Christ knows why. Well, you've got your wish.

BOB [*Turning on him*]: That's all very clever, Ted, but it doesn't mean anything at all. D'you think I'm half-witted?

TED: I told you what I think.

BOB [*Violently*]: Yes, I know! I'm just someone to look down on, aren't I? Teach tricks to! Like a bloody monkey. You're the organ grinder, and I'm the monkey! And that's the way you want people. Well—go home, Ted. Find yourself another monkey!

[DOREEN *returns. A long pause.* BOB *has his back to* TED *and won't turn round.* TED *tries to say something—to patch it up—make a joke—anything—but nothing comes. He gives it up and with a sudden rough gesture walks past* DOREEN *and slams out of the room.*]

DOREEN: Where's he going?

BOB: Home.

DOREEN: Home?

BOB: Yes.

DOREEN: You mean he's not coming back?

BOB: I don't think so, no.

DOREEN [*Unable to take it in*]: You mean he's just gone off like that without even saying good night?

BOB: Well, yes. . . . He had work to do at home, very urgent. Remember, he did say.

DOREEN: Did he?

BOB: Yes. And he won't let anything stand in the way of his work. That's what's called drive.

DOREEN: Have you two had words, then?

BOB: No.

DOREEN: What about?

BOB: Nothing.

DOREEN: Was it about me?

BOB: Of course not! Why should it be?

DOREEN: I don't know I'm sure.

[*She goes to the door, opens it, and disappears onto the landing.*]

BOB: Here—drink your coffee. It's getting cold.

DOREEN [*Returning*]: I think that's the rudest thing I ever heard of. Ever, in my whole life.

BOB: He didn't mean it that way.

DOREEN: Well, what way did he mean it, then?

BOB: Oh, hell, I don't know. Drink your coffee.

DOREEN: I don't want it.

BOB: Then leave it! . . . I'm sorry.

DOREEN: Don't mention it.

BOB: It's my fault really.

DOREEN: Why?

BOB: I've had too much to drink. I can't carry it. Alcohol's not really a stimulant at all, you know—it's a depressant.

DOREEN: I know. I heard.

BOB [*Smiling*]: He means well, you know. He really does. You can't hold things against him.

DOREEN: Why not?

BOB: Because that's the way he is. He's like that in the office—offhand, always joking. . . .

DOREEN: Yes I bet he'll have a joke about me tomorrow.

BOB: Of course not.

DOREEN: I bet. . . . What office would that be, anyway?

BOB: I told you. Export-import.

DOREEN: No, I mean the actual address.

BOB: The address? What for?

DOREEN: Nothing. I just asked. It must be nice having someone in the office. Someone you're close to.

BOB: We're not close.

DOREEN: I thought you were friends.

BOB [*Passionately*]: Well, we're obviously not! Why should we be? We only work in the same office—we've nothing in common. He comes into work, and he's glad to be there. I hate it. Some mornings I can hardly get out of that bed for thinking how I'm going to spend the day. When I wake up I've got so much energy. I could write a whole book—paint great swirling pictures on the ceiling. But what am I *actually* going to do? Just fill in about five hundred invoices.

DOREEN: Well, that's life, isn't it?

BOB: Look. You're a typist. Are you going to spend the rest of your life being somebody else's obedient servant, original and two carbons?

DOREEN: Well, like I say, we haven't got much choice, have we?

BOB: Yes, we have. We must have. We weren't born to do this. Eyes. Complicated things like eyes, weren't made by God just to see columns of pounds, shillings, and pence written up in a ledger. Tongues! Good grief, the woman next to me in the office even sounds like a typewriter. A thin, chipped old typewriter. Do you know how many thousands of years it took to make anything so beautiful, so feeling, as your hand? People say I know something like the back of my hand, but they don't know their hands. They wouldn't recognize a photograph of them. Why? Because their hands are anonymous. They're just tools for filing invoices, turning lathes around. They cramp up from picking slag out of moving belts of coal. If that's not blasphemy, what is?

[*A tiny pause.*]

DOREEN: What's the time?

BOB: Half-past.

DOREEN: Well, I really must be going now. [*She gets up and goes for her coat.*]

BOB [*Urgently*]: You're quite pretty, you know.

DOREEN: Thanks.

BOB: I mean, very pretty really. [*He helps her put on the coat.*] You know, I always thought an ocelot was a bird.

DOREEN: Did you?

BOB: Yes. I must have been thinking of an ostrich.

DOREEN: I'll let you into a secret. It's not really ocelot.

BOB: Isn't it?

DOREEN: No, it's only nylon. It's not really cold enough for fur coats, anyway, is it? I was just showing off.

BOB: I'm glad you were. I'll let *you* into a secret.

DOREEN: What?

BOB: Some nights when I come back here I give Behemoth a record for his supper. That's the way I look at him sometimes, feeding off records, you know. And I conduct it. If it's a concerto I play the solo part, running up and down the keyboard, doing the expressive bits, everything. I imagine someone I love is sitting out in the audience watching; you know, someone I want to admire me. . . . Anyway, it sort of frees things inside me. At great moments I feel shivery all over. It's marvelous to feel shivery like that. What I want to know is—why can't I feel like that in my work? There's something inside me that can be excited. And that means I could excite other people, if I only knew what way. . . . I never met anyone to show me that way.

DOREEN: Well, I really must be going now.

BOB: How about one more record before you go? . . . One for the road, as they say. Something more tuneful and luscious? *Madame Butterfly*? D'you know the Love Duet? You'll like that. I know it's awfully corny, but I do love all that fudgy sort of music. At least I have great sort of craving for it. Like I suppose some people have for chocolates. Try a bit.

DOREEN: Well really, it is getting rather late.

BOB [*Desperately*]: It only takes three minutes.

[*Pause.*]

DOREEN [*Reluctantly*]: All right.

BOB [*excited again, as he switches on the machine*]: You know what's happening, don't you? Pinkerton—that's the American sailor—has married this Japanese girl in spite of her family and the priests and everybody. And this is the first time they're alone together. . . .

[*He puts on the record, not looking at her, at the start of the Love Duet from* Madame Butterfly, *beginning with the quiet orchestral music before* "Vogliatemi bene, un bene piccolino." *Butterfly begins to sing.*

*There now ensues a six-minute sequence in which not a word is spoken. At first both stand—he by the gramophone, she by the door—in attitudes of strain. Then the warmth of the music gives* BOB *the courage to gesture her toward the armchair, and she tiptoes across the room and sits in it.*

*She listens for a moment, and finds it surprisingly pleasant. She smiles. He sits on the stool near the table, then surreptitiously edges it nearer to her. He reaches out his hand to touch the ocelot coat; she notices this, and the boy hastily mimes a gesture to indicate smoking. She nods. He rises eagerly, and gets her the cigarettes: in his nervousness he opens the box of matches upside down, and they scatter all over the floor. They pick them up together.*

*Finally, kneeling, he lights her cigarette—then, fascinated by her prettiness, he stares up at her. The flame of the match burns between them until she gently blows it out. She offers him a puff: he declines—then accepts. He inhales and chokes a little. He takes her hand and begins to study it with intense concentration. The music increases in ardor.*

*Suddenly* DOREEN *is sorry for him. She closes her eyes and lowers her face to be kissed. Lightly, hardly daring, he responds by kissing her forehead. She opens her eyes a little impatiently, and tugs at her ocelot coat: it is rather hot, isn't it? With clumsy fingers he helps her out of it, and she makes herself more comfortable, tucking her legs under her chair. Then again she closes her eyes and invites his kiss.*

*This time he touches her lips. Clumsily, hardly knowing what to do, his arms grope for her body. The eagerness of his response surprises and alarms the girl. She begins to struggle as the boy's excitement grows. Their positions in the chair become increasingly ridiculous, as she seeks to avoid his embrace with her legs trapped under her. Above them the voices of the operatic lovers sing ecstatically of love. Finally,* DOREEN *struggles free:* BOB *is left lying in an absurd position across the armchair.*

*He stands up, rumpled and upset. He is no longer listening to the inhuman, undisturbable lovers: he is desperate. Slowly, his mind full of how* TED *would act under these circumstances, he begins pursuing her: as slowly, she retreats to the corner of the room, and stumbles back on to the bed. The boy falls softly on top of her, and tries with a deep muddled gentleness to show her passion. She tries haplessly to avoid him. Finally she half rises and pushes him to the floor. Then she gets up, adjusts her clothes, and moves away from him across the room.*

BOB *stares at her. Then he, too, gets up, and comes toward her with a gesture at once desperate and supplicating. Puccini's Love Duet rises to its climax. As the final, unifying chord of deliciousness crashes over the room,* DOREEN *slaps the boy's face—then, horrified, takes it between her hands, trying to recall the blow. Slowly* BOB *backs away from her across the width of the room. The music dies away; the record turns itself off. Silence hangs between them.* BOB *speaks at last.*

BOB: I'm sorry.

DOREEN: That's all right.

BOB: No, no, it isn't. It isn't at all. Actually, you see, I've brought you here under false pretenses.

DOREEN: What d'you mean?

BOB: I've got a girl friend of my own already.

DOREEN: You have?

[*On an impulse he looks at the photograph of the girl left in the corner of the mirror by Ted. She follows his look.*]

DOREEN: Is that her?

[*A pause.*]

BOB: Yes.

DOREEN: Can I see?

[*He takes it and passes it to her.*]

She looks lovely.

BOB: Yes, she is. Very. That's really raven black, her hair. It's got tints of blue in it. You can't really judge from a photo.

DOREEN: What's her name?

BOB: Er . . . Lavinia. It's rather an unusual name, isn't it? Lavinia. I think it's rather distinguished.

DOREEN: Yes, it is.

BOB: Like her. She's distinguished. She's got a way with her. Style, you know. It's what they used to call "carriage."

[*She gives him a startled look.*]

We're going to get married.

DOREEN: When?

BOB: Very soon. So you see it wasn't right of me to bring you here. Anyway, no harm done, I suppose.

DOREEN: No, of course not. [*They go to the door.*] Well, it's been lovely. I enjoyed the music. Really.

BOB: Did you?

DOREEN: Perhaps we'll meet again. At a concert or somewhere.

BOB: Yes.

DOREEN: I'm glad about your girl. She looks lovely.

BOB [*Almost out of control*]: She is.

[*He opens the door and lets her out.*]

Fabian and Carter.

DOREEN: Pardon?

BOB: The name of the firm where Ted works. You wanted to know it. Fabian and Carter. Bishopsgate 2437. Goodbye.

DOREEN: Goodbye.

[*She gives him a quick smile and goes. He shuts the door. He turns and surveys the empty room. Then he walks almost aimlessly across it.*
*He stops by the gramophone. He puts it on. We hear the first strains of* Madame Butterfly. *He stands by it as it plays. He looks down at the record turning. He kneels to it, stretching out his arms to enfold it.*
*Suddenly he draws his hands back. He takes off the pickup, and, with a*

*vicious gesture, scratches the record twice, damaging it beyond repair. A pause. The boy replaces the pickup. Again the Love Duet fills the shabby room, but now there is a deep scratch clicking through it, ruining it. The stage darkens.*
BOB *stands rigid beside Behemoth.*]

SLOW CURTAIN

# THE PUBLIC EYE

A COMEDY IN ONE ACT

*For*
*Victor*
*with love*

*The Public Eye* was first presented with *The Private Ear* at the Globe Theatre, London W1, on May 10, 1962, by H. M. Tennent, Ltd., with the following cast:

| | |
|---|---|
| JULIAN | Kenneth Williams |
| CHARLES | Richard Pearson |
| BELINDA | Maggie Smith |

Directed by Peter Wood

The New York production, also directed by Peter Wood, opened at the Morosco Theatre on October 9, 1963, with *The Private Ear*. The cast was as follows:

| | |
|---|---|
| JULIAN | Barry Foster |
| CHARLES | Moray Watson |
| BELINDA | Geraldine McEwan |

---

*The curtain rises on the outer office of* CHARLES SIDLEY, *Chartered Accountant, in Bloomsbury. It is a well-furnished room in white, gold, and russet, with many white bookshelves laden with works of reference bound in leather. There is a desk where a secretary customarily sits, a sofa, and two doors. One leads out into the hall of the building, the other into* CHARLES'*s office and is marked* Private. *When the door is open we can see stairs going up to higher floors.*

*It is midmorning, and sunlight streams brightly through a large window.*

[*On a chair sits* JULIAN CRISTOFOROU, *studying a large turnip watch. He is a man in his middle thirties; his whole air breathes a gentle eccentricity, a nervousness combined with an air of almost meek self-disapprobation, and a certain bright detachment. He is bundled in a white raincoat, with many pockets. Sighing, he drops the watch into a battered leather bag, like a Gladstone, which is beside him. Then he reaches into one inside pocket and extracts a large handkerchief, which he spreads over his knees; from another he produces a packet of raisins and pours them out; from a third, a packet of nuts, and does likewise. He just begins to eat them when he cocks his ear, hastily stuffs the handkerchief away in a fourth pocket and sits upright and unconcerned as the inner door opens and* CHARLES SIDLEY *comes out.*

CHARLES *is a good-looking man of forty, exact and almost finicky in his speech, with a fairly steady line in pompous sarcasm, and another, more immediately concealed, in self-pity.*]

JULIAN: Good morning.

CHARLES [*surprised to see him*]: Good morning.

JULIAN: Mr. Sidley?

CHARLES: Correct.

JULIAN: I'm delighted.

CHARLES: You want to see me?

JULIAN: It's rather more that I have to. Not that I don't want to see you, of course.

CHARLES: Well, I'm sorry, but I was just on my way home. The office isn't really open on Saturday mornings; I was just doing a little work.

JULIAN: I know. I saw you.

CHARLES: I beg your pardon?

JULIAN: I peeped into your office before. But you were so engrossed I didn't like to disturb you.

CHARLES: How long have you been waiting, then?

JULIAN: About half an hour.

CHARLES: Half—

JULIAN: Oh, please don't apologize. It's a positive joy to wait in a room like this. There are so many delights to detain one. Your reference books, for instance. Overwhelming!

CHARLES: Thank you.

JULIAN: I perceive you have a passion for accuracy.

CHARLES: Let's say a respect for fact.

JULIAN: Oh, let's indeed. I do admire that. And in an accountant a first essential, surely. Mind you, one must be careful. Facts can become an obsession. I hope they aren't with you.

CHARLES: I hope so, too. Now, if you don't mind—perhaps I can make an appointment for next week.

JULIAN [*ignoring him, staring at the shelves*]: Websters! Chambers! *Whittakers Almanac*! Even the names have a certain leathery beauty. And how imposing they look on your shelves. Serried ranks of learning!

CHARLES [*brutally*]: Are you a salesman?

JULIAN: Forgive me. I was lapsing. Yes, I was once. But then I was everything once. I had twenty-three positions before I was thirty.

CHARLES: Did you really?

JULIAN: I know what you're thinking. A striking record of failure. But you're wrong. I never fail in jobs, they fail me.

CHARLES: Well, I really must be getting home now. I'm sorry to have kept you waiting, even inadvertently. May I make an appointment for you early next week?

JULIAN: Certainly. If that's what you want.

CHARLES: Well, as I say, I don't receive clients at the weekend. Now let me look at my secretary's book. . . . What about next Tuesday?

JULIAN [*considering*]: I don't really like Tuesdays. They're an indeterminate sort of day.

CHARLES [*with a touch of exasperation*]: Well, you name it, Mr.—

JULIAN: Cristoforou. [*He pronounces it with an accent on the third syllable.*]

CHARLES: Cristoforou?

JULIAN: Yes. It's a little downbeat, I admit. Balkan cigarettes and conspirator mustaches. I don't care for it, but it's not to be avoided. My father was a Rhodes scholar. I mean he was a scholar from Rhodes.

CHARLES [*with desperate politeness*]: Oh yes?

JULIAN: Why don't you call me Julian? That's a good between-the-wars name. Cricket pads and a secret passion for E. M. Forster. That's my mother's influence. She had connections with Bloomsbury. To be precise, a boardinghouse.

CHARLES: Would you please tell me when you would like to see me?

JULIAN: It's rather more when *you* would like, isn't it?

CHARLES: I have no special relationship with the days of the week, Mr. Cristoforou.

JULIAN: Oh, no more have I, in the final analysis. I mean, they don't actually prevent me from doing things on them. They merely encourage or discourage.

CHARLES: I suppose I could squeeze you in late on Monday if it's urgent.

JULIAN: I had imagined it was. In fact, I must admit to feeling disappointed.

CHARLES: I'm sorry—

JULIAN: No, if the truth be known, extremely surprised.

CHARLES: Surprised?

JULIAN: At your being so offhand. I had imagined you differently.

CHARLES: Are you in some kind of trouble?

JULIAN: Your trouble is mine, sir. That's one of my mottoes. Not inappropriate, I think. Still, of course, I mustn't be unreasonable. It's your decision. After all, you're paying.

CHARLES: I'm what?

JULIAN: Paying. [*He makes to go out.*]

CHARLES: Mr. Cristoforou, come here. I had assumed you were here to see me professionally.

JULIAN: Certainly.

CHARLES: Well?

JULIAN: Well, it's more you wishing to see me, isn't it? Or hear from me anyway.

CHARLES: Perhaps you'd better state your business with me very precisely.

JULIAN: You mean to say you don't know what it is?

CHARLES: How can I?

JULIAN: You don't know why I'm here?

CHARLES: I haven't the faintest idea.

JULIAN: How appalling. I'm agonized. I'm really *agonized!* What must you think of me? Chattering away and you not even knowing why I'm here. Well, of course I'd assumed—but then you shouldn't assume anything. Certainly not in my business. I'm afraid it's absolutely typical of me. My wits are scattered when they should be most collected. You haven't got a spoon on you by any chance?

CHARLES: A spoon?

JULIAN: For my yogurt. Forgive me, it's a distressing symptom of nervousness which I've never been able to conquer. I always eat when I'm embarrassed. Or, as in this case, agonized. [*He takes out a carton of yogurt from his pocket.*]

CHARLES: Mr. Cristoforou, I'm not noted for my patient disposition.

JULIAN: I'm glad to hear that. Patience too long controlled turns to cruelty. That's an old Persian proverb. At least I think it's Persian. It could be Hindu. Do you have a dictionary of proverbs?

CHARLES [*bluntly*]: Who are you?

JULIAN: I'm Parkinson's replacement.

CHARLES: Replacement?

JULIAN: From Mayhew and Figgis. Now there are two names which are quite inappropriate for a detective agency. They should be Snuffmakers to the Duke of Cumberland or something like that. Don't you agree?

CHARLES: Are you telling me that you are employed by Mayhew and Figgis as a private detective?

JULIAN [*producing a china canister labeled* Sugar, *and attempting to pour some on his yogurt*]: Of course. What else? I'm here to make our monthly report. The office was to telephone you and say I'd be coming today. They obviously failed. Very embarrassing. For both of us. [*Referring to the canister.*] That's empty.

CHARLES: And you are here in place of Parkinson?

JULIAN: Exactly.

CHARLES: Why? Where is he?

JULIAN: He's not with us any more.

CHARLES: You mean he resigned?

JULIAN: No. He was thrown down a lift shaft in Goodge Street. Do you know it? It's just off the Tottenham Court Road.

CHARLES: I know where it is.

JULIAN: Hazards of the game, you know. No one mourns him more than I. [*He opens the desk drawer and extracts a spoon.*] Where there's a secretary, there's always a teaspoon.

[CHARLES *stares at his visitor in disbelief. Then impulsively he picks up the telephone.*]

What are you doing?

[*Grimly* CHARLES *dials.*]

CHARLES: Hello? Mayhew and Figgis? This is Mr. Sidley. Mr. Charles Sidley. I'd like to speak to Mr. Mayhew. If he's not there I should like his home number. Yes. Good. Thank you.

[*Unconcernedly* JULIAN *eats his carton of yogurt and looks out of the window.*] [*Irritably.*] Hello? Mr. Mayhew? Mr. Sidley here. I have a man in my office at this moment calling himself Cristoforou. He claims to be an employee of yours. What? . . . Yes? . . . Oh, I see. Yes, he told me that. Goodge Street. Yes, *I know where it is!* Very regrettable. A most efficient man. [*Looking at* JULIAN, *surprised.*] He is? Well, I hope I can, Mr. Mayhew. I hope I can. This is a very delicate matter, as you know. What? No, of course I understand that: yours is a firm of the very highest . . . Yes, I say I know: yours is a firm of the very highest . . . Yes, yes, of course: I realize that. Naturally. Yours is a firm of the very highest—[*Pause.*] Well, we'll see, Mr. Mayhew. I am always willing to give people the benefit of the doubt, though I may add that when I say doubt in this case, I mean doubt. Good morning. [*He hangs up.*] You have a garrulous employer.

JULIAN: Only where he feels his honor to be at stake. After all, his is a firm of the very highest. [*He smiles his bright smile.* CHARLES *glares.*] In this case he said I'd been with it for three years and did the most expert work. Yes?

CHARLES: Correct, as it happens.

JULIAN: Well, it happens to be true. At the risk of sounding forward, I am a superb detective. It's one of the few jobs where being nondescript is an advantage. [*He takes off his raincoat to reveal an eye-catching striped suit underneath.*]

CHARLES: One would hardly describe you as nondescript, Mr. Cristoforou.

JULIAN: Oh yes. I attained nondescript a long time ago. Last year I became characterless. This year, superfluous. Next year I shall be invisible. It's rather like one of those American Gain Confidence Courses in reverse. Make Nothing of Yourself in Six Easy Lessons! . . . Actually I've been working on your affair for four weeks. Mayhew's is a large agency, and we often take over each other's assignments. It's quite routine.

CHARLES: All the same, a little high-handed, I'd say.

JULIAN: I'm sorry you'd say that.

CHARLES: In any case, how did you know I was here?

JULIAN: I am a detective, Mr. Sidley. You work here every Saturday morning, and your wife goes to the Cordon Bleu for a cooking lesson.

CHARLES: Correct.

JULIAN: It was an obvious opportunity to come around.

CHARLES: I see. Very thorough, I'm sure. Now perhaps you would oblige me by reading your report.

JULIAN: Of course. That's why I'm here.

CHARLES: One would never know it.

[JULIAN *sits down and gropes in the Gladstone bag. He struggles with it for a moment and produces not the report, but an immense plastic bag of macaroons.*]

JULIAN: Would you like a macaroon? Excuse me. It's really disgusting, this eating business, I know. I have a friend who's a lawyer, and he gets so nervous about speaking in court, he eats sweets all day long. In his last murder case he devoured twenty-six Mars bars in a morning. You're not a lawyer, are you?

CHARLES: No.

JULIAN: Of course not; an accountant. Silly of me. Scattered wits again! That's almost like being a priest today, isn't it? I mean, people do what you tell them without question. [*He takes out his report.*] What did poor Parkinson tell you at your last meeting?

CHARLES: Surely you know that already, if you inherited his assignment.

JULIAN: His report was negative.

CHARLES: Correct.

JULIAN: Your suspicions were unfounded.

CHARLES: So he said. The point is, are they still? A month has gone by since then.

JULIAN: That rather depends on what they were, doesn't it?

CHARLES: You know very well what they were. What they always are when you call in a detective. Are you trying to be humorous?

JULIAN: I sometimes succeed in being humorous, Mr. Sidley, but I never try. Suspicion is a highly subjective word. It refers with exactitude only to the man who entertains it.

CHARLES: Mr. Cristoforou, what do I have to do to get from you the information I am paying for?

JULIAN [*reasonably*]: I don't know what that is, Mr. Sidley. If you wish to know whether your wife is being sexually unfaithful to you, I must point out that it is extremely difficult for a private eye to witness copulation.

CHARLES: How dare you?

JULIAN: It's even difficult to witness the *desire* for copulation. Inevitably, therefore, there is no proof that your wife has slept outside her marriage bed.

CHARLES: No proof.

JULIAN: None whatever.

CHARLES: Then you have nothing to tell me.

JULIAN: I wouldn't say that.

CHARLES: Then what would you say? In a word, what—would—you—say?

JULIAN: I haven't got a word.

CHARLES: *Then find one!*

JULIAN [*hastily*]: Perhaps I'd better read my report. [*The detective picks up his report and tries to open it. Unfortunately the pages seem to be gummed together.*] Oh dear. That's syrup.

CHARLES: What?

JULIAN: I tried to transport a waffle yesterday, but it didn't work.

[*He tries for a long moment to separate the pages of his report. It tears badly. He looks at his employer with hapless eyes.* CHARLES *stares back in a thunderous silence.*]

[*Ingratiatingly.*] Well, I can read the first page anyway. [JULIAN *picks up the first page, which is in two bits, and reads in an official voice.*] "Report by J. Cristoforou on the movements of Mrs. Charles Sidley. Wednesday: September twenty-second." That was my first day, you see.

CHARLES: Never mind about that.

JULIAN: "Ten-forty-eight: subject leaves house. Takes taxi at corner of Walton and Pont Streets." That's always a tricky one, by the way. Have you ever considered what one does if one's quarry hails a taxi and there isn't another one in sight?

CHARLES: I'd always assumed you drove a car.

JULIAN: Ah, sadly, no longer. I used to be the ace driver of the agency. But one day I found myself in my car—a lightning-fast Volkswagen, painted chameleon brown—when I spotted on the pavement a wanted criminal of immense notoriety. Pablo Ibanez—an Iberian burglar—known to the police of six outraged countries as the Spanish Fly. Suddenly he caught my eye focused upon him—always an unnerving experience—and he began to run! I gave chase, still in my car. To evade me he darted through the door of a large church, and I had no choice but to follow.

CHARLES: In your car?

JULIAN: There wasn't a moment to lose!

CHARLES: What happened?

JULIAN: I crashed into the baptismal font and ruined a christening. The baby fainted. The man got clean away, and later sent a jeering letter to the agency from Andalusia. As a result they took away my driving licence.

CHARLES: Would you continue with your report? My wife was in a taxi.

JULIAN: Yes, and on this occasion—most luckily—I was able to hail another. [*Reading.*] "Subject proceeds to Madame Martha, hatmaker, of 32 Marble Street."

CHARLES: Could you see in?

JULIAN: Yes.

CHARLES: Who was there?

JULIAN: Four old ladies.

CHARLES: Any men?

JULIAN: I don't think so.

CHARLES: You don't think?

JULIAN: I mean they may have been dressed as ladies. It's just a possibility in a hat shop.

CHARLES: I see.

JULIAN: "Subject collects hat, which appears to be already ordered, and emerges, wearing it. Hat resembles a wilted lettuce. Very unbecoming."

CHARLES: Watch what you say, please. Everything my wife knows about hats, or clothes of any kind, she learned from me. When I first met her she wore nothing but sweaters and trousers. When you criticize her taste in hats, you are criticizing me.

JULIAN: I'm terribly sorry.

CHARLES: I suppose it's only natural that now she's moved away from me she should revert to type. All this last week she's worn nothing but a hideous black sombrero.

JULIAN: You don't like it?

CHARLES: You do?

JULIAN: I think it has a certain gamin chic.

CHARLES: Continue, please.

JULIAN: "Eleven-thirty: subject in *exquisite* green hat walks up Brompton Road, enters the Michelangelo Coffee Bar. Orders a Leaning Tower of Pisa."

CHARLES: What the hell's that?

JULIAN: A phallic confection of tutti frutti, chocolate chips, nougat, stem ginger, toasted almonds and molasses—the whole cloud-capped with cream! . . . Your wife is rather partial to it. So, as a matter of irrelevant fact, am I. Do you have a sweet tooth?

CHARLES: Never mind about my teeth. What happened next?

JULIAN: "Twelve-seventeen: subject rises and goes into Kensington Gardens. Walks to the statue of Peter Pan."

CHARLES: What did she do?

JULIAN: She looked at it and laughed. A curious reaction, I thought.

CHARLES: Not at all. The first week we were married I showed her that statue and explained to her precisely why it was ridiculous. When you criticize her taste in statuary you criticize me.

JULIAN: Please forgive me. I don't know where to look.

CHARLES: At your report.

JULIAN: Yes . . . certainly . . .

CHARLES: She was waiting for someone, I presume.

JULIAN: On the contrary, she wandered about quite aimlessly.

CHARLES: How do you know it was aimlessly?

JULIAN: At one point she picked up some acorns.

CHARLES: Acorns?

JULIAN: Yes, to throw at the ducks. I got the impression she had nothing better to do.

CHARLES: Charming! That's the result of all my work, trying to teach her to spend her leisure properly.

JULIAN: It was a very nice day.

CHARLES: What's that got to do with it?

JULIAN: I was trying to be indulgent.

CHARLES: You're not paid for indulgence, are you?

JULIAN: No.

CHARLES: Then get on.

JULIAN: Yes. "Twelve-fifty-five: subject leaves park and enters a cinema in Oxford Street. It was showing the film *I Was a Teenage Necrophile.*"

CHARLES: Did you go in after her?

JULIAN: Naturally.

CHARLES: And she sat by herself?

JULIAN: Throughout. Four hours and seventeen minutes.

CHARLES: Four hours . . . ?

JULIAN: She saw it twice.

CHARLES: What did you make of that?

JULIAN: I thought it argued the most amazing capacity to suspend disbelief.

CHARLES: Indeed?

JULIAN: It was a very tasteless film. But worse ones were to follow. I mean on subsequent days.

CHARLES: And that was how she spent her day?

JULIAN: Yes.

CHARLES: After all I've taught her. How dare she? . . . *How dare she??!* . . . [*Upset.*] I beg your pardon. It's not an easy thing to set detectives on your wife. It must seem rather bad form to you—or it would if—well.

JULIAN: If I wasn't one myself. It still does, Mr. Sidley. I must admit I end up despising many of our clients.

CHARLES: Despising? That's rather rich coming from you, isn't it?

JULIAN: Oh yes, I dare say. It's something of a reflex action. They despise me, after all.

CHARLES: What else do you expect?

JULIAN: Nothing. The client looks down on the whore who relieves him. It's a familiar pattern.

CHARLES: Charming image.

JULIAN: But not inappropriate, I think.

CHARLES: If you think like that, why do you do it?

JULIAN: Private reasons. Or, to be exact, public reasons.

CHARLES: I don't understand.

JULIAN: It's not important. At the risk of seeming impertinent, Mr. Sidley, why did you come to us? You really had nothing to go on.

CHARLES: You mean nothing concrete. No letters written in a hot, impetuous hand. No guilty smiles or blushes. My dear man, we live in the twentieth century, which blushes at nothing. The blush has gone out, like the ball card and the billet-doux. Betrayal has become a word with rather quaint connotations.

JULIAN: I think that's just rhetoric, Mr. Sidley. Rather well managed, if I may say so, but not true at all.

CHARLES: No? My wife has no more conception of sexual fidelity than that chair. When I married her, she thought nothing of sleeping with three different men in the same week.

JULIAN: Was one of them you?

CHARLES: I don't think I need to answer that.

JULIAN: Oh, come. If you're like a priest in your profession, I'm like a psychoanalyst in mine. You can't afford to withhold information. Unlike an analyst, I'm not considered a gentleman, so you can tell me everything. If this was true, why did you marry her?

CHARLES: Because . . . I was infatuated with her.

[*A pause.* CHARLES *almost visibly unbends a little.*]

JULIAN: Continue, please.

CHARLES: I don't see what possible bearing this could have on the situation.

JULIAN: Oh! But you must let me be the judge of that. Where did you meet her?

CHARLES: In a place called the Up-to-Date Club in Soho.

JULIAN: It doesn't seem the sort of place you would go to.

CHARLES: I was taken there by a journalist friend. I must say it was very pleasant. It had a dining room upstairs with French cooking and a sort of cellar below where you could dance. I wasn't very good at dancing—at least not all that jungle warfare they call dancing—but the food was delicious, and Belinda served it.

JULIAN: Belinda?

CHARLES: My wife. She didn't serve it very well either. She was always forgetting one's order and having to come back for it, which I found more agreeable than otherwise. . . . I caught myself going there rather often. Finally I asked her out to a theater. She'd never seen anything more complicated in her life than a horror film. She was absolutely obsessed by horror films.

JULIAN: She still is.

CHARLES: Yes . . . It was a curious courtship. Without my demanding it, of course, she surrendered her whole life to me, for remaking. In a way, I suppose it wasn't too surprising. She'd lived in Northampton for the first eighteen years: her father was in shoes—and his ambitions for her extended no further than a job at the library and marriage with a local boy. Very properly she ran away to London, where she led the most extraordinary life, sharing a flat with two artists, one of whom baked his canvases in an oven, while the other spat paint onto his direct from his mouth—thereby expressing contempt for society, I believe. It's not surprising really, since at the time she was comparing them both to El Greco, that she reacted to some tactful reform with enthusiasm. For my part, I taught her everything I could. I'm not an expert, Mr. Cristoforou: I'm that old-fashioned, but I hope not too comical thing, a dilettante. Of course the notion of an accountant with what, in the days when Europe was the world, used to be called a soul, probably strikes you as ludicrous. I'm afraid there's a great deal about this situation which is ludicrous. The moral, of course, is that men of forty shouldn't marry girls of eighteen. It should be a prohibition of the church like consanguinity: only marry in your generation. And yet it began so well . . .

JULIAN: You were happy?

CHARLES: Deeply. She renewed my life. I had someone to share things with: show things to.

JULIAN: And she? Did she show things to you?

CHARLES: She didn't need to. She was young and that was enough. Youth needs only to show itself. It's like the sun in that respect. In company with many men of my age, I found I was slipping away into middle life: journeying, as it were, into a colder latitude. I didn't like it. I didn't like it at all.

JULIAN: So you went after the sun. Tried to bottle a ray or two.

CHARLES: Foolish, imbecile attempt. Within a year I had to recognize that I had married a child. Someone with no sense of her place at all.

JULIAN: Her place?

CHARLES: Certainly. Her place. Belinda is the wife of a professional man in a highly organized city in the twentieth century. That is her place. As I have often explained to her, this would undoubtedly be different if she were wedded to a pop musician, which she seems to think she is. There is no such thing as a perfectly independent person.

JULIAN: Is that what she wants to be?

CHARLES [*irritably*]: I don't know what she wants to be. She doesn't know herself. Things have got steadily worse. Three months ago I invited a very important client to dinner, the president of one of the largest investment companies in the City. My wife presided over my table dressed in what I can only describe as a leather pajama suit. When I remonstrated with her, she said she was sick of stuffy guests.

JULIAN: It's a fair point.

CHARLES [*hotly*]: It's not a fair point! [*Exasperated.*] My friends are not stuffy, Mr. Cristoforou, just because they don't come to dinner disguised as motorcyclists. No doubt they are helplessly out of touch with modern living. They only read, think, travel, and exchange the fruits of doing so pleasurably with each other. Is there anything so utterly boring and ridiculous as the modern worship of youth?

JULIAN: Nothing, no. It's like sun worship. Debasing and superstitious.

CHARLES [*looking at him suspiciously*]: No doubt this is very amusing to you.

JULIAN: How can you think that?

CHARLES: You think it's sour grapes?

JULIAN: Of course not!

CHARLES: Oh yes!

JULIAN: Mr. Sidley, I beg you—

CHARLES [*with real pain*]: Has my wife a lover?

JULIAN: What makes you think she has?

CHARLES [*in a defeated voice*]: Because for three months now she has turned away from me. Just turned away. You know how women avert their faces when they don't want to be kissed. Well, she is averting her face, her look, her mind. Everything. Whole meals go by in silence, and when she talks, she appears not to be listening to what she herself is saying. In the old days she used to stay in bed until long after I'd gone to the office. I used to remonstrate with her about it. Now she's up and out of the house sometimes before eight. As if she can't bear to lie in my bed another minute. . . . Last week one morning she was up at six. When I asked her where she was going, she said she wanted to watch the sun come up on Parliament Hill. [*Explosively.*] Goddamnit, d'you think I'm a fool? She's seeing someone else, isn't she? Look—last night she didn't come in at all!

JULIAN: At all?

CHARLES: Well, not until well past two. And not one word of explanation.

JULIAN: Did you ask her for one?

CHARLES: If I ask her for anything, that's a quarrel in a minute. [*Pause.*] Tell me. There's someone else, isn't there?

JULIAN [*quietly*]: Yes.

CHARLES: Go on.

JULIAN: I find this hard.

CHARLES: Go on. How often do they meet?

JULIAN: Every day.

CHARLES: Every day?

JULIAN: Yes.

CHARLES: Describe him.

JULIAN: Well . . . he's handsome, I'd say.

CHARLES [*bitterly*]: Of course.

JULIAN: Full of a kind of confidence: you know, debonair, well dressed. I'd say he was a diplomat.

CHARLES: A diplomat? . . . There was that party at the Nicaraguan Embassy.

JULIAN: No, he's definitely not Nicaraguan.

CHARLES: How do you know that?

JULIAN: Ah! That's a very fair point. You have an acute mind, Mr. Sidley. I admit that when you meet a complete stranger for the first time there is no definite way of knowing he's not Nicaraguan.

CHARLES: How does he behave to her?

JULIAN: With great politeness. He shows a most striking restraint.

CHARLES: You mean they don't actually kiss in public?

JULIAN: Certainly not!

CHARLES: What *do* they do, then?

JULIAN: Oh . . . stare at each other happily. Exchange looks of deep meaning. Give those little secret glances—you know—I think the

French call them "*oeillades.*" I'm sure that's the word. Shall I look it up?

CHARLES: Secret glances . . .

JULIAN: I'd say, watching from a distance, their relationship was one of the utmost tenderness.

CHARLES: Would you?

JULIAN: Yes, I would.

CHARLES: Damn her!

JULIAN: Mr. Sidley—

CHARLES: Damn her! Damn her!! [*Furiously.*] What's his name?

JULIAN: I don't know.

CHARLES: Where does he live?

JULIAN: I don't know.

CHARLES: Liar!

JULIAN: I don't.

CHARLES [*grabbing him by the lapels*]: Listen to me. You're a private detective, aren't you?

JULIAN: You know I am.

CHARLES: And it's your job to find out names and addresses?

JULIAN: I suppose it is.

CHARLES [*shaking him*]: Well, you find out this man's name and address by tonight, or I'll break your bloody neck! [*He hurls him down onto the sofa.*]

JULIAN: Mr. Sidley! You've no right to handle me like this. I'm a professional man.

CHARLES: You're a sneaking, prying, impertinent little wog!

JULIAN: I didn't want to tell you. You made me. Be honest. You made me.

[*A buzzer sounds. Pause.* CHARLES *goes to the intercom on the desk and speaks.*]

CHARLES: Yes? Who is it?

BELINDA [*through the intercom*]: Surprise, surprise!

CHARLES [*to* JULIAN, *amazed*]: My wife! She hasn't been here in over a year! . . . You'll have to slip out the back way. [*Indicating the inner office.*]

JULIAN: Why?

CHARLES: Do as I say.

JULIAN: No.

[*The buzzer sounds again.*]

BELINDA: Charles?

CHARLES: I'm coming! . . . Through there, down the fire escape, into the mews!

JULIAN: No.

CHARLES: Please. I'm sorry I pushed you. You're quite right, you're a professional man. I apologize. Only please go!

JULIAN: No.

CHARLES: Why not?

JULIAN: I haven't finished my report. There's lots more yet if I can unglue the pages.

CHARLES: Look, come back on Tuesday.

JULIAN: I told you I hate Tuesdays.

CHARLES: Well, Monday then. Six o'clock.

JULIAN: Five o'clock.

CHARLES: Five-thirty.

JULIAN: Done!

[*He stares at* CHARLES *and then goes into the inner office, shutting the door. The buzzer goes again.* CHARLES *answers it.*]

CHARLES: Yes.

BELINDA [*off*]: What's going on up there?

CHARLES: Nothing, my dear.

BELINDA [*off*]: Well, open the door then. It's still locked.

CHARLES: Oh! Yes—I'm sorry.

[JULIAN *rushes back into the room.*]

What is it *now*?

JULIAN: My macaroons!

CHARLES: Oh, for God's sake!

JULIAN: I can't possibly go without them. They're flown in daily from Vienna!

[*He rushes out again just as* BELINDA *appears screened by an enormous armful of yellow flowers. She lowers them to reveal a pretty young girl of twenty-two, wearing a colored blouse, slacks, and a black sombrero.*]

CHARLES [*coldly*]: Why aren't you at the Cordon Bleu?

BELINDA: I got tired of learning the right way to hold a saucepan, so I left.

CHARLES: And came here.

BELINDA: Obviously.

CHARLES: Why?

BELINDA: I was just passing.

CHARLES: Passing?

BELINDA: Yes. I thought I'd collect you. Surprise, lovely surprise! [*Seeing the carton left by mistake on the desk.*] Who eats yogurt?

CHARLES: I do.

BELINDA: Since when? I thought you loathed it.

CHARLES [*picking it up*]: Did you? Aha! Well, you don't know everything about me.

BELINDA: I'll buy some for home.

CHARLES [*tasting it*]: No, thank you.

BELINDA: Why not? If you like it.

CHARLES [*testily*]: I like it in the office. I do not like it at home. It's as simple as that.

BELINDA: Are you feeling all right?

CHARLES: Perfectly.

BELINDA: Well, you don't look it. [*She dumps flowers into the vase.*]

CHARLES: Belinda, this is only my office.

BELINDA: I know where it is, Charles, and it needs them. Aren't they lovely? There was a man at the corner selling them off a barrow. I think he was a Malayan. At any rate he had topaz eyes, so I bought the lot. Two pounds ten with the greenery. The Malayan said if I bought everything, there'd be no monsoon over my temple for a year. Wasn't that a sweet thing to say?

CHARLES: Fairly uninspired, I should say. The gypsy who sold you one sprig of heather last week for five pounds did rather better.

BELINDA: That was because he belonged to a dying race, and I couldn't bear it. How awful it must be to belong to a dying race. Like the Yaghan Indians. I read somewhere there were only nine Yaghans left, right at the bottom of the world. No, honest! South Chile. After a while nature says, "Scrap them," and they just fail, like crops. Isn't it sad? Imagine them. Nine little shrunk people, sitting on green water, waiting to die.

CHARLES [*grimly*]: I am imagining them.

BELINDA: What's the matter with you?

CHARLES: It's a pity I'm not a Yaghan Indian, isn't it? I might get a little attention from you. Yes. Outrageous demand for a husband to make of a wife, isn't it? Attention. Notice.

BELINDA: I notice you, Charles.

CHARLES: Very humorous.

BELINDA: It's not meant to be.

CHARLES: Where were you last night?

BELINDA: Out.

CHARLES: You knew I was bringing someone back.

BELINDA: You said you *might*.

CHARLES: Well, I phoned you from here at six and you weren't home.

BELINDA: Well, so? Did you need me to pour out whisky or cut his cigar?

CHARLES: That's hardly the point.

BELINDA: It's just the point, I'd say. You always say you want me to entertain your friends, and as soon as you can, you get out the port and send me out of the room. It's incredible, anyway, that a man of your age should be pushing decanters of port clockwise round a dining table. It makes you look a hundred. When I tell my friends, they can't believe it.

CHARLES: I'm sure they can't. But then one would hardly accept their notions of etiquette as final, would one?

BELINDA: Oh, please!

CHARLES: What?

BELINDA: Not your iceberg voice. I can't bear it. "One would hardly say." "I scarcely think." "One might hazard, my dear." All that morning-suit language. It's only hiding.

CHARLES: Indeed?

BELINDA: Yes, indeed. Indeed, indeed! People don't say "indeed" any more, Charles. It's got dry rot.

CHARLES: Where were you?

BELINDA: With my friends.

CHARLES: Oh, of course. In some grotesque little coffee bar, I suppose.

BELINDA: Correct, as you would say.

CHARLES: Telling stories about me. The way I talk. The words I use. My behavior at dinner. Very loyal, I must say.

BELINDA: And where were you? In a stuffy old club, surrounded by coughing old men with weak bladders and filthy tempers, scared of women and all mauve with brandy. How lovely!

CHARLES: That's just disgusting.

BELINDA: You're telling me!

CHARLES: And where are you going now? I mean, where are you *passing* to go to? Another coffee bar?

BELINDA: Perhaps.

CHARLES: Belinda, what does "wife" mean?

BELINDA: What?

CHARLES: Perhaps it's a word no one has ever explained to you. Certainly they didn't in that squalid little registry office you insisted on going to, because you couldn't enter a church. Nevertheless, at the risk of appearing still more pompous, my dear, you made a contract with me. A contract of marriage.

BELINDA: Well, what about it? There's nothing in it that says a woman must drop her friends and take her husband's. I know it's always done, but I don't see it should be. I never promised to cherish all those mauve old men in sickness and health. I love my friends: how can I be faithful to you if I'm unfaithful to them?

CHARLES: May I ask what that means?

BELINDA: That you're not my only duty, that's what it means, and I'm not yours. You've got to be faithful to all sorts of people. You can't give everything to just one. Just one can't use everything. And you certainly can't *get* everything from just one. Just because you get sex from a man, it doesn't mean you're going to get jokes as well, or someone who likes jazz. Oh, I know a husband claims the right to be all these things to a woman, but he never is. The strain would be appalling.

CHARLES: Charming.

BELINDA: It's true.

CHARLES: It's not true! You talk about men as if they were hors d'oeuvres: him for the herring, him for the mayonnaise, him for the pickled beetroot.

BELINDA: But that's exactly it! How clever of you to think of a comparison like that. That's marvelous!

CHARLES: Yes, well, it's just stupid and immature. I suppose I really shouldn't expect anything else.

BELINDA: Thanks for nothing.

CHARLES: If you were a real woman, you wouldn't find it hard to receive everything from one man. To see everything in him and hope to be everything in return. But it's beyond you, of course.

BELINDA: Thanks for nothing.

CHARLES: Oh, stop that!

BELINDA: Then *you* stop it!

CHARLES: Listen to me, and try to understand. Stop fiddling with those flowers.

BELINDA: Well?

[*A slight pause.* CHARLES *collects himself.*]

CHARLES: Let me tell you something. Each man has all of these things inside him: sex, jokes, jazz, and many other things than that. He's got the whole of human history in him, only in capsule. But it takes someone who loves him to make those capsules grow. If they don't grow, he's not loved enough. And that kind of love can only be given by an adult.

BELINDA: Which I'm not. Thanks for nothing! Well, if I'm not, whose damn fault is it? This isn't my home. It's my school.

CHARLES: That's not true.

BELINDA: Oh, but yes it is, Charles. Just look at the way you're holding that ruler! [*A pause. She looks at him seriously.*] You *were* everything to me once. I thought you were the most fantastic person I'd ever met. I remember the exact moment I fell in love with you. It was half past three on Thursday afternoon February the nineteenth, two years ago. You had already explained to me the theory of natural selection, the meaning of id, ego and superego, and were halfway through the structure of Bach's *Fugue in C Sharp Minor*, Book One, *Well-Tempered Clavier.* I thought to myself, "How can one head hold so much? He's not showing off, these things come up naturally in his conversation." I adored it. The world seemed so wide suddenly. You were the first person who showed me that an intellectual was a marvelous thing to be. Most of my friends are all feelings. They're just like moles bumping about in dark little burrows of feeling. And that was me too. Feeling, feeling all the time—but never getting to understand anything. When you met me, I'd have said or done anything just to join in. I thought people would like me more if I liked what they liked. So I pretended all the time. In the end I couldn't tell what I really liked from what I said I liked. Do you remember the day we played "Totem Animals" and I said yours was the llama? Well, mine was the chameleon. I made up my enthusiasm to suit my surroundings. [*Frankly.*] You released me from all that. You gave me facts, ideas, reasons for things. You let me out of that hot, black burrow of feeling. I loved you then.

CHARLES [*dully*]: Then.

BELINDA: Yes.

CHARLES: But no longer?

[*A little pause.*]

BELINDA: I don't know. Living with you has taught me to respect my feelings—not alter them under pressure.

CHARLES: And I'm pressure?

BELINDA: Look, I know I was a pupil before. I admit it—it was good. But you were different then. Now I feel that you hate me half the time.

CHARLES: That's ridiculous.

BELINDA: Well, resent me, anyway. Like an awful headmaster. I feel I have to defend myself in front of you. I feel guilty.

CHARLES [*ironic*]: Do you? How extraordinary!

BELINDA: Charles, answer me something.

CHARLES: What?

BELINDA: Do you love me? I don't mean want me, for whatever reason. I mean, love me. Be honest.

[*A little pause.*]

CHARLES: Very much.

BELINDA: Then why the hell don't I feel it? "I'm burning," says the fire. But my cold hands say, "No, you're not!" Love with me is a great burst of joy that someone exists. Just that. Breathes! And with that joy comes a huge great need to go out and greet them. Yes, that's the word: *greet.* I used to greet you, inside me anyway, forty times a day. Now it's once a fortnight. And always when you're not looking. When you've got your hat on at an angle trying to look jaunty, which you can never manage anyway. It's all so dead with us now.

[*Pause.*]

CHARLES: And *he's* made you come alive?

BELINDA [*startled*]: What do you mean?

CHARLES: For someone who puts such a premium on her honesty, you make a pretty awful showing. I *know*, my dear. I *know.* So there's no need for any of this.

BELINDA: Know?

CHARLES: About him. Your man.

BELINDA: But you can't! . . .

CHARLES: But I do.

BELINDA: How?

CHARLES: Never mind how! I may be the pompous headmaster, but I'm not the village idiot. [*Pause.*] Don't you think you'd better tell me?

BELINDA: No.

CHARLES: Is it so painful?

BELINDA: It's not painful at all. But you just wouldn't dig it.

CHARLES: Give me the spade and let me try.

BELINDA [*smiling*]: You're marvelous sometimes!

CHARLES: Thank you.

[*A pause. Husband and wife look at each other.*]

BELINDA: All right. I will. Only you must promise not to interrupt.

CHARLES: Very well.

BELINDA: Just listen and make what sense of it you can.

CHARLES: All right.

BELINDA: I can make none, so we start equal.

CHARLES: Go on.

BELINDA: Well, you know I've been going out by myself for weeks.

CHARLES: I had noticed.

BELINDA: I was trying to think: that's all. Trying to pull myself out of the burrow on my own. I wandered about all over the place, it doesn't matter where. Then one day, about three weeks ago, a man sat down next to me on the bus, turned, and looked me straight in the eye. He was the most extraordinary man.

CHARLES: Handsome. Debonair. The look of a diplomat, no doubt.

BELINDA [*surprised*]: No, not at all like that. He was a goofy-looking man in a white raincoat, eating macaroons out of a polythene bag.

[CHARLES *gives her a startled look.*]

He had the funniest expression I ever saw—sort of witty—as if he wanted to wink, but didn't know how. At first I thought he was trying to pick me up, but it wasn't that. It took me a few minutes to work it out. What I was seeing was approval. Simply that. Do you know, I'd forgotten what it was like to be looked at without criticism? I was so embarrassed I got up and left. He immediately got up too, and followed me. I began to walk very fast down Bond Street, and he walked just as fast behind, until we were both almost running. In the end I dived into the hairdressers and had quite an unnecessary shampoo. When I came out, he was waiting for me, leaning against Cartier's window, sucking an iced lolly. Since then we've been together every day. I don't expect you to believe what I'm going to tell you, but it's every word true.

CHARLES [*grimly*]: Go on, please.

BELINDA: You're getting upset, aren't you?

CHARLES: Never mind me. Just go on.

BELINDA: I don't want to upset you. I really don't.

CHARLES: On!

BELINDA: All right. . . . First let me tell you the oddest thing about this whole affair. I call it an affair because it is one. But do you know, for the whole three weeks since we first saw each other, we haven't exchanged a single word? When I say we meet every day, I don't mean we make a date. All I mean is that like Mary's little lamb, wherever I go he's sure to follow. He's a pure genius at following! You never see him till he decides to show himself. Then he just pops up—click! like that!—in a coffee bar or a cinema, or out from behind a statue in the park. Once I turned round and there he was in the powder room at Fortnums! I suppose at the start I ought to have been scared, but I never was. Isn't that odd? All I knew was here was someone who approved of me. Who got pleasure out of just being in my company. Of course I realized he must be the loneliest man in town, but then in a way I was the loneliest girl, so it was sort of fitting. Who was I to complain if he got his kicks following me around? After a bit—and this is the really kooky thing—I began to get mine by following *him.*

CHARLES: What?

BELINDA: The day came when he took over. I'd stopped outside a cinema where there was a horror film, and looked back, as usual, just to make sure he'd seen me go in. And you know, he shook his head. He wasn't going to see that film! He was like you, you see: he didn't really like horror films. Mind you, he'd had a bit of a go with them: I'd made him sit through eleven that week. Instead he turned round, signed for me to follow and marched off to the next cinema. That was the first time I'd ever seen an Ingmar Bergman film. Charles, they're marvelous! This one has a poor old man driving all over Sweden in a motorcar, looking for the turning he took wrong years before. It's pathetic.

CHARLES: No doubt.

BELINDA: It is really. At one point he sees himself in his own coffin!

CHARLES: And this is all you've got to tell me?

BELINDA: Yes. Anyway, as far as what you're thinking's concerned. After that the whole thing became marvelous. We never knew what each day would bring. Sometimes I would lead. Sometimes he would. Last week I marched into the National Gallery and stopped in front of Bellini's portrait of a Doge. He was terribly grateful: you know, he'd obviously never seen it. He paid me back by leading me out to Syon House, which is hidden away behind all sorts of slummy things in Isleworth and has a huge hall of green marble, and eight statues life-size in gold! I know everything about him now: the things he likes doing, even what he likes to eat. They're all sweet things—he must be a Greek or something. Actually, he looks a bit Greeky. And he knows everything about me. The other day we were in a shop and he laid that out—[*she picks up the sombrero*] for me to buy. And it's the only hat I don't look stupid in.

CHARLES: Thank you.

BELINDA [*gently*]: Oh, Charles, it's not a question of hats. I've had the most intimate relationship of my life with someone I've never spoken to. What does it mean? . . . When I'm with him I live.

[CHARLES *stares at her with a numb expression on his face.*]

And because there aren't any words, everything's easy and possible. I share all the time. I share. . . . Actually, to be honest, I do feel guilty. I wasn't just passing. I wanted to talk to you. No, not talk. I knew that wouldn't be any good. I wanted to—I don't know—give you something. These flowers. . . . Poor things—they look a bit withered, don't they? I'll get them some water.

[BELINDA *opens the office door, goes in—screams loudly—and comes running back into the room. She is followed by* JULIAN, *who stands blinking in the doorway. A pause.*]

CHARLES: Who on earth are *you?*

JULIAN [*surprised*]: My name is Cristoforou . . .

CHARLES: I'm afraid the office is closed on Saturday mornings. If you'd care to make an appointment.

JULIAN: We've done that already.

CHARLES [*furious*]: What did I tell you to do?

JULIAN: Go down the fire escape into the mews.

CHARLES: Well?

JULIAN: I did, but the mews was so blank and abandoned. There was more life up here.

BELINDA: You know each other?

JULIAN: Your husband and I are new acquaintances. I don't think it will blossom beyond that.

CHARLES: How long have you been in there?

JULIAN: All the time. It was very illuminating. I mean you being so intimate. If you'd been discussing topics of general interest, I'd probably have gone away.

CHARLES: You mean you listened?

JULIAN: Of course. Eavesdropping is the second thing one is trained in, Mr. Sidley. First shadow your man with your eye, then with your ear. It's an indispensable ability.

BELINDA: Charles, it's him!

JULIAN: He knows it is.

CHARLES: Don't.

JULIAN: I must.

BELINDA: Don't what?

CHARLES: No, please.

JULIAN: It's inevitable.

CHARLES: I forbid you to speak.

JULIAN: You can't. [*To* BELINDA.] I think you should sit down.

BELINDA: Who are you?

CHARLES: I'm your employer. Leave this office at once!

BELINDA: Employer?

CHARLES: Do you hear?

BELINDA: Employer?

CHARLES: Please . . . I ask you as a friend.

JULIAN: You're not a friend.

BELINDA: Who are you? Tell me.

[*A pause.*]

JULIAN [*matter-of-factly*]: I am a private detective, Mrs. Sidley. Hired by your husband to spy on you.

[*She stares at him in stunned amazement.*]

BELINDA [*faintly*]: No . . . [*She looks at her husband.*]

CHARLES: It was all I could think of to do. I was at my wits' end.

BELINDA: No. Oh no!

CHARLES: I know it was awful. But what else could I do? Your behavior was so odd. You must admit that. Any husband would have been suspicious.

BELINDA [*breaking out*]: No! No! No! No! NO!

CHARLES: Belinda—

BELINDA: Go away! You're filthy! Filthy! . . . I never want to see you again as long as I live!

[*She bursts into tears and collapses on the sofa, sobbing helplessly.* CHARLES *looks on impotently.*]

JULIAN: Well, you heard what she said. Go away.

CHARLES [*turning on him*]: What did you say?

JULIAN: I said go. It's what she wants.

CHARLES: You bloody meddling little wog! I'll teach you to make a fool out of me! Interfere with people's lives! . . .

[*He bounds forward, snatching up a ruler.* JULIAN *snatches up a heavy statuette and threatens him with it. He speaks in a new, sharp tone.*]

JULIAN: One step more, and I'll interfere with your brains!

[CHARLES *glares indecisively.*]

I mean it, Mr. Sidley. Coshing is the third thing a detective's trained in.

[*Warily, breathing hard,* CHARLES *lowers the ruler.*]

That's better. Now, what have I done to upset you like this?

CHARLES: Only stolen my wife's affections, that's all!

JULIAN: Your wife's affections weren't stolen, Mr. Sidley. They were going begging. . . . [*Pause.*] And if you want them back, you must first learn how to get them. For a start, put down that ruler, and go out and walk around the gardens. It's time *you* waited for ten minutes.

[*When* JULIAN'S *back is turned,* CHARLES *makes another attempt to hit him.* JULIAN *whirls round, statue in hand.*]

DO AS I SAY!

[*Even* BELINDA *is startled by this new tone of authority. Speechlessly,* CHARLES *looks from one to the other.*]

BELINDA: Oh, Charles, for God's sake, just go!

[*With an attempt at dignity,* CHARLES *tucks the ruler under his arm and marches abruptly out of the room. There is a pause.*]

JULIAN: So your name is Belinda.

BELINDA: Go away too.

JULIAN: Mine, as you may have heard, is Cristoforou. How strange it was to hear your voice for the first time! Even in a scream it sounded charming.

BELINDA: Go *with* him—go on. You're two of a kind.

JULIAN: You don't know my kind. It's very rare.

BELINDA: It's vile, that's all I know.

JULIAN: Why? What is my crime? The fairy tale prince has turned back into a frog, is that it? Well, it's no fun for me either. I'd rather keep my magic. Though it's only training in how to shadow, you must admit I do it superbly. I should: I worked at it. Surely you'd like to know why? It's a sad and fascinating story: the making of a detective.

BELINDA: I'm not listening.

JULIAN: Nonsense: you're riveted. Briefly, then, I am a middleman. Most of my life has been spent making three where two are company. I was hardly out of puberty before I started becoming attracted to other men's wives. Women who were unattainable obsessed me. Usually, out of guilt, I'd work up a friendship with the husband, and take a painful pleasure in being a constant guest in their home. Masochism, you see: very un-Latin. I was always in the middle, getting nothing and being generally in the way. Finally I made myself so unhappy that I had to sit down and think. One day I asked myself this fateful question: "Would you like to know a beautiful, tender, unattached girl to whom you were everything in the world?" And the answer came back: "No!" . . . Revelation! At that moment I realized something shattering about myself. I wasn't made to bear the responsibility of a private life! Obviously nature never intended me to have one! I had been created to spend all my time in public! . . . This thought simply delighted me! It seemed to account for everything—all the unhappiness I'd ever suffered. Alone, I didn't exist; I came alive only against a background of other people's affairs.

[*She turns and looks at him, fascinated.*]

Once I realized this, of course, it was the simplest thing in the world to select a permanent career. A detective was the obvious solution. I immediately resigned from private life, and became a Public Eye. A dick. Have a macaroon. They ease the heart.

BELINDA: Look: you've got no rights here, so why don't you just dick off to your dick's office?

JULIAN: Oh, how can you talk like that to someone who's been as intimate with you as I have?

BELINDA: Intimate?

JULIAN: Do you deny we have spent three weeks in this city as blissfully as two people ever spent them in its history? Syon House! The Isle of Dogs! Parliament Hill at six in the morning! Beware! There is no sin more unpardonable than denying you were pleased when pleasure touched you. You can die for that.

BELINDA: What the hell are you talking about?

JULIAN: You and I have exchanged our most personal treasures, and that makes rights.

BELINDA: What rights? To make a fool of me?

JULIAN: Is that what I've done?

BELINDA: You know it is.

JULIAN: I don't. I found you aimless in London: I gave you direction. I found you smileless: I gave you joy. Not eternal joy, or even joy for a week. But immediate, particular, bright little minutes of joy—which is all we ever get or should expect. Give up self-pity. It doesn't become you.

BELINDA: Thanks for nothing!

JULIAN: And give up saying that too. It's hideous.

BELINDA: I'll say what I bloody want. It's no business of yours what I say.

JULIAN: Oh, but it is. You are my business. Look into my eye. Come on: look. No, this one.

[*Reluctantly she looks. He stares at her hypnotically, one inch from her face.*]

What do you see? I will tell you. You see one of the Seven Wonders of Nature. The completely Public Eye—which looks entirely outward. Look into it. Beside this eye, the eagle is blind. The puma needs spectacles. Without immodesty I tell you—this eye possesses the most watchful iris, the most attentive cornea, the most percipient retina in the northern hemisphere. [*He suddenly withdraws it from her scrutiny.*] And for almost a month it has been focused exclusively on you. It has seen more in you than anyone you ever met, or ever will meet. Think of that. And, may I add, it belongs in the head of a man of taste and refinement who has been made to sit through more execrable horror films than anyone should be called on to see in a lifetime of duty! How dared you inflict on me *Werewolves from Mars* and *Bloodsuckers from Venus* both on the same day? If that doesn't give me rights, what the hell does?

BELINDA: You're raving mad, aren't you? I should have realized it all along.

JULIAN: It's not a word I can define, and your husband's books aren't much help with it. . . . [*He goes and looks through the window.*] Look at him.

BELINDA: What's he doing?

JULIAN: Beheading the chrysanthemums with his ruler.

BELINDA: That's his way of working off anger. It's why I have to buy all my flowers off barrows. . . . He's always knocking the dahlias about. . . .

[*She starts to cry again. He hastens to her side, and sits down on the sofa. She turns away.*]

JULIAN: Oh, please, don't cry any more. I can't bear tears. They're so excluding! Please! [*He takes her arm.*] Please. Let me dry your eyes. [*Seductively.*] Belinda . . . [*Slowly she turns round.*] A simple service from a simple friend. Eye-drying while you wait. *Voilà!*

[*He pulls out the handkerchief which was stuffed into his pocket at the beginning of the play.* BELINDA *is showered with nuts and raisins. Her crying turns to laughter.*]

I'm *agonized!* Utterly *agonized!* Did I hurt you? I'm sure I did. Nothing can hurt more than a brazil nut aimed with force. [BELINDA *begins to laugh really hard.*] And the carpet! Ohh! Look at them—all over it!

[*He falls to his knees on the carpet and starts picking up the raisins and popping them in his mouth as he talks.*]

And such a *gorgeous rug!* Real Bokhara! I can tell. I used to sell them once, door to door, wearing a fez and stick-on goatee. Some dreadful gimmick of my employers. I looked like an extra out of *Kismet* and sold nothing at all *ever*, not even a welcome mat.

[*She stops laughing. He offers her a raisin from the floor.*]

Would you like one?

BELINDA: Your need is greater than mine!

JULIAN [*seriously*]: Will you give me one more minute before you throw me out?

BELINDA: Well?

[*He squats cross-legged in front of her.*]

JULIAN: Look: this is my last day as a private detective. After your husband gets through with me, I can't hope to go back to Mayhew and Figgis, or anybody else. It's just as well. I was on the point of resigning anyway. You can't imagine how wretched the job is. How unworthy.

BELINDA: I thought you loved it.

JULIAN: I thought I would, too. But I reckoned without my awful desire to be liked. Well, if you're a dick you can't be. If you give your employer bad news he hates you. If you give him good, he thinks his money's been wasted. Either way you can't win.

BELINDA: Well, I don't see how I can help.

JULIAN: Oh, but you can. You can get me back my self-respect.

BELINDA: Me?

JULIAN: Yes, Belinda. I've spent three years helping to break up people's marriages. Don't you think it might make it up to them a little if I helped to preserve yours? Let me be honest with you: I'd like to be the first detective to *cement* a marriage.

BELINDA: That's a lovely thought, but I'm not going to stay with Charles to oblige you.

JULIAN: Why not? You owe me something. You made me betray a job which I've never done in my whole life before.

BELINDA: *I* did?

JULIAN: Certainly. I was paid to follow you, not sit down beside you on a bus.

BELINDA: Why did you, then?

JULIAN: I couldn't help it. You're a witch. You can throw an acorn at a duck and stike the heart of a man with grief at fifty paces. I knew it as soon as ever I saw you, standing all alone in the mists of Hyde Park. There was something about your loneliness that filled my eyes with tears! I tasted at a distance the salt of your solitude! After a week of following you about, staring aimlessly into windows, crumbling endless filthy cakes in endless loathsome coffee bars, I did something which my whole training was powerless to prevent. I sat down beside you in a bus, and smiled. Your hand, Belinda! Darkness shades me! On thy bosom let me rest! . . . I quote, as you may imagine.

BELINDA: Look, there are limits to humoring the mad, and I've reached them.

JULIAN: You love your husband. You admitted it to him before. Or at least all your wish is to find your way to him.

BELINDA: Oh, stop!

JULIAN: What?

BELINDA: All that magaziny language.

JULIAN: I've got a magaziny mind. You've found me out. I should never have talked. When I was dumb we understood each other.

BELINDA: If there's any finding ways back to be done, it's by him—not me. If you'd known him as he was you'd have adored him. He used to be gay—really gay. He used to say hundreds of funny things and then laugh at them himself, which I think's a marvelous sign, to laugh at your own jokes. It means you're *in* life. Now he's sort of out of it, sarcastic and gritty, as if something's drying him up.

JULIAN: It is.

BELINDA: What?

JULIAN: Jealousy.

BELINDA: Jealousy? If anyone should be jealous it's me!

JULIAN: What d'you mean by that?

BELINDA: Nothing.

JULIAN: You mean he's unfaithful to you?

BELINDA: Oh no, not really. He takes himself off to a tart sometimes, somewhere in Ladbroke Grove. That's not really unfaithful. He'd die of shame if he thought I knew.

JULIAN: How *do* you know?

BELINDA: A friend of mine saw him going in one day. Her name's Madame Conchita, which is a lovely name for a tart, isn't it? I mean, you can just see her. Sort of Bayswater Brazilian! He must have found her in the Ladies' Directory.

JULIAN: What on earth's that?

BELINDA: A sort of underground directory of tarts. Privately published. Charles is riveted by it. He keeps a copy in his desk. I found it there one day.

JULIAN: Oh, you poor thing.

BELINDA: Not at all. It served me right for prying.

JULIAN: And you're not jealous?

BELINDA: Of course not. I think it's very sensible of him. Men should have a change from their wives occasionally. It makes for a happy home.

JULIAN: I haven't noticed it in your case.

BELINDA: Neither have I. What do you mean, he's jealous? What's he jealous of?

JULIAN [*gravely*]: All your personal life which he hasn't given you. When you married, you were his pupil. He talked, you listened. Then one day as you said, school closed. The chameleon began to change into a princess. Your own thoughts sprouted, and you turned into yourself.

That's what he can't forgive: your life outside of him. It's not really unusual. Many husbands want to create wives in their own image: they allow a certain growth—so far and no farther. Thereafter they will resent all changes they haven't caused, all experiences they haven't shared, and—with wives brighter than they—all new things they can't keep up with.

BELINDA: But I'm not brighter than Charles.

JULIAN: Oh, Belinda—a million times!

BELINDA [*astonished*]: Me?

JULIAN: Of course. Do you want to know what I think about your Charles?

BELINDA: What?

JULIAN: I think he's pitiful.

BELINDA: He isn't!

JULIAN: He's so afraid of being touched by life, he hardly exists. He's so scared of looking foolish, he puts up words against it for barriers: Good Taste, Morality. What you *should* do, what you *should* feel. He's walled up in Should like a tomb.

BELINDA: What a marvelous comparison!

JULIAN: It's true, isn't it?

BELINDA: I suppose it is. Poor Charles.

JULIAN: Lucky Charles, to have you. Because he's sick and you're well.

BELINDA: He's not sick! He's just a bit stuffy, that's all.

JULIAN: Sick. If you hear a piece of music, you'll either love it or hate it. He won't know what to feel till he knows who it's by. Sick. You can say "nigger" and have black friends. He'll only say "negro"—but dislike them.

BELINDA: That's true.

JULIAN: Sick.

BELINDA [*eagerly*]: Go on! More!

JULIAN: You're Spirit, Belinda, and he's Letter. You've got passion where all he's got is pronouncement.

BELINDA: You're not mad. You're not mad at all. You don't miss anything.

JULIAN: Of course. I have a Public Eye.

BELINDA: What else does it see?

JULIAN: That Charles Sidley is half dead, and only his wife can save him.

BELINDA: How? What can I do?

JULIAN: You're a witch. You can do anything. Don't you know what you did for me?

BELINDA: What?

JULIAN: You gave me a private life. For three weeks I walked through

London, all alone except for you to point the way. And slowly, for the first time since I can remember, I began to feel my own feelings. In the depths of that long silence I began to hear the rustle of my own emotions growing. At first just one or two little shoots, quick to die—then thicker, stronger—my very own feelings, Belinda, my very own reactions! And I was no longer displaced. *I was the being who contained this rustling.* You talked about burrows of feeling without thought. But there's something worse: burrows of not feeling anything. Burrows of deadness! Burrows of numbness! Burrows of sleep and torpor where you hide away from experience because you are afraid of changing! Like him. Clinging to a past self that festers when it's clung to. [*He takes her hand.*] You led me out of those burrows, Belinda. Now lead him the same way. Eurydice leading Orpheus for a change.

BELINDA: Who were they?

JULIAN: Lovers who found their way back from Hades by not looking at each other. Only you do it by not speaking, which is so much better in this babel we're all in. How many more people would stay married if they just shut up, and listened, and heard each other's heartbeat in the daytime? [*A pause. They look at one another. He kisses her hand.*] You gave me the only gift I really needed. Now give it to him.

BELINDA: How?

JULIAN: The same way. In silence.

BELINDA: You mean not speak to him?

JULIAN: Of course. It's his only chance.

BELINDA: But that's impossible!

JULIAN [*excited*]: Of course! Of course! Of course! [*He goes quickly to the window. Calling.*] Mr. Sidley! . . . Yes, you! Come up here at once!

BELINDA: What are you going to do?

JULIAN: Do you trust me?

BELINDA: No!

JULIAN: Do you want to return to your marriage?

BELINDA: Yes, I do.

JULIAN: Then do exactly as I say. Do you promise?

BELINDA: I don't know why I should.

JULIAN: Put yourself completely under my orders for a month. I promise in return it'll work.

BELINDA: For a month?

JULIAN: Unavoidable. Promise.

BELINDA: A month's forever.

JULIAN: It's four weeks. Promise.

BELINDA: And I think you really are mad after all.

JULIAN: Promise.

BELINDA: Yes.

JULIAN: You break it and you'll go to hell. Stand there. When he comes in, don't look at him! And whatever happens don't speak.

BELINDA: Don't speak?

JULIAN: Not a single word.

BELINDA: That's idiotic.

JULIAN: Are you questioning me?

BELINDA: Yes!

JULIAN: Oh, well then, the game's off. There's no fun playing Master and Slave if you're going to question everything.

BELINDA: No, I'm sorry. I'll behave. But not speaking is a bit brutal. You forget I'm a woman.

JULIAN: Well, you'd better get used to it. You're going to have to do it for thirty days.

[*She opens her mouth in surprise.*]

Ssh. Here he comes. Stand up straight. Look proud!

[BELINDA *stands like a statue.* CHARLES *comes storming in.*]

CHARLES: Well, who are *you* shouting at?

JULIAN: You.

CHARLES: Belinda, I think it's time we went home, don't you? We can discuss all this later, at home. Are you coming, dear? [*Pause.*] Belinda, I'm talking to you. [*Pause.*] I'd like you to come home now, do you hear?

JULIAN: It isn't any good, is it, Mr. Sidley?

CHARLES [*angrily*]: Belinda!

JULIAN: It's useless to address her. She will not reply. As far as you are concerned, she has renounced speech. I bear her exact and peremptory ultimatum. She is so shattered by your conduct—setting a low, sneaking, prying little wog of a detective to spy on her—that she is leaving you forever.

CHARLES: Belinda!

[BELINDA *turns to protest, but is gestured to keep silent by* JULIAN.]

JULIAN: Unless. Yes, you are lucky. There's an unless. You have one chance of keeping her. But only one. That is—you will take my place in the streets of London. [*Formally.*] You will follow her every day for a month, at a distance of fifty feet, wherever she chooses to go. You will look at whatever she chooses to point at. You will hear whatever she chooses to listen to. You will sit, stand, skip, slide, or shuffle entirely at her will. And for all this month, neither in study nor street, at table nor in bed, will you exchange a single word. [*More easily.*] If there's anything special you want to see and show her, then you may lead. But it had better be good. This is your will, isn't it, Belinda?

[BELINDA *nods.*]

Inexorable, aren't you, Belinda? The alternative is divorce.

[*Nod.*]

Sunderment!

[*Nod.*]

Eternal separation!

CHARLES: Are you done?

JULIAN: Oh yes. End of words, start of action. [*To* BELINDA, *taking her hand.*] Go forth, Eurydice!

CHARLES: Stay here, Belinda!

[*A long pause.* BELINDA *looks between the two men, choosing. Then she smiles at* JULIAN, *picks up her hat and starts to walk out.*]

JULIAN: I suggest the Michelangelo Coffee Bar for a start. Make him eat a Leaning Tower of Pisa.

CHARLES: Belinda?

JULIAN: No, make him eat two!

[BELINDA *goes.* CHARLES *follows her through the door.*]

CHARLES: This seems a good joke to you, but what are you really doing? You're acting on impulse, that's all. [*He is now out of sight.*] You're living on pure emotion without thought or . . . Belinda . . . Belinda! . . . Belinda? [CHARLES *comes back, slamming door.*] If she thinks I'm going after her, she's mad.

JULIAN: I strongly advise you to follow her, Mr. Sidley.

CHARLES: Do you? Do you indeed? Well, fortunately you don't know my wife as well as you think. She'll get tired of this nonsense in an hour. Now get out. And I may as well tell you I'm going to see to it immediately that you are fired.

JULIAN: I'm agonized. Actually I have a much better job to go to.

CHARLES: Indeed?

JULIAN: Yes. Yours. . . . I've come to a decision. While you are outside doing my job, I'll sit here and do yours. Exchange is no robbery, as they say. And even it if is, robbery can be rather stimulating.

CHARLES: Very humorous.

JULIAN: It may well be. I've always had a hankering after the accountant's life. [*Pompous voice.*] "Good morning, Miss Smith: bring me the Sidley Trust file, please." "My dear sir, you have made a great deal of money.

You must look to pay a great deal of tax. However, there are one or two—what can one say?—loopholes, I believe, is the vulgar word. I prefer 'modes of avoidance.' "

CHARLES: If you are not out of this office in one minute by my watch, I shall call the police.

JULIAN: If you are not out of this office in thirty seconds by my watch—

CHARLES: Well?

JULIAN: I shall tell your wife about Ladbroke Grove.

CHARLES [*startled*]: What did you say?

JULIAN: I'm not a private detective for nothing, Mr. Sidley. And I did give you warning I was a good one. Once I was sure of your wife's innocence, I took to wondering about yours. So I followed you.

CHARLES: I don't believe it.

JULIAN [*lightly*]: Madame Conchita? . . . *Olé!* . . . Not exactly my type. We wogs prefer something more Home Counties. Let's see . . . there ought to be reference books on the subject. I'm sure your superb collection must contain at least one encyclopedia on matters sexual. One Almanac of Arcana? At the very least, a Directory.

CHARLES [*his voice faltering*]: Directory?

JULIAN: Perhaps it's in the Pornographic Section.

[*He moves toward the office door.* CHARLES *puts himself between him and it.*]

Ah, closed to the general public.

CHARLES: How dare you?

JULIAN: Go through your desk? Routine procedure. You have fifteen seconds, Mr. Sidley. [*He takes out of his bag a large grapefruit and knife and the canister of sugar.*] Look: as I told you. I never fail jobs, they always fail me. I can hold the fort here perfectly well for a month. I'll just sit here, turn all comers into corporations, and let them enjoy themselves. To be an accountant nowadays you simply need a highly developed sense of fantasy. And I'm sure you'll admit I've got that. [*He slices through the grapefruit and puts it into a glass ashtray. The telephone rings.*] Hello? No, this is Mr. Sidley's assistant.

[CHARLES *makes a grab for the telephone, but* JULIAN *dodges.*]

He's on holiday for a month. That's right: one month. [CHARLES *makes another effort to grab it.*] One moment, please. [*He puts down the telephone, and shoves the open receiver in a drawer. He looks very seriously at* CHARLES.] Look, my dear man, don't be entirely stupid. Your wife's failing love may not be a deductible expense, but it's the only thing you've got.

[*A pause.* CHARLES *returns his stare, tacitly admitting the truth of this. He lowers his eyes.*]

[*As if to a child.*] Go on. Or you'll lose her. [*Indicating the white raincoat.*] And put that on. It may help. Conditioned reflex, you know. If you find any goodies in it, you're very welcome to them.

[*Stunned,* CHARLES *obeys.* JULIAN *sits at the desk.*]

Remember: one month. I do know your wife, Mr. Sidley, and I know she'll keep at it. But if, by any small chance, she wavers, you must insist. Otherwise—Madame Conchita! . . . Go on, now. [*He watches, smiling amiably, as* CHARLES *retreats to the door.*] I'll have the bill sent here, of course. It's more discreet, isn't it?

CHARLES [*viciously*]: One thing, Mr. Cristoforou. If I may remind you, you said that the man my wife met every day was handsome, well dressed, Mr. Cristoforou. Debonair.

JULIAN: So I did, Mr. Sidley. So I did. I thought it more tactful. I mean any husband can be excused for losing out to a dream figure like that. But to someone like me? . . . [*Taking the receiver from the drawer.*] Hello? Sorry to have kept you waiting. Yes, he felt the need for a complete rest. [*Pointedly at* CHARLES.] Yes, he had to . . . *go!*

[CHARLES *goes out.*]

Well, permit me to introduce myself. My name is Cristoforou. Julian Cristoforou. Diplomas in Accountancy from the Universities of Cairo, Beirut, Istanbul, and Damascus. Author of the well-known handbook *Teach Yourself Tax Evasion.* What seems to be your particular problem? Income tax? . . . Yes? . . . That's monstrous! You haven't paid it, I hope? . . . I'm delighted to hear it. Of course not. Paying any tax that is more than one percent of your total income I consider a desperate imprudence. Yes, of course, we have limitless experience in this field. Cristoforou and Sidley. A firm of the very highest! I think you'd better come round and see me immediately. [*He eats the grapefruit: it is obviously sour. He shakes the canister of sugar: it is obviously empty.*] No, my dear sir, I assure you, we won't let the government touch a penny piece of your money. Not without a battle that will make the Battle of Waterloo look like a scuffle on the village green. Come round in, shall we say, one hour? I look forward to it. In the meantime, don't worry about a thing. And if you could bring round with you a pound of granulated sugar, I'd be greatly obliged. Goodbye to you, sir. Goodbye! [*He hangs up as—*

THE CURTAIN FALLS

# WHITE LIARS

A PLAY IN ONE ACT

*For*
*my parents*
*with love*

*White Liars* opened at the Ethel Barrymore Theatre in New York on February 12, 1967, along with *Black Comedy*. The cast was as follows:

| | |
|---|---|
| SOPHIE, BARONESS LEMBERG | Geraldine Page |
| FRANK | Donald Madden |
| TOM | Michael Crawford |

Directed by John Dexter

*White Liars* was produced at the Lyric Theatre, London, in 1968. The cast was as follows:

| | |
|---|---|
| SOPHIE, BARONESS LEMBERG | Dorothy Reynolds |
| FRANK | James Boham |
| TOM | Ian McKellen |

*The Fortune Teller's Parlor of* SOPHIE, BARONESS LEMBERG, *on the pier of a rundown seaside resort on the south coast of England. Around one* P.M. *late September.*

SOPHIE*'s parlor is set between two levels of the pier. It is reached from above by an iron staircase, and it is set on iron stanchions rising out of the sea. As we look at it, it seems to be suspended against the wet one o'clock sky; a cluttered nest in a tangle of Victorian ironwork. The room is actually divided by a curtain into two: a little anteroom, with a bench for waiting; and the consulting room, which is much larger, and is replete with a covered table on a rotting strip of carpet, and a couple of broken-down chairs. On the table stands the faded photograph of a middle-aged man, in an ornate silver frame. A completed game of patience is laid out on the cloth. On a shelf at the back stands the crystal ball, under a covering. The window, streaked with salt and bird droppings, proclaims in reverse gilt letters:* Baroness Lemberg. Palmist. Clairvoyante. *And in smaller letters underneath:* Lemberg Never Lies. *The place is dirty and claustrophobic, deriving its mystery from the fantasy of its location, hung over the water. Little light bulbs are festooned down the pier, above.*

[*As the curtain rises and the lights come up through the cobweb of rusty iron, we see* SOPHIE *standing at her table, carefully pouring gin from a half-bottle through a funnel into a rose-colored decanter. She is a woman of fifty, once beautiful and still handsome, dressed in the blouse and skirt of a professional working woman. When she speaks her voice is marked by a strong but never incomprehensible German accent. She drops the bottle into a waste basket, picks up a delicate little rose-colored wineglass and pours some gin into it. Seagulls suddenly scream. She raises her glass to them.*]

SOPHIE: *Salut!* Bloody things! Greedy, filthy, middle-class birds. Here's to you! And to another brilliant, dazzling afternoon in Grinmouth-on-Sea! Grinmouth, glorious Grinmouth—Fairyland of the South Coast! [*She swallows her gin.*] You know something, I think they're watering the drink in this country. This is definitely less fortifying than it used to be. But that of course is no surprise. It is one of the iron laws of life: everything gets less fortifying. What Goes Down Must Go Downer! Lemberg's Law of Life . . . ! [*She turns to the photograph. Imploringly, like a little girl.*] Oh, don't look so disapproving, please. What else am I going to do? Improve my mind for the glittering society of Grinmouth-on-Sea? Look at it! [*She goes to the window.*] Not one gleam of sunlight for ten days. Not one soul out walking, jetty to jetty. Nothing but wet sand—rusty iron—plastic bottles all along the shore, and bird shit on the windows. I'm sorry for the language, Papa, but there it is: see for yourself. *Vogeldrecke* on every pane: who needs curtains? And the sea. This ravishing sea! Look at it, if you please—such an exotic color. It's exactly like they've poured out ten million cups of tea. No wonder they call it the English Channel! . . . Grinmouth-on-*Tea,* that's what I name it from now on. [*She laughs sourly.*] You hear that, Papa? That's my joke for today. Grinmouth-on-Tea! I admit it's not one of my best. But then *you* sit here all day entirely by yourself, you're not going to win decorations for your wit either! [*She pours some more gin, and gulps.*] The truth is, my dear, they haven't the faintest idea what water should look like in this country. Do you remember our lake? Our beautiful summer lake, what it was like to come back to each year? Clear, clear water—absolutely still—with the pine trees standing in it, upside down—how was it you called them?—rows of little green soldiers marching on their heads! You had really a good power of description, you know, sometimes. . . . [*She sits at her table.*] Beloved God, this silence! You'd think *someone* would consult me, if only to ask should they kill themselves. Do you realize there hasn't been an actual human being in this room for six days? And then it was only Mr. Fowler with his boring rent book. [*Imitating a "common" accent.*] "I hate to mention it, Baroness, but you owe us more than a little back rent!" More than a little! Only six bloody weeks! "Hate to mention it"—he loves it; boring old swine! . . . Sorry, Papa, your Sophie is getting just a little bad-tempered with the world. Can you really blame her? How would *you* like it to sit here all day in this black little prison, with drafts going up *your* skirts. I'm sorry, I mean trousers! [*She giggles.*] Excuse me, Father, you are absolutely right. A lady shouldn't drink. Though actually, I don't know why. I was under the impression, my dear, that the aristocracy *set* the do's and don'ts, not followed them. That is entirely for the middle classes . . . [*She looks up and out.*] Beloved God, I don't believe it!

[FRANK *and* TOM *appear on the upper level.*]

Two whole clients! Oh, God, oh, my God!

[FRANK *and* TOM *lounge down the iron stairs and stand outside her window, apparently debating whether to come in. She watches them hungrily.*]

Two pounds if they take the cards. Four if they take the crystal ball! Beloved God, make them come in!

[*The two boys start to walk away.*]

Come in, oh, *please!*

[*They turn back and enter the anteroom.*]

TOM: Anyone home?

SOPHIE: One moment, please!

[*She scurries about during the following, stacking the cards, getting the crystal ball and setting it on the table, and adjusting her hair. Finally, she swirls around herself a colored shawl, sits, and opens a fan. Of the two boys,* FRANK *is middle class, soft-spoken, and gentle; his manner is shy, warm, and immediately likable—in great contrast to his companion, who seems casual almost to the point of brutality.* TOM *is dressed very "trendily," in bright colors, wears his hair long, and slumps about. He speaks in a heavy North Country accent.*]

FRANK: I'll go first.

TOM: Why?

FRANK: I've got to get back to the hall. I want to check that sound system.

TOM: Why bother? There's not going to be an audience anyway.

FRANK: And whose fault is that?

TOM: What d'you mean?

FRANK: We wouldn't be here at all, if it wasn't for your stupid astrologer.

TOM: He's not stupid.

FRANK: "Avoid the seaside in the month of August." What d'you call *that?*

TOM: Don't mock what you don't understand.

FRANK: All right, all right. I don't know what I'm doing with you anyway. You don't need a business manager. Why not just hire yourself a crack astrologer, and get him to fix all your engagements for you? He could make sure we'd go broke inside a month.

TOM [*surly*]: Shut up, will you?

FRANK: What are you going to ask *her* now? Where we play next?

TOM: I said, Shut up. O.K.?

FRANK [*appeasingly*]: Look, Tom, I'm not mocking. You've got a right to believe what you please. But really this—this stuff can go too far sometimes. A two-year-old baby could tell you you don't play the seaside in late bloody September. If we'd come here six weeks ago, when they *wanted* us, we'd have cleaned up, and you know it.

SOPHIE [*calling*]: Come in, please!

FRANK: I'm sorry but that's the truth. Astrology or no astrology!

[TOM *brushes by him into the consulting room.* FRANK *follows him quickly.* SOPHIE *is seated regally at her table.*]

SOPHIE: Good evening. One of you at a time, please.

TOM [*dismissing* FRANK]: Right. I'll see you, then.

FRANK [*standing his ground*]: I—well, why don't we toss for it?

TOM [*surprised at being challenged*]: Toss?

FRANK: Well, that's fair, isn't it?

[TOM *shrugs sullenly.* FRANK *pulls a coin from his pocket.*]

Well, it is . . . [*To* SOPHIE, *with a nervous laugh.*] We're both so anxious to see you, it's a bit of a fight. [*To* TOM.] Heads or tails?

TOM: Heads.

[FRANK *tosses.*]

FRANK: Tails! I win! [*Showing it to* SOPHIE.] True?

[SOPHIE *nods in acquiescence.*]

[*To* TOM.] Look, why don't you go for a ride on the dodgems? They'll be glad of the custom.

[TOM *shrugs again.*]

SOPHIE: Come back in ten minutes, please. Expert divination does not take very long.

FRANK: You don't mind, do you?

TOM: You won, didn't you?

[TOM *lounges out, upstairs and out of sight.* FRANK *looks after him.*]

SOPHIE: Come along, then.

FRANK [*staring out of the window*]: It's a rotten old day, isn't it? There isn't a soul out on the prom. Just us and the seagulls. They're all sitting in those little shelters meant for people.

SOPHIE: Like rows of people from a sanitarium, coughing into their coat collars.

FRANK: That's a nasty thought.

SOPHIE: It's a nasty place, mister. It makes you have nasty ideas.

[*He turns to look at her.*]

FRANK: It must feel strange living with the sea all around you.

SOPHIE: It is not a sea at all. It is merely a gutter between here and France. All the same, I prefer it to the land. A third-rate holiday resort is not my idea of a place to reside in. . . . I have known other days, mister.

FRANK: I'd assumed that, of course.

SOPHIE: You had? Why?

FRANK: From your manner. It's very—distinguished. And also of course from—well, your title.

SOPHIE: I am a Baroness of the Holy Roman Empire. I was born with certain powers. Owing to an alteration in my fortune, I am reduced to selling these for money. It is regrettable, but then so is most of contemporary life. . . . You have a special purpose in coming to see me. Please tell me what it is, and don't waste my time.

FRANK: A special purpose?

SOPHIE: Of course.

FRANK: How do you know?

SOPHIE: That wasn't tails, mister.

FRANK: What?

SOPHIE: The coin. It wasn't tails. It was heads.

FRANK [*grinning nervously*]: Oh . . . yes, yes—yes—that's right. I know. I'm sorry about that. But I—I—I had to see you first. I really had . . . It's vital.

SOPHIE: *Ja*?

FRANK [*very ill at ease*]: When we drove into town this morning in the van, I saw your sign right away. It says "Advice and Consultation." It sort of gave me the idea. Well, it gave me hope, actually.

SOPHIE: Go on.

FRANK: I don't know. It seemed like a good idea, then. Now it's perfectly ridiculous. I mean, just embarrassing, really. . . . The thing is, you mustn't be angry.

SOPHIE: Angry?

FRANK: At what I'm going to ask. Promise that, please. You see, I've—I've got a suggestion. A sort of a—little game. A, well, frankly a . . . look, Baroness, I don't really want my fortune told at all. I've come about something entirely different. And you've every right to throw me out, and be very annoyed. Only I hope you won't be.

SOPHIE: Young mister: I have no idea what you are saying. Am I supposed to be clairvoyant, or something? . . . That's my joke. I often make it.

FRANK: Oh . . . Yes . . .

SOPHIE: Sit down for a start. Come—come.

[FRANK *sits*.]

You're very pale. Are you ill?

FRANK: No.

SOPHIE: Worried?

FRANK: Yes.

SOPHIE: Is it your professional life?

FRANK: No. Look, I'll pay you, just like it was a regular session. Actually, I thought I'd offer you a little more. Unless you'd be insulted.

SOPHIE: Why should I be insulted? Advice is as hard as divination. It is your love life? Trouble with a girl? Ha?

[FRANK *shrugs.*]

Of course. And your friend is involved also, *ja, ja, ja . . .*

FRANK: A bit cliché, isn't it?

SOPHIE: It is not exactly unfamiliar, I admit. Two friends in love with the same girl.

FRANK: Except he's *not* in love with her. And she just thinks she's in love with him. She's very easily impressed. Mind you, I see in a way. He's an impressive boy. Susan's always been surrounded by phonies. Suddenly, along comes someone who's completely himself—it's bound to be a turn-on.

SOPHIE: A what?

FRANK: It's bound to excite her.

SOPHIE: This boy is working class, *ja?*

FRANK: He could hardly be more so.

SOPHIE: And the girl is not?

FRANK: You're clever, Baroness. You see things. Sue's bugbear is respectability. Her dad is a nice respectable department manager in John Lewis's. He's got himself a nice, respectable house in Chislehurst, and she's had enough golf and gardening to last her a lifetime. Tom represents everything her parents hate. Rotten slum background. Independence of the kind that really makes them nervous. The kind you can only have when you've truly had nothing to begin with. They'd call it arrogance. Well, you've seen him. He *is* arrogant, of course, he is. He's also extraordinary. [*Pause.*] The trouble with me is, I see everyone's point of view. Here I am, defending him already.

SOPHIE: This boy is an entertainer?

FRANK: Singer. Thanks to me. I found him singing in an East End pub, flat broke. A natural musician. I mean really marvelous. And with absolutely no idea what to do with it. I made a whole group for him. That's my thing, you see: I'm a manager, no point in being modest about it. If he's a natural singer, I'm a natural manager. I created the Liars especially for him.

SOPHIE: The Liars?

FRANK: The White Liars. Four instrumentalists and Tom. I even designed the uniform. White satin—it's wild! Susan helped me, of course.

SOPHIE: She helps you a lot, your girl?

FRANK: I don't know what I'd do without her. She does everything. Drives the van, does the accounts, nursemaids the boys—you'll meet her tonight, if you like. We're doing a show at the Winter Garden. Perhaps you'd like to come.

SOPHIE: Thank you, no. As far as I'm concerned, the birth of electricity meant the death of music.

FRANK [*laughing politely*]: That's good.

SOPHIE: It's not good, mister. It's true. There is no music made today: just noise.

FRANK: If you say so, Baroness.

SOPHIE: Don't condescend to me, please. I come from the one country that created all the music that matters! And I was brought up to *listen* to it, my dear mister. Not just bob my head, or twist my tummy. My father was a *real* natural musician! He was an *amateur* in the true meaning of the word. Do you know what that means? A lover! He played the clarinet like a lover! It is hard to appreciate amateurs in the other sense of the word—bricklayers and plumbers hitting guitars—when one has known the Rosé.

FRANK: Rosé?

SOPHIE: The Rosé String Quartet. No doubt you've never heard of them. Before the war they were the finest chamber players in Austria. My father knew them intimately. He would invite them each summer to our villa in the country, to play with him. And they would come. "Sir," they'd say, "it is an honor to play with someone as good as you!" They would all sit by the lake, by this glorious lake on our beautiful little private estate, and they would play together—the Brahms *Quintet, in B Minor*. I would always be the guest of honor. Ten, eleven, twelve years old, they'd put me in the middle of them, on a special armchair carried out on to the grass, and I would sit *engulfed* in the music! Sentimental, *ja?* Well, other years—other tears.

FRANK: It sounds marvelous.

SOPHIE: My father was a man of great style. It is a way of conduct that has passed entirely from the world.

FRANK [*looking at the photograph*]: Is that him there?

SOPHIE: It is.

FRANK: What are those things he's wearing?

SOPHIE [*loftily: not looking at the picture herself*]: You mean decorations.

The top one is the Order of St. Michael. Next the Golden Spur. Last the papal medal of the Holy Roman Empire. Impressive, *ja?* As you would say—wow!

FRANK: Is he still alive?

SOPHIE: No. He drowned.

FRANK: Drowned?

SOPHIE: *Ja*: in middle-class mediocrity. When the Nazis came, we left Austria. What else could we do? As he observed, no man of civilization could continue to live there. Besides, my mother was of Romany blood. It was from her I derive my gift. Her mother had been a noblewoman of that very ancient race, but of course to the Nazis the Romanies were simply degenerates. We lived together all three in London. My father tried to work, but he'd been trained for nothing practical. All his life he'd been a diplomat—and the new government detested him. The Third Reich only had use for traitors, of course. And so he passed his time mostly sitting by himself in Regent's Park, reading music scores, while first my mother and then I, after she'd taught me properly, practiced our gift of divination. . . . Other years, other tears. We were talking of your girl friend. What is it you want of me? You love her, *ja?*

FRANK: Yes.

SOPHIE: Very much?

FRANK: We've been together two years—and it's been the best time I've ever known.

SOPHIE: But now it is ending?

FRANK: Not if I can help it.

SOPHIE: Because of him? Your friend?

FRANK: Look, when I first met Tom he'd only been down from Yorkshire three weeks. He was living in a filthy little cellar in the slums. He was absolutely miserable.

SOPHIE: So you took him into your house?

FRANK: The stupidest thing I ever did. I gave him a room in my flat, free. The thing about Tom is, he's a monster, I mean that in the Greek way. Like one of those things in a fable. He *lives* on worship. It's his food. I mean it quite literally: he can hardly get through a day without two tablespoons of sticky golden worship poured down his throat, preferably by a girl. Poor Sue walked right into it, you see. I mean because that's a bit her scene—spooning it out. And the awful thing is, she's getting more and more turned on. Every day I watch it happening. It's like I can't stop it. Any moment now she's going to cross that landing from our bedroom to his. I just know it.

SOPHIE: So prevent it! Tell him to go!

FRANK: Well, that's it. I can't—I just can't. I'm just—incapable. Isn't that stupid? . . . For one thing, it's just so corny. Keep Your Hands Off My Girl! I mean he'd laugh. I'd just look so silly, you know, squaring up. . . . It's not me. Anyway, it isn't that simple. The thing is—he's so bloody disarming. I can't explain really. I lie in bed at night beside her, rehearsing scenes I'm going to have with Tom in the morning. I make up whole conversations—brilliant cutting sentences—or maybe ones more in sorrow than in anger, you know—rather noble. And then in the daylight I look at him and he's swabbing crusts round the egg yolk on his plate, and I just can't bring them out. I mean, people aren't in your head, are they? [*Pause.*] The thing is, I can't take any more. He's got to get out! *I've got to get him out!*

[*His vehemence seems to surprise them both.*]

[*After a pause.*] I had this wild idea.

SOPHIE: What kind of idea?

FRANK: That you could—see it all.

SOPHIE: See?

FRANK: In the ball.

SOPHIE [*slowly*]: See all—what?

FRANK [*getting nervous*]: Look, the thing about Tom is, he's fantastically superstitious. I mean, ridiculous. He's always loping off to fortune tellers and palmists, every place he goes. One week it's a woman in Acton, who does it with beans. The next, it's some Chinaman in Clapham who does it with dice.

SOPHIE: And now it's some German in Grinmouth who does it—with what exactly?

FRANK: Well, this, actually, I thought . . . [*He produces an envelope from his pocket.*] The main facts of Tom's life. It's all stuff he's told me over the past year. Yorkshire childhood—coal-mining village—drunken dad who threw his guitar on the fire. They're pretty dismal, really. I thought—

SOPHIE: What? That as I'm a fake, I could not possibly find them out for myself?

FRANK: Of course not! Only using this, you'd be absolutely accurate. I mean absolutely. So exact you'd have him freaked. He'd totally believe you—totally: you can't imagine it. I mean if you were to see something a bit . . .

SOPHIE: *Ja?* A bit . . .?

FRANK: Alarming—in his future.

SOPHIE [*carefully*]: What kind of alarming, mister?

FRANK: Well, like some dangerous relationship.

SOPHIE: With a girl.

FRANK: Yes.

SOPHIE: Which, of course, he should break off immediately. If he doesn't, terrible disaster waits for him. *Ja?* [*Amused.*] Blood and calamity!

FRANK: It sounds ridiculous, I know. Like I said. With anyone else but Tom it would be. But I swear to you, any kind of warning coming from you—because you're very impressive, you really are—he'd actually stop and think. It could work.

SOPHIE: And how much am I to receive for this absurdity?

FRANK: I thought five pounds would be . . .

SOPHIE: Suitable? [*Silence.*] Mister, I know I don't look so prosperous here in this filthy little room, but who do you think I am? Some silly gypsy bitch in a caravan, you can buy for five pounds?

FRANK: No, of course not!

SOPHIE [*with grandeur*]: I practice here in this hideous town an art as old, as sacred as medicine. Look at this! [*She shoots out her hand.*] This hand has held the hand of a royal duchess in intimate spiritual communion. It has held the hand of an Archimandrite—a Prince of the Orthodox Church, who said to me, *bowing* to me, "Baroness, you are not just a fortune teller: you have the divine gift!" All right, I have—what is it?—*"come down"* in the world! Come down to Grinmouth! Down to pizza stalls and grease in the air! Dodge-them cars and rifle guns and all the fun in the fairground! Every day now—if I see anybody at all—my *noble* clients are people like old potatoes wearing paper hats saying "Kiss Me!" Whispering old spinsters, smelling of camphor—old red men with gin in their eyes, begging me to predict just one football pool to make them rich for life! *Rubbish people,* all of them, *killing* me to death with their middle-class dreams! But one thing, mister, I may hate them—but I never cheat them. Lemberg never lies!

[*A pause.* SOPHIE *glares at him:* FRANK *is mortified.*]

FRANK: I'm sorry.

SOPHIE: That's all right. Go now, please.

[FRANK *rises and goes out in silence through the curtain and into the anteroom.* SOPHIE *sits staring after him, clasping her hands together in anxiety.*]

[*sotto voce*] Five pounds! Five pounds, five whole pounds . . . !

[*Suddenly* FRANK *returns, abruptly.*]

FRANK: Look, I really am sorry! It was disgusting to do that. I'm sorry: I see that now . . . but I'm desperate, Baroness. I love this girl. I'd do anything to keep her. Tom is ruthless. You can't understand that. Someone from your world couldn't possibly understand . . . I'm sorry. Goodbye. [*As abruptly, he makes to go again.*]

SOPHIE [*stopping him*]: One moment, please! [*A slight pause.*] I misjudged you, mister. I thought you were like him. The two of you were together in my mind. I thought: tummy twisters! Head-bobbers! No sensitivity or gentleness about them. But I was wrong. . . . [*She rises.*] I see after all you have a faithful nature. I have come to believe that faithfulness in love is like real music—one of the marvels of the past. It is good to find it still exists. Look, there he is: coming back!

[*We hear the sound of* TOM*'s whistling. He strolls into view on the upper level of the pier: in his hand is a large, woolly toy dog.* SOPHIE *and* FRANK *watch him through the window, as he stands looking at the sea, making slight dance movements with an air of confident conceit.*]

[*Grimly.*] Look at him. *Ja:* I see it now. Tummy-twister . . . taker! . . . What you said: the *arrogance!* . . . You're kind about him, because you are a kind man. "Disarming," you call him. Well, mister, he doesn't disarm me! I see what he is. I see them every day, the new savages! I watch them on this pier, whistling up and down with their stupid fuzzy hair, stumbling along in their stupid high shoes, sequins on their shoulders, pretending to be amusing and eccentric—but really, underneath, just thugs! Working-class thugs! They think they own the world. *Ja,* and we let them think it. *We*—you and I—the foolish ones, the romantics, the *square* ones as they see us. Well, for once one of *them* is going to get it! A taker gets it from a giver! . . . [*Briskly.*] I'll help you, mister! I'll keep your girl safe for you. I'll frighten the sequins right off this monster of yours! Give me the envelope.

[SOPHIE *stretches out her hand for the envelope.* TOM *turns to the stairs.* FRANK *hesitates.*]

Quick, quick, quick, quick!

[FRANK *hands it over.*]

It will cost you ten pounds.

FRANK: Ten?!

SOPHIE: Of course, ten. Do you think I compromise my art for nothing? Take it or leave it.

FRANK: All right.

[TOM *comes down the stairs.*]

SOPHIE: Good, then! Sssssh, he's coming. Sit! Sit!

[FRANK *sits at the table. So does she.*]

Now tell me quick, what color is your girl?

FRANK: Blond.

SOPHIE: More.

FRANK: She often wears a pink scarf round her head. She's very fond of that. A pink scarf. You can see it in there—[*pointing to the crystal ball*]—if you like.

SOPHIE: Ssssh!

[*They freeze as* TOM *enters the anteroom.*]

[*Raising her voice.*] And you, my dear, your dominant color is green—your lucky day of the week is Wednesday, and, as I said before, everything in your cards indicates activity, activity, and again activity! That will be two pounds, please.

[FRANK *hands her ten pounds, very reluctantly. She counts them carefully.*]

SOPHIE: It's going to be a very busy year, believe me. Lemberg never lies.

FRANK: Well, thank you, Baroness.

SOPHIE: Thank you. I wonder if your friend has returned.

FRANK: [*raising his voice*]: Tom!

TOM: Yeh.

SOPHIE: Ah: good. Ask him to be kind enough to wait one minute, please. [*Indicating the envelope.*] I'll call when I'm ready.

FRANK: Of course. Goodbye now.

SOPHIE: Goodbye.

FRANK [*for* TOM*'s benefit, at the curtain*]: And thank you again.

[FRANK *goes through into the anteroom. Hastily,* SOPHIE *sits at the table, tears open the envelope, and starts reading it.*]

[*To* TOM.]: Hello.

TOM: Well, how is she?

[*This ensuing scene is sotto voce.*]

FRANK: She's—she's all right . . .

TOM: What did she tell you?

FRANK: Nothing, actually. . . . Actually, she's lousy.

TOM: What d'you mean?

SOPHIE [*calling out*]: One moment, mister, please! I'll be with you immediately! [*Reading the notes.*] "Born nineteen fifty-three . . ." [*She writes it on her fan.*]

TOM: Is she really hopeless?

FRANK: Well, they're all fakes, aren't they?

TOM: Of course they're not!

FRANK: Well, this one didn't get a thing right! If you ask me, they should cancel her witch license.

TOM [*alarmed*]: Ssh!

FRANK: Why?

TOM: You mustn't call them that!

SOPHIE: [*reading the notes: concentrating*]: "Mining village—father drunkard." [*She writes on her fan.*]

FRANK [*seeing the toy dog*]: What the hell's that?

TOM: I won it. There's a rifle stall by the turnstiles. They were so glad to see me, they virtually gave it to me. I'll give it to Sue.

FRANK: He looks drunk to me.

TOM: It's all that fresh air. It's knocked the poor bugger out!

SOPHIE [*to the photograph, whispering*]: Why are you staring at me? It's ten pounds, that's all that matters. . . . And anyway, surely, it is a major duty of the aristocracy to give lessons when necessary. [*She turns the photograph away from her and takes another drink, knocking it back.*]

TOM: What's she doing in there? Is she in a trance or something?

FRANK: I don't know. I think she calls it preparing.

TOM: You mean like meditation. It probably is.

FRANK: I bet she's just taking a quick zizz, poor old cow!

TOM [*furious*]: Ssssh! I *told* you!

SOPHIE [*reading the notes*]: "Boxing Day—ran away from home—Boxing Day." [*She writes it on her fan.*]

FRANK [*in sudden panic*]: Look—why don't you just come back with me?

TOM: What for?

FRANK: Because it really is a waste of money. This *one* is!

TOM [*slyly*]: Here—there's nothing funny about her, is there? Are you sure she didn't tell you something?

FRANK: Nothing, not a damn thing!

TOM: Well, you look a bit funny to me.

FRANK: I'm bored, that's all. I'm just plain bored! You'll hate it!

SOPHIE [*reading*]: "Pink scarf . . ."

TOM: Well, I'm here now, and she's seen me, so I might as well go in.

FRANK: Tom, listen to me—

SOPHIE [*calling out*]: I'm ready, mister. Enter, please! [*Reading the last note again, and putting away the envelope.*] "Pink scarf—*pink scarf* . . ."

TOM [*to* FRANK]: I'll see you back there.

FRANK: All right. Don't say I didn't warn you . . .

TOM [*"setting" the stuffed dog on him*]: Arf! Arf! Arf! . . . You just go and check that system.

[TOM *chucks the dog on a chair, and lounges into the parlor.* FRANK *lingers for a second.*]

SOPHIE: Come in, mister. Sit down. . . .

[TOM *stays by the curtain—turns and lifts it, to find* FRANK *still there.*]

TOM [*coldly, to* FRANK]: Did I eavesdrop on *you?*

[FRANK *leaves in confusion. He goes up the iron stairs and off out of sight.* TOM *lets the curtain fall, and approaches the table where* SOPHIE *is waiting.*]

SOPHIE: So. Here is my scale of charges. [*She hands him a card.*] Two pounds for cards alone. Two pounds fifty, cards and palms. Three pounds for the crystal ball. I recommend the ball. It is more profound.

TOM [*agreeing*]: Yeh.

SOPHIE: You're an addict, I think.

TOM: Addict? You mean drugs?

SOPHIE: Divination. You go often to consult people.

TOM [*surprised*]: That's right, actually. Does it show?

SOPHIE: You have comparing eyes.

TOM: Oh. That's no fun, is it?

SOPHIE [*coldly*]: They don't disturb me, mister. When you are older, you will learn that you can't go *shopping* in the world of the occult. People with the gift do not live in supermarkets, you know. Give me something you wear, please. Your scarf will do. . . .

[*Warily he hands her his scarf.*]

Thank you. Now please sit.

[*He sits.*]

And we begin. [*She takes the cover off the ball.*] There. Just a ball of glass. Except that nothing is *just* anything.

TOM: Of course not.

SOPHIE [*abruptly*]: Sssh! Don't speak, please. [*She puts his scarf on the ball.*] You are a musician.

[TOM *nods, surprised.*]

[*Sarcastically.*] It's not such an amazing guess, mister. I've just finished reading your friend, after all. I hope he was satisfied.

TOM: Oh . . . yes . . .

SOPHIE: He has good emanation. He is going to have a very happy domestic life.

TOM: Yeh?

SOPHIE [*hostile*]: Yeh. [*She stares at him. A pause.*] We begin now. What month were you born?

TOM: May.

SOPHIE: Taurus. Impetuous. Sometimes ruthless.

TOM: Twenty-fifth.

SOPHIE: Gemini. Interesting. [*She removes the handkerchief and peers savagely into the ball.*] It's very disturbed. Much confusion. Nineteen fifty-three. You were born in nineteen fifty-three.

TOM [*amazed*]: Yes!

SOPHIE: It's ritualistic, the ball. Often it gives first the date of birth, and then the place. *Ja,* exactly. Now I see a house—a little narrow house in a dirty street. At the end a huge wheel turning in the sky. A coal wheel!—a coal village . . . I see I'm not too far from the truth.

[TOM *can only nod, speechless. Covertly she consults her fan for more details, and goes on peering into the ball.*]

There is no woman in the house. Your mother is dead, *ja?* Your father, still alive. At least I see a man in working clothes. A bad face. Brutal face. Thick like a drunken man.

[*They exchange stares.* TOM *is very disturbed.*]

And now? I see a child. A little pale face. Eyes of fear, looking here—there—for escape. Such a frightened face. He ill-treated you, this father? He beat you?

[TOM *rises and begins to pace about.*]

What is this now? A fire. Something burning on it—it looks like a guitar. . . .

[*He turns on her, startled.*]

Can that be right, a guitar? What is that? Some symbol of your music talent?

TOM: No . . .

SOPHIE: I disturb you, mister.

TOM: You see that?

SOPHIE: Very plain.

TOM: But you can't. You just *can't*—because it's here—my head. It's in here! . . .

SOPHIE: And for me it is *there!* Mister, you can lock nothing away. Time that happened once for you, happens *now* for me. Why did he do that, your father? To stop you being a musician? To hurt you?

[TOM *suddenly stops short, struck by something.*]

Maybe I should stop now?

TOM: No. Go on. What else do you see?

SOPHIE [*addressing herself again to the ball*]: You left home in the North, came to London.

TOM [*in a dead voice*]: Boxing Day. Lunch in Euston Station. Veal and ham pie!

SOPHIE: But you were fortunate in your friends. Recent time has been good for you. The ball is golden . . . [*peering harder*] but now . . . [*recoiling*] *Oh!*

TOM: What?

SOPHIE: Not any more. Not golden now. Going!

TOM: Can you see anything particular?

SOPHIE: Gold to gray. Dark. Now pink in dark. Hair. Pink hair—no, pink scarf—pink something, running, but into darkness . . . You have a girl friend?

[*He shrugs, then nods.*]

She is in flight. I see her shadow, running in the dark. And after, another shadow: desire running, too. It's—*you,* I think! Running! Running! One shadow trying to take the other! But now—another comes . . . Oh, it's so confused!

TOM: Tell me!

SOPHIE: Ssssh! [*Peering fiercely.*] This new shadow is much bigger. *Ja:* another man. It grows—swarms up over everything, you and her both—enormous red shadow up over everything! Over the gray, over the pink, over the dark, the red—the—red, the—red—*red*—RED!! [*She breaks off with a cry of distress.*]

TOM: What is it?

SOPHIE: No!

TOM: What?

SOPHIE [*in a tone of awe*]: I have seen it. *The blood-flash!* I have seen it.

TOM: The blood—?

SOPHIE: Blood-flash. The most rare vision in divination. Red blood, drowning the ball. I have read about this, but never have I seen it till now, running over the glass . . . It means—the most terrible warning.

TOM: Warning?

[*She rises impressively.*]

SOPHIE [*solemnly*]: You are doing something that is not good, mister. If you continue—disaster will strike at you. Disaster. And very soon. I mean it, mister. I'm sorry.

[*A pause.* TOM *lowers his head, as if he's crying.*]

If there is anything in your emotional life which is not what it should be, I beg of you: beware! If there is a girl in your life at the moment, she is not for you. . . !

[*But she has to break off:* TOM *is not crying—he is laughing! She stares at him, scandalized. He laughs until he nearly chokes. Finally the noise subsides, with difficulty. She waits, outraged.*]

TOM: How much did he pay you?

SOPHIE: Pay?

TOM: Well, how did he set it up? He must have offered you a few quid on the side. He couldn't have expected you to do it for nothing.

SOPHIE: What do you mean, please?

TOM [*rising, wiping his eyes with his scarf*]: All the same, it's fantastic! I mean, what's the point? Is it supposed to be a joke? Fun and games by the sea?

SOPHIE: Mister, are you suggesting I've been bribed?

TOM: I'm not suggesting it. I'm saying it.

SOPHIE: How dare you? How absolutely bloody dare you?

TOM: Because I absolutely bloody know, that's how! There's only one person in the world I've ever told those things about my childhood, and that's Frank.

SOPHIE [*loftily*]: My dear mister, to a professional eye like mine, truth does not have to be told. It is evident.

TOM: I dare say. And what if it *isn't* the truth?

[*A long pause.*]

SOPHIE: I beg your pardon?

TOM: What if it's a zonking great lie? Like every word of that story?

SOPHIE: I don't believe it.

TOM: It's true.

SOPHIE: Impossible. You say this to discredit me.

TOM: Why should I do that?

SOPHIE: Look, mister, what I see, I see. Lemberg never lies!

TOM: No, but *I do!*

[*Another pause.*]

SOPHIE [*carefully*]: You mean—your father is not a miner?

TOM: No. He's a rich accountant living in Leeds. [*He sits again, indolently.*]

SOPHIE: And your mother is not dead?

TOM: Not in the biological sense, no. She likes her game of golf, and gives bridge parties every Wednesday.

SOPHIE: But your accent!

TOM: [*dropping it completely*]: I'm afraid that's as put on as everything else. I mean, there's no point changing your background if you're going to keep your accent, now is there?

SOPHIE [*astounded*]: Beloved God!

TOM: Actually, it slips a bit when I'm drunk, but people just think I'm being affected.

SOPHIE [*trying to grasp it*]: You mean to say—you live your whole life like this? One enormous great *lie* from morning to night?

TOM: Yes, I suppose I do.

SOPHIE: *Unimaginable!*

TOM: Does it worry you?

SOPHIE: Doesn't it worry you?

TOM: Not particularly. I regard it as a sort of . . .

SOPHIE: White lie?

TOM: Yes, very good! A white lie . . .

SOPHIE: But why? In heaven's name, why? Why? . . . WHY?

TOM: Well, it's a question of image, really. When I was a kid, in pop music you had to be working class to get anywhere at all. Middle class was right out. Five years ago no one believed you could sing with the authentic voice of the people if you're the son of an accountant—and here we are!

SOPHIE: Incredible. And your parents, do they know that you have abolished them completely—like they never existed?

TOM: No, but it doesn't matter. They've abolished *me*, after all. How real am I to them? Dad calls me "Minstrel Boy" whenever I go home, because he finds it embarrassing to have a singer for a son. And Mother tells her bridge club I'm in London studying music—because *studying* is a more respectable image for her than performing in a cellar. Both of them are talking about themselves, not me. And that's fine, because that's what everybody's doing all the time, everywhere. Do you dig?

SOPHIE: But at least you've told this girl friend? She knows the truth?

TOM: Sue? No.

SOPHIE: You mean you just go on and on telling her lies about your terrible childhood?

TOM: She likes it. She finds it all very sad.

SOPHIE: That's the most disgusting thing I ever heard! Do you think you can borrow suffering—just to make yourself attractive?

TOM: I know I can.

SOPHIE: He was right, your friend. You're a monster.

[TOM *turns. A pause.*]

TOM: Is that what he said?

SOPHIE: His word exact. A monster.

TOM [*laughing*]: I don't believe it.

SOPHIE: Of course not. All the same, to me it's obvious. I can see it now quite clearly.

TOM: As clearly as you saw my past life in that ball?

SOPHIE: Don't be impertinent. Remember, please, who you are speaking to. You are in the presence of a Baroness of the Holy Roman Empire!

TOM: Am I?

[SOPHIE *glares at him, wrapping her shawl tighter about her. Bewildered, he gets up and goes into the anteroom.*]

SOPHIE [*calling out, very angry*]: There will be no charge!

TOM [*equally upset*]: Oh, thank you!

[*He stands shaking his head, trying to understand. Hastily* SOPHIE *rises and takes a swig from the decanter.*]

*Monster?* What . . . I don't get any of this . . .

[*He returns unexpectedly. She takes the decanter hastily from her lips.*]

I don't understand! What's been going on?

SOPHIE [*trying to recover her dignity*]: Going on?

TOM: You tell me!

SOPHIE: Look, mister: it was a joke. Your friend is a joker. He made up this whole thing to amuse you. He said to me life was a bit grim for you at the moment. The engagement here was not so good—you were both down in the mouth. He suggested I cheered you up . . . !

TOM: No.

SOPHIE: I assure you.

TOM: That's not it.

SOPHIE: Of course it is. Most certainly: what else? Do you imagine I would do such a thing for real? *Ja, ja,* to amuse, why not? But *seriously*—to betray my art? *Do you think I would?*

TOM [*working it out*]: You had to see disaster for me and Sue. If we—she and me got together . . . He's trying to warn me. Warn me off . . . My God! [*His mouth opens in amazement.*]

SOPHIE: So he's jealous. Is that so astounding . . .? He's right to be, isn't he?

TOM: What d'you mean?

SOPHIE: Look, I know you, mister. I know you very well. Don't look at me like that—"Oh, my God!" "What do you mean?" I'm not ashamed of what I did! I took money under false pretenses. Good. Good, good, good—because for a good good purpose.

TOM: What are you talking about?

SOPHIE: Please go now. Absolutely at once! There's no point to discuss further. There really isn't . . .

TOM [*alarmed*]: Just tell me this, first. How long has he known about me and Sue?

[*She looks at him sharply.*]

Did he say? A couple of weeks? A month? I mean, Jesus, to be that *hidden!* Not to give one sign. Just wait, day after day—build up and build up—keep your face smiling all the time. And then come down here for the day, pull a stunt like this, thinking about it all the way down in the van, I suppose . . . I mean, *who is he?*

SOPHIE: A giver.

TOM: What?

SOPHIE: A giver, mister. Impossible for you to imagine, of course, you taker. Someone who just gives, over and over to the end. . . . Hidden, you call him. Of course. Just because he's too proud to show the pain he feels. He is now walking by the sea asking that same question about you: "*Who is he?* What does he want? I gave him everything. Admiration. Not enough! Security. Not enough! I take him out of a slum—absolutely broke—give him my own flat to share, not one penny in rent—not enough! I make him a job. A whole Group I form for him. White satin—engagements—everything so he can fulfill his talent, not just sing for pennies in a filthy pub."

TOM: He told you *that*?

SOPHIE: *Ja,* mister, he told me. The poor idiot. He doesn't know about people like you. Take and take and take until the cows are at home. Take his hope, take his happiness—everything—everything you find!

TOM [*breaking*]: Here, I'm off!

SOPHIE: *Ja,* run! Run! The truth is unbearable, isn't it?

TOM: The what?

SOPHIE: The truth. *The truth,* mister! It's a meaningless word to you, isn't it?

[*A pause.* TOM *stands by the door, controlling himself.* SOPHIE *stands by the table, breathing heavily.*]

TOM [*quietly*]: All right. Just for the record, for the record, that's all—I'll give you three straight facts. Then I'll go. . . . When I met him I wasn't broke. I wasn't living in a slum. And I'd formed my Group a good year before I set eyes on him.

SOPHIE: The White Liars.

TOM: That's right.

SOPHIE: Liars, yes—liars is right!

TOM [*protesting*]: We had a regular gig every Friday at the Iron Duke in the Commercial Road! You can check on that, if you like.

SOPHIE: Black liars! Black! Not white!

TOM [*insistently*]: He used to come every weekend with Sue, and sit in the corner listening to us. I just remember eyes—his brown ones and her big blue ones—and they'd sit there and groove on us for hours, just like they were the only people in the world who knew about us. Yeh—that's it! Like we were simply part of their private world, with no existence anywhere else. . . .

[*He comes back into the room. She is suddenly listening.*]

Then suddenly one night, about six months ago, he comes over to me—says his name's Frank—he's a freelance journalist, and wants to do a whole story on the Liars for one of the Sunday papers. What they call a study in depth. It'll mean living around us for a while—did I mind? Well, it sounded great to me. I said fine. And there it was. I mean that's how it all began—with me chasing publicity! . . . A whole month—no, longer—he just followed us about, *observing*. Endless notes in a little book. Always grinning. Silly, you know, but very likable. He was a mad talker: you couldn't stop him, for anything. I used to tell him, a journalist is supposed to listen, not yap all the time, but he'd just laugh. "I like talking," he'd say. "It's the best thing in the world, after eating." I was living out in Winchmore Hill then, with my Aunt Daisy. Too much glazed chintz, but definitely not a slum. The only kind of music she likes is the sort you can chew tea cakes to. In the end I left and moved in with him. I hadn't been there a week before I discovered he owed three months' rent.

SOPHIE: No!

TOM: Which I paid.

SOPHIE: I don't believe you.

TOM: And a week after that, I found out he wasn't really a journalist at all. He worked with Sue in a boutique in the King's Road.

SOPHIE: That's not true.

TOM: Till he was sacked.

SOPHIE: You're making it up.

TOM: Why should I do that? Look, can't you dig? . . . From the moment Frank came in here he handed you a pack of lies. One after another.

[FRANK *returns, comes down the stairs and enters the anteroom.*]

SOPHIE: Fibs, maybe. That's possible.

TOM: Lies.

SOPHIE: Stories.

TOM: *Lies!* Zonking great *lies!*

SOPHIE [*suddenly furious*]: All right, lies, so what? *So what?* So he did, so he tells a couple of—of tales just to make himself a little more important. You dare! *You* dare talk about liars! You, with your coal mines, guitar on the fire—your whole disgusting childhood!

TOM: *His!*

SOPHIE: What?

TOM: *His! His* lies! All of them.

SOPHIE: *His* lies? About *your* childhood?

TOM [*more softly*]: His and hers together. Theirs.

[*Gulls and wind are heard.* FRANK, *standing by the curtain in the anteroom, listens intently.*]

SOPHIE [*carefully*]: Mister, I don't know what the hell you are saying.

TOM: If I said they'd made me up, would you get it? If I said they'd made *me* make me up. That's nearer . . . I don't know. Sometimes I see it, just for a second, a bit of it. Then it clouds over, just like in your ball—and becomes a nightmare. . . . [*He moves slowly to the crystal ball on the table.*] If only that thing really worked. If it could really show why. Why things happen.

SOPHIE: That's what it does, mister.

TOM: Yes, but to me. [*He picks the ball up.*] If I had the gift—just for five minutes to see the whole thing—her and him and me . . . How does it work? Colors, isn't that it? Red for rage, black for death? What for fake? Brown? That's good. Butch brown: the sound of my accent: the phony Yorkshire I put on when I came south, mainly because I couldn't stand my own voice. [*In a Yorkshire accent.*] Butch brown! Color of the moors . . . !

[FRANK *reacts, startled.* TOM *sits at the table, holding the ball.*]

[*Dropping the accent*] My grandpa used to talk like that, much to my mother's shame: I worked it up from him. It's what first turned them on: especially Frank. He used to sit on the end of my bed with his pencil and notebook, just grooving on it. Bogus journalist interviewing bogus miner! "You're so lucky," he'd say: "so lucky to be born a prole. The working class is the last repository of instinct." I'd just shrug. Shrugs are perfect. You can imply anything with a good shrug: repository of instinct—childhood misery—whatever's wanted. [*He sets down the ball.*] What color's that? The Want? The crazy Want in someone for an image to turn him on? Yeh—and the crazy way you play to it, just to make him feel good! Green, I bet you. Green for nausea . . . [*Simply.*] I watched him make up my childhood. "Where were you born?" he'd ask me. Then right away, he'd answer himself. "Some godawful little cottage in the North, I suppose: no loo, I suppose, no electric light, I suppose." "I suppose" meaning "I want." And me, I'd shrug. Shrug, shrug: up goes his slum. Shrug, shrug: down comes Dad's belt: ow! Anything. I made bricks out of shrugs. Slagheaps. Flagellant fathers and blanketless winters, and stolen crusts gnawed in the outside lav! His eyes would pop. "My God, how we treat kids in this country!" Hers, too—Sue's: no, hers were worse. They'd brim with tears. She was the world's champion brimmer! . . . She cried the first night we ever . . .

[FRANK *gives a start; his hand flies up to his mouth; he strains to hear more.* TOM *rises and grows more urgent.*]

She had this flat on her own, right near the boutique. One night I'd been over for spaghetti, and I'd played a bit to her after. Suddenly—chord of E major still fading into the Chelsea drizzle—she's looking down at me, and her voice is all panty. "You were *born* with that," she says. "There's the natural music of working people in your hands!" And down comes her hair—curtain of buttermilk over my mouth. And there it is. The Want. I knew it right away; the same Want as his, all desperate under her hair—"Give it me. An image. Give me an image! Turn me on!" . . . What do you do? Buttermilk hair across your aching mouth, what do you do? Mouth opens—starts to speak—how do you stop it? [*In his Yorkshire accent.*] "You *understand,*" it says, dead sincere. "Christ, you understand! . . . I'll tell you. The only encouragement my dad ever gave me was to throw my guitar on the fire. It wasn't much of an instrument, of course, but it was all I could afford. . . ." [*Dropping the accent.*] Oh, green! Green for nausea! And blue, blue, blue for all the tears in her sky—dropping on me! Spattering me! Lashing the Swedish rug like rain on a Bank Holiday beach! I was soaked. I really was. I went to bed with her to get dry. Honest.

[*A slight pause.* TOM *starts to walk about the room. His voice betrays increasingly more desperation.* FRANK *stands rigid now. The light has faded considerably.*]

That was three months ago. When did he find out? *She* didn't tell him. She wouldn't dare . . . he guessed. Well, of *course* he guessed! They know each other completely. They *are* each other! . . . Yes.

[*A pause.* TOM *and* SOPHIE *look at each other.*]

Once I'd spoken—actually spoken a lie out loud—I was theirs. They got excited, like lions after meat, sniffing about me, drooling. I suppose I could have stopped it any time. Just by using my own voice—telling them who I was. But I didn't. Color the ball yellow. I told myself I didn't want to hurt them. But why not? Who was I? I didn't exist for them. I don't *now!* [*Excitedly.*] They want *their* Tom: not me. Tom the idol. Tom the turn-on. Tom the yob god, born in a slum, standing in his long-suffering, maltreated skin—all tangled hair and natural instinct—to be hung by his priests in white satin! . . . Yeh: that's the real color for it all. *White.* Our uniform for the Liars. He designed it—she made it—I wear it! You should see me in it! Frothy white lace round the working-class throat! [*In his Yorkshire accent.*] "I look right handsome in it!"

SOPHIE [*crying out*]: Stop it, now, mister! Stop it! Words on words on words on words. What *he* did—what *she* did—what *they* did! And all to escape the guilt of what *you* did!

TOM: I?

SOPHIE: Of course, you! *You* told the lies, didn't you? *You* needed the worship. The fact remains. Mr. Taker, he gave you everything he had.

TOM: He gave me a role, that's what he gave! Can't you see that? I'm just acting in a film projected out of their eyes. *I Was a Prisoner on Wet Dream Island!*

SOPHIE: Oh, ha, ha, ha. Very funny! The truth is much simpler than that, mister. Simpler and much more nasty.

TOM: Is it?

SOPHIE: A boring, familiar, nasty old story! You had a friend. He had a girl. You stole her. And that's all. [*Pause.*] Actually he has not guessed you have been sleeping with her three months. He just feared you might, one day soon. . . . It's why he came here with his stupid game. Poor fellow. Poor stupid fellow . . . *Ja,* but people in love do many desperate things. You wouldn't understand that, of course. Goodbye, mister.

[*A pause.*]

TOM [*simply*]: Love, you really are in the wrong business, aren't you?

SOPHIE: What do you mean?

TOM: Excuse me.

[TOM *goes out suddenly into the anteroom.*]

SOPHIE [*calling out after him*]: What do you mean, please?

[TOM *sees* FRANK *standing there, in the gloom.* FRANK *is very upset.*]

TOM: How long have you been there?

FRANK: Few minutes.

SOPHIE [*to herself*]: Beloved God! [*She stands rigidly, trying to listen.*]

TOM: You heard.

FRANK: No. No. Nothing . . . Heard what? I—I—I've just this second come in. . . .

TOM: Goodbye, Frank.

[TOM *goes out of the anteroom and on to the pier.*]

FRANK: Where are you going? Tom!

[FRANK *follows* TOM *outside.*]

Where are you going?

TOM [*in a very posh accent*]: Back to Lichfield, old boy—back home.

FRANK: No! You can't . . . All right, it was disgusting—it was a stupid bloody trick: I'm sorry. It was plain awful, I know—I know. But you just can't go like this. You can't just go!

TOM: What else do you suggest?

FRANK: Well, we could—we could—surely we . . .

TOM: I've had it, Frank. With you. With her. With me, actually. You were right about one thing. The word you used. "Monster."

FRANK: I didn't mean that.

TOM: You should.

FRANK: That was the heat of the moment!

TOM: Tara, Frank. [*He puts out his hand.*]

FRANK: Tom, please. Can't we talk about this?

[TOM *shakes his head, smiles awkwardly, then suddenly turns and runs up the steps and out of sight.*]

[*Calling after him.*] Tom! You've got the concert! [*Howling suddenly.*] TOM! [*He stands still. Gulls and wind. Then slowly he goes back inside.* SOPHIE *has seen* TOM *running away. Now she hears* FRANK *return and stand in the anteroom.*]

SOPHIE: Mister, mister, won't you come in here, please?

[FRANK *stays where he is. She addresses him, unseen, from the darkening parlor.*]

I'm sorry. It's not gone so well, our little trick. It exploded, didn't it? I'm afraid that is sometimes the way with tricks . . . Still, it's not so bad, is it? After all, it's what you wanted really—him to go away. "Make him go," you asked me. "Get rid of him for me." Well, I can't claim I did it myself, but it's been done, mister. He's gone. You won't see him again. It's not such a bad day's work, after all. Your girl is quite safe now: that's the important thing.

[*A great sob comes from the anteroom.*]

Mister? . . . Mister . . . ?

[*The sobs grow louder.* FRANK *is in agony.* SOPHIE *moves across the parlor to the anteroom, draws the curtain, and enters it.* FRANK *turns away from her.*]

Oh, come now, please. I don't understand.

FRANK: No, you don't, do you?

SOPHIE: You wanted him to go.

[*He turns on her.*]

FRANK: I wanted him to leave her alone! . . . And to stay with me. In—my—bed.

[*She stares at him.*]

He'd been there six months.

[*A pause. Slowly* SOPHIE *retreats from the anteroom, back into the parlor. She stands by the curtain, deeply upset.*]

SOPHIE: He's right, your friend. I'm in the wrong business. I see nothing.

I understand nothing, any more. I'm in the wrong place. The wrong world. Who are you all? You weird people—you young, weird, mad people! I was brought up in a proper world. People were clear, what they were—what they wanted! People were decent! I don't understand this world now—freaks and frauds and turn me on! *I don't understand anything any more!* It's all so ugly! [*She grows more and more desperate.*] I was born into a world of order and beauty! That's what it meant to be noble—to give order to the world, and beautiful things. Not just tummy-twisting and wow-wow-wow like sick dogs! There was beauty, mister. My father brought me up in beauty, to respect beauty—to respect *people*—not make jokes of them—not dress like lunatics and make fun of people! I knew the Old World, mister! I knew the real world! My father, he knew the real world! He taught me how to live—my father; he taught me beauty—he taught me truth—he knew everything, my father—beauty and music and loving—he knew everything, everything—he knew NOTHING!

[*With a sudden swipe she smashes the photograph off the table on to the floor.* FRANK *is startled by the noise. She stares at the picture with hatred. Her speech gets more and more upset, but does not lose rapidity.*]

Weak, stupid little man! Folded his hands in front of the world, and said nothing. Just nothing! Every day on the twenty-seven bus, for fourteen years. Eight-forty-five leave the house, back at seven smelling of gherkins! Gherkins have a smell, mister—you know that smell? The smell of delicatessens? I said he was what to you? A Baron? Don't believe it. Take comfort, mister—here's a bit of comfort. It's not only the young who lie, whatever I said, it's not true—the old are worse. They are the biggest liars of them all! He was not a Baron; I am not a Baroness; my mother was not a Romany noblewoman, she was just a gypsy—and not even interesting. Just a quarter-gypsy, not colorful with scarves and lovers—just dull. Dull lady, always frightened. Both of them, always frightened! He had no estates, my dear: his estate was a kosher delicatessen in the town of Innsbruck. After Hitler, he worked exactly at the same trade in London. Gherkins in Innsbruck, gherkins in Crawford Street—the Prater Deli: Proprietor Harry Plotkin. That is my real name: *Plotkin!* I started the fortune telling because I could not bear to stand behind a counter and spoon out pickles! My mother said, "It's beneath you to tell fortunes." *Beneath!* Do you hear? Better of course to ladle out gherkins all your life into little cartons! "Thank you, madame, that will be two pounds forty . . . Thank you, sir! Thank you, thank you!"

[FRANK *suddenly makes a move: he cannot bear any more. He starts for the door—suddenly he notices the toy dog. He picks it up.*]

The photograph you saw, that is a costume. [*She takes the crystal ball, re-covers it, and carries it back to its shelf.*] The Paddington Opera Society presented *The Count of Luxembourg,* and my father got into the chorus. I found the medals myself for him, in the Portobello Road. They are not exactly accurate.

[FRANK *walks slowly out of the door, and away up the stairs, holding the dog. He disappears into the evening.* SOPHIE *does not realize he has left. She kneels down and picks up the photograph. Her speech grows a little more tender but no slower.*]

One thing I told you was true. His clarinet. After he came here he never touched it; but in Austria he played quite well. And there *was* a lake. It wasn't ours, but we went there every year, two weeks in the summer, and stayed at a guest house on the shore. One year the Rosé Quartet was staying there also for a couple of nights, appearing at the Salzburg Festival. And one evening, for a quarter of an hour, they let him play with them: the slow movement of the Brahms. I sat on a chair on the grass. I watched him. He looked unbelievable. He narrowed his eyes behind his pince-nez, and he concentrated everything inside him, and he made no mistakes at all. Not one. They let him play the whole movement. And just as he finished the sun went down, just like that, went absolutely out like a light, exactly as if it had been arranged. And that was the best moment of his life . . . [*She gets up, and replaces the photograph. She is half crying.*] Well, well, well: other years, other tears . . .

[*The lights on the pier suddenly come on: a bright string of little bulbs. She raises her voice in the gloom, to the anteroom.*]

Why are you crying, mister? For *whom?* Your lover? What lover? There never *was* one! *Who did you lose, you stupid boy?* . . . You hear me, mister? You want my advice? Advice and Consultation! Go home now—go home and find someone *real!* That's my advice to you, mister—and it's good. It's the best. I tell you something: *Plotkin Never Lies!* Do you hear me, mister? That's my joke for today. *Plotkin Never Lies!* [*She pours herself a drink.*] That's my joke for tomorrow.

[*Gulls and wind.* SOPHIE *salutes the gulls with her glass, and drinks. The light fades on her, into darkness, as*

THE CURTAIN FALLS

# BLACK COMEDY

A FARCE IN ONE ACT

*In memory*
*of Jerry Weinstein*
*who laughed*

*and to*
*John Dexter*
*who helped so much*
*to make the laughter*

*Black Comedy* was first presented at Chichester by the National Theatre on July 27, 1965, and subsequently at the Old Vic Theatre, London, with the following cast:

| | |
|---|---|
| BRINDSLEY MILLER | Derek Jacobi |
| CAROL MELKETT | Louise Purnell |
| MISS FURNIVAL | Doris Hare |
| COLONEL MELKETT | Graham Crowden |
| HAROLD GORRINGE | Albert Finney |
| SCHUPPANZIGH | Paul Curran |
| CLEA | Maggie Smith |
| GEORG BAMBERGER | Michael Byrne |

Directed by John Dexter

The New York production opened at the Ethel Barrymore Theatre on February 12, 1967, along with *White Liars.* The cast was as follows:

| | |
|---|---|
| BRINDSLEY MILLER | Michael Crawford |
| CAROL MELKETT | Lynn Redgrave |
| MISS FURNIVAL | Camila Ashland |
| COLONEL MELKETT | Peter Bull |
| HAROLD GORRINGE | Donald Madden |
| SCHUPPANZIGH | Pierre Epstein |
| CLEA | Geraldine Page |
| GEORG BAMBERGER | Michael Miller |

Directed by John Dexter

## THE SETTING

The action of the play takes place in BRINDSLEY's apartment in South Kensington, London. This forms the ground floor of a large house now divided into flats. HAROLD GORRINGE lives opposite; MISS FURNIVAL lives above. Right means stage right. Left means stage left.

There are four ways out of the room. A door at the left, upstage, leads directly across the passage to HAROLD's room. The door to this, with its mat laid tidily outside, can clearly be seen. A curtain, upstage center, screens BRINDSLEY's studio: when it is parted we glimpse samples of his work in metal. To the right of this an open stair shoots steeply up to his bedroom above, reached through a door at the top. To the left, downstage, a trap in the floor leads down to the cellar.

It is a gay room, when we finally see it, full of color and space and new shapes. It is littered with marvelous objects—mobiles, manikins, toys, and dotty bric-à-brac—the happy paraphernalia of a free and imaginative mind. The total effect is of chaos tidied in honor of an occasion, and of a temporary elegance created by the furniture borrowed from HAROLD GORRINGE and arranged to its best advantage.

This consists of three elegant Regency chairs in gold leaf; a Regency chaise longue to match; a small Queen Anne table bearing a fine opaline lamp, with a silk shade; a Wedgwood bowl in black basalt; a good Coalport vase containing summer flowers; and a fine porcelain Buddha.

The only things which actually belong to BRINDSLEY are a cheap square table bearing the drinks; an equally cheap round table in the middle of the room, shrouded by a cloth and decorated with the Wedgwood bowl; a low stool downstage center, improved by the Buddha; a record player; and his own artistic creations. These are largely assumed to be in the studio awaiting inspection; but one of them is visible in this room. On the dais stands a bizarre iron sculpture dominated by two long detachable metal prongs, and hung with metal pieces which jangle loudly if touched.

On the wall hang paintings, some of them presumably by CLEA. All are nonfigurative: colorful geometric designs, splashes, splodges, and splats of color; whirls and whorls and wiggles—all testifying more to a delight in handling paint than to an ability to achieve very much with it.

## THE TIME

9:30 on a Sunday night.

## THE LIGHT

On the few occasions when a lighter is lit, matches are struck, or a torch is put on, the light on stage merely gets dimmer. When these objects are extinguished, the stage immediately grows brighter.

---

[*Complete darkness. Two voices are heard:* BRINDSLEY *and* CAROL. *They must give the impression of two people walking round a room with absolute confidence, as if in the light. We hear sounds as of furniture being moved. A chair is dumped down.*]

BRINDSLEY: There! How do you think the room looks?

CAROL [*quacking*]: Fabulous! I wish you could always have it like this. That lamp looks divine there. And those chairs are just the right color. I told you green would look well in here.

BRINDSLEY: Suppose Harold comes back?

CAROL: He is not coming back till tomorrow morning.

[*We hear* BRINDSLEY *pacing nervously.*]

BRINDSLEY: I know. But suppose he comes tonight? He's mad about his antiques. What do you think he'll say if he goes into his room and finds out we've stolen them?

CAROL: Don't dramatize. We haven't stolen *all* his furniture. Just three chairs, the sofa, that table, the lamp, the bowl, and the vase of flowers, that's all.

BRINDSLEY: And the Buddha. That's more valuable than anything.

CAROL: Oh, do stop worrying, darling.

BRINDSLEY: Well, you don't know Harold. He won't even let anyone *touch* his antiques.

CAROL: Look, we'll put everything back as soon as Mr. Bamberger leaves. Now stop being dreary.

BRINDSLEY: Well, frankly, I don't think we should have done it. I mean—*anyway*, Harold or no.

CAROL: Why not, for heaven's sake? The room looks divine now. Just look at it!

BRINDSLEY: Darling, Georg Bamberger's a multimillionaire. He's lived all his life against this sort of furniture. Our few stolen bits aren't going to impress him. He's coming to see the work of an unknown sculptor. If you ask me, it would look much better to him if he found me exactly as I really am: a poor artist. It might touch his heart.

CAROL: It might—but it certainly won't impress Daddy. Remember, he's coming too.

BRINDSLEY: As if I could forget! Why you had to invite your monster father tonight, I can't think!

CAROL: Oh, not again!

BRINDSLEY: Well, it's too bloody much. If he's going to be persuaded I'm a fit husband for you, just by watching a famous collector buy some of my work, he doesn't deserve to have me as a son-in-law!

CAROL: He just wants some proof you can earn your own living.

BRINDSLEY: And what if Bamberger *doesn't* like my work?

CAROL: He will, darling. Just stop worrying.

BRINDSLEY: I can't. Get me a whisky.

[*She does. We hear her steps, and a glass clink against a bottle—then the sound of a soda syphon.*]

[*Grimly.*] I've got a foreboding. It's all going to be a disaster. An A1, copper-bottomed, twenty-four-carat disaster!

CAROL: Look, darling, you know what they say. Faint heart never won fair ladypegs!

BRINDSLEY: How true.

CAROL: The trouble with you is you're what Daddy calls a Determined Defeatist.

BRINDSLEY: The more I hear about your daddy, the more I hate him. I loathe military men anyway . . . and in any case, he's bound to hate me.

CAROL: Why?

BRINDSLEY: Because I'm a complete physical coward. He'll smell it on my breath.

CAROL: Look, darling, all you've got to do is stand up to him. Daddy's only a bully when he thinks people are afraid of him.

BRINDSLEY: Well, I am.

CAROL: You haven't even met him.

BRINDSLEY: That doesn't make any difference.

CAROL: Don't be ridiculous. [*Hands him a drink.*] Here.

BRINDSLEY: Thanks.

CAROL: What can he do to you?

BRINDSLEY: For one thing, he can refuse to let me marry you.

CAROL: Ah, that's sweetipegs!

[*We hear them embrace.*]

BRINDSLEY: I like you in yellow. It brings out your hair.

CAROL: Straighten your tie. You look sloppy.

BRINDSLEY: Well, you look divine.

CAROL: Really?

BRINDSLEY: I mean it. I've never seen you look so lovely.

CAROL: Tell me, Brin—have there been many before me?

BRINDSLEY: Thousands.

CAROL: Seriously!

BRINDSLEY: Seriously—none.

CAROL: What about that girl in the photo?

BRINDSLEY: She lasted about three months.

CAROL: When?

BRINDSLEY: Two years ago.

CAROL: What was her name?

BRINDSLEY: Clea.

CAROL: What was she like?

BRINDSLEY: She was a painter. Very honest. Very clever. And just about as cozy as a steel razor blade.

CAROL: When was the last time you saw her?

BRINDSLEY [*evasively*]: I told you . . . two years ago.

CAROL: Well, why did you still have her photo in your bedroom drawer?

BRINDSLEY: It was just there. That's all. Give me a kiss . . .[*Pause.*] No one in the world kisses like you.

CAROL [*murmuring*]: Tell me something. . . . Did you like it better with her—or me?

BRINDSLEY: Like what?

CAROL: Sexipegs.

BRINDSLEY: Look, people will be here in a minute. Put a record on. It had better be something for your father. What does he like?

CAROL [*crossing to the record player*]: He doesn't like anything except military marches.

BRINDSLEY: I might have guessed. . . . Wait—I think I've got some! That last record on the shelf. The orange cover. It's called "Marching and Murdering with Sousa," or something.

CAROL: This one?

BRINDSLEY: That's it.

CAROL [*getting it*]: "The Band of the Coldstream Guards."

BRINDSLEY: Ideal. Put it on.

CAROL: How'd you switch on?

BRINDSLEY: The last knob on the left. That's it. . . . Let us pray! . . . Oh, God, let this evening go all right! Let Mr. Bamberger like my sculpture and buy some! Let Carol's monster father like me! And let my neighbor Harold Gorringe never find out that we borrowed his precious furniture behind his back! Amen.

[*A Sousa march; loud. Hardly has it begun, however, when it runs down—as if there is a failure of electricity. The sound stops.*

*Brilliant light floods the stage. The rest of the play, save for the times when matches are struck or a flashlight is switched on, is acted in this light, but as if in pitch darkness.*

*They freeze:* CAROL *by the end of the sofa;* BRINDSLEY *by the drinks table. The girl's dress is a silk flag of chic wrapped round her greyhound's body. The boy's look is equally cool: narrow, contained, and sexy. Throughout the evening, as things slide into disaster for him, his crisp, detached shape degenerates progressively into sweat and rumple—just as the elegance of his room gives way relentlessly to its usual near-slum appearance. For the place, as for its owner, the evening is a progress through disintegration.*]

God! We've blown a fuse!

[*The structure and appearance of* BRINDSLEY'*s room is described in the note at the beginning of the play.*]

CAROL: *Oh no!*

BRINDSLEY: It must be. [*He blunders to the light switch, feeling ahead of him, trying to part the darkness with his hands. Finding the switch, he flicks it on and off.*]

CAROL: It is!

BRINDSLEY: Oh no!

CAROL: Or a power cut. Where's the box?

BRINDSLEY: In the hall.

CAROL: Have you any candles?

BRINDSLEY: No. Damn!

CAROL: Where are the matches?

BRINDSLEY: They should be on the drinks table. [*Feeling round the bottles*] No. Try on the record player.

[*They both start groping about the room, feeling for matches.*]

Damn, damn, damn, damn, damn, damn!

[CAROL *sets a maraca rattling off the record player.*]

CAROL: There! [*Finding it.*] No . . .

[*The telephone rings.*]

BRINDSLEY: Would you believe it! [*He blunders his way toward the sound of the bell. Just in time he remembers the central table—and stops himself colliding into it with a smile of self-congratulation.*] All right: I'm coming! [*Instead he trips over the dais, and goes sprawling—knocking the phone onto the floor. He has to grope for it on his knees, hauling the receiver back to him by the wire. Into receiver.*] Hello? . . . [*In sudden horror.*] *Hello!* . . . No, no, no, no—I'm fine, just fine! . . . You? . . . [*His hand over the receiver: to* CAROL.] Darling—look in the bedroom, will you?

CAROL: I haven't finished in here yet.

BRINDSLEY: Well, I've just remembered there's some fuse wire in the bedroom. In that drawer where you found the photograph. Go and get it, will you?

CAROL: I don't think there is. I didn't see any there.

BRINDSLEY [*snapping*]: Don't argue. Just look!

CAROL: All right. Keep your hairpiece on!

[*During the following she gropes her way cautiously up the stairs—head down, arms up the banisters, silken bottom thrust out with the effort.*]

BRINDSLEY [*controlling himself*]: I'm sorry. I just know it's there, that's all. You must have missed it.

CAROL: What about the matches?

BRINDSLEY: We'll have to mend it in the dark, that's all. Please hurry, dear.

CAROL [*climbing*]: Oh, God, how dreary! . . .

BRINDSLEY [*taking his hand off the receiver and listening to hear* CAROL *go*]: Hello? . . . Well, well, well, well! How are you? Good. That's just fine. Fine, fine! . . . Stop saying what?

[CAROL *reaches the top of the stairs—and from force of habit pulls down her skirt before groping her way into the bedroom.*]

BRINDSLEY [*hand still over the receiver*]: Carol? . . . Darling? . . . [*Satisfied she has gone; in a rush into the telephone, his voice low.*] Clea! What are you doing here? I thought you were in Finland. . . . But you've hardly been gone six weeks. . . . Where are you speaking from? . . . The air terminal? . . . Well, no, that's not a good idea tonight. I'm terribly busy, and I'm afraid I just can't get out of it. It's business.

CAROL [*calling from the bedroom door, above*]: There's nothing there except your dreary socks. I told you.

BRINDSLEY [*calling back*]: Well, try the other drawers! . . . [*He rises as he speaks, turning so that the wire wraps itself around his legs.*]

[CAROL *returns to her search.*]

[*Low and rapid, into phone.*]: Look: I can't talk now. Can I call you tomorrow? Where will you be? . . . Look, I told you *no*, Clea. Not tonight. I know it's just around the corner, that's not the point! You can't come round. . . . Look, the situation's changed. Something's happened this past month—

CAROL [*off*]: I can't see anything. Brin, *please!*

BRINDSLEY: Clea, I've got to go. . . . Look, I can't discuss it over the phone. . . . Has it got to do with what? Yes, of course it has. I mean you can't expect things to stay frozen, can you?

CAROL [*emerging from the bedroom*]: There's nothing here. Haven't we any matches at all?

BRINDSLEY: Oh, stop wailing! [*Into phone.*] No, not you. I'll call you tomorrow. Goodbye. [*He hangs up sharply—but fails to find the rest of the telephone so that he bangs the receiver hard on the table first. Then he has to disentangle himself from the wire. Already* BRINDSLEY *is beginning to be fussed.*]

CAROL [*descending*]: Who was that?

BRINDSLEY: Just a chum. Did you find the wire?

CAROL: I can't find anything in this. We've *got* to get some matches!

BRINDSLEY: I'll try the pub. Perhaps they'll have some candles as well.

[*Little screams are heard approaching from above. It is* MISS FURNIVAL *groping her way down in a panic.*]

MISS FURNIVAL [*squealing*]: Help! Help! . . .Oh, please someone help me!

BRINDSLEY [*calling out*]: Is that you, Miss Furnival?

MISS FURNIVAL: Mr. Miller? . . .

BRINDSLEY: Yes?

MISS FURNIVAL: Mr. Miller!

BRINDSLEY: Yes!

[*She gropes her way in.* BRINDSLEY *crosses to find her, but narrowly misses her.*]

MISS FURNIVAL: Oh, thank God, you're there; I'm so frightened!

BRINDSLEY: Why? Have your lights gone too?

MISS FURNIVAL: Yes!

BRINDSLEY: It must be a power cut.

[*He finds her hand and leads her to the chair downstage left.*]

MISS FURNIVAL: I don't think so. The street lights are on in the front. I saw them from the landing.

BRINDSLEY: Then it must be the main switch of the house.

CAROL: Where is that?

[MISS FURNIVAL *gasps at the strange voice.*]

BRINDSLEY: It's in the cellar. It's all sealed up. No one's allowed to touch it but the electricity people.

CAROL: What are we going to do?

BRINDSLEY: Get them—quick!

CAROL: Will they come out at this time of night?

BRINDSLEY: They've got to.

[BRINDSLEY *accidentally touches* MISS FURNIVAL's *breasts. She gives a little scream.* BRINDSLEY *gropes his way to the phone.*]

Have you by any chance got a match on you, Miss Furnival?

MISS FURNIVAL: I'm afraid I haven't. So improvident of me. And I'm absolutely terrified of the dark!

BRINDSLEY: Darling, this is Miss Furnival, from upstairs. Miss Furnival—Miss Melkett.

MISS FURNIVAL: How do you do?

CAROL [*extending her hand in the darkness*]: How do you do?

MISS FURNIVAL: Isn't this frightful?

[BRINDSLEY *picks up the phone and dials O.*]

CAROL: Perhaps we can put Mr. Bamberger off.

BRINDSLEY: Impossible. He's dining out and coming on here after. He can't be reached.

CAROL: Oh, flip!

BRINDSLEY [*sitting on the dais, and speaking into the phone*]: Hello, Operator, can you give me the London Electricity Board, please? Night Service . . . I'm sure it's in the book, Miss, but I'm afraid I can't see. . . . There's no need to apologize. No, I'm not blind—I just can't see! We've got a fuse. . . . No, we *haven't* got any matches! [*Desperate.*] Miss, *please*: this is an emergency! . . . Thank you! . . . [*To the room.*] London is staffed with imbeciles!

MISS FURNIVAL: Oh, you're so right, Mr. Miller.

BRINDSLEY [*rising, frantic: into the phone*]: Miss, I *don't want* the number: I can't dial it! . . . Well, have *you* ever tried to dial a number in the dark? . . . [*Trying to keep control.*] I just want to be connected . . . thank you. [*To* MISS FURNIVAL] Miss Furnival, do you by any remote chance have any candles?

MISS FURNIVAL: I'm afraid not, Mr. Miller.

BRINDSLEY [*mouthing nastily at her*]: "I'm afraid not, Mr. Miller." . . . [*Briskly, into phone.*] Hello? Look, I'd like to report a main fuse at 18 Scarlatti Gardens. My name is Miller. [*Exasperated.*] Yes, yes! All right . . . ! [*Maddened: to the room.*] Hold on! Hold bloody on! . . .

MISS FURNIVAL: If I might suggest, Harold Gorringe opposite might have some candles. He's away for the weekend, but always leaves his key under the mat.

BRINDSLEY: What a good idea. That's just the sort of practical thing he would have. [*To* CAROL.] Here—take this . . . I'll go and see, love. [*He hands her the telephone in a fumble—then makes for the door—only to collide with his sculpture.*] Bugger!

MISS FURNIVAL: Are you all right, Mr. Miller?

BRINDSLEY: I knew it! I bloody knew it. This is going to be the worst night of my life! . . . [*He collides with the door.*]

CAROL: Don't panic, darling. Just don't panic!

[*He stumbles out and is seen groping under* HAROLD's *mat for the key. He finds it and enters the room opposite.*]

MISS FURNIVAL: You're so right, Miss Melkett. We must none of us panic.

CAROL [*on the phone*]: Hello? Hello? [*To* MISS FURNIVAL.] This would have to happen tonight. It's just Brindsley's luck.

MISS FURNIVAL: Is it something special tonight then, Miss Melkett?

CAROL: It couldn't be more special if it tried.

MISS FURNIVAL: Oh dear. May I ask why?

CAROL: Have you ever heard of a German called Georg Bamberger?

MISS FURNIVAL: Indeed, yes. Isn't he the richest man in the world?

CAROL: Yes. [*Into phone.*] Hello? . . . [*To* MISS FURNIVAL.] Well, he's coming here tonight.

MISS FURNIVAL: Tonight!

CAROL: In about twenty minutes, to be exact. And to make matters worse, he's apparently stone deaf.

MISS FURNIVAL: How extraordinary! May I ask why he's coming?

CAROL: He saw some photos of Brindsley's work and apparently got madly excited about it. His secretary rang up last week and asked if he could come and see it. He's a great collector. Brin would be absolutely *made* if Bamberger bought a piece of his.

MISS FURNIVAL: Oh, how exciting!

CAROL: It's his big break. Or was—till a moment ago.

MISS FURNIVAL: Oh, my dear, you *must* get some help. Jiggle that thing.

CAROL [*jiggling the phone*]: Hello? Hello? . . . Perhaps the Bomb's fallen, and everyone's dead.

MISS FURNIVAL: Oh, please don't say things like that—even in levity.

CAROL [*someone answers her at last*]: Hello? Ah! This is Number 18, Scarlatti Gardens. I'm afraid we've had the most dreary fuse. It's what's laughingly known as the main switch. We want a *little man!* . . . Well, they can't *all* have flu . . . Oh, please try! It's screamingly urgent. . . . Thank you. [*She hangs up.*] Sometime this evening, they hope. That's a lot of help.

MISS FURNIVAL: They're not here to help, my dear. In my young days you paid your rates and you got satisfaction. Nowadays you just get some foreigner swearing at you. And if they think you're of the middle class, that only makes it worse.

CAROL: Would you like a drink?

MISS FURNIVAL: I don't drink, thank you. My dear father, being a Baptist minister, strongly disapproved of alcohol.

*[A scuffle is heard among milk bottles off, followed by a stifled oath.]*

COLONEL MELKETT *[off]*: Damn and blast!! . . . *[Barking.]* Is there anybody there?

CAROL *[calling]*: In here, daddypegs!

COLONEL: Can't you put the light on, dammit? I've almost knocked meself out on a damn milk bottle.

CAROL: We've got a fuse. Nothing's working.

[COLONEL MELKETT *appears, holding a lighter which evidently is working—we can see the flame, and, of course, the lights go down a little.*]

MISS FURNIVAL: Oh, what a relief! A light!

CAROL: This is my father, Colonel Melkett, Miss Furnival. She's from upstairs.

COLONEL: Good evening.

MISS FURNIVAL: I'm taking refuge for a moment with Mr. Miller. I'm not very good in the dark.

COLONEL: When did this happen?

[MISS FURNIVAL, *glad for the light, follows it pathetically as the* COLONEL crosses the room.]

CAROL: Five minutes ago. The main just blew.

COLONEL: And where's this young man of yours?

CAROL: In the flat opposite. He's trying to find candles.

COLONEL: You mean he hasn't got any?

CAROL: No. We can't even find the matches.

COLONEL: I see. No organization. Bad sign!

CAROL: Daddy, please. It could happen to any of us.

COLONEL: Not to me.

*[He turns to find* MISS FURNIVAL *right behind him and glares at her balefully. The poor woman retreats to the sofa and sits down.]*

[COLONEL MELKETT *gets his first sight of* BRINDSLEY'*s sculpture.*] What the hell's that?

CAROL: Some of Brindsley's work.

COLONEL: Is it, by Jove? And how much does that cost?

CAROL: I think he's asking fifty pounds for it.

COLONEL: My God!

CAROL *[nervously]*: Do you like the flat, Daddy? He's furnished it very well, hasn't he? I mean it's rich, but not gaudipegs.

COLONEL: Very elegant—good: I can see he's got excellent taste. *[Seeing the Buddha]* Now that's what I understand by a real work of art—you can see what it's meant to be.

MISS FURNIVAL: Good heavens!

CAROL: What is it?

MISS FURNIVAL: Nothing . . . it's just that Buddha—it so closely resembles the one Harold Gorringe has.

[CAROL *looks panic-stricken.*]

COLONEL: It must have cost a pretty penny, what? He must be quite well off. . . . By Jove—it's got pretty colors. [*He bends to examine it.*]

CAROL [*sotto voce, urgently, to* MISS FURNIVAL]: You *know* Mr. Gorringe?

MISS FURNIVAL: Oh, very well indeed! We're excellent friends. He has such lovely things . . . [*For the first time she notices the sofa on which she is sitting*] Oh . . .

CAROL: What?

MISS FURNIVAL: This furniture . . . [*Looking about her.*] Surely?—my goodness!

CAROL [*hastily*]: Daddy, why don't you look in there? It's Brin's studio. There's something I particularly want you to see before he comes back.

COLONEL: What?

CAROL: It—it—er—it's a surprise, go and see.

COLONEL: Very well, Dumpling. Anythin' to oblige. [*To* MISS FURNIVAL.] Excuse me.

[*He goes off into the studio, taking his lighter with him. The light instantly gets brighter on stage.* CAROL *sits beside the spinster on the sofa, crouching like a conspirator.*]

CAROL [*low and urgent*]: Miss Furnival, you're a sport, aren't you?

MISS FURNIVAL: I don't know. What is this furniture doing in here? It belongs to Harold Gorringe.

CAROL: I know. We've done something absolutely frightful. We've stolen all his best pieces and put Brin's horrid old bits in *his* room.

MISS FURNIVAL: But why? It's disgraceful!

CAROL [*sentimentally*]: Because Brindsley's got nothing. Miss Furnival. Nothing at all. He's as poor as a churchmouse. If Daddy had seen this place as it looks normally, he'd have forbidden our marriage on the spot. Mr. Gorringe wasn't there to ask—so we just took the chance.

MISS FURNIVAL: If Harold Gorringe knew that anyone had touched his furniture or his porcelain, he'd go out of his mind! And as for that Buddha—[*pointing in the wrong direction*] it's the most precious piece he owns. It's worth hundreds of pounds.

CAROL: Oh, please, Miss Furnival—you won't give us away, will you? We're desperate! And it's only for an hour. . . . Oh, please! *please!*

MISS FURNIVAL [*giggling*]: Very well! . . . I won't betray you!

CAROL: Oh, thank you!

MISS FURNIVAL: But it'll have to go back exactly as it was, just as soon as Mr. Bamberger and your father leave.

CAROL: I swear! Oh, Miss Furnival, you're an angel! Do have a drink. Oh, no, you don't. Well, have a bitter lemon.

MISS FURNIVAL: Thank you. That I won't refuse.

[*The* COLONEL *returns, still holding his lighter. The stage darkens a little.*]

COLONEL: Well, they're certainly a surprise. And that's supposed to be sculpture?

CAROL: It's not supposed to be. It is.

COLONEL: They'd make good garden implements. I'd like 'em for turnin' the soil.

[MISS FURNIVAL *giggles.*]

CAROL: That's not very funny, Daddy.

[MISS FURNIVAL *stops giggling.*]

COLONEL: Sorry, Dumpling. Speak as you find.

CAROL: I wish you wouldn't call me Dumpling.

COLONEL: Well, there's no point wastin' this. We may need it!

[*He snaps off his lighter.* MISS FURNIVAL *gives her little gasp as the stage brightens.*]

CAROL: Don't be nervous, Miss Furnival. Brin will be here in a minute with the candles.

MISS FURNIVAL: Then I'll leave, of course. I don't want to be in your way.

CAROL: You're not at all. [*Hearing him.*] Brin?

[BRINDSLEY *comes out of* HAROLD*'s room—returns the key under the mat.*]

BRINDSLEY: Hello?

CAROL: Did you find anything?

BRINDSLEY [*coming in*]: You can't find anything in this! If there's candles there, *I* don't know where they are. Did you get the electric people?

CAROL: They said they might send someone around later.

BRINDSLEY: How much later?

CAROL: They don't know.

BRINDSLEY: That's a lot of help. What a lookout! Not a bloody candle in the house. A deaf millionaire to show sculpture to—and your monster father to keep happy. Lovely!

COLONEL [*grimly lighting his lighter*]: Good evenin'.

[BRINDSLEY *jumps.*]

CAROL: Brin, this *is* my father—Colonel Melkett.

BRINDSLEY [*wildly embarrassed*]: Well, well, well, well, well! . . . [*Panic.*] Good evening, sir. Fancy you being there all the time! I—I'm expecting some dreadful neighbors, some neighbor monsters, monster neighbors, you know. . . . They rang up and said they might look round . . . Well, well, well! . . .

COLONEL [*darkly*]: Well, well.

MISS FURNIVAL [*nervously*]: Well, well!

CAROL [*brightly*]: Well!

[*The* COLONEL *rises and advances on* BRINDSLEY, *who retreats before him across the room.*]

COLONEL: You seem to be in a spot of trouble.

BRINDSLEY [*with mad nervousness*]: Oh, not really! Just a fuse—nothing really, we have them all the time . . . I mean, it won't be the first fuse I've survived, and I dare say it won't be the last! [*He gives a wild braying laugh.*]

COLONEL [*relentless*]: In the meantime, you've got no matches. Right?

BRINDSLEY: Right.

COLONEL: No candles. Right?

BRINDSLEY: Right.

COLONEL: No basic efficiency, right?

BRINDSLEY: I wouldn't say that, exactly . . .

COLONEL: By basic efficiency, young man, I mean the simple state of being At Attention in life, rather than At Ease. Understand?

BRINDSLEY: Well, I'm certainly not at ease.

COLONEL: What are you goin' to do about it?

BRINDSLEY: Do?

COLONEL: Don't echo me, sir. I don't like it.

BRINDSLEY: You don't like it . . . I'm sorry.

COLONEL: Now look you here. This is an emergency. Anyone can see that.

BRINDSLEY: No one can see anything: that's the emergency! [*He gives his braying laugh again.*]

COLONEL: Spare me your humor, sir, if you don't mind. Let's look at the situation objectively. Right?

BRINDSLEY: Right.

COLONEL: Good. [*He snaps off the lighter.*] Problem: Darkness. Solution: Light.

BRINDSLEY: Oh, very good, sir.

COLONEL: Weapons: Matches: none! Candles: none! What remains?

BRINDSLEY: Search me.

COLONEL [*triumphantly*]: Torches. Torches, sir! what?

BRINDSLEY: Or a set of early Christians.

COLONEL: What did you say?

BRINDSLEY: I'm sorry. I think I'm becoming unhinged. Very good. Torches—brilliant.

COLONEL: Routine. Well, where would you find one?

BRINDSLEY: The pub. What time is it?

[*The* COLONEL *lights his lighter, but now not at the first try. The stage lights flickers up and down accordingly.*]

COLONEL: Blasted thing. It's beginnin' to go. [*He consults his watch.*] Quarter to ten. You can just make it, if you hurry.

BRINDSLEY: Thank you, sir. Your clarity of mind has saved the day!

COLONEL: Well, get on with it, man.

BRINDSLEY: Yes, sir! Back in a minute!

[*The* COLONEL *sits in the Regency chair, downstage right.*]

CAROL: Good luck, darling.

BRINDSLEY: Thank you, my sweet.

[*She blows him a kiss. He blows her one back.*]

COLONEL [*irritated*]: Stop that at once!

[BRINDSLEY *starts for the door, but as he reaches it,* HAROLD GORRINGE *is heard, off.*]

HAROLD [*broad Lancashire accent*]: Hello? Hello? Anyone there?

BRINDSLEY [*freezing with horror*]: HAROLD!!

HAROLD: Brindsley?

BRINDSLEY [*meant for* CAROL]: It's Harold! He's back!

CAROL: Oh no!

BRINDSLEY: THE FURNITURE!!

HAROLD: What's going on here?

[HAROLD *appears. He wears a smart raincoat and carries a weekend suitcase. His hair falls over his brow in a flossy attempt at elegance.*]

BRINDSLEY: Nothing, Harold. Don't go in there—come in here! We've had a fuse. It's dark—it's all over the house.

HAROLD: Have you phoned the electric? [*Reaching out.*]

BRINDSLEY [*reaching out and grabbing him*]: Yes. Come in here.

HAROLD [*grabbed*]: Ohh! . . . [*He takes* BRINDSLEY'S *hand and enters the room cozily on his arm.*] It's rather cozy in the dark, isn't it?

BRINDSLEY [*desperately*]: Yes! I suppose so. . . . So, you're back from your weekend then . . .

HAROLD: I certainly am, dear. Weekend! Some weekend! It rained the whole bloody time. I feel damp to my knickers.

BRINDSLEY [*nervously*]: Well, have a drink and tell us all about it.

HAROLD: Us? [*Disengaging himself.*] Who's here, then?

MISS FURNIVAL [*archly*]: I am, Mr. Gorringe.

HAROLD: Ferny?

MISS FURNIVAL: Taking refuge, I'm afraid. You know how I hate the dark.

COLONEL [*attempting to light his lighter*]: Blasted thing! . . . [*He succeeds.*] There we are! [*Raising it to* GORRINGE'*s face, with distaste.*] Who are you?

BRINDSLEY: May I present my neighbor. This is Harold Gorringe—Colonel Melkett.

HAROLD: How do?

COLONEL: How d'ye do?

BRINDSLEY: And this is Carol Melkett, Harold Gorringe.

CAROL [*giving him a chilly smile*]: Hello!? . . .

[HAROLD *nods coldly.*]

BRINDSLEY: Here, let me take your raincoat, Harold.

HAROLD [*taking it off and handing it to him*]: Be careful, it's sopping wet.

[*He is wearing a tight, modish, gray suit and a brilliant strawberry shirt. Adroitly,* BRINDSLEY *drops the raincoat over the Wedgwood bowl on the table.*]

COLONEL: You've got no candles, I suppose?

HAROLD: Would you believe it, Colonel, but I haven't! Silly me!

[BRINDSLEY *crosses and blows out the* COLONEL'*s lighter, just as* HAROLD *begins to look around the room. The stage brightens.*]

COLONEL: What the devil did you do that for?

BRINDSLEY: I'm saving your wick, Colonel. You may need it later and it's failing fast.

[*The* COLONEL *gives him a suspicious look.* BRINDSLEY *moves quickly back, takes up the coat and drops it over the right end of the sofa, to conceal as much of it as possible.*]

HAROLD: It's all right. I've got some matches.

CAROL [*alarmed*]: Matches!

HAROLD: Here we are! I hope I've got the right end. [*He strikes one.*]

[BRINDSLEY *immediately blows it out from behind, then moves swiftly to hide the Wedgwood bowl under the table and drop the tablecloth over the remaining end of the sofa.* MISS FURNIVAL *sits serenely unknowing between the two covers.*]

Hey, what was that?

BRINDSLEY [*babbling*]: A draft. No match stays alight in this room. It's impossible. Crosscurrents, you know! Old houses are full of them. They're almost a permanent feature in *this* house. . . .

HAROLD [*bewildered*]: I don't know what you're on about. [*He strikes another match.*]

[BRINDSLEY *agains blows it out as he nips over to sit in the chair downstage left, but this time is seen.*]

HAROLD: What's up with you?

BRINDSLEY: Nothing!

HAROLD: Have you got a dead body in here or something?

BRINDSLEY: NO! [*He starts his maniacal laughter.*]

HAROLD: Here, have you been drinking?

BRINDSLEY: No. Of course not.

[HAROLD *strikes another match.* BRINDSLEY *dashes up to him and yet again blows it out. All these strikings and blowings are of course accompanied by swift and violent alterations of the light.*]

HAROLD [*exasperated*]: Now look here! What's up with you?

BRINDSLEY [*inspired*]: Dangerous!

HAROLD: What?

BRINDSLEY [*frantically improvising*]: Dangerous! It's dangerous! . . . We can all die! . . . Naked flames! Hideous accidents can happen with naked flames!

HAROLD: I don't know what you're on about—what's up with you?

[BRINDSLEY *clutches* HAROLD *and backs him bewilderedly across to the center table.*]

BRINDSLEY: I've just remembered! It's something they always warn you about. In old houses the fuse box and the gas meter are in the same cupboard. They are here!

COLONEL: So what about it?

BRINDSLEY: Well . . . electrical blowouts can damage the gas supply. They're famous for it! They do it all the time! And they say you've got to avoid naked flames till they're mended.

COLONEL [*suspicious*]: I've never heard of that.

HAROLD: Me neither.

BRINDSLEY: Well, take my word for it. It's fantastically dangerous to burn naked flames in this room!

CAROL [*catching on*]: Brin's absolutely right. In fact, they warned me about it on the phone this evening when I called them. They said, "Whatever you do, don't strike a match till the fuse is mended."

BRINDSLEY: There, you see!—it's terribly dangerous.

COLONEL [*grimly*]: Then why didn't you warn me, Dumpling?

CAROL: I—I forgot.

COLONEL: Brilliant!

MISS FURNIVAL: Oh, goodness, we must take care!

BRINDSLEY: We certainly must! . . . [*Pause.*] Let's all have a drink. Cheer us up! . . .

CAROL: Good idea! Mr. Gorringe, would you like a drink?

HAROLD: Well, I must say, that wouldn't come amiss. Not after the journey I've had tonight. I swear to God there was thirty-five people in that compartment if there was one—babes in arms, toddlers, two nuns, three yapping poodles, and not a sausage to eat from Leamington to London. It's a bloody disgrace.

MISS FURNIVAL: You'd think they'd put on a restaurnat car, Mr. Gorringe.

HAROLD: Not them, Ferny. They don't care if you perish once they've got your fare. Excuse me. I'll just go and clean up.

BRINDSLEY [*panic*]: You can do that here!

HAROLD: Well, I must unpack anyway.

BRINDSLEY: Do it later.

HAROLD: No, I hate to keep clothes in a suitcase longer than I absolutely have to. If there's one thing I can't stand, it's a creased suit.

BRINDSLEY: Five more minutes won't hurt, surely?

HAROLD: Ooh, you aren't half bossy!

CAROL: What will you have? Winnie, Vera, or Ginette?

HAROLD: Come again?

CAROL: Winnie Whisky, Vera Vodka, or dear old standby Ginette.

HAROLD [*yielding*]: I can see you're the camp one! . . . If it's all the same to you, I'll have a drop of Ginette, please, and a little lime juice.

COLONEL [*irritated*]: Young man, do I have to keep reminding you that you are in an emergency? You have a guest arrivin' any second.

BRINDSLEY: Oh, God, I'd forgotten!

COLONEL: Try the pub. Try the neighbor's. Try who you damn well please, sir—but *get a torch!*

BRINDSLEY: Yes . . . yes! . . . [*Airily.*] Carol, can I have a word with you, please?

CAROL: I'm here.

[*She gropes toward him and* BRINDSLEY *leads her to the stairs.*]

COLONEL: What now?

BRINDSLEY: Excuse us just a moment, please. Colonel.

[*He pulls her quickly after him, up the stairs.*]

MISS FURNIVAL [*as they do this*]: Oh, Mr. Gorringe, it's so exciting. You'll never guess who's coming here tonight.

HAROLD: Who?

MISS FURNIVAL: Guess.

HAROLD: The Queen!

MISS FURNIVAL: Oh, Mr. Gorringe, you are ridiculous!

[BRINDSLEY *arrives at the top of the stairs, then opens the bedroom door and closes it behind them.*]

BRINDSLEY: What are we going to do?

CAROL [*behind the door*]: I don't know!

BRINDSLEY [*behind the door*]: Think!

CAROL: But—

BRINDSLEY: *Think!*

COLONEL: Is that boy touched or somethin'?

HAROLD: Touched? He's an absolute poppet.

COLONEL: A what?

HAROLD: A duck. I've known him for years, ever since he came here. There's not many secrets we keep from each other, I can tell you.

COLONEL [*frostily*]: Really?

HAROLD: Yes, really. He's a very sweet boy.

[BRINDSLEY *and* CAROL *emerge from behind the bedroom door.*]

BRINDSLEY: We'll have to put all Harold's furniture back in his room.

CAROL: *Now?!*

BRINDSLEY: We'll have to! I can't get a torch till we do.

CAROL: We can't!

BRINDSLEY: We must. He'll go *mad* if he finds out what we've done!

HAROLD: Well, come on, Ferny: don't be a tease. Who is it? Who's coming?

MISS FURNIVAL: I'll give you a clue. It's someone with money.

HAROLD: Money? . . . Let me think.

COLONEL [*calling out*]: Carol!

CAROL: Look, can't you just tell him it was a joke?

BRINDSLEY: You don't know him. He can't bear anyone to touch his treasures. They're like children to him. He cleans everything twice a day with a special swansdown duster. He'd wreck everything. Would you like him to call me a thief in front of your father?

CAROL: Of course not!

BRINDSLEY: Well, he would. He gets absolutely hysterical. I've seen him.

COLONEL: Brindsley!

CAROL: Well, how the hell can we do it?

HAROLD: It's no good. You can't hear up there.

BRINDSLEY [*stripping off his jacket*]: Look, you hold the fort. Serve them drinks. Just keep things going. Leave it all to me. I'll try and put everything back in the dark.

CAROL: It won't work.

BRINDSLEY: It's *got* to!

CAROL [*roaring*]: *Brindsley!!*

BRINDSLEY [*dashing to the door*]: Coming, sir. . . .[*With false calm.*] I'm just getting some empties to take to the pub.

COLONEL: Say what you like. That boy's touched.

BRINDSLEY [*to* CAROL, *intimately*]: Trust me, darling.

[*They kiss.*]

COLONEL: At the double, Miller.

BRINDSLEY: Yes, sir! Yes, sir! [*He rushes out and in his anxiety he misses his footing and falls neatly down the entire flight of stairs. Picking himself up.*] I'm off now, Colonel! Help is definitely on the way.

COLONEL: Well, hurry it up, man.

BRINDSLEY: Carol will give you drinks. If Mr. Bamberger arrives, just explain the situation to him.

HAROLD [*feeling for his hand*]: Would you like me to come with you?

BRINDSLEY: No, no, no—good heavens: stay and enjoy yourself!

[HAROLD *kisses his hand.* BRINDSLEY *pulls it away.*]

I mean, you must be exhausted after all those poodles. A nice gin and lime will do wonders for you. I shan't be a minute. [*He reaches the door, opens it, then slams it loudly, remaining on the inside. Stealthily he opens it again, stands dead still for a moment, center, silently indicating to himself the position of the chairs he has to move—then he finds his way to the first of the Regency chairs, downstage left, which he lifts noiselessly.*]

CAROL [*with bright desperation*]: Well now, drinks! What's everyone going to have? It's Ginette for Mr. Gorringe and I suppose Winnie for Daddy.

COLONEL: And how on earth are you going to do that in the dark?

CAROL: I remember the exact way I put out the bottles.

[BRINDSLEY *bumps into her with the chair and falls back, gored by its leg.*]

CAROL: It's very simple.

HAROLD: Oh, look, luv, let me strike a match. I'm sure it's not that dangerous, just for a *minute!* [*He strikes a match.*]

CAROL: Oh no! . . .

[BRINDSLEY *ducks down, chair in hand, and Carol blows out the match.*]

Do you want to blow us all up, Mr. Gorringe? . . . All poor Mr. Bamberger would find would be teensy-weensy bits of us. Very messypegs!

[*She snatches the box of matches, feels for the ice bucket, and drops them into it.* BRINDSLEY *steals out, Felix-the-cat-like, with the chair as* CAROL *fumblingly starts to mix drinks. He sets it down, opens* HAROLD*'s door, and disappears inside it with the chair.*]

HAROLD: Bamberger? Is that who's coming? Georg Bamberger?

MISS FURNIVAL: Yes. To see Mr. Miller's work. Isn't it exciting?

HAROLD: Well, I never! I read an article about him last week in the Sunday paper. He's known as the mystery millionaire. He's almost completely deaf—deaf as a post—and spends most of his time indoors alone with his collection. He hardly ever goes out, except to a gallery or a private studio. Thats the life! If I had money that's what I'd do. Just collect all the china and porcelain I wanted.

[BRINDSLEY *returns with a poor, broken-down chair of his own and sets it down in the same position as the one he has taken out. The second chair presents a harder challenge. It sits right across the room, upstage right. Delicately he moves toward it—but he has difficulty finding it. We watch him walk round and round it in desperately narrowing circles till he touches it and with relief picks it up.*]

MISS FURNIVAL: I've never met a millionaire. I've always wondered if they feel different to us. I mean their actual skins.

COLONEL: Their skins?

MISS FURNIVAL: Yes. I've always imagined they must be softer than ours. Like the skins of ladies when I was a girl.

CAROL: What an interesting idea.

HAROLD: Oh, she's very fanciful is Ferny. Real imagination, I always say.

MISS FURNIVAL: Very kind of you, Mr. Gorringe. You're always so generous with your compliments.

[*As she speaks her next speech staring smugly into the darkness, hands clasped in maidenly gentility, the second Regency chair is being moved slowly across what should be her field of vision, two inches from her face. During the following,* BRINDSLEY *unfortunately misaims and carries the chair past the door, bumps into the wall, retreats from it, and inadvertently shuts the door softly with his back. Now he cannot get out of the room. He has to set down the chair, grope for the door handle, turn it, then open the door—then refind the chair, which he has quite lost. This takes a long and frantic time. At last he triumphs, and staggers from the room, nearly exhausted.*]

But this is by no means fancy. In my day, softness of skin was quite the sign of refinement. Nowadays, of course, it's hard enough for us middle classes to keep ourselves decently clothed, let alone soft. My father used to say, even before the bombs came and burned our dear little house at Wendover: 'The game's up, my girl. We middle classes are as dead as the dodo.' Poor Father, how right he was.

[Note: *Hopefully, if the counterpoint of farce action goes well,* MISS FURNIVAL *may have to ad-lib a fair bit during all this, and not mind too much if nobody hears her. The essential thing for all four actors during the furniture moving is to preserve the look of ordinary conversation.*]

COLONEL: Your father was a professional man?

MISS FURNIVAL: He was a man of God, Colonel.

COLONEL: Oh.

[BRINDSLEY *returns with a broken-down rocking chair of his own. He crosses gingerly to where the* COLONEL *is sitting.*]

How are those drinks coming, Dumpling?

CAROL: Fine, Daddy. They'll be one minute.

COLONEL [*speaking directly into* BRINDSLEY'*s face*]: Let me help you.

[BRINDSLEY *staggers back, startled.*]

CAROL: You can take this bitter lemon to Miss Furnival if you want.

[BRINDSLEY *sets down the rocker immediately next to the* COLONEL'*s chair.*]

COLONEL: Very well.

[*He rises just as* BRINDSLEY'*s hand pulls it from beneath him. With his other hand* BRINDSLEY *pulls the rocker into the identical position. The* COLONEL *moves slowly across the room, arms outstretched for the bitter lemon. Unknowingly* BRINDSLEY *follows him, carrying the third chair. The* COLONEL *collides gently with the table. At the same moment* BRINDSLEY *reaches it upstage of him, and searches for the Wedgwood bowl. Their hands narrowly miss. Then* BRINDSLEY *remembers the bowl is under the table. Deftly he reaches down and retrieves it—and carrying it in one hand and the chair in the other, triumphantly leaves the room through the arch unconsciously provided by the outstretched arms of* CAROL *and the* COLONEL, *giving and receiving a glass of Scotch—which they think is lemonade.*]

CAROL: Here you are, Daddy. Bitter lemon for Miss Furnival.

COLONEL: Right you are, Dumpling. [*To* MISS FURNIVAL.] So your father was a minister, then?

MISS FURNIVAL: He was a saint, Colonel. I'm only thankful he never lived to see the rudeness and vulgarity of life today.

[*The* COLONEL *sets off to find her but goes much too far to the right.*]

HAROLD [*sits on the sofa beside her*]: Oooh, you're so right, Ferny. Rudeness and vulgarity—that's it to a T. The manners of some people today are beyond belief. Honestly. Did I tell you what happened in my shop last Friday? I don't think I did.

MISS FURNIVAL: No, Mr. Gorringe, I don't think so.

[*Her voice corrects the* COLONEL'*s direction. During the following he moves slowly up toward her.*]

HAROLD: Well, I'd just opened up—it was about quarter to ten and I was dusting off the teapots—you know, Rockingham collects the dust something shocking!—when who should walk in but that Mrs. Levitt, you know—the ginger-haired bit I told you about, the one who thinks she's God's gift to bachelors.

COLONEL [*finding her head with his hand and presenting her with the Scotch*]: Here's your lemonade.

MISS FURNIVAL: Oh, thank you. Most kind.

[*Throughout* HAROLD'*s story,* MISS FURNIVAL *nurses the glass, not drinking. The* COLONEL *finds his way slowly back to the chair he thinks he was sitting on before, but which is now a rocker.* BRINDSLEY *reappears triumphantly carrying one of the original Regency chairs he took out. He moves slowly across the room getting his bearings.*]

HAROLD: Anyway, she's got in her hand a vase I'd sold her last week—it was a birthday present for an old geezer she's having a bit of a ding-dong with somewhere in Earl's Court, hoping to collect all his lolly when he dies, as I read the situation. I'm a pretty good judge of character, Ferny, as you know—and she's a real grasper if ever I saw one.

[*The* COLONEL *sits heavily in the rocking chair which overbalances backwards, spilling him onto the floor.*]

COLONEL: Dammit to hell!

CAROL: What's the matter, Daddy?

[*A pause.* BRINDSLEY *sits down panic-stricken on the chair he has carried in. The* COLONEL *feels the chair and sets it on its feet.*]

COLONEL [*unbelieving*]: It's a blasted rockin' chair! I didn't see a blasted rockin' chair here before! . . .

[*Astounded, the* COLONEL *remains on the floor.* BRINDSLEY *rises and moves the chair to the original position of the second chair he moved.*]

HAROLD: Oh yes, you want to watch that. It's in a pretty ropey condition. I've told Brin about it several times. Anyway, this vase. It's a nice bit of Kang Tsi, blue and white with a good orange-peel glaze, absolutely authentic—I'd let her have it for forty-five pounds, and she'd got infinitely the best of the bargain, no arguments about that!

[HAROLD *rises and leans against the center table to tell his story more effectively. The* COLONEL *seats himelf again, gingerly.*]

Well, in she prances, her hair all done up in one of them bouffon hair-dos, you know, tarty—French-like—it would have looked fancy on a girl half her age with twice her looks—

[BRINDSLEY *mistakenly lifts the end of the sofa.* MISS FURNIVAL *gives a little scream at the jolt.*]

HAROLD: Exactly! You know the sort.

[BRINDSLEY *staggers in the opposite direction downstage onto the rostrum.*]

And d'you know what she says to me? "Mr. Gorringe," she says, "I've been cheated."

MISS FURNIVAL: No!

HAROLD: Her very words. "Cheated."

[BRINDSLEY *collides with the sculpture on the dais. It jangles violently.*]

[*To it.*] Hush up, I'm talking!

CAROL [*covering up*]: I'm frightfully sorry.

[HAROLD *whirls round, surprised.*]

HAROLD: Anyway—"Oh," I say, "and how exactly has that occurred, Mrs. Levitt?" "Well," she says, "quite by chance I took this vase over to Bill Everett in the Portobello, and he says it's not what you called it at all, Chinese and very rare. He says it's a piece of nineteenth-century English trash!"

[BRINDSLEY *finds the lamp on the downstage table and picks it up. He walks with it round the rocking chair, on which the* COLONEL *is now sitting again.*]

"Does he?" I say. "Does he?" I keep calm. I always do when I'm riled. "Yes," she says. "He does. And I'd thank you to give me my money back!"

[*The wire of the lamp has followed* BRINDSLEY *round the bottom of the rocking chair. It catches.* BRINDSLEY *tugs it gently. The chair moves. Surprised, the* COLONEL *jerks forward.* BRINDSLEY *tugs it again, much harder. The rocking chair is pulled forward, spilling the* COLONEL *out of it, again onto the floor, and then falling itself on top of him. The shade of the lamp comes off. During the ensuing dialogue* BRINDSLEY *gets to his knees and crawls right across the room following the flex of the lamp. He finds the plug, pulls it out, and—still on his knees—retraces his steps, winding up the wire around his arm, and becoming helplessly entangled in it. The* COLONEL *remains on the floor, now really alarmed.*]

MISS FURNIVAL: How dreadful, Mr. Gorringe. What did you do?

HAROLD: I counted to ten, and then I let her have it. "In the first place," I said, "I don't expect my customers to go checking up on my honesty behind my back. In the second, Bill Everett is ignorant as Barnsley dirt; he doesn't know Tang from Ting. And in the third place, that applies to you, too, Mrs. Levitt."

MISS FURNIVAL: You didn't!

HAROLD: I certainly did—and worse than that. "You've got in your hand," I said, "a minor masterpiece of Chinese pottery. But in point of fact," I said, "you're not even fit to hold a 1953 Coronation mug. Don't you ever come in here again," I said, "don't you cross my threshold. Because, if you do, Mrs. Levitt, I won't make myself responsible for the consequences."

CAROL [*with two drinks in her hand*]: My, Mr. Gorringe, how splendid of you. Here's your gin and lime. You deserve it. [*She hands him the bitter lemon.*]

HAROLD [*accepting it*]: Ta. I was proper blazing, I didn't care!

CAROL: Where are you? Where are you, Daddy? Here's your Scotch.

COLONEL: Here, Dumpling!

[*He gets up dazedly and fumbles his way to the glass of gin and lime.* BRINDSLEY *meanwhile realizes he has lost the shade of the lamp. On his knees, he begins to look for it.*]

HAROLD: Carroty old bitch— telling *me* about pottery! *Oooh!!* [*He shakes himself indignantly at the recollection of it.*]

MISS FURNIVAL: Do you care for porcelain yourself, Colonel?

COLONEL: I'm afraid I don't know very much about it, madam. I like some of that Chinese stuff—you get some lovely colors, like on that statue I saw when I came in here—very delicate.

HAROLD: What statue's that, Colonel?

COLONEL: The one on the packing case, sir. Very fine.

HAROLD: I didn't know Brin had any Chinese stuff. What's it of then, this statue?

[BRINDSLEY *freezes.*]

CAROL [*desperately*]: Well, we've all got drinks, I'd like to propose Daddy's regimental toast. Raise your glasses everyone! "To the dear old Twenty-fifth Horse. Up the British, and Down with the Enemy!"

MISS FURNIVAL: I'll drink to that! Up the British!

HAROLD: Up the old Twenty-fifth!!

[*Quickly* BRINDSLEY *finds the Buddha, moves it from the packing case to the table, then gets* HAROLD'*s raincoat from the sofa, and wraps the statue up in it, leaving it on the table.*]

COLONEL: Thank you, Dumpling. That was very touchin' of you. Very touchin' indeed. [*He swallows his drink.*] Dammit, that's gin!

HAROLD: I've got lemonade!

MISS FURNIVAL: Oh! Horrible! . . .Quite horrible! That would be alcohol, I suppose! . . .Oh dear, how unpleasant! . . .

HAROLD [*to* MISS FURNIVAL]: Here, luv, exchange with me. No—you get the lemonade—but I get the gin. Colonel—

COLONEL: Here, sir.

[*Seizing her chance* MISS FURNIVAL *downs a huge draft of Scotch. They all exchange drinks.* BRINDSLEY *resumes his frantic search for the shade.*]

HAROLD: Here, Ferny.

[*The* COLONEL *hands her the gin and lime. He gets instead the bitter lemon from* HAROLD. HAROLD *gets the Scotch.*]

MISS FURNIVAL: Thank you.

HAROLD: Well, let's try again. Bottoms up!

COLONEL: Quite.

[*They drink. Triumphantly,* BRINDSLEY *finds the shade. Unfortunately at the same moment the* COLONEL *spits out his lemonade in a fury all over him, as he marches toward him on his knees.*]

Look here—I can't stand another minute of this! [*He fishes his lighter out of his pocket and angrily tries to light it.*]

CAROL: Daddy, please!

COLONEL: I don't care, Dumpling. If I blow us up, then I'll blow us up! This is *ridiculous!* . . .

[*His words die in the flame. He spies* BRINDSLEY *kneeling at his feet, wound about with lamp wire.*]

What the devil are you doin' there?

BRINDSLEY [*blowing out his lighter*]: Now don't be rash, Colonel! Isn't the first rule of an officer "Don't involve your men in unnecessary danger?" [*Quickly he steals, still on his knees, to the table downstage right.*]

COLONEL: Don't be impertinent. Where's the torch?

BRINDSLEY: Er . . . the pub was closed.

HAROLD: You didn't go to the pub in that time, surely? You couldn't have done.

BRINDSLEY: Of course I did.

MISS FURNIVAL: But it's five streets away, Mr. Miller.

BRINDSLEY: Needs must when the Devil drives, Miss Furnival. Whatever that means. [*Quickly he lifts the table, and steals out of the room with it and the wrecked lamp.*]

COLONEL: [*who thinks he is still kneeling at his feet*]: Now look here: there's somethin' very peculiar goin' on in this room. I may not know about art, Miller, but I know men. I know a liar in the light, and I know one in the dark.

CAROL: Daddy!

COLONEL: I don't want to doubt your word, sir. All the same, I'd like your oath you went out to that public house. *Well?*

CAROL [*realizing he isn't there, raising her voice*]: Brin, Daddy's talking to you!

COLONEL: What are you shoutin' for?

BRINDSLEY [*rushing back from* HAROLD'*s room, still entangled in the lamp*]: Of course! I know! He's absolutely right. I was—just thinking it over for a moment.

COLONEL: Well? What's your answer?

BRINDSLEY: I . . . I couldn't agree with you more, sir.

COLONEL: What?

BRINDSLEY: That was a very perceptive remark you made there. Not everyone would have thought of that. Individual. You know. Almost witty. Well, it *was* witty. Why be ungenerous? . . .

COLONEL: Look, young man, are you trying to be funny?

BRINDSLEY [*ingratiatingly*]: Well, I'll try anything once . . .

HAROLD: I say, this is becoming a bit unpleasant, isn't it?

CAROL: It's becoming drearypegs.

COLONEL: Quiet, Dumpling. Let me handle this.

BRINDSLEY: What's there to handle, sir?

COLONEL: If you think I'm going to let my daughter marry a born liar, you're very much mistaken.

HAROLD: Marry!

CAROL: Well, that's the idea.

HAROLD: You and this young lady, Brin?

CAROL: Are what's laughingly known as engaged. Subject of course to Daddy's approval.

HAROLD: Well! [*Furious at the news, and at the fact that* BRINDSLEY *hasn't confided in him.*] What a surprise! . . .

BRINDSLEY: We were keeping it a secret.

HAROLD: Evidently. How long's this been going on, then?

BRINDSLEY: A few months.

HAROLD: You old slyboots.

BRINDSLEY [*nervous*]: I hope you approve, Harold.

HAROLD: Well, I must say, you know how to keep things to yourself.

BRINDSLEY [*placatingly*]: I meant to tell you, Harold . . . I really did. You were the one person I was going to tell.

HAROLD: Well, why didn't you, then?

BRINDSLEY: I don't know. I just never got around to it.

HAROLD: You saw me every day.

BRINDSLEY: I know.

HAROLD: You could have mentioned it at any time.

BRINDSLEY: I know.

HAROLD [*huffy*]: Well, it's your business. There's no obligation to share confidences. I've only been your neighbor for three years. I've always assumed there was more than a geographical closeness between us, but I was obviously mistaken.

BRINDSLEY: Oh, don't start getting huffy, Harold!

HAROLD: I'm not getting anything! I'm just saying it's surprising, that's all. Surprising and somewhat disappointing.

BRINDSLEY: Oh, look, Harold, please understand—

HAROLD [*shrill*]: There's no need to say anything! It'll just teach me in future not to bank too much on friendship. It's silly me again! Silly, stupid, trusting me!

[MISS FURNIVAL *rises in agitation and gropes her way to the drinks table.*]

COLONEL: Good God!

CAROL [*wheedling*]: Oh, come, Mr. Gorringe. We haven't told anybody. Not one single soulipegs. Really.

COLONEL: At the moment, Dumpling, there's nothing to tell. And I'm not sure there's going to be!

BRINDSLEY: Look, sir, we seem to have got off on the wrong foot. If it's my fault, I apologize.

MISS FURNIVAL [*groping about on the drinks table*]: My father always used to say, "To err is human: to forgive divine."

CAROL: I thought that was somebody else.

MISS FURNIVAL [*blithely*]: So many people copied him. [*She finds the open bottle of gin, lifts it and sniffs it eagerly.*]

CAROL: May I help you, Miss Furnival?

MISS FURNIVAL: No, thank you, Miss Melkett. I'm just getting myself another bitter lemon. That is—if I may, Mr. Miller?

BRINDSLEY: Of course. Help yourself.

MISS FURNIVAL: Thank you, most kind! [*She pours more gin into her glass and returns slowly to sit upstage on the edge of the rostrum.*]

COLONEL: Well, sir, wherever you are—

BRINDSLEY: Here, Colonel.

COLONEL: I'll overlook your damn peculiar behavior this once, but understand this, Miller. My daughter's dear to me. You show me you can look after her, and I'll consider the whole thing most favorably. I can't say fairer than that, can I?

BRINDSLEY: No, sir. Most fair, sir. Most fair. [*He pulls a hideous face one inch from the* COLONEL'*s.*]

CAROL: Of course he can look after me, Daddy. His works are going to be world famous. In five years I'll feel just like Mrs. Michelangelo.

HAROLD [*loftily*]: There wasn't a Mrs. Michelangelo, actually.

CAROL [*irritated*]: Wasn't there?

HAROLD: No. *He* had passionate feelings of a rather different nature.

CAROL: Really, Mr. Gorringe. I didn't know that. [*She puts out her tongue at him.*]

BRINDSLEY: Look, Harold, I'm sorry if I've hurt your feelings.

HAROLD [*loftily*]: You haven't.

BRINDSLEY: I know I have. Please forgive me.

CAROL: Oh do, Mr. Gorringe. Quarreling is so dreary. I hope we're all going to be great friends.

HAROLD: I'm not sure that I can contemplate a friendly relationship with a viper.

MISS FURNIVAL: Remember: to err is human, to forgive divine!

COLONEL [*irritated*]: You just said that, madam.

[CLEA *enters, wearing dark glasses and carrying an air-bag. She stands in the doorway, amazed by the dark. She takes off her glasses, but this doesn't improve matters.*]

MISS FURNIVAL [*downing her gin happily*]: Did I?

CAROL: Brin's not really a viper. He's just artistic, aren't you, darling?

BRINDSLEY: Yes, darling.

[CAROL *sends him an audible kiss across the astonished* CLEA. *He returns it, equally audibly.*]

CAROL [*winningly*]: Come on, Mr. Gorringe. It really is a case of forgive and forgettipegs.

HAROLD: Is it reallypegs?

CAROL: Have another Ginette and lime. I'll have one with you. [*She rises and mixes the drink.*]

HAROLD [*rising*]: Oh, all right. I don't mind if I do.

CAROL: Let me mix it for you.

HAROLD: Ta. [*He crosses to her, narrowly missing* CLEA *who is now crossing the room to the sofa, and gets his drink.*] I must say there's nothing nicer than having a booze-up with a pretty girl.

CAROL [*archly*]: You haven't seen me yet.

HAROLD: Oh, I just know it. Brindsley always had wonderful taste. I've often said to him, you've got the same taste in ladies as I have in porcelain. Ta.

[HAROLD *and* BRINDSLEY—*one from upstage, one from across the room—begin to converge on the sofa. On the word "modest" all three,* CLEA *in the middle, sit on it.* BRINDSLEY *of course imagines he is sitting next to* HAROLD.]

BRINDSLEY: Harold!

CAROL: Oh, don't be silly, Brin. Why be so modest? I found a photograph of one of his bits from two years ago, and I must say she was pretty stunning, in a blowsy sort of way.

HAROLD: Which one was that, then? I suppose she means Clea.

CAROL: Did you know her, Mr. Gorringe?

HAROLD: Oh yes. She's been around a long time.

[BRINDSLEY *nudges* CLEA *warningly—imagining she is* HAROLD. CLEA *gently bumps against* HAROLD.]

CAROL [*surprised*]: Has she?

HAROLD: Oh yes, dear. Or am I speaking out of turn?

BRINDSLEY: Not at all. I've told Carol all *about* Clea.

[*He bangs* CLEA *again, a little harder—who correspondingly bumps against* HAROLD.]

Though I must say, Harold, I'm surprised you call three months "a long time."

[CLEA *shoots him a look of total outrage at this lie.* HAROLD *is also astonished.*]

CAROL: What was she like?

BRINDSLEY [*meaningfully, into* CLEA'*s ear*]: I suppose you can hardly remember her, Harold.

HAROLD [*speaking across her*]: Why on earth shouldn't I?

BRINDSLEY: Well, since it was two years ago, you've probably forgotten.

HAROLD: Two years?!

BRINDSLEY: *Two years ago!*

[*He punches* CLEA *so hard that the rebound knocks* HAROLD *off the sofa, drink and all.*]

HAROLD [*picking himself up. Spitefully*]: Well, now since you mention it, I remember her perfectly. I mean, she's not one you can easily forget!

CAROL: Was she pretty?

HAROLD: No, not at all. In fact, I'd say the opposite. Actually she was rather plain.

BRINDSLEY: She wasn't!

HAROLD: I'm just giving my opinion.

BRINDSLEY: You've never given it before.

HAROLD [*leaning over* CLEA]: I was never *asked!* But since it's come up, I always thought she was ugly. For one thing, she had teeth like a picket fence—yellow and spiky. And for another, she had bad skin.

BRINDSLEY: She had nothing of the kind!

HAROLD: She did. I remember it perfectly. It was like a new pink wallpaper, with an old gray crumbly paper underneath.

MISS FURNIVAL: Quite right, Mr. Gorringe. I hardly ever saw her, but I do recall her skin. It was a strange color, as you say—and very coarse. . . . Not soft, as the skins of young ladies should be, if they *are* young ladies.

[CLEA *rises in outrage.*]

HAROLD: Aye, that's right. Coarse.

MISS FURNIVAL: And rather lumpy.

HAROLD: Very lumpy.

BRINDSLEY: This is disgraceful.

HAROLD: You knew I never liked her, Brindsley. She was too clever by half.

MISS FURNIVAL: And so tiresomely Bohemian.

CAROL: You mean she was as pretentious as her name?

[CLEA, *who has been reacting to this last exchange of comments about her like a spectator at a tennis match, now reacts to* CAROL *openmouthed.*]

I bet she was. That photograph I found showed her in a dirndl and a sort of sultry peasant blouse. She looked like *The Bartered Bride* done by Lloyds Bank.

[*They laugh,* BRINDSLEY *hardest of all. Guided by the noise,* CLEA *aims her hand and slaps his face.*]

BRINDSLEY: Ahh!

CAROL: What's wrong?

MISS FURNIVAL: What is it, Mr. Miller?

BRINDSLEY [*furiously*]: That's not very funny, Harold. What the hell's the matter with you?

[CLEA *makes her escape.*]

HAROLD [*indignant*]: With *me?*

BRINDSLEY: Well, I'm sure it wasn't the Colonel.

COLONEL: What wasn't, sir?

[BRINDSLEY, *groping about, catches* CLEA *by the bottom, and instantly recognizes it.*]

BRINDSLEY: *Clea!* . . .[*In horror.*] Clea!

[CLEA *breaks loose and moves away from him. During the following he tries to find her in the dark, and she narrowly avoids him.*]

COLONEL: What?

BRINDSLEY: I was just remembering her, sir. You're all talking the most awful nonsense. She was beautiful. . . . And anyway, Harold, you just said I was famous for my taste in women.

HAROLD: Aye, but it had its lapses.

BRINDSLEY [*frantically moving about*]: Rubbish! She was beautiful and tender and considerate and kind and loyal and witty and adorable in every way!

CAROL: You told me she was as cozy as a steel razor blade.

BRINDSLEY: Did I? Surely not! No. What I said was . . . something quite different . . . utterly different . . . entirely different . . . As different as chalk from cheese. Although when you come to think of it, cheese isn't all that different from chalk! [*He gives his braying laugh.*]

COLONEL: Are you sure you know what you're talking about?

[*During this* CLEA *has reached the table, picked up a bottle of Scotch, and rejected it in favor of vodka, which she takes with her.*]

CAROL: You said to me in this room when I asked you what she was like, "She was a painter. Very honest. Very clever, and just about as cozy—"

BRINDSLEY [*stopping, exasperated*]: As a steel razor blade! Well then, I said it! So bloody what? . . .

CAROL: So nothing!

[*He throws out his hands in a gesture of desperate exhaustion and bumps straight into* CLEA. *They instantly embrace,* CLEA *twining herself around him, her vodka bottle held aloft. A tiny pause.*]

COLONEL: If that boy isn't touched, I don't know the meaning of the word!

CAROL: What's all this talk about her being kind and tender, all of a sudden?

BRINDSLEY [*tenderly, holding* CLEA]: She could be. On occasion. *Very.*

CAROL: Very rare occasions, I imagine.

BRINDSLEY: Not so rare. [*He kisses* CLEA *again.*] Not so rare at all. [*He leads her softly past the irritated* CAROL, *toward the stairs.*]

CAROL: Meaning what, exactly? . . .[*Shouting.*] *Brindsley, I'm talking to you!!*

BRINDSLEY [*sotto voce, into* CLEA's *ear as they stand just behind* HAROLD]: I can explain. Go up to the bedroom. Wait for me there.

HAROLD [*in amazement: thinking he is being addressed*]: *Now?* . . . Do you think this is quite the moment?

BRINDSLEY: Oh, God! . . . I wasn't talking to you!

CAROL: What did you say?

HAROLD [*to* CAROL]: I think he wants *you* upstairs. [*Slyly.*] For what purpose, I can't begin to imagine.

COLONEL: They're going to do some more of that plotting, I dare say.

MISS FURNIVAL: Lovers' talk, Colonel.

COLONEL: Very touching, I'm sure.

[BRINDSLEY *pushes* CLEA *ahead of him up the stairs.*]

MISS FURNIVAL: "Journeys end in lovers meeting," as my father always used to say.

COLONEL [*grimly*]: What a strikingly original father you seem to have had, madam!

[CAROL *joins the other two on the stairs. We see all three groping blindly up to the bedroom,* BRINDSLEY's *hands on* CLEA's *hips,* CAROL's *hands on* BRINDSLEY's *hips.*]

CAROL [*with a conspirator's stage whisper*]: What is it, darling? Has something gone wrong? What can't you move?

[*This next dialogue sotto voce on the stairs.*]

BRINDSLEY: Nothing. It's all back—every bit of it—except the sofa, and I've covered that up.

CAROL: You mean, we can have lights?

BRINDSLEY: Yes . . .NO!!

CAROL: Why not?

BRINDSLEY: Never mind!

CAROL: Why do you want me in the bedroom?

BRINDSLEY: I don't! Go away!

CAROL: Charming!

BRINDSLEY: I didn't mean that.

COLONEL: There you are. They *are* plotting again. [*Calling up.*] What the hell is going on up there?

BRINDSLEY: Nothing, Colonel. I've just remembered—there may be a torch under my bed. I keep it to blind the burglars with. Have another drink, Colonel!

[*He pushes* CLEA *into the bedroom and shuts the door.*]

COLONEL: What d'you mean another? I haven't had *one* yet!

MISS FURNIVAL: Oh! Poor Colonel! Let me get you one.

COLONEL [*rising*]: I can get one for myself, thank you. Let me get you another lemonade.

MISS FURNIVAL [*rising*]: No, thank you, Colonel, I'll manage myself. It's good practice!

[*They grope toward the drinks table. Above,* CLEA *and* BRINDSLEY *sit on the bed.*]

CLEA: So this is what they mean by a blind date! What the hell is going on?

BRINDSLEY [*sarcastic*]: Nothing! Georg Bamberger is only coming to see my work tonight, and we've got a main fuse.

CLEA: Is that the reason for all this furtive clutching?

BRINDSLEY: Look, I can't explain things at the moment.

CLEA: Who's that—[*debutante accent*] "frightful gel"?

BRINDSLEY: Just a friend.

CLEA: She sounded more than that.

BRINDSLEY: Well, if you must know, it's Carol. I've told you about her.

CLEA: The Idiot Deb?

BRINDSLEY: She's a very sweet girl. As a matter of fact we've become very good friends in the last six weeks.

CLEA: How good?

BRINDSLEY: Just good.

CLEA: And have you become friends with her father too?

BRINDSLEY: If it's any of your business, they just dropped in to meet Mr. Bamberger.

CLEA: What was it you wanted to tell me on the phone tonight?

BRINDSLEY: Nothing.

CLEA: You're lying!

BRINDSLEY: Look, Clea, if you ever loved me, just slip away quietly with no more questions, and I'll come round later and explain everything, I promise.

CLEA: I don't believe you.

BRINDSLEY: Please, darling . . . please . . . please . . . please!

[*They kiss, passionately, stretched out on the bed.*]

COLONEL [*pouring*]: At last . . . a decent glass of Scotch. Are you getting your lemonade?

MISS FURNIVAL [*cheerfully pouring herself an enormous gin*]: Oh yes, thank you, Colonel!

COLONEL: I'm just wonderin' if this Bamberger fellow is goin' to show up at all. He's half an hour late already.

HAROLD: Oh! That's nothing, Colonel. Millionaires are always late. It's their thing.

MISS FURNIVAL: I'm sure you're right, Mr. Gorringe. That's how *I* imagine them. Hands like silk, and always two hours late.

CAROL: Brin's been up there a long time. What can he be doing?

HAROLD: Maybe he's got that Clea hidden away in his bedroom, and they're having a tête-à-tête!!

CAROL: What a fragrant suggestion, Mr. Gorringe.

BRINDSLEY [*disengaging himself*]: No one in the world kisses like you.

CLEA: I missed you so badly, Brin. I had to see you. I've thought about nothing else these past six weeks. Brin, I made the most awful mistake walking out.

BRINDSLEY: Clea—*please!*

CLEA: I mean we've known each other for four years. We can't just throw each other away like old newspapers.

BRINDSLEY: I don't see why not. You know my politics, you've heard my gossip, and you've certainly been through all my entertainment section.

CLEA: Well, how about a second edition?

BRINDSLEY: Darling, we simply can't talk about this now. Can't you trust me just for an hour?

CLEA: Of course I can, darling. You don't want me down there?

BRINDSLEY: No.

CLEA: Then I'll get undressed and go quietly to bed. When you've got rid of them all, I'll be waiting.

BRINDSLEY: That's a terrible idea!

CLEA [*reaching for him*]: I think it's lovely. A little happy relaxation for us both.

BRINDSLEY [*falling off the bed*]: I'm perfectly relaxed!

CAROL: Brindsley!

CLEA: "Too solemn for day, too sweet for night. Come not in darkness, come not in light." That's me, isn't it?

BRINDSLEY: Of course not. I just can't explain now, that's all.

CLEA: Oh, very well, you can explain later . . . in bed!

BRINDSLEY: Not tonight, Clea.

CLEA: Either that or I come down and discover your sordid secret.

BRINDSLEY: There *is* no sordid secret!

CLEA: Then you won't mind my coming down!

CAROL, COLONEL [*roaring together*]: BRINDSLEY!!!

BRINDSLEY: Oh, God!! . . . All right, stay. Only keep quiet. . . . Blackmailing bitch! [*He emerges at the top of the stairs.*] Yes, my sweet?

CAROL: What are you doing up there? You've been an eternity!

BRINDSLEY: I . . . I . . . I'm just looking in the bathroom, my darling. You never know what you might find in that clever little cabinet!

COLONEL [*moving to the stairs*]: Are you trying to madden me, sir? Are you trying to put me in a fury?

BRINDSLEY: Certainly not, sir!

COLONEL: I warn you, Miller, it's not difficult! In the old days in the regiment I was known for my furies! I was famous for my furies! . . . Do you hear?

CLEA: I may sing! [*She goes off into the bathroom.*]

BRINDSLEY: I may knock your teeth in!

COLONEL: What did you say?

CAROL: Brin! How dare you talk to Daddy like that!

BRINDSLEY: Oh!! I . . . I . . . I wasn't talking to Daddy like that . . .

CAROL: Then who *were* you talking to?

BRINDSLEY: I was talking to no one! Myself I was talking to! I was saying . . ."If I keep groping about up here like this, I might knock my teeth in!"

COLONEL: Mad! . . . Mad! . . . Mad as the south wind! It's the only explanation—you've got yourself engaged to a lunatic.

CAROL: There's something going on up there, and I'm coming up to find out what it is. Do you hear me, Brin?

BRINDSLEY: Carol—no!

CAROL [*climbing the stairs*]: I'm not such a fool as you take me for. I know when you're hiding something. Your voice goes all deceitful—very, very foxipegs!

BRINDSLEY: Darling, please. That's not very ladylike . . . I'm sure the Colonel won't approve of you entering a man's bedroom in the dark!

[*Enter* SCHUPPANZIGH. *He wears the overcoat and peaked cap of the London Electricity Board and carries a large toolbag, similarly labeled.*]

CAROL: I'm comin' up, Brindsley, I'm comin' up!!!

BRINDSLEY [*scrambling down*]: I'm coming down . . . . We'll all have a nice cozy drink . . .

SCHUPPANZIGH [*German accent*]: 'Allo, please? Mr. Miller? Mr. Miller? I've come as was arranged.

BRINDSLEY: My God . . . it's Bamberger!

CAROL: Bamberger?

BRINDSLEY: Yes, Bamberger. [BRINDSLEY *rushes down the remaining stairs, pulling Carol with him.*]

SCHUPPANZIGH: You must have thought I was never coming! [*He takes off his overcoat and cap.*]

BRINDSLEY: Not at all. I'm delighted you could spare the time. I know how busy you are. I'm afraid we've had the most idiotic disaster. We've had a fuse.

HAROLD: You'll have to speak up, dear, he's stone deaf!

BRINDSLEY [*yelling*]: We've had a fuse—not the best conditions for seeing sculpture.

SCHUPPANZIGH: Please not to worry. Here!

[*He produces a torch from his pocket and "lights" it. The light on stage dims a little, as usual, to indicate this. All relax with audible sighs of pleasure.* SCHUPPANZIGH *at once places his toolbag on the Regency chair, and puts his coat and cap on top of it, concealing the fact that it is one of* HAROLD'*s chairs.*]

CAROL: Oh, what a relief!

BRINDSLEY [*hastily dragging the sheet over the rest of the sofa*]: Do you always travel with a torch?

SCHUPPANZIGH: Mostly, yes. It helps to see details. [*Seeing the others.*] You are holding a private view?

MISS FURNIVAL: Oh no! I was just going, I'd hate to distract you.

SCHUPPANZIGH: Please not on my account, dear lady, I am not so easily distracted.

MISS FURNIVAL [*charmed*]: Oh! . . .

BRINDSLEY [*yelling in his ear*]: May I present Colonel Melkett?

COLONEL [*yelling in his other ear*]: A great honor, sir!

SCHUPPANZIGH [*banging his ear, to clear it*]: No, no, mine—mine!

BRINDSLEY: Miss Carol Melkett!

CAROL [*screeching in his ear*]: I say: hello. So glad you got here! It's terribly kind of you to take such an interest!

SCHUPPANZIGH: Not at all. *Vous êtes très gentil.*

CAROL [*yelling*]: What would you like to drink?

SCHUPPANZIGH [*bewildered*]: A little vodka would be beautiful!

CAROL: Of course!

BRINDSLEY: Harold Gorringe—a neighbor of mine!

HAROLD [*shouting*]: How do? Very honored, I'm sure.

SCHUPPANZIGH: Enchanted.

HAROLD: I must say it's a real thrill, meeting you!

BRINDSLEY: And another neighbor, Miss Furnival!

SCHUPPANZIGH: Enchanted.

MISS FURNIVAL [*hooting in his ear*]: I'm afraid we've all been taking refuge from the *storm*, as it were. [*Exclaiming as she holds* SCHUPPANZIGH'*s hand.*] Oh! It *is* true! They *are* softer! Much, much softer!

SCHUPPANZIGH [*utterly confused as she strokes his hand*]: Softer? Please?

[BRINDSLEY *and* HAROLD *pull her away, and she subsides onto the sofa.*]

BRINDSLEY: Miss Furnival, please!

CAROL [*at the drinks table*]: Darling, where's the vodka?

BRINDSLEY: It's on the table.

CAROL: No, it isn't.

BRINDSLEY: It must be!

[*Above,* CLEA *reenters wearing the top half of* BRINDSLEY'*s pajamas and nothing else. She gets into bed, still clutching the vodka bottle and carrying a plastic toothmug.*]

CAROL: Well, see for yourself. There's Winnie and Ginette, and Vera has quite vanished, the naughty girl!

BRINDSLEY: She can't have done.

SCHUPPANZIGH: Please don't concern yourselves. I am pressed for time. If I might just be shown where to go.

BRINDSLEY: Of course. It's through the studio there. Darling, if you would just show our guest into the studio—*with his torch.*

CAROL: What?? . . .

BRINDSLEY [*sotto voce*]: *The sofa!* . . .Get him out of here!

CAROL: Oh yes!! . . .

SCHUPPANZIGH [*sighting the sculpture*]: Oh! Good gracious! What an extraordinary object!

BRINDSLEY: Oh, that's just a spare piece of my work I keep in here!

SCHUPPANZIGH: Spare, maybe, but fascinating!

BRINDSLEY: You really think so?

SCHUPPANZIGH [*approaching it*]: I do! *Ja!*

BRINDSLEY: Well, in that case you should see my main collection. It's next door. My fiancée will show you!

[MISS FURNIVAL *sits on the sofa. She is now quite drunk.*]

SCHUPPANZIGH: One amazement at a time, if you please! In this gluttonous age it is easy to get visual indigestion—hard to find visual Alka Seltzer. . . . Permit me to digest this first!

BRINDSLEY: Oh, by all means. . . . Good, yes. . . . There's no hurry—no hurry at all . . . . Only . . . [*inspired*], why don't you digest it *in the dark?*

SCHUPPANZIGH: I beg your pardon?

BRINDSLEY: You'll never believe it, sir, but I actually made that piece to be appreciated in the dark. I was working on a very interesting theory. You know how the Victorians said, "Children should be seen and not heard"? Well, I say, "Art should be felt and not seen."

SCHUPPANZIGH: Amazing.

BRINDSLEY: Yes, isn't it. I call it my theory of Factual Tactility. If it doesn't stab you to the quick—it's not art. Look! Why don't you give me that torch, and try for yourself?

SCHUPPANZIGH: Very well, I will! [*He hands* BRINDSLEY *the torch.*]

BRINDSLEY: Thank you!

[*He turns off the torch and hands it to* CAROL. *At the same moment* MISS FURNIVAL *quietly lies down, her full length on the sofa.*]

Now just stretch out your arms and feel it all over, sir. [*He steals toward the studio.*] Have a good long feel!

[SCHUPPANZIGH *embraces the metal sculpture with a fervent clash. He pulls at the two metal prongs.*]

Do you see what I mean? [*Silently he opens the curtains.*]

SCHUPPANZIGH: Amazing! . . . Absolutely incredible! . . . It's quite true . . . Like this, the piece becomes a masterpiece at once.

BRINDSLEY [*astonished*]: It does?

SCHUPPANZIGH: But of course! I feel it here—and here—the two needles of man's unrest! . . .Self-love and self-hate, leading to the same point! That's the meaning of the work, isn't it?

BRINDSLEY: Of course. You've got it in one! You're obviously a great expert, sir!

[*Quietly he pulls the sofa into the studio, bearing on it the supine* MISS FURNIVAL, *who vaguely waves goodbye as she disappears.*]

SCHUPPANZIGH: Not at all. *Vous êtes très gentil*—but it is evident! . . .Standing here in the dark, one can feel the vital thrust of the argument! The essential anguish! The stress and the torment of our times! It is simple but not simpleminded! Ingenious, but not ingenuous! Above all, it has real moral force! Of how many modern works can one say that, good people?

CAROL [*gushing*]: Oh, none, none at all really!

SCHUPPANZIGH: I hope I do not lecture. It can be a fault with me.

CAROL: Not at all! I could listen all night, it's so profound.

HAROLD: Me too. Really deep!

COLONEL: I don't know anything about this myself, sir, but it's an honor to listen to you.

[*He starts off upstage in search of the sofa, seating himself tentatively in the air, then moving himself along in a sitting position, trying to find it with his rear end. At the same moment* BRINDSLEY *emerges from the studio, closes the curtains behind him, and gropes his way to the upstage corner where there stands a small packing case. This he carries forward, hopefully to do duty for the missing sofa. Just as he places it on the ground the traveling* COLONEL *sits on it, trapping* BRINDSLEY'*s hand beneath his weight. During the following,* BRINDSLEY *tries frantically to free himself.*]

SCHUPPANZIGH: *Vous êtes très gentil!*

HAROLD: You mean to say you see all that in a bit of metal?

SCHUPPANZIGH: A *tiny* bit of metal, that's the point. A miracle of compression. You want my opinion, this boy is a genius. A master of the miniature. In the space of a matchbox he can realize anything he wants—the black virginity of Chartres! The white chorale of the Acropolis! *Wunderbar!*

CAROL: Oh, how super!

SCHUPPANZIGH: You should charge immense sums for work like this, Mr. Miller. They should be very, very expensive! This one, for example, how much is this?

BRINDSLEY: Fifty—

CAROL: Five hundred guineas!

SCHUPPANZIGH: Ah so! Very cheap.

HAROLD: Cheap!

CAROL: I think so, Mr. Gorringe. Well . . . so will you have it, then?

SCHUPPANZIGH: Me?

BRINDSLEY: Darling . . . aren't you rushing things just a little? Perhaps you would like to see the rest of my work.

SCHUPPANZIGH: Alas, I have no more time. To linger would be pleasant, but alas, I must work . . . Also, as Moses discovered, it is sufficient to *glimpse* milk and honey. One does not have to wolf them down!

BRINDSLEY: Well.

COLONEL: Well . . .

HAROLD: Well . . .

CAROL: Well . . . would you like it then?

SCHUPPANZIGH: Very much.

COLONEL [*rising.* BRINDSLEY *is freed at last*]: For five hundred guineas?

SCHUPPANZIGH: Certainly—if I had it!

HAROLD: According to the Sunday paper, you must be worth at least seventeen million pounds.

SCHUPPANZIGH: The Sunday papers are notoriously ill-informed. According to my last bank statement, I was worth one hundred pounds, eight shillings, and fourpence.

HAROLD: You mean you've gone broke?

SCHUPPANZIGH: No. I mean I never had any more.

COLONEL: Now look, sir, I know millionaires are supposed to be eccentric, but this is gettin' tiresome.

CAROL: Daddy, ssh!

SCHUPPANZIGH: Millionaires? Who do you think I am?

COLONEL: Dammit, man! You must know who you are!

CAROL: Mr. Bamberger, is this some kind of joke you like to play?

SCHUPPANZIGH: Excuse me. That is not my name.

BRINDSLEY: It isn't?

SCHUPPANZIGH: No. My name is Schuppanzigh. Franz Schuppanzigh. Born in Weimar, 1905. Student of philosophy at Heidelberg, 1934. Refugee to this country, 1938. Regular employment ever since with the London Electricity Board!

[*All rise.*]

CAROL: Electricity?

MISS FURNIVAL: Electricity!

BRINDSLEY: You mean you're not—?

HAROLD: Of course he's not!

SCHUPPANZIGH: But who did you imagine I was?

HAROLD [*furious*]: How dare you? [*He snatches the electrician's torch.*]

SCHUPPANZIGH [*retreating before him*]: Please?

HAROLD: Of all the nerve, coming in here, giving us a lecture about needles and virgins, and all the time you're simply here to mend the fuses!

COLONEL: I agree with you, sir. It's monstrous!

SCHUPPANZIGH [*bewildered*]: It is?

[*The* COLONEL *takes the torch and shines it pitilessly in the man's face.*]

COLONEL: You come in here, a public servant, and proceed to harangue your employers, unasked and uninvited.

SCHUPPANZIGH [*bewildered*]: Excuse me. But I *was* invited.

COLONEL: Don't answer back. In my day you would have been fired on the spot for impertinence.

CAROL: Daddy's absolutely right! Ever since the Beatles, the lower classes think they can behave exactly as they want.

COLONEL [*handing the torch to* BRINDSLEY]: Miller, will you kindly show this feller his work?

BRINDSLEY: The mains are in the cellar. There's a trapdoor. [*Indicating.*] Do you mind?

SCHUPPANZIGH [*snatching the torch furiously*]: Why should I mind? It's why I came, after all! [*He takes his coat, cap, and bag off* HAROLD'*s Regency chair . . . seeing it*] Now there is a really beautiful chair!

[BRINDSLEY *stares at the chair aghast—and in a twinkling seats himself in it to conceal it.*]

BRINDSLEY [*exasperated*]: Why don't you just go into the cellar?

SCHUPPANZIGH: *How?* Where is it?

BRINDSLEY [*to* CAROL]: Darling, will you open the trap, please.

CAROL: Me? [*Understanding—as he indicates the chair*] Oh—yes! [*She kneels and struggles to open the trap.*]

COLONEL [*to* BRINDSLEY]: Well, I must say, that's very gallant of you, Miller.

BRINDSLEY: I've got a sudden touch of lumbago, sir. It often afflicts me after long spells in the dark.

CAROL [*very sympathetic*]: Oh, darling! Has it come back?

BRINDSLEY: I'm afraid it has, my sweet.

HAROLD [*opening the trap*]: Here, let me. I'm not as frail as our wilting friend. [*To* SCHUPPANZIGH.] Well, down you go, you!

SCHUPPANZIGH [*shrugging*]: So. Farewell. I leave the light of Art for the dark of Science.

HAROLD: Let's have a little less of your lip, shall we?

SCHUPPANZIGH: Excuse me.

[SCHUPPANZIGH *descends through the trap, taking the torch with him.* HAROLD *slams the trapdoor down irritably after him, and of course the lights immediately come up full. There is a long pause. All stand about embarrassed. Suddenly they hear the noise of* MISS FURNIVAL *singing "Rock of Ages" in a high drunken voice from behind the curtain. Above, attracted by the noise of the slam,* CLEA *gets out of bed, still clutching the vodka and toothmug, opens the door, and stands at the top of the stairs listening.*]

BRINDSLEY: None of this evening is happening.

CAROL: Cheer up, darling. In a few minutes everything will be all right. Mr. Bamberger will arrive in the light—he'll adore your work and give you twenty thousand pounds for your whole collection.

BRINDSLEY [*sarcastic*]: Oh, yes!

CAROL: Then we can buy a super Georgian house and live what's laughingly known as happily ever after. I want to leave this place just as soon as we're married.

[CLEA *hears this. Her mouth opens wide.*]

BRINDSLEY [*nervously*]: Sssh!

CAROL: Why? I don't want to live in a slum for our first couple of years—like other newlyweds.

BRINDSLEY: Sssh! Ssssh! . . .

CAROL: What's the matter with you?

BRINDSLEY: The gods listen, darling. They've given me a terrible night so far. They may do worse.

CAROL [*cooing*]: I know, darling. You've had a filthy evening. Poor babykins. But I'll fight them with you. I don't care a fig for those naughty old Goddipegs! [*Looking up.*] Do you hear? Not a single little fig!

[CLEA *aims at the voice and sends a jet of vodka splashing down over* CAROL.]

Ahh!!!

BRINDSLEY: What is it?

CAROL: It's raining!

BRINDSLEY: Don't be ridiculous.

CAROL: I'm all wet!

BRINDSLEY: How can you be?

[CLEA *throws vodka over a wider area.* HAROLD *gets it.*]

HAROLD: Hey, what's going on?

BRINDSLEY: What?

COLONEL: What the devil's the matter with you all? What are you hollerin' for? [*He gets a slug of vodka in the face.*] Ahh!!

BRINDSLEY [*inspired*]: It's a leak—the water mains must have gone now!

HAROLD: Oh, good God!

BRINDSLEY: It must be!

[*Mischievously,* CLEA *raps her bottle loudly on the top stair. There is a terrified silence. All look up.*]

HAROLD: Don't say there's someone else here.

BRINDSLEY: Good Lord!

COLONEL: Who's there?

[*Silence from above.*]

Come on! I know you're there!

BRINDSLEY [*improvising wildly*]: I—I bet you it's Mrs. Punnet.

[CLEA *looks astonished.*]

COLONEL: Who?

BRINDSLEY [*for* CLEA*'s benefit*]: Mrs. Punnet. My cleaning woman.

HAROLD: Cleaning woman?

BRINDSLEY: She does for me on Mondays, Wednesdays, and Fridays.

CAROL: Well, what would she be doing here now?

BRINDSLEY: I've just remembered—she rang up and said she'd look in about six to tidy up the place.

COLONEL: Dammit, man, it's almost eleven.

HAROLD: She's not that conscientious. She couldn't be!

CAROL: Not these days!

COLONEL: Well, we'll soon see. [*Calling up.*] Mrs. Punnet?

BRINDSLEY [*desperately*]: Don't interrupt her, sir. She doesn't like to be disturbed when she's working. Why don't we just leave her to potter around upstairs with her duster?

COLONEL: Let us first just see if it's her. Is that you, Mrs. Punnet? . . .

[CLEA *keeps still.*]

COLONEL [*roaring*]: MRS. PUNNET!

CLEA [*deciding on a cockney voice of great antiquity*]: 'Allo! Yes?

BRINDSLEY [*weakly*]: It is. Good heavens, Mrs. Punnet, what on earth are you doing up there?

CLEA: I'm just giving your bedroom a bit of a tidy, sir.

BRINDSLEY: At this time of night?

[*The mischief in* CLEA *begins to take over.*]

CLEA: Better late than never, sir, as they say. I know how you like your bedroom to be nice and inviting when you're giving one of your parties.

BRINDSLEY: Yes, yes, yes, of course . . .

CAROL: When did you come, madam?

CLEA: Just a few minutes ago, sir. I didn't like to disturb you, so I come on up 'ere.

HAROLD: Was it you pouring all that water on us, then?

CLEA: Water? Good 'eavens, I must have upset something. It's as black as Newgate's Knocker up 'ere. Are you playing one of your saucy games, Mr. Miller?

BRINDSLEY: No, Mrs. Punnet. We've had a fuse. It's all over the house.

CLEA: Oh! A *fuse!* I thought it might be one of them saucy games in the dark, sir: Sardines or Piccadilly. The kind that end in a general squeeze-up. I know you're rather partial to kinky games, Mr. Miller, so I just wondered. [*She starts to come down the stairs.*]

BRINDSLEY [*distinctly*]: It is a fuse, Mrs. Punnet. The man's mending it now. The lights will be on *any minute!*

CLEA: Well, that'll be a relief for you, won't it? [*She dashes the vodka accurately in his face, passes him by, and comes into the room.*]

BRINDSLEY: Yes, of course. Now why don't you just go on home?

CLEA: I'm sorry I couldn't come before, sir. I was delayed, you see. My Rosie's been taken queer again.

BRINDSLEY: I quite understand! [*He gropes around trying to hide her, but she continuously evades him.*]

CLEA [*relentlessly*]: It's her tummy. There's a lump under her belly button the size of a grapefruit.

HAROLD: Oh, how nasty!

CLEA: Horrid. Poor little Rosie. I said to her this evening, I said, "There's no good your being mulish, my girl. You're going to the hospital first thing tomorrow morning and getting yourself ultraviolated!"

BRINDSLEY: Well, hadn't you better be getting back to poor little Rosie? She must need you, surely? And there's really nothing you can do here tonight.

CLEA [*meaningfully*]: Are you sure of that, sir?

BRINDSLEY: Positive, thank you.

[*They are close now.*]

CLEA: I mean, I know what this place can be like after one of your evenings. A gypsy caravan isn't in it. Gin bottles all over the floor! Bras and panties in the sink! And God knows what in the—

[BRINDSLEY *muzzles her with his hand. She bites it hard, and he drops to his knees in silent agony.*]

COLONEL: Please watch what you say, madam. You don't know it, but you're in the presence of Mr. Miller's fiancée.

CLEA: Fiancée?

COLONEL: Yes, and I am her father.

CLEA: Well, I never! . . . Oh, Mr. Miller! I'm so 'appy for you! . . . Fiancée! Oh, sir! And you never *told* me!

BRINDSLEY: I was keeping it a surprise.

CLEA: Well, I never! Oh, how lovely! . . . May I kiss you, sir, please?

BRINDSLEY [*on his knees*]: Well, yes, yes, of course . . .

[CLEA *gropes for his ear, finds it, and twists it.*]

CLEA: Oh, sir, I'm so pleased for you! And for *you*, miss, too!

CAROL: Thank you.

CLEA [*to* COLONEL MELKETT]: And for *you*, sir.

COLONEL: Thank you.

CLEA: You must be Miss Clea's father.

COLONEL: Miss Clea? I don't understand.

[*Triumphantly she sticks out her tongue at* BRINDSLEY, *who collapses his length on the floor, face down, in a gesture of total surrender. For him it is the end. The evening can hold no further disasters for him.*]

CLEA [*to* CAROL]: Well, I never! So you've got him at last! Well done, Miss Clea! I never thought you would—not after four years . . .

BRINDSLEY: No—no—no—no . . .

CLEA: Forgive me, sir, if I'm speaking out of turn, but you must admit four years is a long time to be courting one woman. Four days is stretching it a bit nowadays!

BRINDSLEY [*weakly*]: Mrs. Punnet, *please!*

CAROL: Four years!

CLEA: Well, yes, dear. It's been all of that and a bit more really, hasn't it? [*In a stage whisper.*] And of course it's just in time. It was getting a bit prominent, your little bun in the oven.

[CAROL *screeches with disgust.* BRINDSLEY *covers his ears.*]

Oh, miss, I don't mean that's why he popped the question. Of course it's not. He's always been stuck on you. He told me so, not one week ago, in this room. [*Sentimentally.*] "Mrs. Punnet," he says, "Mrs. Punnet, as far as I'm concerned you can keep the rest of them—Miss Clea will always be on top of the heap for me." "Oh," I says, "then what about that debutante bit, Carol, the one you're always telling me about?" "Oh, 'er," he says, "she's just a bit of Knightsbridge candyfloss. A couple of licks and you've 'ad 'er."

[*There is a long pause.* CLEA *is now sitting on the table, swinging her vodka bottle in absolute command of the situation.*]

COLONEL [*faintly; at last grappling with the situation*]: Did you say four years, madam?

CLEA [*in her own voice, quiet*]: Yes, Colonel. Four years, in this room.

HAROLD: I know that voice. It's Clea!

MISS FURNIVAL [*surprised*]: Clea!

CAROL [*horrified*]: Clea!

BRINDSLEY [*unconvincingly*]: Clea!

CLEA: Surprised, Brin?

CAROL [*understanding*]: Clea! . . .

COLONEL: I don't understand anything that's going on in this room!

CLEA: I know. It is a very odd room, isn't it? It's like a magic dark room, where everything happens the wrong way round. Rain falls indoors, the daily comes at night, and turns in a second from a nice maid into nasty mistress.

BRINDSLEY: Be quiet, Clea!

CLEA: At last! One real word of protest! Have you finished lying, then? Have you eaten the last crumb of humble pie? Oh, you coward, you bloody coward! Just because you didn't want to marry me, did you have to settle for this lot?

CAROL: Marry!

COLONEL: Marry?

CLEA: Four years of meaning to end in this triviality! Miss Laughingly-Known-As and her Daddipegs!

CAROL: Stop her! She's disgusting!

COLONEL: How can I, for God's sake?

CAROL: Well, where's all that bloody resource you keep talking about?

[*The* COLONEL *goes to her but takes* CLEA*'s hand by mistake.*]

COLONEL: Now calm down, Dumpling. Keep your head. . . . There—hold my hand, that's it, now Daddy's here. Everything is under control. All right?

CLEA: Are you sure that is your daughter's hand you're holding, Colonel?

COLONEL: What? Carol, isn't this your hand?

CAROL: No.

CLEA: You must have lived with your daughter for well over twenty years, Colonel. What remarkable use you've made of your eyes.

[*There is another pause. The* COLONEL *moves away in embarrassment.*]

CLEA [*wickedly*]: All right! Kinky game time! . . . Let's all play Guess the Hand.

HAROLD: Oh, good God!

CLEA: Or would you rather Guess the Lips, Harold?

CAROL: How disgusting!

CLEA: Well, that's me, dear. [CAROL*'s accent.*] I'm Queen Disgustipegs! [*She seizes* CAROL*'s hand and puts it into* HAROLD*'s.*] Who's that?

CAROL: I don't know.

CLEA: Guess.

CAROL: I don't know, and I don't care.

CLEA: Oh, go on. Have a go!

CAROL: It's Brin, of course: You can't trick me like that! It's Brindsley's stupid hand.

HAROLD: I'm afraid you're wrong. It's me.

CAROL [*struggling*]: It's not. You're lying.

HAROLD [*holding on*]: I'm not. I don't lie.

CAROL: You're lying! . . .You're lying!

HAROLD: I'm not.

[CAROL *breaks away and blunders upstage. She is becoming hysterical.*]

CLEA: You try it, Harold. Take the hand on your right.

HAROLD: I'm not playing. It's a bloody silly game.

CLEA: Go on . . .[*She seizes his hand and puts it into* BRINDSLEY'*s.*] Well?

HAROLD: It's Brin.

BRINDSLEY: Yes.

CLEA: Well done! [*She sits on the low stool.*]

CAROL [*outraged*]: How does he know that? How does *he* know your hand and I don't?

BRINDSLEY: Calm down, Carol.

CAROL: Answer me! I want to know!

BRINDSLEY: Stop it!

CAROL: I won't!

BRINDSLEY: You're getting hysterical!

CAROL: Leave me alone! I want to go home.

[*And suddenly* MISS FURNIVAL *gives a sharp short scream and blunders out through the curtains.*]

MISS FURNIVAL: Prams! Prams! Prams—in the supermarket! . . .

[*They all freeze. She is evidently out of control in a world of her own fears. She speaks quickly and strangely.*]

All those hideous wire prams full of babies and bottles—"Cornflakes over there" is all they say—and then they leave you to yourself. Biscuits over there—cat food over there—fish cakes over there—Airwick over there! Pink stamps, green stamps, free balloons—television dinners—pay as you go out—oh, Daddy, it's *awful!* . . . And then the godless ones, the heathens in their leather jackets—laughing me to scorn! But not for long. Oh, no! Who shall stand when He appeareth? He'll strike them from their motorcycles! He'll dash their helmets to the ground! Yes, verily, I say unto thee—there shall be an end of gasoline! An end to cigarette puffing and jostling with hips. . . . Keep off . . . Keep off! Keep off! . . .[*She runs drunkenly across the room and collides with* HAROLD.]

HAROLD: Come on, Ferny, I think it's time we went home.

MISS FURNIVAL [*pulling herself together*]: Yes. You're quite right. . . .[*With an attempt at grandeur.*] I'm sorry I can't stay any longer, Mr. Miller; but your millionaire is unpardonably late. So typical of modern manners. . . . Express my regrets, if you please.

BRINDSLEY: Certainly.

[*Leaning heavily on* HAROLD'*s arm she leaves the room. He shuts the door after them.*]

Thank you, Clea. Thank you very much.

CLEA: Any time.

BRINDSLEY: You had no right.

CLEA: No?

BRINDSLEY: *You* walked out on *me*. [*He joins her on the low stool.*]

CLEA: Is that what I did?

BRINDSLEY: You said you never wanted to see me again.

CLEA: I never saw you at all—how could you be walked out on? You should *live* in the dark, Brindsley. It's your natural element.

BRINDSLEY: Whatever that means.

CLEA: It means you don't really want to be seen. Why is that, Brindsley? Do you think if someone really saw you, they would never love you?

BRINDSLEY: Oh, go away.

CLEA: I want to know.

BRINDSLEY: Yes, you always want to know. Pick-pick-pick away! Why is *that*, Clea? Have you ever thought why you need to do it? Well?

CLEA: Perhaps because I care about you.

BRINDSLEY: Perhaps there's nothing to care about. Just a fake artist.

CLEA: Stop pitying yourself. It's always your vice. I told you when I met you: you could either be a good artist, or a chic fake. You didn't like it, because I refused just to give you applause.

BRINDSLEY: God knows, you certainly did that!

CLEA: Is that what *she* gives you? Twenty hours of ego-massage every day?

BRINDSLEY: At least our life together isn't the replica of the Holy Inquisition you made of ours. I didn't have an affair with you: it was just four years of nooky with Torquemada!

CLEA: And don't say you didn't enjoy it!

BRINDSLEY: Enjoy it? I hated every second of it.

CLEA: Yes, I remember.

BRINDSLEY: Every second!

CLEA: I recall.

BRINDSLEY: When you left for Finland, it was the happiest day of my life.

CLEA: Mine, too!

BRINDSLEY: I sighed with relief.

CLEA: So did I.

BRINDSLEY: I went out dancing that very night.

CLEA: So did I. It was out with the lyre and the timbrel.

BRINDSLEY: Good. Then that's all right.

CLEA: Fine.

BRINDSLEY: Super!

CLEA: Duper!

BRINDSLEY: It's lovely to see you looking so happy.

CLEA: You too. Radiant with self-fulfillment.

[*A pause.*]

BRINDSLEY: If you felt like this, why did you come back?

CLEA: If *you* felt like this, why did you tell Mrs. Punnet I was still at the top of the heap?

BRINDSLEY: I never said that!

CLEA: You did.

BRINDSLEY: Never!

CLEA: You *did!*

BRINDSLEY: Of course I didn't. You invented that ten minutes ago, when you were *playing* Mrs. Punnet.

CLEA: I—oh! So I did! . . .

[*They both giggle. She falls happily against his shoulder.*]

BRINDSLEY: You know something—I'm not sure she's not right.

[*During this exchange the* COLONEL *and* CAROL *have been standing frozen with astonished anger. Now the outraged father takes over. He is very angry.*]

COLONEL: No doubt this is very funny to you two.

CLEA: It is, quite, actually.

COLONEL: I'm not so easily amused, however, madam.

BRINDSLEY: Now look, Colonel—

COLONEL: Hold your tongue, sir, I'm talking. Do you know what would have happened to a young man in my day who dared to treat a girl the way you have treated my Dumpling?

BRINDSLEY: Well, I assume, Colonel—

COLONEL: Hold your tongue, I'm talking!

CAROL: Oh, leave it, Daddy. Let's just go home.

COLONEL: In a moment, Dumpling. Kindly leave this to me.

BRINDSLEY: Look, Carol, I can explain—

CAROL: Explain what?

BRINDSLEY: It's impossible here.

COLONEL: You understate, sir.

BRINDSLEY: Carol, you don't understand.

CAROL: What the hell's to understand? All the time you were going with me, she was in the background—that's all there is to it. What were you doing? Weighing us up? . . . Here! [*She pulls off her engagement ring.*]

BRINDSLEY: What?

CAROL: Your ring. Take the bloody thing back!

[*She throws it. It hits the* COLONEL *in the eye.*]

COLONEL: My eye! My damned eye!

[CLEA *starts to laugh again.*]

[*In mounting fury, clutching his eye.*] Oh, very droll, madam! Very droll indeed! Laugh your fill! . . . Miller! I asked you a question. Do you know what would have happened to a young lout like you in my day?

BRINDSLEY: Happened, sir?

COLONEL [*quietly*]: You'd have been thrashed, sir.

BRINDSLEY [*nervous*]: Thrashed—

[*The man of war begins to go after him, feeling his way in the dark, like some furious robot.*]

COLONEL: You'd have felt the mark of a father's horsewhip across your seducer's shoulders. You'd have gone down on your cad's bended knees, and begged my daughter's pardon for the insults you've offered her tonight.

BRINDSLEY [*retreating before the* COLONEL*'s groping advance*]: Would I, sir?

COLONEL: You'd have raised your guttersnipe voice in a piteous scream for mercy and forgiveness!

[*A terrible scream is indeed heard from the hall. They freeze, listening as it comes nearer and nearer, then the door is flung open and* HAROLD *plunges into the room. He is wild-eyed with rage: a lit and bent taper shakes in his furious hand.*]

HAROLD: Ooooooh! You villain!

BRINDSLEY: Harold—

HAROLD: You skunky, conniving little villain!

BRINDSLEY: What's the matter?

HAROLD [*raging*]: Have you seen the state of my room? My room? My lovely room, the most elegant and cared for in this entire district? One chair turned absolutely upside down, one chair on top of another like a Portobello junkshop! And that's not all, is it, Brindsley? Oh no, that's not the worst by a long chalk, is it, Brindsley?

BRINDSLEY: Long chalk?

HAROLD: Don't play the innocent with me! I thought I had a friend living here all these years. I didn't know I was living opposite a Light-fingered Lenny!

BRINDSLEY: Harold!

HAROLD [*hysterical*]: This is my reward, isn't it? After years of looking after you, sweeping and tidying up this place, because you're too much of a slut to do it for yourself—to have my best pieces stolen from me to impress your new girl friend and her daddy. Or did she help you?

BRINDSLEY: Harold, it was an emergency.

HAROLD: Don't talk to me: I don't want to know! I know what you think of me now. . . . "Don't tell Harold about the engagement. He's not to be trusted. He's not a friend. He's just someone to steal things from!"

BRINDSLEY: You know that's not true.

HAROLD [*shrieking—in one hysterical breath*]: I know I was the last one to know—that's what I know! I have to find it out in a room full of strangers. Me, who's listened to more of your miseries in the small hours of the morning than anyone else would put up with! All your boring talk about women, hour after hour, as if no one's got troubles but you!

CLEA: She's getting hysterical, dear. Ignore her.

HAROLD: It's you who's going to be ignored, Clea. [*To* BRINDSLEY.] As for you, all I can say about your engagement is this: you deserve each other, you and that little nit.

[CAROL *gives a shriek.*]

BRINDSLEY: Carol!

HAROLD: Oh, so you're there, are you? Skulking in the shadows!

BRINDSLEY: Leave her alone!

HAROLD: I'm not going to touch her! I just want my things and I'll be off. Did you hear me, Brindsley? You give me my things now, or I'll call the police.

BRINDSLEY: Don't be ridiculous.

HAROLD [*grimly*]: Item: One lyre-back Regency chair, in lacquered mahogany with ormolu inlay and appliqué work on the cushions.

BRINDSLEY: In front of you.

[*HAROLD thrusts the taper at it to see it.*]

HAROLD: Ta. Item: One half-back sofa—likewise Regency—supported by claw legs and upholstered in a rich silk of bottle green to match the aforesaid chair.

BRINDSLEY: In the studio.

HAROLD: Unbelievable! Item: One Coalport vase, dated 1809, decorated on the rim with a pleasing design of daisies and peonies.

BRINDSLEY: On the floor.

HAROLD: Ta.

[BRINDSLEY *hands it to him.*]

Ooooh! You've even taken the flowers! I'll come back for the chair and sofa in a minute. [*Drawing himself up with all the offended dignity of which a* HAROLD GORRINGE *is capable.*] This is the end of our relationship, Brindsley. We won't be speaking again, I don't think.

[*He twitches his raincoat off the table. Inside it, of course, is the Buddha, which falls on the floor and smashes beyond repair. There is a terrible silence. Trying to keep his voice under control.*]

Do you know what that statue was worth? Do you? More money than you'll ever see in your whole life, even if you sell every piece of that nasty, rusty rubbish. [*With the quietness of the very angry.*] I think I'm going to have to smash you, Brindsley.

BRINDSLEY [*nervously*]: Now steady on, Harold . . . don't be rash . . .

HAROLD: Yes, I'm very much afraid I'll have to smash you. . . . Smash for smash—that's fair do's. [*He pulls one of the long metal prongs out of the sculpture.*] Smash for smash. Smash for *smash!* [*Insanely he advances on* BRINDSLEY, *holding the prong like a sword, the taper burning in his other hand.*]

BRINDSLEY [*retreating*]: Stop it, Harold. You've gone mad!

COLONEL: Well done, sir. I think it's time for the reckoning. [*The* COLONEL *grabs the other prong and also advances.*]

BRINDSLEY [*retreating from them both*]: Now just a minute, Colonel. Be reasonable! . . . Let's not revert to savages! . . . Harold, I appeal to you—you've always had civilized instincts! Don't join the Army! . . .

CAROL [*grimly advancing also*]: Get him, Daddy! Get him! Get him!

BRINDSLEY [*horrified at her*]: Carol!

CAROL [*malevolently*]: Get him! Get him! Get . . .

BRINDSLEY: *Clea!*

[CLEA *leaps up and blows out the taper. Lights up.*]

COLONEL: Dammit!

[CLEA *grabs* BRINDSLEY*'s hand and pulls him out of danger.*]

[*To* CLEA.] Careful, my little Dumpling. Keep out of the way.

HAROLD [*to* CAROL]: Hush up, Colonel. We'll be able to hear them breathing.

COLONEL: Clever idea! Smart tactics, sir!

[*Silence. They listen.* BRINDSLEY *climbs carefully onto the table and silently pulls* CLEA *up after him.* HAROLD *and the* COLONEL, *prodding and slashing the darkness with their swords, grimly hunt their quarry. Twenty seconds pass. Suddenly, with a bang* SCHUPPANZIGH *opens the trap from below. Both men advance on it warily. The electrician disappears again below. They have almost reached it, on tiptoe, when there is another crash—this time from the hall. Someone has again tripped over the milk bottles.* HAROLD *and the* COLONEL *immediately swing round and start stalking upstage, still on tiptoe. Enter* GEORG BAMBERGER. *He is quite evidently a millionaire. Dressed in the Gulbenkian manner, he wears a beard, an eyeglass, a frock coat, a top hat, and an orchid. He carries a large deaf aid. Bewildered, he advances into the room. Stealthily, the two armed men stalk him upstage as he silently gropes his way downstage and passes between them.*]

BAMBERGER [*speaking in a middle-aged German voice, as near to the voice of* SCHUPPANZIGH *as possible*]: Hello, please! Mr. Miller?

[HAROLD *and the* COLONEL *spin round in a third direction.*]

HAROLD: Oh, it's the electrician!

BAMBERGER: Hello, please?

COLONEL: What the devil are you doing up here?

[SCHUPPANZIGH *appears at the trap.*]

Have you mended the fuse?

HAROLD: Or are you going to keep us in the dark all night?

SCHUPPANZIGH: Don't worry. The fuse is mended.

[*He comes out of the trap.* BAMBERGER *goes round the stage, right.*]

HAROLD: Thank God for that.

BAMBERGER [*still groping around*]: Hello, please? Mr. Miller—vere are you? Vy zis darkness? Is a joke, yes?

SCHUPPANZIGH [*incensed*]: Ah, no! That is not very funny, good people—just because I am a foreigner, to imitate my voice. You English can be the rudest people on earth!

BAMBERGER [*imperiously*]: Mr. Miller! I have come here to give attention to your sculptures!

SCHUPPANZIGH: *Gott in Himmel!*

BAMBERGER: *Gott in Himmel!*

BRINDSLEY: God, it's him! *Bamberger!*

CLEA: He's come!

HAROLD: Bamberger!

COLONEL: Bamberger!

[*They freeze. The millionaire sets off, left, toward the open trap.*]

BRINDSLEY: Don't worry. Mr. Bamberger. We've had a fuse, but it's mended now.

BAMBERGER [*irritably*]: Mr. Miller!

CLEA: You'll have to speak up. He's deaf.

BRINDSLEY [*shouting*]: Don't worry, Mr. Bamberger! We've had a fuse, but it's all right now! . . .

[*Standing on the table, he clasps* CLEA *happily.* BAMBERGER *misses the trap by inches.*]

Oh, Clea, that's true. Everything's all right now! Just in the nick of time!

[*But as he says this* BAMBERGER *turns and falls into the open trapdoor.* SCHUPPANZIGH *slams it to with his foot.*]

SCHUPPANZIGH: So! Here's now an end to your troubles! Like Jehovah in the Sacred Testament, I give you the most miraculous gift of the Creation! Light!

CLEA: Light!

BRINDSLEY: Oh, thank God. *Thank God!*

[SCHUPPANZIGH *goes to the switch.*]

HAROLD [*grimly*]: I wouldn't thank Him too soon, Brindsley, if I were you!

COLONEL: Nor would I, Brindsley, if I were you!

CAROL: Nor would I, Brinnie Winnie, if I were you!

SCHUPPANZIGH [*grandly*]: Then thank *me!* For I shall play God for this second! [*Clapping his hands.*] Attend all of you. God said: "Let there be light!" And there was, good people, suddenly!—astoundingly!—instantaneously—inconceivably—inexhaustibly—inextinguishably and eternally—LIGHT!

[SCHUPPANZIGH, *with a great flourish, flicks the light switch. Instant darkness. The turntable of the record player starts up again, and with an exultant crash the Sousa March falls on the audience—and blazes away in the black.*]

END

# THE ROYAL HUNT OF THE SUN

*For*
*Alan and Paula*
*with love*

*The Royal Hunt of the Sun* was first presented by the National Theatre at Chichester on July 7, 1964, with the following cast:

| | |
|---|---|
| MARTIN RUIZ | Robert Lang |
| MARTIN RUIZ as a boy | Roy Holder |
| FRANCISCO PIZARRO | Colin Blakely |
| DIEGO DE TRUJILLO | Mike Gambon |
| SALINAS | Dan Meaden |
| RODAS | Rod Beacham |
| FRAY VINCENTE DE VALVERDE | Peter Cellier |
| VASCA | Robert Russell |
| DOMINGO | Lewis Fiander |
| JUAN CHAVEZ | Christopher Timothy |
| PEDRO CHAVEZ | Gerald McNally |
| HERNANDO DE SOTO | Michael Turner |
| FELIPILLO | Derek Jacobi |
| FRAY MARCOS DE NIZZA | Edward Caddick |
| MIGUEL ESTETE | James Mellor |
| MANCO | Neil Fitzpatrick |
| ATAHUALLPA | Robert Stephens |
| VILLAC UMU | Edward Petherbridge |
| CHALLCUCHIMA | Edward Hardwicke |
| PEDRO DE CANDIA | Frank Wylie |
| CHIEFTAIN | Peter John |
| HEADMAN | Bruce Purchase |
| INTI COUSSI | Louise Purnell |
| OELLO | Jeanette Landis |
| PERUVIAN INDIANS | Michael Byrne, Christopher Chittell, Kurt Christian, Anton Darby, Nicholas Edmett, William Hobbs, Alan Ridgway, John Rogers, Clive Rust |

Production by John Dexter, Desmond O'Donovan
Scenery and costumes by Michael Annals
Music by Marc Wilkinson
Movement by Claude Chagrin
Lighting by John Read

Subsequently this production played at the Old Vic Theatre, London, in the repertory of the National Theatre.

The New York production opened at the ANTA Theatre on October 26, 1965, with the following cast:

| | |
|---|---|
| MARTIN RUIZ | George Rose |
| MARTIN RUIZ as a boy | Paul Collins |
| FRANCISCO PIZARRO | Christopher Plummer |
| DIEGO DE TRUJILLO | Michael Lamont |
| SALINAS | Nelson Phillips |
| RODAS | Jake Dengel |
| FRAY VINCENTE DE VALVERDE | Ben Hammer |
| VASCA | Tony Capodilupo |
| DOMINGO | George Sampson |
| JUAN CHAVEZ | Clyde Burton |
| PEDRO CHAVEZ | John Church |
| HERNANDO DE SOTO | John Vernon |
| FELIPILLO | Gregory Rozakis |
| FRAY MARCOS DE NIZZA | Michael Levin |
| MIGUEL ESTETE | Thayer David |
| MANCO | Marc Maskin |
| ATAHUALLPA | David Carradine |
| VILLAC UMU | Mylo Quam |
| CHALLCUCHIMA | Clayton Corbin |
| PEDRO DE CANDIA | Cal Bellini |
| CHIEFTAIN | Robert Berdeen |
| HEADMAN | Judd Jones |
| INTI COUSSI | Julie Sheppard |
| OELLO | Sandy Leeds |
| PERUVIAN INDIANS | Barry Burns, Paul Charles, Kurt Christian, Edilio Ferraro, Roy Lozano, Hector Mercado, Ken Novarro, B. J. Desimone, Don Silber |

Directed by John Dexter

## AUTHOR'S NOTES

### THE TEXT

Each act contains twelve sections, marked by Arabic numerals. These are solely for reference, and do not indicate pauses or breaks of any kind. The action is continuous.

### THE SET

In this version of the play I refer throughout to the set used by the National Theatre Company at the Chichester Festival, 1964. Essentially, all that is required for a production of *The Royal Hunt of the Sun* is a bare stage and an upper level. However, the setting by Michael Annals was so superb, and so brilliantly succeeded in solving the visual problems of the play, that I wish to recall it here in print.

Basically this design consisted of a huge aluminum ring, twelve feet in diameter, hung in the center of a plain wooden back wall. Around its circumference were hinged twelve petals. When closed, these interlocked to form a great medallion on which was incised the emblem of the Conquistadors; when opened, they formed the rays of a giant golden sun, emblem of the Incas. Each petal had an inlay of gold magnetized to it: when these inlays were pulled out (in Act Two, Scene vi) the great black frame remaining symbolized magnificently the desecration of Peru. The center of this sun formed an acting area above the stage, which was used in Act One to show Atahuallpa in majesty, and in Act Two served for his prison and subsequently for the treasure chamber.

This simple but amazing set was for me totally satisfying on all levels: scenically, aesthetically, and symbolically.

### THE MUSIC

The musical excerpts at the end of the play represent the three most easily detached pieces from the remarkable score composed for the play by Marc

Wilkinson. This extraordinary music I believe to be an integral part of any production of *The Royal Hunt of the Sun*. It embraces bird cries; plainchant; a fantasia for organ; freezing sounds for the Mime of the Great Ascent, and frightening ones for the Mime of the Great Massacre. To me its most memorable items are the exquisitely doleful lament which opens Act Two, and, most amazing of all, the final Chant of Resurrection, to be whined and whispered, howled and hooted, over Atahuallpa's body in the darkness, before the last sunrise of the Inca Empire.

The full score can be obtained from Liz Keys, London Management, 235–241 Regent Street, London, WIA 2JT, England.

## THE PRODUCTION

There are, no doubt, many ways of producing this play, as there are of setting it. My hope was always to realize on stage a kind of "total" theater, involving not only words but rites, mimes, masks, and magics. The text cries for illustration. It is a director's piece, a pantomimist's piece, a musician's piece, a designer's piece, and of course an actor's piece, almost as much as it is an author's. In this edition, as with the set, I have included as many details of the Chichester production as possible, partly because I was deeply involved in its creation, but mainly as a tribute to the superb achievement of John Dexter.

P.S.

# CHARACTERS

## THE SPANIARDS

*The Officers*

| | |
|---|---|
| FRANCISCO PIZARRO | Commander of the Expedition |
| HERNANDO DE SOTO | Second-in-Command |
| MIGUEL ESTETE | Royal Veedor, or Overseer |
| PEDRO DE CANDIA | Commander of Artillery |
| DIEGO DE TRUJILLO | Master of Horse |

*The Men*

| | |
|---|---|
| OLD MARTIN | |
| YOUNG MARTIN | Pizarro's Page: Old Martin as a boy |
| SALINAS | Blacksmith |
| RODAS | Tailor |
| VASCA | |
| DOMINGO | |
| JUAN CHAVEZ | |
| PEDRO CHAVEZ | |

*The Priests*

| | |
|---|---|
| FRAY VINCENTE DE VALVERDE | Chaplain to the Expedition (Dominican) |
| FRAY MARCOS DE NIZZA | Franciscan Friar |

## THE INDIANS

| | |
|---|---|
| ATAHUALLPA | Sovereign Inca of Peru |
| VILLAC UMU | High Priest of Peru |
| CHALLCUCHIMA | An Inca General |
| A CHIEFTAIN | |

A HEADMAN OF A THOUSAND FAMILIES

FELIPILLO — An Indian boy, employed by Pizarro as Interpreter

MANCO — A Chasqui, or Messenger

INTI COUSSI — Step-sister of Atahuallpa

nonspeaking

OELLO — A wife of Atahuallpa

SPANISH SOLDIERS AND PERUVIAN INDIANS

PLACE

*Apart from two early scenes in Spain and Panama, the play is set in the Upper Province of the Inca Empire: what is now South Ecuador and northwestern Peru. The whole of Act Two takes place in the town of Cajamarca.*

TIME

June 1529–August 1533

# ACT ONE

## THE HUNT

*A bare stage. On the back wall, which is of wood, hangs a huge metal medallion, quartered by four black crucifixes, sharpened to resemble swords.*

### 1

[*Darkness.* OLD MARTIN, *grizzled, in his middle fifties, appears. He wears the black costume of a Spanish hidalgo in the mid-sixteenth century.*]

OLD MARTIN [*to the audience*]: Save you all. My name is Martin. I'm a soldier of Spain and that's it. Most of my life I've spent fighting for land, treasure, and the cross. I'm worth millions. Soon I'll be dead, and they'll bury me out here in Peru, the land I helped ruin as a boy. This story is about ruin. Ruin and gold. More gold than any of you will ever see even if you work in a countinghouse. I'm going to tell you how one hundred and sixty-seven men conquered an empire of twenty-four million. And then things that no one has ever told: things to make you groan and cry out I'm lying. And perhaps I am. The air of Peru is cold and sour like in a vault, and wits turn easier here even than in Europe. But grant me this: I saw him closer than anyone, and had cause only to love him. He was my altar, my bright image of salvation. Francisco Pizarro! Time was when I'd have died for him, or for any worship.

[YOUNG MARTIN *enters dueling an invisible opponent with a stick. He is* OLD MARTIN *as an impetuous boy of fifteen.*]

If you could only imagine what it was like for me at the beginning, to be allowed to serve him. But boys don't dream like that any more—

service! Conquest! Riding down Indians in the name of Spain! The inside of my head was one vast plain for feats of daring. I used to lie up in the hayloft for hours reading my Bible—Don Cristobal on the Rules of Chivalry. And then he came and made them real. And the only wish of my life is that I had never seen him.

[FRANCISCO PIZARRO *comes in. He is a man in late middle age: tough, commanding, harsh, wasted, secret. The gestures are blunt and often violent; the expression intense and energetic, capable of fury and cruelty, but also of sudden melancholy and sardonic humor. At the moment he appears more neatly than he is ever to do again: hair and beard are trimmed, and his clothes quite grand, as if he is trying to make a fine impression.*

*He is accompanied by his Second-in-Command,* HERNANDO DE SOTO, *and the Dominican* FRAY VINCENTE DE VALVERDE. DE SOTO *is an impressive figure in his forties: his whole air breathes an unquestioning loyalty: to his profession, his faith, and to accepted values. He is an admirable soldier and a staunch friend.* VALVERDE, *on the other hand, is a peasant priest whose zeal is not greatly tempered by intelligence, nor sweetened by any anxiety to please.*]

PIZARRO: I was suckled by a sow. My house is the oldest in Spain—the pigsty.

OLD MARTIN: He'd made two expeditions to the New World already. Now at over sixty years old he was back in Spain, making one last try. He'd shown the King enough gold to get sole right of discovery in Peru and the title of Viceroy over anything he conquered. In return he was to fit out an army at his own expense. He started recruiting in his own birthplace, Trujillo.

[*Lights up below as he speaks. Several Spanish villagers have entered, among them* SALINAS, *a blacksmith,* RODAS, *a tailor,* VASCA, DOMINGO, *and the* CHAVEZ *brothers.* PIZARRO *addresses* DIEGO, *a young man of twenty-five.*]

PIZARRO: What's your name?

DIEGO: Diego, sir.

PIZARRO: What do you know best?

DIEGO: Horses, I suppose, if I was to name anything.

PIZARRO: How would you feel to be Master of Horse, Diego?

DIEGO [*eagerly*]: Sir!

PIZARRO: Go over there. Who's smith here?

SALINAS: I am.

PIZARRO: Are you with us?

SALINAS: I'm not against you.

PIZARRO: Who's your friend?

RODAS: Tailor, if it's your business.

PIZARRO: Soldiers never stop mending and patching. They'll be grateful for your assistance.

RODAS: Well, find some other fool to give it to them. I'm resting here.

PIZARRO: Rest. [*To* YOUNG MARTIN.] Who's this?

DIEGO: Martin Ruiz, sir. A good lad. He knows all his codes of chivalry by heart. He's aching to be a Page, sir.

PIZARRO: How old?

OLD MARTIN: Seventeen.

PIZARRO: Don't lie.

YOUNG MARTIN: Fifteen, sir.

[OLD MARTIN *goes off.*]

PIZARRO: Parents?

YOUNG MARTIN: Dead, sir.

PIZARRO: Can you write?

YOUNG MARTIN: Two hundred Latin words. Three hundred Spanish.

PIZARRO: Why do you want to come?

YOUNG MARTIN: It's going to be glorious, sir.

PIZARRO: Look you, if you served me, you'd be Page to an old slogger: no titles, no traditions. I learned my trade as a mercenary, going with who best paid me. It's a closed book to me, all that Chivalry! But then, not reading or writing, all books are closed to me. If I took you, you'd have to be my reader and writer, both.

YOUNG MARTIN: I'd be honored, my Lord. Oh, *please,* my Lord!

PIZARRO: General will do. Let's see your respect. Greet me. [*The boy bows.*] Now to the Church. That's Brother Valverde, our Chaplain.

VALVERDE: The blessing of God on you, my son. And on all who come with us to alter the heathen.

PIZARRO: Now to our Second-in-Command, Cavalier de Soto. I'm sure you all know the Cavalier well by reputation: a great soldier. He has fought under Cordoba! No expedition he seconds can fail! [*He takes a roll of cloth, woven with the design of a llama, from* DE SOTO *and exhibits it.*] Now look at this! Indian stuff! Ten years ago standing with the great Balboa, I saw a chieftain draw this beast on the leaf of an aloe. And he said to me: "Where this roams is uncountable wealth!"

RODAS [*sourly*]: Oh yes, uncountable! Ask Sanchez the farrier about that. He listened to talk like that from him five years ago.

DIEGO: Who cares about him?

RODAS: Uncountable pissing wealth? It rained six months and his skin rotted on him! They lost twenty-seven out of fifty.

PIZARRO [*sharply*]: And so we may again. What do you think I'm offering? A walk in the country? Jellies and wine in a basket, your hand round your girl? No, I'm promising you swamps. A forest like the beard of the world. Sitting half buried in earth to escape the mouths of insects. You may live for weeks on palm tree buds and soup made out of leather straps. And at night you will sleep in thick wet darkness with snakes hung over your heads like bell ropes—and black men in that blackness: men that eat each other. And why should you endure all this? Because I believe that beyond this terrible place is a kingdom where gold is as common as wood is here! I took only two steps in and found cups and pans made out of it solid!

[*He claps his hands.* FELIPILLO *comes in. He is a slim, delicate Indian from Ecuador, loaded with golden ornaments. In actuality* FELIPILLO *is a treacherous and hysterical creature, but at the moment, under his master's eye, he sways forward before the stupefied villagers with a demure grace.*]

I present Felipillo, captured on my last trip! Look close at his ornaments. To him they are no more than feathers are to us, but they are all gold, my friends. Examine him. *Down!*

[FELIPILLO *kneels. The villagers examine him.*]

VALVERDE: Look at him well. This is a heathen. A being condemned to eternal flame unless you help him. Don't think we are merely going to destroy his people and lift their wealth. We are going to take from them what they don't value, and give them instead the priceless mercy of heaven. He who helps me lift this dark man into light I absolve of all crimes he ever committed.

PIZARRO: Well?

SALINAS: That's gold right enough!

PIZARRO: And for your taking! . . . I was like you once. Sitting the afternoon away in this same street, drunk in the inn, to bed in the sty. Stink and mud and nothing to look for. Even if you die with me, what's so tender precious to hold you here?

VASCA: You're pissing right!

PIZARRO: I tell you, man: over there you'll be the masters—that'll be your slave.

VASCA: Well, there's a thought: talk about the slave of slaves!

DOMINGO [*timidly*]: Do you think it's true?

PIZARRO: Do you say I lie?

DOMINGO: Oh no, sir . . .

VASCA: Even if he does, what's to keep you here? You're a cooper: how many casks have you made this year? That's no employment for a dog!

PIZARRO: How about you? You're brothers, aren't you?

DIEGO: That's the Chavez brothers, Juan and Pedro.

JUAN: Sir.

PEDRO: Sir.

PIZARRO: Well, what d'you say?

JUAN: I say right, sir.

PEDRO: Me too!

VASCA: And me. I'm going to get a slave or two like him!

DOMINGO: And me. Vasca's right, you can't do worse than stay here.

RODAS: Well, not me, boys. Just you catch Rodas marching through any pissing jungle!

SALINAS: Oh, shut your ape's face. Are you going to sit here for ever and pick fleas? He'll come, sir.

PIZARRO: Make your way to Toledo for the muster. Diego, enroll them all and take them along.

DIEGO: Sir!

[YOUNG MARTIN *makes to go off with the rest.* PIZARRO *stays him.*]

PIZARRO: Boy.

YOUNG MARTIN: Sir.

[*A pause.*]

PIZARRO: Master me the names of all officers and men so far listed.

YOUNG MARTIN [*overwhelmed*]: *Oh, sir!* . . . Yes, sir! Thank you, sir!

PIZARRO: You're a Page now, so act like one. Dignity at all times.

YOUNG MARTIN [*bowing*]: Yes, sir.

PIZARRO: Respect.

YOUNG MARTIN [*bowing*]: Yes, sir.

PIZARRO: And obedience.

YOUNG MARTIN [*bowing*]: Yes, sir.

PIZARRO: And it isn't necessary to salute every ten seconds.

YOUNG MARTIN: [*bowing*]: No, sir.

VALVERDE: Come, my son, there's work to do.

[*They go off. A pause.*]

PIZARRO: Strange sight, yourself, just as you were in this very street.

DE SOTO: Do you like it?

PIZARRO: No, I was a fool. Dreamers deserve what they get.

DE SOTO: And what are you dreaming about now?

PIZARRO: Gold.

DE SOTO: Oh, come. Gold is not enough lodestone for you, not any more, to drag you back to the New World.

PIZARRO: You're right. At my age things become what they really are. Gold turns into metal.

DE SOTO: Then why? You could stay here now and be hero for a province. What's left to endure so much for—especially with your infirmity? You've earned the right to comfort. Your country would gladly grant it to you for the rest of your life.

PIZARRO: My country, where is that?

DE SOTO: Spain, sir.

PIZARRO: Spain and I have been strangers since I was a boy. The only spot I know in it is here—this filthy village. This is Spain to me. Is this where you wish me comfort? For twenty-two years I drove pigs down this street because my father couldn't own to my mother. Twenty-two years without one single day of hope. When I turned soldier and dragged my arquebus along the roads of Italy, I was so famished I was beyond eating. I got nothing and I gave nothing, and though I groaned for that once I'm glad with it now. Because I owe nothing. . . . Once the world could have had me for a petty farm, two rocky fields and a Señor to my name. It said "No." Ten years on it could have had me for double—small estate, fifty orange trees and a Sir to them. It said "No." Twenty years more and it could still have had me cheap: Balboa's trusty lieutenant, marched with him into the Pacific and claimed it for Spain: state pension and dinner once a week with the local mayor. But the world said "No." Said "No" and said "No." Well, now it's going to know me. If I live this next year I'm going to get me a name that won't ever be forgotten! A name to be sung here for centuries in your ballads, out there under the cork trees where I sat as a boy with bandages for shoes. I amuse you.

DE SOTO: Surely you see you don't.

PIZARRO: Oh yes, I amuse you, Cavalier de Soto. The old pigherd lumbering after fame. You inherited your honor—I had to root for mine like the pigs. It's amusing.

2

*[Lights whiter, colder. He kneels. An organ sounds: the austere polyphony of Spanish celebration.* VALVERDE *enters, bearing an immense wooden Christ. He is accompanied by his assistant,* FRAY MARCOS DE NIZZA, *a Franciscan, a man of far more serene temper and intellectual maturity. All the villagers come in also, wearing the white cloaks of chivalry and carrying banners.*

*Among them is* PEDRO DE CANDIA, *a Venetian captain, wearing a pearl in one ear and walking with a lazy stealth that at once suggests danger.* OLD MARTIN *comes in and as usual addresses the audience.*]

OLD MARTIN: On the day of St. John the Evangelist, our weapons were consecrated in the Cathedral Church of Panama. Our muster was one hundred and eighty-seven, with horses for twenty-seven.

VALVERDE: You are the huntsmen of God! The weapons you draw are sacred! Oh, God, invest us all with the courage of Thy unflinching Son. Show us our way to beat the savage out of his dark forests on to the broad plain of Thy Grace.

DE NIZZA: And comfort, we pray, all warriors that shall be in affliction from this setting out.

OLD MARTIN: Fray Marcos de Nizza, Franciscan, appointed to assist Valverde.

DE NIZZA: You are the bringers of food to starving peoples. You go to break mercy with them like bread, and outpour gentleness into their cups. You will lay before them the inexhaustible table of free spirit, and invite to it all who have dieted on terror. You will bring to all tribes the nourishment of pity. You will sow their fields with love, and teach them to harvest the crop of it, each yield in its season. Remember this always: we are their New World.

VALVERDE: Approach all and be blessed.

[*During this, the men kneel and are blessed in turn.*]

OLD MARTIN: Pedro de Candia, Cavalier from Venice, in charge of weapons and artillery. These villagers you know already. There were many others, of course. Almagro, the General's partner, who stayed to organize reinforcements and follow in three months. Riquelme the Treasurer. Pedro of Ayala and Blas of Atienza. Herrada the Swordsman and Gonzales of Toledo. And Juan de Barbaran whom everyone called the Good Servant out of love for him. And many smaller men. Even its youngest member saw himself with a following of Indians and a province for an orchard. It was a tumbled company, none too noble, but ginger for wealth!

[*Enter* ESTETE: *a stiff, haughty man, dressed in the black of the Spanish court.*] And chiefly there was—

ESTETE: Miguel Estete. Royal Veedor, and Overseer in the name of King Carlos the Fifth! You should not have allowed anyone to be blessed before me.

PIZARRO: Your pardon, Veedor, I don't understand affairs of Before and After.

ESTETE: That is evident. General, on this expedition my name is the law: it is spoken with the King's authority.

PIZARRO: Your pardon, but on this expedition *my* name is the law: there will be no other.

ESTETE: In matters military.

PIZARRO: In all matters.

ESTETE: In all that do not infringe the majesty of the King.

PIZARRO: What matters could?

ESTETE: Remember your duty to God, sir, and to the throne, sir, and you will not discover them.

PIZARRO [*furious*]: De Soto! In the name of Spain our holy country, I invest you as Second-in-Command to me. Subject only to me. In the name of Spain our holy country—I—I— [*He falters, clutching his side in pain. A pause. The men whisper among themselves.*] Take the banners out. . . .

DE SOTO: Take up your banners. March!

[*The organ music continues: all march out, leaving* PIZARRO *and his* PAGE *alone on the stage. Only when all the rest are gone does the General collapse. The boy is frightened and concerned.*]

YOUNG MARTIN: What is it, sir?

PIZARRO: A wound from long ago. A knife to the bone. A savage put it into me for life. It troubles me at times . . . You'll start long before me with your wounds. With your killing too. I wonder how you'll like that.

YOUNG MARTIN: You watch me, sir!

PIZARRO: I will. You deal in deaths when you are a soldier, and all your study should be to make them clean, what scratches kill and how to cut them.

YOUNG MARTIN: But surely, sir, there's more to soldiering than that?

PIZARRO: You mean honor, glory—traditions of the service?

YOUNG MARTIN: Yes, sir.

PIZARRO: Dungballs. Soldiers are for killing: that's their reason.

YOUNG MARTIN: But, sir—

PIZARRO: What?

YOUNG MARTIN: It's not just killing. . . .

PIZARRO: Look, boy: know something. Men cannot just stand as men in this world. It's too big for them and they grow scared. So they build themselves shelters against the bigness, do you see? They call the shelters Court, Army, Church. They're useful against loneliness, Martin, but they're not true. They're not *real*, Martin. Do you see?

YOUNG MARTIN: No, sir. Not truthfully, sir . . .

PIZARRO [*savagely*]: No, sir. Not truthfully, sir! . . . Why must you be so young? Look at you. Only a quarter formed. A colt the world will break for its sightless track. Listen once. Army loyalty is blasphemy. The world of soldiers is a yard of ungrowable children. They play with ribbons and make up ceremonies just to keep out the rest of the world. They add up the number of their blue dead and their green dead and call that their History. But all this is just the flower the bandit carves on his knife before shoving it into a man's side. . . . What's Army tradition? Nothing but years of Us against Them. Christ-men against Pagan-men. Men against men. I've had a life of it, boy, and let me tell you it's nothing but a nightmare game, played by brutes to give themselves a reason.

YOUNG MARTIN: But, sir, a noble reason can make a fight glorious.

PIZARRO: Give me a reason that stays noble once you start hacking off limbs in its name. There isn't a cause in the world to set against this pain. Noble's a word. Leave it for the books.

YOUNG MARTIN: I can't believe that, sir.

PIZARRO: Look at you—hope, lovely hope, it's on you like dew. . . . Do you know where you're going? Into the forest. A hundred miles of dark and screaming. The dark we all came out of, hot. Things flying, fleeing, falling dead—and their death unnoticed. Take your noble reasons there, Martin. Pitch your silk flags in that black and wave your crosses at the wild cats. See what awe they command. Be advised, boy. Go back to Spain.

YOUNG MARTIN: No, sir. I'm coming with you! I can learn, sir.

PIZARRO: You will be taught. Not by me. The forest. [*He stumps out.*]

## 3

[*The boy is left alone. The stage darkens and the huge medallion high on the back wall begins to glow. Great cries of "Inca!" are heard. The boy bolts offstage. Exotic music mixes with the chanting. Slowly the medallion opens outward to form a huge golden sun with twelve great inlaid rays. In the center stands* ATAHUALLPA, *sovereign Inca of Peru, masked, crowned, and dressed in gold and feathers. When he speaks, his voice, like the voices of all the Incas, is strangely formalized.*

*Enter below the Inca court:* VILLAC UMU, *the High Priest,* CHALLCUCHIMA, MANCO, *and others, all masked, and robed in terracotta. They prostrate themselves.*]

MANCO: Atahuallpa! God!

ATAHUALLPA: God hears!

MANCO: Manco your Chasqui speaks! I bring truth from many runners what has been seen in the Farthest Province. White men sitting on huge sheep! The sheep are red! Everywhere their leader shouts aloud, "Here is God!"

ATAHUALLPA [*astounded*]: The White God!

VILLAC UMU: Beware, beware Inca!

ATAHUALLPA: All-powerful spirit who left this place before my ancestors ruled you! . . . The White God returns!

CHALLCUCHIMA: You do not know this.

ATAHUALLPA: He has been long waited for. If he comes, it is with blessing. Then my people will see I did well to take the crown.

VILLAC UMU: Ware you! Your mother Moon wears a veil of green fire. An eagle fell on to the temple in Cuzco.

MANCO: It is true, Capac. He fell out of the sky.

VILLAC UMU: Out of a green sky.

CHALLCUCHIMA: On to a house of gold.

VILLAC UMU: When the world ends, small birds grow sharp claws.

ATAHUALLPA: Cover your mouth.

[*All cover their mouths.*]

If the White God comes to bless me, all must see him.

[*The court retires.* ATAHUALLPA *remains onstage, motionless in his sunflower. He stays in this position until the end of Scene* 7.]

4

[*Mottled light. Province of Tumbes. Screams and whoops of alarm imitating tropical bird cries. A horde of Indians rushes across the stage pursued by all the Spanish soldiers.*]

DE CANDIA: Grab that one! That's the chief!

[*They capture the chieftain. At the sight of this, all the Indians fall silent and passive.* DE CANDIA *approaches him with drawn sword.*] Now, you brownie bastard, show us gold!

PIZARRO: Gently, De Candia. You'll get nothing from him in terror.

DE CANDIA: Let's see.

PIZARRO: God's wounds! Put up! . . . Felipillo, ask for gold.

[FELIPILLO *adopts a set of stylized gestures for his interpreting, in the manner of sign language.*]

CHIEF: We have no gold. All was taken by the great King in his war.

PIZARRO: What King?

CHIEF: Holy Atahuallpa, Inca of earth and sky. His kingdom is the widest in the world.

DE SOTO: How wide?

CHIEF: A man can run in it every day for a year.

DE SOTO: More than a thousand miles.

ESTETE: Poor savage, trying to impress us with his little tribe!

PIZARRO: I think we've found more than a little tribe, Veedor. Tell me of this King. Who did he fight?

CHIEF: His brother Huascar. His father the great Inca Huayana grew two sons. One by a wife, one by a not-wife. At his death he cut the kingdom in two for them. But Atahuallpa wanted all. So he made war, and killed his brother. Now he is lord of earth and sky.

PIZARRO [*interested*]: And he's the bastard?

[*All the* INDIANS *cry out.*]

Answer! He's the bastard?

CHIEF: He is Son of the Sun. He needs no wedded mother. He is God.

INDIANS [*chanting*]: Sapa Inca! Inca Capac!

PIZARRO: God?

CHIEF: God!

PIZARRO: God on earth?

VALVERDE [*horrified*]: Christ defend us!

DE SOTO: Do you believe this?

CHIEF: It is true. The sun is God. Atahuallpa is his child, sent to shine on us for a few years of life. Then he will return to his father's palace and live forever.

PIZARRO [*wondering*]: God on earth!

VALVERDE: Oh, my brothers, where have we come? The land of Anti-Christ! . . . Do your duty, Spaniards! Take each an Indian and work to shift his soul! Go to them. Show them rigor! No softness to gentle idolatry! [*To the* INDIANS.] The cross, you pagan dust!

[*They try to escape.*]

Stay them!

[*The* SPANIARDS *ring them with drawn swords.*]

Repeat. Jesus Christ Inca!

INDIANS [*uncertainly*]: Jesus Christ Inca! . . .

ESTETE: Jesus Christ Inca!

INDIANS [*repeating*]: Jesus Christ Inca!

[*The soldiers herd them offstage. Their cries punctuate the end of the scene. All below go off after them, save* PIZARRO *and* DE SOTO.]

ATAHUALLPA: He surely is a God. He teaches my people to praise him.

PIZARRO: He's a god all right. They're scared to hell of him. And a bastard too. That's civil war—bastards against bastards!

ATAHUALLPA: I will see him. Let no one harm these men!

PIZARRO: Let's see you, then! What's it look like to be Son of the Sun?

DE SOTO: That's something in Europe no one's ever dared call himself.

PIZARRO: God on earth, living forever. . . .

DE SOTO: He's got a shock coming. [*He goes off.*]

PIZARRO [*calling up*]: Do you hear that, God? You're not going to like that! Because we've got a god worth a thousand of yours. A gentle god with gentle priests, and a couple of big cannon to blow you out of the sky!

VALVERDE [*off*]: Jesus Christ Inca!

PIZARRO: Christ the Merciful, with his shackles and stakes! . . . So enjoy yourself while you can. Have a glorious shine! [*He makes the sign of the cross.*] Take that, Anti-Christ! [*He runs off, laughing.*]

VALVERDE [*off*]: Jesus Christ Inca!

[INDIANS *(off) cry out.*]

[*Enter* VILLAC UMU *and* CHALLCUCHIMA, *below.*]

VILLAC UMU: Your people groan!

ATAHUALLPA: They groan with my voice!

CHALLCUCHIMA: Your people weep!

ATAHUALLPA: They weep with my tears!

CHALLCUCHIMA: He searches all the houses. He seeks your crown. Remember the prophecy! *The twelfth Lord of the Four Quarters shall be the last!* . . . Inca, ware you!

VILLAC UMU: Inca, ware you!

ATAHUALLPA [*to* CHALLCUCHIMA]: Go to him. Take him my word. Tell him to greet me at Cajamarca, behind the great mountains. If he is a god he will find me. If he is no god, he will die.

[*Lights down on him. Priest and noblemen retire.*]

## 5

[*Night. Wild bird cries.* DOMINGO *and* VASCA *on sentry duty.*]

VASCA: There must be a pissing thousand of 'em, every night we halt.

DOMINGO: Why don't they just come and get us?

VASCA: They're waiting.

DOMINGO: What for?

VASCA: Maybe they're cannibals and there's a feast day coming up.

DOMINGO: Very funny. . . . Six weeks in this pissing forest and not one smell of gold. I think we've been had.

VASCA: Unless they're hiding it, like the General says.

DOMINGO: I don't believe it. Goddamned place. I'm starting to rust.

VASCA: We all are. It's the damp. Another week and we'll have to get the blacksmith to cut us out.

[*Enter* ESTETE *with* DE CANDIA *carrying an arquebus*.]

VASCA: Who's there?

DE CANDIA: Talk on duty again and *I'll* cut you out.

DOMINGO: Yes, sir.

VASCA: Yes, sir.

[*They separate and go off*.]

DE CANDIA: They're right. Everything's rusting. Even you, my darling [*the gun*]. Look at her, Strozzi's most perfect model. She can stop a horse at five hundred paces. You're too good for brownies, my sweet.

ESTETE: What are they waiting for? Why don't they just attack and be done with it?

DE CANDIA: They'd find nothing against them. A hundred and eighty terrified men, nine of these, and two cannon. If your King wasn't so mean, we might just stand a chance out here.

ESTETE: Hold your tongue, De Candia.

DE CANDIA: Good: loyalty. That's what I like to see. The only thing that puzzles me is what the hell *you* get out of it. They tell me royal overseers get nothing.

ESTETE: Any man without self-interest must puzzle a Venetian. If you serve a King you must kill personal ambition. Only then can you become a channel between the people and its collective glory—which otherwise it would never feel. In Byzantium court officials were castrated to resemble the Order of Angels. But I don't expect you to understand.

DE CANDIA: You Spaniards! You men with missions! You just can't bear to think of yourselves as the thieves you are.

ESTETE: How dare you, sir!

[*Enter* PIZARRO *and* YOUNG MARTIN.]

DE CANDIA: Our noble General. They say in the Indies he traded his immortal part to the Devil.

ESTETE: For what, pray? Health? Breeding? Handsomeness?

DE CANDIA: That they don't tell.

ESTETE: I only wonder His Majesty could give command to such a man. I believe he's mad.

DE CANDIA: No, but still dangerous.

ESTETE: What do you mean?

DE CANDIA: I've served under many men: but this is the first who makes me afraid. Look into him, you'll see a kind of death.

[*Bird cries fill the forest.* PIZARRO *talks to* YOUNG MARTIN.]

PIZARRO: Listen to them. There's the world. The eagle rips the condor; the condor rips the crow. And the crow would blind all the eagles in the sky if once it had the beak to do it. The clothed hunt the naked; the legitimates hunt the bastards, and put down the word gentleman to blot up the blood. Your chivalry rules don't govern me, Martin. They're for Belonging Birds—like them [*indicating* ESTETE *and* DE CANDIA]: legitimate birds with claws trim on the perch their fathers left to them. . . . Make no error; if I could once peck them off it, I'd tear them into gobbets to feed cats. Don't ever trust me, boy.

YOUNG MARTIN: Sir? I'm your man.

PIZARRO: Don't ever trust me.

YOUNG MARTIN: Sir?

PIZARRO: Or if you must, never say I deceived you. Know me.

YOUNG MARTIN: I do, sir. You are all I ever want to be.

PIZARRO: I am nothing you could ever want to be, or any man alive. Believe this: if the time ever came for you to harry me, I'd rip you too, easy as look at you. Because you belong too, Martin.

YOUNG MARTIN: I belong to you, sir!

PIZARRO: You belong to hope. To faith. To priests and pretenses. To dipping flags and ducking heads. To laying hands and licking rings. To prostraters and saluters, and the whole vast stupid congregation of cringers and cross-kissers! You're a worshiper, Martin. A groveler. You were born with feet but you prefer your knees. It's you who make Bishops—Kings—Generals . . . You trust me, I'll hurt you past believing. [*A pause.*] Have the sentries changed?

YOUNG MARTIN [*distressed*]: Not yet, sir.

PIZARRO: Little Lord of Hope, I'm harsh with you. You own everything I've lost. I despise the keeping, and I loathe the losing. Where can a man live, between two hates? [*He goes toward the two officers.*] Gentlemen.

ESTETE: How is your wound tonight, General?

PIZARRO: The calmer for your inquiring, Veedor.

DE CANDIA: Well, and what's your plan, sir?

PIZARRO: To go on until I'm stopped.

DE CANDIA: Admirable simplicity.

ESTETE: What kind of plan is that?

PIZARRO: You have a better? It's obvious they've been ordered to hold off.

ESTETE: Why?

PIZARRO: If it's wickedness, I'm sure the crown can guess it as soon as the Army.

ESTETE: Sir, I know your birth hasn't fitted you for much civility, but remember, in me speaks your King.

PIZARRO: Well, go and write to him. Set down more about my unfitness in your report. Then show it to the birds.

[*He goes off.* ESTETE *goes off another way.* DE CANDIA *laughs and follows him.*]

## 6

[*Light brightens to morning. Enter* OLD MARTIN.]

OLD MARTIN: We were in the forest for six weeks, but at last we escaped and found on the other side our first witness of a great empire. There was a road fifteen feet wide, bordered with mimosa and blue glories, with walls on both sides the height of a man. We rode it for days, six horses abreast: and all the way, far up the hillsides, were huge fields of corn laid out in terraces, and a net of water in a thousand canals.

[*Lights up on* ATAHUALLPA, *above.* OLD MARTIN *goes out.*]

MANCO: Manco your Chasqui speaks! They move on the road to Ricaplaya.

ATAHUALLPA: What do they do?

MANCO: They walk through the field terraces. They listen to toil-songs. They clap their hands at fields of llama!

[*Enter groups of* INDIANS, *singing a toil-song and miming their work of sowing and reaping.* PIZARRO, *the* PRIESTS, FELIPILLO, *and* SOLDIERS, *among them* DE SOTO, DE CANDIA, DIEGO, ESTETE, *and* YOUNG MARTIN, *enter and stand watching.* YOUNG MARTIN *carries a drum.*]

DE NIZZA: How beautiful their tongue sounds!

YOUNG MARTIN: I'm trying to study it, but it's very hard. All the words seem to slip together.

FELIPILLO: Oh, very hard, yes! But more hard for Indian to learn Spanish.

DE NIZZA: I'm sure. See how contented they look.

DIEGO: It's the first time I've ever seen people glad at working.

DE SOTO: This is their headman.

PIZARRO: You are the Lord of the Manor?

[FELIPILLO *interprets.*]

HEADMAN: Here all work together in families: fifty, a hundred, a thousand. I am head of a thousand families. I give out to all food. I give out to all clothes. I give out to all confessing.

DE NIZZA: Confessing?

HEADMAN: I have priest power . . . I confess my people of all crimes against the laws of the sun.

DE NIZZA: What laws are these?

HEADMAN: It is the seventh month. That is why they must pick corn.

ATAHUALLPA [*intoning*]: In the eighth month you will plow! In the ninth, sow maize! In the tenth, mend your roofs!

HEADMAN: Each age also has its tasks.

ATAHUALLPA: Nine years to twelve, protect harvests. Twelve to eighteen, care for herds. Eighteen to twenty-five, warriors for *me*—Atahuallpa Inca!

FELIPILLO: They are stupid; always do what they are told.

DE SOTO: This is because they are poor?

FELIPILLO: Not poor. Not rich. All same.

ATAHUALLPA: At twenty-five all will marry. All will receive one *tupu* of land.

HEADMAN: What may be covered by one hundred pounds of maize.

ATAHUALLPA: They will never move from there. At birth of a son one more *tupu* will be given. At birth of a daughter, half a *tupu*. At fifty all people will leave work forever, and be fed in honor till they die.

DE SOTO: I have settled several lands. This is the first I've entered which shames our Spain.

ESTETE: Shames?

PIZARRO: Oh, it's not difficult to shame Spain. Here shames every country which teaches we are born greedy for possessions. Clearly we're made greedy when we're assured it's natural. But there's a picture for a Spanish eye! There's nothing to covet, so covetousness dies at birth.

DE SOTO: But don't you have any nobles or grand people?

HEADMAN: The King has great men near him to order the country. But they are few.

DE SOTO: How then can he make sure so many are happy over so large a land?

HEADMAN: His messengers run light and dark, one after one, over four great roads. No one else may move on them. So he has eyes everywhere. He sees you now.

PIZARRO: Now?

ATAHUALLPA: *Now!*

[CHALLCUCHIMA *enters with* MANCO, *bearing the image of the Sun on a pole.* FELIPILLO *interprets.*]

CHALLCUCHIMA: I bring greeting from Atahuallpa Inca, Lord of the Four Quarters, King of the earth and sky.

ESTETE: I will speak with him. A King's man must always greet a King's man. We bring greeting from King Carlos, Emperor of Spain and Austria. We bring blessing from Jesus Christ, the Son of God.

ATAHUALLPA: Blessing!

CHALLCUCHIMA: *I* am sent by the Son of God. He orders *you* to visit him!

ESTETE: Orders? Does he take us for servants?

CHALLCUCHIMA: All men are his servants.

ESTETE: Does he think so? He's got awakening coming.

CHALLCUCHIMA: *Awakening?*

PIZARRO: Veedor, under pardon, let my peasant tongue have a word . . . Where is your King?

CHALLCUCHIMA: Cajamarca. Behind the great mountains. Perhaps they are too high for you.

ESTETE: There isn't a hill in your whole country a Spaniard couldn't climb in full armor.

CHALLCUCHIMA [*ironically*]: That is wonderful.

PIZARRO: How long should we march before we find him?

CHALLCUCHIMA: One life of Mother Moon.

FELIPILLO: A month.

PIZARRO: For us, two weeks. Tell him we come.

ATAHUALLPA: He gives his word with no fear!

CHALLCUCHIMA: Ware you! It is great danger to take back your word.

PIZARRO: I do not fear danger. What I say I do.

CHALLCUCHIMA: So. Do.

[CHALLCUCHIMA *and* MANCO *go off.*]

ATAHUALLPA: He speaks with a God's tongue! Let us take his blessing.

DE SOTO: Well, God help us now.

DE CANDIA: He'd better. I don't know who else will get us out of this. Certainly not the artillery.

FELIPILLO [*imitating* CHALLCUCHIMA'*s walk and voice*]: So! Do!

DE SOTO: Be still. You're too free.

ESTETE: My advice to you now is to wait for the reinforcements.

PIZARRO: I thank you for it.

DE SOTO: There's no telling when they'll come, sir. We daren't stay till then.

PIZARRO: But *you* of course will.

ESTETE: I?

PIZARRO: I cannot hazard the life of a royal officer.

ESTETE: My personal safety has never concerned me, General. My master's service is all I care for.

PIZARRO: That's why we must ensure its continuance. I'll give you twenty men. You can make a garrison.

ESTETE: I must decline, General. If you go—I go also.

PIZARRO: I'm infinitely moved, Veedor, but my orders remain. You stay here. [*To his* PAGE.] Call Assembly.

YOUNG MARTIN: [*banging his drum*]: Assembly! . . . Assembly!

[ESTETE *goes off angrily.*]

7

[*The company pelts on.* PIZARRO *addresses them.*]

PIZARRO: We are commanded to court by a brown King, more powerful than any you have ever heard of, sole owner of all the gold we came for! We have three roads. Go back, and he kills us. Stay here, and he kills us. Go on, and he still may kill us. Who fears to meet him can stay here with the Veedor and swell a garrison. He'll have no disgrace, but no gold neither. Who stirs?

RODAS: Well, I pissing stir for one! I'm not going to be chewed up by no pissing heathen king. What do you say, Vasca, lad?

VASCA: I don't know. I reckon if he chews us first, he chews you second. We're the eggs and you're the stew!

RODAS: Ha, ha, day of a hundred jokes!

SALINAS: Come on, friend, for God's sake! Who's going to sew us up if you desert?

RODAS: You can all rot for all I care, breeches and what's bloody in 'em!

SALINAS: Bastard!

RODAS: To hell with the lot of you!

[*He walks off.*]

PIZARRO: Anyone else?

DOMINGO: Well, I don't know . . . maybe he's right.

JUAN: Hey, Pedro, what do you think?

PEDRO: Hell, no! Vasca's right. It's as safe to go as stay here.

SALINAS: That's right.

VASCA: Anyway, I didn't come to keep no pissing garrison!

PEDRO: Nor me. I'm going on!

JUAN: Right, boy.

SALINAS: And me!

DOMINGO: Well, I don't know . . .

VASCA: Oh, close your mouth! You're like a pissing girl! [*To* PIZARRO.] We're coming. Just find us the gold.

PIZARRO: All right then! [*To* YOUNG MARTIN.] You stay here.

YOUNG MARTIN: No, sir. The place of a squire is at all times by his knight's side. Laws of chivalry.

PIZARRO [*touched*]: Get them in rank. *Move!*

YOUNG MARTIN: Company in rank. *Move!*

[*The soldiers form up in rank. They stand stiffly.*]

PIZARRO: Stand firm. Firmer! . . . Look at you—you could be dead already! If he sees you like that you will be! Make no error, he's watching every step you take. You're not men any longer, you're gods now. Eternal gods, each one of you. Two can play this immortality game, my lads! I want to see you move over his land like figures from a Lent procession. He must see gods walk on earth. Indifferent! Uncrushable! No death to be afraid of! I tell you, one shiver dooms the lot of us. One yelp of fright and we'll never be heard of again. He'll serve us like cheeseworms you crush with a knife. So come on, you tattered trash—shake out the straw! Forget your village magic: fingers in crosses, saints under your shirts. You can *grant* prayers now—no need to answer them. Come on! Fix your eyes! Follow the pig-boy to his glory! I'll have an empire for my farm! A million boys driving in the pigs at night! And each one of you will own a share—juicy black earth a hundred mile apiece—and golden plows to cut it! Get up, you god-boys—*March!*

[MARTIN *bangs his drum. The Spaniards begin to march in slow motion. Above, masked Indians move on to the upper level and address the still immobile Inca.*]

MANCO: They move, Inca! They come! One hundred and sixty and seven.

ATAHUALLPA: Where?

MANCO: Zaran.

VILLAC UMU: Ware! Ware, Inca!

MANCO: They move all in step. Not fast, not slow. They keep straight on from dark to dark.

VILLAC UMU: Ware! Ware, Inca!

MANCO: They are at Motupe, Inca! They do not look on left or right.

VILLAC UMU: Ware! this is great danger.

ATAHUALLPA: No danger. He is coming to bless me. A God and all his priests. Praise Father Sun!

ALL ABOVE [*chanting*]: Viracoch'an Aticsi.

ATAHUALLPA: Praise Sapa Inca!

ALL ABOVE: Sapa Inca! Inca Capac!

ATAHUALLPA: Praise Inti Cori!

ALL ABOVE: Cayalla Int'i Cori!

CHALLCUCHIMA: They come to the *mountains!*

VILLAC UMU: Kill them now!

ATAHUALLPA: Praise Atahuallpa!

VILLAC UMU: Destroy them! Teach them *death!*

ATAHUALLPA: Praise Atahuallpa!

ALL ABOVE: Atahuallpa! Sapa Inca! Huaccha Cuyak!

ATAHUALLPA [*crying out*]: *Let them see my mountains!*

[*A crash of primitive instruments. The lights snap out and, lit from the side, the rays of the metal sun throw long shadows across the wooden wall. All the Spaniards fall down. A cold blue light fills the stage.*]

DE SOTO: God in heaven!

[*Enter* OLD MARTIN.]

OLD MARTIN: You call them the Andes. Picture a curtain of stone hung by some giant across your path. Mountains set on mountains: cliffs on cliffs. Hands of rock a hundred yards high, with flashing nails—where the snow never moved, scratching the gashed face of the sun. For miles around the jungle lay black in its shadow. A freezing cold fell on us.

PIZARRO: Up, my godlings! Up, my little gods! Take heart, now. He's watching you. *Get to your feet!* [*To* DIEGO.] Master, what of the horses?

DIEGO: D'you need them, sir?

PIZARRO: They're vital, boy.

DIEGO: Then you'll have 'em, sir. They'll follow you as we will.

PIZARRO: Up we go, then! We're coming for you, Atahuallpa! [*Shouting up.*] Show me the toppest peak-top you can pile—show me the lid of the world—I'll stand tiptoe on it and pull you right out of the sky! I'll grab you by the legs, you Son of the Sun, and smash your flaming crown on the rocks! . . . Bless them, Church!

VALVERDE: God stay you, and stay with you all.

DE NIZZA: Amen.

[*While* PIZARRO *is calling his last speech to the Inca, the silent King thrice beckons to him, and retires backward out of the sun into blackness. In the cold light there now ensues:*

## 8

### THE MIME OF THE GREAT ASCENT

*As* OLD MARTIN *describes their ordeal, the men climb the Andes. It is a terrible progress: a stumbling, tortuous climb into the clouds, over ledges and giant chasms, performed to an eerie, cold music made from the thin whine of huge metal saws.*]

OLD MARTIN: Have you ever climbed a mountain in full armor? That's what we did, him going first the whole way up a tiny path into the clouds, with drops sheer on both sides into nothing. For hours we crept forward like blind men, the sweat freezing on our faces, lugging skittery leaking horses, and pricked all the time for the ambush that would tip us into death. Each turn of the path it grew colder. The friendly trees of the forest dropped away, and there were only pines. Then they went too, and there were just scrubby little bushes standing up in ice. All round us the rocks began to whine with cold. And always above us or below us, those filthy condor birds, hanging on the air with great tasseled wings.

[*It grows darker. The music grows colder yet. The men freeze and hang their heads for a long moment, before resuming their desperate climb.*]

Then night. We lay down twos and threes together on the path, and hugged like lovers for warmth in that burning cold. And most cried. We got up with cold iron for bones and went on. Four days like that; groaning, not speaking; the breath a blade in our lungs. Four days, slowly, like flies on a wall; limping flies, dying flies, up an endless wall of rock. A tiny army lost in the creases of the moon.

INDIANS [*off: in echo*]: Stand!

[*The Spaniards whirl round.* VILLAC UMU *and his attendants appear, clothed entirely in white fur. The High Priest wears a snow-white llama head on top of his own.*]

VILLAC UMU: You see Villac Umu. Chief Priest of the Sun. Why do you come?

PIZARRO: To see the Great Inca.

VILLAC UMU: Why will you see him?

PIZARRO: To give him blessing.

VILLAC UMU: Why will you bless him?

PIZARRO: He is a God. I am a God.

VALVERDE [*protesting sotto voce*]: General!

PIZARRO: Be still.

VILLAC UMU: Below you is the town of Cajamarca. The Great Inca orders: rest there. Tomorrow, early, he will come to you. Do not move from the town. Outside it is his anger.

[*He goes off with his attendants.*]

VALVERDE: What have you done, sir?

PIZARRO: Sent him news to amaze him.

VALVERDE: I cannot approve blasphemy.

PIZARRO: To conquer for Christ, one can surely usurp his name for a night, Father. [*To the men.*] Set on!

9

[*A dreary light. The Spaniards fan out over the stage.* DE SOTO *goes off.*]

OLD MARTIN: So down we went from ledge to ledge, and out onto a huge plain of eucalyptus trees, all glowing in the failing light. And there, at the other end, lay a vast white town with roofs of straw. As night fell, we entered it. We came into an empty square, larger than any in Spain. All round it ran long white buildings, three times the height of a man. Everywhere was grave quiet. You could almost touch the silence. Up on the hill we could see the Inca's tents, and the lights from his fires ringing the valley. [*Exit.*]

[*Some sit. All look up at the hillside.*]

DIEGO: How many do you reckon there's up there?

DE CANDIA: Ten thousand.

DE SOTO [*reentering*]: The town's empty. Not even a dog.

DOMINGO: It's a trap. I know it's a trap!

PIZARRO: Felipillo! Where's that little rat? . . . *Felipillo!*

FELIPILLO: General, Lord.

PIZARRO: What does this mean?

FELIPILLO: I don't know. Perhaps it is order of welcome. Great people. Much honor.

VALVERDE: Nonsense, it's a trick! A brownie trick. He's got us all marked for death.

DE NIZZA: He could have killed us at any time. Why should he take such trouble with us?

PIZARRO: Because we're gods, Father. He'll change soon enough when he finds out different.

DE SOTO: Brace up, boy! It's what you came for, isn't it? Death and glory?

YOUNG MARTIN [*faintly*]: Yes, sir.

PIZARRO: De Soto. De Candia. [*They go to him.*] It's got to be ambush. That's our only hope.

DE SOTO: Round the square?

PIZARRO: Lowers the odds. Three thousand at most.

DE CANDIA: Thirty to one. Not low enough.

PIZARRO: It'll have to do. We're not fighting ten thousand or three. *One man: that's all.* Get him, the rest collapse.

DE SOTO: Even if we can, they'll kill us all to get him back.

PIZARRO: If there's a knife at his throat? It's a risk, sure. But what do worshipers do when you snatch their god?

DE CANDIA: Pray to you instead.

DIEGO: It's wonderful. Grab the King, grab the kingdom!

DE NIZZA: It would avoid bloodshed.

PIZARRO: What do you say?

DE CANDIA: It's the only way. It could work.

DE SOTO: With God's help.

PIZARRO: Then pray all. Disperse. Light fires. Make confession. Battle orders at first light.

[*Most disperse. Some lie down to pray and sleep.*]

DE NIZZA [*to* DE CANDIA]: Shall I hear your confession now, my son?

DE CANDIA: You'd best save all that for tomorrow, Father. For the men who are left. What have we got to confess tonight but thoughts of murder?

DE NIZZA: Then confess those.

DE CANDIA: Why? Should I feel shame for them? What would I say to God if I refused to destroy His enemies?

VALVERDE: More Venetian nonsense!

DE NIZZA: God has no enemies, my son. Only men nearer to Him or farther from Him.

DE CANDIA: Well, my job is to aim at the far ones. I'll go and position the guns. Excuse me. [*He goes off.*]

PIZARRO: Diego, look to the horses. I know they're sorry, but we'll need them brisk.

VALVERDE: Come my brother, we'll pray together.

[*Both priests go too.*]

PIZARRO [*to* DE SOTO]: The cavalry will split and hide in the buildings, there and there.

DE SOTO: And the infantry in file—there, and round there.

PIZARRO: Perfect. Herrada can command one flank, De Barbaran the other. Everyone hidden.

DE SOTO: They'll suspect then.

PIZARRO: No, the Church will greet them.

DE SOTO: We'll need a watchword.

PIZARRO: San Jago.

DE SOTO: San Jago. Good.

[*The old man comes upon his Page who is sitting huddled by himself.*]

PIZARRO: Are you scared?

YOUNG MARTIN: No, sir . . . [*Pause.*] Yes, sir.

PIZARRO: You're a good boy. If ever we get out of this, I'll make you a gift of whatever you ask me. Is that chivalrous enough for you?

YOUNG MARTIN: Being your Page is enough, sir.

PIZARRO: And there's nothing else you want?

YOUNG MARTIN: A sword, sir.

PIZARRO: Of course . . . Take what rest you can. Call Assembly at first light.

YOUNG MARTIN: Yes, sir. Good night, sir.

DE SOTO: Good night, Martin. Try and sleep.

[*The boy lies down to sleep. The singing of prayers is heard, off, all around.*]

PIZARRO: Hope, lovely hope. A sword's no mere bar of metal for him. His world still has sacred objects. How remote . . .

DIEGO [*Praying*]: Holy Virgin, give us victory. If you do, I'll make you a present of a fine Indian cloak. But you let us down, and I'll leave you for the Virgin of the Conception, and I mean that.

[*He lies down also. The prayers die away. Silence.*]

## 10

[*Semidarkness.*]

PIZARRO: This is probably our last night. If we die, what will we have gone for?

DE SOTO: Spain. Christ.

PIZARRO: I envy you, Cavalier.

DE SOTO: For what?

PIZARRO: Your service. God. King. It's all simple for you.

DE SOTO: No, sir, it's not simple. But it's what I've chosen.

PIZARRO: Yes. And what have I chosen?

DE SOTO: To be a King yourself. Or as good, if we win here.

PIZARRO: And what's that at my age? Not only swords turn into bars of metal. Scepters too. What's left, De Soto?

DE SOTO: What you told me in Spain. A name for ballads. The man of honor has three good lives: The Life Today. The Life to Come. The Life of Fame.

PIZARRO: Fame is long. Death is longer. . . . Does anyone ever die for anything? I thought so once. Life was fierce with feeling. It was all hope, like on that boy. Swords shone and armor sang, and cheese bit you, and kissing burned, and death—ah, death was going to make an exception in my case! I couldn't believe I was ever going to die. But once you know it—really know it—it's all over. You know you've been cheated, and nothing's the same again.

DE SOTO: Cheated?

PIZARRO: Time cheats us all the way. Children, yes—having children goes some steps to defeating it. Nothing else. It would have been good to have a son.

DE SOTO: Did you never think to marry?

PIZARRO: With my parentage? The only women who would have had me weren't the sort you married. Spain's a pile of horse dung. . . . When I began to think of a world here, something in me was longing for a new place like a country after rain, washed clear of all the badges and barriers, the pebbles men drop to tell them where they are, on a plain that's got no landmarks. I used to look after women with hope, but they didn't have much time for me. One of them said—what was it?—my soul was frostbitten. That's a word for you—frostbitten. How goes it, man?

VASCA [*off*]: A clear night, sir. Everything clear.

PIZARRO: I had a girl once, on a rock by the southern ocean. I lay with her one afternoon in winter, wrapped up in her against the cold, and the seafowl screaming, and it was the best hour of my life. I felt then that seawater, and bird droppings, and the little pits in human flesh were all linked together for some great end right out of the net of words to catch. Not just my words, but anyone's. Then I lost it. Time came back. For always.

[*He moves away, feeling his side.*]

DE SOTO: Does it pain you?

PIZARRO: Oh, yes: *that's* still fierce.

DE SOTO: You should try to sleep. We'll need our strength.

PIZARRO: Listen! Listen! Everything we feel is made of Time! All the beauties of life are shaped by it. Imagine a fixed sunset: the last note of a song that hung an hour, or a kiss for half of it. Try and halt a moment in our lives and it becomes maggoty at once. Even that word "moment" is wrong, since that would mean a *speck* of time, something you could pick up on a rag and peer at. . . . But that's the awful trap of life. You can't escape maggots unless you go with Time, and if you go, they wriggle in you anyway.

DE SOTO: This is gloomy talk.

[YOUNG MARTIN *groans in his sleep.*]

PIZARRO: For a gloomy time. You were talking women. I loved them with all the juice in me—but oh, the cheat in that tenderness! What is it but a lust to own their beauty, not them, which you never can: like trying to own the beauty of a goblet by paying for it. And even if you could, it would become *you* and get soiled. . . . I'm an old man,

Cavalier, I can explain nothing. What I mean is: Time whipped up the lust in me and Time purged it. I was dandled on Time's knee and made to gurgle, then put to my sleep. I've been cheated from the moment I was born because there's death in everything.

DE SOTO: Except in God.

[*A pause.*]

PIZARRO: When I was young, I used to sit on the slope outside the village and watch the sun go down, and I used to think, if only I could find the place where it sinks to rest for the night, I'd find the source of life, like the beginning of a river. I used to wonder what it could be like. Perhaps an island—a strange place of white sand, where the people never died. Never grew old, or felt pain, and never died.

DE SOTO: Sweet fancy.

PIZARRO: It's what your mind runs to when it lacks instruction. If I had a son, I'd kill him if he didn't read his book. . . . Where does the sun rest at night?

DE SOTO: Nowhere. It's a heavenly body set by God to move round the earth in perpetual motion.

PIZARRO: Do you know this?

DE SOTO: All Europe knows it.

PIZARRO: What if they were wrong? If it settled here each evening, somewhere in those great mountains, like a god laid down to sleep? To a savage mind it must make a fine god. I myself can't fix anything nearer to a thought of worship than standing at dawn and watching it fill the world. Like the coming of something eternal against going flesh. What a fantastic wonder that anyone on earth should dare to say: "That's my father. My father: the sun!" It's silly—but tremendous. . . . You know—strange nonsense: since first I heard of him I've dreamed of him every night. A black King with glowing eyes, sporting the sun for a crown. What does it mean?

DE SOTO: I've no skill with dreams. Perhaps a soothsayer would tell you: "The Inca's your enemy. You dream his emblem to increase your hate."

PIZARRO: But I feel no enemy.

DE SOTO: Surely you do?

PIZARRO: No. Only that of all meetings I have made in my life, this with him is the one I have to make. . . . Maybe it's my death. Or maybe new life. I feel just this: all my days have been a path to this one morning.

OLD MARTIN: The sixteenth of November, 1532. First light, sir.

## 11

[*Lights brighten slowly.*]

VALVERDE [*singing, off*]: Exsurge Domine.

SOLDIERS [*singing in unison*]: Exsurge Domine.

[*All the company comes on, chanting.*]

VALVERDE: Deus meus eripe me de manu peccatoris.

SOLDIERS: Deus meus eripe me de manu peccatoris.

[*All kneel, spread across the stage.*]

VALVERDE: Many strong bulls have compassed me.

DE NIZZA: They have gaped upon me with their mouths, as a lion ravening.

VALVERDE: I am poured out like water, and all my bones are scattered.

DE NIZZA: My heart is like wax, melting in the midst of my bowels. My tongue cleaves to my jaws, and thou hast brought me into the dust of death.

[*All freeze.*]

OLD MARTIN: The dust of death. It was in our noses. The full scare came to us quickly, like plague.

[*All heads turn.*]

Then men were crammed in buildings all round the square.

[*All stand.*]

They stood there shivering, making water where they stood. An hour went by. Two. Three.

[*All remain absolutely still.*]

Five. Not a move from the Indian camp. Not a sound from us. Only the weight of the day. A hundred and sixty men in full armor, cavalry mounted, infantry at the ready, standing in dead silence—glued in a trance of waiting.

PIZARRO: Hold fast now. Come on—you're gods! Take heart. Don't blink your eyes, that's too much noise.

OLD MARTIN: Seven.

PIZARRO: Stiff! Stiff! . . . You're your own masters, boys. Not peasant any more. This is your time. Own it. Live it.

OLD MARTIN: Nine. Ten hours passed. There were few of us then who didn't feel the cold begin to crawl.

PIZARRO [*whispering*]: *Send him, send him, send him, send him!*

OLD MARTIN: Dread comes with the evening air. Even the priest's arm fails.

PIZARRO: The sun's going out!

OLD MARTIN: No one looks at his neighbor. Then—with the shadow of night already running toward us—

YOUNG MARTIN: *They're coming! Look! Down the hill—*

DE SOTO: How many?

YOUNG MARTIN: Hundreds, sir.

DE CANDIA: Thousands—two or three.

PIZARRO: Can you see *him?*

DE CANDIA: No, not yet.

DOMINGO: What's that?—out there in front—they're doing something.

VASCA: Looks like sweeping—

DIEGO [*amazed*]: They're sweeping the road!

DOMINGO: For *him!* They're sweeping the road for him! Five hundred of 'em *sweeping the road!*

SALINAS: God in Heaven!

PIZARRO: Are they armed?

DE CANDIA: To the teeth!

DE SOTO: How?

DE CANDIA: Axes and spears.

YOUNG MARTIN: They're all glittering, glittering red!

DIEGO: It's the sun! Like someone's stabbed it!

VASCA: Squirting blood all over the sky!

DOMINGO: It's an omen!

SALINAS: Shut up!

DOMINGO: It must be. The whole country's bleeding. Look for yourself. *It's an omen!*

VALVERDE: This is the day foretold you by the Angel of the Apocalypse! Satan reigns on the altars, jeering at the true God. The earth teems with corrupt kings!

DOMINGO: Oh, God! Oh, God! Oh, God! Oh, God!

DE SOTO: Control yourself!

DE CANDIA: They're stopping!

YOUNG MARTIN: They're throwing things down, sir!

PIZARRO: What things?

DE CANDIA: Weapons.

PIZARRO: No!

DIEGO: Yes, sir. I can see. All their weapons. They're throwing them down in a pile.

VASCA: They're laying down their arms.

SALINAS: I don't believe it!

VASCA: They are. They are leaving everything!

DOMINGO: It's a miracle.

DE SOTO: Why? *Why?*

PIZARRO [*half laughing*]: *Because we're gods!* You see? You don't approach gods with weapons!

[*Strange music faintly in the distance. Through all the ensuing it grows louder and louder.*]

DE SOTO: What's that?

YOUNG MARTIN: It's *him.* He's coming, sir.

PIZARRO: Where?

YOUNG MARTIN: *There, sir.*

DIEGO: Oh, look, *look.* God Almightly, it's not happening!

DE SOTO: Steady man.

PIZARRO: You're coming! Come on, then! *Come on!*

DE SOTO: General, it's time to hide.

PIZARRO: Yes, quick now. No one must be seen but the priests. Out there in the middle, Fathers: everyone else in hiding.

DE SOTO: Quick! Jump to it!

[*Only now do the men break, scatter, and vanish.*]

PIZARRO [*to* YOUNG MARTIN]: You too.

YOUNG MARTIN: Until the fighting, sir?

PIZARRO: All the time for you, fighting or no.

YOUNG MARTIN: Oh no, sir!

PIZARRO: Do as I say. Take him, De Soto.

DE SOTO: Save you, General.

PIZARRO: And you, De Soto. San Jago!

DE SOTO: San Jago! Come on.

DE CANDIA: There are seven gunners on the roof. And three over there.

PIZARRO: Watch the crossfire.

DE CANDIA: I'll wait for your signal.

PIZARRO: Then sound yours.

DE CANDIA: You'll hear it!

PIZARRO [*to* FELIPILLO]: Felipillo! Stand there! Now . . . now . . . NOW!

[*He hurries off.*]

## 12

[*The music crashes over the stage as the Indian procession enters in an astonishing explosion of color. The King's attendants—many of them playing musical instruments: reed pipes, cymbals, and giant maracas—are as gay as parrots. They wear costumes of orange and yellow, and fantastic headdresses of gold and feathers, with eyes embossed on them in staring black enamel. By contrast,* ATAHUALLPA INCA *presents a picture of utter simplicity. He is dressed from head to foot in white: across his eyes is a mask of jade mosaic, and round his head a circlet of plain gold. Silence falls. The King glares about him.*]

ATAHUALLPA [*Haughtily*]: Where is the god?

VALVERDE [*through* FELIPILLO]: I am a Priest of God.

ATAHUALLPA: I do not want the priest. I want the god. Where is he? He sent me greeting.

VALVERDE: That was our General. Our God cannot be seen.

ATAHUALLPA: *I* may see him.

VALVERDE: No. He was killed by men and went into the sky.

ATAHUALLPA: A god cannot be killed. [*Pointing to the sunset.*] See my father! You cannot kill him. He lives forever and looks over his children every day.

VALVERDE: I am the answer to all mysteries. Hark, pagan, and I will expound.

OLD MARTIN: And so he did, from the Creation to Our Lord's ascension. [*He goes off.*]

VALVERDE [*walking among the Indians to the right*]: And when he went he left the Pope as Regent for him.

DE NIZZA [*walking among the Indians to the left*]: And when he went he left the Pope as Regent for him.

VALVERDE: He has commanded our King to bring all men to belief in the true God.

DE NIZZA: He has commanded our King to bring all men to belief in the true God.

VALVERDE / DE NIZZA [*together*]: In Christ's name therefore I charge you: yield yourself his willing vassal.

ATAHUALLPA: I am the vassal of no man! I am the greatest prince on earth. Your King is great. He has sent you far across the water. So he is my brother. But your Pope is mad. He gives away countries that are not his. His faith also is mad.

VALVERDE: Beware!

ATAHUALLPA: Ware you! You kill my people; you make them slaves. By what power?

VALVERDE: By this. [*He offers a Bible.*] The Word of God.

[ATAHUALLPA *holds it to his ear. He listens intently. He shakes it.*]

ATAHUALLPA: No word. [*He smells the book, and then licks it. Finally he throws it down impatiently.*] God is angry with your insults.

VALVERDE: Blasphemy!

ATAHUALLPA: God is angry!

VALVERDE [*calling*]: Francisco Pizarro, do you stay your hand when Christ is insulted? Let this pagan feel the power of your arm. I absolve you all! San Jago!

[PIZARRO *appears above with drawn sword, and in a great voice sings out his battle cry.*]

PIZARRO: SAN JAGO Y CIERRA ESPAÑA!

[*Instantly from all sides the soldiers rush in, echoing the great cry.*]

SOLDIERS: SAN JAGO!

[*There is a tense pause. The Indians look at this ring of armed men in terror. A violent drumming begins, and there ensues:*

THE MIME OF THE GREAT MASSACRE

*To a savage music, wave upon wave of Indians are slaughtered and rise again to protect their lord, who stands bewildered in their midst. It is all in vain. Relentlessly the Spanish soldiers hew their way through the ranks of feathered attendants toward their quarry. They surround him.* SALINAS *snatches the crown off his head and tosses it up to* PIZARRO, *who catches it and to a great shout crowns himself. All the Indians cry out in horror. The drum hammers on relentlessly while* ATAHUALLPA *is led off at sword point by the whole band of Spaniards. At the same time, dragged from the middle of the sun by howling Indians, a vast bloodstained cloth bellies out over the stage. All rush off; their screams fill the theater. The lights fade out slowly on the rippling cloth of blood.*]

# ACT TWO

## THE KILL

### 1

[*Darkness. A bitter Inca lament is intoned, above. Lights up a little. The bloodstained cloth still lies over the stage. In the sun chamber* ATAHUALLPA *stands in chains, his back to the audience, his white robe dirty with blood. Although he is unmasked, we cannot yet see his face, only a tail of black hair hanging down his neck.*

OLD MARTIN *appears. From opposite,* YOUNG MARTIN *comes in, stumbling with shock. He collapses on his knees.*]

OLD MARTIN: Look at the warrior where he struts. Glory on his sword. Salvation in his new spurs. One of the knights at last. The very perfect knight Sir Martin, tender in virtue, bodyguard of Christ. Jesus, we are all eased out of kids' dreams; but who can be ripped out of them and live loving after? Three thousand Indians we killed in that square. The only Spaniard to be wounded was the General, scratched by a sword while protecting his royal prisoner. That night, as I knelt vomiting into a canal, the empire of the Incas stopped. The spring of the clock was snapped. For a thousand miles men sat down, not knowing what to do.

[*Enter* DE SOTO.]

DE SOTO: Well, boy, what is it? They weren't armed, is that it? If they had been we could be dead now.

YOUNG MARTIN: Honorably dead! Not alive and shamed.

DE SOTO: And Christ would be dead here too, scarcely born. When I first breathed blood, it was in my lungs for days. But the time comes when you won't even sniff when it pours over your feet. See, boy, here and now it's kill or get killed. And if we go, we betray Christ, whose coming we are here to make.

YOUNG MARTIN: You talk as if we're butlers, sent to open the door for him.

DE SOTO: So we are.

YOUNG MARTIN: No! He's with us now—at all times—or never.

DE SOTO: He's with us, yes, but not with them. After he is, there will be time for mercy.

YOUNG MARTIN: When there is no danger! Some mercy!

DE SOTO: Would you put Christ in danger, then?

YOUNG MARTIN: He can look after himself.

DE SOTO: He can't. That's why he needs servants.

YOUNG MARTIN: To kill for him?

DE SOTO: If necessary. And it was. My parish priest used to say: There must always be dying to make new life. I think of that whenever I draw the sword. My constant thought is: I must be winter for Our Lord to be spring.

YOUNG MARTIN: I don't understand.

[PIZARRO *and* FELIPILLO *come in.*]

PIZARRO [*roughly*]: Stand up when the Second addresses you! What are you, a defiled girl? [*To* DE SOTO] I've sent De Candia back to the garrison. Reinforcements should be there presently. Come now: let's meet this King.

## 2

[*Lights up more. They move upstage and bow. Above the women* OELLO *and* INTI COUSSI *come in and kneel on either side of the Inca, who ignores the embassy below.*]

PIZARRO: My lord, I am Francisco Pizarro, General of Spain. It is an honor to speak with you. [*Pause.*] You are very tall, my lord. In my country are no such tall men. [*Pause.*] My lord, won't you speak?

[ATAHUALLPA *turns. For the first time we see his face, carved in a mold of serene arrogance. His whole bearing displays the most entire dignity and natural grace. When he moves or speaks, it is always with the consciousness of his divine origin, his sacred function, and his absolute power.*]

ATAHUALLPA [*to* FELIPILLO]: Tell him I am Atahuallpa Capac, Son of the Sun, Son of the Moon, Lord of the Four Quarters. Why does he not kneel?

FELIPILLO: The Inca says he wishes he had killed you when you first came.

PIZARRO: Why didn't he?

ATAHUALLPA: He lied to me. He is not a god. I came for blessing. He sharpened his knives on the shoulders of my servants. I have no word for *him* whose word is evil.

FELIPILLO: He says he wants to make slaves of your best warriors, then kill all the others. Especially you he would kill because you are old: no use as slave.

PIZARRO: Tell him he will live to rue those intentions.

FELIPILLO: You make my master angry. He will kill you tomorrow. Then he will give that wife [*he indicates* OELLO] to me for my pleasure.

[OELLO *rises in alarm.*]

ATAHUALLPA: How dare you speak this before my face?

YOUNG MARTIN: General.

PIZARRO: What?

YOUNG MARTIN: Excuse me, sir, but I don't think you're being translated aright.

PIZARRO: You don't?

YOUNG MARTIN: No, sir. Nor the King to you. I know a little of the language and he said nothing about slaves.

PIZARRO: You! What are you saying?

FELIPILLO: General Lord. This boy know nothing how to speak.

YOUNG MARTIN: I know more than you think. I know you're lying. . . . He's after the woman, General. I saw him before, in the square, grabbing at her.

PIZARRO: Is that true?

YOUNG MARTIN: As I live, sir.

PIZARRO: What do you say?

FELIPILLO: General Lord, I speak wonderful for you. No one speak so wonderful.

PIZARRO: What about that girl?

FELIPILLO: You give her as present to me, yes?

PIZARRO: The Inca's wife?

FELIPILLO: Inca has many wives. This one small, not famous.

PIZARRO: Get out.

FELIPILLO: General Lord!

PIZARRO: You work another trick like this and I'll swear I'll hang you. Out!

[FELIPILLO *spits at him and runs off.*]

PIZARRO: Could you take his place?

YOUNG MARTIN: With work, sir.

PIZARRO: Work, then. Come, let's make a start. Ask him his age.

YOUNG MARTIN: My lord [*hesitantly*], how old are him? I mean "you."

ATAHUALLPA: I have been on earth thirty and three years. What age is your master?

YOUNG MARTIN: Sixty-three.

ATAHUALLPA: All those years have taught him nothing but wickedness.

YOUNG MARTIN: That's not true.

PIZARRO: What does he say?

YOUNG MARTIN [*diplomatically*]: I don't quite understand, my lord. . . .

[YOUNG MARTIN *bows and goes off.*]

OLD MARTIN: So it was I became the General's interpreter and was privy to everything that passed between them during the next months. The Inca tongue was very hard, but to please my adored master I worked at it for hours, and with each passing day found out more of it.

[PIZARRO *leaves, followed by* DE SOTO.]

## 3

[*Reenter* YOUNG MARTIN *above. He produces a pack of playing cards, and sits on the floor.* OLD MARTIN *watches below before going off.*]

YOUNG MARTIN: Good day, my lord. I have a game here to amuse you. No Spaniard is complete without them. I take half and you take half. Then we fight. These are the Churchmen with their pyxes. The Nobility with their swords. The Merchants with their gold, and the Poor with their sticks.

ATAHUALLPA: What are the poor?

YOUNG MARTIN: Those who've got no gold. They suffer for this.

ATAHUALLPA [*crying out*]: Aiyah!

YOUNG MARTIN: What are you thinking, my lord?

ATAHUALLPA: That my people will suffer.

[*Enter* PIZARRO *and* DE SOTO.]

PIZARRO: Good day, my lord. How are you this morning?

ATAHUALLPA: You want gold. That is why you came here.

PIZARRO: My lord—

ATAHUALLPA: You cannot hide from me. [*Showing him the card of the Poor.*] You want gold. I know. Speak.

PIZARRO: You have gold?

ATAHUALLPA: It is the sweat of the sun. It belongs to me.

PIZARRO: Is there much?

ATAHUALLPA: Make me free. I would fill this room.

PIZARRO: Fill?

DE SOTO: It's not possible.

ATAHUALLPA: I am Atahuallpa and I say it.

PIZARRO: How long?

ATAHUALLPA: Two showings of my Mother Moon. But it will not be done.

PIZARRO: Why not?

ATAHUALLPA: You must swear to free me and you have no swear to give.

PIZARRO: You wrong me, my lord.

ATAHUALLPA: No, it is in your face, no swear.

PIZARRO: I never broke word with you. I never promised you safety. If once I did, you would have it.

ATAHUALLPA: Do you now?

DE SOTO: Refuse, sir. You could never free him.

PIZARRO: It won't come to that.

DE SOTO: It could.

PIZARRO: Never. Can you think how much gold it would take? Even half would drown us in riches.

DE SOTO: General, you can only give your word where you can keep it.

PIZARRO: I'll never have to break it. It's the same case.

DE SOTO: It's not.

PIZARRO: Oh, God's wounds, your niceties! He's offering more than any conqueror has ever seen. Alexander, Tamberlaine, or who you please. I mean to have it.

DE SOTO: So. At your age gold is no lodestone!

PIZARRO: No more is it. I promised my men gold. Yes? He stands between them and that gold. If I don't make this bargain now he'll die; the men will demand it.

DE SOTO: And what's that to you if he does?

PIZARRO: I want him alive. At least for a while.

DE SOTO: You're thinking of how you dreamed of him.

PIZARRO: Yes. He has some meaning for me, this man-god. An immortal man in whom all his people live completely. He has an answer for Time.

DE SOTO: If it was true.

PIZARRO: Yes, if . . .

DE SOTO: General, be careful. I don't understand you in full, but I know this: what you do now can never be undone.

PIZARRO: Words, my dear Cavalier. They don't touch me. This way I'll have gold for my men and him there safe. That's enough for the moment. [*To* ATAHUALLPA.] Now you must keep the peace meanwhile, not strive to escape, nor urge your men to help you. So swear.

ATAHUALLPA: I swear!

PIZARRO: Then I swear too. Fill that room with gold and I will set you free.

DE SOTO: General!

PIZARRO: Oh, come, man! He never will.

DE SOTO: I think this man performs what he swears. Pray God we don't pay bitterly for this.

[*He goes off. Enter* OLD MARTIN.]

PIZARRO: My lord—[ATAHUALLPA *ignores him.*] Well spoken, lad. Your services increase every day.

YOUNG MARTIN: Thank you, sir.

[*The General leaves the stage and the boy goes out of the Sun Chamber, leaving* ATAHUALLPA *alone in it.*]

OLD MARTIN: The room was twenty-two feet long by seventeen feet wide. The mark on the wall was nine feet high.

[*The Inca adopts a pose of command and calls out.*]

ATAHUALLPA: Atahuallpa speaks!

[*A crash of instruments.*]

Atahuallpa needs!

[*Crash.*]

Atahuallpa commands!

[*Crash.*]

Bring him gold. From the palaces. From the temples. From all buildings in the great places. From walls of pleasure and roofs of omen. From floors of feasting and ceilings of death. Bring him the gold of Quito and Pachamacac! [*Drums mark each name.*] Bring him the gold of Cuzco and Coricancha! Bring him the gold of Vilcanota! Bring him the gold of Colae! Of Aymaraes and Arequipa! Bring him the gold of the Chimu! Put up a mountain of gold and free your Sun from his prison of clouds!

[*Lights down above.* ATAHUALLPA *leaves the chamber.*]

OLD MARTIN: It was agreed that the gold collected was not to be melted beforehand into bars, so that the Inca got the benefit of the space between them. Then he was moved out of his prison to make way for the treasure, and given more comfortable state.

## 4

[*Lights fade above, and brighten below. Slowly the great cloth of blood is dragged off by two Indians as* ATAHUALLPA *appears. He advances to the middle of the stage. He claps his hands, once. Immediately a gentle hum is heard and Indians appear with new clothing. From their wrists hang tiny golden cymbals and small bells; to the soft clash and tinkle of these little instruments his servants remove the Inca's bloodstained garments and put clean ones on him.*]

OLD MARTIN: He was allowed to audience his nobles. The little loads they bore were a sign of reverence.

[VILLAC UMU *and* CHALLCUCHIMA *come in.*]

He was dressed in his royal cloak, made from the skins of vampire birds, and his ears were hung again with the weight of noble responsibility.

[ATAHUALLPA *is cloaked, a collar of turquoises is placed round his neck, and heavy gold rings are placed in his ears. While this is happening there is a fresh tinkling and more Indians appear, carrying his meal in musical dishes—plates like tambourines from whose rims hang bells, or in whose lower shelves are tiny golden balls. The stage is filled with chimes and delicate clatter, and above it is the perpetual humming of masked servants.*]

OLD MARTIN: His meals were served as they always had been. I remember his favorite food was stewed lamb, garnished with sweet potatoes.

[*The food is served to the Inca in this manner.* OELLO *takes meat out of a bowl, places it in her hands and* ATAHUALLPA *lowers his face to it, while she turns her own face away from him out of respect.*]

OLD MARTIN: What he didn't eat was burned, and if he spilled any on himself, his clothes were burned also. [*Exit.*]

[OELLO *rises and quietly removes the dish. Suddenly* FELIPILLO *rushes on and knocks it violently from her hand.*]

FELIPILLO: You're going to burn it? Why? Because your husband is a god? How stupid! stupid! stupid!

[*He grabs her and flings her to the ground. A general cry of horror.*]

[*To* ATAHUALLPA.] Yes, I touch her! Make me dead! You are a god. Make me dead with your eyes!

VILLAC UMU: What you have said kills you. You will be buried in the earth alive.

[*A pause. For a moment* FELIPILLO *half believes this. Then he laughs and kisses the girl on the throat. As she screams and struggles,* YOUNG MARTIN *rushes in.*]

YOUNG MARTIN: Felipillo—stop!

[VALVERDE *comes in from another side, with* DE NIZZA.]

VALVERDE: Felipillo! Is it for this we saved you from Hell? Your old god encouraged lust. Your new God will damn you for it. Leave him!

[FELIPILLO *runs off*.]

[*To the* INDIANS.] Go!

[*A pause. No one moves until* ATAHUALLPA *claps his hands twice. Then all the servants bow and leave. Young* MARTIN *interprets, but by now using the hand movements very unobtrusively*.]

Now, my lord, let us take up our talk again. Tell me—I am only a simple priest—as an undoubted god, do you live forever here on earth?

VILLAC UMU: Here on earth gods come one after another, young and young again, to protect the people of the Sun. Then they go up to his great place in the sky, at his will.

VALVERDE: What if they are killed in battle?

VILLAC UMU: If it is not the Sun's time for them to go, he will return them to life again in the next day's light.

VALVERDE: How comforting. And has any Inca so returned?

VILLAC UMU: No.

VALVERDE: Curious.

VILLAC UMU: This means only that all Incas have died in the Sun's time.

VALVERDE: Clever.

VILLAC UMU: No. True.

VALVERDE: Tell me this, how can the Sun have a child?

VILLAC UMU: How can your god have a child, since you say he has no body?

VALVERDE: He is spirit—inside us.

VILLAC UMU: Your god is inside you? How can this be?

ATAHUALLPA: They eat him. First he becomes a biscuit, and then they eat him. [*The Inca bares his teeth and laughs soundlessly*.] I have seen this. At praying they say "This is the body of our God." Then they drink his blood. [*Loftily*.] It is very bad. Here in my empire we do not eat men. My family forbade it many years past.

VALVERDE: You are being deliberately stupid.

VILLAC UMU: Why do you eat your god? To have his strength?

DE NIZZA: Yes, my lord.

VILLAC UMU: But your god is weak. He fights with no man. That is why he was killed.

DE NIZZA: He wanted to be killed, so he could share death with us.

ATAHUALLPA: So he needed killers to help him, though you say killing is bad.

VALVERDE: This is the Devil's tongue.

DE NIZZA: My lord must see that when God becomes man, he can no longer act perfectly.

ATAHUALLPA: Why?

DE NIZZA: He joins us in the prison of our sin.

ATAHUALLPA: What is sin?

DE NIZZA: Let me picture it to you as a prison cell, the bars made of our imperfections. Through them we glimpse a fair country where it is always morning. We wish we could walk there, or else forget the place entirely. But we cannot snap the bars, or if we do, others grow in their stead.

ATAHUALLPA: All your pictures are of prisons and chains.

DE NIZZA: All life is chains. We are chained to food, and fire in the winter. To innocence lost but its memory unlost. And to needing each other.

ATAHUALLPA: I need no one.

DE NIZZA: That is not true.

ATAHUALLPA: I am the Sun. I need only the sky.

DE NIZZA: That is not true, Atahuallpa. The sun is a ball of fire. Nothing more.

ATAHUALLPA: *How?*

DE NIZZA: Nothing more.

[*With terrible speed, the* INCA *rises to strike* DE NIZZA.]

VALVERDE: Down! Do you dare lift your hand against a priest? Sit! Now!

[ATAHUALLPA *does not move.*]

DE NIZZA: You do not feel your people, my lord, because you do not love them.

ATAHUALLPA: Explain—love.

DE NIZZA: It is not known in your kingdom. At home we can say to our ladies, "I love you," or to our native earth. It means we rejoice in their lives. But a man cannot say this to the woman he must marry at twenty-five; or to the strip of land allotted to him at birth which he must till till he dies. Love must be free, or else it alters away. Command it to your court: it will send a deputy. Let God order it to fill our hearts, it becomes useless to him. It is stronger than iron: yet in a fist of force it melts. It is a coin that sparkles in the hand; yet in the pocket it turns to rust. Love is the only door from the prison of ourselves. It is the eagerness of God to enter that prison: to take on pain, and imagine lust, so that the torn soldier, or the spent lecher, can call out in his defeat, "You know this too, so help me from it."

[*A further music of bells and humming. Enter* OLD MARTIN.]

## THE FIRST GOLD PROCESSION

[*Guarded closely by Spanish soldiers, a line of Indian porters comes in, each carrying a stylized gold object: utensils and ornaments. They cross the stage and disappear. Almost simultaneously, above, similar objects are hung up by Indians in the middle of the sun.*]

OLD MARTIN [*during this*]: The first gold arrived. Much of it was in big plates weighing up to seventy-five pounds, the rest in objects of amazing skill. Knives of ceremony; collars and fretted crowns; funeral gloves, and red-stained death masks, goggling at us with profound enamel eyes. Some days there were things worth thirty or forty gold pesos— but we weren't satisfied with that. [*Exit.*]

[*Enter* PIZARRO *and* DE SOTO.]

PIZARRO: Atahuallpa, I find you wanting in honesty. A month has passed: the room isn't a quarter full.

ATAHUALLPA: My kingdom is great; porters are slow. You will see more gold before long.

PIZARRO: The rumor is we'll see a rising before long.

ATAHUALLPA: Not a leaf stirs in my kingdom without my leave. If you do not trust me, send to Cuzco, my capital. See how quiet my people sit.

PIZARRO [*to* DE SOTO]: Good. You leave immediately with a force of thirty.

CHALLCUCHIMA: God is tied by his word, like you. But if he raised one nail of one finger of one hand, you would all die that same raising.

PIZARRO [*to* ATAHUALLPA]: So be it. If you play us false, both these will die before us.

ATAHUALLPA: There are many priests, many generals. These can die.

VALVERDE: Mother of God! There's no conversion possible for this man.

DE SOTO: You cannot say that, sir.

VALVERDE: Satan has many forms and there sits one! As for his advisers, it is you, Priest, who stiffen him against me. You, General, who whisper revolt.

CHALLCUCHIMA: You lie.

VALVERDE: Leave him!

[*As before, they do not move until* ATAHUALLPA *has clapped his hands twice. Then, immediately, the two Indians bow and leave.*]

Pagan filth.

DE SOTO: I'll make inspection. Goodbye, my lord, we'll meet in a month. [*Exit* DE SOTO.]

VALVERDE: Beware, Pizarro. Give him the slack, he will destroy us all. [*He goes out another way.*]

DE NIZZA: The Father has great zeal.

PIZARRO: Oh yes, great zeal to see the Devil in a poor dark man.

DE NIZZA: Not so poor, General. A man who is the soul of his kingdom. Look hard, you *will* find Satan here, because here is a country which denies the right to hunger.

PIZARRO: You call hunger a *right?*

DE NIZZA: Of course. It gives life meaning. Look around you: happiness has no feel for men here since they are forbidden unhappiness. They have everything in common so they have nothing to give each other. They are part of the seasons, no more; as indistinguishable as mules, as predictable as trees. All men are born unequal: this is a divine gift. And want is their birthright. Where you deny this and there is no hope of any new love—where tomorrow is abolished, and no man ever thinks "I can change myself"—there you have the rule of Anti-Christ. Atahuallpa, I will not rest until I have brought you to the true God.

ATAHUALLPA: No! He is not true! . . . Where is he? *There* is my Father-*Sun!* You see now only by his wish—yet try to see into him and he will darken your eyes forever! With hot burning he pulls up the corn and we feed. With cold burning he shrinks it and we starve. These are his burnings and our life. Do not speak to me again of your god. He is nowhere.

[PIZARRO *laughs. Hurriedly* DE NIZZA *leaves.* YOUNG MARTIN *stays on.*]

5

PIZARRO: You said you'd hear the Holy Men.

ATAHUALLPA: They are fools.

PIZARRO: They are not fools.

ATAHUALLPA: Do you believe them?

PIZARRO: For certain.

ATAHUALLPA: Look into me.

PIZARRO: Your eyes are smoking wood.

ATAHUALLPA: You do not believe them.

PIZARRO: You dare not say that to me . . .

ATAHUALLPA: You do not believe them. Their god is not in your face.

[PIZARRO *retreats from* ATAHUALLPA, *who begins to sing in a strange voice:*]

You must not rob, O little finch.
The harvest maize, O little finch.

The trap is set, O little finch.
To seize you quick, O little finch!

Ask that black bird, O little finch.
Nailed on a branch, O little finch.
Where is her heart, O little finch?
Where are her plumes, O little finch?

She is cut up, O little finch.
For stealing grain, O little finch.
See, see the fate, O little finch.
Of robber birds, O little finch!

This is a harvest song. For you.

PIZARRO: For me?

ATAHUALLPA: Yes.

PIZARRO: Robber birds.

ATAHUALLPA: Yes.

PIZARRO: You're a robber bird yourself.

ATAHUALLPA: Explain this.

PIZARRO: You killed your brother to get the throne.

ATAHUALLPA: He was a fool. His body was a man. His head was a child.

PIZARRO: But he was the rightful King.

ATAHUALLPA: I was the rightful god. My Sky Father shouted "Rise up! In you lives your Earth Father, Huayana the Warrior. Your brother is fit only to tend herds, but you were born to tend my people." So I killed him, and the land smiled.

PIZARRO: That was my work long ago. Tending herds.

ATAHUALLPA: It was not your work. You are a warrior. It is in your face.

PIZARRO: You see much in my face.

ATAHUALLPA: I see my father.

PIZARRO: You do me honor, lad.

ATAHUALLPA: Speak true. If in your home your brother was King, but fit only for herds, would you take his crown?

PIZARRO: If I could.

ATAHUALLPA: And then you would kill him.

PIZARRO: No.

ATAHUALLPA: If you could not keep it for fear of his friends, unless he was dead, you would kill him.

PIZARRO: Let me give you another case. If I come to a country and seize the King's crown, but for fear of his friends cannot keep it unless I kill him, what do I do?

ATAHUALLPA: So.

PIZARRO: So.

[ATAHUALLPA *moves away, offended.*]

Oh, it is only a game we play! Tell me—did you hate your brother?

ATAHUALLPA: No. He was ugly like a llama, like his mother. My mother was beautiful.

PIZARRO: I did not know my mother. She was not my father's wife. She left me at the church door for anyone to find. There's talk in the village still, how I was suckled by a sow.

ATAHUALLPA: You are not then . . . ?

PIZARRO: Legitimate? No, my lord. No more than you.

ATAHUALLPA: So.

PIZARRO: So.

[*A pause.*]

ATAHUALLPA: To be born so is a sign for a great man.

PIZARRO [*smiling*]: I think so too.

[ATAHUALLPA *removes one of his golden earrings and hangs it on* PIZARRO'*s ear.*]

And what is that?

ATAHUALLPA: The sign of a nobleman. Only the most important men may wear them. The most near to me.

YOUNG MARTIN: Very becoming, sir. Look.

[*He hands him a dagger. The General looks at himself in the blade.*]

PIZARRO: I have never seemed so distinguished to myself. I thank you.

ATAHUALLPA: Now you must learn the dance of the *aylu.*

YOUNG MARTIN: The dance of a nobleman, sir.

ATAHUALLPA: Only he can do this. I will show you.

[PIZARRO *sits.* ATAHUALLPA *dances a ferocious mime of a warrior killing his foes. It is very difficult to execute, demanding great litheness and physical stamina. As suddenly as it began, it is over.*]

You dance.

PIZARRO: I can't dance, lad.

ATAHUALLPA [*imperiously*]: *You dance!*

[*He sits to watch. Seeing there is no help for it,* PIZARRO *rises and clumsily tries to copy the dance. The effect is so grotesque that* YOUNG MARTIN *cannot help laughing. The General tries again, lunges, slips, slides, and finally starts to laugh himself. He gives up the attempt.*]

PIZARRO [*to* ATAHUALLPA]: You make me laugh! [*In sudden wonder.*] *You make me laugh!*

[ATAHUALLPA *consults his young interpreter, who tries to explain. The Inca nods gravely. Tentatively* PIZARRO *extends his hand to him.* ATAHUALLPA *takes it and rises. Quietly they go off together.*]

## 6

[*Enter* OLD MARTIN.]

OLD MARTIN: Slowly the pile increased. The Army waited nervously and licked its lips. Greed began to rise in us like a tide of sea.

[*A music of bells and humming.*]

### THE SECOND GOLD PROCESSION AND THE RAPE OF THE SUN

[*Another line of Indian porters comes in, bearing gold objects. Like the first, this installment of treasure is guarded by Spanish soldiers, but they are less disciplined now. Two of them assault an Indian and grab his headdress. Another snatches a necklace at sword point.*

*Above, in the chamber, the treasure is piled up as before.* DIEGO *and the* CHAVEZ *brothers are seen supervising. They begin to explore the sun itself, leaning out of the chamber and prodding at the petals with their halberds. Suddenly* DIEGO *gives a cry of triumph, drives his halberd into a slot in one of the rays, and pulls out the gold inlay. The sun gives a deep groan, like the sound of a great animal being wounded. With greedy yelps, all the soldiers below rush at the sun and start pulling it to bits; they tear out the gold inlays and fling them on the ground, while terrible groans fill the air. In a moment only the great gold frame remains; a broken, blackened sun.*

*Enter* DE SOTO.]

DIEGO: Welcome back, sir.

DE SOTO: Diego, it's good to see you.

DIEGO: What's it like, sir? Is there trouble?

DE SOTO: It's grave quiet. Terrible. Men just standing in fields for hundreds of miles. Waiting for their god to come back to them.

DIEGO: Well, if he does they'll be fighters again, and we're for the limepit.

DE SOTO: How's the General?

DIEGO: An altered man. No one's ever seen him so easy. He spends hours each day with the King. He's going to find it hard when he has to do it.

DE SOTO: Do what?

DIEGO: Kill him, sir.

DE SOTO: He can't do that. Not after a contract witnessed before a whole Army.

DIEGO: Well, he can't let him go, that's for certain. . . . Never mind, he'll find a way. He's as cunning as the Devil's granddad, save your pardon, sir.

DE SOTO: No, you're right, boy.

DIEGO: Tell us about their capital, then. What's it like?

[*During the preceding, a line of Indians, bent double, has been loaded with the torn-off petals from the sun. Now, as* DE SOTO *describes Cuzco, they file slowly round the stage and go off, staggering under the weight of the great gold slabs. When he reaches the account of the garden, the marvelous objects he tells of appear in the treasure chamber above, borne by Indians, and are stacked up until they fill it completely. The interior of the sun is now a solid mass of gold.*]

DE SOTO: Completely round. They call it the navel of the earth and that's what it looks like. In the middle was a huge temple, the center of their faith. The walls were plated with gold, enough to blind us. Inside, set out on tables, golden platters for the sun to dine off. Outside, the garden: acres of gold soil planted with gold maize. Entire apple trees in gold. Gold birds on the branches. Gold geese and ducks. Gold butterflies in the air on silver strings. And—imagine this—away in a field, life-size, twenty golden llamas grazing with their kids. The garden of the Sun at Cuzco. A wonder of the earth. . . . Look at it now.

DIEGO [*rushing in below*]: Hey! The room's full!

DOMINGO: It isn't!

SALINAS: It is. Look!

JUAN: He's right. It's *full!*

DIEGO: We can start the share-out now! [*Cheers.*]

PEDRO: What'll you do with your lot, Juan, boy?

JUAN: Buy a farm.

PEDRO: Me, too. I don't work for nobody ever again.

DOMINGO: Ah, you can buy a palace, easy, with a share of that. Never mind a pissing farm! What d'you say, Diego?

DIEGO: Oh, I want a farm. A good stud farm, and a stable of Arabs just for me to ride! What will you have, Salinas?

SALINAS: Me? A bash-house! [*Laughter.*] Right in the middle of Trujillo, open six to six, filled with saddle-backed little fillies from Andalusia! . . .

[*Enter* VASCA *rolling a huge gold sun, like a hoop.*]

VASCA: Look what I got, boys! The sun! . . . He ain't public any more, the old sun. He's private property!

DOMINGO: There's no private property, till share-out.

VASCA: Well, here's the exception. I risked my life to get this, a hundred feet up!

JUAN: Dungballs!

VASCA: I did! Off the temple roof.

PEDRO: Come on, boy, get it up there with the rest.

VASCA: No. Finding's keepings. That's the law.

JUAN: What law?

VASCA: My law! Do you think you'll see any of this once the share-out starts? Not on your pissing life! You leave it up there, boy, you won't see nothing again.

PEDRO [*to his brother*]: He's right there.

JUAN: Do you think so?

VASCA: Of course. Officers first, then the Church. You'll get pissing nothing. [*A pause.*]

SALINAS: So let's have a share-out now, then!

DOMINGO: Why not? We're all entitled.

VASCA: Of course we are.

JUAN: All right. I'm with you!

PEDRO: Good boy!

SALINAS: Come on, then!

[*They all make a rush for the Sun Chamber.* DE SOTO *interposes himself.*]

DE SOTO: Where do you think you're going?! . . . You know the General's orders. Nothing till share-out. Penalty for breach, death. . . . Disperse now. I'll go and see the General.

[*They hesitate.*]

[*Quietly*] Get to your posts.

[*Reluctantly, they disperse.*]

And keep a sharp watch. The danger's not over yet.

DIEGO: I'd say it had only just begun, sir.

[*He goes.* DE SOTO *remains.*]

## 7

[*Enter* PIZARRO *and* ATAHUALLPA *dueling furiously;* YOUNG MARTIN *behind. The Inca is a magnificent fighter and launches himself vigorously on the old man, finally knocking the sword from his hand.*]

PIZARRO: Enough! You exhaust me . . .

ATAHUALLPA: I fight well—"ye-es"? [*From the difficulty he has with this word, it is evident that it is in Spanish.*]

PIZARRO [*imitating him*]: "Ye-es"! . . . Like a hidalgo!

YOUNG MARTIN: Magnificent, my lord.

PIZARRO: I'm proud of you.

ATAHUALLPA [*calling*]: Chica!

YOUNG MARTIN: Maize wine, sir.

PIZARRO: De Soto! A drink, my dear Second.

DE SOTO: With pleasure. General, the room is full.

PIZARRO [*casually*]: I know it.

DE SOTO: My advice to you is to share out right away. The men are just on the turn.

PIZARRO: I think so too.

DE SOTO: We daren't delay.

PIZARRO: Agreed. Now I shall astound you, Cavalier. Atahuallpa, you have learned how a Spaniard fights. Now you will learn his honor. Martin, your pen. [*Dictating*] "Let this be known throughout my Army. The Inca Atahuallpa has today discharged his obligation to General Pizarro. He is therefore a free man."

DE SOTO [*toasting him*]: My lord, your freedom!

[ATAHUALLPA *kneels. Silently he mouths words of gratitude to the sun.*]

ATAHUALLPA: Atahuallpa thanks the lord De Soto, the lord Pizarro, all lords of honor. You may touch my joy.

[*He extends his arms. Both Spaniards help to raise him.*]

DE SOTO: What happens now?

PIZARRO: I release him. He must swear first, of course, not to harm us.

DE SOTO: Do you think he will?

PIZARRO: For me he will.

ATAHUALLPA [*curious: to the boy*]: What is that you have done?

YOUNG MARTIN: Writing, my lord.

ATAHUALLPA: Explain this.

YOUNG MARTIN: These are signs: This is "Atahuallpa," and this is "ransom."

ATAHUALLPA: You put this sign, and he will see and know "ransom"?

YOUNG MARTIN: Yes.

ATAHUALLPA: No.

YOUNG MARTIN: Yes, my lord. I'll do it again.

ATAHUALLPA: Here, on my nail. Do not say what you put.

[YOUNG MARTIN *writes on his nail.*]

YOUNG MARTIN: Now show it to Cavalier de Soto.

[*He does so.* DE SOTO *reads and whispers the word to* ATAHUALLPA.]

ATAHUALLPA [*to the boy*]: What is put?

YOUNG MARTIN: God.

ATAHUALLPA [*amazed*]: God! . . . [*He stares at his nail in fascination then bursts into delighted laughter, like a child.*] Show me again! Another sign!

[*The boy writes on another nail.*]

PIZARRO: Tell Salinas to take five hundred Indians and melt everything down.

DE SOTO: Everything?

PIZARRO: We can't transport it as it is.

DE SOTO: But there are objects of great beauty, sir. In all my service I've never seen treasure like this. Work subtler than anything in Italy.

PIZARRO: You're a tender man.

ATAHUALLPA [*extending his nail to* PIZARRO]: What is put?

PIZARRO [*who of course cannot read*]: Put?

ATAHUALLPA: Here.

PIZARRO: This is a foolish game.

YOUNG MARTIN: The General never learned the skill, my lord. [*An embarrassed pause.*] A soldier does not need it.

[ATAHUALLPA *stares at him.*]

ATAHUALLPA: A King needs it! There is great power in these marks. *You* are the King in this room. You must teach us two. We will learn together—like brothers!

PIZARRO: You would stay with me here, to learn?

[*Pause.*]

ATAHUALLPA: No. Tomorrow I will go.

PIZARRO: And then? What will you do then?

ATAHUALLPA: I will not hurt you.

PIZARRO: Or my Army?

ATAHUALLPA: That I do not swear.

PIZARRO: You must.

ATAHUALLPA: You do not say this till now.

PIZARRO: Well, now I say it. Atahuallpa, you must swear to me that you will not hurt a man in my Army if I let you go.

ATAHUALLPA: I will not swear this.

PIZARRO: For my sake.

ATAHUALLPA: Three thousand of my servants they killed in the square! Three thousand, without arms. I will avenge them.

PIZARRO: There is a way of mercy, Atahuallpa.

ATAHUALLPA: It is not my way. It is not your way.

PIZARRO: Well, show it to me, then!

ATAHUALLPA: Keep your swear first.

PIZARRO: That I cannot do.

ATAHUALLPA: *Cannot?*

PIZARRO: Not immediately. . . . You must see: you are many, we are few.

ATAHUALLPA: This is not important.

PIZARRO: To me it is.

[ATAHUALLPA *hisses with fury. He strides across the room and before* PIZARRO's *face makes a violent gesture with his hand between their two mouths.*]

ATAHUALLPA [*violently*]: You gave a *word!*

PIZARRO: And will keep it! . . . Only not now. Not today.

ATAHUALLPA: When?

PIZARRO: Soon.

ATAHUALLPA: When?

PIZARRO: Very soon.

ATAHUALLPA [*falling on his knees and beating the ground*]: *When!*

PIZARRO: As soon as you promise not to hurt my Army.

ATAHUALLPA [*with wild rage*]: I will kill every man of them! I will make drums of their bodies! I will beat music on them at my great feasts!

PIZARRO [*provoked*]: Boy—what have I put?

YOUNG MARTIN: "He is therefore a free man."

PIZARRO: Continue: "But for the welfare of the country, he will remain for the moment as guest of the Army."

DE SOTO: What does that mean?

ATAHUALLPA: What does he say?

PIZARRO: Don't translate.

DE SOTO: So it's started. My warning was nothing to you.

PIZARRO: Well, gloat, gloat!

DE SOTO: I don't gloat.

ATAHUALLPA: What does he say?

PIZARRO: Nothing.

ATAHUALLPA: There is fear in his face!

PIZARRO: *Be quiet!* . . . [*to* DE SOTO.] I want all the gold in blocks! Leave nothing unmelted. Attend to it yourself, *personally!*

[DE SOTO *goes abruptly.* OLD MARTIN *appears in the background.* PIZARRO *is trembling.*]

[*To the* PAGE.] Well, what are you staring at, Little Lord Chivalry? Get out!

YOUNG MARTIN: He trusts you, sir.

PIZARRO: Trust: what's that? Another word! Honor . . . glory . . . trust: your word-Gods!

YOUNG MARTIN: You can see it, sir. He trusts you.

PIZARRO: I told you: out.

YOUNG MARTIN [*greatly daring*]: You can't betray him, sir. You can't.

PIZARRO: Damn you—impertinence!

YOUNG MARTIN: I don't care, sir. You just can't! [*He stops.*]

PIZARRO [*coldly*]: In all your study of those admirable writers, you never learned the duty a Page owes his master. I am sorry you have not better fulfilled your first office. There will be no other.

[*The boy makes to go out.*]

A salute, if you please.

[*He bows.*]

Time was when we couldn't stop you.

[YOUNG MARTIN *leaves.* PIZARRO *stares after him, shaking.*]

OLD MARTIN: I went out into the night—the cold high night of the Andes, hung with stars like crystal apples—and dropped my first tears as a man. My first and last. That was my first and last worship too. Devotion never came again. [*Exit.*]

[*With a moan,* PIZARRO *collapses on the floor and lies writhing in pain.* ATAHUALLPA *contemplates his captor with surprised disdain. But slowly, as the old man's agony continues, contempt in the King is replaced by a gentler emotion. Curious, he kneels. Uncertain what to do, he extends his hands, first to the wound, and then to* PIZARRO's *head, which he holds with a kind of remote tenderness. The lights go down all around them.*]

PIZARRO: Leave it now. There's no cure or more easing for it. Death's entered the house, you see. It's half down already, like an old barn. What can you know about that? Youth's in you like a spring of blood, to spurt forever. Your skin is singing: "I will never get old." But it will. Time is stalking you, as I did. That gold flesh will cold and blacken. Your eyes will curdle—those wet living eyes. . . . They'll make a mummy of your body—I know the custom—and wrap you in robes of vicuna wool, and carry you through all your empire down to Cuzco. And then they'll fold you in two and sit you on a chair in darkness. . . . *Atahuallpa, I'm going to die!* And the thought of that dark has for years rotted everything for me, all simple joy in life. All through old age, which is so much longer and more terrible than anything in youth, I've watched the circles of nature with hatred. The leaves pop out, the leaves fall. Every year it's piglet time, calving time, time for children in a gush of blood and water. Women dote on this. A birth, any birth, fills them with love. They clap with love, and my soul shrugs. Round and round is all I see: an endless sky of birds, flying and ripping and nursing their young to fly and rip and nurse their young—*for what?* Listen, boy. That prison the priest calls Sin Original, I know as Time. And seen in Time everything is trivial. Pain. Good. God is trivial in that seeing. Trapped in this cage we cry out, "There's a jailer; there must be. At the last, last, last of lasts he will let us out. He will! He will!" . . . But, oh, my boy, no one will come for all our crying. [*Pause.*] I'm going to kill you, Atahuallpa. What does it matter? Words kept, words broken, it all means nothing. Nothing. You go to sleep earlier than me, that's all. Do you see? Look at your eyes, like coals from the sun, glowing forever in the deep of your skull. Like my dream. . . . Sing me your little song. [*Singing*] "O little finch . . ."

[ATAHUALLPA *intones a few lines of the song.*]

Nothing. Nothing . . . [*In sudden anguish, almost hatred.*] Oh, lad, what am I going to do with you?

## 8

[*A red light up above.* OLD MARTIN *appears above in the Sun Chamber. Violent music, the sound of destruction. The light fades and comes up on stage where the soldiers assemble.*]

OLD MARTIN: Nine forges were kept alight for three weeks. The masterwork of centuries was banged down into fat bars, four hundred and forty pounds each day. The booty exceeded all other known in history: the sack of Genoa, Milan, or even Rome. Share-out started at once.

[*Exit.*]

DIEGO: General Francisco Pizarro, 57,220 gold pesos. Hernando de Soto, 17,740 gold pesos. The Holy Church 2,220 gold pesos.

[*Enter* ESTETE *and* DE CANDIA.]

ESTETE: And a fifth of everything, of course, to the crown!

PIZARRO: You come in good time, Veedor.

ESTETE: So it seems! Cavalier.

DE SOTO: Veedor.

PIZARRO: Welcome, De Candia.

DE CANDIA: Thank you. [*Indicating the earring.*] I see the living's become soft here already. The men hung with jewels like fops at court.

PIZARRO: You set the fashion: I only follow.

DE CANDIA: I'm flattered.

PIZARRO: What news of the reinforcements?

DE CANDIA: None.

ESTETE: I sent runners back to the coast. They saw nothing.

PIZARRO: So we're cut off, here. How's my garrison?

DE CANDIA: Spanish justice reigns supreme. They hang Indians for everything. How's your royal friend? When do we hang him?

[*Pause.* PIZARRO *tears off his earring and flings it on the floor.*]

PIZARRO: Finish the share-out.

[*Violently he leaves them. The men stare after him.*]

DE SOTO: Go on, Diego. Tell us the rest. . . . *Go on,* man!

DIEGO: The remainder—cavalry, infantry, clerks, farriers, coopers, and the like—will divide a total of 971,000 gold pesos!

[*Cheers. Enter* RODAS.]

SALINAS: Well, look. Our little tailor! How are you, friend?

RODAS: Hungry. What do I get?

SALINAS: A kick up the tunnel.

RODAS: Ha, ha. Day of a hundred jokes! I got a right to a share.

DOMINGO: What for?

RODAS: I stayed behind and guarded your pissing rear, that's what for!

DE SOTO: You've no right, Rodas. As far as you cared we could all rot, remember? Well, now you get nothing: the proper wage for cowardice.

[*General agreement. The men settle upstage to a game of dice.*]

[*To* ESTETE.] I must wait on the General.

ESTETE: I am sorry to see him still subject to distresses. I had hoped that victory would have brought him calmer temper.

DE CANDIA: It must be his new wealth, Veedor. So much, so sudden, must be a great burden to him.

DE SOTO: The burdens of the General, sir, are care for his men, and for our present situation. Let us try to lighten them for him as we can. [*He goes off.*]

DE CANDIA: Let us indeed. One throat cut and we're all lightened . . .

ESTETE: It would much relieve the crown if you'd cut it.

DE CANDIA: If I . . . ? You mean I'm not Spanish. I don't have to trouble with honor.

ESTETE: You're not a subject. It could be disowned by my King. And you have none.

DE CANDIA: So the Palace of Disinterest has a shithouse after all! Look, man, you're the overseer here, so do your job. Go to the General and tell him the brownie must go. And add this from me: if Spain waits any longer, Venice will act for herself.

[*They go off. Enter* OLD MARTIN.]

## 9

[*A scene of tension and growing violence. The soldiers, now dirty almost beyond recognition, but wearing ornaments, earrings, and headdresses stolen from the treasure, dice for gold. They are watched silently from above by a line of seated Indians carrying instruments for making bird noises. A drum begins to beat.* PIZARRO *stumbles in, and during the whole ensuing scene limps to and fro across the stage like a caged animal, ignoring everything but his own mental pain.*]

OLD MARTIN: Morale began to go fast. Day after day we watched his private struggle, and the brownies watched us, waiting one sign from the frozen boy to get up and kill the lot of us.

DOMINGO: Play up, then!

PEDRO: Two fours.

[JUAN *throws successfully.*]

JUAN [*grabbing a gold bar belonging to* PEDRO]: That's mine, boy!

PEDRO: No—Juan!

JUAN: Give it! [*He snatches it.*]

DOMINGO: They say there's an army gathering in the mountains. At least five thousand of them.

VASCA: I heard that too.

DOMINGO: Blas says there's some of them cannibals.

[*Bird cries.*]

SALINAS: That's just stories. Pissing stupid stories. You don't want to listen to 'em.

RODAS: I'd like to see you when they tie you to the spit.

VASCA [*rolling the dice*]: Turn up! Turn up! Turn up!

RODAS: Come on, boys, cut me in.

VASCA: Piss off! No stake, no play.

RODAS: Bloody bastards!

DOMINGO: They say it's led by the Inca's top general. The brownies are full of his name.

VASCA: What is it? Rumi . . . Rumi . . . ?

DOMINGO: That's it. Ruminagui, something like that.

[*The Indians above repeat the name in a low menacing chant:* RUMIN-Ã-GUI! *The soldiers look fearfully about them. The bird cries sound again.*]

SALINAS: Come on, then, let's play.

VASCA: What for? The sun?

SALINAS: The sun!

VASCA: Turn up! Turn up! Turn up! Turn up! [*He throws.*] King and ten. Beat that!

SALINAS: Holy Mary, Mother of Christ, save my soul and bless my dice! [*He throws.*] Two Kings . . . I did it! I'm sorry, lads, but that's your sun gone.

VASCA: Go on, then. Let's see you pick it up.

[SALINAS *bends and tries to shift the huge gold wheel.* VASCA *laughs. The bird cries grow wilder.*]

RODAS: He can't even lift it, but I can't play!

SALINAS: I'll settle for these.

[*He picks up three gold bars and walks off with them.* RODAS *trips him up and he goes sprawling.*]

Christ damn you, Rodas—that's the pissing last I take from you!

[*He springs at* RODAS *and clouts him with a gold bar. The tailor howls, picks up another, and a fight starts between them which soon becomes a violent free-for-all. The men shout; the birds scream; the General paces to and fro, ignoring everything. Finally* DE SOTO *rushes on just in time as* SALINAS *tries to strangle* RODAS. *He is followed by* ESTETE *and the two priests, who attend to the wounded.*]

DE SOTO: *Stop this!* . . . Do you want to start it all off?

[*Silence. All the Indians rise, above. Uneasily the soldiers stare up at them.*]

You—night watch! You, you go with him! You take the east gate! The rest to quarters. Move!

[*They disperse.* ESTETE *and the priests remain.*]

10

DE SOTO [*to* PIZARRO]: Mutiny's smoking. Act now or it'll be a blaze you'll not put out.

PIZARRO: What do I do?

DE SOTO: Take our chances, what else *can* we do? You have to let him go.

PIZARRO: And what happens then? A tiny Army is wiped out in five minutes, and the whole story lost for always. Later someone else will conquer Peru, and no one will even remember my name.

DE SOTO: What kind of name will they remember if you kill him?

PIZARRO: A conqueror. That at least.

DE SOTO: A man who butchered his prisoner after giving his word. There's a name for your ballads.

PIZARRO: I'll never live to hear them. What do I care? What does it matter? Whatever I do, what does it matter?

DE SOTO: Nothing, if you don't feel it. But I think you do.

PIZARRO: Let me understand you. As Second-in-Command, you counsel certain death for this Army?

DE SOTO: I'll not counsel his.

PIZARRO: Then you counsel the death of Christ in this country, as you told my pageboy months ago?

DE SOTO: That's not known.

PIZARRO: As good.

DE SOTO: No. Christ is love. Love is—

PIZARRO: What? *What?*

DE SOTO: Now in him. He trusts you, trust him. It's all you can do.

PIZARRO: Have you gone soft in the head? What's this chorus now? "Trust! trust!" You know the law out here: kill or get killed. You said it yourself. The mercies come later.

DE SOTO: Not for you. I wish to God you'd never made this bargain. But you did. Now you've no choice left.

PIZARRO: No, this is my kingdom. In Peru I am absolute. I have choice always.

DE SOTO: You had it. But you made it.

PIZARRO: Then I'll take it back.

DE SOTO: Then you never made it. I'm not playing words, General. There's no choice where you don't stick by it.

PIZARRO: I can *choose* to take it back.

DE SOTO: No, sir. That would only be done on orders from your own fear. That's not choosing.

ESTETE: May the crown be allowed a word?

PIZARRO: I know your word. Death.

ESTETE: What else can it be?

VALVERDE: Your Army is in terror. Do you care nothing for them?

PIZARRO: Well, Cavalier. Do you?

DE SOTO: I care for them. But less than I care for you . . . God knows why.

[*He goes off.* ESTETE *approaches* PIZARRO.]

ESTETE: The issue is simple. You are Viceroy here, ruling in the name of the King who sent you. You have no right to risk his land for any reason at all.

PIZARRO: And what did this King ever do for me? Granted me salary if I found money to pay it. Allowed me governance if I found land to govern. Magnificent! For years I strove to make this expedition: years of scars and hunger. While I sweated, your Holy Roman vulture turned away his beak till I'd shaken out enough gold to tempt his greed. If I'd failed this time he'd have cast me off with one shrug of his royal feathers. Well, now I cast him! Francisco Pizarro casts off Carlos the Fifth. Go and tell him.

ESTETE: This is ridiculous.

PIZARRO: No doubt, but you'll have to give me better argument before I give him up.

ESTETE: Perverse man, what is Atahuallpa to you?

PIZARRO: Someone I promised life.

ESTETE [*sneering*]: Promised life? How quaint. The sort of chivalry idea you pretend to despise. If you want to be an absolute King, my man, you must learn to act out of personal will. Break your word just *because* you gave it. Till then, you're only a pig-man trying to copy his betters.

[PIZARRO *rounds on him angrily.* VALVERDE *interposes himself.*]

VALVERDE: My son, listen to me. No promise to a pagan need bind a Christian. Simply think what's at stake: the lives of a hundred and seventy of the faithful. Are you going to sacrifice them for one savage?

PIZARRO [*impatiently*]: You know lives have no weight, Father. Ten can't be added up to outbalance one.

VALVERDE: Ten good can against one evil. And this man is evil. His people kiss his hands as the source of life.

PIZARRO: As we do yours. All your days you play at being God. You only hate my Inca because he does it better.

VALVERDE: *What?*

PIZARRO: Dungballs to all churches that are or ever could be! How I hate you. "Kill who I bid you kill and I will pardon it!" *You* with your milky fingers forcing in the blade! How dare you priests bless any man who goes slicing into battle? But no: you slice with him! "Rip!" you scream, "tear! blind! in the name of Christ!" . . . Tell me, soft Father, if Christ was here now, do you think he would kill my Inca? [*Pause.*] Well, Brother de Nizza, you're the lord of answers: let's hear you. Do I kill him?

DE NIZZA: Don't try and trap me. I know as well as you how terrible it is to kill. But worse is to spare evil. When I came here first I thought I had found Paradise. Now I know it is Hell. A country which castrates its people. What are your Inca's subjects? A population of eunuchs, living entirely without choice.

PIZARRO: And what are your Christians? Unhappy hating men. Look: I'm a peasant, I want value for money. If I go marketing for gods, who do I buy? The God of Europe with all its death and blooding, or Atahuallpa of Peru? His spirit keeps an empire sweet and still as corn in the field.

DE NIZZA: And you're content to be a stalk of corn?

PIZARRO: Yes, yes! They're no fools, these sun men. They know what cheats you sell on your barrow. Choice. Hunger. Tomorrow. They've looked at your wares and passed on. They live here as part of nature: no hope and no despair.

DE NIZZA [*earnestly*]: And no life. Why must you be so dishonest? You are not only part of nature, and you know it. There is something in you at *war* with nature: there is in all of us. Something that does not belong in you the animal. What do you think it is? What is this pain in you that month after month makes you hurl yourself against the cage of time? . . . This is God, driving you to accept divine eternity! Take it, General: not this pathetic copy of eternity the Incas have tried to make on earth. Peru is a sepulchre of the soul. For the sake of the free spirit in each of us it must be destroyed.

PIZARRO: So there is Christian charity. To save my own soul I must kill another man!

DE NIZZA: To save love in the world you must kill lovelessness.

PIZARRO: Hail to you, sole judge of love! No salvation outside your church: and no love either! Oh, you arrogance! . . . [*Simply*] I do not know love, Father, but what can I ever know, if I feel none for him?

DIEGO [*rushing on after a pause*]: Sir! Sir! Another fight broke out, sir. There's one dead.

PIZARRO: Who?

DIEGO: Blas. He drew a knife. I only meant to split his leg, but he slipped and got it through the guts.

PIZARRO: You did well to punish fighting.

DIEGO: May I speak free, sir?

PIZARRO: What? I've got to kill him, is that it?

DIEGO: What other way is there? The men are out of their wits. They feel death all around them.

PIZARRO: So it is and let them face it! I promised them gold, not life. Well, they've got gold. The cripples have gold crutches. The coughers spit gold snot. The bargain's over.

DIEGO: No, sir, not with me. To me you're the greatest General in the world. And we're the greatest company.

PIZARRO: Pizarro's Boys, is that it?

DIEGO: Yes, sir. Pizarro's Boys.

PIZARRO: Ah, the old band! The dear old regiment! . . . *Fool!* . . . Look, you were born a man. Not a Blue man, or a Green man, but A MAN. You are able to feel a thousand separate loves unordered by fear or solitude. Are you going to trade them all in for Gang-love? Flag-love? Carlos-the-Fifth-love? Jesus-the-Christ-love? All that has been *tied* on you. It is only this that makes you bay for death.

VALVERDE: I'll give you death! When I get back to Spain, a commission will hale you to the stake for what you have said today.

PIZARRO [*slyly*]: If I let the Inca go, Father, you'll never get back to Spain.

ESTETE: You madman: see here, you put him underground by sunset or I'll take the knife to him myself.

PIZARRO: ATAHUALLPA!

[ATAHUALLPA *enters with* YOUNG MARTIN.]

They ache for your death. They want to write psalms to their god in your blood. But they'll all die before you—that I promise. [*He binds* ATAHUALLPA'*s arm to his own with a long cord of rope last used to tie some gold. The Inca pulls back.*] There. No, no, come here! . . . Now no one will kill you unless they kill me first.

ESTETE: De Candia!

[*Enter* DE CANDIA, *with a drawn sword.*]

DE CANDIA [*coldly*]: A touching game—jailers and prisoners. But it's over now. General, do you think I'm going to die so that you can dance with a darkie?

[PIZARRO *pulls the sword from* YOUNG MARTIN'*s scabbard.*]

DIEGO [*drawing*]: Sorry, sir, but it's got to be done.

ESTETE [*drawing*]: There's nothing you can do, Pizarro. The whole camp's against you.

PIZARRO: De Soto!

DE CANDIA: If De Soto raises his sword, he'll lose the arm that swings it.

PIZARRO: You'll lose yours first! Come on!

[*He rushes at* DE CANDIA *but* ATAHUALLPA *gives a growl and pulls him back by the rope. A pause.*]

ATAHUALLPA: I have no eyes for you. You are nothing.

PIZARRO: I command here still. They will obey me.

ATAHUALLPA: They will kill me though you cry curses of earth and sky. [*To them all.*] Leave us. I will speak with him.

[*An uneasy pause. Then, impressed by the command in his voice, all leave the stage save the General—now roped to his prisoner—and* YOUNG MARTIN.]

## 11

ATAHUALLPA [*calmly*]: It is no matter. They cannot kill me.

PIZARRO: Cannot?

ATAHUALLPA: Man who dies cannot kill a god who lives forever.

PIZARRO: I wouldn't bet on it, my lord.

ATAHUALLPA: Only my father can take me from here. And he would not accept me, killed by men like you. Men with no word. You may be King in this land, but never God. I am God of the Four Quarters, and if you kill me tonight I will rise at dawn when my father first touches my body with light. [*Pause.*]

PIZARRO [*in wonder*]: You believe this?

ATAHUALLPA: All my people know it—it is why they have let me stay with you.

PIZARRO: They knew you could not be harmed . . .

ATAHUALLPA: So.

PIZARRO [*with grinning excitement*]: Was this the meaning? The meaning of my dream? . . . You were choosing *me?*

YOUNG MARTIN: My lord, it's just a boast. Beyond any kind of reason.

PIZARRO: Is it?

YOUNG MARTIN: How can a man die, then get up and walk away?

PIZARRO: Let's hear your creed, boy. "I believe in Jesus Christ, the Son of God, that He suffered under Pontius Pilate, was crucified, dead and buried" . . . and what?

YOUNG MARTIN: Sir?

PIZARRO: *What?*

YOUNG MARTIN: "He descended into Hell, and on the third day He rose again from the dead . . ."

[*His voice dies out. The Inca watches calmly.*]

PIZARRO: You don't believe it!

YOUNG MARTIN: I do! On my soul! I believe with perfect faith!

PIZARRO: But Christ's to be the only one, is that it? [*Urgently.*] What if it's possible, here in a land beyond all maps and scholars, guarded by mountains up to the sky, that there were true gods on earth, creators of true peace? Think of it! Gods, free of time!

YOUNG MARTIN: It's impossible, my lord.

PIZARRO: It's the only way to give life meaning! To blast out of Time and live forever, *us*, in our own persons! This is the law: die in despair or be a god yourself! . . . Look at him: always so calm as if the teeth of life never bit him . . . or the teeth of death. What if it was really true, Martin? That I've gone god-hunting and caught one. A being who can renew his life over and over?

YOUNG MARTIN: But how can he do that, sir? How could any man?

PIZARRO: By returning over and over again to the source of life—*to the Sun!*

YOUNG MARTIN: No, sir . . .

PIZARRO: Why not? What else is a god but what we know we can't do without? The flowers that worship it, the sunflowers in their soil, are us after night, after cold and lightless days, turning our faces to it adoring. The sun is the only god I know! We eat you to walk. We drink you to sing. Our reins loosen under you and we laugh. Even I laugh, here! [*He starts to laugh exhaustedly.*]

YOUNG MARTIN: General, you need rest, sir.

[*Pause.*]

PIZARRO: Yes. Yes. . . . Yes. [*Bitterly.*] How clever. He's understood everything I've said to him these awful months—all the secret pain he's heard—and this is his revenge. This futile joke. How he must hate me. [*Tightening the rope.*] Oh yes, you cunning bastard! Look, Martin—behold, my God. I've got the Sun on a string! I can make it rise—[*he pulls the Inca's arm up*]—or set! [*He throws the* INCA *to his knees.*]

YOUNG MARTIN: General . . . !

PIZARRO [*wildly*]: I'll make you set forever! Two can joke as well as one! You want your freedom? All right, you're free! [*He starts circling round* ATAHUALLPA.] Walk out of the camp! They may stop you, but what's that to you? You're invulnerable. They'll knock you down but your father the Sun will pick you up again. Go on! Get up! . . . Go on! . . . Get up! . . . Go on! . . . Go on! . . . Go on! . . . Go on! . . . Go on! . . . Go on!

[*He breaks into a frantic gallop round and round the Inca, the rope at full stretch,* ATAHUALLPA *turning with him, somersaulting, then holding him, his teeth bared with the strain, as if breaking a wild horse, until the old man tumbles exhausted to the ground. Silence follows, broken only by deep moaning from the stricken man. Quietly the Inca pulls in the rope. Then at last he speaks.*]

ATAHUALLPA: Pizarro. You will die soon and you do not believe in your god. That is why you tremble and keep no word. Believe in me. I will give you a word and fill you with joy. For you I will do a great thing. I will swallow death and spit it out of me.

[*Pause. This whole scene stays very still.*]

PIZARRO: [*whispering*]: You cannot.

ATAHUALLPA: Yes, if my father wills it.

PIZARRO: How if he does not?

ATAHUALLPA: He will. His people still need me. Believe.

PIZARRO: Impossible.

ATAHUALLPA: Believe.

PIZARRO: How? . . . How? . . .

ATAHUALLPA: First you must take my priest-power.

PIZARRO [*quietly*]: Oh no! You go or not as you choose, but I take nothing more in this world.

ATAHUALLPA: Take my word. Take my peace. I will put water to your wound, old man. Believe.

[*A long silence. The lights are now fading round them.*]

PIZARRO: What must I do?

[*Enter* OLD MARTIN.]

OLD MARTIN: How can I speak now and hope to be believed? As night fell, like a hand over the eye, and great white stars sprang out over the snow-rim of our world, Atahuallpa confessed Pizarro. He did it in the Inca manner. He took Ichu grass and a stone. Into the Ichu grass the General spoke for an hour or more. None heard what he said save the King, who could not understand it. Then the King struck him on the back with the stone, cast away the grass, and made the signs for purification.

PIZARRO: If any blessing is in me, take it and go. Fly up, my bird, and come to me again.

[*The* INCA *takes a knife from* YOUNG MARTIN *and cuts the rope. Then he walks upstage. All the* OFFICERS *and* MEN *enter. During the following a pole is set up above, in the sun, and* ATAHUALLPA *is hauled up into it.*]

12

OLD MARTIN: The Inca was tried by a court quickly mustered. He was accused of usurping the throne and killing his brother; of idolatry and of having more than one wife. On all these charges he was found—

ESTETE: Guilty.

VALVERDE: Guilty.

DE CANDIA: Guilty.

DIEGO: Guilty.

OLD MARTIN: Sentence to be carried out the same night.

ESTETE: Death by burning.

[*Lights up above in the sun.* ATAHUALLPA *gives a great cry.*]

PIZARRO: No! He must not burn! His body must stay in *one piece!*

VALVERDE: Let him repent his idolatry and be baptized a Christian. He will receive the customary mercy.

OLD MARTIN: Strangling instead.

PIZARRO: You must do it! Deny your father! If you don't, you will be burned to ashes. There will be no flesh left for him to warm alive at dawn.

[YOUNG MARTIN *screams and runs from the stage in horror.*]

You must do it.

[*In a gesture of surrender the Inca King kneels.*]

OLD MARTIN: So it was that Atahuallpa came to Christ.

[*Enter* DE NIZZA, *above, with a bowl of water.*]

DE NIZZA: I baptize you Juan de Atahuallpa, in honor of Juan the Baptist, whose sacred day this is.

ESTETE: The twenty-ninth of August, 1533.

VALVERDE: And may Our Lord and His angels receive your soul with joy!

SOLDIERS: Amen!

[*The Inca suddenly raises his head, tears off his clothes and intones in a great voice*]:

ATAHUALLPA: INTI! INTI! INTI!

VALVERDE: What does he say?

PIZARRO [*intoning also*]: The Sun. The Sun. The Sun.

VALVERDE: *Kill him!*

[*Soldiers haul* ATAHUALLPA *to his feet and hold him to the stake.* RODAS *slips a string over his head and while all the Spaniards recite the Latin creed below, and great howls of "Inca!" come from the darkness, the Sovereign King of Peru is garroted. His screams and struggles subside; his body falls slack. His executioners hand the corpse down to the soldiers below, who carry it to the center of the stage and drop it at* PIZARRO'*s feet. Then all leave save the old man, who stands as if turned to stone. A drum beats. Slowly, in semidarkness, the stage fills with all the Indians, robed in black and terracotta, wearing the great golden funeral masks of ancient Peru. Grouped round the prone body, they intone a strange Chant of Resurrection, punctuated by hollow beats on the drums and by long, long silences in which they turn their immense triangular eyes inquiringly up to the sky. Finally, after three great cries appear to summon it, the sun rises. Its rays fall on the body.* ATAHUALLPA *does not move. The masked men watch in amazement—disbelief—finally, despair. Slowly, with hanging, dejected heads, they shuffle away.* PIZARRO *is left alone with the dead King. He sits. He contemplates him. A silence. Then suddenly he slaps it viciously, and the body rolls over on its back.*]

PIZARRO: Cheat! You've cheated me! Cheat . . .

[*For a moment his old body is racked with sobs; then, surprised, he feels tears on his cheek. He examines them. The sunlight brightens on his head.*]

What's this? What is it? In all your life you never made one of these, I know, and I not till this minute. Look. [*He kneels to show the dead Inca.*] Ah, no. You have no eyes for me now, Atahuallpa: they are dusty balls of amber I can tap on. You have no peace for me, Atahuallpa: the birds still scream in your forest. You have no joy for me, Atahuallpa, my boy: the only joy is in death. I lived between two hates: I die between two darks: blind eyes and a blind sky. And yet you saw once. The sky sees nothing, but you saw. Is there comfort there? The sky knows no feelings, but we know them, that's sure. Martin's hope, and De Soto's honor, and your trust—your trust which hunted me: we alone make these. That's some marvel, yes, some marvel. To sit in a great cold silence, and sing out sweet with just our own warm breath: that's some marvel, surely. To make water in a sand world: surely, surely . . . God's just a name on your nail; and naming begins cries and cruelties. But to live without hope of after, and make whatever God there is, oh, that's some immortal business surely! . . . I'm tired. Where are you? You're so cold. I'd warm you if I could. But there's no warming now, not ever now. I'm colding too. There's a snow of death falling all round us. You can almost see it. It's over, lad, I'm coming after you. There's nothing but peace to come. We'll be put into the same earth, father and son in our own land. And that sun will roam uncaught over his empty pasture.

[*Enter* OLD MARTIN.]

OLD MARTIN: So fell Peru. We gave her greed, hunger, and the cross: three gifts for the civilized life. The family groups that sang on the terraces are gone. In their place slaves shuffle underground and they don't sing there. Peru is a silent country, frozen in avarice. So fell Spain, gorged with gold; distended; now dying.

PIZARRO [*singing*]: "Where is her heart, O little finch?"

OLD MARTIN: And so fell you, General, my master, whom men called the Son of His Own Deeds. He was killed later in a quarrel with his partner who brought up the reinforcements. But to speak truth, he sat down that morning and never really got up again.

PIZARRO [*singing*]: "Where are her plumes, O little finch?"

OLD MARTIN: I'm the only one left now of that company: landowner—slaveowner—and forty years from any time of hope. It put out a good blossom, but it was shaken off rough. After that I reckon the fruit always comes sour, and doesn't sweeten up much with age.

PIZARRO [*singing*]: "She is cut up, O little finch. For stealing grain, O little finch."

OLD MARTIN: General, you did for me, and now I've done for you. And there's no joy in that. Or in anything now. But then there's no joy in the world could match for me what I had when I first went with you across the water to find the gold country. And no pain like losing it. Save you all.

[*He goes out.* PIZARRO *lies beside the body of* ATAHUALLPA *and quietly sings to it.*]

PIZARRO [*singing*]:

See, see the fate, O little finch,
Of robber birds, O little finch.

[*The sun glares at the audience.*]

END OF PLAY

# SHRIVINGS

*In memory of*
*James Mossman*

## A NOTE ON THE PLAY, 1974

As of now, this play has never been acted.

It is a much rewritten version of another play of mine called *The Battle of Shrivings,* which has never been printed.

This first version was presented at the Lyric Theatre, London, in February 1970, by five fine actors: John Gielgud, Patrick Magee, Wendy Hiller, ebullient young Dorothy Lyman, and compelling young Martin Shaw. It was directed with cool precision by Peter Hall, and placed by John Bury in a set so bone-white that a bowl of green apples placed suddenly on a table—"the buttons of original sin"—riveted every eye. The action of the play was lightly formalized throughout, so that it could make an austere gesture somewhat at variance with the aesthetic standards prevailing on Shaftesbury Avenue. I found this gesture beautiful, since my intention from the start had always been to stage a fairly abstract proceeding, and theatrically I am strongly drawn to the cold which burns, However, it is possible that the proceeding was not abstract enough, or not cold enough to burn effectively. At any rate the play fell somewhere between domesticity and grandeur—a bad kind of fall—and though some critics found it exciting, many more received it with an almost jubilant hostility.

For myself, the more I saw *The Battle of Shrivings* performed, the more I wanted to change it. I do not mean that I just wanted to make it work. "Working," in the sense intended by many theatrical professionals, far too often simply means a certain effectiveness purchased at the price of any ambiguous insight, or of any qualifying perception not immediately accessible to a dozing audience sullenly suspicious of language. Other plays of mine had relied for their completion on elaborate stretches of physical action: in this one I wanted the electricity to be sparked almost exclusively from the spoken words—though of course there was a physical set-piece as well in the shape of the Apple Game. My dissatisfaction with the play, therefore, had nothing to do with its rhetoric, which if anything I wanted to intensify; nor with its verbal dueling, which if anything I wanted to extend. I desired only to make the piece more purely *itself*.

Successful plays of large scope die for their authors with a pleasant expiration, wrapped in a sheet of public approval: unsuccessful ones are apt to be left naked to the sky—particularly plays of a turbulent nature—writhing under an obloquy which never quite covers them and so turns into oblivion. I remember how in the first hard weeks after its public maiming, I became obsessed with considering what further writing was needed to give the play its quietus in my mind. I had loved it a great deal, but had I allowed it to speak entirely in its own voice? I suspected that the intransigence of the argument had been blunted by an almost conventional turn it had taken, toward the end, into domestic bickering. Certain furious passages between the husband and the wife had been undeniably useful in humanizing action otherwise largely concerned with debate, but I wondered whether fundamentally they had not constituted an easy way around the rigorous path which the piece should properly have followed. The first thing I did, when I started to rewrite, was to remove altogether the character of Enid Petrie, the pacifist's unhappy wife, thereby changing a quintet into a quartet.

The creation of Lady Petrie in the first place had been largely due to some speculation I once entertained concerning the household of Mahatma Gandhi. I had read in a famous life of the great man how at the age of forty he had summoned his wife and informed her of his irrevocable decision to give up all sexual activity, since he had come to recognize in it the source of aggression in himself. This startling act of renunciation certainly impressed me; but I could not stop wondering at the same time about the reaction to it of Mrs. Gandhi. Her possible sufferings seemed so extremely relevant to my theme, and to the doings in the Petrie household. Indeed some years later I received a passionate letter from a woman psychiatrist, warmly congratulating me on perceiving how often idealism of the lofty Petrie kind is fed by the life-blood of humble domestic victims. However, despite my speculation about Gandhi's wife (and the encouraging letter from this doctor) I could not finally avoid the insistent conclusion that Enid Petrie was a dramatic cliché, and that the scene where she was finally struck by her husband was simply no fitting climax for the play.

Obviously the horror of this story, in any version of it, has to be Gideon's lapse into violence after so many years of self-restraint. But with Enid removed, a more dramatically interesting target for the pacifist's blow instantly appeared: Lois, his idealistic and worshiping young secretary. An assault on a committed girl seemed to me in this situation even more appalling than one on an aggrieved wife. The fact that the girl was also an American clinched the matter for me.

*Shrivings* has always been an "American" play. I associate it most strongly with sojourns in New York City in 1968 and 1969. The encounter between Mark and Gideon naturally sprang out of a division of feeling in myself, but it was charged with the violence of this angry city during one of her angriest times, when streets were choked with raging protesters against the Vietnam War, newspapers were filled with the killings at Kent State University, and there drifted through our midst the fantastic army of Flower People, now already turned into ghosts. So quickly does time run on, their passionate confronting of public brutality with public gentleness now seems almost totally unreal. The savage alignments of those days had about them such a relieving simplicity. I am aware that to many people in England the excesses of the Peace Movement occasioned feelings of near-amusement; but then near-amusement of this kind is one of the more obvious symptoms of an English strangeness.

As a foreigner in America, I became too possessed by the fever of that time, and the baffling contradictions it set off in my head. Obsessively I wanted to set out on paper the conflicting ideas which sprang up everywhere I looked—often enough taking the form of elaborate interior duologues. Over and over I returned to the apparent truth that an absolute nonaggressive position seems unattainable by Man without tangible loss of warmth and cherishable humanity (what warm man will spare the Ruffian with the Pistol threatening his beloved?), and yet a relative, "human" attitude which permits retaliating under extreme provocation inescapably leads to horrors unenvisaged and unintended at the start of it: witness Hiroshima at the end of the Second World War.

Man squeezed like a nut between an ideal choice and a practical one, and cracked in bits by either, is scarcely a novel image; yet the discovering of it for oneself, the coming to any sort of awareness of tragic ambiguity, must always be new and painful. I remember how angry I felt with my many opposed thoughts, and yet how also exciting I found the idea of Insoluble Situation. Walking around Manhattan, I was accompanied everywhere by the nagging exhilaration of irresolvable argument. As I contemplated the pop-eyed King of Sassania in the Metropolitan Museum, Mark Askelon contemplated him too over my shoulder, and voiced his mocking comments in my ear. (Mark himself, of course, has clear "American" ancestors: brilliant Ezra Pound, or magnificent Orson Welles, living half-fulfilled and half-wasted by the Mediterranean Sea.) The actual figure of the young student with hair torn out of his head appeared to me suddenly one evening in the apartment of a friend, a few hours after a savage clash had occurred near Wall Street between a band of youngsters and a gang of construction workers. I can still see vividly the patch of white on his head.

I remember starting *The Battle of Shrivings* high up in a tiny workroom in the roof of the Dakota building on West Seventy-second Street. For relief, I would walk out and breathe fresh air on a small gargoyle-bordered terrace overlooking glorious Central Park. If it has ever energized you at all, it is impossible to resist the anguish of this most urgent and beautiful of cities. Over me its spell has long been unbreakable. In those days of early work on the play, its concerns seemed to me so immense that flying from Kennedy to Heathrow Airport felt like flying out of the twentieth century back to the nineteenth. A truly multiracial society would be receding, in all the torment of its birth; approaching would be one chiefly insular, condescending, and frigid. This impression was of course unfair, and confessing it makes one seem self-righteous, but I was never happy in swinging, satirical London; the constant drizzle of put-down and small-minded preoccupation tended to dampen my spirits far too often.

I recall this feeling now because only now do I realize how living so much out of the country at that time enabled me to become infected with the need to discuss onstage, with flourish and head-on explicitness, the idea of human improvability. English dramatic taste rather deplores the large theme, largely broached: it tends to prefer—sometimes with good sense, but often with a really dangerous fear of grossness—the minute fragment, minutely observed. I am not saying that I did the job (or have redone it) well. I simply reflect that had I remained a constant Londoner during that period, I doubt if I would have done it at all.

This said, I must confess that this second version of the play—composed three years ago, and now simply called *Shrivings* as earnest of plain intent—is much nearer to my original goal than was the first. I would like to thank my original publisher, André Deutsch, deeply for letting me see it in print, laid out between hard and handsome covers, even though not interred in public acclaim. It is, after all, a brave act for a man of business to bring out a play which has yet to be produced on the stage. May the Protective God of Dramatists rain benefits upon him! And may the play itself now give me at last some kind of peace.

P.S.

## THE SETTING

(All directions are given from the viewpoint of the audience)

In the Middle Ages, Shrivings was a House of Retreat. Now it shows a wide, austere, light-filled interior of whitewashed wall and crude timber, divided into two levels.

Below: the main living area of the house.

Two huge arches, left and right. That to the left frames the door to Gideon's study; that to the right frames the staircase. Between them, the room goes back under the lip of Mark's bedroom, to the back wall of the house, which contains a window. The front door is assumed to be offstage right, in this same wall.

Two doors, downstage, left and right. That to the left leads to the garden; that to the right, to the kitchen.

Two tables, left and right. That to the left—standing diagonally to the audience—serves as a desk: a chair, behind it; two stools before it, a telephone on it and a pile of letters, half opened. That to the right, a long refectory table for dining: a bench on the upstage side of it.

All the furniture has been made by David, which gives to the place an original look: cool, and beautiful.

At the head of the stairs, one can either turn right, to the other bedrooms, or left to Mark's.

Above: this room hangs over the playing area below, framed by the top half of the two large arches. It contains a bed and a table. Its window is assumed to be out front. The bathroom is off, to the left.

The whole atmosphere of this place is one of tranquillity and dedication.

## ACT ONE

### SCENE 1

*Friday evening.*

*Five o'clock.* DAVID, *a boy of nineteen, sits in the middle of the room, carving the leg of a small table, which is upside down on a sheet. He wears a frayed blue shirt and frayed blue jeans; his hair is long, and there are woodshavings in it. He concentrates very hard on the work.*
*The telephone rings. He pays no attention. Finally* LOIS *comes in calmly, carrying a cup of tea. She is a pretty American girl of twenty-five; tidy, efficient, and cheerful. She too wears her hair long and is dressed informally.*

LOIS [*picking up the phone*]: Sir Gideon Petrie's secretary . . . No, I'm afraid he always spends this hour after tea completely alone. Beg pardon? Yes, sir; the vigil will go ahead exactly as announced. Sir Gideon will sit in Parliament Square from two o'clock till eight, tomorrow and Sunday. All who care to join him we welcome. Peace. [*She hangs up and sits at the table, opening the letters.*] Why didn't you answer the phone?

DAVID: It didn't sound interesting. It had that ring to it which said "World Organization."

LOIS: It's one of the neurotic symptoms of our time, you know, an inability to live in the real world.

DAVID: And where's that?

LOIS: O.K.

DAVID: No; where is it?

LOIS [*pointing to the desk*]: This is the real world, David.

DAVID: Letters?

LOIS: *These* letters, yes.

DAVID: This is the real world. Here. [*He throws up a handful of shavings over his head.*]

LOIS: Ha, ha, ha. [*She turns to the desk.*]

DAVID: Hey!

LOIS [*impatiently*]: What?

DAVID: Hey!

LOIS: Hay is for horses. [*The phone rings. She answers it.*] Sir Gideon Petrie's secretary. Beg pardon? . . . No, sir, there is no conflict in any way. The vigil ends on Sunday night. The Award will take place on Monday morning. Sir Gideon receives it for his twenty-fifth book *Explorations*—and Mr. Askelon to mark the appearance of his *Collected Poems* . . . Well, I would have thought the award of a world-famous prize to two world-famous figures was Human Interest enough . . . No, I'm sorry. Shrivings is a place of quiet, and we like to keep it that way. Peace. [*She hangs up, gently.*]

DAVID: You're beautiful.

LOIS: Me?

DAVID: You're so firm. It's marvelous to be firm like that.

LOIS: It sounds awful. "Firm"'s a disgusting word for a girl.

DAVID: It's great when applied to breasts. And even greater when applied to moral outline. That's what you've got. Moral outline.

LOIS [*amused*]: Yeah, well, why don't you just tidy all that away now, before your dad comes?

DAVID: Why? It creates an impression of industry, and dedication.

LOIS: It makes a grundgy impression.

DAVID: What a beautiful word!

LOIS: You know, I really can't believe I'm finally going to meet him. The great Mark Askelon! Do you think I should tell him I've been in love with him ever since I read *Wafers of Death* in Doubleday's bookshop, the first day I arrived in New York?

DAVID: "Grundgy"! That's perfect!

LOIS: He wrote about Catholicism like it was a disease. If my dad read any one of those poems, they'd have to take him straight to the hospital . . . What about your mother? She must have hated them.

DAVID: I bet she just laughed.

LOIS: But she was a believer?

DAVID: Giulia laughed about everything.

LOIS: Why do you call her that?

DAVID: Why not?

LOIS: She was your mother.

DAVID: Once. Since then, Father immortalized her in poetry. Now she belongs wholly to Penguin Books.

LOIS: She must have been incredible. I mean, to make a great poet give up writing revolutionary poems, and do all his writing about love!

DAVID: That's bad?

LOIS: Of course not. It's just irrelevant. Do you realize that some parts of this world are actually getting poorer? When you're faced with a fact like that, people's sex lives come to look a bit trivial, don't they?

DAVID: Absolutely. [*He tries to kiss her. She turns away very coolly, slits open another letter with great dexterity.* DAVID *shrugs.*

The door opens. SIR GIDEON PETRIE *comes in. He is a gentle, noble man of over sixty. One senses a great toughness, both of intellect and staying-power. His manner shows a charm composed of clarity, courtesy, and gaiety of spirit.*

*There is about him a sort of sparkling serenity: a delicate earnestness, through which one glimpses a deep and passionate involvement. He contemplates the youngsters lovingly.*]

GIDEON: Peace, my fliers.

LOIS: Peace, Giddy.

DAVID: Peace, Giddy.

LOIS: You're out early. It's not six yet.

GIDEON: I'm too excited to settle. When I think he'll be here any time now! My goodness! [*To* DAVID.] Are you up to it?

DAVID: No.

GIDEON: Nor me. He sets such standards, your father. Everything has to be so memorable.

DAVID: Yes.

GIDEON: How's the afternoon post?

LOIS: I've laid them out. [*Indicating piles of letters.*] Requests to speak. Requests to write.

GIDEON [*sitting at the desk*]: Yes, yes, yes to all requests today! I can't refuse anybody on the day Mark Askelon first comes to Shrivings! Do you think we did right in closing it this weekend? It's been bothering me.

LOIS: Why not? We've all got to be selfish sometimes.

GIDEON: Have we?

LOIS: You're too hard on yourself, Giddy!

GIDEON: You know, I haven't been working in there at all. Just lying on my bed, remembering him. Seeing him on his terrace in the sunshine. The Sage of Corfu, under his trellis of vines! Like a Roman pugilist gone to seed.

LOIS: You mean fat?

GIDEON: Of course.

LOIS: Oh no!

GIDEON: He was always a mountain! A *sacred* mountain, of course. Everybody came from miles to sit round the foothills and listen!

[LOIS *laughs.*]

And what wonderful talk it was, my goodness!

LOIS: What kind?

GIDEON: Well, the last thing I remember him discussing—and it was all of eleven years ago, mind you—was whether the heart's blood the Furies dropped on Athens in the *Oresteia* was really their menstrual fluid.

LOIS [*a little shocked: trying not to show it*]: Gee! Oh my!

DAVID: He really put a spell on you, didn't he?

GIDEON [*glancing through the letters and ticking some*]: From the first day he became my student at Cambridge! You know, the summer we met we went for our first walking tour. Even then, he moved through the Mediterranean as if he owned it.

DAVID: Do you see Giulia there too, under the trellis?

GIDEON: Whenever I picture your mother, it's always in movement.

DAVID: Me too. She used to dance me to sleep, like other mothers sing. She'd light a candle and I'd have to watch her shadow on the wall. Up and down, up and down, till I went off.

GIDEON: How exquisite.

LOIS: D'you know the last thing *I'd* see at night when I was a kid? A beautiful plastic Jesus, like the ones they have in taxis to prevent crashes, only bigger. It had these great ruby tears on its face, and I'd have to pray to it before turning out the light: "Dear Lord, make me a Good Catholic and a Good American. Amen!" We all have different backgrounds, I guess.

GIDEON [*laughing*]: And yours made you the fierce Falcon you are today!

LOIS [*smiling*]: Oh, sure! [*Scooping up the letters.*] I'll do these now. While I've got the energy. [*She looks fondly at* GIDEON.] You're looking great, d'you know that?

GIDEON: I feel great; thank you. So are you, I may say.

LOIS: Really?

GIDEON: Prettier each day.

LOIS [*flattered*]: Ha, ha, ha!

[*Smiling, she takes the letters into* GIDEON'S *study, shutting the door.*]

GIDEON: You know, you two are absolutely complementary. A Falcon and an Owl. She can give you the gifts of the day. You can give her the gifts of the night.

DAVID: Oh, Giddy!

GIDEON: What, my dear?

DAVID: I can't give anybody anything. Sometimes I think all the opposite things I feel should just cancel me out, and make me invisible. Like all colors make up white.

GIDEON: You know, your father's going to be very impressed with you.

DAVID: Why not? I'm very impressive. It's not everyone who can drop out of two public schools, and Cambridge University, all in the space of five years.

GIDEON: Do you think Mark cares a fig about academic conformity?

DAVID: I don't know. I don't even know what he feels about me being here.

GIDEON: If *I* had a son, there's nowhere in the world I'd rather think of him than in your father's villa.

DAVID: Six years' silence, punctuated by telegrams. "Regret still not convenient you return. Father."

GIDEON: We've talked about this a great deal, my dear. Perhaps he did not feel able to write. It happens.

DAVID: And why does he come now? Certainly not just to get a prize. He's had hundreds offered, and never accepted one.

GIDEON: Perhaps he needs us. Have you thought of that?

DAVID [*startled*]: Needs?

GIDEON: Yes

[*Suddenly* DAVID *shudders violently.*]

David! What's the matter?

DAVID: Nothing.

GIDEON: But there is. Tell me.

DAVID: Nothing. Why do you listen to me? It's all nonsense!

GIDEON: Listen to me, then. Life hasn't been so easy for him these past years. People say hard things of him, I know. How heartless to forbid you the house all the time your mother was so ill. Was it so heartless to want to spare you the horror of watching her go? The paralysis claiming more of her each day?

DAVID: And afterward? Staying there quite alone?

GIDEON: Your mother's death was an end of a world for Mark. I wonder if even you can quite conceive the end of a world. . . . [*Warmly.*] My dear, let's offer him this house these few days to be his home. Let's offer him Shrivings, with all its tradition of Peace. What d'you say? Oh, my goodness; isn't that lovely work?

DAVID: Your goodness. [*Abruptly.*] I'll take this back to the stables.

[*He picks up the table.*]

GIDEON: What are you trying to tell me?

[*Pause. Then the boy shrugs.* LOIS *comes in.*]

LOIS: I've just typed the two for your personal signature.

GIDEON: I'll sign them.

[*With a look at* DAVID, GIDEON *retires to his study.*]

LOIS [*tidying up*]: Dinner's at eight. I've decided to make Roman eggs in honor of your father. Do you think he'll appreciate the subtle compliment?

DAVID: I don't know.

[*He goes out into the garden with the unfinished table. She looks after him, puzzled, then sits at the desk and starts sorting out some more papers. Pause. A voice is heard calling wooingly.*]

MARK [*off*]: Gideon! . . . Gideon! . . .

[LOIS *looks up.* MARK *appears from the back, carrying a large package done up in sacking and a small parcel in brown paper. In his early fifties, he is the relic of an enormous man. A mass of hair falls from a massive head; eyes stare from an eroded face. He wears a Greek shepherd's cloak with a hood. His voice is still powerful.*]

LOIS: Peace.

MARK: What?

LOIS: Peace.

MARK: If possible. [*He moves into the room, looking about him.*] Stupendous!

LOIS: Can I help you?

MARK: Is that Lyssop Ridge up there behind the house?

LOIS: I'm afraid I don't know.

MARK: Those woods lie on it like a silver fox on a nigger's shoulder.

LOIS [*offended*]: May I ask who you are, please?

MARK: A shepherd, as my cloak proclaims. I suspect permanently without a flock. The name is Mark.

LOIS [*amazed*]: Not Mark *Askelon!*

MARK: Exactly so.

LOIS: How did you get here?

MARK: A hired Humber car in leatherette. It's just gone away.

LOIS [*excited and suddenly nervous*]: Oh, gee! I didn't expect you to . . . well to . . . look exactly like that! I didn't know what you'd look like really! . . . Where's your luggage?

MARK: In the hall. The maid can fetch it in later.

LOIS: We have no maids at Shrivings, sir. Sir Gideon does not approve of servants. Here everybody has to do his own room. I do this and the kitchen. Of course you won't have to—I'll do yours, of course!

MARK: How many people stay here, then?

LOIS: Oh, it's just like a hotel. We've got fifteen bedrooms, and we hope they'll be filled every night. They're mostly kids on their way someplace. We try not to turn anyone away who genuinely wants a place to sleep.

MARK: You mean it's a sort of Commune for Transients?

LOIS [*laughing*]: Oh now, don't get scared! There's no one coming this weekend. Giddy asked me to accept nobody for the three days you're here. He figured you'd like some quiet.

MARK: And you do all the supervising?

LOIS: Sure! Giddy calls me a general factota! . . . My actual name's Lois. Lois Neal . . . I'll get your case.

[*She runs off, and returns with a battered suitcase.*]

MARK: Where did he find you?

LOIS [*proudly*]: In jail, after a march! Two years ago. We talked all night. In the morning he asked me to work for him. I was terribly proud. I could type some, but I didn't know any shorthand at all. So I took one of those Courses in Speedwriting for With-It Girls. Do you know, after four weeks I could do a hundred words a minute?

MARK: But surely there was a secretary here already?

LOIS: Oh, there was a grundgy old woman called Miss Crawford. She looked like one of those feminists from the 1910s. You know—white cuffs, and tits like dried apples. She was going to retire anyway. One look at me, and she fled.

MARK: I bet she did.

LOIS: I think Giddy was glad to see her go—but of course he'd never say.

MARK: You admire him very much, don't you?

LOIS: He's a saint. [*Pause.*] Well, let me show you your room. [*She turns and picks up the package wrapped in sacking.*]

MARK [*with a hint of sharpness*]: Please—let me carry that.

LOIS [*pleasantly*]: O.K.!

[*She picks up the case instead, and goes upstairs.* MARK *follows, leaving the small parcel behind on the table. They enter the bedroom above.*]

In here.

MARK: Thank you. [*He puts his package on the table, down front.*]

LOIS: It's nice, isn't it?

MARK: Excellent. [*He takes off his cloak. Underneath he is wearing a baggy old suit and a cheap cotton shirt.*]

LOIS: The bathroom's through there. I hope you like lemon soap. I put in a great cake of it. [*He throws his cloak on the bed.*]

MARK: What's a saint?

LOIS: A man who doesn't know what it is to reject people.

MARK: And that's Gideon?

LOIS: He has no hostility left in him for anyone in the world.

MARK: Do you really believe that?

LOIS: Absolutely. He's proved it can be done.

MARK: You have American eyes.

LOIS: Is that good?

MARK: Eyes are inherited. Who gave you yours?

LOIS: I don't know. My father, I guess. He's a doctor in Chicago.

MARK: Does he approve your working for the President of the World League of Peace?

LOIS: God, no! All he thinks about is how to get me home, away from the enemies of the American way of life! . . . [*Gleefully.*] Oh, gee, it's so great you're here! I'm making a special dinner in your honor. We're vegetarian here, you know.

MARK: We?

LOIS: Well, it's me really, I'm afraid. I'm a health food nut. Since I've come, Shrivings does without meat. Giddy entirely endorses this, I may say. I hope you don't mind. It's much better for you. . . . I'm going to try and make a cream-cheese soufflé for dessert. It can be spectacular, but it's a bastard to get right.

MARK: You do all the cooking here?

LOIS: Sure. I enjoy it.

MARK: Yes, but do the diners?

LOIS [*laughing*]: Well, they say they do!

[GIDEON *comes out of the study, and walks to the foot of the stairs.*]

Giddy says I should publish my recipes altogether and call it *The Protester's Cookbook*. I think that sounds just a little pompous, don't you?

GIDEON [*calling upstairs*]: Mark?

[MARK *comes out of the room. He looks down the stairs, and sees* GIDEON. *He descends.*]

MARK: Gideon.

[*They embrace, very warmly.*]

GIDEON: My dear, you look marvelous!

MARK [*coming into the living room*]: You mean slimmer? It's true. God knows how, with my alcoholic ingestion. Behold! [*He swirls across the room.*] Man is a reed—but a drinking reed!

[GIDEON *laughs delightedly.* LOIS *comes down also.*]

As for you—you haven't changed a hair. Not one hair since I last saw you—eleven years ago, in Corfu harbor!

GIDEON: I wish that were true. Alas, my dear, at my age the last hairs fall even quicker than the last illusions. You've met Miss Neal, I see. More than a secretary—she's a conscience.

LOIS: Nonsense, Giddy!

MARK: Oh, I sensed that right away. My moral hazel twig pointed straight at her!

GIDEON [*embarrassed for* LOIS]: You had a good flight, I hope?

MARK: Did I? We annihilated the Appenines, the Alps, and the Dordogne in less than three hours. Is that good? . . . No matter. This room is compensation for anything!

GIDEON: It used to be a House of Retreat, you know.

MARK: Of confession, surely? Is that not what Shriving means? Confession and penance?

GIDEON: Oh well, I hope it won't be found too inappropriate for a thoroughgoing atheist.

MARK: I daresay a thoroughgoing rationalist has exorcized its spirit not a little.

[*They bow to each other.*]

Coming up your drive is an unforgettable experience. That long tunnel of elm trees, and at the end a great stone porch shouting "Stop!"

GIDEON: Shouting "Come!" my dear. "Come."

MARK: Is it? [*Slight pause. Then abruptly indicating the parcel.*] Please open that. My present to your house.

GIDEON: My goodness! Whatever can it be?

MARK [*to* LOIS]: Do you have wine?

LOIS: I've got a little for cooking. It's not very good, I guess.

MARK: So much the better. Household gods cherish the ordinary.

LOIS [*admiringly*]: Out of sight!

MARK: Please fetch it.

LOIS: Right!

[*She darts out to the kitchen.* GIDEON *lifts from the smaller package an ancient Greek drinking cup of clay.*]

GIDEON: Oh, my dear! How exquisite!

MARK: A libation cup from the sixth century Before Cant!

GIDEON: I'm overwhelmed.

MARK: Wine was poured into that to toast the gods.

GIDEON: I'm afraid it's been years since I drank wine.

MARK: What do you need with it? Your spirit is the last of the wine. After you, all is vinegar! . . . I shall put that into my speech about you.

GIDEON: Speech?

MARK: At the prize-giving. I assume you are preparing one about me.

GIDEON: No. Surely that isn't part of the ceremony, that we eulogize each other?

MARK: If it isn't, I shall make it so.

GIDEON: Oh, my goodness, I hope not!

[LOIS *returns with an open wine bottle.*]

LOIS: Here!

MARK: Splendid! Giddy, you pour. [*Extending the cup.*] Fill it to the brim.

GIDEON: Very well, my dear. [*He takes the bottle.*] I can always rely on you to make a delicious ceremony out of everything! [*He pours the wine into the cup.*]

MARK: There now. Thank you. . . . Attention, please! [*He raises the cup.*] I lift this cup of many consecrations! I drink to your house!

LOIS: Wow!

MARK: To Shrivings—in whose cool chambers the dangling soul was once tied to the trellis of confession, and so helped to flower.

[DAVID *comes in from the garden, carrying a great object wrapped in a white sheet.*]

Here was sheath in time of swords! Silence in a time of muskets! And now, in a time of bombs—

DAVID: Peace.

[*All look at him. A pause. He sets the object down. Then abruptly,* MARK *turns away and thrusts the cup at* GIDEON.]

MARK: Complete the toast.

GIDEON: I couldn't, my dear. I'm afraid it would make my head swim.

MARK: You must—or there will be perturbation in the house.

DAVID: I'll drink for him.

[MARK *contemplates him, then hands him the cup.* DAVID *drinks, wincing.*]

LOIS: I guess it's been open a few days.

MARK: Haven't we all? Well, not him perhaps. . . . Well, I did not expect to see you so soon. It's charming of you to come all this way over from Cambridge.

DAVID [*avoiding his eyes*]: I . . . live here.

MARK: Live?

DAVID: I wrote to you.

MARK: I don't read letters.

DAVID [*embarrassed*]: I gave up Cambridge. And then Giddy—Gideon—suggested I move in here. So I did. I've been here since November.

MARK: You gave up?

DAVID: Well, it would have given me up. I just got in first . . .

GIDEON: Philosophy is not David's metier. He prefers at the moment to make furniture for philosophers. A decision I selfishly encourage.

MARK: I don't understand.

GIDEON: All the furniture in this room was made by David.

[*Pause.* MARK *looks about him. He has difficulty in digesting this news.*]

MARK: Extraordinary. Where did you learn?

DAVID [*darting glances at his father, but unable to look him fully in the face*]: I took woodwork at my last school. Then Giddy had an old stable here. I felt I wanted . . .

MARK: What?

DAVID: To do something with my hands.

MARK: Well, why not? . . . It's a noble profession, carpentry. The only one with an indisputable patron saint!

[DAVID *laughs.*]

What's that you've got there? Something for my arrival?

GIDEON [*confidently to* MARK]: It's something special, I'm sure! He's been rather secretive lately. Are you going to show it to us?

DAVID [*embarrassed*]: Not now.

GIDEON: Of course now. Why ever not?

DAVID: Later. Tomorrow. I'll take it back. [*He moves to pick the object up again.*]

GIDEON [*in great surprise*]: David! . . . Please show us. We're all dying of curiosity.

[DAVID *stands staring at the ground.*]

LOIS: Come on, David, don't be so dopey!

[*He still stands not replying.*]

O.K.—*I'll* do it!

DAVID: No! [*To* GIDEON.] You! [*He smiles at* GIDEON.]

GIDEON [*smiling back, intimately*]: Me? I'm honored. [*He approaches the object.*] Hey presto! One—two—three!

[*He takes off the sheet. Underneath stands a throne of marvelous austerity. A pause.*]

GIDEON: How beautiful! Oh, how beautiful, David! It's the most lovely thing you've done yet.

DAVID [*pleased*]: Really?

LOIS: Wow!

DAVID [*eagerly to her*]: D'you like it?

LOIS: It's out of sight! . . . Honest!

GIDEON: What do you say, Mark? Isn't it fine?

MARK: I say felicitations to my son on his sense of things. He obviously sees what is lacking here. A true Cathedral needs a true Cathe*dra!*

LOIS: Cathedral?

MARK: That's where we are, isn't it? Shrivings, the Cathedral of Humanism.

GIDEON: Don't be naughty, Mark!

MARK [*to* DAVID]: I'm right, aren't I? It is a throne?

DAVID [*low*]: Yes.

MARK: And for Giddy?

DAVID: Yes.

MARK [*to* GIDEON]: Exactly so! All for *you!* The Chair of Paternal Wisdom. I would hope to earn one myself in time. Such objects have to be earned, eh, David?

[DAVID *shrugs haplessly.*]

GIDEON: You sit on it. It would become you far better, a throne.

MARK: Maybe—but it hasn't been offered! We're here to witness *your* coronation. So please get up there and sit down as impressively as you can manage!

GIDEON [*grimacing modestly*]: Very well. Thank you, David. [*He sits on the throne.*]

[MARK *claps.*]

MARK: Hail, Gideon! First Pope of Reason! Hail!

GIDEON [*embarrassed*]: Stop it now, Mark, really!

LOIS: Hail, Giddy! Hail, Giddy! Hail, Giddy!

GIDEON: Now, please! Really! Really! . . .

LOIS: You look absolutely wonderful there! Doesn't he, Mr. Askelon?

MARK: Exactly in place!

GIDEON: Perhaps I should take it with me on the vigil. Set it up in Parliament Square. It would evoke irreverent comparisons with the one in Westminster Abbey!

MARK: Vigil? What vigil?

LOIS: We're all sitting, tomorrow and Sunday afternoon.

MARK [*alarmed*]: You mean a demonstration?

LOIS: Yes. It's been in all the papers!

MARK: I don't read newspapers. In the end, that is the only truly obscene four-letter word: NEWS!

LOIS: We're hoping for at least ten thousand people. Why don't you come too? It'd be the most tremendous help to the cause!

GIDEON: She's right. I'm known as a crank—but you would really be a catch.

MARK: Oh no, I don't think so.

LOIS: Oh, why not, Mr. Askelon? It would be so *great* having you!

MARK [*lightly*]: Let's say, I hate to be old-fashioned.

LOIS [*bewildered*]: Old-fashioned?

MARK: Peaceful protest is absolutely Out, my dear. The really modern young have quite abandoned vigils. Especially in your fair country.

GIDEON: Which is why she left it, Mark; for the moment. Until there's another real peace movement, and not just Young Violence joining with Old.

LOIS: Which will be never.

GIDEON: Oh, come now. All revolutionaries idealize their movement's early days. Don't fall into the same trap. The Flower Children shouted some simple truths. Home has to be found: it's not the place you're born in. Country can be a mental prison, and patriotism an ape's adrenaline. Do you think that'll be forgotten?

LOIS [*warmly*]: Not when you speak, no!

MARK [*ironic*]: And what did the flowers shout?

LOIS: Beg pardon?

MARK: If those daffodils could speak, which the flower boys handed out to policemen—if they could tell about their birth, through layers of icy spring soil, d'you know what they'd say? They'd open their yellow mouths and yell "Violence! Violence!" at the top of their stalks.

LOIS [*laughing*]: No, they would not! They'd shout "Effort!" That's not the same thing at all.

GIDEON: Well said, Lois!

MARK: *Touché!* . . . What would I have to do at your vigil? Sit in front of the House of Commons and chant Down with the Bomb!?

LOIS: We're concerned to ban all weapons, you know. Not just the bomb.

MARK [*playfully*]: Even penknives?

LOIS: Beg pardon?

MARK: Even vegetable knives? Those clever little knives which dice carrots for your joy-giving, life-enhancing salads?

LOIS: Well, that would be a dreadful idea!

MARK: What is not a weapon? The tongue, Miss Neal, can be a dreadful weapon. Should we have them all cut out?

LOIS [*becoming a little confused*]: I mean, here at Shrivings we think it is wrong to fight in any circumstances.

MARK: Any whatever?

LOIS: Any whatever!

[*She looks at* GIDEON *for approval.*]

MARK: Even Hitler?

LOIS: Well, it is hard to adjust to that particular concept, I admit. But once you start fighting, you become as guilty as your enemy.

MARK [*blandly*]: You mean, the men who freed Belsen were as guilty as the men who made it?

LOIS: No, of course not.

MARK: Then what? The evil you don't fight, you enlarge.

GIDEON [*softly*]: No, my dear. The evil you do fight you enlarge. That's surely the point. You arm yourself to destroy gas chambers in Poland. Five years later, you are melting the eyeballs of fishermen on the Yellow Sea. We've had centuries of fighting back for Freedom and Justice. It doesn't work. We've had centuries of trying to *limit* fighting back: battle by mercenaries; truces on Christmas Eve. It doesn't work either. So long as boys can continue to hose each other down with fire on Boxing Day, their Christmas Day truce is an obscenity; a sop to the unseeing.

[*Pause. Reassuringly he squeezes* LOIS'*s hand.*]

MARK [*brusquely*]: If a ruffian with a pistol entered this room, and was definitely going to kill Miss Neal—assuming you had a pistol too, would you use it on him?

GIDEON: No.

MARK: You would let him kill her?

GIDEON: I have no choice, unless I wish to become him.

MARK [*to* LOIS]: Same situation. Would you let him kill Giddy?

LOIS: Yes.

MARK: Touching loyalty you have for each other here at Shrivings!

LOIS: We *do!*

MARK: Apparently.

LOIS: Shrivings *is* the loyalty!

MARK [*to* DAVID]: What would you do, my son?

[*Pause.*]

DAVID: Is it a girl ruffian or a man?

LOIS: What difference does *that* make?

DAVID: I think I'd use the gun.

MARK: Why?

DAVID: Because I'd rather have Lois alive than somebody I didn't know.

MARK: Unreasonable boy! And she's not even flattered, are you?

LOIS [*to* DAVID]: How can you be so subjective about everything? It's like you can't grasp the simplest general idea!

MARK: Don't blame him too harshly, Miss Neal. Beauty, after all, confuses the best of us!

LOIS [*embarrassed*]: Oh! Well! Gee! . . .

MARK: I must confess that I myself, seeing you threatened by this ruffian, would have a hard time leaving you to your fate.

LOIS: Thank you!

MARK: But I would, of course. Out of deference to your principles.

LOIS [*nervously*]: Oh, of course!

MARK [*his tone darkening*]: I would—with the utmost regret—abandon you to his pistol. Or to his razor. Or to the dungeons of the Inquisition. Or the locomotives of Chiang Kai-shek, who, I have been told, fed his prisoners into their furnaces in order to keep them running. Or for that matter, to the hands of New York construction workers . . .[*He stops suddenly.*]

GIDEON [*puzzled*]: Mark?

MARK [*his tone totally changed*]: Have you seen the Ruffian at work? Really seen him? Have you, Giddy? You sit here so calmly. . . . Have you seen a boy scalped? I have. Last year—in the civilized city of Manhattan . . . [*Pause.*] I'd gone there after Giulia died, to keep busy, as they say.

GIDEON: Yes, I heard that you went.

MARK: To declaim poems to college students, written twenty years before they were born. . . . They were in fact swarming all over the city the day I arrived: yet again protesting the Vietnam War—in this instance, the invasion of Cambodia. Isn't it amazing the way the Young simply won't give up? There they all were, in their velvets and zippy boots—haircuts like so many liberty bells—still handing out pamphlets, still squeaking "Stop Killing" in desperate little voices. And the next day their elders—as if the murder of four children in Ohio had not been enough—decided to punish their impertinence in New York. [*Pause.*] I was sitting with my lawyer in his office in Wall Street. Suddenly we heard this roar outside—it was about noon: a sea of approaching fury. We walked to the window. Four floors below us, a terrified group of youngsters was standing quite still. On both sides of them stood massed ranks of workers from the building trade—men whose present affluence has apparently compelled them into the right wing. Dreadful-looking thugs, with faces like huge steaks, wearing hard yellow hats. And then we watched *their* protest: *their* statement of human dignity. For fifteen minutes, they beat the children into pulp. They bashed them with their fists. They kicked them in the balls and the breasts with steel toes. They tore cheeks from faces. They danced on vomiting girls. And then they swept on, shouting "America! America!"—round the corner, to the next gang-bang. And all the while, not moving, not doing anything, stood policemen–their Irish potato faces barely concealing smiles. [*Pause.*] My lawyer, a fellow of infinite social conscience, had dashed into the street, leaving me alone. Suddenly the place was quiet again, and there was only one figure visible. A boy, sitting on the curb, wearing a sort of eiderdown. Lumps of hair had been torn from his head. Can you imagine the force that needed?—and he was moaning in unspeakable pain. But with some kind of instinct for city tidiness, he was carefully dropping what blood he could into a drain. I stood in the window watching him, a dry martini in my hand. It was a day of April. Clouds of pollen were streaming down the street between us. Golden dust tumbling through the air. It seemed to be settling over him, like dandruff. . . . And then he raised his head and looked at me.

LOIS: What did you do?

MARK [*brutally*]: I raised my glass.

LOIS [*confused*]: But . . . but couldn't you have—?

MARK: What?

LOIS: Well, gotten him an ambulance?

MARK: I could. But I wanted another drink.

[*A shocked pause.*

*Abruptly he goes upstairs into his bedroom, and bangs the door.* GIDEON *moves after him, but suddenly the door is loudly locked from the inside.* MARK *sits on the bed, his face in his hands.*]

LOIS: He's nuts! He's completely *nuts!*

GIDEON: Lois, please.

LOIS: What's that supposed to mean? What's he *talking* about?

GIDEON: He was always addicted to drama. You know that.

LOIS: Drama?

GIDEON: Why don't you just start dinner?

LOIS: Jesus! . . .[*Regaining control.*] O.K.!

[*She goes out to the kitchen.* DAVID *stands unmoving, staring at the stairs.*]

GIDEON: It's just fatigue. That's all. He'll be down for dinner. . . . Why don't we take a walk in the garden? What do you say? . . . *David* . . . he's simply tired—

[DAVID *turns and goes abruptly into the garden. Puzzled,* GIDEON *follows him. Above,* MARK *springs up from the bed. He opens his case and takes out two bottles of brandy, which he places on the shelf. Then he returns and extracts another two, which he also puts on the shelf. Then he takes out one shirt, closes the case, and kicks it under the bed. He turns to the package in its sacking on the table. He places his hands on it.*]

MARK: *Proteggimi. Proteggimi. Proteggimi!* . . . And him. Keep him safe from me. By your limbs, I beg you. By your murdered limbs, keep them all out of harm from me: Gideon—David our son—that silly girl. [*He unties the string and stuffs it into his pocket. Then he lowers the sacking to reveal a black wooden box with doors. On the top is a little pediment in pink wood: this he erects, with a deliberate delicacy.*] My wife. My own true wife. Santissima, Beatissima Giulia! [*Standing behind it, he opens the doors of the box to reveal, staring straight at us, the head in effigy of a young woman painted in naïve style. The whole shrine is colored in the gay, crude manner of peasant work from Southern Italy: on the inside flaps of the doors are bright, little gilded saints. Mark moves round and kneels to it, reverently.*] I'll not go down there again. I'll keep in here till the prize-giving. Then straight back to Corfu—hurting no one. I swear it, my darling. *Te lo juro! Te lo juro, mia moglie! Santa Giulia Paralytica!*

SLOW BLACKOUT

## SCENE 2

*Friday night.*

*Ten-thirty. As the lights come up,* LOIS *is clearing the dinner table.* DAVID *sits cross-legged on the floor, rolling a joint. Upstairs,* MARK *lies on his bed. One hand holds a half-empty bottle.*

DAVID: I saw an armored car today.

LOIS: What?

DAVID: In Trister village, just before dinner. Well, it was one of those converted ones. At first I thought it was full of chrysanthemums. Then just as they passed me, they all separated, and turned out to be four shaggy male heads and four shaggy female, all the same color bronze. If I'd chosen the next street, there'd have been no car. If I'd seen them at the next corner, they'd already have separated.

LOIS: Are you stoned?

*[He does not reply.*

*She gives him a bewildered face, and goes into the kitchen with her tray.* DAVID *lights his joint.* MARK *sits on the bed.]*

MARK: Brilliant. Absolutely brilliant! Not ten minutes in the house, go off like that—bang! Just for one pretentious American slit. . . . *[He sits up and looks at the shrine.]* No, it was his fault, the boy. Coming in like that—your eyes in his head! . . . Who knew he was here? . . . Standing there like some medieval halfwit, all shrugs and shavings in the hair. Who the hell is he? Master carpenter to Gideon Petrie. I sent him to England for *that?*—to carve his throne! "Hail to my new daddy—Lord of the twenty-five books!" My old daddy only wrote four, and they were just poetry! That doesn't count . . .

*[*LOIS *returns with a bowl containing four green apples. She piles the remaining plates on the tray.* DAVID *watches her.]*

And what about his eyes, eh? Gideon's? Did you see all that white gum in the corners? My God, he's aged!

*[He lifts the bottle to his lips, and drinks.]*

DAVID: Smash one.

LOIS: Huh?

DAVID: Say Let this Plate be Dad, and smash it. Banish the Demon Uptight.

LOIS: It wouldn't.

*[She goes on piling the plates.]*

MARK *[half to himself]*: "Peace!" "Peace!" What's that supposed to mean? Well, of course, you could hear it—defiance. "I'm Giddy's boy now. Let's not mistake . . . Son and heir of Shrivings . . ." Sagging Jesus!

DAVID *[warmly]*: I'm sorry.

LOIS: I mean, O.K., I just wish you'd warned me in advance. I wish you'd told me; please overlook my Dad's behavior, because he's clinically insane. I'd have been prepared.

DAVID: He's not.

LOIS: Yeah, well, like what's he doing up there now, locked in his room all night? No dinner—nothing.

DAVID: Your elbows are very upset.

LOIS: What?

DAVID: They're up in arms.

LOIS: Ha, ha, ha. *[She picks up the full tray.]*

DAVID: Hey.

LOIS: Hay is for horses. *[She goes into the kitchen.]*

MARK [*to the shrine*]: All right, dance for him. You dance for him. [*He gets off the bed, and stands glaring at the shrine.*] You go in there and dance him to sleep *now!* Try it, why don't you? Get out of bed, and try it! . . .

[*He begins a drunk parody "dance," singing to himself. Sitting below,* DAVID *looks upward. The dance stops.*]

[*Shouting at the shrine.*] All right, stop it! Just stop . . . sad looks. Reproach . . . Well, well! Can't you ever cry? Can't you ever fight me like a woman, not fucking saint? . . .

[*He starts pacing about.* DAVID *rises anxiously to his feet.*]

That damn book. Always that prayer book! Can't you see it's disgusting? Filthy colored pictures—Christ the Sheperdess! Have you got no dignity at all, praying to a Bearded Lady? Signora Gesù, Little Bo-Peep of Souls!

[*He starts to laugh—snatches up a large white towel, and lurches off to the bathroom.*

*Below,* DAVID *suddenly shudders.* LOIS *comes in with a cloth to wipe the table.*]

LOIS: What's the matter?

DAVID [*not looking at her*]: On the terrace.

LOIS: What?

DAVID: He'd sit and watch me for hours. Straw hat—eyes . . .

LOIS: What are you talking about?

DAVID: When I used to play . . . I'd go la-la-la, pretending to sing.

LOIS: I thought you adored him. You sort of said . . .

[*He turns and shrugs, hopelessly.*]

Look, why don't you go up there now? It's obviously what he'd like.

DAVID: It isn't.

LOIS: Of course it is. It must be.

DAVID: It isn't.

LOIS: How do you know?

[*He shrugs again.*]

Well then, what does he *want?*

DAVID: I'll whisper it. Here.

[*She approaches, puzzled. He kisses her abruptly. She lets herself be kissed, but remains inert.*]

Thank you.

LOIS: You're welcome.

DAVID: You know something? You're so uptight, it's a joke.

LOIS: A person is not uptight, my dear, just because she doesn't happen to want that.

DAVID: I think she is. I think that's exactly what she is.

LOIS [*gently*]: Or because she respects somebody else's opinions. I know it's me being pompous again. O.K. But we've talked about this one hundred times. This is Giddy's place. His whole meaning. Don't you realize this is where he did it? Probably in this very room.

DAVID [*sarcastic*]: Wow! . . .

LOIS: Do you think it was easy for a normal man to go to his wife on his forty-fifth birthday and tell her he can't have sex any more?

DAVID: It certainly wasn't easy for her, was it? She buggered off, and maybe that's exactly what I should do too.

LOIS [*alarmed*]: What d'you mean?

DAVID: Piss off, that's what I mean. Exit. Is that what you want? Come on, tell me. Is that what you'd like—for me to go, as she did?

LOIS: Don't be silly. You know I'd hate it.

DAVID [*warmly*]: Would you?

LOIS: I'm simply asking you to respect the spirit of a great man in his own house, that's all.

DAVID [*playfully*]: Because he's a vegetarian, we all have to be?

LOIS: Yes.

DAVID: Even though he doesn't mind?

LOIS: Yes. Because I do. On his behalf.

DAVID: You know what you are? You are a Disciple.

LOIS: And proud of it.

DAVID: I don't know a word that means so many boring things.

LOIS: O.K. I'm boring. I know it. You're not saying anything new.

DAVID: I didn't mean that.

LOIS: It doesn't matter.

DAVID: I don't know what I mean. Not from one second to the next!

LOIS: If you could ever get involved, you might just find out. Till then you're like a sort of ghost, tapping on the window. Do you know?

[*He pulls "ghost faces" on her.*]

I'm serious, David. I mean it! . . .[*She breaks up laughing.*] Oh, cut it out!

[*She returns the faces. They are both playing, when* GIDEON *comes out of his study.*]

GIDEON: I suppose Mark hasn't been down?

LOIS: No sign of him.

GIDEON: Then I'd better go up.

DAVID: D'you think you should?

GIDEON: We're starting a Vigil of Peace tomorrow. We can't leave distress at home. . . . Are you coming with us?

LOIS: Of course he is! Oh, Giddy, it's going to be wild! I heard on the radio they're expecting twenty-five thousand people. Isn't that crazy? You'll have to address them.

GIDEON: Will I?

LOIS: Well, of course. The eyes of England will be upon you!

GIDEON: Oh, my goodness.

LOIS: You'll have to say something witty and profound.

DAVID: And very loud: the open air.

GIDEON: Very well. I shall say, "Go home, the lot of you! What the devil do you think you're doing here, parading the streets in fancy dress, and annoying the police who have far more important things to do than take care of you lot!"

[*Both the youngsters laugh.* GIDEON *ascends his throne with an air.*]

"What it is you want? We have educated you, at vast expense, in all the wisdom at our disposal. You've been given expert courses in all the right subjects. Mangerism, or worship of Family; Flaggism, or worship of Tribe; Thingism, or worship of Money. In our theaters and on our screens, we have taught you to find the act of killing men exciting, and the act of creating them obscene. You can go to church, and respect the stopped mind. You can go to war memorials, and respect the stopped body. What more do you want?"

[*Both youngsters laugh and clap.*]

LOIS: Oh, Giddy, that's great! You've got to say it—just like that!

GIDEON: And then, perhaps I'll ask them what they *really* want. If they are honest, they'll reply: "A point to our lives. A meaning." "Very well, then," I'll say, "ask yourselves who you are. Look at each other. What do you see there? A crowd of weird beings, standing half-in, half-out of nature. Animals possessed of powers completely nonanimal. Powers to symbolize, to imagine, to laugh with self-ridicule. What could they be, these powers, if not tools to help free you from the violent, circular force which dominates all other life? [*He sits.*] Scientists go about the world looking for the Missing Link. It is staring them in the face. [*Pointing to* DAVID.] *You* are the Missing Link. [*Pointing to* LOIS.] *You* are the link between animals and what must appear if we are not to be sucked back into annihilation. Remember, as animals we are failures, and as aggressive beings also. We have to come at last to see Ego in a new way. As a pod, evolved for our protection during our years through prehistory, but which has now become our prison. If we are not to suffocate in it, we have to burst it open."

LOIS: Wow!

GIDEON: We know more and more about our aggressions. We can't ever hope to remove them by reason alone; but if we don't make the attempt, not merely to concentrate their fury on to ever-lessening objects, but absolutely to starve them to death, we are doomed. Let me simplify it for you to the point of a crazy imperative. The drug children of today cry: "Unite with Nature!" I say: "Resist her. Spit out the anger in your daddy's sperm! The bile in your mother's milk! The more you starve out aggression, the more you will begin yourselves!"

DAVID: Oh, that's beautiful!

GIDEON: "Fight your instinctive dislike of other people. Fight the clinging to possession. Fight the need to invent enemies. If you want fights, I have them for you in plenty! I tell you, you must fight all the preserving mechanisms which you have inherited from evolution. Only so can you fulfill your Destiny. I detest that word. It is fascist, and Siegfriedish, and faintly embarrassing. But I can't think of another. Man *has* a Destiny: to be a loving creator, or a dead duck!". . . How about that?

DAVID [*laughing*]: You're a mad old ham, aren't you?

LOIS: David!

GIDEON: Not too mad, I hope.

DAVID: I don't know.

GIDEON: Anyway, I've made a huge decision. I'm going to fast, all weekend!

LOIS: Fast? Whatever for?

GIDEON [*getting up*]: I've been thinking what his father was saying: how vigils and protests are out of date. Well, there's really nothing I can do about that, since war and violence are even more out of date. But the least I can do is pep things up a bit. Inject a little show business into proceedings! Hence the fast. If I were to faint from hunger on the pavement, the effect could be sensational.

DAVID: I don't like it.

GIDEON: Oh, come. Pathos still remains the best way of influencing the middle class.

LOIS: I think it's out of sight! Why don't we ask everyone who comes to fast too?

DAVID: And pass out too, all at the same time! You could blow your nose as a signal, and twenty-five thousand people could collapse, holding their tummies.

LOIS: Ha, ha, ha!

GIDEON: No, she's got a good idea, David. [*To* LOIS.] Look, why don't you ring the newspapers? We can make the first editions if we hurry. Say I'm announcing a two-day hunger protest and would like everyone who's coming tomorrow to stay hungry as well. The press will love it. It's so sensationally vulgar.

LOIS [*getting up*]: Great!

GIDEON: They always say my head's in the clouds. They'll have to admit this is pretty nifty.

LOIS: I'll get started right away. And you two go to bed. You'll need your strength. Both of you, now. [*She goes out into the study.*]

GIDEON: What's the matter?

[*Pause.*]

DAVID: Starving people aren't protected.

GIDEON [*puzzled*]: Protected? Against what? . . . Why should I need protection?

[*Pause.* DAVID *shrugs, looking at the floor.*]

GIDEON: Are you being fanciful again? . . . I'll go and see your father. You go to bed. Things will look fine in the morning.

[*He goes to the stairs.* DAVID *rises anxiously.* GIDEON *turns, aware of this.*]

[*Amusedly.*] I should think pot is allowed on a fast, wouldn't you? Does that make you any happier?

DAVID: Peace.

[*The boy walks rapidly past him, and runs upstairs, out of sight. To the right* GIDEON *ascends after him. He knocks on* MARK'*s door.*]

GIDEON: Mark! . . . Mark!

[MARK *appears slowly from the bathroom.*]

Let me see you, please. Just for a moment.

[MARK *moves into the room, without replying.*]

I beg you. Please let me in.

[MARK *stands before the shrine.*]

Mark . . .

MARK [*whispering to the shrine*]: *Se viene, non ne sono responsabile!*

GIDEON: I'll not go away till I've seen you. There. What do you think of that? I'll stay here all night. It'll be the start of my vigil.

[MARK *laughs aloud.*]

Come on, now! Let me in! [*He rattles the door handle.*]

MARK: *Non ne sono.*

[*He moves to shut the doors of the shrine—then pauses and mischievously opens them again. Then he goes to the door, unlocks it, and retreats to the bed, where he sits.* GIDEON *enters.*]

GIDEON: Peace.

MARK: I am surprised.

GIDEON: By what?

MARK: To find locks at Shrivings.

GIDEON: People require privacy at times.

MARK [*sarcastically*]: You mean for lovemaking?

GIDEON [*imperturbably*]: Among other things.

MARK: And who makes love here?

GIDEON: Youngsters stay every night. I imagine they're at it all the time.

MARK: How does Miss Neal regard that? Is she delighted by all that hippie coition?

GIDEON [*smiling*]: I think she tends to turn a blind eye.

MARK: Yes, I've seen that blind eye. It's magnificent. A great improvement on your ex-wife's, to be honest.

GIDEON: Really?

MARK: Enid's eyes were like two pebbles in a January stream. I can say that now.

GIDEON: You've lost none of your naughtiness, my dear!

[*He turns and sees the shrine.*]

MARK: Giulia's, of course, you remember. Around them flared that corona. Invisible there, of course. But quite detectable in David.

GIDEON: Yes.

MARK: I had her made by a craftsman in Corfu, from an old photograph. As a souvenir, she works well. Also as a reliquary.

GIDEON: Reliquary?

MARK: For her ashes.

[*Pause.*]

GIDEON: How beautiful.

MARK: Yes, well, there we are. Two old men with dead wives.

GIDEON: To be pedantic—you are still young, and Enid is still alive.

MARK: Married to an accountant I believe.

GIDEON: Yes. In Berkshire.

MARK: Isn't that death?

GIDEON [*laughing*]: You really are outrageous!

MARK: Do you miss her?

GIDEON: Very much.

MARK: Still?

GIDEON: Yes.

MARK: I leave tomorrow.

GIDEON: Leave?

MARK: For Corfu.

GIDEON: I won't hear of it. Why?

MARK: I'm out of practice at being a guest.

GIDEON [*gently*]: There are no guests at Shrivings. You're part of a family, and have to work at it.

MARK: Is my son part of this family?

GIDEON: Everybody is who stays here.

MARK: And he's stayed six months. He must enjoy it. Naturally. The more unreal the place, the more he would thrive.

GIDEON: Unreal?

MARK: We are not Place People, David or I. My father was not called Askelon, but Ashkenazy. Israel Ashkenazy, of the ghetto face. He bequeathed me no home on earth: only envy of home in others. That boy will never walk a Dorset lane like an Englishman—rock on a Vermont porch like a Yankee—doze under a Corfu cypress like a Greek. He's a mongrel! Russo-Jewish-English-Neapolitan! Whelped in one island, weaned in another.

GIDEON [*with energy*]: Then lucky him! He at least has no chance to fool himself with illusion! We are all mongrels, Mark. Don't hunt for your home in the bloodstream! Home is an act of will.

MARK: Do you imagine?

GIDEON: Make no mistake: Shrivings is real. It would still be real if it were a tent or a set of shacks. Ask the people who come here, the hopeful young, who flood in every night. It's not a family, as so many people know it—a box of boredom for man and wife—a torture chamber for the children. That idea of family must soon be obsolete, surely?—a miserable little group, marked off by a flat door, or a garden fence! . . .[*Ardently.*] No, my dear. Here is a new place of love. Stay with us, not just till Monday. See it for yourself . . .This one weekend, for your sake, I broke all rules and closed it—just to give us time alone. I believe I was wrong. [*He extends his hand.*]

MARK [*coldly*]: I leave tomorrow. No more questions.

GIDEON [*very gently*]: We simply will not allow it.

MARK: Please go.

GIDEON: I can't believe you mean this.

MARK: Go!

[*Pause.*]

GIDEON: Peace.

[GIDEON *leaves the room.* MARK *sits on for a moment, takes a swig from his bottle—then suddenly rushes downstairs after him. Startled,* GIDEON *turns.*]

MARK [*blurting it out*]: All right! *Save me!*

[*Pause.*

LOIS *comes out of the study.* MARK *immediately turns away.*]

LOIS: Oh, excuse me.

GIDEON: It's all right, my dear.

LOIS: I talked with six papers. They're all printing something in their first editions.

GIDEON: Good girl. [*He silently signs for her to go upstairs.*]

LOIS: Don't stay up too late. Good night, Mr. Askelon. [*Tenderly.*] Peace.

[*He nods. She goes upstairs. Pause.*]

GIDEON: Save you from what?

MARK: Dust.

GIDEON: Dust?

MARK: Pollen.

GIDEON: That morning you spoke of. In New York. The riot in New York.

MARK: Yes?

GIDEON: There was pollen in the streets.

MARK: Yes.

GIDEON: Well? What of it?

MARK: It's hard.

GIDEON: Yes?

[*A long pause.*]

MARK: It was there between us. Me and that student. Between us in a long stream. I remained at my lawyer's window, looking down at him. He sat there on the curb looking up at me, through that curtain of pollen. We lasted like that forever. I mean, five minutes. Five centuries in another sense, until I saw him transformed to an earlier time, five hundred years at least, when Wall Street was just a granite ledge padded by Redskin feet, and he another human sack, holding its scalped head. . . . Five hundred years and no change. Five thousand, and still the identical horror. The tearers and the torn. The orderers. The Penalizers. The Joyless, returning and returning like the spring. Unalterable. . . . Do you know the taste of Unalterable? That boy sat glued to the earth, with the pollen twirling round his red scalp—clouds of glinting dust—round and round the blood patch, like flies. . . . I leaned out, and it flew up to my mouth. I breathed it. I chewed it. It entered my stomach like powdered drug: dead spring—round, dead, unalterable spring, with its meaningless glints of hope! On and on we glared at each other, and on and on his blood dripped into the drain, and the pollen twirled inside me, and the years turned, till I was sick. Till I vomited down the side of that smart new building. I saw my sick running down the glass walls, and the boy began to laugh.

GIDEON: Oh, my dear Mark! My poor man!

MARK: There he sat—blond puppet, in his eiderdown! There he sat on the curb—my wife, in her canvas jacket, staring at me, those fixed eyes, "*Gesù! Gesù!*"

GIDEON: Your wife?

MARK: Yes! . . .YES! . . .[*Pause.*] Public murder or private: it's all the same.

GIDEON [*bewildered*]: Murder?

MARK: Pull the hair out—pull the life. It's all the same. Takes longer, of course. Ten years longer. But it's all the same.

GIDEON: What do you mean, Mark? Murder?

MARK [*dryly*]: Killing. Taking the life of.

GIDEON: What are you saying?

MARK: I'm saying I killed my wife. Is that hard to understand?

GIDEON: Oh, look—my dear . . .

MARK: Yes?

GIDEON: This is entirely my fault. I should never have left you alone in that villa! I should have come out myself and brought you back here. I ask you to forgive my selfishness. . . . Sometimes one makes the most terrible mistakes; just for fear of intruding on grief.

MARK: Grief? Is that all you see, then? *Grief?!*

GIDEON: It is the most warping emotion in the world.

MARK: The great poet, grieving for his love! Sagging Jesus! . . . Look at you. What can you see? [*Viciously.*] Gummy worried old eyes. What can you really see, Giddy, through all that white gum?

[*Pause.*]

GIDEON [*imperturbably*]: I like to think of it as spirit gum.

[*Pause.*]

MARK [*lower*]: Twelve years ago, you couldn't see. Even when you were in Corfu, I'd already started to kill her. You couldn't see it.

GIDEON [*distressed*]: My dear—my dear, dear man . . .

MARK: Even if I told you every detail. If I described to you exactly how I finished her off—what I actually *did* to her on her last night on earth . . . you wouldn't believe me. I'm your darling. Your first flier.

GIDEON: Of course you are.

MARK: Your eagle.

GIDEON: Yes.

MARK: No, Giddy.

GIDEON [*passionately*]: Yes, my eagle! The most marvelous pupil I ever had. The most marvelous friend!

MARK [*quietly*]: Stop it.

GIDEON: That's what you could never quite believe: that everything you did was a *marvel* to me.

MARK: Please stop it, Giddy.

GIDEON: Now I've found you again I'm not going to let you go until I've mended those damaged wings and sent you soaring up again into the sky of action—your proper element—your *real place!*

MARK: *Stop it! Will you stop it?* [*Pause. He draws* GIDEON *gently to him, and stares into his face.*] [*Softly.*] Believe me, old master, I could tear the faith out of your head, as easily as they tore the hair out of that boy.

GIDEON [*levelly*]: My goodness.

[GIDEON *smiles. They remain unmoving, very close together, staring at each other.*]

MARK: Poor Mark. Grief has made him quite dotty, hasn't it?

GIDEON: A little unfair on himself, I think.

MARK [*quietly*]: Is there no way of convincing you of your danger?

GIDEON: From you? . . .

MARK [*intensely*]: It isn't grief, Giddy! Be warned.

GIDEON: Then what, my dear?

MARK: The dust. It seeks converts. . . . Do you know how long it took me to fall finally from your faith? The time it takes vomit to slide down a wall. Now I know—and have to make others know.

GIDEON: What do you know?

MARK: That the Gospel According to Saint Gideon is a lie. That we as men cannot alter for the better in any particular that matters. That we are totally and forever unimprovable.

GIDEON: No.

MARK: We will kill forever. We will persecute forever. We will break our lust forever on enemies we invent for the purpose.

GIDEON: No.

MARK: We are made of hostility as the spring is made of pollen. And each birth renews it, as the spring renews the year.

GIDEON: No.

MARK: Prove it.

GIDEON: Impossible. It is a faith, like others.

MARK [*ironically*]: Faith! Saint Gideon Petrie on his peacock throne of Reason, ringed by the irises of adolescence! Do you know what they say about you? Your discipline alone can save the world—because you alone have withered out of yourself entirely the roots of hate. Is it possible? [*Slyly.*] How if I showed them their delusion—Miss Neal, and my doting son? . . . "Stay with us," you say, "in this Commune of Love." I say, if I chose, they would see you drive me out of it with hate.

GIDEON: Never.

MARK: Within one week.

GIDEON: Never.

MARK: Within one weekend.

GIDEON [*serenely*]: Never. Never. Never.

[*Pause.*]

MARK [*hard*]: Very well. Let's see. . . . I propose a battle. It is now Friday night. I say by Monday morning—day of our joint award for Humane Letters—you will have thrown me out of Shrivings. How about that?

GIDEON: You would lose.

MARK: *I want to lose!* Because, if you lose, it'll be an end for both of us. . . . If you can survive me with all your gentleness intact, I will stay here and work as your disciple. But you succumb—order me out of here in hate, for whatever reason—and you will not again be able to preach Improvability. As for me, once you slam that door upon me, I will stagger down your tunnel of elm trees into the arms of Mother Church. Whether Roman or Greek to be later determined. So. I give you the Battle of Shrivings. [*He drinks.*]

GIDEON: You know, my dear, you really are the naughtiest man in the world!

MARK: Aren't I?

GIDEON: I think you'd say anything for the sake of drama!

MARK: I come out of the dust. Into the Church of Man. Do I join it, or pull it down? . . . You're right. I'm ridiculous. Goodbye. [*He strides to the door.*]

GIDEON: Mark!

[MARK *pauses; turns.*]

Stay in this house as long as you wish. Shrivings will never reject you.

MARK: So be it.

GIDEON: Now it's very late. We can resume this tomorrow, surely?

MARK: You have no choice, now.

GIDEON [*amused*]: Oh, my goodness.

[MARK *goes to the stairs, then turns.*]

MARK: Don't you know who I am?

GIDEON: Who?

MARK: The Ruffian with the Pistol. Shoot me, and *you're* dead.
GIDEON: Peace, my friend.
MARK: Impossible. Battle has begun.

[*He goes upstairs.* GIDEON *stares after him, then goes into his bedroom. The light fades.*]

## ACT TWO

### SCENE 1

*Saturday night.*

*Eleven o'clock.* MARK *sits alone at the desk, listening to a large transistor radio.*

B.B.C. ANNOUNCER: In the debate which followed, Mr. Lucas Brangwyn, the Member for Bloomsbury, called the wholesale destruction of Devonshire Square "nothing less than a national scandal." In his reply the Minister of Housing said nobody regretted the passing of old London more than he, but he sincerely believed the demolition had been carried out in what would ultimately be the best interests of the British public. [*Pause.*] This afternoon at two o'clock, Sir Gideon Petrie sat down in Parliament Square, Westminster, to begin the first of his two six-hour vigils outside the House of Commons in protest against the manufacture of all arms in the United Kingdom. He was accompanied by members of the World League of Peace, of which Sir Gideon is president: as well as many students and well-wishers. Minor outbreaks of violence occurred when a group representing the League of Empire Loyalists threw bags of refuse over the sitting figures. They were moved on by the police.

[MARK *smiles.*]

Sir Gideon, who is also on a two-day fast, appeared composed and smiling throughout. [*Pause.*] The forecasters say that the easterly winds sweeping the country are dying down and it will become warmer tomorrow, but with a chance of showers—

[MARK *twiddles the dial. Loud rock music comes out of the radio. He turns it off contemptuously. The front door slams.* MARK *rises, hearing the voices of the returning protesters. He tiptoes out into the kitchen. Into the room come* GIDEON, LOIS, *and* DAVID, *flushed and excited, taking off their thick outdoor clothes.*

*Chattering, they peel off scarves and boots.* DAVID *relieves* GIDEON *of his overcoat and beret, and hangs it up on the peg by the garden door.*]

LOIS: Yeah, that was great! *That* was the best!

DAVID: No, the old man in the top hat was the best!

LOIS: Yeah, but did you see the old woman in the fur coat dancing the Hare Krishna with those kids? I acted dumb, you know—pretending not to know, and I asked her what she was doing. Do you know what she said? [*Cockney accent.*] "I don't know, love. It's a new religion. Ride-a-Christian!"

GIDEON [*laughing*]: That's delightful! I wish I'd heard that.

LOIS: Isn't it great?

DAVID: D'you know who I really liked best? You probably didn't notice him. A short, fat man carrying a pork pie with a flag in it, saying "Peace for all Pigs!" It turned out he was from the Society of Vegetarians.

[LOIS *laughs.*]

GIDEON: Oh, that's marvelous! Yes, that's really the best!

LOIS: They were all fasting, you know. Everyone in that square, I bet you.

DAVID: That girl in the string mini looked like she'd been fasting for a month.

LOIS: What's that smell?

[*Pause. They sniff.*]

DAVID: Cooking.

LOIS: It can't be.

GIDEON: Oh, I think it can. [*Slight pause. He calls.*] Mark!

[MARK *enters from the kitchen, wearing an apron, a chef's hat made out of newspaper, and carrying a cooking slice.*]

MARK: You called for me, sir?

GIDEON: Peace.

MARK: How are you? Rumor reached me that people threw things at you.

GIDEON [*calmly*]: Only a few. It's not the first time the League of Empire Loyalists has emptied its rubbish over the British public. Besides, I was in wonderful hands. These two looked after me all day, like the brave fliers they are!

LOIS: Nonsense, Giddy. He was just great, Mr. Askelon! You should have seen him! His head was like the still center of that whole huge crowd!

GIDEON: Well, it didn't feel very still, or very central, come to that!

MARK: Why? Did you fast badly?

GIDEON: Not at all. I saw two Members of Parliament, who had obviously just left the dining room of the House of Commons. I thought they looked at me with envy.

LOIS: You should have a good hot bath and go straight to bed. I'll run it for you.

GIDEON [*staring at* MARK]: In a moment. You appear to be cooking something.

MARK: Yes. I'm a weak brother, I regret to say. I held out all day, out of sympathy. But just fifteen minutes ago, I yielded. I'm afraid I started to make myself the very smallest repast. Of course, I'll eat it out of sight, in there. [*He makes to go back to the kitchen.*]

GIDEON: Mark.

MARK: Yes?

GIDEON: Bring your very small repast in here. Please.

MARK [*grinning*]: Certainly.

[*He goes out. They all watch the kitchen.* DAVID *squats on the floor.* MARK *reappears, without his hat and apron, and carrying a laden tray.*]

Here we are. [*He seats himself at the table, shakes out a white napkin, and tucks it under his chin.*]

A couple of lamb chops. What could be more sustaining?

LOIS [*shocked*]: Lamb?

MARK: Bought in the village, this afternoon! [*He uncovers them.*] Behold them—beautifully crisped in the English manner. With them, one salad of watercress prepared in the French. One hot roll, leaking butter into a sympathetic napkin. One bottle of Corton, 1964. Your bin is woefully Spartan, Giddy. I took the liberty of replenishing it by telephone. [*He raises the Greek cup.*] Well, here's to famine! Self-willed famine, of course.

[*He drinks.* DAVID *laughs.* LOIS *throws him a look of outrage.*]

[*To* GIDEON.] So. Were you impressive? Did you change hearts and collect minds?

[GIDEON *comes and sits next to him.*]

GIDEON: I hope so. In one way or another.

LOIS: He was cheered all day.

MARK: Were you?

GIDEON: Well, it was more people cheering up themselves, really. It keeps out the damp.

LOIS [*smiling*]: That's not true. When he got up to go, it was just deafening.

Tomorrow they say there's going to be an even bigger crowd.

MARK: Are you going tomorrow, David?

LOIS: Of course he is! Why don't you change your mind and come too?

MARK: Were you fasting, David?

DAVID: I don't know. I didn't get anything to eat, anyway.

LOIS: What do you mean? Of course you were fasting. You agreed to it.

DAVID: I didn't say anything, actually. You told me I was.

MARK [*blandly*]: Well, would you like something now? There's this other chop here.

LOIS [*indignantly*]: He certainly would not! . . . [*To* GIDEON.] I saw this man from the *Observer* taking pictures like crazy. He was trying to get you to turn your head for half an hour. He'll be there again tomorrow.

GIDEON: Perhaps I should faint for him.

LOIS: Into my arms!

GIDEON: Excellent idea. It should make a brilliant poster. A Pietà, with the ages reversed!

[DAVID *rises.*]

DAVID [*to* MARK]: Thanks. I'll have it. [*Pause.*] The chop. [*He goes to the table.*]

MARK: By all means. Here—

[*He forks one of the chops to* GIDEON, *who sniffs it, interestedly, and passes it to* DAVID.]

GIDEON [*imperturbably*]: *Bon appetit.*

DAVID: Thank you.

[*He sits.* LOIS *glares at him.*]

MARK: Have some wine.

DAVID: No, thanks. Actually, I don't like alcohol much.

LOIS: He prefers pot.

MARK: You do?

DAVID: Yes. I think it's better for you. Or anyway, it does you less harm.

MARK: I've heard that argument before, my dear boy. It's merely pot calling the bottle black.

[DAVID *laughs.*]

LOIS: I'll run your bath, Giddy. Please come upstairs. [*She moves to the stairs.*]

GIDEON: Very well. [*To* DAVID.] You find that repulsive, don't you?

DAVID [*his mouth full*]: Yes.

LOIS: I hope it chokes you. [*She goes upstairs.*]

MARK: Pacifism makes people so generous.

DAVID: She's all right.

GIDEON: She takes things very seriously, our Falcon.

MARK: Wisely.

[*He smiles at* GIDEON.]

GIDEON: Excuse me. [*He goes upstairs.*]

MARK: Well. Alone at last.

DAVID: Yes.

MARK: Am I . . . as you remember me?

DAVID: You've lost weight a bit.

MARK: With whom? [*He laughs.*] It's well known, no one reads me any more. Mind you, there hasn't been that much to read recently. Unlike the productions from Shrivings. It's a veritable philosophy factory here! [*Raising the cup.*] To home!

[*He drinks and hands it to his son, who also drinks.*]

DAVID: Home.

MARK: You're happy here, aren't you?

DAVID: Yes.

MARK: That's good. All the same, of course, you can hardly intend to remain forever. I mean, sooner or later, Shrivings is going to be full of furniture. Unless you are intending to start a workshop, and supply the area.

DAVID [*smiling*]: I'm not going to be a carpenter all my life, you know.

MARK: I hadn't actually imagined you were. What do you really want to be?

DAVID: I don't know.

MARK: You must have some ideas.

DAVID: They keep changing.

MARK: Well, let's hear some of them.

DAVID: Last week I wanted to be an old woman.

MARK: Yes?

DAVID: Living near here. It's strange, but the Cotswolds mean more to me than the Mediterranean. I suppose green turns me on, and yellow doesn't. . . . I'd gone for a walk the other side of Trister. And there was this brick house with a sign saying "Jam for Sale." The door was open and the wireless was playing. I could see it through the window. It was a real wireless—one of those Gothic ones, with fretwork on the front. I rang the bell and this woman came. She had red knuckles and hairgrips—you know, the old-fashioned, wavy ones. She saw me and smiled. Just like that. A huge smile, all National Health teeth: the way you can only smile, I bet you, if you've been there four hundred years. She was absolutely *there*. She wore great carpet slippers, cut out at the toe for her corns, and they were part of the corridor, like the flagging. She weighed everything very solid in her hand, the jar of jam, the money I gave her, the latch on the door, and, you know something—the only word she said the whole time was "Thank you." Over and over. "Thank you." It was like a little flat song. "Thank you for shillings. Thank you for cold. Thank you for greengages and hairgrips and the wireless. Thank you for asking the way." . . . And suddenly I wanted to be her, more than anything else.

MARK: Good. I deserved it.

DAVID: What?

MARK: Mind your own business, Father. You've forfeited the right to inquire.

DAVID: I didn't mean that!

MARK: I had no idea I had such a witty son. A charming way of telling me.

DAVID: That's not true!

MARK: Sssh! Not another word. I understand. . . . Doubtless you find it easier to converse with Gideon. Well, naturally. Over a few months a giant intellect can learn anything, even the parlance of the young.

DAVID: You must know what I'm talking about. You *must!*

MARK: Well, I can learn. You'll have to teach me, of course. It's a new language—it always is—*young* English!

DAVID: *Don't!*

MARK: What?

DAVID: You said "Home!"

MARK [*hard*]: And you've found it. Good!

[*Silence.* DAVID *looks away.* LOIS *comes downstairs and crosses to the study with* GIDEON*'s clothes.*]

MARK: Ah, Miss Neal. The sage is laving himself?

LOIS: Sir Gideon is having his bath, Mr. Askelon.

MARK: Washing the fascist tomatoes out of his hair!

LOIS [*coming out of the study*]: I'm afraid I don't find that very funny, sir. The man is quite exhausted.

MARK: It's entirely his own fault. He is hardly of an age to sit about on wet pavements.

LOIS: There are some things more important than physical comfort, sir.

MARK: What things in particular? What exactly has been achieved by today's nonsense? One old man lying dizzy in the bathtub, instead of sitting down here eating a nice Welsh rarebit.

LOIS: That's plain silly! Excuse me, but it is.

MARK: Then what did he really do today? Tell me that.

LOIS: He made a sign.

MARK: And that's sufficient?

LOIS: When the first monk set himself on fire in Saigon, everyone in the so-called civilized world was suddenly aware of Vietnam. That was a sign. O.K.? Well, in a small way that man, walking out of that square tonight, being touched by hundreds of people—that was a sign too.

MARK: I declare you believe in the People, Miss Neal. How moving. It has a sublime simplicity—like Doric pillars, or bread and jam!

LOIS: Huh?

MARK: The poor tormented People, who left to themselves would make such a loving world! Exquisite.

LOIS [*with an attempt at calm*]: It is very easy, Mr. Askelon, to put a person down by calling her simple. O.K. I'm simple. I'm a naïve, simpleminded American. I believe in the people, yes. And I believe that most of them don't want any part of the world they've been given. They don't want war. Or politics. Or organized religion. They've been taught to want these things by the ruling class, just desperate to keep its power. If they could ever get their heads straight, ordinary people would realize what history is all about. How it's just the story of a great big lie factory, where we've all been made to work every day, printing up labels: Serf. Heretic. Catholic. Communist. Middle class. And when we're through, we're made to paste them over each other till the original person disappears, and nobody knows who the hell he is any more!

DAVID [*admiringly*]: Yes!

LOIS: Till we can't ever tear them off us again and just be the great thing you despise, Mr. Askelon. People.

DAVID: Oh, when she talks like this I can listen all night.

MARK: I agree. It's better than the opera!

DAVID [*Yorkshire accent*]: Will ya marry me, Lois, lass?

LOIS [*upset*]: Oh, cut it out, David!

MARK: I'd take him up on it, if I were you. Not many girls get proposed to on the strength of their rhetoric.

LOIS: *Ha, ha, ha!* . . .Why did you come here, Mr. Askelon? What do you want? . . . I used to admire you so much. I used to think you were one of the few real people in the world . . .

MARK: Used to!

LOIS: Boy, can you ever be wrong!

MARK: *Used to!*

LOIS [*very near tears*]: I must have been out of my mind!

MARK: *Used to admire! Used to!*

LOIS: I don't care what suffering you've had in your life! It doesn't excuse a damn thing!

MARK: Sagging Jesus—*Once!* The crucifixion of Once! You *said!* You *wrote!* You did *once!* . . . Nail a man to Once and cry when he drops, leaving his fingers on the wall! You arrogant little beast, do you imagine I live my life to be approved by *you?*

[LOIS *turns away, dabbing furiously at her eyes.*]

DAVID: Stop it. Please!

MARK [*hard*]: What?

DAVID [*embarrassed*]: I mean . . . well, that's not fair. Really.

LOIS [*suddenly turning back on* MARK]: Boy, oh boy, are you contemptible! The Grand Old Man, destroyed by suffering! When you're my age, you'll understand. Till then I can kick your head in all I like!

DAVID: Hey, hey!

LOIS [*to* DAVID]: I tell you I don't know one person over fifty—except Giddy—who isn't full of shit!

[MARK *rises in apparent fury. She falls quiet. He approaches her. Pause.*]

MARK [*gently*]: Who gave you those eyes?

LOIS: Huh? . . .

MARK: Blue as the jeans of innocence. Blue as fall sky above your Elysian Field, where the unicorn masses crop the grass of Universal love—till they're taken out by wicked keepers and shot. . . . It's a lovely vision, Miss Neal. Many of us dreamed it once. And then woke.

LOIS: You didn't wake, Mr. Askelon. You went to sleep for good.

[*Pause.*]

MARK [*still very calm*]: In 1920 the greatest psychiatrist in Europe analyzed the dreams of five hundred patients. From them, he slowly made out—detail by detail—the appalling shape of the Nazi beast. It was there, waiting to spring out of the black cave of the Common Unconscious. . . . Out of that deep pit, stinking of orgasm, economical soup, and the halitosis of mediocrity, have risen all the terrors of the earth. All the kings who now sit in museums, glaring at the tourists. The rulers of Assyria tearing lions in half. The despots of Asia, with their cold lozenge faces, forever denying forgiveness. The pop-eyed Lord of Sassania, primping his silver beard, saying "Behold perfection! I have no petty thoughts. No hemorrhoids. No moments when I fail to get erection.

Long live the King! The King *must* live forever!" . . . Who would make such objects? God cannot make anything infallible. Who needs Forever? Who raised these idols from the anonymous dust—hysterical puppets of Nineveh or Nuremberg? Who linked the wires? Started the scepter arms flailing, the saluting arms of self-abuse? Who opened their anthem-yelling metal mouths? Who if not I? Him. You. [*Pause.*] You walk royal portrait galleries as if you are attending identity parades for murderers. Start looking for yourself there, Miss Neal. You might just begin to understand history better.

[LOIS *stares at him, fascinated.*]

DAVID: Oh, hey! Thank you! Wow!

LOIS: What do you mean?

DAVID: The words.

LOIS: What do you mean, "wow"?

DAVID: The words . . .

LOIS: So it's wow for Giddy and wow for him and wow for me and wow for everybody with you?

DAVID: Yes!

LOIS: No distinctions! No differences at all?

DAVID: Well, you screw up your mouth too much. It doesn't do a thing for your face.

LOIS: What?

DAVID: You don't have enough moments that only happen once. You should have more.

LOIS: I think you're mad.

DAVID: I mean, to turn tummies over.

LOIS: I really do! Life's just a set of pictures to you, isn't it? What we say here doesn't connect with you at all.

DAVID: Pictures connect.

LOIS: You know what that means?

DAVID: Pictures are real.

LOIS: It means you have a complete inability to feel anything not related to personal gratification.

DAVID: Really?

LOIS: Yes, really. I'm sorry for you, David.

DAVID: Thank you.

LOIS: I really am. Anyone who can't feel social injustice is sick. I mean it!

DAVID [*exploding*]: All right! You mean it! You really pity me! Poor me! Poor bloody me! [*He springs up and pulls a "mad" face at her.*]

LOIS: David. Ssh!

DAVID: All right, I'm insane! [*He rushes to the table, stands on it, grabs some watercress out of the salad bowl, and puts it on his head. He flicks some watercress at her.*] Deficient Dan, the Insane Man!

LOIS: Stop it!

DAVID: Couldn't feel things, so away he ran!

LOIS: Stop it, David! Cut it out!

DAVID [*quietly*]: You stop it. Stop picking. . . . Mad people shouldn't be picked on!

MARK: No, but heretics should. [*Standing up.*] And that's what you are, my boy. A raving, flagrant heretic, ripe for the burning. Don't you realize what you have just admitted?

DAVID [*shyly*]: No.

[MARK *moves to* DAVID.]

MARK: A sense of the Unalterable. Oh, my poor, demented son: in this house that is enough to get you stoned to death and buried in the midden! [*Kindly.*] Give me some watercress too! Let me go down with you under the knives of optimism! [*He plunges in his hand, takes out some watercress and jams it on his head too.*] Acolytes of the unalterable: unite! Let's wear our green with courage! Green for nature! For the returning cycles of our agony! The grazing green of God!

[DAVID *laughs.* MARK *begins to walk about, enjoying himself, crowned with greens.*]

Ssh! You'll upset Torquemada. . . . Isn't it amusing how the fashions in Inquisition stay the same? They all have one thing in common. A passion for invisible gods! First we had vengeful Daddy, wrapped in clouds. Then Mobile Mary, whizzing up to Heaven. Now it's Self-Raising Man, jumping himself out of nature: what an astonishing sight! . . .

[GIDEON *appears on the stairs, dressed in a long white linen bathrobe. He halts, staring at the scene—then comes down into the room.*]

But perhaps I'm being unfair. No one ever saw Airborne Intacta on her jet flight to Jehovah—but with the God of Shrivings we may be luckier. Any time now we might see something. Maybe today! Who knows? In a few hours the birds up there on Lyssop Ridge will be piping up a new morning. And the hands of perfectible Man will flutter out of sleep to begin again his wonderful work of self-creation. The hands of police will stir and pick up clubs. The hands of nuns will resume whipping fables into frightened children. The hands of patriots will tie some more electrodes on to partisan balls. The hands of the envious will load fresh guns, to assassinate hands more graceful than their own. And the delicate, nicotined hands of genius will continue to stuff all ages together—dark, middle, and decayed—into one metal, lethal sausage. Hail to Man! *Homo Improvabilis!*

GIDEON: Smug!

MARK: What?

GIDEON: Smugness! The endless smugness of pessimism! Under all that litany of woe I heard only one note: *relish!* Comfort in the idea of your own perpetual failure. How can you receive that, and still have anything to live for?

MARK: [*grandly*]: I do not require anything to live for!

GIDEON: Then you are unique in the world.

MARK On the contrary, like everybody else, I live NOT to understand!

GIDEON [*sharper*]: Then why demand of me a Faith you *can?* You want an Indefinable God, but *I* must produce a definable Man. Trot him out of a shed for your inspection, like one of your icons on a trolley! How unfair you are! . . . I offer you what you want. An indefinable mystery. This hand.

[*He extends it.*]

MARK: Offer me first one proof it can do better.

GIDEON: Its change of ownership.

MARK: What d'you mean?

GIDEON: Two thousand years ago, when it chained men all their lives to galley ships—one thousand, when it blinded an entire Byzantine army—five hundred, when it pushed men on to fires, and gutted whole towns to impose True Religion—it was the Gods' hand: plural or singular! Its crimes were accepted. They were God's will—God's scourge—God's anything, so long as they kept its owners from shame. Since we started to abolish Independent God, we have become measurably less callous.

MARK [*sarcastic*]: Oh, good!

GIDEON: It *is* good! Concern has its evolution. That's good.

MARK: Marvelous! We weep more—we war more. What a liberating equation! Agonize while you atomize!

GIDEON: We do not war more. It is only techniques that bring us to holocaust.

MARK [*derisively*]: Only!

GIDEON [*bursting out*]: Yes, only! Only! . . . I say again: concern has its evolution. Everything in *us* can have *unending* evolution. That is our glory—our amazement! . . . [*Scornfully.*] How *can* you dish out that gloating old rubbish about the Unalterable? You ought to be ashamed!

If we know *one thing* about Man, it is that he cannot *stop* altering—that's his condition! He is unique on earth in that he has *no* fixed behavior patterns! Look at the world. At the differences in families—in tribes and nations. Some are paternal: some are not. Some are predatory: some are not. Some are aggressive, sustained by the desire to dominate others. All right, but equally others are not. Oh yes, they can be *made* to be. These differences are social—but they are not inherent. They are not *biological.* Do you follow, children? . . . [*He turns to them.*] There is no proof whatever that man is born inherently aggressive.

MARK [*ironically*]: No proof?

GIDEON [*sternly*]: None. And I deny it, absolutely. Man is born free to make himself . . .

[*He approaches* MARK, *again extending his hand.*]

[*Urgently.*] This hand—this is your proper focus for worship. Not glaring idols, or ancestor poles, or mothy banners hanging in cathedrals. This. This tool, for making. . . . And soon to be extinct if we pursue our blasphemies against ourselves much longer.

[*He is moved, and stands staring at* MARK *as if challenging him not to agree.* MARK *takes* GIDEON's *hand, and inspects it closely.*]

MARK [*with disgusted interest*]: In the Middle West of America, I watched this thing kill a man, seventeen times in succession.

GIDEON: You saw a man killed seventeen times?

MARK [*dropping the hand*]: Yes. What kind of evolution do you call that?

GIDEON: How?

MARK: In the psychology department of a major university, where they were working on aggression. The professor had set up a board with six buttons. These were allegedly controlled by electrical wires attached to an actor, sitting across the laboratory, bound and gagged. Members of the public, chosen off the street, completely at random, were admitted one by one and asked to assist at a scientific experiment of an undisclosed nature. They were told the first button would give the man a mild electric shock, the second more—and so on, up to the sixth, which was, in fact, a death button. It was clearly explained to all that if they pressed that button the man would die. They were then left alone for an hour each, to play. . . . A simple scene: one helpless man at the mercy of a complete stranger who was his absolute master in the matter of the punishment given him.

GIDEON: And seventeen pressed the death button?

MARK: Exactly so.

GIDEON: Out of how many?

MARK: Seventeen.

LOIS: I don't believe it.

GIDEON [*patiently*]: My dear, there is a famous experiment of this sort; but it wasn't exactly as you described. There was no death button. And the people were not left alone. They had two pseudocolleagues—fake scientists whose job it was to provoke them. The result was that more than half agreed to vote for painful shock. Depressing, I admit, but scarcely as final as you make it out.

MARK: That was one experiment. I watched another.

GIDEON [*dryly*]: I see.

LOIS: I don't believe you. Go on, admit it. You made it up. You're reduced to making up stupid lies! How incredible.

MARK: Am I?

LOIS: Yes, you are!

GIDEON: Lois, please!

MARK [*staring at her*]: It's easily proved.

LOIS: Proved? How?

MARK: Sit down. We'll play my game here.

GIDEON: Here?

MARK: Why not? These apples will do very well. [*He takes them from the bowl on the table, and lays them out in a straight line, parallel to the audience.*] The buttons of Original Sin! Ouch—oucher—oucher—Death! What do you say? Will you play? I'll be the victim.

LOIS: You mean you'll act?

MARK: Exactly so.

LOIS: You've got to be kidding.

MARK: Try me and see. David?

DAVID: I'd like to see you act.

MARK: Good. Giddy? I can devise a short version for you, if you are tired.

GIDEON: I don't see how you can devise *any* version, my dear. We know you will be acting—and those are apples. The illusion that we can actually kill you being destroyed, there seems little point in the exercise.

MARK: Well, I would have to claim a few rights in compensation, denied to the original victim.

GIDEON: Of what nature?

MARK: Speech.

GIDEON: That seems fair.

MARK: Free speech. Complete license, no matter how provoking. Strictly of course for the purpose of the game.

GIDEON: That could be interesting.

LOIS: I don't see how.

MARK: Shall we try?

LOIS: I think it's time Giddy was in bed.

GIDEON: All the same, I would like to see what Mark intends.

MARK: Of course you would. . . . All right, then. [*He pulls from his pocket the string with which he had wrapped the shrine.*] Ah now, this will do very well! Come, David; tie me to your throne of reason.

[*He sits in it, and offers the string.* DAVID *approaches.*]

Come on. Tie down the wrists.

[DAVID *takes the string. He begins to tie.*]

LOIS: I don't see the point of this. I don't see the point of it at all. It's just plain stupid.

MARK: The head of the house wishes it. As I understand things, what he wants, so want the rest of you. Isn't that true?

LOIS: Ha, ha, ha!

GIDEON: Come on now, you fierce Falcon; it's only a game. An after-fast entertainment!

MARK: Exactly; only a game. Whatever that word means. . . . Tighter, David; anyone can see I can get out of *that*. . . .You do allow me complete license of speech, by the way, Gideon?

GIDEON: Yes.

MARK: Miss Neal?

LOIS: Why not? I guess there won't be any difference from the sort of things you say normally.

MARK: David?

DAVID: Anything you want. . . . Can you move?

MARK [*wriggling about*]: No, that's fine. You might have made this chair especially for the purpose. To incapacitate your old dad! All right, join the others.

[DAVID *goes to the others, standing by the table.*]

You are, of course, all playing at once. The solo, masturbatory element has been eliminated. You must admit, I'm making it very difficult for myself.

GIDEON: I certainly admit that. Yes.

LOIS: What are you going to do? Just insult us till one of us bangs this last apple?

MARK: More or less.

LOIS: Jesus! I've never heard anything so stupid! Grown people standing up in the middle of the night, playing with apples.

GIDEON: Which is the mildest one?

MARK: The far one from me.

[GIDEON *goes to it and raises his hand to touch it.*]

LOIS [*with sudden alarm*]: Giddy—don't.

GIDEON: Why not?

LOIS: Well . . . it's just so childish. [*Pause.*] Goddamn childish, that's all.

GIDEON: Let's oblige our guest. Don't you want to see how he acts?

[LOIS *shrugs her acquiescence.*]

LOIS: O.K. Go ahead.

[GIDEON *delicately presses the first apple.* MARK *writhes a little.*]

MARK: Ah! Ah! Stop it, please.

[GIDEON *stops pressing.*]

GIDEON: Excellent. Thank you.

[*The two men bow at each other.*]

LOIS: I don't think it's excellent! I think it's lousy. I've seen people under electric shock. It doesn't look at all like that.

MARK: Trust you to introduce a boring, factual note into the proceedings.

GIDEON: Really, Mark!

MARK [*apologetically*]: License, Giddy! License!

LOIS: What does the second button do?

MARK: Push it and see.

LOIS: I don't want to waste my money. What do you do? Twice as much?

MARK: Push it and see.

LOIS: Because that would only be twice nothing!

MARK: Push it and see.

LOIS: O.K. Just this next one. Just to see how you make out. Look everybody—Acting Class Number Two! Bang! [*She bangs the second apple.*]

[MARK *writhes more.*]

Presenting Mark Askelon, the greatest actor of our time, in "The Electrified Man!" . . .

[MARK *stops writhing.*]

Why are you stopping, Mr. Askelon? I haven't taken my hand off the button!

[MARK *resumes writhing.*]

MARK: Ah! Ah! . . .

LOIS: There we go! Now you, Giddy! You press number one again, and let's watch the subtle way he changes!

[GIDEON *hesitates.*]

Go on, it's only a game. Like you said!

GIDEON: True.

LOIS: O.K., then!

[*He presses the first apple again, and she takes her hand off the second.* MARK*'s convulsions lessen.*]

Oh, beautiful! Beautiful! . . . Now mine again!

[GIDEON *stops pressing and she resumes.* MARK *writhes more energetically, and his cries increase.*]

Now you, David! Press number three. He should really blow his mind on number three! [*To* MARK.] Go on, keep it up! I'm still pressing! . . . Come *on*, David!

[DAVID *hesitates.*]

What's the matter with you? We're just having fun!

[DAVID *shrugs, smiles, shakes his head.* LOIS *takes her hand off her apple.* MARK *relaxes.*]

You really are a pain in the ass, aren't you?

MARK: You certainly are, David. For once I agree with Miss Neal. I was enjoying myself hugely. And it is only a game, after all. That's why Miss Neal could afford to reveal herself so completely.

LOIS: What do you mean?

MARK: For one moment there, when you realized that I had to keep writhing for just so long as you kept pressing, you became interested.

LOIS: Sure, I did. The longer I did it, the bigger fool you looked.

MARK: That's not the reason you did it, Miss Neal. Not by any means.

LOIS: Well, what other reason could there be, Mr. Askelon?

DAVID [*distressed*]: Oh, stop it, Lois!

LOIS: What?

DAVID: Stop it.

LOIS: Thanks! Thanks very much. That's great. That really is great! . . .You tell me I'm so serious, and I'm too serious, and when I play a game you say stop it.

DAVID: You weren't playing a game.

LOIS: Well, what the hell else was I doing? . . . I'm bored with this, Giddy. Why don't we go to bed?

MARK: Ah, that's sweet. "Why don't we go to bed?" Can you really mean that seriously—to a man you've selected entirely because he can't?

GIDEON: Mark, really!

MARK: Well, it's true, isn't it? Look at her—Miss Lois Neal! What the hell is she doing in this house? Making the beds, making the eggs, making the laws round here like a sort of Earth Mother—or, sorry, Earth Auntie. Unmarried, of course.

GIDEON: Mark, I must protest.

MARK: License, Giddy—license!

GIDEON: All the same!

MARK: Who is she, this Illinois idiot, creaming her committed little panties every time you enter the room? [*American accent.*] "Oh, Giddy, you're so great! Gee, Giddy, you're so wonderful! You're a fuckin' saint, boy, honest!" . . . Is that what you really want? A sticky little acolyte plunging after a man three times her age, just because he's safe?

[*All the others stay rigid:* DAVID, *head lowered,* LOIS *looking away.*]

What's in your mind, Lois? His wife couldn't stand it, could she? Stuck it three years after his famous vow of chastity—then ups and bloody goes. But you're made of sterner stuff than that, aren't you? You're going to last forever! Forever deliciously unsatisfied! Forever a Vestal Virgin, waving the flag of Humanity high over your frozen Mount of Venus! Sagging Jesus, protect me from all Liberal American Virgins!

GIDEON: David, please untie your father. I find I am tireder than I thought.

MARK: You granted me license.

GIDEON: Yes, and now withdraw it. Good night.

MARK [*sotto voce, to* DAVID, *who is approaching the chair*]: Keep still.

GIDEON: Come, Lois.

MARK: Yes, come, Lois—before you hear any more. Before you hear, for example, why exactly Enid left! . . . Do you imagine it was because of that boring vow of chastity? You must, as they say, be joking! Enid Petrie never cared about sex. To her it was always "nasties"! She's much happier now with her middle-aged accountant. One dry kiss at night before they skin the Ovaltine! She didn't leave Shrivings for *that*! . . . It was the hypocrisy she couldn't take. Poor old stick, in her own way she had a sort of maidenly integrity.

GIDEON [*facing him directly*]: What are you talking about?

MARK: Do you have to ask? . . . Why do you imagine, Miss Neal, that your employer gave up sex? Because he found you ladies such a block on his path to virtue? Don't you know the only sex Gideon ever really enjoyed was with boys? Slim brown boys with sloping shoulders. He used to chase them all over Italy on our walking tours. And then, of course, the guilt would chase him; and I'd have to endure boring vows of repentance all the next day— to be broken again, naturally, all the next night, in the very next piazza! In the end he gave everything up. Guilt, nothing but guilt! The world saw only a Great Renunciation on the grandest philosophic grounds: but not so Enid. All she saw was a self-accusing pederast, pretending to be Gandhi!

DAVID [*low*]: Stop it.

MARK: Mind you, old habits die hard. Once you grow accustomed to having Mediterranean boys, I suppose you get to need them. Send for them. Import them. Steal them, if necessary, from your friends!

DAVID [*in pain*]: Shut up.

MARK: Make my chairs! Make my tables! Make my bed, and we will lie on it together!

DAVID [*moving forward*]: Shut up!

MARK: Not, my dear boy—my flyer! my *owl!*—that I would suspect *you* of anything so bizarre! Innocent to the last breath, I make no doubt!

[DAVID *rushes to the table, picks up the "death apple," and smashes it down over and over again. Pieces fly about the room.*]

DAVID: SHUT UP! SHUT UP! SHUT UP! SHUT UP!

MARK [*triumphantly*]: *What?!* Oh!—AAAHHH!!!

[*He "dies" in elaborate convulsions. All freeze. Pause.*
*Then, with a violent motion,* MARK *snaps the ropes from his wrists and rises from the throne. With a grin at* GIDEON, *he flaps like a great eagle up the stairs into his room. Pause again. Then* DAVID *drops the bit of apple still in his hand and walks very stiffly out of the house. The front door slams.* LOIS *turns round at this.* GIDEON *approaches her, his arms outstretched—but with a stifled cry, she avoids them, and runs into the garden.* GIDEON *is left standing alone. He bows his head over the table. The lights go down a little below, and come up above, where* MARK *is kneeling to the shrine.*]

MARK: I begged him! You heard. I *begged* him, over and over. "Let me go. No questions." He wouldn't believe me. Like you. You never saw me, either. I was literally invisible to you. [*Piteously.*] The two of you. *You can't see!* [*Pause.*] And then when it happens, you look at me with that stare of unbelievable pain. *He* will, too. Soon now.

[*He stands up.* GIDEON *moves toward his study. He is upset and alarmed. He pauses at the throne, fingering the ropes that still hang from it.* MARK *pours himself a glass of brandy.*]

Thing is, I didn't believe me either, last night. I only half meant it, the battle. My usual half-meant, *you know*. . . . And now it's here. The knife's in. Suddenly there's blood dripping in the house. Surprised blood. . . . No return . . .

[GIDEON *moves slowly to his study door, opens it—looks back at the room, and disappears.*]

[*Darkly, to the shrine.*] I begged you, too. "*Proteggimi*"—remember? Look after me. What does that mean? Look after? What language do you speak, then, Saint? . . . [*Bitterly.*] Saint . . . Saint . . . SAINTS!

[*He throws the brandy in the face of the statue. It drips from the shrine as* MARK *turns away from it, and stands with head sharply averted.*]

SLOW BLACKOUT

## SCENE 2

*Sunday morning.*

*Ten o'clock. The telephone rings insistently.* LOIS *is tidying the room—picking pieces of apple off the floor. She ignores the telephone. Finally it stops. Her whole manner is shocked and cold.*

GIDEON *comes in from his study and looks at her. He appears tired, and is dressed very casually; as if he has become involved with his clothes by accident.*

*Above,* MARK *lies inert on his bed.*

GIDEON: Peace.

LOIS: Sure.

GIDEON: Who was that on the phone?

LOIS: I don't know.

GIDEON: Oh. How are you feeling?

LOIS: Fine. You?

GIDEON: It hasn't been a very pleasant night for any of us, I imagine. Where's David?

LOIS: I don't know. [*Pause.*] I want you to do something for me.

GIDEON: Certainly. What?

LOIS [*hard*]: Tell that man to go.

GIDEON: I can't do that, my dear.

LOIS: You have to.

GIDEON: There is no have to. We can't throw people out of here. Least of all him. If this house can't overcome what's happened to Mark, then it's useless.

[*Pause. She dusts.*]

Look: he asked us all yesterday what would happen if a Ruffian came in here with a pistol. We all said we wouldn't fire back, didn't we?

LOIS [*short*]: Yeah.

GIDEON: Well, it's as simple as that. As complex as that.

LOIS: Yeah.

GIDEON: What can we do, but try and disarm him another way? Aggression is like a fire: smother it in blankets, it dies for want of air. Our blanket is acceptance.

LOIS: Yeah. O.K.

GIDEON: I know it sounds hopelessly abstract, after last night—but what else are we here for? You left America for one reason; the Peace men were joining in the violence. Well, is that what you want me to do now?

[*She goes on dusting.*]

Or is it something else? What he said about me.

LOIS [*flat*]: Don't be ridiculous.

GIDEON: No, be honest now.

[DAVID *comes downstairs.*]

DAVID: Hello. How are you feeling?

GIDEON: Peckish.

DAVID: Me too. [*To* LOIS.] Good morning.

[*No reply.*]

Peace.

LOIS [*to* GIDEON]: I've got some letters to do. Excuse me, please. The car will collect you at twelve, same as yesterday. The assembly point will again be the statue of Charles the Third.

GIDEON: First.

LOIS: Big deal.

GIDEON [*sympathetically*]: Lois!

DAVID: What the hell's the matter with you?

LOIS: If you don't know, I'm not telling.

DAVID: Well, I don't know.

[*She pauses a second, then marches across and picks up a piece of apple.*]

LOIS: This, then. This, David.

DAVID: The apple?

LOIS: You really think that was a smart, civilized thing you did last night?

DAVID: Well, it stopped the voice.

LOIS: Voice?

DAVID: That was supposed to be the point.

LOIS: The point, David, was not to touch the goddamn thing. You deliberately played his game.

DAVID: It shut him up, didn't it?

LOIS: Ha, ha, ha!

DAVID: Well, didn't it?

LOIS: O.K. It shut him up! Well done! Great.

DAVID: So what's the matter? It was just an apple.

LOIS: "Just" an apple!

DAVID: Yes! An apple is an apple is an apple.

LOIS: And an idiot is an idiot!

GIDEON [*mildly*]: Children, please. I beg you.

DAVID: I'm sorry, Giddy.

LOIS: I'll go answer letters. [*She moves to the study.*]

GIDEON [*calmly*]: Before you go, I would like to make a brief observation about homosexuality. I mean, my own.

[*Slight pause.*]

DAVID: I think that's a boring subject.

GIDEON: Nevertheless, since it's been raised.

LOIS: O.K. What about it?

[*Pause.*]

GIDEON: How to put it? . . . When I was young, I had, as they say, sex on the brain. I meant by that, that even when I worked on equations, or read political science, the impulse of my attention was somehow sexual. Sex was everywhere. A girl's hair bobbing down the street. The sudden fur of a boy's neck. The twitching lope of a red-setter dog. In flowers, even—the smell of cow parsley in a field of poppies would almost make me faint. To say I was bisexual would have been a ludicrous understatement. I was trisexual. Quadri. Quinti. Sexisexual, you might say!

[DAVID *laughs and sits on the floor, happily interested.*]

I tell you this, just in case you've been wondering about the guilt attributed to me last night. So far was I from feeling that particular emotion, I confess throughout my twenties I cheerfully, and indeed gratefully, engaged in repeated encounters with both sexes.

DAVID [*gleefully*]: Which did you prefer?

GIDEON: Boys were physically more attractive to me; their lines are more economical. But for sex I preferred girls. In that department, at least, God got his mathematics right!

[DAVID *laughs again.* LOIS *does not laugh.*]

However—after fifteen years' abstinence, I find the whole area of experience somewhat remote. That is why, my Owl, though you are extremely attractive, I hope you won't find it unforgivable in me not to have responded more vigorously to your charms. You too, of course, my Falcon.

[DAVID *springs up happily.*]

DAVID: I'm not sure. I think we should both be very offended! [*Warmly.*] Oh, that's lovely! . . . You're lovely. You are! [*He hugs the old man.*]

LOIS: All the same, you stopped.

GIDEON: True.

LOIS: It couldn't have been that great, if you stopped.

GIDEON: I describe intensity, not joy. You might not conceive it of me, but in those days I knew great violence. It grew, I think, from what used to be called Despair. The great myth of sex told of coitus and transfiguration. Comingling of spirits! I found the reality to be very different. This supreme experience of union appeared to me with more and more force each time, to be simply a twin act of masturbation, accompanied by murmurs designed to disguise the fact. Out of that realization, slowly, came a sort of cruelty. Having and discarding. Searching ever more mechanically, in a savorless frenzy of disappointment. I grew to hate the very shape of desire. Its parody of closeness. Its separating climax. Finally, I came to know that, for me, it was the main source of aggression. That before I could even start on my innocence, I would have to give it up. . . . My wife left me for the reason I have always told you. The decision was too rigorous for her. I didn't blame her. How could I? I myself found it . . . very difficult. . . .Almost unendurable, in fact. [*Pause.*] The youngsters who come here find this all absurd, no doubt. Sex is no problem to them. Or so they tell us, anyway, with their tulip heads like emblems for tenderness. Can it be true? I pray so. If they can really kiss without the taste of conquest, then they've done more than all generations before them: detached the whip at their belts, and hung a flower. . . . So. . . . Everyone has a struggle. That was something of mine.

DAVID: Thank you. [*Pause. Enthusiastically.*] Let's go for a walk. All three of us! [MARK *stirs on his bed.*]

GIDEON [*to* LOIS]: Yes! We have the time, my dear.

LOIS: You two go. There's too much I've got to do here.

DAVID: Well, leave it.

LOIS: I'm afraid I can't do that.

DAVID: Oh, balls!

LOIS: Shrivings does not run itself, David. Excuse me. [*She goes into the study.*]

GIDEON: What's wrong?

DAVID: She's shocked.

GIDEON: Impossible. By what? My language? But she's such a free girl. She couldn't be shocked just by words. Not a liberal girl like my Falcon! Do you really think she found me coarse?

DAVID: I love you. I wish I could keep you from harm.

GIDEON: Am I in danger?

DAVID: Don't you feel it?

GIDEON: I feel . . . a little unnerved. Perhaps it's the fast.

[MARK *gets off his bed and comes to the window. He stares out front.*]

DAVID: You didn't sleep last night.

GIDEON: No.

DAVID: You're changing.

GIDEON: What d'you mean?

DAVID: So's Lois. [*Pause.*] That's the thing.

GIDEON: What?

[DAVID *shudders.*]

David!

DAVID: He changes you. But he can't change himself.

GIDEON: I don't think that's true. He's changed more than any of us. I never realized he had become so desperate.

DAVID: Become?

GIDEON: Well, yes, in the last few years. Was that what you were trying to tell me, before he arrived? You suspected this had happened?

DAVID: Not become.

GIDEON: What d'you mean? He was always like this? . . . That's nonsense, my dear. He was often trying—bombastic—egocentric—all of that. But never . . . never like this.

[DAVID *shrugs.*]

What did you mean before? You wanted to stop the voice?

DAVID: The thing in it.

GIDEON: What thing?

[DAVID *shrugs again.*]

I'm not sure I understand you.

DAVID [*fiercely*]: The thing!

[*Pause.*]

GIDEON [*perplexed*]: He would never hurt you. You know that.

DAVID: Let's go for our walk.

[*He goes abruptly over to the garden exit, where the coats hang, and takes* GIDEON's *scarf and beret.*]

GIDEON: David . . .

DAVID [*handing him the beret*]: Here.

GIDEON: Thank you. [*He puts it on.*] If I asked him to leave Shrivings, would you like that?

DAVID: You can't.

GIDEON: You mean, I mustn't.

DAVID: I mean, you can't.

[GIDEON *stares at him.* DAVID *takes his hand.*]

[*Quietly.*] Come on.

[*They go out together. Above,* MARK *stares out front.*]

MARK: Well, there they go. Father and son—hand in hand up the meadow. Touching! The whole hippie dream in one frame: old and young, leaping the generation gap like mountain goats! . . . Look, he's dancing. Our boy! [*He turns away. Bitterly.*] Dances with Giddy, and I stay here with you. No, with myself. Alone. You'd be up there with them leading the dance. "*Venga, vengate!* Dance with me, San Marco!" [*Pompously.*] "No, no, my dear Giulia, good heavens—*dance*, with my girth? You must be mad! . . . *You* dance: I'll watch." *You* laugh: I'll watch. You live: I'll watch and turn it all into literature. Literature counts, after all! It's so much more important than life . . .

[*The telephone rings.* LOIS *comes in from the study and answers it.*]

LOIS: Look, mister: a vigil *is* a public statement. What more do you want?

[*She hangs up and goes listlessly to the refectory table.*]

MARK: So who's left downstairs? The Innocent Abroad, savaging her typewriter! Bashing out manifestos of love, with hating little touch-type fingers!

[LOIS *sits at the table, staring miserably ahead.*]

I must say I'd like to give her some touch-typing myself. One hour could change her life. What's she ever known, after all, but student fumbling? [*He sits on the bed.*] Why not? Superb move! Life in Shrivings would hardly be the same ever after, that's for sure. How would the old man take it? How would David—? [*He breaks the thought, snapping at the shrine.*] Ah, don't be idiotic! I couldn't do it, anyway. Look at her! The odds are a thousand to one. Richard the Third had better with that dreary Lady Anne! . . . [*Slyly.*] All the same. There she sits—tighter than a Labrador limpet. Here I sit, the well-known blade, not entirely rusted yet. One could always see. The most anyone can say in the end, to God or Man, is "Let us see!" [*He gets up. He smiles.*] My move, I think. [*He leaves the room and tiptoes down. At the bottom of the stairs he pauses, contemplating the girl.*] All alone, with your Remingtone?

[*She ignores him. He advances into the room.*]

Are you still angry with me for last night? You shouldn't be. Truth hurts—but in a house of Shriving, one should tell nothing else. And then one should forgive. Isn't that the point of this house?

LOIS: Why don't you just get out of here?

MARK: Where? Back to Corfu?

LOIS: So long as it's away from me, I don't give a damn.

MARK: Now that, I'm afraid, is *untrue*. I think you lie in bed at night thinking a great deal about me.

LOIS: You're right. I do think a lot about you. Not necessarily in bed. Would you like to hear what I think about you, Mr. Askelon?

MARK: Not at all. Mediocre descriptive powers are not necessarily improved by having a great subject to work on.

LOIS: You think you're the last representative of the Grand Manner, don't you?—all cooking and quotations! You wear your learning lightly. You got style. Well, let me tell you—most of the kids I know have more style in their assholes than you have in your whole drunken body.

MARK: And Gideon? Do they have more style than Gideon?

LOIS: Damn you, Mr. Askelon! We were happy before you came.

MARK: Liar! I saw you the day I arrived, Anxious Annie clutching her nervous little fistful of attitudes. Happy? You haven't even been goosed by happy!

LOIS: Screw you!

MARK: What was my real crime? Showing your saint in a real light?

LOIS: Get out of here—that's all I want.

MARK: Look, stop hiding from it. Giddy is completely queer, for what that's worth. He never slept with a woman in his life.

LOIS: That's not true.

MARK: It's not in the least important. Who cares, after all?

LOIS: It's not true!

MARK: It's just a question of the facts. Boring, unilluminating facts.

LOIS: *It's not true!*

MARK: You have proof to the contrary?

LOIS: Yes.

[*Pause.*]

MARK: How beautiful. What a delicious discovery! Women can be as gallant as men. *More* gallant in this instance. I didn't exactly think Giddy displayed much last night. The way he came to your protection.

LOIS: You're not worthy to wipe his ass.

MARK: Or rather—didn't.

LOIS [*tight*]: I don't need any protection.

MARK: "I find I'm tireder than I thought."

LOIS: What?

MARK: That was the most he could manage to say. "I find I'm tireder than I thought!" Hardly the last word in gallantry.

LOIS: You couldn't begin to understand him. You couldn't begin!

MARK [*admiringly*]: You really are remarkable.

LOIS: What d'you mean?

MARK: After a scene like that—to defend him like that. Eyes sparkling. Breasts heaving. . . . You're a Valkyrie.

LOIS: Get fucked.

MARK: All right, I'm joking, a little. But it's true, when you say you don't need protection. You have an integrity that is absolutely scary. You know, you are the first person I've met—since I first met myself—who can really treat abstractions like lovers.

LOIS [*dryly*]: Great.

MARK: I mean kiss them. Beat them for infidelity.

LOIS: Ha, ha, ha.

MARK: It's what my wife never dug. She couldn't cope with the simplest general idea.

LOIS: Her son has the same problem.

MARK: She would have adored you. Honesty excited her above everything. Her eyes would have widened on you. They were quite miraculous, you know. Round the pupils flared a sun ring. In all other ways she was quite ordinary. A spindly, red-haired dancer from the Rome Opera, not actually very good. When she retired to live with me on pasta and poems, she grew less shapely—but her eyes never lost their light. God knows where she got them. Her father was a gray civil servant with eyes like a carp. Her mother's, two clams on a plate of spaghetti. I can only conclude, therefore, that Giulia's were miraculous. Like yours.

LOIS: Oh sure.

MARK: Who gave you those eyes? Some baby-faced doctor from the plains of Illinois? Not on your Midwestern life! Eyes are the sequins of grace. The angel sews them, when she calls.

[*Long pause.*]

LOIS [*calmly*]: Giddy's eyes are disgusting.

MARK: What?

LOIS: That white stuff. It's really awful. Why doesn't he do something about it? And the way they're never really *on you*.

MARK [*slyly*]: As if they're . . . out of focus?

LOIS: You're really very clever, aren't you?

[*He grins.*]

MARK: I was.

LOIS: Yeah, sure.

MARK: You don't know how clever I was.

LOIS: "Once," you mean? Once?

MARK [*staring at her*]: Yes. Once. [*Pause.*]

LOIS [*softer*]: Will you go now, please?

MARK: I was someone amazing!

LOIS: Just leave me alone . . .

MARK: I was the world!

LOIS: Please! Get out of here! . . .

MARK: I knew an Encyclopedic Sympathy: there was nobody outside of *me!* I was the arriving lecturer—and the doorman who admits him, cringing. I was the Fabergé Prince—the traveler in undies—the teagirl who stands for eight repetitive hours between two steaming urns. I went to parade grounds, brisk in khaki. Returned at night, tired dandruff in an aching bus. I was the arch of the morning—Cream of Corelli—the indigestion of a wasted day! I was a replete, complete Man . . . but for one thing. I was never quite alive. [*Pause.*] Inside me, from my first day on earth, was a cancer. An incapacity for Immediate Life. When I was a boy, the crowd at football matches jumped to its feet, shouting. All I could see was a ball and legs. At student dances, I hopped in silence. They all said: Isn't it exciting, the music? I grinned, but heard nothing. The only music I ever heard was words, and the clear thought of Gideon Petrie. When I yoked them, I became your admired Poet. I slew Generals. I drowned Presidents in spit. The insane Popes! The Rabbis of Repression! Oh, they kept me going for years, good hates—*the scapegoats for myself*. The only thing was, they ran out. Even atheism itself ran out, the moment I felt one poem as an act of worship. The next second—when I realized how worship demands the Present—then hell began. I was no longer a Revolutionary Poet. I was a self-ordained priest without a faith. [*Pause.*] Do you know what I'm saying? I have never lived *Now*. And that "Never" makes crueler murderers, even than Christ or Country. Look into my eyes. What do you see? The envy? The endless living through others? Jealousy squinting through the glare of commitment? . . . There is where Vietnam starts. Don't sit on pavements to ban armaments: sit, if you must, to ban these eyes. They would kill Gideon, if they could, for his goodness. They would kill David for his instinct. Yes, my own son—as they killed his mother: Giulia. Poor girl, you are looking at a murderer. But don't be afraid. You're quite safe. You have nothing I want, you see.

[*She kisses him gently on the mouth. He draws back, then kisses her passionately. She throws her arms round him.*]

## ACT THREE

*Sunday night.*

*Eleven-thirty. Above,* LOIS *lies in* MARK'S *bed, naked, under a sheet. Behind her stands* MARK, *also naked and wrapped in a large white towel. He holds a bottle.*

MARK: Are you awake?

LOIS: Mmm.

MARK: Then listen, Miss America. Go home. Forget Europe. She's old, wicked, and useless—like me. Purge her. Get her right out of you, if you want to live. Believe me, everything bad started here. The pox. The subjugation of woolly heads. The social layer cake, which God's hand alone is allowed to crumble. Above all, the Police State. That's our main gift to the world. We've never been without it. The helmeted thugs of Prussia. Hohenstauffen—Hohenzollern. All those Bourbon nights. The shadows of agents everywhere—Fouché spies in the arcades—Metternich men—the soutanes of insane Priests slipping through the twilight—Rome, with her tinkling bells, summoning us to avoid ourselves. Giddy's quite right. . . . [*Fiercer.*] Never forgive them. The kneelers! The followers of carriage axles. The motorcade boys. The smart saluters. The slow lookers through documents. The postilions of the state in dark glasses, now not even bobbing on cream horses, just on mobikes! Not even in plumes, just in Perspex, crackling with transistors. Disembodied, uninteresting as the astronauts, their heroes. Assembled men! . . . We taught you the tricks, and you've made them shoddier. Get us out of you entirely! The hell with Europe. Get us out of you! . . . I'm pissed.

[*He hands her the bottle.*]

LOIS: You're fantastic. Do you know you've been talking all day?

MARK: And you keep sleeping. Well, naturally. Speeches of such preternatural tedium.

LOIS: Don't be silly. Hold my hand.

[*He moves to the bed, and holds it.*]

MARK: Look at your eyes. It's a joke.

LOIS: What is?

MARK: Your mouth all day long shouts Equality! But your eyes keep singing Uniqueness! You won't hear *them* demanding Equal Eyes For All Women!

[*She giggles, and drinks from the bottle.*]

If I could once make them in a poem, I'd never open my mouth again. Consider that.

LOIS: Sssh!

[DAVID *comes from his room, pauses a second on the landing, then runs down the stairs.* LOIS *freezes.*

*The boy is naked, save for a white towel: he carries another. He goes straight to* GIDEON's *study and knocks on the door.*]

GIDEON [*inside*]: Hello?

MARK [*kissing* LOIS's *hand*]: Firm, typewriter-bashing little hand. I think I'd quite like to be that Remington.

LOIS: Oh, stop it now.

[MARK *laughs.* GIDEON *opens the door. He is wearing his white dressing gown.*]

DAVID: You're still wet.

GIDEON [*coming out into the room*]: I am a bit.

DAVID: Sit down, I'll dry you.

GIDEON: No, it's all right.

DAVID: Sit!

[GIDEON *sits.* DAVID *starts to towel his head.*]

MARK: We'll have to go down in a minute.

LOIS: No.

MARK: We must.

LOIS: I don't want to.

MARK: You're just going to stay here?

LOIS: Yes.

[*She turns away from him and throws the sheet over her head.*]

GIDEON: It was noble of you to sit with me today.

DAVID: Don't be silly.

GIDEON: You got even wetter than I did. You looked like an otter.

DAVID: I enjoyed it.

GIDEON: Did you?

DAVID: I think because Lois wasn't there. I mean, yesterday she looked at me the whole time, like she was challenging me to find it boring.

GIDEON: Your opinion matters to her.

DAVID: Do you mean that?

GIDEON: Of course. Otherwise you wouldn't have such power to upset her.

DAVID: I really am naïve, aren't I?

GIDEON: Yes, if you mean unconscious of your charm. Now, you will be more conscious, therefore less charming.

DAVID: Life's depressing, isn't it?

GIDEON: No denying it.

[MARK *stands up.*]

MARK: Come on, now. It's time you got up.

LOIS [*under the sheet*]: No.

MARK: They've been back fifteen minutes. Gideon will be wanting his dinner. He must be starving.

LOIS: He can get it himself.

MARK: That's not a very nice thing to say.

LOIS: Oh, leave me alone!

DAVID: Where the hell can she be?

GIDEON: I don't understand it.

DAVID: We held the car for ages.

GIDEON: She must have been walking, and not realized the time.

DAVID: I don't believe it.

GIDEON: Why not? It's a natural explanation. She wasn't exactly pleased with either of us.

DAVID: Lois would never forget a vigil.

MARK: Lois.

GIDEON: Then what? You mean, she did it deliberately?

MARK [*insistently*]: Lois.

GIDEON: But why? Why on earth would she? . . .

[DAVID *towels harder.*]

Gently, my dear!

DAVID: What's going on, Giddy?

GIDEON: Going on?

DAVID: What is it? What has he said to you?

MARK: Here!

[*He jabs her. She sits up.*]

LOIS: Cut it out!

[*They glare at each other.*]

GIDEON [*gently*]: Trust me, my dear.

DAVID: What about? Trust you what about?

GIDEON: You know, they say there are seven meals between Man and Revolution. I've missed six already.

DAVID: Poor Giddy. I'm sorry . . . I'll get you something right now. Let's see what there is. [*He crosses to the kitchen.*]

GIDEON: She didn't even leave us any food ready. I can't think why.

DAVID: Because she's a selfish cow.

GIDEON: Sssh!

MARK: Get out of bed.

LOIS: No.

DAVID: You're all right, aren't you?

GIDEON: I think so. How about you! You haven't eaten either.

DAVID: I'll be better after a snack. Excuse me.

[*He goes out.*

MARK *comes over to* LOIS.]

MARK [*hard*]: Get up, Lois!

LOIS: What's the matter with you?

MARK: I need you downstairs.

LOIS: Need?

MARK: Exactly.

LOIS: What *is* this? What game are you playing?

MARK: My own. As always.

LOIS: But I figure in it, don't I? You want me downstairs very much. Why?

MARK: Press it and see.

LOIS [*realizing it*]: You're going to tell, aren't you? You're going to *tell, right now!* . . . You are, aren't you? Why? . . . *Why?*

MARK: Stop questioning me, you silly bitch! Put on your panties and get downstairs.

LOIS: You've *planned* it! . . . You've planned the whole thing!

MARK: Let's have no hysterics, please.

LOIS: Every bit of it . . .

MARK: Lois—

LOIS: Every bit!

MARK [*quietly*]: I'll open the door. You can scream again.

[*He moves to the door.*]

LOIS: I'm not leaving this room. I'm staying right here.

MARK: As you please. [*He leaves the bedroom and comes downstairs.*] Good evening.

GIDEON: Peace.

MARK: How was your vigil? A smash hit, I should imagine. You *are* clever, making that addition to the story. I mean the fast. Add the possibility that the leading actor might pass out at any minute, and you turn the inevitable anticlimax of a second-night performance into pure thriller. Congratulations.

GIDEON: I again missed you among the audience.

MARK: And Lois. You must have missed her too.

GIDEON: I did. Where is she?

[DAVID *comes in, carrying a can of soup.*]

DAVID: I've found some lentil soup. It's only a tin—

[*He stares at his father.*]

MARK: Would you lay a place for me also? After all, it's an occasion—the breaking of the Great Man's fast. Perhaps we should call it the First Supper!

DAVID: It'll be five minutes, Giddy.

[*He starts to go back to the kitchen.*]

GIDEON: Lay a place for your father too, please.

DAVID: All right.

MARK: And for Lois too, please. She will be hungry also. [*He smiles.*] It's not only vigils that make man hungry.

DAVID: What?

MARK: Lay for your father, and he will lay for you.

[*Pause.*]

DAVID: Where is she?

[*They stare at one another. Intuitively,* DAVID *moves to the foot of the stairs.*]

[*Calling up.*] Lois? . . . *Lois!*

[*The girl starts up in bed.*]

MARK: Perhaps she's asleep.

DAVID: Lois!

[*The girl gets quickly out of bed, wrapping the sheet about her. Standing there, she drinks elaborately from the bottle.*]

GIDEON [*to* DAVID]: Gently, David, I beg you.

DAVID: Lois!!!

[*Carefully, she puts down the bottle, winds the sheet around her, and comes slowly downstairs: a white figure joining three others.*]

GIDEON: Peace.

LOIS: Good evening. [*To* DAVID.] Good evening. [*To* MARK.] Good evening. [*To* GIDEON.] You got wet.

GIDEON: I'm afraid I did.

LOIS: Well, that's all right. It was that kind of a day. Everybody got wet! . . . [*She starts to wander round the room.*] Actually, it was an ordinary day. Absolutely ordinary. Some people got chicken in their gut, and some people got a bullet, and some other people—the lucky ones they *say*—got something else. And it's all explicable only in the eyes of God. [*To* MARK.] Right? . . . [*To* DAVID.] What are you doing with that? Are you going to give that to Giddy? Is that all he gets after two whole days' starvation—is that all he gets in *his* gut?—a lousy plate of canned soup? Ah, poor Giddy! I stop looking after you for one day, and see what happens. You see—you still need me! [*She gives a strained laugh.*] Well, actually no one needs anyone. That's just a word—*needs*, one of those crazy words . . . mess up your head . . .

DAVID: Lois . . .

LOIS [*fiercely snatching the can of soup out of his hand*]: *Give me that!*

[*She turns and goes with it into the kitchen.*]

GIDEON [*to* MARK: *cold.*]: What have you done?

MARK [*innocently*]: I?

GIDEON: I can't believe . . .

MARK: What?

GIDEON: Even . . . even within the context. . . . *No, Mark.*

MARK: What? What, Gideon?

GIDEON [*bursting out*]: That even you—!

MARK: "Would stoop so low"?

[*He laughs.* DAVID *turns and stares at him.*]

MARK [*to his son*]: What are you gaping at? An old wreck still attractive to women? Disgusting, isn't it? Pleasure's for the young. Everyone knows that! . . . Portrait of a teenager discovering the world not made entirely in his own image! [*Pause.* MARK *sits on the throne.*] Don't worry, boy! You didn't miss much. It wasn't exactly the sex act of the era. She's as cold as haddock, you must know that. Deep Freeze Dora, the Tundra Gash!

GIDEON: Be quiet!

MARK: Still, I gave her *something*. What do you think she wanted from you, eh? Drugs and shrugs, and a pleady kiss once a week. D'you think that satisfies a girl? I know you pot babies. It's all wow and wee-wee, with you, isn't it? You can't get it up to save your stoned lives!

GIDEON: Be quiet! Be quiet, this instant!

MARK [*ignoring him*]: No wonder she couldn't stand you—your mother.

Even in her, deep down, was the natural Italian horror of the Unmale.

GIDEON: Mark, I beg you!

[MARK *gets up again. He approaches his son, and puts his arm intimately around his neck.*]

MARK: Now don't fret, boy. We're two of a kind, you and I. I could never dominate a woman either. You don't want to believe all that stuff about me, the Great Lover. It was all rubbish. I failed just as early with Giulia. Well, of course. All she wanted was the ancestral Roman pattern. Smashed fist: smashed plate. How else do you know you are loved? I was hopeless at it! Her "big shy Englishman"! It was my fault, really, she had to turn elsewhere for comfort.

[DAVID *turns to him sharply.* GIDEON *rises, appalled.*]

Oh, well, yes! What's so new about that? What's the big surprise? You must have realized! No? . . . You mustn't be too hard on her. After all, what else was she going to do? She was a hot lady, your mum. What I couldn't supply, she had to get somewhere. So she found it in Corfu harbor. A vulgar choice, but there you are.

GIDEON [*in pain*]: *Mark!*

MARK [*roughly*]: Oh, come on now, Giddy. Stop playacting! It's time we told him.

GIDEON: "We"?

MARK: My snot son, who claims no kinship with the Mediterranean! It's time he knew our little secret.

GIDEON: Secret? . . . What secret? . . . There's no—no—no secret! . . .

DAVID [*soft: dead*]: Stop it.

GIDEON [*desperate and confused*]: I know no secret, David!

[DAVID *stands rigid, looking at neither of them.*]

DAVID: Just stop it, Giddy.

GIDEON: I know nothing, David. Believe me: nothing. He's inventing every scrap of this!

MARK: Oh, come now: you can do better than that! You don't have to resort to lies, Gideon. Protect him, if you want—but don't lie! It's shocking when *you* do it!

GIDEON [*urgently*]: David? . . .

MARK: It's really obscene!

GIDEON: Dear boy?

DAVID [*low: stiffly*]: Just stop it. Just stop the voice. The voice . . . the voice! . . . *Please!* . . .

MARK: Look at you! Is that my face? Dirty olive out of the standard wop jar! Is that my body? Slack-waisted camel walk: the harbor hump! Get with it, you lump of Italy—it took a lot of pasta to make you!

GIDEON [*breaking out*]: Be silent! Abominable—abominable man! Close your mouth!

MARK: You know it's true.

GIDEON: I know nothing of the sort. There's not one word of truth in any of this, and you know it. Believe me, David, not one!

MARK: Why, what's the tragedy? Some matelot lowered his flap to his mum under the arcade. So what? We're all God's bambini, aren't we?

GIDEON: Liar!

MARK: I forgave her. Gave you my name!

GIDEON: Liar!

MARK: My glorious *name*—which some girls still conjure with! . . . All right, when you were young. But come thirteen, when she saw her little Corsican stoker or whatever he was, start to slouch round the villa, memory-sized—ah, then she got the Gods! Suddenly she couldn't bear to look at you any more! Started calling you her punishment. God's retribution on a Catholic girl who had strayed! You had to go, and I had to do it. Send you to England for your education. Keep you away from Corfu. Telegrams every few months—"Still not convenient you return. Your loving father."

[DAVID *looks at him in horror.*]

GIDEON: Listen to me, David. All of this is part of a game. A hideous, disgusting game. Your father is simply trying to provoke me, that's all. That is all it's about.

DAVID [*in anguish*]: Just stop the voice, Giddy! Stop it, that's all I want!

MARK [*raising his voice*]: Why else should I keep you away from Corfu all those years? Answer me that! Why else should I keep you away for six whole years—if she hadn't begged me to? Why else would I do that, Giddy? Perhaps you can tell!?

GIDEON: I don't know. I don't care!

MARK: Why else?

GIDEON: Hold your tongue.

MARK [*to* DAVID]: Why else? Why else? Give me one reason, my dear little bastard!

GIDEON [*exploding*]: *No!* . . . I order you! I order you—YES! . . .

MARK [*jeeringly*]: What?

[*Pause.*]

GIDEON [*controlling himself with great effort*]: To be quiet.

[*Suddenly* DAVID *runs to the garden exit, snatches up his boots, and shoves his feet into them.*]

David! . . . Where are you going?

DAVID: Away.

GIDEON: Where?

DAVID: Out of the voice.

GIDEON: No!

[DAVID *runs toward the front door.*]

Stay here.

DAVID: I can't.

GIDEON: Please, David. *Please!*

DAVID: I can't, Giddy. No more!

GIDEON: All of this is lies. Every bit of it. Everything he says is a lie!

DAVID [*in great anguish*]: I KNOW! I KNOW! . . . *I KNOW!*

[*Slight pause.*]

GIDEON [*with desperate quietness*]: *Then why?*

DAVID: I've got to get out. That's all.

GIDEON: No. Not you! . . . Not *you!*

MARK: Then who? Who's got to get out, then, Giddy? . . . *Who?*

[*A pause.* GIDEON *wrings his hands.*]

GIDEON: No one. Everyone must stay. No one must leave this house. No one.

[*He stands, looking straight ahead.*]

DAVID [*dead*]: That's right. No one. In the end, there's no one. "Be silent. Hold your tongue." That's all you can do. You can't stop it. The voice goes on and on—and all you've got against it is words. Lovely words. And theories—lovely theories. And fasts!

GIDEON: Owl!

DAVID: Theories and hopes and vigils and fasts! And *nothing! Lovely nothing!*

GIDEON: David! . . .

DAVID [*savagely*]: No one and nothing!

[*He turns on his heel and moves to the stairs.* GIDEON *pursues him.*]

GIDEON: David! . . . Listen to me, I beg you. Please, David, look at me, at least. My dear, dear boy—look at me. Please . . . won't you look?

[DAVID *turns.*]

DAVID [*howling*]: FUCK OFF!

[*He dashes upstairs. A pause.* GIDEON *begins to move slowly downstage.* MARK *comes up to him.*]

MARK: Congratulations. The battle's over. You win. I see there is nothing I can do will make Shrivings reject me. You will even help torture a boy to maintain its foundations. [*He opens his arms wide.*] Master—Receive your Disciple!

[GIDEON *stares at him, then crumples in a faint on to the floor.* MARK *crouches over him in horror.*]

MARK [*in a whisper*]: Giulia! . . . [*He looks wildly about him, then retreats in panic to the stairs, calling aloud.*] Lois! . . . LOIS!

LOIS [*off*]: What is it? [*She rushes in.*] Giddy!

MARK [*moving to the table*]: Water . . .

LOIS [*kneeling*]: Giddy! . . . Jesus! . . . Giddy! . . . [*She pulls him to a sitting position.*] . . . *Giddy!*

MARK [*approaching with the water*]: Give him this.

LOIS: No!

MARK: It's only water.

LOIS [*ferociously*]: Get away! Don't you touch him! Get away!

[MARK *scrambles to the foot of the stairs where he watches her revive* GIDEON.]

Hey . . . hey now . . . hey now, Giddy . . . hey now. . . . Open your eyes. Open your eyes for me, Giddy. Come on now: be good. Be good with me, Giddy . . . be good . . . [*She starts to rock him to and fro in her arms.*] Come on, now, be my Giddy; my own Giddy; my darling! Come on, now, be my Giddy; my own Giddy; my darling! Come on, now, be my Giddy; my own Giddy; my darling!

[GIDEON *opens his eyes, and stirs.*]

Hi! You fell. It's all right. I'm here. Try and stand. Come on. Lean on me. Up we go. . . . That's it . . .

[*She helps him to rise.* MARK *moves up the stairs into his bedroom, leaving the door open.*]

Now we'll sit over there. Come on. It's only a few steps. . . . There we are . . . come along now. . . . That's it.

[*She leads him tenderly across the room to the table, and helps him sit behind it, facing front.*]

Now I'll make you some soup. It won't take a minute.

GIDEON [*faintly*]: No.

LOIS: Of course, my dear. You're very hungry. That's why you fell.

GIDEON: No.

LOIS: I'll bring you some bread, first. Just while I heat it.

GIDEON: Please leave me alone.

[MARK *suddenly raises his head and calls out.*]

MARK: David!

[GIDEON *half rises.*]

LOIS: Giddy, please sit down. You haven't any strength at all. Go on, now.

[*He obeys her.*]

LOIS: You just sit there. I'll be right back. [*She goes into the kitchen.*]

MARK [*roaring*]: David!

[GIDEON *lowers his head and puts his hands over his ears. Suddenly* DAVID *dashes out of his bedroom, crosses violently into* MARK's *room, and slams the door behind him. He glares.*]

[*Throwing out his arms.*] All right—I'm here. Look. Look. *Look!* Keep them on me, your eyes—your mother's—yes! Ruined by me! Who the hell else could I be but your dad? Keep looking. This is it. The last time. You'll hear the voice just once more—then never again. I'll go back to Corfu for life!

[*Father and son stare at each other, each dressed in white towels.*]

Now. Now—I'll tell you why I kept you out of your home.

[*He raises a bottle to his lips—then suddenly chucks it on the bed instead.* DAVID *keeps looking at him.*]

Your first week on earth you stared at me like that. Before you could even see properly, you heard the voice. The dead man's voice, singing a lullaby. Your face wrinkled in fear. [*Pause.*] When you were six, I watched you race your bike through the olive trees. Your mother was standing beside me. Your mouth opened with glee. Hers too. All I got were the mouths opening and shutting. No glee. Just physical movements. I stood there hating you both. Filling up with hate. And you, twisting the handlebars, turned and caught my eye, you shook—and fell off. Giulia screamed and ran to you. I didn't . . . Do you still shake?

[DAVID *stands unmoving.* MARK *turns away. Below,* LOIS *comes in with a board of bread and a dish of butter.*]

LOIS: Here now. Have a slice of this.

[GIDEON *does not move.*]

Don't give me a hard time, Giddy. Sit up.

GIDEON [*raising himself*]: Please go away.

[*Determinedly, she cuts the bread and butters it.*]

LOIS: There. I want you to finish that by the time I bring the soup. O.K.?

[GIDEON *does not move. She goes back into the kitchen.*]

MARK: Do you know what it's like to be worshiped by a saint? She truly believed that I—this object in front of you—because a writer, was actually *better*, actually superior to her, mere creature of instinct! What could I do? I encouraged her. I got her to regard herself as entirely frivolous. Trivial! Unworthy of her important husband! . . . And the more she cringed in awe, the more I hated her. . . . Well, naturally . . . [*He goes to the bed, snatches up the bottle, and drinks.*] My Son-Confessor. You were never fooled. You saw him only too clear: the killer in me. It's why I had to get rid of you. You knew how he'd finish the brandy alone at night in the villa—then stand in the bathroom, sticking pins of Seconal into his face, saying: "Let this be the Young! The hateful Young!" How he'd tear his own hair in front of the mirror—hit himself with his own construction worker's hand, screaming inside: "Why was I born without joy? Why do others have it, and not me?" [*Softer.*] And later, lying beside her in morning light, watching her wake. The only girl I ever knew who smiled first thing on waking. Watching the smile come, a second before the eyes open. Spill over me their bright love . . . watching her in such anger. [*Pause.*] Till one morning, she doesn't smile. She groans instead. One morning—after one particular night.

[*He turns away.* GIDEON *begins to murmur below. He is very disturbed.*]

GIDEON [*low*]: No one.

MARK: And I've got to . . . tell you . . .

[*He sits on the bed.*]

GIDEON: No one and nothing . . . just words . . . words and nothing.

MARK: How does a dancer die, who doesn't want to live?

GIDEON: No! . . .

MARK: I watched my hate creep up her legs. It was as if I was needling it into her veins.

GIDEON: Theories . . . lovely theories . . .

MARK: She goes to bed. The hips suddenly won't move. Don't want to any more.

GIDEON [*agitated: half to himself*]: Well, what else could I *do?* Join in? Bang, bang! "Get out. Shrivings can't cope with you!"—is that what you want? . . . "Stop it," you say. "Stop the voice!" All right! That's easy to say. The hard thing *is not to!* Let it go on! Let it die of itself. Can't you see that? *It must die of itself!* [*He springs up and starts pacing the room, speaking feverishly.*] The hard thing is to do nothing. Almost impossible. . . . Well, we've spoken of it often enough. . . . Answer me this! How could we throw him out, and live here afterward ourselves? Doesn't it—in the end—doesn't it just—*just*—come down to *that?* To the sheer impossibility of that? . . . In the end, to shift at all—make any change that *is* a change—to *shove*, if you like, evolution on—and that's the task: no less!—*there have to be priorities!* . . . All right. Abstraction! That's just another bogey word! . . . I'm talking about a new kind of honor. Holding on to priorities. Do you see? . . .[*He continues to walk up and down the room, hands clasped, caged in pain.*]

MARK: Finally, nothing moves. Except her mouth, praying. Just sits there in a canvas jacket, praying.

GIDEON: Yes. . . . *Exactly!* . . . That's what's needed. . . . A new kind of *honor*. . . .

MARK: Shoving the book under the pillow whenever she hears me coming. "Sorry, Gesù! Must go now! *He* won't understand!"

GIDEON: When we say Faith, it's *that*. . . . What is worth honoring? Really worth it? . . . Really? . . . *Really?* [*He stops short.*] You real people, what will you really honor?

MARK [*shouting at the shrine*]: Oh, you martyrs! You martyrs! [*He springs to his feet and over to the shrine.*] Why couldn't you ever fight me like a woman?

GIDEON [*rapidly*]: You speak of love all the time. But what will you honor? . . . Everyone says love: you've got to fight for your love. All right! But what does that mean? Do you think silence can't be fight? Do you judge a love only by the *bashing* you do for it? [*Bitterly.*] Oh yes! Stand up! Square up! Come outside! Come on the battlefield! History of the World! Put your fists where your faith is! Marvelous! . . . [*Harshly.*] And that's what you want too, with all your long hair, sweet looks! . . . All of you, just the same . . . [*Pause. He stands for a moment, with eyes closed. Quieter: very calm.*] To let go. Just to let go that *indulgence*. Fill up instead with true passiveness. A feeling so total, it's *like* violence. An immense Nothing inside you. A sledgehammer Nothing which alone can break that crust of Ego. . . . Fasts—vigils—all those tricks: what are they about, except this?—to fill up in a new way! [*Pause. He stands very still, like a statue.*] You have to stand there, my dear, and take it. Bang—and no reply. None. [*Dead.*] None. None . . . [*He starts to tremble. Suddenly he begins to imitate himself, in a new and bitter, spinsterish voice.*] "Be quiet, Mark, please. Be silent, Mark. Mark, I forbid you. Mark, I beg you." [*Savagely.*] Words! Words and nothing! Lovely nothing! [*Crying out.*] *Oh, David!*

MARK [*standing before the shrine: low*]: Giulia!

GIDEON: *David!*

MARK: My dancer!

GIDEON: *David! My David! . . . My owl! . . .*

[LOIS *comes in with a bowl of steaming soup. She stares at* GIDEON. *He becomes aware of her. Slowly he sits again at the table. She places the soup in front of him.*]

LOIS: Eat.

[*He does not move, or look at her.*]

Eat, Giddy. [*Pause.*] Look, if you're mad at me, O.K., let me have it. Anything but the noble act. Sitting there all wounded. That's just shit, Giddy.

[*He remains motionless, as do father and son above.*]

O.K., I did it! So what does that make me? A Scarlet Woman? . . . O.K., say it, if that's what you think. And it is exactly what you think! Only it's too aggressive to say it right out, isn't it? . . . Wow! [*Pause.*] Gee, I'm disappointed in you. Who'd have thought that you, of all people in the world, would be jealous? Anything so *ordinary!* . . . Sagging Jesus, as my lover would say! . . . Well, you live and learn. Or do you? I don't learn a damn thing, except that everyone's full of shit, and that's not much to learn. Every classroom cynic you meet in college tells you that. It's funny to find out they're right. That's funny . . . [*Pause.*] Say something, for Christ's sake! Who d'you think you are, some kind of a priest or something? Mark's right—he's absolutely right! It's the Pope! I've offended the Pope! The lowly acolyte has displeased the Pope of Reason! [*Mock humble.*] All right, I did it, Your Holiness. I have sinned. I did it, Your Holiness. I have sinned. I did it. So what? [*Angry.*] Sex, sex, sex! So what? Supposed to be so great! What's great? *He's* the famous lover—he didn't find it great. It took him forever! Just a fat old man, dropping his sweat on me! And that's supposed to be beautiful! . . . *What are they all lying about?*

[*Pause. Still* GIDEON *does not move.*]

MARK [*softly*]: *Perdonna. Perdonna me. Perdonna.*

[LOIS *laughs.*]

LOIS: No, that's not why you're angry, is it? It's not the fuck, is it? It's him! The Enemy! I went off with the Opposition! [*False English accent.*] "Isn't that the end, my deah? She doesn't do it for two whole years, and when she *does,* who does she choose? A nice Progressive fuck with an approved young boy? Oh no. She has to have a beastly, reactionary fuck with his old man!" [*She laughs: then coolly.*] You don't care at all, do you? I'm kidding. I know it's not jealousy. It's nothing. It's absolutely nothing—right? You don't give a damn who I go to bed with! As far as you are concerned, I could go to bed with Hitler! . . . [*She laughs.*] Boy, you really are a mess! I mean it. Like you sit there with your nose up in the air, preaching all the time—Nonattachment—Get Beyond the Possessive Scene—all that beautiful new humanist shit!—and all there is is *you,* making a great cause out of not caring. A way of life, yeah, a whole religion—out of not feeling anything personal at all! [*She comes closer.*] I saw you last night, when he attacked me. Oh, you were distressed, all right. It was a distressing scene. Difficult to handle, even for a saint. But you managed. You managed, Giddy. You handled it O.K.! [*Grandly.*] "Come, Lois, I am tireder than I thought." [*Pause: coldly.*] You bastard.

[*He looks at her in amazement. She speaks with deep hostility.*]

I think you actually enjoyed it. Like it was a test of your virtue. "Poor Lois. Horrid for her, of course; but good for her too. You gotta be tested, after all. Everyone's got to be tested." Right? Just stand there and take it. Right . . . ? [*Leaning into his face.*] *Isn't that right?*

[GIDEON *puts his hands over his ears and turns away from her. For a second she falters and stops.*]

MARK [*dead*]: All right. Let me give it to you in the face. How I actually killed her, your mother. How I actually finished her off. Short and physical.

LOIS: At least, he knows! He's the filthiest man I've met, but he knows something!

MARK: One night . . .

LOIS: He's not a phony.

MARK: One night . . .

LOIS: He's garbage, but at least he's not a complete phony.

MARK [*with sudden violence*]: Take your eyes off me! Get out of here! I can't speak! [*He turns away.*]

LOIS [*now relentless*]: Do you know what a phony is, Giddy? A person who says the family is obsolete, and all he really wishes is that David Askelon was his own son!

[GIDEON *turns to look at her.*]

Do you know what a phony is? Someone who says Peace because there's no war in him. I don't mean he drove it out—I mean he never had it. It's easy to be chaste when you've got no cock, Giddy. It's easy to give up bloodshed, if you've got no blood to shed! Right? Dig that! I made an epigram! You see, I'm not so pompous as everyone says! . . . [*Icy.*] You know something? I don't believe your word on anything. Like when you say when you were young, you were attracted to boys and dogs and shit knows what? I tell you, I don't believe a fucking word. *I think you're exactly like me. You can't stand it!* You made that whole thing up just to teach a point. [*English accent.*] "Sex Freedom is a jolly good thing!" But I'm willing to bet my ass you never did it at all. Everyone says how noble you were to give it up—just *imagine* what he went through to do it! . . . Well, yeah, I can imagine. It was like nothing! No wonder she left you, your wife. No wonder she just got out, poor stupid Enid. She found out what a phony she was hitched to. What a phony! Christ, at least he's alive up there! Not dead—as good as dead! Dead thing! Dead old thing! Dead! Boring—dead!—ridiculous—dead! phony—dead!—old—dead! dead! dead! DEAD!

[*Deliberately,* GIDEON *strikes her as she leans over him. She recoils. He rises. She retreats. He strikes her again more violently. She stares at him in horror.*

*Pause.*]

GIDEON: Are you satisfied? In your deep heart, are you satisfied?

[*She turns from him. Then he turns from her. They stand frozen.*

*Pause.*]

MARK [*flatly*]: One night. She lying upstairs; I below, turning over my book of love poems. I get up. I drive into town. I sit in the arcade. I see a girl. I signal. I drive her back to the villa. I go up with her, into your mother's room. She lying there, drinking Coca-Cola her favorite way, out of the bottle. Now barely able to speak, she turns to me with her usual smile for any new thing. The girl giggles. "Don't be afraid," I say. "My wife enjoys this. It's for her we do it." [*Pause.*] And so. Slowly. On the floor. At the foot of the bed from which she could not move. I saluted her with my ecstasies. [*Pause.*] During the whole time she held the bottle before her, as if she were offering me refreshment. It was next morning she groaned first thing on waking. Very exactly: once. As if she were clearing her throat. [*Pause.*] She didn't live three weeks after that. I remember she held the cola bottle night and day. Like a doll to a sick child.

[*Silence. Then* DAVID *moves, quickly. His hands fly up, join violently above his head. For a long moment they stay up there, poised to smash his father down. Then he begins to tremble. Slowly his arms are lowered over his father's head. He pulls* MARK *to him, and kisses him on the face. They stay still.*

*Below neither* LOIS *nor* GIDEON *moves.*]

LOIS [*low*]: Don't ever forgive me.

[DAVID *releases* MARK. *He moves, and shuts the shrine on his mother's image.*]

Don't ever.

DAVID: Go down to him.

MARK: No.

DAVID: You *have* to.

MARK: You. You're his son where it matters.

DAVID: No. You are. [*Pause.*] *Padre.*

MARK: *Figlio.*

[*They stare at each other.*]

DAVID: *Va.*

MARK: *Si.*

[MARK *leaves the bedroom, and comes slowly downstairs.* DAVID *sits on the bed, exhausted.*]

LOIS [*quietly*]: That night we met him in jail. I was reading John Stuart Mill. Where he asked himself that question: if all the wrongs in the world were put right, would you yourself be any happier?—and the answer came back "No." You said, for you it would be "Yes." [*Pause.*] I never heard anything better than that.

[*She turns and sees* MARK *watching them both. He moves toward them. She ignores him, and walks straight by him up the stairs.* GIDEON *does not move. The girl hesitates outside the bedroom door—looks in—sees* DAVID—*enters.* DAVID *does not look at her.*

*Pause.*]

MARK [*seeing the bowl of soup*]: You haven't even eaten.

LOIS: Hey.

DAVID: Hay is for horses.

LOIS: Sure.

MARK: I warned you. I did. [*With fury.*] *You talk about life!*

[LOIS *turns her face to the wall, but does not leave.*]

No. *We* talk about life—the knowers. And look at us. You are the only possible thing I've ever met. D'you wonder I hate you?

DAVID [*woodenly*]: Why, Lois?

MARK: D'you wonder I love you?

DAVID: Why?

LOIS [*as woodenly*]: I don't know.

DAVID: Did you enjoy it, at least?

LOIS [*quietly: with absolute frankness*]: I don't know what enjoy means.

MARK: I wish I was an animal, and could live without a dream. I wish I was a child, and could live in a church. But I'm a man, and I've known you. Where else can I go?

LOIS: I don't know who I am, David.

[MARK *moves forward and thrusts his outstretched hand before the motionless* GIDEON.]

MARK: Here! This. This tool for making. A killer's hand. It's all you've got. . . . Take it.

[GIDEON *ignores it, staring straight ahead.*]

What will it do without you? Squeeze some more napalm out of my cock? Drive some more Red tanks over dreaming heads? Wear the Pope's ring, and dip a gold pen in the sick of starving children it's helped create. Sign me Governor of Louisibama, and decree at parties for the blind, white guests must be separated from black by charitable hands, since they can't see to do God's work for themselves. Don't leave me with this God's hand, Giddy.

[GIDEON *says nothing and does not move.*]

LOIS [*quietly*]: I'm no place, David. No place at all.

DAVID: Shrivings is a place.

LOIS: No.

DAVID: It has to be.

LOIS: It's nowhere.

DAVID [*violently*]: It has to be! IT HAS TO BE!

[*The girl turns. He turns round to her. They stare at one another.*]

MARK: Have you no word for me? No word at all?

GIDEON: Dust.

[*Appalled,* MARK *sits down at the table. He takes up a spoon. He dips it in the soup, and presents it to* GIDEON.]

MARK: Peace!

[GIDEON *sits rigid.*

*Above,* DAVID *suddenly stretches out his arm to* LOIS. *She looks at it without expression: motionless.*

*A long pause.*

*Then, very slowly,* GIDEON *begins to lower his head to the spoon held before him. He does not look at* MARK. *He opens his mouth, and drinks.*

*The light fades.*]

CURTAIN

# EQUUS

*For*
*Paul*
*with love*

*Equus* was first presented by the National Theatre at the Old Vic Theatre on July 26, 1973, with the following cast:

| | |
|---|---|
| MARTIN DYSART | Alec McCowen |
| NURSE | Louie Ramsay |
| HESTHER SALOMON | Gillian Barge |
| ALAN STRANG | Peter Firth |
| FRANK STRANG | Alan MacNaughtan |
| DORA STRANG | Jeanne Watts |
| HORSEMAN | Nicholas Clay |
| HARRY DALTON | David Healy |
| JILL MASON | Doran Godwin |

and

Neil Cunningham, David Graham, David Kincaid, Maggie Riley, Rosalind Shanks, Veronica Sowerby, Harry Waters

Directed by John Dexter

The New York production of *Equus* was first performed at the Plymouth Theatre on October 24, 1974, with the following cast:

| | |
|---|---|
| MARTIN DYSART | Anthony Hopkins |
| ALAN STRANG | Peter Firth |
| NURSE | Mary Doyle |
| HESTHER SALOMON | Marian Seldes |
| FRANK STRANG | Michael Higgins |
| DORA STRANG | Frances Sternhagen |
| HORSEMAN/NUGGET | Everett McGill |
| HARRY DALTON | Walter Mathews |
| JILL MASON | Roberta Maxwell |
| HORSES | Gus Kaikkoen, Philip Kraus, Gabriel Oshen, David Ramsey, John Tyrrell |

Directed by John Dexter

The main action of the play takes place in Rokeby Psychiatric Hospital in southern England. The time is the present.

The play is divided into numbered scenes, indicating a change of time or locale or mood. The action, however, is continuous.

## A NOTE ON THE PLAY

One weekend over two years ago, I was driving with a friend through bleak countryside. We passed a stable. Suddenly he was reminded by it of an alarming crime which he had heard about recently at a dinner party in London. He knew only one horrible detail, and his complete mention of it could barely have lasted a minute—but it was enough to arouse in me an intense fascination.

The act had been committed several years before by a highly disturbed young man. It had deeply shocked a local bench of magistrates. It lacked, finally, any coherent explanation.

A few months later my friend died. I could not verify what he had said, or ask him to expand it. He had given me no name, no place, and no time. I don't think he knew them. All I possessed was his report of a dreadful event, and the feeling it engendered in me. I knew very strongly that I wanted to interpret it in some entirely personal way. I had to create a mental world in which the deed could be made comprehensible.

Every person and incident in *Equus* is of my own invention, save the crime itself; and even that I modified to accord with what I feel to be acceptable theatrical proportion. I am grateful now that I have never received confirmed details of the real story, since my concern has been more and more with a different kind of exploration.

I have been lucky, in doing final work on the play, to have enjoyed the advice and expert comment of a distinguished child psychiatrist. Through him I have tried to keep things real in a more naturalistic sense. I have also come to perceive that psychiatrists are an immensely varied breed, professing immensely varied methods and techniques. Martin Dysart is simply one doctor in one hospital. I must take responsibility for him, as I do for his patient.

P.S.

## THE SETTING

A square of wood set on a circle of wood.

The square resembles a railed boxing ring. The rail, also of wood, encloses three sides. It is perforated on each side by an opening. Under the rail are a few vertical slats, as if in a fence. On the downstage side there is no rail. The whole square is set on ball bearings, so that by slight pressure from actors standing round it on the circle, it can be made to turn round smoothly by hand.

On the square are set three little plain benches, also of wood. They are placed parallel with the rail, against the slats, but can be moved out by the actors to stand at right angles to them.

Set into the floor of the square, and flush with it, is a thin metal pole, about a yard high. This can be raised out of the floor, to stand upright. It acts as a support for the actor playing Nugget, when he is ridden.

In the area outside the circle stand benches. Two downstage left and right are curved to accord with the circle. The left one is used by Dysart as a listening and observing post when he is out of the square, and also by Alan as his hospital bed. The right one is used by Alan's parents, who sit side by side on it. (Viewpoint is from the main body of the audience.)

Further benches stand upstage, and accommodate the other actors. All the cast of *Equus* sits on stage the entire evening. They get up to perform their scenes, and return when they are done to their places around the set. They are witnesses, assistants—and especially a Chorus.

Upstage, forming a backdrop to the whole, are tiers of seats in the fashion of a dissecting theater, formed into two railed-off blocks, pierced by a central tunnel. In these blocks sit members of the audience. During the play, Dysart addresses them directly from time to time, as he addresses the main body of the theater. No other actor ever refers to them.

To left and right, downstage, stand two ladders on which are suspended horse masks.

The color of all benches is olive green.

Above the stage hangs a battery of lights, set in a huge metal ring. Light cues, in this version, will be only of the most general description.

## THE HORSES

The actors wear tracksuits of chestnut velvet. On their feet are light strutted hooves, about four inches high, set on metal horseshoes. On their hands are gloves of the same color. On their heads are tough masks made of alternating bands of silver wire and leather; their eyes are outlined by leather blinkers. The actors' own heads are seen beneath them: no attempt should be made to conceal them.

Any literalism which could suggest the cozy familiarity of a domestic animal—or worse, a pantomime horse—should be avoided. The actors should never crouch on all fours, or even bend forward. They must always—except on the one occasion where Nugget is ridden—stand upright, as if the body of the horse extended invisibly behind them. Animal effect must be created entirely mimetically, through the use of legs, knees, neck, face, and the turn of the head which can move the mask above it through all the gestures of equine wariness and pride. Great care must also be taken that the masks are put on before the audience with very precise timing—the actors watching each other, so that the masking has an exact and ceremonial effect.

## THE CHORUS

References are made in the text to the Equus Noise. I have in mind a choric effect, made by all the actors sitting round upstage, and composed of humming, thumping, and stamping—though never of neighing or whinnying. This Noise heralds or illustrates the presence of Equus the God.

# ACT ONE

## SCENE 1

*Darkness.*

*Silence.*

*Dim light up on the square. In a spotlight stands* ALAN STRANG, *a lean boy of seventeen, in sweater and jeans. In front of him, the horse* NUGGET. ALAN'*s pose represents a contour of great tenderness: his head is pressed against the shoulder of the horse, his hands stretching up to fondle its head. The horse in turn nuzzles his neck.*
*The flame of a cigarette lighter jumps in the dark. Lights come up slowly on the circle. On the left bench, downstage,* MARTIN DYSART, *smoking. A man in his mid-forties.*

DYSART: With one particular horse, called Nugget, he embraces. The animal digs its sweaty brow into his cheek, and they stand in the dark for an hour—like a necking couple. And of all nonsensical things—I keep thinking about the *horse!* Not the boy: the horse, and what it may be trying to do. I keep seeing that huge head kissing him with its chained mouth. Nudging through the metal some desire absolutely irrelevant to filling its belly or propagating its own kind. What desire could that be? Not to stay a horse any longer? Not to remain reined up forever in those particular genetic strings? Is it possible, at certain moments we cannot imagine, a horse can add its sufferings together—the nonstop jerks and jabs that are its daily life—and turn them into grief? What use is grief to a horse?

[ALAN *leads* NUGGET *out of the square and they disappear together up the tunnel, the horse's hooves scraping delicately on the wood.*

DYSART *rises, and addresses both the large audience in the theater and the smaller one onstage.*]

You see, I'm lost. What use, I should be asking, are questions like these to an overworked psychiatrist in a provincial hospital? They're worse than useless; they are, in fact, subversive. [*He enters the square. The light grows brighter.*] The thing is, I'm desperate. You see, I'm wearing that horse's head myself. That's the feeling. All reined up in old language and old assumptions, straining to jump clean-hoofed on to a whole new track of being I only suspect is there. I can't see it, because my educated, average head is being held at the wrong angle. I can't jump because the bit forbids it, and my own basic force—my horsepower, if you like—is too little. The only thing I know for sure is this: a horse's head is finally unknowable to me. Yet I handle children's heads—which I must presume to be more complicated, at least in the area of my chief concern. . . . In a way, it has nothing to do with this boy. The doubts have been there for years, piling up steadily in this dreary place. It's only the extremity of this case that's made them active. I know that. The *extremity* is the point! All the same, whatever the reason, they are now, these doubts, not just vaguely worrying—but intolerable. . . . I'm sorry. I'm not making much sense. Let me start properly; in order. It began one Monday last month, with Hesther's visit.

## SCENE 2

[*The light gets warmer.*

*He sits.* NURSE *enters the square.*]

NURSE: Mrs. Salomon to see you, Doctor.

DYSART: Show her in, please.

[NURSE *leaves and crosses to where* HESTHER *sits.*]

Some days I blame Hesther. She brought him to me. But of course that's nonsense. What is he but a last straw? a last symbol? If it hadn't been him, it would have been the next patient, or the next. At least, I suppose so.

[HESTHER *enters the square: a woman in her mid-forties.*]

HESTHER: Hello, Martin.

[DYSART *rises and kisses her on the cheek.*]

DYSART: Madam Chairman! Welcome to the torture chamber!

HESTHER: It's good of you to see me right away.

DYSART: You're a welcome relief. Take a couch.

HESTHER: It's been a day?

DYSART: No—just a fifteen-year-old schizophrenic, and a girl of eight thrashed into catatonia by her father. Normal, really. . . . You're in a state.

HESTHER: Martin, this is the most shocking case I ever tried.

DYSART: So you said on the phone.

HESTHER: I mean it. My bench wanted to send the boy to prison. For life, if they could manage it. It took me two hours' solid arguing to get him sent to you instead.

DYSART: Me?

HESTHER: I mean, to hospital.

DYSART: Now look, Hesther. Before you say anything else, I can take no more patients at the moment. I can't even cope with the ones I have.

HESTHER: You must.

DYSART: Why?

HESTHER: Because most people are going to be disgusted by the whole thing. Including doctors.

DYSART: May I remind you I share this room with two highly competent psychiatrists?

HESTHER: Bennett and Thoroughgood. They'll be as shocked as the public.

DYSART: That's an absolutely unwarrantable statement.

HESTHER: Oh, they'll be cool and exact. And underneath they'll be revolted, and immovably English. Just like my bench.

DYSART: Well, what am I? Polynesian?

HESTHER: You know exactly what I mean! . . . [*Pause.*] Please, Martin. It's vital. You're this boy's only chance.

DYSART: Why? What's he done? Dosed some little girl's Pepsi with Spanish Fly? What could possibly throw your bench into two-hour convulsions?

HESTHER: He blinded six horses with a metal spike.

[*A long pause.*]

DYSART: Blinded?

HESTHER: Yes.

DYSART: All at once, or over a period?

HESTHER: All on the same night.

DYSART: Where?

HESTHER: In a riding stable near Winchester. He worked there at weekends.

DYSART: How old?

HESTHER: Seventeen.

DYSART: What did he say in court?

HESTHER: Nothing. He just sang.

DYSART: Sang?

HESTHER: Any time anyone asked him anything. [*Pause.*] Please take him, Martin. It's the last favor I'll ever ask you.

DYSART: No, it's not.

HESTHER: No, it's not—and he's probably abominable. All I know is, he needs you badly. Because there really is nobody within a hundred miles of your desk who can handle him. And perhaps understand what this is about. Also . . .

DYSART: What?

HESTHER: There's something very special about him.

DYSART: In what way?

HESTHER: Vibrations.

DYSART: You and your vibrations.

HESTHER: They're quite startling. You'll see.

DYSART: When does he get here?

HESTHER: Tomorrow morning. Luckily there was a bed in Neville Ward. I know this is an awful imposition, Martin. Frankly I didn't know what else to do.

[*Pause.*]

DYSART: Can you come in and see me on Friday?

HESTHER: Bless you!

DYSART: If you come after work I can give you a drink. Will six-thirty be all right?

HESTHER: You're a dear. You really are.

DYSART: Famous for it.

HESTHER: Goodbye.

DYSART: By the way, what's his name?

HESTHER: Alan Strang.

[*She leaves and returns to her seat.*]

DYSART [*to audience*]: What did I expect of him? Very little, I promise you. One more dented little face. Once more adolescent freak. The usual unusual. One great thing about being in the adjustment business: you're never short of customers.

[NURSE *comes down the tunnel, followed by* ALAN. *She enters the square.*]

NURSE: Alan Strang, Doctor.

[*The boy comes in.*]

DYSART: Hello. My name's Martin Dysart. I'm pleased to meet you. [*He puts out his hand. Alan does not respond in any way.*] That'll be all, Nurse, thank you.

## SCENE 3

[NURSE *goes out and back to her place.*
DYSART *sits, opening a file.*]

So: did you have a good journey? I hope they gave you lunch at least. Not that there's much to choose between a British Rail meal and one here.

[ALAN *stands staring at him.*]

DYSART: Won't you sit down? [*Pause. He does not.* DYSART *consults his file.*] Is this your full name? Alan Strang?

[*Silence.*]

And you're seventeen. Is that right? Seventeen? . . . Well?

ALAN [*singing low*]: Double your pleasure,
Double your fun
With Doublemint, Doublemint,
Doublemint gum.

DYSART [*unperturbed*]: Now, let's see. You work in an electrical shop during the week. You live with your parents, and your father's a printer. What sort of things does he print?

ALAN [*singing louder*]: Double your pleasure
Double your fun
With Doublemint, Doublemint,
Doublemint gum.

DYSART: I mean does he do leaflets and calendars? Things like that?

[*The boy approaches him, hostile.*]

ALAN [*singing*]: Try the taste of Martini
The most beautiful drink in the world.
It's the right one—
The bright one—
That's Martini!

DYSART: I wish you'd sit down, if you're going to sing. Don't you think you'd be more comfortable?

[*Pause.*]

ALAN [*singing*]: There's only one "T" in Typhoo!
In packets and in teabags too.
Any way you make it, you'll find it's true:
There's only one "T" in Typhoo!

DYSART [*appreciatively*]: Now that's a good song. I like it better than the other two. Can I hear that one again?

[ALAN *starts away from him, and sits on the upstage bench.*]

ALAN [*singing*]: Double your pleasure
Double your fun
With Doublemint, Doublemint,
Doublemint gum.

DYSART [*smiling*]: You know I was wrong. I really do think that one's better. It's got such a catchy tune. Please do that one again. [*Silence. The boy glares at him.*] I'm going to put you in a private bedroom for a little while. There are one or two available, and they're rather more pleasant than being in a ward. Will you please come and see me tomorrow? . . . [*He rises.*] By the way, which parent is it who won't allow you to watch television? Mother or father? Or is it both? [*Calling out of the door.*] Nurse!

[ALAN *stares at him.* NURSE *comes in.*]

NURSE: Yes, Doctor?

DYSART: Take Strang here to Number Three, will you? He's moving in there for a while.

NURSE: Very good, Doctor.

DYSART [*to* ALAN]: You'll like that room. It's nice.

[*The boy sits staring at* DYSART.
DYSART *returns the stare.*]

NURSE: Come along, young man. This way . . . I said this way, please.
[*Reluctantly* ALAN *rises and goes to* NURSE, *passing dangerously close to* DYSART, *and out through the left door.* DYSART *looks after him, fascinated.*]

## SCENE 4

[NURSE *and patient move on to the circle, and walk downstage to the bench where the doctor first sat, which is to serve also as* ALAN'*s bed.*]

NURSE: Well now; isn't this nice? You're lucky to be in here, you know, rather than the ward. That ward's a noisy old place.

ALAN [*singing*]: Let's go where you wanna go—Texaco!

NURSE [*contemplating him*]: I hope you're not going to make a nuisance of yourself. You'll have a much better time of it here, you know, if you behave yourself.

ALAN: Fuck off.

NURSE [*tight*]: That's the bell there. The lav's down the corridor.
[*She leaves him, and goes back to her place.*
ALAN *lies down.*]

## SCENE 5

[DYSART *stands in the middle of the square and addresses the audience. He is agitated.*]

DYSART: That night, I had this very explicit dream. In it I'm a chief priest in Homeric Greece. I'm wearing a wide gold mask, all noble and bearded, like the so-called Mask of Agamemnon found at Mycenae. I'm standing by a thick round stone and holding a sharp knife. In fact, I'm officiating at some immensely important ritual sacrifice, on which depends the fate of the crops or of a military expedition. The sacrifice is a herd of children. About five hundred boys and girls. I can see them stretching away in a long queue, right across the plain of Argos. I know it's Argos because of the red soil. On either side of me stand two assistant priests, wearing masks as well: lumpy, pop-eyed masks, such as also were found at Mycenae. They are enormously strong, these other priests, and absolutely tireless. As each child steps forward, they grab it from behind and throw it over the stone. Then, with a surgical skill which amazes even me, I fit in the knife and slice elegantly down to the navel, just like a seamstress following a pattern. I part the flaps, sever the inner tubes, yank them out and throw them hot and steaming on to the floor. The other two then study the pattern they make, as if they were reading hieroglyphics. It's obvious to me that I'm tops as chief priest. It's this unique talent for carving that has got me where I am. The only thing is, unknown to them, I've started to feel distinctly nauseous. And with each victim, it's getting worse. My face is going green behind the mask. Of course, I redouble my efforts to look professional—cutting and snipping for all I'm worth: mainly because I know that if ever those two assistants so much as glimpse my distress—and the implied doubt that this repetitive and smelly work is doing any social good at all—I will be the next across the stone. And then, of course—the damn mask begins to slip. The priests both turn and look at it—it slips some more—they see the green sweat running down my face—their gold pop eyes suddenly fill up with blood—they tear the knife out of my hand . . . and I wake up.

## SCENE 6

[HESTHER *enters the square. Light grows warmer.*]

HESTHER: That's the most indulgent thing I ever heard.

DYSART: You think?

HESTHER: Please don't be ridiculous. You've done the most superb work with children. You must know that.

DYSART: Yes, but do the children?

HESTHER: Really!

DYSART: I'm sorry.

HESTHER: So you should be.

DYSART: I don't know why you listen. It's just professional menopause. Everyone gets it sooner or later. Except you.

HESTHER: Oh, of course. I feel totally fit to be a magistrate all the time.

DYSART: No, you don't—but then that's you feeling unworthy to fill a job. I feel the job is unworthy to fill me.

HESTHER: Do you seriously?

DYSART: More and more. I'd like to spend the next ten years wandering very slowly around the *real* Greece. . . . Anyway, all this dream nonsense is your fault.

HESTHER: Mine?

DYSART: It's that lad of yours who started it off. Do you know it's his face I saw on every victim across the stone?

HESTHER: Strang?

DYSART: He has the strangest stare I ever met.

HESTHER: Yes.

DYSART: It's exactly like being accused. Violently accused. But what of? . . . Treating him is going to be unsettling. Especially in my present state. His singing was direct enough. His speech is more so.

HESTHER [*surprised*]: He's talking to you, then?

DYSART: Oh yes. It took him two more days of commercials, and then he snapped. Just like that—I suspect it has something to do with his nightmares.

[NURSE *walks briskly round the circle, a blanket over her arm, a clipboard of notes in her hand.*]

HESTHER: He has nightmares?

DYSART: Bad ones.

NURSE: We had to give him a sedative or two, Doctor. Last night it was exactly the same.

DYSART [*to* NURSE]: What does he do? Call out?

NURSE [*to desk*]: A lot of screaming, Doctor.

DYSART [*to* NURSE]: Screaming?

NURSE: One word in particular.

DYSART [*to* NURSE]: You mean a special word?

NURSE: Over and over again. [*Consulting clipboard.*] It sounds like "Ek."

HESTHER: Ek?

NURSE: Yes, Doctor. Ek . . ."Ek!" he goes. "Ek!"

HESTHER: How weird.

NURSE: When I woke him up he clung to me like he was going to break my arm.

[*She stops at* ALAN*'s bed. He is sitting up. She puts the blanket over him, and returns to her place.*]

DYSART: And then he bursts in—just like that—without knocking or anything. Fortunately, I didn't have a patient with me.

ALAN [*jumping up*]: *Dad!*

HESTHER: What?

DYSART: The answer to a question I'd asked him two days before. Spat out with the same anger as he sang the commercials.

HESTHER: Dad what?

ALAN: Who hates telly.

[*He lies downstage on the circle, as if watching television.*]

HESTHER: You mean his dad forbids him to watch?

DYSART: Yes.

ALAN: It's a dangerous drug.

HESTHER: Oh, really!

[FRANK *stands up and enters the scene downstage on the circle. A man in his fifties.*]

FRANK [*to* ALAN]: It may not look like that, but that's what it is. Absolutely fatal mentally, if you receive my meaning.

[DORA *follows him on. She is also middle-aged.*]

DORA: That's a little extreme, dear, isn't it?

FRANK: You sit in front of that thing long enough, you'll become stupid for life—like most of the population. [*To* ALAN.] The thing is, it's a *swiz*. It seems to be offering you something, but actually it's taking something away. Your intelligence and your concentration, every minute you watch it. That's a true swiz, do you see?

[*Seated on the floor,* ALAN *shrugs.*]

I don't want to sound like a spoilsport, old chum—but there really is no substitute for reading. What's the matter: don't you like it?

ALAN: It's all right.

FRANK: I know you think it's none of my beeswax, but it really is, you know. . . . Actually, it's a disgrace when you come to think of it. You the son of a printer, and never opening a book! If all the world was like you, I'd be out of a job, if you receive my meaning!

DORA: All the same, times change, Frank.

FRANK [*reasonably*]: They change if you let them change, Dora. Please return that set in the morning.

ALAN [*crying out*]: No!

DORA: Frank—no!

FRANK: I'm sorry, Dora, but I'm not having that thing in the house a moment longer. I told you I didn't want it to begin with.

DORA: But, dear, everyone watches television these days!

FRANK: Yes, and what do they watch? Mindless violence! Mindless jokes! Every five minutes some laughing idiot selling you something you don't want, just to bolster up the economic system. [*To* ALAN.] I'm sorry, old chum.

[*He leaves the scene and sits again in his place.*]

HESTHER: He's a Communist, then?

DYSART: Old-type Socialist, I'd say. Relentlessly self-improving.

HESTHER: They're *both* older than you'd expect.

DYSART: So I gather.

DORA [*looking after* FRANK]: Really, dear, you are very extreme!

[*She leaves the scene too, and again sits beside her husband.*]

HESTHER: She's an ex-schoolteacher, isn't she?

DYSART: Yes. The boy's proud of that. We got on to it this afternoon.

ALAN [*belligerently, standing up*]: She knows more than you.

[HESTHER *crosses and sits by* DYSART. *During the following, the boy walks round the circle, speaking to* DYSART *but not looking at him.* DYSART *replies in the same manner.*]

DYSART: [*to* ALAN]: Does she?

ALAN: I bet I do too. I bet I know more history than you.

DYSART [*to* ALAN]: Well, I bet you don't.

ALAN: All right: who was the Hammer of the Scots?

DYSART [*to* ALAN]: I don't know: who?

ALAN: King Edward the First. Who never smiled again?

DYSART [*to* ALAN]: I don't know: who?

ALAN: You don't know anything, do you? It was Henry the First. I know all the Kings.

DYSART [*To* ALAN]: And who's your favorite?

ALAN: John.

DYSART [*to* ALAN]: Why?

ALAN: Because he put out the eyes of that smarty little—

[*Pause.*]

[*Sensing he has said something wrong.*] Well, he didn't really. He was prevented, because the jailer was merciful!

HESTHER: Oh dear.

ALAN: *He was prevented!*

DYSART: Something odder was to follow.

ALAN: Who said "Religion is the opium of the people?"

HESTHER: Good Lord!

[ALAN *giggles.*]

DYSART: The odd thing was, he said it with a sort of guilty snigger. The sentence is obviously associated with some kind of tension.

HESTHER: What did you say?

DYSART: I gave him the right answer. [*To* ALAN.] Karl Marx.

ALAN: No.

DYSART [*to* ALAN]: Then who?

ALAN: Mind your own beeswax.

DYSART: It's probably his dad. He may say it to provoke his wife.

HESTHER: And you mean she's religious?

DYSART: She could be. I tried to discover—none too successfully.

ALAN: Mind your own beeswax!

[ALAN *goes back to bed and lies down in the dark.*]

DYSART: However, I shall find out on Sunday.

HESTHER: What do you mean?

DYSART [*getting up*]: I want to have a look at his home, so I invited myself over.

HESTHER: Did you?

DYSART: If there's any tension over religion, it should be evident on a Sabbath evening! I'll let you know.

[*He kisses her cheek and they part, both leaving the square.* HESTHER *sits in her place again;* DYSART *walks round the circle, and greets* DORA, *who stands waiting for him downstage.*]

## SCENE 7

DYSART [*shaking hands*]: Mrs. Strang.

DORA: Mr. Strang's still at the press, I'm afraid. He should be home in a minute.

DYSART: He works Sundays as well?

DORA: Oh yes. He doesn't set much store by Sundays.

DYSART: Perhaps you and I could have a little talk before he comes in.

DORA: Certainly. Won't you come into the living room? [*She leads the way into the square. She is very nervous.*] Please . . . [*She motions him to sit, then holds her hands tightly together.*]

DYSART: Mrs. Strang, have you any idea how this thing could have occurred?

DORA: I can't imagine, Doctor. It's all so unbelievable! . . . Alan's always been such a gentle boy. He loves animals! Especially horses.

DYSART: Especially?

DORA: Yes. He even has a photograph of one up in his bedroom. A beautiful white one, looking over a gate. His father gave it to him a few years ago, off a calendar he'd printed—and he's never taken it down. . . . And when he was seven or eight, I used to have to read him the same book over and over, all *about* a horse.

DYSART: Really?

DORA: Yes; it was called Prince, and no one could ride him.

[ALAN *calls from his bed, not looking at his mother.*]

ALAN [*excited, younger voice*]: Why not? . . . Why not? . . . Say it! In his voice!

DORA: He loved the idea of animals talking.

DYSART: Did he?

ALAN: *Say it! Say it! . . . Use his voice!*

DORA [*"proud" voice*]: "Because I am faithful!"

[ALAN *giggles.*]

"My name is Prince, and I'm a Prince among horses! Only my young Master can ride me! Anyone else—I'll *throw off!*"

[ALAN *giggles louder.*]

And then I remember I used to tell him a funny thing about falling off horses. Did you know that when Christian cavalry first appeared in the New World, the pagans thought horse and rider was one person?

DYSART: Really?

ALAN [*sitting up, amazed*]: One person?

DORA: Actually, they thought it must be a god.

ALAN: *A god!*

DORA: It was only when one rider fell off, they realized the truth.

DYSART: That's fascinating. I never heard that before. . . . Can you remember anything else like that you may have told him about horses?

DORA: Well, not really. They're in the Bible, of course. "He saith among the trumpets, Ha, ha."

DYSART: Ha, ha?

DORA: The Book of Job. Such a noble passage. *You* know—[*Quoting.*] "Hast thou given the horse strength?"

ALAN [*responding*]: "Hast thou clothed his neck with thunder?"

DORA [*to* ALAN]: "The glory of his nostrils is terrible!"

ALAN: "He swallows the ground with fierceness and rage!"

DORA: "He saith among the trumpets—"

ALAN [*trumpeting*]: "Ha! Ha!"

DORA [*to* DYSART]: Isn't that splendid?

DYSART: It certainly is.

ALAN [*trumpeting*]: Ha! Ha!

DORA: And then, of course, we saw an awful lot of Westerns on the television. He couldn't have enough of those.

DYSART: But surely you don't have a set, do you? I understood Mr. Strang doesn't approve.

DORA [*conspiratorially*]: He doesn't . . . I used to let him slip off in the afternoons to a friend next door.

DYSART [*smiling*]: You mean without his father's knowledge?

DORA: What the eye does not see, the heart does not grieve over, does it? Anyway, Westerns are harmless enough, surely?

[FRANK *stands up and enters the square.* ALAN *lies back under the blanket.*]

[*To* FRANK]: Oh, hello, dear. This is Dr. Dysart.

FRANK [*shaking hands*]: How d'you do?

DYSART: How d'you do?

DORA: I was just telling the doctor, Alan's always adored horses.

FRANK [*tight*]: We assumed he did.

DORA: You know he did, dear. Look how he liked that photograph you gave him.

FRANK [*startled*]: What about it?

DORA: Nothing, dear. Just that he pestered you to have it as soon as he saw it. Do you remember? [*To* DYSART.] We've always been a horsy family. At least my side of it has. My grandfather used to ride every morning on the downs behind Brighton, all dressed up in bowler hat and jodhpurs! He used to look splendid. Indulging in equitation, he called it.

[FRANK *moves away from them and sits wearily.*]

ALAN [*trying the word*]: Equitation . . .

DORA: I remember I told him how that came from *equus,* the Latin word for horse. Alan was fascinated by that word, I know. I suppose because he'd never come across one with two "u"s together before.

ALAN [*savoring it*]: *Equus!*

DORA: I always wanted the boy to ride himself. He'd have so enjoyed it.

DYSART: But surely he did?

DORA: No.

DYSART: Never?

DORA: He didn't care for it. He was most definite about not wanting to.

DYSART: But he must have had to at the stables? I mean, it would be part of the job.

DORA: You'd have thought so, but no. He absolutely wouldn't, would he, dear?

FRANK [*dryly*]: It seems he was perfectly happy raking out manure.

DYSART: Did he ever give a reason for this?

DORA: No. I must say we both thought it most peculiar, but he wouldn't discuss it. I mean, you'd have thought he'd be longing to get out in the air after being cooped up all week in that dreadful shop. Electrical and kitchenware! Isn't *that* an environment for a sensitive boy, Doctor? . . .

FRANK: Dear, have you offered the doctor a cup of tea?

DORA: Oh dear, no, I haven't! . . . And you must be dying for one.

DYSART: That would be nice.

DORA: Of course it would . . . excuse me . . .

[*She goes out—but lingers on the circle, eavesdropping near the right door.* ALAN *stretches out under his blanket and sleeps.* FRANK *gets up.*]

FRANK: My wife has romantic ideas, if you receive my meaning.

DYSART: About her family?

FRANK: She thinks she married beneath her. I daresay she did. I don't understand these things myself.

DYSART: Mr. Strang, I'm fascinated by the fact that Alan wouldn't ride.

FRANK: Yes, well, that's him. He's always been a weird lad, I have to be honest. Can you imagine spending your weekends like that—just cleaning out stalls—with all the things that he could have been doing in the way of Further Education?

DYSART: Except he's hardly a scholar.

FRANK: How do we know? He's never really tried. His mother indulged him. She doesn't care if he can hardly write his own name, and she a schoolteacher that was. Just as long as he's happy, she says . . .

[DORA *wrings her hands in anguish.* FRANK *sits again.*]

DYSART: Would you say she was closer to him than you are?

FRANK: They've always been thick as thieves. I can't say I entirely approve—especially when I hear her whispering that Bible to him hour after hour, up there in his room.

DYSART: Your wife is religious?

FRANK: Some might say excessively so. Mind you, that's her business. But when it comes to dosing it down the boy's throat—well, frankly, he's my son as well as hers. She doesn't see that. Of course, that's the funny thing about religious people. They always think their susceptibilities are more important than nonreligious.

DYSART: And you're nonreligious, I take it?

FRANK: I'm an atheist, and I don't mind admitting it. If you want my opinion, it's the Bible that's responsible for all this.

DYSART: Why?

FRANK: Well, look at it yourself. A boy spends night after night having this stuff read into him; an innocent man tortured to death—thorns driven into his head—nails into his hands—a spear jammed through his ribs. It can mark anyone for life, that kind of thing. I'm not joking. The boy was absolutely fascinated by all that. He was always mooning over religious pictures. I mean real kinky ones, if you receive my meaning. I had to put a stop to it once or twice! . . . [*Pause.*] Bloody religion—it's our only real problem in this house, but it's insuperable; I don't mind admitting it.

[*Unable to stand any more,* DORA *comes in again.*]

DORA [*pleasantly*]: You must excuse my husband, Doctor. This one subject is something of an obsession with him, isn't it, dear? You must admit.

FRANK: Call it what you like. All that stuff to me is just bad sex.

DORA: And what has that got to do with Alan?

FRANK: Everything! . . . [*Seriously.*]. Everything, Dora!

DORA: I don't understand. What are you saying?

[*He turns away from her.*]

DYSART [*calmingly*]: Mr.Strang, exactly how informed do you judge your son to *be* about sex?

FRANK [*tight*]: I don't know.

DYSART: You didn't actually instruct him yourself?

FRANK: Not in so many words, no.

DYSART: Did *you*, Mrs. Strang?

DORA: Well, I spoke a little, yes. I had to. I've been a teacher, Doctor, and I know what happens if you don't. They find out through magazines and dirty books.

DYSART: What sort of thing did you tell him? I'm sorry if this is embarrassing.

DORA: I told him the biological facts. But I also told him what I believed. That sex is not *just* a biological matter, but spiritual as well. That if God willed, he would fall in love one day. That his task was to prepare himself for the most important happening of his life. And after that, if he was lucky, he might come to know a higher love still. . . . I simply . . . don't understand . . . *Alan!* . . .

[*She breaks down in sobs. Her husband gets up and goes to her.*]

FRANK [*embarrassed*]: There now. There now, Dora. Come on!
DORA [*with sudden desperation*]: All right—laugh! Laugh, as usual!
FRANK [*kindly*]: No one's laughing, Dora.

[*She glares at him. He puts his arms round her shoulders.*]

No one's laughing, are they, Doctor?

[*Tenderly, he leads his wife out of the square, and they resume their places on the bench. Lights grow much dimmer.*]

## SCENE 8

[*A strange noise begins.* ALAN *begins to murmur from his bed. He is having a bad nightmare, moving his hands and body as if frantically straining to tug something back.* DYSART *leaves the square as the boy's cries increase.*]

ALAN: Ek! . . . Ek! . . . *Ek!* . . .

[*Cries of* Ek! *on tape fill the theater, from all around.* DYSART *reaches the foot of* ALAN*'s bed as the boy gives a terrible cry—*

EK!

*—and wakes up. The sounds snap off.* ALAN *and the doctor stare at each other. Then abruptly* DYSART *leaves the area and reenters the square.*]

## SCENE 9

[*Lights grow brighter.* DYSART *sits on his bench, left, and opens his file.* ALAN *gets out of bed, leaves his blanket, and comes in. He looks truculent.*]

DYSART: Hello. How are you this morning?

[ALAN *stares at him.*]

Come on: sit down.

[ALAN *crosses the stage and sits on the bench, opposite.*]

Sorry if I gave you a start last night. I was collecting some papers from my office, and I thought I'd look in on you. Do you dream often?

ALAN: Do *you?*
DYSART: It's my job to ask the questions. Yours to answer them.
ALAN: Says who?
DYSART: Says me. Do you dream often?
ALAN: Do you?
DYSART: Look—Alan.
ALAN: I'll answer if you answer. In turns.

[*Pause.*]

DYSART: Very well. Only we have to speak the truth.

ALAN [*mocking*]: Very well.

DYSART: So. Do you dream often?

ALAN: Yes. Do you?

DYSART: Yes. Do you have a special dream?

ALAN: No. Do you?

DYSART: Yes. What was your dream about last night?

ALAN: Can't remember. What's yours about?

DYSART: I said the truth.

ALAN: That is the truth. What's yours about? The special one.

DYSART: Carving up children.

[ALAN *smiles.*]

My turn!

ALAN: What?

DYSART: What is your first memory of a horse?

ALAN: What d'you mean?

DYSART: The first time one entered your life, in any way.

ALAN: Can't remember.

DYSART: Are you sure?

ALAN: Yes.

DYSART: You have no recollection of the first time you noticed a horse?

ALAN: I told you. Now it's my turn. Are you married?

DYSART [*controlling himself*]: I am.

ALAN: Is she a doctor too?

DYSART: It's my turn.

ALAN: Yes, well what?

DYSART: What is Ek?

[*Pause.*]

You shouted it out last night in your sleep. I thought you might like to talk about it.

ALAN [*singing*]: Double Diamond works wonders, works wonders, works wonders!

DYSART: Come on, now. You can do better than that.

ALAN [*singing louder*]: Double Diamond works wonders, works wonders for you!

DYSART: All right. Good morning.

ALAN: What d'you mean?

DYSART: We're finished for today.

ALAN: But I've only had ten minutes.

DYSART: Too bad.

[*He picks up a file and studies it.* ALAN *lingers.*]

Didn't you hear me? I said, Good morning.

ALAN: That's not fair!

DYSART: No?

ALAN [*savagely*]: The government pays you twenty quid an hour to see me. I know. I heard downstairs.

DYSART: Well, go back there and hear some more.

ALAN: *That's not fair!*

[*He springs up, clenching his fists in a sudden violent rage.*]

You're a—you're a—you're a swiz! . . . Bloody swiz! . . . Fucking swiz!

DYSART: Do I have to call Nurse?

ALAN: She puts a finger on me, I'll bash her!

DYSART: She'll bash you much harder, I can assure you. Now go away.

[*He reads his file.* ALAN *stays where he is, emptily clenching his hands. He turns away. A pause. A faint hum starts from the* CHORUS.]

ALAN [*sullenly*]: On a beach . . .

## SCENE 10

[*He steps out of the square, upstage, and begins to walk round the circle. Warm light glows on it.*]

DYSART: What?

ALAN: Where I saw a horse. Swizzy.

[*Lazily he kicks at the sand, and throws stones at the sea.*]

DYSART: How old were you?

ALAN: How should I know? . . . Six.

DYSART: Well, go on. What were you doing there?

ALAN: Digging.

[*He throws himself on the ground, downstage center of the circle, and starts scuffing with his hands.*]

DYSART: A sandcastle?

ALAN: Well, what else?

DYSART [*warningly*]: And?

ALAN: Suddenly I heard this noise. Coming up behind me.

[*A young* HORSEMAN *issues in* slow motion *out of the tunnel. He carries a riding crop with which he is urging on his invisible horse, down the right side of the circle. The hum increases.*]

DYSART: What noise?

ALAN: Hooves. Splashing.

DYSART: Splashing?

ALAN: The tide was out and he was galloping.

DYSART: Who was?

ALAN: This fellow. Like a college chap. He was on a big horse—urging him on. I thought he hadn't seen me. I called out: Hey!

[*The* HORSEMAN *goes into* natural time, *charging fast round the downstage corner of the square straight at* ALAN.]

And they just swerved in time!

HORSEMAN [*reining back*]: Whoa! . . . Whoa there! *Whoa!* . . . Sorry! I didn't see you! . . . Did I scare you?

ALAN: No!

HORSEMAN [*looking down on him*]: That's a terrific castle!

ALAN: What's his name?

HORSEMAN: Trojan. You can stroke him, if you like. He won't mind.

[*Shyly* ALAN *stretches up on tiptoe, and pats an invisible shoulder.*]

[*Amused.*] You can hardly reach down there. Would you like to come up?

[ALAN *nods, eyes wide.*]

All right. Come round this side. You always mount a horse from the left. I'll give you a lift. O.K.?

[ALAN *goes round on the other side.*]

Here we go, now. Just do nothing. Upsadaisy!

[ALAN *sets his foot on the* HORSEMAN'*s thigh, and is lifted by him up on to his shoulders. The hum from the* CHORUS *becomes exultant. Then stops.*]

All right?

[ALAN *nods.*]

Good. Now all you do is hold onto his mane.

[*He holds up the crop, and* ALAN *grips on to it.*]

Tight now. And grip with your knees. All right? All set? . . . Come on, then, Trojan. Let's go!

[*The* HORSEMAN *walks slowly upstage round the circle, with* ALAN'*s legs tight round his neck.*]

DYSART: How was it? Was it wonderful?

[ALAN *rides in silence.*]

Can't you remember?

HORSEMAN: Do you want to go faster?

ALAN: Yes!

HORSEMAN: O.K. All you have to do is say, "Come on, Trojan—bear me away!" . . . Say it, then!

ALAN: Bear me away!

*[The* HORSEMAN *starts to run with* ALAN *round the circle.]*

DYSART: You went fast?

ALAN: Yes!

DYSART: Weren't you frightened?

ALAN: No!

HORSEMAN: Come on now, Trojan! Bear us away! Hold on! Come on now! . . .

*[He runs faster.* ALAN *begins to laugh. Then suddenly, as they reach again the right downstage corner,* FRANK *and* DORA *stand up in alarm.]*

DORA: Alan!

FRANK: Alan!

DORA: Alan, stop!

[FRANK *runs round after them.* DORA *follows behind.]*

FRANK: Hey, you! *You!* . . .

HORSEMAN: Whoa, boy! . . . Whoa! . . .

*[He reins the horse round, and wheels to face the parents. This all goes fast.]*

FRANK: What do you imagine you are doing?

HORSEMAN *[ironic]*: "Imagine"?

FRANK: What is my son doing up there?

HORSEMAN: Waterskiing!

[DORA *joins them, breathless.]*

DORA: Is he all right, Frank? . . . He's not hurt?

FRANK: Don't you think you should ask permission before doing a stupid thing like that?

HORSEMAN: What's stupid?

ALAN: It's lovely, Dad!

DORA: Alan, come down here!

HORSEMAN: The boy's perfectly safe. Please don't be hysterical.

FRANK: Don't you be la-di-da with me, young man! Come down here, Alan. You heard what your mother said.

ALAN: No.

FRANK: Come down at once. Right this moment.

ALAN: No . . . NO!

FRANK *[in a fury]*: I said—this moment!

*[He pulls* ALAN *from the horseman's shoulders. The boy shrieks, and falls to the ground.]*

HORSEMAN: Watch it!

DORA: Frank!

[*She runs to her son, and kneels. The* HORSEMAN *skitters.*]

HORSEMAN: Are you mad? D'you want to terrify the horse?

DORA: He's grazed his knee. Frank—the boy's hurt!

ALAN: I'm not! I'm *not!*

FRANK: What's your name?

HORSEMAN: Jesse James.

DORA: Frank, he's bleeding!

FRANK: I intend to report you to the police for endangering the lives of children.

HORSEMAN: Go right ahead!

DORA: Can you stand, dear?

ALAN: Oh, *stop* it! . . .

FRANK: You're a public menace, d'you know that? How dare you pick up children and put them on dangerous animals?

HORSEMAN: Dangerous?

FRANK: Of course dangerous. Look at his eyes. They're rolling!

HORSEMAN: So are yours!

FRANK: In my opinion that is a dangerous animal. In my considered opinion you are both dangers to the safety of this beach.

HORSEMAN: And in my opinion, you're a stupid fart!

DORA: Frank, leave it!

FRANK: What did you say?

DORA: It's not important, Frank—really!

FRANK: *What did you say?*

HORSEMAN: Oh, bugger off! Sorry, chum! Come on, Trojan!

[*He urges his horse straight at them, then wheels it and gallops off round the right side of the circle and away up the tunnel, out of sight. The parents cry out, as they are covered with sand and water.* FRANK *runs after him, and round the left side of the circle, with his wife following after.*]

ALAN: Splash, splash, splash! All three of us got covered with water! Dad got absolutely soaked!

FRANK [*shouting after the* HORSEMAN]: Hooligan! Filthy hooligan!

ALAN: I wanted to laugh!

FRANK: Upper-class riffraff! That's all they are, people who go riding! That's what they *want*—trample on ordinary people!

DORA: Don't be absurd, Frank!

FRANK: It's why they do it. It's why they bloody do it!

DORA [*amused*]: Look at you. You're covered!

FRANK: Not as much as you. There's sand all over your hair!

[*She starts to laugh.*]

[*Shouting.*] Hooligan! Bloody hooligan!

[*She starts to laugh more. He tries to brush the sand out of her hair.*]

What are you laughing at? It's not funny at all, Dora!

[*She goes off, right, still laughing.* ALAN *edges into the square, still on the ground.*]

It's just not funny! . . .

[FRANK *returns to his place on the beach, sulky. Abrupt silence.*]

ALAN: And that's all I remember.

DYSART: And a lot, too. Thank you. . . . You know, I've never been on a horse in my life.

ALAN [*not looking at him*]: Nor me.

DYSART: You mean, after that?

ALAN: Yes.

DYSART: But you must have done at the stables?

ALAN: No.

DYSART: Never?

ALAN: No.

DYSART: How come?

ALAN: I didn't care to.

DYSART: Did it have anything to do with falling off like that, all those years ago?

ALAN [*tight*]: I just didn't care to, that's all.

DYSART: Do you think of that scene often?

ALAN: I suppose.

DYSART: Why, do you think?

ALAN: 'Cos it's funny.

DYSART: Is that all?

ALAN: What else? My turn. . . . I told you a secret; now you tell me one.

DYSART: All right. I have patients who've got things to tell me, only they're ashamed to say them to my face. What do you think I do about that?

ALAN: What?

DYSART: I give them this little tape recorder. [*He takes a small tape recorder and microphone from his pocket.*] They go off to another room, and send me the tape through Nurse. They don't have to listen to it with me.

ALAN: That's stupid.

DYSART: All you do is press this button, and speak into this. It's very simple. Anyway, your time's up for today. I'll see you tomorrow.

ALAN [*getting up*]: Maybe.

DYSART: Maybe?

ALAN: If I feel like it.

[*He is about to go out. Then suddenly he returns to* DYSART *and takes the machine from him.*]

It's stupid. [*He leaves the square and goes back to his bed.*]

## SCENE 11

DORA [*calling out*]: Doctor!

[DORA *reenters and comes straight on to the square from the right. She wears an overcoat, and is nervously carrying a shopping bag.*]

DYSART: That same evening, his mother appeared.

DORA: Hello, Doctor.

DYSART: Mrs. Strang!

DORA: I've been shopping in the neighborhood. I thought I might just look in.

DYSART: Did you want to see Alan?

DORA [*uncomfortably*]: No, no. . . . Not just at the moment. Actually, it's more you I wanted to see.

DYSART: Yes?

DORA: You see, there's something Mr. Strang and I thought you ought to know. We discussed it, and it might just be important.

DYSART: Well, come and sit down.

DORA: I can't stay more than a moment. I'm late as it is. Mr. Strang will be wanting his dinner.

DYSART: Ah. [*Encouragingly.*] So, what was it you wanted to tell me?

[*She sits on the upstage bench.*]

DORA: Well, do you remember that photograph I mentioned to you? The one Mr. Strang gave Alan to decorate his bedroom a few years ago?

DYSART: Yes. A horse looking over a gate, wasn't it?

DORA: That's right. Well, actually, it took the place of another kind of picture altogether.

DYSART: What kind?

DORA: It was a reproduction of Our Lord on his way to Calvary. Alan found it in Reeds Art Shop, and fell absolutely in love with it. He insisted on buying it with his pocket money, and hanging it at the foot of his bed where he could see it last thing at night. My husband was very displeased.

DYSART: Because it was religious?

DORA: In all fairness I must admit it was a little extreme. The Christ was loaded down with chains, and the centurions were really laying on the stripes. It certainly would not have been my choice, but I don't believe in interfering too much with children, so I said nothing.

DYSART: But Mr. Strang did?

DORA: He stood it for a while, but one day we had one of our tiffs about religion, and he went upstairs, tore it off the boy's wall and threw it in the dustbin. Alan went quite hysterical. He cried for days without stopping—and he was not a crier, you know.

DYSART: But he recovered when he was given the photograph of the horse in its place?

DORA: He certainly seemed to. At least, he hung it in exactly the same position, and we had no more of that awful weeping.

DYSART: Thank you, Mrs. Strang. That *is* interesting. . . . Exactly how long ago was that? Can you remember?

DORA: It must be five years ago, Doctor. Alan would have been about twelve. How is he, by the way?

DYSART: Bearing up.

[*She rises.*]

DORA: Please give him my love.

DYSART: You can see him any time you want, you know.

DORA: Perhaps if I could come one afternoon without Mr. Strang. He and Alan don't exactly get on at the moment, as you can imagine.

DYSART: Whatever you decide, Mrs. Strang. . . . Oh, one thing.

DORA: Yes?

DYSART: Could you describe that photograph of the horse in a little more detail for me? I presume it's still in his bedroom?

DORA: Oh yes. It's a most remarkable picture, really. You very rarely see a horse taken from that angle—absolutely head-on. That's what makes it so interesting.

DYSART: Why? What does it look like?

DORA: Well, it's most extraordinary. It comes out all eyes.

DYSART: Staring straight at you?

DORA: Yes, that's right . . . [*An uncomfortable pause.*] I'll come and see him one day very soon, Doctor. Goodbye. [*She leaves, and resumes her place by her husband.*]

DYSART [*to audience*]: It was then—that moment—I felt real alarm. What was it? The shadow of a giant head across my desk? . . . At any rate, the feeling got worse with the stable-owner's visit.

## SCENE 12

[DALTON *comes in to the square: heavyset, mid-fifties.*]

DALTON: Dr. Dysart?

DYSART: Mr. Dalton. It's very good of you to come.

DALTON: It is, actually. In my opinion the boy should be in prison. Not in a hospital at the taxpayers' expense.

DYSART: Please sit down.

[DALTON *sits.*]

This must have been a terrible experience for you.

DALTON: Terrible? I don't think I'll ever get over it. Jill's had a nervous breakdown.

DYSART: Jill?

DALTON: The girl who worked for me. Of course, she feels responsible in a way. Being the one who introduced him in the first place.

DYSART: He was introduced to the stable by a girl?

DALTON: Jill Mason. He met her somewhere, and asked for a job. She told him to come and see me. I wish to Christ she never had.

DYSART: But when he first appeared he didn't seem in any way peculiar?

DALTON: No, he was bloody good. He'd spend hours with the horses cleaning and grooming them, way over the call of duty. I thought he was a real find.

DYSART: Apparently, during the whole time he worked for you, he never actually rode.

DALTON: That's true.

DYSART: Wasn't that peculiar?

DALTON: Very . . . *if* he didn't.

DYSART: What do you mean?

[DALTON *rises.*]

DALTON: Because on and off, that whole year, I had the feeling the horses were being taken out at night.

DYSART: At night?

DALTON: There were just odd things I noticed. I mean too often one or other of them would be sweaty first thing in the morning, when it wasn't sick. Very sweaty, too. And its stall wouldn't be near as mucky as it should be if it had been in all night. I never paid it much mind at the time. It was only when I realized I'd been hiring a loony, I came to wonder if he hadn't been riding all the time, behind our backs.

DYSART: But wouldn't you have noticed if things had been disturbed?

DALTON: Nothing ever was. Still, he's a neat worker. That wouldn't prove anything.

DYSART: Aren't the stables locked at night?

DALTON: Yes.

DYSART: And someone sleeps on the premises?

DALTON: Me and my son.

DYSART: Two people?

DALTON: I'm sorry, Doctor. It's obviously just my fancy. I tell you, this thing has shaken me so bad, I'm liable to believe anything. If there's nothing else, I'll be going.

DYSART: Look, even if you were right, why should anyone do that? Why would any boy prefer to ride by himself at night, when he could go off with others during the day?

DALTON: Are you asking me? He's a loony, isn't he?

[DALTON *leaves the square and sits again in his place.* DYSART *watches him go.*]

ALAN: It was *sexy.*

DYSART: His tape arrived that evening.

## SCENE 13

[ALAN *is sitting on his bed holding the tape recorder.* NURSE *approaches briskly, takes the machine from him—gives it to* DYSART *in the square—and leaves again, resuming her seat.* DYSART *switches on the tape.*]

ALAN: That's what you want to know, isn't it? All right: it was. I'm talking about the beach. That time when I was a kid. What I told you about . . .

[*Pause. He is in great emotional difficulty.* DYSART *sits on the left bench listening, file in hand.* ALAN *rises and stands directly behind him, but on the circle, as if recording the ensuing speech. He never, of course, looks directly at the doctor.*]

I was pushed forward on the horse. There was sweat on my legs from his neck. The fellow held me tight, and let me turn the horse which way I wanted. All that power going any way you wanted. . . . His sides were all warm, and the smell . . . then suddenly I was on the ground, where Dad pulled me. I could have bashed him . . . [*Pause.*] Something else. When the horse first appeared, I looked up into his mouth. It was huge. There was this chain in it. The fellow pulled it, and cream dripped out. I said "Does it hurt?" And he said—the horse said—said—

[*He stops, in anguish.* DYSART *makes a note in his file.*]

[*Desperately.*] It was always the same, after that. Every time I heard one clop by, I had to run and see. Up a country lane or anywhere. They sort of pulled me. I couldn't take my eyes off them. Just to watch their skins. The way their necks twist, and sweat shines in the folds . . .[*Pause.*] I can't remember when it started. Mum reading to me about Prince who no one could ride, except one boy. Or the white horse in Revelation. "He that sat upon him was called Faithful and True. His eyes were as flames of fire, and he had a name written that no man knew but himself." . . . Words like reins. Stirrup. Flanks. . . . "Dashing his spurs against his charger's flanks!" . . . Even the words made me feel— Years, I never told anyone. Mum wouldn't understand. She likes "Equitation." Bowler hats and jodhpurs! "My grandfather dressed for the horse," she says. What does that mean? The horse isn't dressed. It's the most naked thing you ever saw! More than a dog or a cat or anything. Even the most broken-down old nag has got its *life!* To put a bowler on it is *filthy!* . . . Putting them through their paces! Bloody gymkhanas! . . . No one understands! . . . Except cowboys. They do. I wish I was a cowboy. They're free. They just swing up and then it's miles of grass . . . I bet all cowboys are *orphans!* . . . I bet they are!

NURSE: Mr. Strang to see you, Doctor.

DYSART [*in surprise*]: Mr. Strang? Show him up, please.

ALAN: No one ever says to cowboys, "Receive my meaning"! They wouldn't dare. Or "God" all the time. [*Mimicking his mother.*] "God sees you, Alan. God's got eyes everywhere—" [*He stops abruptly.*] I'm not doing any more! . . . I hate this! . . . You can whistle for any more. I've had it!

[*He returns angrily to his bed, throwing the blanket over him.* DYSART *switches off the tape.*]

## SCENE 14

[FRANK STRANG *comes into the square, his hat in his hand. He is nervous and embarrassed.*]

DYSART [*welcoming*]: Hello, Mr. Strang.

FRANK: I was just passing. I hope it's not too late.

DYSART: Of course not. I'm delighted to see you.

FRANK: My wife doesn't know I'm here. I'd be grateful to you if you didn't enlighten her, if you receive my meaning.

DYSART: Everything that happens in this room is confidential, Mr. Strang.

FRANK: I hope so . . . I hope so . . .

DYSART [*gently*]: Do you have something to tell me?

FRANK: As a matter of fact I have. Yes.

DYSART: Your wife told me about the photograph.

FRANK: I know, it's not that! It's *about* that, but it's—worse. . . . I wanted to tell you the other night, but I couldn't in front of Dora. Maybe I should have. It might show her where all that stuff leads to, she drills into the boy behind my back.

DYSART: What kind of thing is it?

FRANK: Something I witnessed.

DYSART: Where?

FRANK: At home. About eighteen months ago.

DYSART: Go on.

FRANK: It was late. I'd gone upstairs to fetch something. The boy had been in bed hours, or so I thought.

DYSART: Go on.

FRANK: As I came along the passage I saw the door of his bedroom was ajar. I'm sure he didn't know it was. From inside I heard the sound of this chanting.

DYSART: Chanting?

FRANK: Like the Bible. One of those lists his mother's always reading to him.

DYSART: What kind of list?

FRANK: Those Begats. So-and-so begat, you know. Genealogy.

DYSART: Can you remember what Alan's list sounded like?

FRANK: Well, the *sort* of thing. I stood there absolutely astonished. The first word I heard was . . .

ALAN [*rising and chanting*]: *Prince!*

DYSART: Prince?

FRANK: Prince begat Prince. That sort of nonsense.

[ALAN *moves slowly to the center of the circle, downstage.*]

ALAN: And Prance begat Prankus! And Prankus begat Flankus!

FRANK: I looked through the door, and he was standing in the moonlight in his pajamas, right in front of that big photograph.

DYSART: The horse with the huge eyes?

FRANK: Right.

ALAN: Flankus begat Spankus. And Spankus begat Spunkus the Great, who lived three score years!

FRANK: It was all like that. I can't remember the exact names, of course. Then suddenly he knelt down.

DYSART: In front of the photograph?

FRANK: Yes. Right there at the foot of his bed.

ALAN [*kneeling*]: And Legwus begat Neckwus. And Neckwus begat Fleckwus, the King of Spit. And Fleckwus spoke out of his chinkle-chankle!

[*He bows himself to the ground.*]

DYSART: What?

FRANK: I'm sure that was the word. I've never forgotten it. Chinkle-chankle.

[ALAN *raises his head and extends his hands up in glory.*]

ALAN: And he said "Behold—I give you Equus, my only begotten son!"

DYSART: Equus?

FRANK: Yes. No doubt of that. He repeated that word several times. "Equus, my only begotten son."

ALAN [*reverently*]: Ek . . . wus!

DYSART [*suddenly understanding: almost "aside"*]: Ek . . . Ek . . .

FRANK [*embarrassed*]: And then . . .

DYSART: Yes: what?

FRANK: He took a piece of string out of his pocket. Made up into a noose. And put it in his mouth.

[ALAN *bridles himself with invisible string, and pulls it back.*]

And then with his other hand he picked up a coat hanger. A wooden coat hanger, and—and—

DYSART: Began to beat himself?

[ALAN, *in mime, begins to thrash himself, increasing the strokes in speed and viciousness. Pause.*]

FRANK: You see why I couldn't tell his mother . . . Religion. Religion's at the bottom of all this!

DYSART: What did you do?

FRANK: Nothing. I coughed—and went back downstairs.

[*The boy starts guiltily—tears the string from his mouth—and scrambles back to bed.*]

DYSART: Did you ever speak to him about it later? Even obliquely?

FRANK [*unhappily*]: I can't speak of things like that, Doctor. It's not in my nature.

DYSART [*kindly*]: No. I see that.

FRANK: But I thought you ought to know. So I came.

DYSART [*warmly*]: Yes. I'm very grateful to you. Thank you.

[*Pause.*]

FRANK: Well, that's it . . .

DYSART: Is there anything else?

FRANK [*even more embarrassed*]: There is actually. One thing.

DYSART: What's that?

FRANK: On the night that he did it—that awful thing in the stable—

DYSART: Yes?

FRANK: That very night, he was out with a girl.

DYSART: How d'you know that?

FRANK: I just know.

DYSART [*puzzled*]: Did he tell you?

FRANK: I can't say any more.

DYSART: I don't quite understand.

FRANK: Everything said in here is confidential, you said.

DYSART: Absolutely.

FRANK: Then ask him. Ask him about taking a girl out, that very night he did it . . . [*Abruptly*] Goodbye, Doctor.

[*He goes.* DYSART *looks after him.*

FRANK *resumes his seat.*]

## SCENE 15

[ALAN *gets up and enters the square.*]

DYSART: Alan! Come in. Sit down. [*Pleasantly.*] What did you do last night?

ALAN: Watched telly.

DYSART: Any good?

ALAN: All right.

DYSART: Thanks for the tape. It was excellent.

ALAN: I'm not making any more.

DYSART: One thing I didn't quite understand. You began to say something about the horse on the beach talking to you.

ALAN: That's stupid. Horses don't talk.

DYSART: So I believe.

ALAN: I don't know what you mean.

DYSART: Never mind. Tell me something else. Who introduced you to the stable to begin with?

[*Pause.*]

ALAN: Someone I met.

DYSART: Where?

ALAN: Bryson's.

DYSART: The shop where you worked?

ALAN: Yes.

DYSART: That's a funny place for you to be. Whose idea was that?

ALAN: Dad.

DYSART: I'd have thought he'd have wanted you to work with him.

ALAN: I haven't the aptitude. And printing's a failing trade. If you receive my meaning.

DYSART [*amused*]: I see. . . . What did your mother think?

ALAN: Shops are common.

DYSART: And you?

ALAN: I loved it.

DYSART: Really?

ALAN [*sarcastic*]: Why not? You get to spend every minute with electrical things. It's fun.

[NURSE, DALTON, *and the actors playing horses call out to him as* CUSTOMERS, *seated where they are. Their voices are aggressive and demanding. There is a constant background mumbling, made up of trade names, out of which can clearly be distinguished the italicized words, which are shouted out.*]

CUSTOMER: *Philco!*

ALAN [*to* DYSART]: Of course it might just drive you off your chump.

CUSTOMER: I want to buy a hotplate. I'm told the *Philco* is a good make!

ALAN: I think it is, madam.

CUSTOMER: *Remington* ladies' shavers?

ALAN: I'm not sure, madam.

CUSTOMER: *Robex* tableware?

CUSTOMER: *Croydex?*

CUSTOMER: *Volex?*

CUSTOMER: *Pifco* automatic toothbrushes?

ALAN: I'll find out, sir.

CUSTOMER: Beautiflor!

CUSTOMER: Windowlene!

CUSTOMER: I want a *Philco* transistor radio!

CUSTOMER: This isn't a *Remington!* I wanted a *Remington!*

ALAN: Sorry.

CUSTOMER: Are you a dealer for *Hoover?*

ALAN: Sorry.

CUSTOMER: I wanted the heat-retaining *Pifco!*

ALAN: *Sorry!*

[JILL *comes into the square; a girl in her early twenties, pretty and middle class. She wears a sweater and jeans. The mumbling stops.*]

JILL: Hello.

ALAN: Hello.

JILL: Have you any blades for a clipping machine?

ALAN: Clipping?

JILL: To clip horses.

*[Pause. He stares at her, openmouthed.]*

What's the matter?

ALAN: You work at Dalton's stables. I've seen you.

*[During the following, he mimes putting away a pile of boxes on a shelf in the shop.]*

JILL: I've seen you too, haven't I? You're the boy who's always staring into the yard around lunchtime.

ALAN: Me?

JILL: You're there most days.

ALAN: Not me.

JILL *[amused]*: Of course it's you. Mr. Dalton was only saying the other day, "Who's that boy keeps staring in at the door?" Are you looking for a job or something?

ALAN *[eagerly]*: Is there one?

JILL: I don't know.

ALAN: I can only do weekends.

JILL: That's when most people ride. We can always use extra hands. It'd mainly be mucking out.

ALAN: I don't mind.

JILL: Can you ride?

ALAN: No. . . . No . . . I don't want to.

*[She looks at him curiously.]*

Please.

JILL: Come up on Saturday. I'll introduce you to Mr. Dalton.

*[She leaves the square.]*

DYSART: When was this? About a year ago?

ALAN: I suppose.

DYSART: And she did?

ALAN: Yes.

*[Briskly he moves the three benches to form three stalls in the stable.]*

## SCENE 16

*[Rich light falls on the square. An exultant humming from the* CHORUS. *Tramping is heard. Three actors playing horses rise from their places. Together they unhook three horse masks from the ladders to left and right, put them on with rigid timing, and walk with swaying horse motion into the square. Their metal hooves stamp on the wood. Their masks turn and*

*toss high above their heads—as they will do sporadically throughout all horse scenes—making the steel gleam in the light. For a moment they seem to converge on the boy as he stands in the middle of the stable, but then they swiftly turn and take up positions as if tethered by the head, with their invisible rumps toward him, one by each bench.*

ALAN *is sunk in this glowing world of horses. Lost in wonder, he starts almost involuntarily to kneel on the floor in reverence—but is sharply interrupted by the cheery voice of* DALTON, *coming into the stable, followed by* JILL. *The boy straightens up guiltily.*]

DALTON: First thing to learn is drill. Learn it and keep to it. I want this place neat, dry, and clean at all times. After you've mucked out, Jill will show you some grooming. What we call strapping a horse.

JILL: I think Trooper's got a stone.

DALTON: Yes? Let's see. [*He crosses to the horse by the left bench, who is balancing one hoof on its tip. He picks up the hoof.*] You're right. [*To* ALAN.] See this? This V here. It's what's called a frog. Sort of shock absorber. Once you pierce that, it takes ages to heal—so you want to watch for it. You clean it out with this. What we call a hoof-pick. [*He takes from his pocket an invisible pick.*] Mind how you go with it. It's very sharp. Use it like this. [*He quickly takes the stone out.*] See?

[ALAN *nods, fascinated.*]

You'll soon get the hang of it. Jill will look after you. What she doesn't know about stables, isn't worth knowing.

JILL [*pleased*]: Oh yes, I'm sure!

DALTON [*handing* ALAN *the pick*]: Careful how you go with that. The main rule is, anything you don't know: ask. Never pretend you know something when you don't. [*Smiling.*] Actually, the main rule is: enjoy yourself. All right?

ALAN: Yes, sir.

DALTON: Good lad. See you later.

[*He nods to them cheerfully, and leaves the square.* ALAN *clearly puts the invisible hoof-pick on the rail, downstage left.*]

JILL: All right, let's start on some grooming. Why don't we begin with him? He looks as if he needs it.

[*They approach* NUGGET, *who is standing to the right. She pats him.* ALAN *sits and watches her.*]

This is Nugget. He's my favorite. He's as gentle as a baby, aren't you? But terribly fast if you want him to be. [*During the following, she mimes both the actions and the objects, which she picks up from the right bench.*] Now this is the dandy, and we start with that. Then you move on to the body brush. This is the most important, and you use it with this currycomb. Now you always groom the same way: from the ears downward. Don't be afraid to do it hard. The harder you do it, the more the horse loves it. Push it right through the coat: like this.

[*The boy watches in fascination as she brushes the invisible body of* NUGGET, *scraping the dirt and hair off on to the invisible currycomb. Now and then the horse mask moves very slightly in pleasure.*]

Down toward the tail and right through the coat. See how he loves it? I'm giving you a lovely massage, boy, aren't I? . . .You try.

[*She hands him the brush. Gingerly he rises and approaches* NUGGET. *Embarrassed and excited, he copies her movements, inexpertly.*]

Keep it nice and easy. Never rush. Down toward the tail and right through the coat. That's it. Again. Down toward the tail and right through the coat. . . . Very good. Now you keep that up for fifteen minutes and then do old Trooper. Will you?

[ALAN *nods.*]

You've got a feel for it. I can tell. It's going to be nice teaching you. See you later.

[*She leaves the square and resumes her place.* ALAN *is left alone with the horses. They all stamp. He approaches* NUGGET *again, and touches the horse's shoulder. The mask turns sharply in his direction. The boy pauses, then moves his hand gently over the outline of the neck and back. The mask is reassured. It stares ahead unmoving. Then* ALAN *lifts his palm to his face and smells it deeply, closing his eyes.* DYSART *rises from his bench, and begins to walk slowly upstage round the circle.*]

DYSART: Was that good? Touching them.

[ALAN *gives a faint groan.*]

ALAN: Mmm.

DYSART: It must have been marvelous, being near them at last. . . . Stroking them . . . making them fresh and glossy. . . . Tell me . . .

[*Silence.* ALAN *begins to brush* NUGGET.]

How about the girl? Did you like her?

ALAN [*tight*]: All right.

DYSART: Just all right?

[ALAN *changes his position, moving round* NUGGET'*s rump so that his back is to the audience. He brushes harder.* DYSART *comes downstage around the circle, and finally back to his bench.*] Was she friendly?

ALAN: Yes.

DYSART: Or standoffish?

ALAN: Yes.

DYSART: Well which?

ALAN: What?

DYSART: Which was she?

[ALAN *brushes harder.*]

Did you take her out? Come on now: tell me. Did you have a date with her?

ALAN: What?

DYSART [*sitting*]: Tell me if you did.

[*The boy suddenly explodes in one of his rages.*]

ALAN [*yelling*]: TELL ME!

[*All the masks toss at the noise.*]

DYSART: What?

ALAN: *Tell me, tell me, tell me, tell me!*

[ALAN *storms out of the square, and downstage to where* DYSART *sits. He is raging. During the ensuing, the horses leave by all three openings.*]

On and on, sitting there! Nosy Parker! That's all you are! Bloody Nosy Parker! Just like Dad. On and on and bloody on! Tell me, tell me, tell me! . . . Answer this. Answer that. Never stop!

[*He marches round the circle and back into the square.* DYSART *rises and enters it from the other side.*]

## SCENE 17

[*Lights brighten.*]

DYSART: I'm sorry.

[ALAN *slams about in what is now the office again, replacing the benches to their usual position.*]

ALAN: All right, it's my turn now. You tell me! Answer me!

DYSART: We're not playing that game now.

ALAN: We're playing what I say!

DYSART: All right. What do you want to know?

[*He sits.*]

ALAN: Do *you* have dates?

DYSART: I told you. I'm married.

[ALAN *approaches him, very hostile.*]

ALAN: I know. Her name's Margaret. She's a dentist! You see, I found out! What made you go with her? Did you use to bite her hands when she did you in the chair?

[*The boy sits next to him, close.*]

DYSART: That's not very funny.

ALAN: Do you have girls behind her back?

DYSART: No.

ALAN: Then what? Do you fuck her?

DYSART: That's enough now.

[*He rises and moves away.*]

ALAN: Come on, tell me! Tell me, tell me!

DYSART: I said that's enough now.

[ALAN *rises too and walks around him.*]

I bet you don't. I bet you never touch her. Come on, tell me. You've got no kids, have you? Is that because you don't fuck?

DYSART [*sharp*]: Go to your room. Go on: quick march.

[*Pause.* ALAN *moves away from him, insolently takes up a packet of* DYSART'*s cigarettes from the bench, and extracts one.*]

Give me those cigarettes.

[*The boy puts one in his mouth.*]

[*Exploding.*] Alan, *give them to me!*

[*Reluctantly* ALAN *shoves the cigarette back in the packet, turns and hands it to him.*]

*Now go!*

[ALAN *bolts out of the square, and back to his bed.* DYSART, *unnerved, addresses the audience.*]

Brilliant! Absolutely brilliant! The boy's on the run, so he gets defensive. What am *I*, then? . . . Wicked little bastard—he knew exactly what questions to try. He'd actually marched himself round the hospital, making inquiries about my wife. Wicked and—of course, perceptive. Ever since I made that crack about carving up children, he's been aware of me in an absolutely specific way. Of course, there's nothing novel in that. Advanced neurotics can be dazzling at that game. They aim unswervingly at your area of maximum vulnerability. . . . Which I suppose is as good a way as any of describing Margaret.

[*He sits.* HESTHER *enters the square. Light grows warmer.*]

## SCENE 18

HESTHER: Now stop it.

DYSART: Do I embarrass you?

HESTHER: I suspect you're about to.

[*Pause.*]

DYSART: My wife doesn't understand me, Your Honor.

HESTHER: Do you understand her?

DYSART: No. Obviously I never did.

HESTHER: I'm sorry. I've never liked to ask but I've always imagined you weren't exactly compatible.

[*She moves to sit opposite.*]

DYSART: We were. It actually worked for a bit. I mean for both of us. We worked for each other. She actually for me through a kind of briskness. A clear, redheaded, inaccessible briskness which kept me keyed up for months. Mind you, if you're kinky for Northern Hygienic, as I am, you can't find anything much more compelling than a Scottish Lady Dentist.

HESTHER: It's *you* who are wicked, you know!

DYSART: Not at all. She got exactly the same from me. Antiseptic proficiency. I was like that in those days. We suited each other admirably. I see us in our wedding photo: Doctor and Doctor Mac Brisk. We were brisk in our wooing, brisk in our wedding, brisk in our disappointment. We turned from each other briskly into our separate surgeries: and now there's damn-all.

HESTHER: You have no children, have you?

DYSART: No, we didn't go in for them. Instead, she sits beside our salmon-pink, glazed brick fireplace, and knits things for orphans in a home she helps with. And I sit opposite, turning the pages of art books on Ancient Greece. Occasionally, I still trail a faint scent of my enthusiasm across her path. I pass her a picture of the sacred acrobats of Crete leaping through the horns of running bulls—and she'll say: [*Scots accent*] "Och, Martin, what an *absurred* thing to be doing! The Highland Games, now there's *norrmal* sport!" Or she'll observe, just after I've told her a story from the *Iliad*: "You know, when you come to think of it, Agamemnon and that lot were nothing but a bunch of ruffians from the Gorbals, only with fancy names!" [*He rises.*] You get the picture. She's turned into a Shrink. The familiar domestic monster. Margaret Dysart: the Shrink's Shrink.

HESTHER: That's cruel, Martin.

DYSART: Yes. Do you know what it's like for two people to live in the same house as if they were in different parts of the world? Mentally, she's always in some drizzly kirk of her own inheriting: and I'm in some Doric temple—clouds tearing through pillars—eagles bearing prophecies out of the sky. She finds all that repulsive. All my wife has ever taken from the Mediterranean—from that whole vast intuitive culture—are four bottles of Chianti to make into lamps, and two china condiment donkeys labeled Sally and Peppy. [*Pause. More intimately.*]

I wish there was one person in my life I could show. One instinctive, absolutely unbrisk person I could take to Greece, and stand in front of certain shrines and sacred streams and say "Look! Life is only comprehensible through a thousand local Gods. And not just the old dead ones with names like Zeus—no, but living Geniuses of Place and Person! And not just Greece but modern England! Spirits of certain trees, certain curves of brick wall, certain chip shops, if you like, and slate roofs—just as of certain frowns in people and slouches." . . . I'd say to them, "Worship as many as you can see—and more will appear!" . . . If I had a son, I bet you he'd come out exactly like his mother. Utterly worshipless. Would you like a drink?

HESTHER: No, thanks. Actually, I've got to be going. As usual . . .

DYSART: Really?

HESTHER: Really. I've got an Everest of papers to get through before bed.

DYSART: You never stop, do you?

HESTHER: Do you?

DYSART: This boy, with his stare. He's trying to save himself through me.

HESTHER: I'd say so.

DYSART: What am I trying to do to him?

HESTHER: Restore him, surely?

DYSART: To what?

HESTHER: A normal life.

DYSART: Normal?

HESTHER: It still means something.

DYSART: Does it?

HESTHER: Of course.

DYSART: You mean a normal boy has one head: a normal head has two ears?

HESTHER: You know I don't.

DYSART: Then what else?

HESTHER [*lightly*]: Oh, stop it.

DYSART: No, what? You tell me.

HESTHER [*rising: smiling*]: I won't be put on the stand like this, Martin. You're really disgraceful! . . . [*Pause.*] You know what I mean by a normal smile in a child's eyes, and one that isn't—even if I can't exactly define it. Don't you?

DYSART: Yes.

HESTHER: Then we have a duty to that, surely? Both of us.

DYSART: *Touché* . . . I'll talk to you.

HESTHER: Dismissed?

DYSART: You said you had to go.

HESTHER: I do . . . [*She kisses his cheek.*] Thank you for what you're doing. . . . You're going through a rotten patch at the moment. I'm sorry . . . I suppose one of the few things one can do is simply hold on to priorities.

DYSART: Like what?

HESTHER: Oh—children before grownups. Things like that.

[*He contemplates her.*]

DYSART: You're really quite splendid.

HESTHER: Famous for it. Good night.

[*She leaves him.*]

DYSART [*to himself—or to the audience*]: Normal! . . . Normal!

## SCENE 19

[ALAN *rises and enters the square. He is subdued.*]

DYSART: Good afternoon.

ALAN: Afternoon.

DYSART: I'm sorry about our row yesterday.

ALAN: It was stupid.

DYSART: It was.

ALAN: What I said, I mean.

DYSART: How are you sleeping?

[ALAN *shrugs.*]

You're not feeling well, are you?

ALAN: All right.

DYSART: Would you like to play a game? It could make you feel better.

ALAN: What kind?

DYSART: It's called *Blink*. You have to fix your eyes on something: say, that little stain over there on the wall—and I tap this pen on the desk. The first time I tap it, you close your eyes. The next time you open them. And so on. Close, open, close, open, till I say stop.

ALAN: How can that make you feel better?

DYSART: It relaxes you. You'll feel as though you're talking to me in your sleep.

ALAN: It's stupid.

DYSART: You don't have to do it, if you don't want to.

ALAN: I didn't say I didn't want to.

DYSART: Well?

ALAN: I don't mind.

DYSART: Good. Sit down and start watching that stain. Put your hands by your sides, and open the fingers wide.

*[He opens the left bench and* ALAN *sits on the end of it.]*

The thing is to feel comfortable, and relax absolutely. . . . Are you looking at the stain?

ALAN: Yes.

DYSART: Right. Now try and keep your mind as blank as possible.

ALAN: That's not difficult.

DYSART: Ssh. Stop talking. . . . On the first tap, close. On the second, open. Are you ready?

*[*ALAN *nods.* DYSART *taps his pen on the wooden rail.* ALAN *shuts his eyes.* DYSART *taps again.* ALAN *opens them. The taps are evenly spaced. After four of them the sound cuts out, and is replaced by a louder, metallic sound, on tape.* DYSART *talks through this, to the audience—the light changes to cold—while the boy sits in front of him, staring at the wall, opening and shutting his eyes.]*

The Normal is the good smile in a child's eyes—all right. It is also the dead stare in a million adults. It both sustains and kills—like a God. It is the Ordinary made beautiful: it is also the Average made lethal. The Normal is the indispensable, murderous God of Health, and I am his Priest. My tools are very delicate. My compassion is honest. I have honestly assisted children in this room. I have talked away terrors and relieved many agonies. But also—beyond question—I have cut from them parts of individuality repugnant to this God, in both his aspects. Parts sacred to rarer and more wonderful Gods. And at what length. . . . Sacrifices to Zeus took at the most, surely, sixty seconds each. Sacrifices to the Normal can take as long as sixty months.

*[The natural sound of the pencil resumes. Light changes back.]*

*[To* ALAN.*]* Now your eyes are feeling heavy. You want to sleep, don't you? You want a long, deep sleep. Have it. Your head is heavy. Very heavy. Your shoulders are heavy. Sleep.

*[The pencil stops.* ALAN'*s eyes remain shut and his head has sunk on his chest.]*

Can you hear me?

ALAN: Mmm.

DYSART: You can speak normally. Say "Yes," if you can.

ALAN: Yes.

DYSART: Good boy. Now raise your head, and open your eyes. *[He does so.*] Now, Alan, you're going to answer questions I'm going to ask you. Do you understand?

ALAN: Yes.

DYSART: And when you wake up, you are going to remember everything you tell me. All right?

ALAN: Yes.

DYSART: Good. Now I want you to think back in time. You are on that beach you told me about. The tide has gone out, and you're making sandcastles. Above you, staring down at you, is that great horse's head, and the cream dropping from it. Can you see that?

ALAN: Yes.

DYSART: You ask him a question. "Does the chain hurt?"

ALAN: Yes.

DYSART: Do you ask him aloud?

ALAN: No.

DYSART: And what does the horse say back?

ALAN: "Yes."

DYSART: Then what do you say?

ALAN: "I'll take it out for you."

DYSART: And he says?

ALAN: "It never comes out. They have me in chains."

DYSART: Like Jesus?

ALAN: Yes!

DYSART: Only his name isn't Jesus, is it?

ALAN: No.

DYSART: What is it?

ALAN: No one knows but him and me.

DYSART: You can tell me, Alan. Name him.

ALAN: Equus.

DYSART: Thank you. Does he live in all horses or just some?

ALAN: All.

DYSART: Good boy. Now: you leave the beach. You're in your bedroom at home. You're twelve years old. You're in front of the picture. You're looking at Equus from the foot of your bed. Would you like to kneel down?

ALAN: Yes.

DYSART [*encouragingly*]: Go on, then.

[ALAN *kneels.*]

Now tell me. Why is Equus in chains?

ALAN: For the sins of the world.

DYSART: What does he say to you?

ALAN: "I see you." "I will save you."

DYSART: How?

ALAN: "Bear you away. Two shall be one."

DYSART: Horse and rider shall be one beast?

ALAN: One person!

DYSART: Go on.

ALAN: "And my chinkle-chankle shall be in thy hand."

DYSART: Chinkle-chankle? That's his mouth chain?

ALAN: Yes.

DYSART: Good. You can get up. . . . Come on.

[ALAN *rises.*]

Now: think of the stable. What is the stable? His Temple? His Holy of Holies?

ALAN: Yes.

DYSART: Where you wash him? Where you tend him, and brush him with many brushes?

ALAN: Yes.

DYSART: And there he spoke to you, didn't he? He looked at you with his gentle eyes, and spake unto you?

ALAN: Yes.

DYSART: What did he say? "Ride me"? "Mount me, and ride me forth at night"?

ALAN: Yes.

DYSART: And you obeyed?

ALAN: Yes.

DYSART: How did you learn? By watching others?

ALAN: Yes.

DYSART: It must have been difficult. You bounced about?

ALAN: Yes.

DYSART: But he showed you, didn't he? Equus showed you the way.

ALAN: No!

DYSART: He didn't?

ALAN: He showed me nothing! He's a mean bugger! Ride—or fall! That's Straw Law.

DYSART: Straw Law?

ALAN: He was born in the straw, and this is his law.

DYSART: But you managed? You mastered him?

ALAN: Had to!

DYSART: And then you rode in secret?

ALAN: Yes.

DYSART: How often?

ALAN: Every three weeks. More, people would notice.

DYSART: On a particular horse?

ALAN: No.

DYSART: How did you get into the stable?

ALAN: Stole a key. Had it copied at Bryson's.

DYSART: Clever boy.

[ALAN *smiles.*]

Then you'd slip out of the house?

ALAN: Midnight! On the stroke!

DYSART: How far's the stable?

ALAN: Two miles.

[*Pause.*]

DYSART: Let's do it! Let's go riding! . . . Now!

[*He stands up, and pushes in his bench.*]

You are there now, in front of the stable door.

[ALAN *turns upstage.*]

That key's in your hand. Go and open it.

## SCENE 20

[ALAN *moves upstage, and mimes opening the door. Soft light on the circle. Humming from the* CHORUS: *the Equus noise. The horse actors enter, raise high their masks, and put them on all together. They stand around the circle*—NUGGET *in the mouth of the tunnel.*]

DYSART: Quietly as possible. Dalton may still be awake. Sssh. . . . Quietly. . . . Good. Now go in.

[ALAN *steps secretly out of the square through the central opening on to the circle, now glowing with a warm light. He looks about him. The horses stamp uneasily; their masks turn toward him.*]

You are on the inside now. All the horses are staring at you. Can you see them?

ALAN [*excited*]: Yes!

DYSART: Which one are you going to take?

ALAN: Nugget.

[ALAN *reaches up and mimes leading* NUGGET *carefully round the circle downstage with a rope, past all the horses on the right.*]

DYSART: What color is Nugget?

ALAN: Chestnut.

[*The horse picks his way with care.* ALAN *halts him at the corner of the square.*]

DYSART: What do you do, first thing?

ALAN: Put on his sandals.

DYSART: Sandals?

[*He kneels, downstage center.*]

ALAN: Sandals of Majesty! . . . Made of sack. [*He picks up the invisible sandals, and kisses them devoutly.*] Tie them round his hooves.

[*He taps* NUGGET'*s right leg; the horse raises it and the boy mimes tying the sack round it.*]

DYSART: All four hooves?

ALAN: Yes.

DYSART: Then?

ALAN: Chinkle-chankle. [*He mimes picking up the bridle and bit.*] He doesn't like it so late, but he takes it for my sake. He bends for me. He stretches forth his neck to it.

[NUGGET *bends his head down.* ALAN *first ritually puts the bit into his own mouth, then crosses, and transfers it into* NUGGET'*s. He reaches up and buckles on the bridle. Then he leads him by the invisible reins, across the front of the stage and up round the left side of the circle.* NUGGET *follows obediently.*]

ALAN: Buckle and lead out.

DYSART: No saddle?

ALAN: Never.

DYSART: Go on.

ALAN: Walk down the path behind. He's quiet. Always is, this bit. Meek and mild legs. At least till the field. Then there's trouble.

[*The horse jerks back. The mask tosses.*]

DYSART: What kind?

ALAN: Won't go in.

DYSART: Why not?

ALAN: It's his place of Ha Ha.

DYSART: What?

ALAN: Ha Ha.

DYSART: Make him go into it.

ALAN [*whispering fiercely*]: Come on! . . . Come on! . . .

[*He drags the horse into the square as* DYSART *steps out of it.*]

## SCENE 21

[NUGGET *comes to a halt staring diagonally down what is now the field. The Equus noise dies away. The boy looks about him.*]

DYSART [*from the circle*]: Is it a big field?

ALAN: Huge!

DYSART: What's it like?

ALAN: Full of mist. Nettles on your feet. [*He mimes taking off his shoes—and the sting.*] *Ah!*

DYSART [*going back to his bench*]: You take your shoes off?

ALAN: Everything.

DYSART: All your clothes?

ALAN: Yes. [*He mimes undressing completely in front of the horse. When he is finished, and obviously quite naked, he throws out his arms and shows himself fully to his God, bowing his head before* NUGGET.]

DYSART: Where do you leave them?

ALAN: Tree hole near the gate. No one could find them.

[*He walks upstage and crouches by the bench, stuffing the invisible clothes beneath it.* DYSART *sits again on the left bench, downstage beyond the circle.*]

DYSART: How does it feel now?

ALAN [*holds himself*]: Burns.

DYSART: Burns?

ALAN: The mist!

DYSART: Go on. Now what?

ALAN: The Manbit. [*He reaches again under the bench and draws out an invisible stick.*]

DYSART: Manbit?

ALAN: The stick for my mouth.

DYSART: Your mouth?

ALAN: To bite on.

DYSART: Why? What for?

ALAN: So's it won't happen too quick.

DYSART: Is it always the same stick?

ALAN: Course. Sacred stick. Keep it in the hole. The Ark of the Manbit.

DYSART: And now what? . . . What do you do now?

[*Pause. He rises and approaches* NUGGET.]

ALAN: Touch him!

DYSART: Where?

ALAN [*in wonder*]: All over. Everywhere. Belly. Ribs. His ribs are of ivory. Of great value! . . . His flank is cool. His nostrils open for me. His eyes shine. They can see in the dark . . . *Eyes!* [*Suddenly he dashes in distress to the farthest corner of the square.*]

DYSART: *Go on!* . . . Then?

[*Pause.*]

ALAN: Give sugar.

DYSART: A lump of sugar?

[ALAN *returns to* NUGGET.]

ALAN: His Last Supper.

DYSART: Last before what?

ALAN: Ha Ha. [*He kneels before the horse, palms upward and joined together.*]

DYSART: Do you say anything when you give it to him?

ALAN [*offering it*]: Take my sins. Eat them for my sake. . . . He always does.

[NUGGET *bows the mask into* ALAN'*s palm, then takes a step back to eat.*]

And then he's ready.

DYSART: You can get up on him now?

ALAN: Yes!

DYSART: Do it, then. Mount him.

[ALAN, *lying before* NUGGET, *stretches out on the square. He grasps the top of the thin metal pole embedded in the wood. He whispers his God's name ceremonially.*]

ALAN: Equus! . . . Equus! . . . Equus!

[*He pulls the pole upright. The actor playing* NUGGET *leans forward and grabs it. At the same instant all the other horses lean forward around the circle, each placing a gloved hand on the rail.* ALAN *rises and walks right back to the upstage corner, left.*]

*Take me!*

[*He runs and jumps high on to* NUGGET'*s back.*]

[*Crying out.*] *Ah!*

DYSART: What is it?

ALAN: Hurts!

DYSART: Hurts?

ALAN: Knives in his skin! Little knives—all inside my legs.

[NUGGET *mimes restiveness.*]

ALAN: Stay, Equus! No one said Go! . . . That's it. He's good. Equus the Godslave, Faithful and True. Into my hands he commends himself—naked in his chinkle-chankle. [*He punches* NUGGET.] Stop it! . . . He wants to go so badly.

DYSART: Go, then. Leave me behind. Ride away now, Alan. Now! . . . Now you are alone with Equus.

[ALAN *stiffens his body.*]

ALAN [*ritually*]: Equus—son of Fleckwus—son of Neckwus—*Walk.*

[*A hum from the* CHORUS. *Very slowly the horses standing on the circle begin to turn the square by gently pushing the wooden rail.* ALAN *and his mount start to revolve. The effect, immediately, is of a statue being slowly turned round on a plinth. During the ride, however, the speed increases, and the light decreases until it is only a fierce spotlight on horse and rider, with the overspill glinting on the other masks leaning in toward them.*]

Here we go. The King rides out on Equus, mightiest of horses. Only I can ride him. He lets me turn him this way and that. His neck comes out of my body. It lifts in the dark. Equus, my Godslave! . . . Now the King commands you. Tonight, we ride against them all.

DYSART: Who's all?

ALAN: My foes and His.

DYSART: Who are your foes?

ALAN: The Hosts of Hoover. The Hosts of Philco. The Hosts of Pifco. The House of Remington and all its tribe!

DYSART: Who are His foes?

ALAN: The Hosts of Jodhpur. The Hosts of Bowler and Gymkhana. All those who show him off for their vanity. Tie rosettes on his head for their vanity! Come on, Equus. Let's get them! . . . *Trot!*

[*The speed of the turning square increases.*]

*Stead-y! Stead-y! Stead-y! Stead-y!* Cowboys are watching! Take off their stetsons. They know who we are. They're admiring us! Bowing low unto us! Come on now—show them! *Canter!* . . . CANTER!

[*He whips* NUGGET.]

And Equus the Mighty rose against All!
His enemies scatter, his enemies fall!
TURN!
Trample them, trample them,
Trample them, trample them,
TURN!
TURN!!
TURN!!!

[*The Equus noise increases in volume.*]

[*Shouting.*] WEE! . . . WAA! . . . WONDERFUL! . . .
I'm stiff! Stiff in the wind!
*My* mane, stiff in the wind!
*My* flanks! *My* hooves!
Mane on my legs, on my flanks, like whips!

Raw!
Raw!
*I'm raw! Raw!*
Feel me on you! *On* you! *On* you! *On* you!
I want to be *in* you!
I want to BE you forever and ever!—
*Equus, I love you!*
Now!—
Bear me away!
Make us One Person!

[*He rides* EQUUS *frantically.*]

*One Person! One Person! One Person! One Person!*

[*He rises up on the horse's back, and calls like a trumpet.*]

Ha-HA! . . . Ha-HA! . . . Ha-HA!

[*The trumpet turns to great cries.*]

HA-HA! HA-HA! HA-HA! HA-HA! HA! . . . HA! . . . HAAAAA!

[*He twists like a flame. Silence. The turning square comes to a stop in the same position it occupied at the opening of the act. Slowly the boy drops off the horse's back on to the ground. He lowers his head and kisses* NUGGET'*s hoof. Finally he flings back his head and cries up to him.*]

AMEN!

[NUGGET *snorts, once.*]

BLACKOUT

# ACT TWO

## SCENE 1

*Darkness.*

*Lights come slowly up on* ALAN *kneeling in the night at the hooves of* NUGGET. *Slowly he gets up, climbing lovingly up the body of the horse until he can stand and kiss it.*

DYSART *sits on the downstage bench where he began Act One.*

DYSART: With one particular horse, called Nugget, he embraces. He showed me how he stands with it afterward in the night, one hand on its chest, one on its neck, like a frozen tango dancer, inhaling its cold sweet breath. "Have you noticed," he said, "about horses: how they'll stand one hoof on its end, like those girls in the ballet?"

[ALAN *leads* NUGGET *out of the square.* DYSART *rises. The horse walks away up the tunnel and disappears. The boy comes downstage and sits on the bench* DYSART *has vacated.* DYSART *crosses downstage and moves slowly up round the circle, until he reaches the central entrance to the square.*]

Now he's gone off to rest, leaving me alone with Equus. I can hear the creature's voice. It's calling me out of the black cave of the Psyche. I shove in my dim little torch, and there he stands—waiting for me. He raises his matted head. He opens his great square teeth, and says—[*mocking*] *"Why?* . . . Why *Me?* . . . Why—ultimately—*Me?* . . . Do you really imagine you can account for Me? Totally, infallibly, inevitably account for Me? . . . Poor Dr. Dysart! [*He enters the square.*] Of course I've stared at such images before. Or been stared at by them, whichever way you look at it. And weirdly often now with me the feeling is that *they* are staring at *us*—that in some quite palpable way they precede us. Meaningless, but unsettling. . . . In either case, this one is the most alarming yet. It asks questions I've avoided all my professional life. [*Pause.*] A child is born into a world of phenomena all equal in their power to enslave. It sniffs—it sucks—it strokes it eyes over the whole uncomfortable range. Suddenly one strikes. Why? Moments snap together like magnets, forging a chain of shackles. Why? I can trace them. I can even, with time, pull them apart again. But why at the start they were ever magnetized at all—just those particular moments of experience and no others—I don't know. *And nor does anyone else.* Yet *if* I don't know—if I can never know that—then what am I doing here? I don't mean clinically doing or socially doing—I mean *fundamentally!* These questions, these Whys, are fundamental—yet they have no place in a consulting room. So then, do I? . . . This is the feeling more and more with me—No Place. Displacement . . . "Account for me," says staring Equus. "First account for Me! . . ." I fancy this is more than menopause.

[NURSE *rushes in.*]

NURSE: Doctor! . . . Doctor! There's a terrible scene with the Strang boy. His mother came to visit him, and I gave her the tray to take in. He threw it at her. She's saying the most dreadful things.

[ALAN *springs up, down left.* DORA *springs up, down right. They face each other across the bottom end of the stage. It is observable that at the start of this act* FRANK *is not sitting beside his wife on their bench. It is hopefully not observable that he is placed among the audience upstage, in the gloom, by the central tunnel.*

DORA: Don't you dare! *Don't you dare!*

DYSART: Is she still there?

NURSE: Yes!

[*He quickly leaves the square, followed by the* NURSE. DORA *moves toward her son.*]

DORA: Don't you look at me like that! I'm not a doctor, you know, who'll take anything. Don't you dare give me that stare, young man!

[*She slaps his face.* DYSART *joins them.*]

DYSART: Mrs. Strang!

DORA: I know your stares. They don't work on me!

DYSART [*to her*]: Leave this room.

DORA: What did you say?

DYSART: I tell you to leave here at once.

[DORA *hesitates. Then:*]

DORA: Goodbye, Alan.

[*She walks past her son, and round into the square.* DYSART *follows her. Both are very upset.* ALAN *returns to his bench and* NURSE *to her place.*]

## SCENE 2

[*Lights up on the square.*]

DYSART: I must ask you never to come here again.

DORA: Do you think I want to? Do you think I want to?

DYSART: Mrs. Strang, what on earth has got into you? Can't you see the boy is highly distressed?

DORA [*ironic*]: Really?

DYSART: Of course! He's at a most delicate stage of treatment. He's totally exposed. Ashamed. Everything you can imagine!

DORA [*exploding*]: *And me? What about me? . . . What do you think I am? . . .* I'm a parent, of course—so it doesn't count. That's a dirty word in here, isn't it, "parent"?

DYSART: You know that's not true.

DORA: Oh, I know. I know, all right! I've heard it all my life. It's *our* fault. Whatever happens, *we* did it. Alan's just a little victim. He's really done nothing at all! [*Savagely.*] What do you have to do in this world to get any sympathy—blind animals?

DYSART: Sit down, Mrs. Strang.

DORA [*ignoring him: more and more urgently*]: Look, Doctor: you don't have to live with this. Alan is one patient to you: one out of many. He's my son. I lie awake every night thinking about it. Frank lies there beside me. I can hear him. Neither of us sleeps all night. You come to us and say, who forbids television? who does what behind whose back?—as if we're criminals. Let me tell you something. We're not criminals. We've done nothing wrong. We loved Alan. We gave him the best love we could. All right, we quarrel sometimes—all parents quarrel—we always make it up. My husband is a good man. He's an upright man, religion or no religion. He cares for his home, for the world, and for his boy. Alan had love and care and treats, and as much fun as any boy in the world. I know about loveless homes: I was a teacher. Our home wasn't loveless. I know about privacy too—not invading a child's privacy. All right, Frank may be at fault there—he digs into him too much—but nothing in excess. He's not a bully . . . [*Gravely.*] No, Doctor. Whatever's happened has happened *because of Alan.* Alan is himself. Every soul is itself. If you added up everything we ever did to him, from his first day on earth to this, you wouldn't find why he did this terrible thing—because that's *him*; not just all of our things added up. Do you understand what I'm saying? I want you to understand, because I lie awake and awake thinking it out, and I want you to know that I deny it absolutely what he's doing now, staring at me, attacking me for what *he's* done, for what *he* is! [*Pause: calmer.*] You've got your words, and I've got mine. You call it a complex, I suppose. But if you knew God, Doctor, you would know about the Devil. You'd know the Devil isn't made by what mummy says and daddy says. The Devil's *there.* It's an old-fashioned word, but a true thing . . . I'll go. What I did in there was inexcusable. I only know he was my little Alan, and then the Devil came.

[*She leaves the square, and resumes her place.* DYSART *watches her go, then leaves himself by the opposite entrance, and approaches* ALAN.]

## SCENE 3

[*Seated on his bench, the boy glares at him.*]

DYSART: I thought you liked your mother. [*Silence.*] She doesn't know anything, you know. I haven't told her what you told me. You do know that, don't you?

ALAN: It was lies anyway.

DYSART: What?

ALAN: You and your pencil. Just a con trick, that's all.

DYSART: What do you mean?

ALAN: Made me say a lot of lies.

DYSART: Did it? . . . Like what?

ALAN: All of it. Everything I said. Lot of lies.

[*Pause.*]

DYSART: I see.

ALAN: You ought to be locked up. Your bloody tricks.

DYSART: I thought you liked tricks.

ALAN: It'll be the drug next. I know.

[DYSART *turns, sharply.*]

DYSART: What drug?

ALAN: I've heard. I'm not ignorant. I know what you get up to in here. Shove needles in people, pump them full of truth drug, so they can't help saying things. That's next, isn't it?

[*Pause.*]

DYSART: Alan, do you know why you're here?

ALAN: So you can give me truth drugs.

[*He glares at him.*

DYSART *leaves abruptly, and returns to the square.*]

## SCENE 4

[HESTHER *comes in simultaneously from the other side.*]

DYSART [*agitated*]: He actually thinks they exist! And of course he wants one.

HESTHER: It doesn't sound like that to me.

DYSART: Of course he does. Why mention them otherwise? He wants a way to speak. To finally tell me what happened in that stable. Tape's too isolated, and hypnosis is a trick. At least that's the pretense.

HESTHER: Does he still say that today?

DYSART: I haven't seen him. I canceled his appointment this morning, and let him stew in his own anxiety. Now I am almost tempted to play a real trick on him.

HESTHER [*sitting*]: Like what?

DYSART: The old placebo.

HESTHER: You mean a harmless pill?

DYSART: Full of *alleged* truth drug. Probably an aspirin.

HESTHER: But he'd deny it afterward. Same thing all over.

DYSART: No. Because he's ready to abreact.

HESTHER: Abreact?

DYSART: Live it all again. He won't be able to deny it after that, because he'll have shown me. Not just told me—but acted it out in front of me.

HESTHER: Can you get him to do that?

DYSART: I think so. He's nearly done it already. Under all that glowering, he trusts me. Do you realize that?

HESTHER [*warmly*]: I'm sure he does.

DYSART: Poor bloody fool.

HESTHER: Don't start that again.

[*Pause.*]

DYSART [*quietly*]: Can you think of anything worse one can do to anybody than take away their worship?

HESTHER: Worship?

DYSART: Yes, that word again!

HESTHER: Aren't you being a little extreme?

DYSART: Extremity's the point.

HESTHER: Worship isn't destructive, Martin. I know that.

DYSART: I don't. I only know it's the core of his life. What else has he got? Think about him. He can hardly read. He knows no physics or engineering to make the world real for him. No paintings to show him how others have enjoyed it. No music except television jingles. No history except tales from a desperate mother. No friends. Not one kid to give him a joke, or make him know himself more moderately. He's a modern citizen for whom society doesn't exist. He lives *one hour* every three weeks—howling in a mist. And after the service kneels to a slave who stands over him obviously and unthrowably his master. With my body I thee worship! . . . Many men have less vital with their wives.

[*Pause.*]

HESTHER: All the same, they don't usually blind their wives, do they?

DYSART: Oh, come on!

HESTHER: Well, do they?

DYSART [*sarcastically*]: You mean he's dangerous? A violent, dangerous madman who's going to run round the country doing it again and again?

HESTHER: I mean he's in pain, Martin. He's been in pain for most of his life. That much, at least, you *know.*

DYSART: Possibly.

HESTHER: *Possibly?!* . . . That cut-off little figure you just described must have been in pain for years.

DYSART [*doggedly*]: Possibly.

HESTHER: And you can take it away.

DYSART: Still—possibly.

HESTHER: Then that's enough. That simply has to be enough for you, surely?

DYSART: No!

HESTHER: Why not?

DYSART: Because it's his.

HESTHER: I don't understand.

DYSART: His pain. His own. He made it. [*Pause. Earnestly.*] Look . . . to go through life and call it yours—*your life*—you first have to get your own pain. Pain that's unique to you. You can't just dip into the common bin and say "That's enough!" . . . He's done that. All right, he's sick. He's full of misery and fear. He was dangerous, and could be again, though I doubt it. But that boy has known a passion more ferocious than I have felt in any second of my life. And let me tell you something: I envy it.

HESTHER: You can't

DYSART [*vehemently*]: Don't you see? That's the Accusation? That's what his stare has been saying to me all this time. *"At least I galloped! When did you?"* . . . [*Simply.*] I'm jealous, Hesther. Jealous of Alan Strang.

HESTHER: That's absurd.

DYSART: Is it? . . . I go on about my wife. That smug woman by the fire. Have you thought of the fellow on the other side of it? The finicky, critical husband looking through his art books on mythical Greece. What worship has *he* ever known? Real worship! Without worship you shrink, it's as brutal as that . . . I shrank my *own* life. No one can do it for you. I settled for being pallid and provincial, out of my own eternal timidity. The old story of bluster, and do bugger-all. . . . I imply that we can't have children; but actually, it's only me. I had myself tested behind her back. The lowest sperm count you could find. And I never told her. That's all I need—her sympathy mixed with resentment. . . . I tell everyone Margaret's the puritan, I'm the pagan. Some pagan! Such wild returns I make to the womb of civilization. Three weeks a year in the Peleponnese, every bed booked in advance, every meal paid for by vouchers, cautious jaunts in hired Fiats, suitcase crammed with Kaopectate! Such a fantastic surrender to the primitive! And I use that word endlessly: "primitive." "Oh, the primitive world," I say. "What instinctual truths were lost in it!" And while I sit there, baiting a poor unimaginative woman with the word, that freaky boy tries to conjure the reality! I sit looking at pages of centaurs trampling the soil of Argos—and outside my window he is trying to *become one,* in a Hampshire field! . . . I watch that woman knitting, night after night—a woman I haven't *kissed* in six years—and he stands in the dark for an hour, sucking the sweat off his God's hairy cheek! [*Pause.*] Then in the morning, I put away my books on the cultural shelf, close up the Kodachrome snaps of Mount Olympus, touch my reproduction statue of Dionysus for luck—and go off to hospital to treat him for insanity. Do you see?

HESTHER: The boy's in pain, Martin. That's all I see. In the end . . . I'm sorry.

[*He looks at her.* ALAN *gets up from his bench and stealthily places an envelope in the left-hand entrance of the square, then goes back and sits with his back to the audience, as if watching television.* HESTHER *rises.*]

HESTHER: That stare of his. Have you thought it might not be accusing you at all?

DYSART: What then?

HESTHER: Claiming you.

DYSART: For what?

HESTHER [*mischievously*]: A new God.

[*Pause.*]

DYSART: Too conventional, for him. Finding a religion in psychiatry is really for very ordinary patients.

[*She laughs.*]

HESTHER: Maybe he just wants a new dad. Or is that too conventional, too? . . . Since you're questioning your profession anyway, perhaps you ought to try it and see.

DYSART [*amused*]: I'll talk to you.

HESTHER: Goodbye.

[*She smiles, and leaves him.*]

## SCENE 5

[DYSART *becomes aware of the letter lying on the floor. He picks it up, opens and reads it.*]

ALAN [*speaking stiffly, as* DYSART *reads*]: "It is all true, what I said after you tapped the pencil. I'm sorry if I said different. Post Scriptum: I know why I'm in here."

[*Pause.*]

DYSART [*calling, joyfully*]: Nurse!

[NURSE *comes in.*]

NURSE: Yes, Doctor?

DYSART [*trying to conceal his pleasure*]: Good evening!

NURSE: You're in late tonight.

DYSART: Yes! . . . Tell me, is the Strang boy in bed yet?

NURSE: Oh no, Doctor. He's bound to be upstairs looking at television. He always watches to the last possible moment. He doesn't like going to his room at all.

DYSART: You mean he's still having nightmares?

NURSE: He had a bad one last night.

DYSART: Would you ask him to come down here, please?

NURSE [*faint surprise*]: Now?

DYSART: I'd like a word with him.

NURSE [*puzzled*]: Very good, Doctor.

DYSART: If he's not back in his room by lights out, tell Night Nurse not to worry. I'll see he gets back to bed all right. And would you phone my home and tell my wife I may be in late?

NURSE: Yes, Doctor.

DYSART: Ask him to come straight away, please.

[NURSE *goes to the bench, taps* ALAN *on the shoulder, whispers her message in his ear, and returns to her place.* ALAN *stands up and pauses for a second—then steps into the square.*]

## SCENE 6

[*He stands in the doorway, depressed.*]

DYSART: Hello.

ALAN: Hello.

DYSART: I got your letter. Thank you. [*Pause.*] Also the Post Scriptum.

ALAN [*defensively*]: That's the right word. My mum told me. It's Latin for "After-writing."

DYSART: How are you feeling?

ALAN: All right.

DYSART: I'm sorry I didn't see you today.

ALAN: You were fed up with me.

DYSART: Yes. [*Pause.*] Can I make it up to you now?

ALAN: What d'you mean?

DYSART: I thought we'd have a session.

ALAN [*startled*]: Now?

DYSART: Yes! At dead of night! . . . Better than going to sleep, isn't it?

[*The boy flinches.*]

Alan—look. Everything I say has a trick or a catch. Everything I do is a trick or a catch. That's all I know to do. But they work—and you know that. Trust me.

[*Pause.*]

ALAN: You got another trick, then?

DYSART: Yes.

ALAN: A truth drug?

DYSART: If you like.

ALAN: What's it do?

DYSART: Make it easier for you to talk.

ALAN: Like you can't help yourself?

DYSART: That's right. Like you have to speak the truth at all costs. And all of it.

[*Pause.*]

ALAN [*slyly*]: Comes in a needle, doesn't it?

DYSART: No.

ALAN: Where is it?

DYSART [*indicating his pocket*]: In here.

ALAN: Let's see.

[DYSART *solemnly takes a bottle of pills out of his pocket.*]

DYSART: There.

ALAN [*suspicious*]: That really it?

DYSART: It is. . . . Do you want to try it?

ALAN: No.

DYSART: I think you do.

ALAN: I don't. Not at all.

DYSART: Afterward you'd sleep. You'd have no bad dreams all night. Probably many nights, from then on . . .

[*Pause.*]

ALAN: How long's it take to work?

DYSART: It's instant. Like coffee.

ALAN [*half believing*]: It isn't!

DYSART: I promise you. . . . Well?

ALAN: Can I have a fag?

DYSART: Pill first. Do you want some water?

ALAN: No.

[DYSART *shakes one out onto his palm.* ALAN *hesitates for a second—then takes it and swallows it.*]

DYSART: Then you can chase it down with this. Sit down.

[*He offers him a cigarette, and lights it for him.*]

ALAN [*nervous*]: What happens now?

DYSART: We wait for it to work.

ALAN: What'll I feel first?

DYSART: Nothing much. After a minute, about a hundred green snakes should come out of that cupboard singing the "Hallelujah Chorus."

ALAN [*annoyed*]: *I'm serious!*

DYSART [*earnestly*]: You'll feel nothing. Nothing's going to happen now but what you want to happen. You're not going to say anything to me but what you want to say. Just relax. Lie back and finish your fag.

[ALAN *stares at him. Then accepts the situation, and lies back.*]

DYSART: Good boy.

ALAN: I bet this room's heard some funny things.

DYSART: It certainly has.

ALAN: I like it.

DYSART: This room?

ALAN: Don't you?

DYSART: Well, there's not much to like, is there?

ALAN: How long am I going to be in here?

DYSART: It's hard to say. I quite see you want to leave.

ALAN: No.

DYSART: You don't?

ALAN: Where would I go?

DYSART: Home . . .

[*The boy looks at him.* DYSART *crosses and sits on the rail upstage, his feet on the bench. A pause.*]

Actually, I'd like to leave this room and never see it again in my life.

ALAN [*surprise*]: Why?

DYSART: I've been in it too long.

ALAN: Where would you go?

DYSART: Somewhere.

ALAN: Secret?

DYSART: Yes. There's a sea—a great sea—I love. . . . It's where the Gods used to go to bathe.

ALAN: What Gods?

DYSART: The old ones. Before they died.

ALAN: Gods don't die.

DYSART: Yes, they do. [*Pause.*] There's a village I spent one night in, where I'd like to live. It's all white.

ALAN: How would you Nosy Parker, though? You wouldn't have a room for it any more.

DYSART: I wouldn't mind. I don't actually enjoy being a Nosy Parker, you know.

ALAN: Then why do it?

DYSART: Because you're unhappy.

ALAN: So are you.

[DYSART *looks at him sharply.* ALAN *sits up in alarm.*]

Oooh, I didn't mean that!

DYSART: Didn't you?

ALAN: Here—is that how it works? Things just slip out, not feeling anything?

DYSART: That's right.

ALAN: But it's so quick!

DYSART: I told you; it's instant.

ALAN [*delighted*]: It's wicked, isn't it? I mean, you can say anything under it.

DYSART: Yes.

ALAN: Ask me a question.

DYSART: Tell me about Jill.

[*Pause. The boy turns away.*]

ALAN: There's nothing to tell.

DYSART: Nothing?

ALAN: No.

DYSART: Well, for example—is she pretty? You've never described her.

ALAN: She's all right.

DYSART: What color hair?

ALAN: Dunno.

DYSART: Is it long or short?

ALAN: Dunno

DYSART [*lightly*]: You must know that.

ALAN: I don't remember. *I don't!*

[DYSART *rises and comes down to him. He takes the cigarette out of his hand.*]

DYSART [*firmly*]: Lie back. . . . Now listen. You have to do this. And now. You are going to tell me everything that happened with this girl. And not just *tell* me—*show* me. Act it out, if you like—even more than you did when I tapped the pencil. I want you to feel free to do absolutely anything in this room. The pill will help you. I will help you. . . . Now, where does she live?

[*A long pause.*]

ALAN [*tight*]: Near the stables. About a mile.

[DYSART *steps down out of the square as* JILL *enters it. He sits again on the downstage bench.*]

## SCENE 7

[*The light grows warmer.*]

JILL: It's called the China Pantry.

[*She comes down and sits casually on the rail. Her manner is open and lightly provocative. During these scenes* ALAN *acts directly with her, and never looks over at* DYSART *when he replies to him.*]

When Daddy disappeared, she was left without a bean. She had to earn her own living. I must say she did jolly well, considering she was never trained in business.

DYSART: What do you mean, "disappeared"?

ALAN [*to* DYSART]: He ran off. No one ever saw him again.

JILL: Just left a note on her dressing table saying, "Sorry. I've had it." Just like that. She never got over it. It turned her right off men. All my dates have to be sort of secret. I mean, she knows about them, but I can't ever bring anyone back home. She's so rude to them.

ALAN [*to* DYSART]: She was always looking.

DYSART: At you?

ALAN [*to* DYSART]: Saying stupid things.

[*She jumps off the bench.*]

JILL: You've got super eyes.

ALAN [*to* DYSART]: Anyway, *she* was the one who had them.

[*She sits next to him. Embarrassed, the boy tries to move away as far as he can.*]

JILL: There was an article in the paper last week saying what points about boys fascinate girls. They said Number One is bottoms. I think it's eyes every time. . . . They fascinate you too, don't they?

ALAN: Me?

JILL [*sly*]: Or is it only horses' eyes?

ALAN [*startled*]: What d'you mean?

JILL: I saw you staring into Nugget's eyes yesterday for ages. I spied on you through the door!

ALAN [*hotly*]: There must have been something in it!

JILL: You're a real Man of Mystery, aren't you?

ALAN [*to* DYSART]: Sometimes, it was like she knew.

DYSART: Did you ever hint?

ALAN [*to* DYSART]: 'Course not!

JILL: I love horses' eyes. The way you can see yourself in them. D'you find them sexy?

ALAN [*outraged*]: What?!

JILL: Horses.

ALAN: Don't be daft!

[*He springs up, and away from her.*]

JILL: Girls do. I mean, they go through a period when they pat them and kiss them a lot. I know *I* did. I suppose it's just a substitute, really.

ALAN [*to* DYSART]: That kind of thing, all the time. Until one night . . .

DYSART: Yes? What?

ALAN [*to* DYSART: *defensively*]: She did it! Not me. It was her idea, the whole thing! . . . She got me into it!

DYSART: What are you saying? "One night": go on from there.

[*A pause.*]

ALAN [*to* DYSART]: Saturday night. We were just closing up.

JILL: How would you like to take me out?

ALAN: What?

JILL [*coolly*]: How would you like to take me out tonight?

ALAN: I've got to go home.

JILL: What for?

[*He tries to escape upstage.*]

ALAN: They expect me.

JILL: Ring up and say you're going out.

ALAN: I can't.

JILL: Why?

ALAN: They expect me.

JILL: Look. Either we go out together and have some fun, or you go back to your boring home, *as usual,* and I go back to mine. That's the situation, isn't it?

ALAN: Well . . . where would we go?

JILL: The pictures! There's a skinflick over in Winchester! I've never seen one, have you?

ALAN: No.

JILL: Wouldn't you like to? *I* would. All those heavy Swedes, panting at each other! . . . What d'you say?

ALAN [*grinning*]: Yeh! . . .

JILL: Good! . . .

[*He turns away.*]

DYSART: Go on, please.

[*He steps off the square.*]

ALAN [*to* DYSART]: I'm tired now!

DYSART: Come on now. You can't stop there.

[*He storms round the circle to* DYSART, *and faces him directly.*]

ALAN: I'm *tired!* I want to go to bed!

DYSART [*sharply*]: Well, you can't. I want to hear about the film.

ALAN [*hostile*]: Hear what? . . . *What?* . . . It was bloody awful!

[*The actors playing horses come swiftly on to the square, dressed in sports coats or raincoats. They move the benches to be parallel with the audience, and sit on them—staring out front.*]

DYSART: Why?

ALAN: Nosy Parker!

DYSART: *Why?*

ALAN: *Because* . . . Well—we went into the cinema!

## SCENE 8

[*A burst of rock music, instantly fading down. Lights darken.*
ALAN *reenters the square.* JILL *rises and together they grope their way to the downstage bench, as if in a dark auditorium.*]

ALAN [*to* DYSART]: The whole place was full of men. Jill was the only girl. [*They push by a patron seated at the end, and sit side by side, staring up at the invisible screen, located above the heads of the main audience. A spotlight hits the boy's face.*] We sat down and the film came on. It was daft. Nothing happened for ages. There was this girl Brita, who was sixteen. She went to stay in this house, where there was an older boy. He kept giving her looks, but she ignored him completely. In the end she took a shower. She went into the bathroom and took off all her clothes. The lot. Very slowly. . . . What she didn't know was the boy was looking through the door all the time. . . . [*He starts to become excited.*] It was fantastic! The water fell on her breasts, bouncing down her . . .

[FRANK *steps into the square furtively from the back, hat in hand, and stands looking for a place.*]

DYSART: Was that the first time you'd seen a girl naked?

ALAN [*to* DYSART]: Yes! You couldn't see everything, though. . . . [*Looking about him.*] All round me they were all looking. All the men—staring up like they were in church. Like they were a sort of congregation. And then—[*He sees his father.*] *Ah!*

[*At the same instant* FRANK *sees him.*]

FRANK: Alan!

ALAN: God!

JILL: What is it?

ALAN: *Dad!*

JILL: *Where?*

ALAN: At the back! *He saw me!*

JILL: You sure?

ALAN: Yes!

FRANK [*calling*]: Alan!

ALAN: Oh, God!

[*He tries to hide his face in the girl's shoulder. His father comes down the aisle toward him.*]

FRANK: Alan! You can hear me! Don't pretend!

PATRONS: *Ssssh!*

FRANK [*approaching the row of seats*]: Do I have to come and fetch you out? . . . Do I? . . .

[*Cries of "Sssh!" and "Shut up!"*]

Do I, Alan?

ALAN [*through gritted teeth*]: Oh, fuck!

[*He gets up as the noise increases.* JILL *gets up too and follows him.*]

DYSART: You went?

ALAN [*to* DYSART]: What else could I do? He kept shouting. Everyone was saying "Shut up!"

[*They go out, right, through the group of* PATRONS, *who rise protesting as they pass, quickly replace the benches and leave the square.* DYSART *enters it.*]

## SCENE 9

[*Light brightens from the cinema, but remains cold: streets at night. The three walk round the circle downstage in a line:* FRANK *leading, wearing his hat. He halts in the middle of the left rail, and stands staring straight ahead of him, rigid with embarrassment.*

ALAN *is very agitated.*]

ALAN [*to* DYSART]: We went into the street, all three of us. It was weird. We just stood there by the bus stop—like we were three people in a queue, and we didn't know each other. Dad was all white and sweaty. He didn't look at us at all. It must have gone on for about five minutes. I tried to speak. I said—[*To his father.*] I—I—I've never been there before. Honest . . . Never . . . [*To* DYSART.] He didn't seem to hear. Jill tried.

JILL: It's true, Mr. Strang. It wasn't Alan's idea to go there. It was mine.

ALAN [*to* DYSART]: He just went on staring, straight ahead. It was awful.

JILL: I'm not shocked by films like that. I think they're just silly.

ALAN [*to* DYSART]: The bus wouldn't come. We just stood and stood. . . . Then suddenly he spoke.

[FRANK *takes off his hat.*]

FRANK [*stiffly*]: I'd like you to know something. Both of you. I came here tonight to see the manager. He asked me to call on him for business purposes. I happen to be a printer, miss. A picture house needs posters. That's entirely why I'm here. To discuss posters. While I was waiting I happened to glance in, that's all. I can only say I'm going to complain to the council. I had no idea they showed films like this. I'm certainly going to refuse my services.

JILL [*kindly*]: Yes, of course.

FRANK: So long as that's understood.

ALAN [*to* DYSART]: Then the bus came along.

FRANK: Come along now, Alan.

[*He moves away downstage.*]

ALAN: No.

FRANK [*turning*]: No fuss, please. Say good night to the young lady.

ALAN [*timid but firm*]: No. I'm stopping here. . . . I've got to see her home. . . . It's proper.

[*Pause.*]

FRANK [*as dignified as possible*]: Very well. I'll see you when you choose to return. Very well then . . . yes . . .

[*He walks back to his original seat, next to his wife. He stares across the square at his son—who stares back at him. Then, slowly, he sits.*]

ALAN [*to* DYSART]: And he got in, and we didn't. He sat down and looked at me through the glass. And I saw . . .

DYSART [*soft*]: What?

ALAN [*to* DYSART]: His face. It was scared.

DYSART: Of you?

ALAN [*to* DYSART]: It was terrible. We had to walk home. Four miles. I got the shakes.

DYSART: You were scared too?

ALAN [*to* DYSART]: It was like a hole had been drilled in my tummy. A hole—right here. And the air was getting in!

[*He starts to walk upstage, round the circle.*]

## SCENE 10

[*The girl stays still.*]

JILL [*aware of other people looking*]: Alan . . .

ALAN [*to* DYSART]: People kept turning round in the street to look.

JILL: Alan!

ALAN [*to* DYSART]: I kept seeing him, just as he drove off. Scared of me. . . . And me scared of him . . . I kept thinking—all those airs he put on! . . . "Receive my meaning. Improve your mind!" . . . All those nights he said he'd be in late. "Keep my supper hot, Dora!" "Your poor father: he works so hard!" . . . Bugger! Old bugger! . . . Filthy old bugger!

[*He stops, clenching his fists.*]

JILL: Hey! Wait for me!

[*She runs after him. He waits.*]

What are you thinking about?

ALAN: Nothing.

JILL: Mind my own beeswax?

[*She laughs.*]

ALAN [*to* DYSART]: And suddenly she began to laugh.

JILL: I'm sorry. But it's pretty funny, when you think of it.

ALAN [*bewildered*]: What?

JILL: Catching him like that! I mean, it's terrible—but it's very funny.

ALAN: Yeh!

[*He turns from her.*]

JILL: No, wait! . . . I'm sorry. I know you're upset. But it's not the end of the world, is it? I mean, what was he doing? Only what we were. Watching a silly film. It's a case of like father like son, I'd say! . . . I mean, when that girl was taking a shower, you were pretty interested, weren't you?

[*He turns round and looks at her.*]

We keep saying old people are square. Then when they suddenly aren't—we don't like it!

DYSART: What did you think about that?

ALAN [*to* DYSART]: I don't know. I kept looking at all the people in the street. They were mostly men coming out of pubs. I suddenly thought—*they all do it! All of them!* . . . They're not just dads—they're people with pricks! . . . And Dad—he's not just Dad either. He's a man with a prick too. You know, I'd never thought about it. [*Pause.*] We went into the country.

[*He walks again.* JILL *follows. They turn the corner and come downstage, right.*]

We kept walking. I just thought about Dad, and how he was nothing special—just a poor old sod on his own.

[*He stops.*]

[*To* JILL*: realizing it.*] Poor old sod!

JILL: That's right!

ALAN [*grappling with it*]: I mean, what else has he got? . . . He's got Mum, of course, but well—she—she—she—

JILL: She doesn't give him anything?

ALAN: That's right. I bet you . . . she doesn't give him anything. That's right . . . that's really right! . . . She likes ladies and gentlemen. Do you understand what I mean?

JILL [*mischievously*]: Ladies and gentlemen aren't naked?

ALAN: That's right! Never! . . . *Never!* That would be disgusting! She'd have to put bowler hats on them! . . . Jodhpurs!

[*She laughs.*]

DYSART: Was that the first time you ever thought anything like that about your mother? . . . I mean, that she was unfair to your dad?

ALAN [*to* DYSART]: Absolutely!

DYSART: How did you feel?

ALAN [*to* DYSART]: Sorry. I mean for him. Poor old sod, that's what I felt—he's just like me! He hates ladies and gents just like me! Posh things—and la-di-da. He goes off by himself at night, and does his own secret thing which no one'll know about, just like me! There's no difference—he's just the same as me—just the same!—[*He stops in distress, then bolts back a little upstage.*] Christ!

DYSART [*sternly*]: Go on.

ALAN [*to* DYSART]: I can't.

DYSART: Of course you can. You're doing wonderfully.

ALAN [*to* DYSART]: No, please. *Don't make me!*

DYSART [*firm*]: Don't think: just answer. You were happy at that second, weren't you? When you realized about your dad. How lots of people have secrets, not just you?

ALAN [*to* DYSART]: Yes!

DYSART: You felt sort of free, didn't you? I mean, free to do anything?

ALAN [*to* DYSART, *looking at* JILL]: Yes!

DYSART: What was she doing?

ALAN [*to* DYSART]: Holding my hand.

DYSART: And that was good?

ALAN [*to* DYSART]: Oh yes!

DYSART: Remember what you thought. *As if it's happening to you now. This very moment. . . .* What's in your head?

ALAN [*to* DYSART]: Her eyes. *She's* the one with eyes! . . . I keep looking at them, because I really want—

DYSART: To look at her breasts?

ALAN [*to* DYSART]: Yes.

DYSART: Like in the film.

ALAN [*to* DYSART]: Yes. . . . Then she starts to scratch my hand.

JILL: You're really very nice, you know that?

ALAN [*to* DYSART]: Moving her nails on the back. Her face so warm. Her eyes.

DYSART: You want her very much?

ALAN [*to* DYSART]: Yes . . .

JILL: I love your eyes.

[*She kisses him.*]

[*Whispering.*] Let's go!

ALAN: Where?

JILL: I know a place. It's right near here.

ALAN: Where?

JILL: Surprise! . . . Come on! [*She darts away round the circle, across the stage and up the left side.*] Come *on!*

ALAN [*to* DYSART]: She runs ahead. I follow. And then—and then—!

[*He halts.*]

DYSART: What?

ALAN [*to* DYSART]: I see what she means.

DYSART: What? . . . Where are you? . . . Where has she taken you?

ALAN [*to* JILL]: *The Stables?*

JILL: Of course!

## SCENE 11

[CHORUS *makes a warning hum. The horses actors enter, and ceremonially put on their masks—first raising them high above their heads.* NUGGET *stands in the central tunnel.*]

ALAN [*recoiling*]: No!

JILL: Where else? They're perfect!

ALAN: No!

[*He turns his head from her.*]

JILL: Or do you want to go home now and face your dad?

ALAN: No!

JILL: Then come on!

[*He edges nervously past the horse standing at the left, which turns its neck and even moves a challenging step after him.*]

ALAN: Why not your place?

JILL: I can't. Mother doesn't like me bringing back boys. I told you. . . . Anyway, the barn's better.

ALAN: No!

JILL: All that straw. It's cozy.

ALAN: No.

JILL: *Why not?*

ALAN: Them!

JILL: Dalton will be in bed. . . . What's the matter? . . . Don't you want to?

ALAN [*aching to*]: Yes!

JILL: So?

ALAN [*desperate*]: *Them! . . . Them! . . .*

JILL: *Who?*

ALAN [*low*]: Horses.

JILL: *Horses?* . . . You're really dotty, aren't you? . . . What do you mean?

[*He starts shaking.*]

Oh, you're freezing. . . . Let's get under the straw. You'll be warm there.

ALAN [*pulling away*]: No!

JILL: What on earth's the matter with you?

[*Silence. He won't look at her.*]

Look, if the sight of horses offends you, my lord, we can just shut the door. You won't have to see them. All right?

DYSART: What door is that? In the barn?

ALAN [*to* DYSART]: Yes.

DYSART: So what do you do? You go in?

ALAN [*to* DYSART]: Yes.

## SCENE 12

[*A rich light falls.*

*Furtively* ALAN *enters the square from the top end, and* JILL *follows. The horses on the circle retire out of sight on either side.* NUGGET *retreats up the tunnel and stands where he can just be glimpsed in the dimness.*]

DYSART: Into the Temple? The Holy of Holies?

ALAN [*to* DYSART: *desperate*]: What else can I do? . . . I can't say! I can't tell her . . . [*To* JILL.] Shut it tight.

JILL: All right . . . You're crazy.

ALAN: Lock it.

JILL: Lock?

ALAN: Yes.

JILL: It's just an old door. What's the matter with you? They're in their boxes. They can't get out. . . . Are you all right?

ALAN: Why?

JILL: You look weird.

ALAN: *Lock it!*

JILL: Ssssh! D'you want to wake up Dalton? . . . Stay there, idiot.

[*She mimes locking a heavy door, upstage.*]

DYSART: Describe the barn, please.

ALAN [*walking round it: to* DYSART]: Large room. Straw everywhere. Some tools . . . [*As if picking it up off the rail where he left it in Act One.*] A hoof-pick! . . .

[*He "drops" it hastily, and dashes away from the spot.*]

DYSART: Go on.

ALAN [*to* DYSART]: At the end this big door. Behind it—

DYSART: Horses.

ALAN [*to* DYSART]: Yes.

DYSART: How many?

ALAN [*to* DYSART]: Six.

DYSART: Jill closes the door so you can't see them?

ALAN [*to* DYSART]: Yes.

DYSART: And then? . . . What happens now? . . . Come on, Alan. Show me.

JILL: See, it's all shut. There's just us. . . . Let's sit down. Come on.

[*They sit together on the same bench, left.*]

Hello.

ALAN [*quickly*]: Hello.

[*She kisses him lightly. He responds. Suddenly a faint trampling of hooves, offstage, makes him jump up.*]

JILL: What is it?

[*He turns his head upstage, listening.*]

Relax. There's no one there. Come here.

[*She touches his hand. He turns to her again.*]

You're very gentle. I love that . . .

ALAN: So are you . . . I mean . . .

[*He kisses her spontaneously. The hooves trample again, harder. He breaks away from her abruptly toward the upstage corner.*]

JILL [*rising*]: What is it?

ALAN: Nothing!

[*She moves toward him. He turns and moves past her. He is clearly distressed. She contemplates him for a moment.*]

JILL [*gently*]: Take your sweater off.

ALAN: What?

JILL: I will, if you will.

[*He stares at her. A pause.*

*She lifts her sweater over her head; he watches—then unzips his. They each remove their shoes, their socks, and their jeans. Then they look at each other diagonally across the square, in which the light is gently increasing.*]

ALAN: You're . . . you're very . . .

JILL: So are you. . . . [*Pause.*] Come here.

[*He goes to her. She comes to him. They meet in the middle, and hold each other, and embrace.*]

ALAN [*to* DYSART]: She put her mouth in mine. It was lovely! *Oh, it was lovely!*

[*They burst into giggles. He lays her gently on the floor in the center of the square, and bends over her eagerly.*

*Suddenly the noise of* EQUUS *fills the place. Hooves smash on wood.* ALAN *straightens up, rigid. He stares straight ahead of him over the prone body of the girl.*]

DYSART: Yes, what happened then, Alan?

ALAN [*to* DYSART: *brutally*]: I put it in her!

DYSART: Yes?

ALAN [*to* DYSART]: I put it in her.

DYSART: You did?

ALAN [*to* DYSART]: Yes!

DYSART: Was it easy?

ALAN [*to* DYSART]: Yes.

DYSART: Describe it.

ALAN [*to* DYSART]: I told you.

DYSART: More exactly.

ALAN [*to* DYSART]: I put it in her!

DYSART: Did you?

ALAN [*to* DYSART]: All the way!

DYSART: Did you, Alan?

ALAN [*to* DYSART]: All the way. I shoved it. I put it in her all the way.

DYSART: Did you?

ALAN [*to* DYSART]: Yes!

DYSART: Did you?

ALAN [*to* DYSART]: Yes! . . . Yes!

DYSART: Give me the TRUTH! . . . Did you? . . . *Honestly?*

ALAN [*to* DYSART]: Fuck off!

[*He collapses, lying upstage on his face.* JILL *lies on her back motionless, her head downstage, her arms extended behind her. A pause.*]

DYSART [*gently*]: What was it? You couldn't? Though you wanted to very much?

ALAN [*to* DYSART]: I couldn't . . . see her.

DYSART: What do you mean?

ALAN [*to* DYSART]: Only Him. Every time I kissed her—*He* was in the way.

DYSART: Who?

[ALAN *turns on his back.*]

ALAN [*to* DYSART]: You *know* who! . . . When I touched her, I felt *Him.*

Under me. . . . His side, waiting for my hand . . . his flanks . . . I refused him. I looked. I looked right at her . . . and I couldn't do it. When I shut my eyes, I saw him at once. The streaks on his belly . . . [*With more desperation.*] I couldn't feel *her* flesh at all! I wanted the foam off his neck. His sweaty hide. Not flesh. *Hide! Horsehide!* . . . Then I couldn't even kiss her.

[JILL *sits up.*]

JILL: What is it?

ALAN [*dodging her hand*]: No!

[*He scrambles up and crouches in the corner against the rails, like a little beast in a cage.*]

JILL: Alan!

ALAN: Stop it!

[JILL *gets up.*]

JILL: It's all right. . . . It's all right. . . . Don't worry about it. It often happens—honest. . . . There's nothing wrong. I don't mind, you know . . . I don't at all.

[*He dashes past her downstage.*]

Alan, look at me . . . Alan? . . . Alan!

[*He collapses again by the rail.*]

ALAN: Get out! . . .

JILL: What?

ALAN [*soft*]: Out!

JILL: There's nothing wrong—believe me! It's very common.

ALAN: *Get out!*

[*He snatches up the invisible pick.*]

GET OUT!

JILL: Put that down!

ALAN: Leave me alone!

JILL: Put that down, Alan. It's very dangerous! Go on, please—drop it.

[*He "drops" it, and turns from her.*]

ALAN: You ever tell anyone. Just you tell . . .

JILL: Who do you think I am? . . . I'm your friend—Alan . . . [*She goes toward him.*] Listen: you don't have to do anything. Try to realize that. Nothing at all. Why don't we just lie here together in the straw. And talk.

ALAN [*low*]: Please . . .

JILL: Just talk.

ALAN: *Please!*

JILL: All right, I'm going. . . . Let me put my clothes on first.

[*She dresses, hastily.*]

ALAN: You tell anyone! . . . Just tell and see . . .

JILL: *Oh, stop it!* . . . I wish you could believe me. It's not in the least important. [*Pause.*] Anyway, I won't say anything. You know that. You know I won't . . .

[*Pause. He stands with his back to her.*]

Good night, then, Alan . . . I wish—I really wish—

[*He turns on her, hissing. His face is distorted—possessed.*

*In horrified alarm she turns—fumbles the door open—leaves the barn—shuts the door hard behind her, and dashes up the tunnel out of sight, past the barely visible figure of* NUGGET.]

## SCENE 13

[ALAN *stands alone, and naked.*

*A faint humming and drumming. The boy looks about him in growing terror.*]

DYSART: What?

ALAN [*to* DYSART]: He was there. Through the door. The door was shut, but he was there! . . . He'd seen everything. I could hear him. He was laughing.

DYSART: Laughing?

ALAN [*to* DYSART]: Mocking! . . . *Mocking!* . . .

[*Standing downstage he stares up toward the tunnel. A great silence weighs on the square.*]

[*To the silence: terrified.*] Friend . . . Equus the Kind . . . The Merciful! . . . Forgive me! . . .

[*Silence.*]

It wasn't me. Not really me. *Me!* . . . Forgive me! . . . Take me back again! Please! . . . PLEASE!

[*He kneels on the downstage lip of the square, still facing the door, huddling in fear.*]

I'll never do it again. I swear . . . I swear! . . .

[*Silence.*]

[*In a moan.*] *Please!!!* . . .

DYSART: And He? What does He say?

ALAN [*to* DYSART: *whispering*]: "Mine! . . . You're mine! . . . I am yours and you are mine!" . . . Then I see his eyes. They are rolling!

[NUGGET *begins to advance slowly, with relentless hooves, down the central tunnel.*]

"I see you. I see you. Always! Everywhere! Forever!"

DYSART: Kiss anyone and I will see?

ALAN [*to* DYSART]: Yes!

DYSART: Lie with anyone and I will see?

ALAN [*to* DYSART]: Yes!

DYSART: And you will fail! Forever and ever you will *fail!* You will see ME— and you will FAIL!

[*The boy turns round, hugging himself in pain. From the sides two more horses converge with* NUGGET *on the rails.*

*Their hooves stamp angrily. The* EQUUS *noise is heard more terribly.*]

The Lord thy God is a Jealous God. He sees you. He sees you forever and ever, Alan. He sees you! . . . *He sees you!*

ALAN [*in terror*]: Eyes! . . . White eyes—never closed! Eyes like flames—coming—coming! . . . God seest! God seest! . . . NO! . . .

[*Pause. He steadies himself. The stage begins to blacken.*]

[*Quieter.*] No more. No more, Equus.

[*He gets up. He goes to the bench. He takes up the invisible pick. He moves slowly upstage toward* NUGGET, *concealing the weapon behind his naked back, in the growing darkness. He stretches out his hand and fondles* NUGGET*'s mask.*]

[*Gently.*] Equus . . . Noble Equus . . . Faithful and True . . . God-slave . . . Thou—God—Seest—NOTHING!

[*He stabs out* NUGGET*'s eyes. The horse stamps in agony. A great screaming begins to fill the theater, growing ever louder.* ALAN *dashes at the other two horses and blinds them too, stabbing over the rails. Their metal hooves join in the stamping.*

*Relentlessly, as this happens, three more horses appear in cones of light: not naturalistic animals like the first three, but dreadful creatures out of nightmare. Their eyes flare—their nostrils flare—their mouths flare. They are archetypal images—judging, punishing, pitiless. They do not halt at the rail, but invade the square. As they trample him, the naked boy leaps desperately at them, jumping high and naked in the dark, slashing at their heads with arms upraised.*

*The screams increase. The other horses follow into the square. The whole place is filled with cannoning, blinded horses—and the boy dodging among them, avoiding their slashing hooves as best he can. Finally they plunge off into darkness and away out of sight. The noise dies abruptly, and all we hear is* ALAN *yelling in hysteria as he collapses on the ground—stabbing at his own eyes with the invisible pick.*]

ALAN: Find me! . . . Find me! . . . Find me! . . .

KILL ME! . . . KILL ME! . . . KILL ME! . . . KILL ME! . . . KILL ME! . . .

## SCENE 14

[*The light changes quickly back to brightness.*

DYSART *enters swiftly, hurls a blanket on the left bench, and rushes over to* ALAN. *The boy is having convulsions on the floor.* DYSART *grabs his hands, forces them from his eyes, scoops him up in his arms and carries him over to the bench.* ALAN *hurls his arms around* DYSART *and clings to him, gasping and kicking his legs in a dreadful frenzy.*

DYSART *lays him down and presses his head back on the bench. He keeps talking—urgently talking—soothing the agony as he can.*]

DYSART: Here . . . Here . . . Ssssh . . . Ssssh . . . Calm now . . . Lie back. *Just lie back!* Now breathe in deep. Very deep. In . . . Out . . . In . . . Out . . . That's it . . . In. *Out . . . In . . . Out . . .*

[*The boy's breath is drawn into his body with a harsh rasping sound, which slowly grows less.* DYSART *puts the blanket over him.*]

Keep it going. . . . That's a good boy. . . . Very good boy. . . . It's all over now, Alan. It's all over. He'll go away now. You'll never see him again, I promise. You'll have no more bad dreams. No more awful nights. Think of that! . . . You are going to be well. I'm going to make you well, I promise you. . . . You'll be here for a while, but I'll be here too, so it won't be so bad. Just trust me. . . .

[*He stands upright. The boy lies still.*]

Sleep now. Have a good long sleep. You've earned it. . . . Sleep. Just sleep. . . . I'm going to make you well. [*He steps backward into the center of the square. The light brightens some more. A pause.*]

DYSART: I'm lying to you, Alan. He won't really go that easily. Just clop away from you like a nice old nag. Oh no! When Equus leaves—if he leaves at all—it will be with your intestines in his teeth. And I don't stock replacements. . . . If you knew anything, you'd get up this minute and run from me fast as you could.

[HESTHER *speaks from her place.*]

HESTHER: The boy's in pain, Martin.

DYSART: Yes.

HESTHER: And you can take it away.

DYSART: Yes.

HESTHER: Then that has to be enough for you, surely? . . . In the end!

DYSART [*crying out*]: *All right! I'll take it away!* He'll be delivered from madness. *What then?* He'll feel himself acceptable! *What then?* Do you think feelings like his can be simply reattached, like plasters? Stuck on to other objects we select? *Look at him!* . . . My desire might be to make this boy an ardent husband—a caring citizen—a worshiper of abstract and unifying God. My achievement, however, is more likely to make a ghost! . . . Let me tell you exactly what I'm going to do to him!

[*He steps out of the square and walks round the upstage end of it, storming at the audience.*]

I'll heal the rash on his body. I'll erase the welts cut into his mind by flying manes. When that's done, I'll set him on a metal miniscooter and send him puttering off into the concrete world and he'll never touch hide again! With any luck his private parts will come to feel as plastic to him as the products of the factory to which he will almost certainly be sent. Who knows? He may even come to find sex funny. Smirky funny. Bit of grunt funny. Trampled and furtive and entirely in control. Hopefully, he'll feel nothing at his fork but Approved Flesh. *I doubt, however, with much passion!* . . . Passion, you see, can be destroyed by a doctor. It cannot be created.

[*He addresses* ALAN *directly, in farewell.*]

You won't gallop any more, Alan. Horses will be quite safe. You'll save your pennies every week, till you can change that scooter in for a car, and put the odd fifty pence on the gee-gees, quite forgetting that they were ever anything more to you than bearers of little profits and little losses. You will, however, be without pain. More or less completely without pain.

[*Pause. He speaks directly to the theater, standing by the motionless body of* ALAN STRANG, *under the blanket.*]

And now for me it never stops: that voice of Equus out of the cave— "Why Me? . . . Why Me? . . . Account for Me!" . . . All right— I say it! . . . In an ultimate sense I cannot know what I do in this place— yet I do ultimate things. Irreversible, terminal things. I stand in the dark with a pick in my hand, striking at heads!

[*He moves away from* ALAN, *back to the downstage bench, and finally sits.*]

I need—more desperately than my children need me—a way of seeing in the dark. What way is this? . . . *What dark is this?* . . . I cannot call it ordained of God: I can't get that far. I will, however, pay it so much homage. There is now, in my mouth, this sharp chain. And it never comes out.

[*A long pause.*

DYSART *sits staring.*]

BLACKOUT

# AMADEUS

*For*
*Robert with love*

*Amadeus* was first presented by the National Theatre in London on November 2, 1979, with the following cast:

| | |
|---|---|
| ANTONIO SALIERI | Paul Scofield |
| THE VENTICELLI | Dermont Crowley and Donald Gee |
| GREYBIG | Philip Locke |
| JOSEPH II, EMPEROR OF AUSTRIA | John Normington |
| JOHANN KILLIAN VON STRACK | Basil Henson |
| COUNT ORSINI-ROSENBERG | Andrew Cruickshank |
| BARON VAN SWIETEN | Nicholas Selby |
| CONSTANZE WEBER | Felicity Kendal |
| MAJOR-DOMO | William Sleigh |
| WOLFGANG AMADEUS MOZART | Simon Callow |
| CITIZENS OF VIENNA | Glyn Baker, Nigel Bellairs, Leo Dove, Jane Evers, Susan Filmore, Robin McDonald, Peggy Marshall, Robin Meredith, Ann Sedgwick, Glenn Williams |
| VALETS | Nik Forster, David Morris, Louis Selwyn, Steven Slater |

Directed by Peter Hall

The New York production opened at the Broadhurst Theatre on December 17, 1980, with the following cast:

| | |
|---|---|
| ANTONIO SALIERI | Ian McKellen |
| THE VENTICELLI | Gordon Gould and Edward Zang |
| SALIERI'S VALET | Victor Griffin |
| SALIERI'S COOK | Haskell Gordon |
| JOSEPH II, EMPEROR OF AUSTRIA | Nicholas Kepros |
| JOHANN KILLIAN VON STRACK | Paul Harding |
| COUNT ORSINI-ROSENBERG | Patrick Hines |

| | |
|---|---|
| BARON VAN SWIETEN | Louis Turenne |
| PRIEST | Michael McCarty |
| GUISEPPE BONNO AND MAJOR-DOMO | Philip Pleasants |
| TERESA SALIERI | Linda Robbins |
| KATHERINA CAVALIERI | Carls Corfman |
| CONSTANZE WEBER | Jane Seymour |
| WOLFGANG AMADEUS MOZART | Tim Curry |
| CITIZENS OF VIENNA | Carls Corfman, Michele Farr, Russell Gold, Haskell Gordon, Victor Griffin, Martin LaPlatney, Warren Manzi, Michael McCarty, Philip Pleasants, and Linda Robbins |
| VALETS | Ronald Bagden, Rich Hamilton, Richard Jay Alexander, Peter Kingsley, Mark Nelson, and Mark Torres |

Directed by Peter Hall

## AUTHOR'S NOTE

The asterisks which now and then divide the page indicate changes of scene but there is to be no interruption. The scenes must flow into one another without pause from the beginning to the end of the play.

P.S.

## THE SETTING

Amadeus can and should be played in a variety of settings. What is described in this text is to a large extent based on the exquisite formulation found for the play by the designer John Bury, helped into being by the director, Peter Hall. I was of course in enthusiastic agreement with this formulation, and set it down here as a tribute to admirable work.

The set consisted basically of a handsome rectangle of patterned wood, its longest sides leading away from the viewer, set into a stage of ice-blue plastic. This surface shifted beguilingly under various lights played upon it, to show gunmetal gray, or azure, or emerald green, and reflected the actors standing upon it. The entire design was undeniably modern, yet it suggested without self-consciousness the age of the rococo. Costumes and objects were sumptuously of the period, and should always be so wherever the play is produced.

The rectangle largely represented interiors: especially those of Salieri's salon; Mozart's last apartment; assorted reception rooms, and opera houses. At the back stood a grand proscenium sporting gilded cherubs blowing huge trumpets, and supporting grand curtains of sky-blue, which could rise and part to reveal an enclosed space almost the width of the area downstage. Into this space superb backdrops were flown, and superb projections thrown, to show the scarlet boxes of theaters, or a vast wall of gold mirrors with an immense golden fireplace, representing the encrusted Palace of Schönbrunn. In it also appeared silhouettes of scandalmongering citizens of Vienna, or the formal figures of the Emperor Joseph II of Austria and his brocaded courtiers. This wonderful upstage space, which was in effect an immense rococo peepshow, will be referred to throughout this text as the Light Box.

Onstage, before the lights are lowered in the theater, four objects are to be seen by the audience. To the left, on the wooden rectangle, stands a small table, bearing a cake stand. In the center, farther upstage and also on the wood, stands a wheelchair of the Eighteenth Century, with its back to us. To the right, on the reflecting plastic, stands a beautiful fortepiano in a marquetry case. Above the stage is suspended a large chandelier showing many globes of opaque glass.

All directions will be given from the viewpoint of the audience.

Changes of time and place are indicated throughout by changes of light.

In reading the text it must be remembered that the action is wholly continuous. Its fluidity is ensured by the use of servants played by actors in Eighteenth-Century livery, whose role it is to move the furniture and carry on props with ease and correctness, while the action proceeds around them. Though a pleasant paradox of theater their constant coming and going, bearing tables, chairs, or cloaks, should render them virtually invisible, and certainly unremarkable. This will aid the play to be acted throughout in its proper manner—with the sprung line, gracefulness, and energy for which Mozart is so especially celebrated.

# ACT ONE

VIENNA

*Darkness.*

*Savage whispers fill the theater. We can distinguish nothing at first from this snakelike hissing save the word SALIERI! repeated here, there, and everywhere around the theater. Also, the barely distinguishable word ASSASSIN!*
*The whispers overlap and increase in volume, slashing the air with wicked intensity. Then the light grows upstage to reveal the silhouettes of* MEN AND WOMEN *dressed in the top hats and skirts of early nineteenth century*—CITIZENS OF VIENNA, *all crowded together in the Light Box, and uttering their scandal.*

WHISPERERS: *Salieri! . . . Salieri! . . . Salieri!*

[*Downstage in the wheelchair with his back to us, sits an* OLD MAN. *We can just see, as the light grows a little brighter, the top of his head encased in an old cap, and perhaps a shawl wrapped around his shoulders.*]

*Salieri! . . . Salieri! . . . Salieri!*

[TWO MIDDLE-AGED GENTLEMEN *hurry in from either side, also wearing the long cloaks and tall hats of the period. These are the* TWO VENTICELLI: *purveyors of fact, rumor, and gossip throughout the play. They speak rapidly—in this first appearance extremely rapidly—so that the scene has the air of a fast and dreadful overture. Sometimes they speak to each other; sometimes to us—but always with the urgency of men who have ever been first with the news.*]

VENTICELLO 1: I don't believe it.

VENTICELLO 2: I don't believe it.

V.1.: I don't believe it.

V.2.: I don't believe it.

WHISPERERS: *Salieri!*
V.1.: They say.
V.2.: I hear.
V.1.: I hear.
V.2.: They say.
V.1. & V.2.: *I don't believe it!*
WHISPERERS: *Salieri!*
V.1.: The whole city is talking.
V.2.: You hear it all over.
V.1.: The cafés.
V.2.: The Opera.
V.1.: The Prater.
V.2.: The gutter.
V.1.: They say even Metternich repeats it.
V.2.: They say even Beethoven, his old pupil.
V.1.: But why now?
V.2.: After so long?
V.1.: Thirty-two years!
V.1. & V.2.: *I don't believe it!*
WHISPERERS: SALIERI!
V.1.: They say he shouts it out all day!
V.2.: I hear he cries it out all night!
V.1.: Stays in his apartments.
V.2.: Never goes out.
V.1.: Not for a year now.
V.2.: Longer. Longer.
V.1.: Must be seventy.
V.2.: Older. Older.
V.1.: Antonio Salieri—
V.2.: The famous musician—
V.1.: Shouting it aloud!
V.2.: Crying it aloud!
V.1.: Impossible.
V.2.: Incredible!
V.1.: I don't believe it!
V.2.: I don't believe it!
WHISPERERS: SALIERI!
V.1.: I know who *started* the tale!
V.2.: *I* know who started the tale!

[*Two old men—one thin and dry, one very fat—walk onstage, from either side: Salieri's* VALET *and* PASTRY COOK.]

V.1. [*indicating him*]: The old man's Valet!

V.2. [*indicating him*]: The old man's Cook!

V.1.: The Valet hears him shouting!

V.2.: The Cook hears him crying!

V.1.: What a story!

V.2.: What a scandal!

[*The* VENTICELLI *move quickly upstage, one on either side, and each collects a silent informant.* VENTICELLO ONE *walks down eagerly with the* VALET; VENTICELLO TWO *walks down eagerly with the* COOK.]

V.1. [*to* VALET]: What does he say, your Master?

V.2. [*to* COOK]: What does he cry, the Kapellmeister?

V.1.: Alone in his house—

V.2.: All day and all night—

V.1.: What sins does he shout?

V.2.: The old fellow—

V.1.: The recluse—

V.2.: What horrors have you heard?

V.1. & V.2.: *Tell us! Tell us! Tell us at once! What does he cry? What does he cry? What does he cry?*

[VALET *and* COOK *gesture toward* SALIERI.]

SALIERI [*in a great cry*]: MOZART!

[*Silence.*]

V.1. [*whispering*]: Mozart!

V.2. [*whispering*]: Mozart!

SALIERI: *Perdonami, Mozart! Il tuo assassino ti chiede perdono!*

V.1. [*in disbelief*]: Pardon, Mozart!

V.2. [*in disbelief*]: Pardon your Assassin!

V.1. & V.2.: *God preserve us!*

SALIERI [moaning]: *Pietà, Mozart. Mozart, pietà!*

V.1.: Mercy, Mozart!

V.2.: Mozart, have mercy!

V.1.: He speaks in Italian when excited!

V.2.: German when not!

V.1.: *Perdonami, Mozart!*

V.2.: Pardon your Assassin!

[*The* VALET *and the* COOK *walk to either side of the stage, and stand still. Pause. The* VENTICELLI *cross themselves, deeply shocked.*]

V.1.: There was talk once before, you know.

V.2.: Thirty-two years ago.

V.1.: When Mozart was dying.

V.2.: He claimed he'd been poisoned.

V.1.: Some said he accused a man.

V.2.: Some said that man was Salieri.

V.1.: But no one believed it.

V.2.: They *knew* what he died of!

V.1.: Syphilis, surely.

V.2.: Like everybody else.

[*Pause.*]

V.1. [*slyly*]: But what if Mozart was right?

V.2.: If he really *was* murdered?

V.1.: And by him. Our First Kapellmeister!

V.2.: Antonio Salieri!

V.1.: It can't possibly be true.

V.2.: It's not actually credible.

V.1.: Because *why?*

V.2.: Because why?

V.1. & V.2.: *Why on earth would he do it?*

V.1.: And why confess *now?*

V.2.: After thirty-two years!

WHISPERERS: SALIERI!

SALIERI: *Mozart! Mozart! Perdonami! . . . Il tuo assassino ti chiede perdono!*

[*Pause. They look at him—then at each other.*]

V.1.: What do you think?

V.2.: What do you think?

V.1.: I don't believe it!

V.2.: *I* don't believe it!

V.1.: All the same . . .

V.2.: Is it just possible?

V.1. & V.2. [*whispering*]: *Did he do it after all?!*

WHISPERERS: SALIERI!

[*The* VENTICELLI *go off. The* VALET *and the* COOK *remain, on either side of the stage.* SALIERI *swivels his wheelchair around and stares at us. We see a man of seventy in an old stained dressing gown, shawled. He rises and squints at the Audience as if trying to see it.*]

* * * *

SALIERI'S APARTMENT

*November 1823. The small hours.*

SALIERI [*calling to Audience*]: *Vi Saluto! Ombri del Futuro! Antonio Salieri—a vostro servizio!*

[*A clock outside in the street strikes three.*]

I can almost see you in your ranks—waiting for your turn to live. Ghosts of the Future! Be visible. I beg you. Be visible. Come to this dusty old room—this time, the smallest hours of dark November, eighteen hundred and twenty-three—and be my Confessors! Will you not enter this place and stay with me till dawn? Just till dawn—till six o'clock!

WHISPERERS: *Salieri! . . . Salieri! . . .*

[*The curtains slowly descend on the* CITIZENS OF VIENNA. *Faint images of long windows are projected on the silk.*]

SALIERI: Can you hear them? Vienna is a City of Slander. Everyone tells tales here: even my servants. I keep only two now— [*indicating them*]—they've been with me ever since I came here, fifty years ago. The Keeper of the Razor: the Maker of the Cakes. One keeps me tidy, the other keeps me full. [*To them.*] Leave me, both of you! Tonight I do not go to bed at all!

[*They react in surprise.*]

Return here tomorrow morning at six precisely—to shave, to feed, your capricious master! [*He smiles at them both and claps his hands in gentle dismissal.*] *Via. Via, via, via! Grazie!*

[*They bow, bewildered, and leave the stage.*]

How surprised they are! . . . They'll be even more surprised tomorrow: indeed they will! [*He peers hard at the Audience, trying to see it.*] Oh, won't you appear? I need you—desperately! Those about to die implore you! What must I do to make you visible? Raise you up in the flesh to be my last, last audience? . . . Does it take an Invocation? That's how it's always done in Opera! Ah yes, of course: that's it. An *Invocation.* The only way. [*He rises.*] Let me try to conjure you *now*—Ghosts of the distant Future—so I can see you. [*He gets out of the wheelchair and over to the fortepiano. He stands at the instrument and begins to sing in a high cracked voice, interrupting himself at the end of each sentence with figurations on the keyboard in the manner of a* Recitativo Secco. *During this the House Lights slowly come up to illuminate the Audience.*]

[*Singing*]:

Ghosts of the Future!
Shades of Time to come!
So much more unavoidable than those of Time gone by!
Appear with what sympathy Incarnation may endow you!
Appear you—
The yet-to-be-born!
The yet-to-hate!

The yet-to-*kill!*
Appear—Posterity!

[*The light on the Audience reaches its maximum. It stays like this during all the following.*]

[*Speaking again.*] There! It worked. I can see you! That is the result of proper training. I was taught invocation by Chevalier Gluck, who was a true master at it. He had to be. In his day that is what people went to the Opera for: the raising of Gods, and Ghosts. . . . Nowadays, since Rossini became the rage, they prefer to watch the antics of hairdressers. [*Pause.*] *Scusate.* Invocation is an exhausting business. I need refreshment. [*He goes to the cake stand.*] It's a little repellent, I admit—but actually the first sin I have to confess to you is Gluttony. Sticky gluttony at that. Infantine—Italian gluttony! The truth is that all my life I have never been able to conquer a lust for the sweetmeats of Northern Italy where I was born. From the ages of three to seventy-three my entire career has been conducted to the taste of almonds sprinkled with sifted sugar. [*Lustfully.*] Milanese biscuits! Sienna macaroons! Snow dumplings with pistachio sauce! . . . Do not judge me too harshly for this. All men harbor patriotic feelings of some kind. . . . My parents were Italian subjects of the Austrian Empire, a Lombardy merchant and his Lombardy wife. Their notion of Place was the tiny town of Legnago—which I could not wait to leave. Their notion of God was a superior Hapsburg Emperor inhabiting a heaven only slightly farther off than Vienna. All they asked of Him was to keep them forever unnoticed—preserved in mediocrity. My own requirements were very different. [*Pause.*] I wanted Fame. Not to deceive you. I wanted to *blaze*, like a comet, across the firmament of Europe. Yet only in one especial way. Music. Absolute music! A note of music is either right or wrong—*absolutely!* Not even Time can alter that: music is God's art. [*Excited by the recollection.*] Already when I was ten, a spray of sounded notes would make me dizzy almost to falling! By twelve I was stumbling about under the poplar trees, humming my arias and anthems to the Lord! My one desire was to join all the composers who had celebrated God's glory through the long Italian past! . . . Every Sunday I saw Him in church, painted on the flaking wall. I don't mean Christ. The Christs of Lombardy are simpering sillies with lambkins on their sleeves. No: I mean an old candle-smoked God in a mulberry robe, staring at the world with dealer's eyes. Tradesmen had put him up there. Those eyes made bargains, real and irreversible. "You give me so—I'll give you so! No more. No less!" . . . One night I went to see

Him—and made a bargain with Him myself! I was a sober sixteen, filled with a desperate sense of right. I knelt before the God of Bargains, and I prayed with all my soul.

[*He kneels. The lights in the Audience go out slowly.*]

"*Signore,* let me be a Composer! Grant me sufficient fame to enjoy it. In return I will live with virtue. I will be chaste. I will strive to better the lot of my fellows. And I will honor You with much music all the days of my life!" As I said 'Amen,' I saw his eyes flare. [*As "God."*] "*Bene.* Go forth, Antonio. Serve Me and Mankind—and you will be blessed!" . . . "*Grazie!*" I called back. "I am Your Servant for life!"

[*He gets to his feet again.*]

The very next day, a family friend suddenly appeared—out of the blue—took me off to Vienna and paid for me to study music! [*Pause.*] Shortly afterward I met the Emperor of Austria, who favored me. *Clearly my bargain had been accepted!* [*Pause.*] The same year I left Italy, a young prodigy was touring Europe. A miraculous virtuoso aged ten years. Wolfgang Amadeus Mozart. [*Pause. He smiles at the Audience. Pause.*] And now—Gracious Ladies! Obliging Gentlemen! I present to you—for one performance only—my last composition, entitled *The Death of Mozart,—or Did I Do It?* . . . dedicated to Posterity on this—the last night of my life!

[*He bows deeply, undoing as he does so the buttons of his old dressing gown. When he straightens himself—divesting himself of this drab outer garment and his cap—he is a young man in the prime of life, wearing a sky-blue coat and the elegant decent clothes of a successful composer of the 1780s.*]

* * * *

TRANSFORMATION TO THE EIGHTEENTH CENTURY

[*Music sounds softly in the background: a serene piece for strings by Salieri.* SERVANTS *enter. One takes away the dressing gown and shawl; another places on the table a wig stand bearing a powdered wig; a third brings on a chair and places it at the left, upstage.*

*At the back the blue curtains rise and part to show the* EMPEROR JOSEPH II *and his* COURT *bathed in golden light, against a golden background of mirrors and an immense golden fireplace. His Majesty is seated, holding a rolled paper, listening to the music. Also listening are* COUNT VON STRACK; COUNT ORSINI-ROSENBERG; BARON VAN SWIETEN; *and an anonymous* PRIEST *dressed in a soutane. An old wigged* COURTIER *enters and takes his place at the keyboard:* KAPELLMEISTER BONNO. SALIERI *takes his wig from the stand.*]

SALIERI [*in a young man's voice; vigorous and confident*]: The place throughout is Vienna. The year—to begin with—1781. The age still that of the Enlightenment: that clear time before the guillotine fell in France and cut all our lives in half. I am thirty-one. Already a prolific composer to the Hapsburg Court. I own a respectable house and a respectable wife—Teresa.

[*Enter* TERESA: *a padded placid lady who seats herself uprightly in the upstage chair.*]

I do not mock her, I assure you. I required only one quality in a domestic companion: lack of fire. And in that omission Teresa was conspicuous. [*Ceremoniously he puts on his powdered wig.*] I also had a prize pupil: Katherina Cavalieri.

[KATHERINA *swirls on from the opposite side: a beautiful girl of twenty. The music becomes vocal: faintly, we hear a* SOPRANO *singing a concert aria. Like* TERESA'*s,* KATHERINA'*s part is mute, but as she enters she stands by the fortepiano and energetically mimes her rapturous singing. At the keyboard old* BONNO *accompanies her appreciatively.*]

She was a bubbling student with merry eyes and a sweet, eatable mouth. I was very much in love with Katherina—or at least in lust. But because of my vow to God, I had never laid a finger upon the girl—except occasionally to depress her diaphragm in the way of teaching her to sing. My ambition burned with an unquenchable flame. Its chief goal was the post of First Royal Kapellmeister, then held by Giuseppe Bonno—[*indicating him*]—seventy years old, and apparently immortal.

[*All on stage, save* SALIERI, *suddenly freeze. He speaks very directly to the Audience.*]

You, when you come, will be told that we musicians of the Eighteenth Century were no better than servants: the willing slaves of the well-to-do. This is quite true. It is also quite false. Yes, we were servants. But we were learned servants! And we used our learning to celebrate men's average lives!

[*A grander music sounds. The* EMPEROR *remains seated, but the other four men in the Light Box*—STRACK, ROSENBERG, VAN SWIETEN, *and the* PRIEST—*come slowly out on to the main stage and process imposingly down it, and around it, and up it again to return to their places. Only the* PRIEST *goes off, as do* TERESA *on her side and* KATHERINA *on hers.*]

[*Over this.*]: We took unremarkable men: usual bankers, run-of-the-mill priests, ordinary soldiers and statesmen and wives—and sacramentalized their mediocrity. We smoothed their noons with strings *divisi!* We pierced their nights with *chittarini!* We gave them processions for their strutting—serenades for their rutting—high horns for their hunting, and drums for their wars! Trumpets sounded when they entered the world, and trombones groaned when they left it! The savor of their days remains behind because of *Us,* our music still remembered while their politics are long forgotten.

[*The* EMPEROR *hands his rolled paper to* STRACK *and goes off. In the Light Box are left standing, like three icons,* ORSINI-ROSENBERG, *plump and supercilious, aged sixty;* VON STRACK, *stiff and proper, aged fifty-five;* VAN SWIETEN, *cultivated and serious, aged fifty. The lights go down on them a little.*]

Tell me, before you call us servants, who served whom? And who I wonder, in your generations, will immortalize *you?*

[*The* TWO VENTICELLI *come on quickly downstage, from either side. They are now bewigged also, and are dressed well, in the style of the late Eighteenth Century. Their manner is more confidential than before.*]

V.1. [*to* SALIERI]: Sir!

V.2. [*to* SALIERI]: Sir!

V.1.: Sir. Sir.

V.2.: Sir. Sir. Sir.

[SALIERI *bids them wait for a second.*]

SALIERI: I was the most successful young musician in the city of musicians. And now suddenly, without warning—

[*They approach him eagerly, from either side.*]

V.1.: Mozart!

V.2.: Mozart!

V.1. & V.2.: Mozart has come!

SALIERI: These are my *Venticelli.* My "Little Winds" as I call them. [*He gives each a coin from his pocket.*] The secret of successful living in a large city is always to know to the minute what is being done behind your back.

V.1.: He's left Salzburg.

V.2.: Means to give concerts.

V.1.: Asking for subscribers.

SALIERI: I'd known of him for years, of course. Tales of his prowess were told all over Europe.

V.2.: They say he wrote his first symphony at five.

V.2.: I hear his first concerto at four.

V.1.: A full opera at fourteen.

V.2.: *Mitridate, King of Pontus.*

SALIERI [*to them*]: How old is he now?

V.2.: Twenty-five.

SALIERI [*carefully*]: And how long is he remaining?

V.1.: He's not departing.

V.2.: He's here to stay.

[*The* VENTICELLI *glide off.*]

* * * *

THE ROYAL PALACE

[*Lights come up on the three stiff figures of* ROSENBERG, STRACK, *and* VAN SWIETEN, *standing upstage in the Light Box. The* CHAMBERLAIN *hands the paper he has received from the* EMPEROR *to the* DIRECTOR OF THE OPERA. SALIERI *remains downstage.*]

STRACK [*to* ROSENBERG]: You are required to commission a comic opera in German from Herr Mozart.

SALIERI [*to Audience*]: Johann Von Strack. Royal Chamberlain. A Court official to his collarbone.

ROSENBERG [*loftily*]: Why in German? Italian is the only possible language for opera!

SALIERI: Count Orsini-Rosenberg. Director of the Opera. Benevolent to all things Italian—especially myself.

STRACK [*stiffly*]: The idea of a National Opera is dear to His Majesty's heart. He desires to hear pieces in good plain German.

VAN SWIETEN: Yes, but why comic? It is not the function of music to be funny.

SALIERI: Baron Van Swieten. Prefect of the Imperial Library. Ardent Freemason. Yet to find anything funny. Known for his enthusiasm for old-fashioned music as "Lord Fugue."

VAN SWIETEN: I heard last week a remarkable *serious* opera from Mozart: *Idomeneo, King of Crete.*

ROSENBERG: I heard that too. A young fellow trying to impress beyond his abilities. Too much spice. Too many notes.

STRACK [*firmly, to* ROSENBERG]: Nevertheless, kindly convey the commission to him today.

ROSENBERG [*taking the paper reluctantly*]: I believe we are going to have trouble with this young man.

[ROSENBERG *leaves the Light Box and strolls down the stage to* SALIERI.]

He was a child prodigy. That always spells trouble. His father is Leopold Mozart, a pedantic Salzburg musician in the service of the Archbishop. He dragged the boy endlessly around Europe making him play the keyboard blindfold, with one finger, and that sort of thing. [*To* SALIERI.] All prodigies are hateful—*non è vero, Compositore?*

SALIERI: *Divengono sempre sterili con gli anni.*

ROSENBERG: *Precisamente. Precisamente.*

STRACK [*calling suspiciously*]: What are you saying?

ROSENBERG [*airily*]: Nothing, Herr Chamberlain! . . . *Niente, Signore Pomposo!* . . .

[*He strolls out.* STRACK *strides off, irritated.* VAN SWIETEN *now comes downstage.*]

VAN SWIETEN: We meet tomorrow, I believe, on your committee to devise pensions for old musicians.

SALIERI [*deferentially*]: It's most gracious of you to attend, Baron.

VAN SWIETEN: You're a worthy man, Salieri. You should join our Brotherhood of Masons. We would welcome you warmly.

SALIERI: I would be honored, Baron!

VAN SWIETEN: If you wished I could arrange initiation into my lodge.

SALIERI: That would be more than my due.

VAN SWIETEN: Nonsense. We embrace men of talent of all conditions. I may invite young Mozart also: dependent on the impression he makes.

SALIERI [*Bowing*]: Of course, Baron.

[VAN SWIETEN *goes out.*]

[*To Audience.*] Honor indeed. In those days almost every man of influence in Vienna was a Mason, and the Baron's lodge by far the most fashionable. As for young Mozart, I confess I was alarmed by his coming. He was praised altogether too much.

[*The* VENTICELLI *hurry in from either side.*]

V.1.: Such gaiety of spirit!

V.2.: Such ease of manner!

V.1.: Such natural charm!

SALIERI [*to the* VENTICELLI]: Really? Where does he live?

V.1.: Peter Platz.

V.2.: Number eleven.

V.1.: The landlady is Madame Weber.

V.2.: A real bitch.

V.1.: Takes in male lodgers, and has a tribe of daughters.

V.2.: Mozart was engaged to one of them before!

V.1.: A soprano called Aloysia.

V.2.: She jilted him.

V.1.: Now he's after another sister.

V.2.: Constanze!

SALIERI: You mean he was actually engaged to one sister and now wants to marry another?

V.1. & V.2. [*together*]: Exactly!

V.1.: Her mother's pushing marriage.

V.2.: His *father* isn't!

V.1.: Daddy is worried sick!

V.2.: Writes him every day from Salzburg!

SALIERI [*to them*]: I want to meet him.

V.1.: He'll be at the Baroness Waldstädten's tomorrow night.

SALIERI: *Grazie.*

V.2.: Some of his music is to be played.

SALIERI [*to both*]: *Restiamo in contatto.*

V.1. & V.2.: *Certamente, Signore!*

[*They go off.*]

SALIERI [*to Audience*]: So to the Baroness Waldstädten's I went. That night changed my life.

* * * *

THE LIBRARY OF THE BARONESS WALDSTÄDTEN

[*In the Light Box, two elegantly curtained windows surrounded by handsome subdued wallpaper.*

TWO SERVANTS *bring on a large table loaded with cakes and desserts. Two more carry on a grand high-backed wing chair, which they place ceremoniously downstage at the left.*]

SALIERI [*to Audience*]: I entered the library to take first a little refreshment. My generous hostess always put out the most delicious confections in that room whenever she knew I was coming. *Sorbetti—caramelli—*and most especially a miraculous *crema al mascarpone*—which is simply cream cheese mixed with granulated sugar and suffused with rum—that was totally irresistible!

[*He takes a little bowl of it from the cake stand and sits in the wing chair, facing out front. Thus seated, he is invisible to anyone entering from upstage.*]

SALIERI: I had just sat down in a high-backed chair to consume this paradisal dish—unobservable as it happened to anyone who might come in.

[*Offstage, noises are heard.*]

CONSTANZE [*off*]: Squeak! Squeak! Squeak!

[CONSTANZE *runs on from upstage: a pretty girl in her early twenties, full of high spirits. At this second she is pretending to be a mouse. She runs across the stage in her gay party dress, and hides under the fortepiano.*

*Suddenly a small, pallid, large-eyed man in a showy wig and a showy set of clothes runs in after her and freezes—center—as a cat would freeze, hunting a mouse. This is* WOLFGANG AMADEUS MOZART.

*As we get to know him through his next scenes, we discover several things about him: he is an extremely restless man, his hands and feet in almost continuous motion; his voice is light and high; and he is possessed of an unforgettable giggle—piercing and infantile.*]

MOZART: Miaouw!

CONSTANZE [*betraying where she is*]: Squeak!

MOZART: Miaouw! Miaouw! Miaouw!

*The composer drops on all fours and, wrinkling his face, begins spitting and stalking his prey. The mouse—giggling with excitement—breaks her cover and dashes across the floor. The cat pursues. Almost at the chair where* SALIERI *sits concealed, the mouse turns at bay. The cat stalks her—nearer and nearer—in its knee breeches and elaborate coat.*]

MOZART: I'm going to pounce-bounce! I'm going to scrunch-munch! I'm going to chew-poo my little mouse-wouse! I'm going to tear her to bits with my paws-claws!

CONSTANZE: No!

MOZART: Paws-claws! . . . Paws-claws! . . . Paws-claws! . . . AHH!

[*He falls on her. She screams.*]

SALIERI [*to Audience*]: Before I could rise, it had become difficult to do so.

MOZART: I'm going to bite you in half with my fangs-wangs! My little Stanzerl-wanzerl-banzerl!

[*She giggles delightedly, lying prone beneath him.*]

You're trembling! . . . I think you're frightened of puss-wuss! . . . I think you're scared to death! [*Intimately.*] I think you're going to shit yourself.

[*She squeals, but is not really shocked.*]

In a moment it's going to be on the floor!

CONSTANZE: Ssh! Someone'll hear you!

[*He imitates the noise of a fart.*]

Stop it, Wolferl! Ssh!

MOZART: Here it comes now! I can hear it *coming!* . . .Oh, what a melancholy note! Something's dropping from your boat!

[*Another fart noise, slower.* CONSTANZE *shrieks with amusement.*]

CONSTANZE: Stop it now! It's stupid! Really *stupid!*

[SALIERI *sits appalled.*]

MOZART: Hey—hey—what's Trazom!

CONSTANZE: What?

MOZART: T-R-A-Z-O-M. What's that mean?

CONSTANZE: How should *I* know?

MOZART: It's Mozart spelled backward—shit-wit! If you ever married me, you'd be Constanze Trazom.

CONSTANZE: No, I wouldn't.

MOZART: Yes, you would. Because I'd want everything backward once I was married. I'd want to lick my wife's arse instead of her face.

CONSTANZE: You're not going to lick anything at this rate. Your father's never going to give his consent to us.

[*The sense of fun deserts him instantly.*]

MOZART: And who cares about his consent?

CONSTANZE: *You* do. You care very much. You wouldn't do it without it.

MOZART: Wouldn't I?

CONSTANZE: No, you wouldn't. Because you're too scared of him. I know what he says about me. [*Solemn voice.*] "If you marry that dreadful girl, you'll end up lying on straw with beggars for children."

MOZART [*impulsively*]: Marry me!

CONSTANZE: Don't be silly.

MOZART: Marry me!

CONSTANZE: Are you serious?

MOZART [*defiantly*]: Yes! . . . Answer me this minute: yes or no! Say yes, then I can go home, climb into bed—shit over the mattress and shout "I *did* it!"

[*He rolls on top of her delightedly, uttering his high whinnying giggle. The* MAJOR-DOMO *of the house stalks in, upstage.*]

MAJOR-DOMO [*imperviously*]: Her Ladyship is ready to commence.

MOZART: Ah! . . . Yes! . . . Good! [*He picks himself up, embarrassed, and helps* CONSTANZE *to rise. With an attempt at dignity.*] Come, my dear. The music waits!

CONSTANZE [*suppressing giggles*]: Oh, by all means—Herr Trazom!

[*He takes her arm. They prance off together, followed by the disapproving* MAJOR-DOMO.]

SALIERI [*shaken, to Audience*]: And then, right away, the concert began. I heard it through the door—some serenade: at first only vaguely—too horrified to attend. But presently the sound insisted—a solemn adagio, in E flat.

[*The* Adagio from the Serenade for Thirteen Wind Instruments (K. 361) *begins to sound. Quietly and quite slowly, seated in the wing chair,* SALIERI *speaks over the music.*]

It started simply enough: just a pulse in the lowest registers—bassoons and basset horns—like a rusty squeezebox. It would have been comic except for the slowness, which gave it instead a sort of serenity. And then suddenly, high above it, sounded a single note on the oboe.

[*We hear it.*]

It hung there unwavering—piercing me through—till breath could hold it no longer, and a clarinet withdrew it out of me, and sweetened it into a phrase of such delight it had me trembling. The light flickered in the room. My eyes clouded! [*With ever-increasing emotion and vigor.*] The squeezebox groaned louder, and over it the higher instruments wailed and warbled, throwing lines of sound around me—long lines of pain around and through me—ah, the pain! Pain as I had never known it. I called up to my sharp old God *"What is this? . . . What?!"* But the squeezebox went on and on, and the pain cut deeper into my shaking head until suddenly I was running—

[*He bolts out of the chair and runs across the stage in a fever, to center. Behind him in the Light Box the Library fades into a street scene at night: small houses under a rent sky. The music continues, fainter, underneath.*]

—dashing through the side door, stumbling downstairs into the street, into the cold night, gasping for life. [*Calling up in agony.*] *"What?! What is this? Tell me, Signore!* What is this *pain?* What is this *need* in the sound? Forever unfulfillable yet fulfilling him who hears it, utterly! Is it *Your* need? . . . *Can it be Yours?* . . . [ *Pause.*] Dimly the music sounded from the salon above. Dimly the stars shone on the empty street. I was suddenly frightened. It seemed to me I had heard a voice of God—and that it issued from a creature whose own voice I had also heard—and it was the voice of an obscene child!

[*Light change. The street scene fades.*]

* * * *

SALIERI'S APARTMENT

[*It remains dark.*]

I ran home and buried my fear in work. More pupils—till there were thirty and forty. More Committees—toiling long hours to help musicians! More motets and anthems to God's glory. And at night I prayed for just one thing. [*He kneels desperately.*] "Let your voice enter *me!* Let *me* be your conduct! . . . *Let* me!" [*Pause. He rises.*] As for Mozart, I avoided meeting him—and sent out my Little Winds for whatever scores of his could be found.

[*The* VENTICELLI *come in with manuscripts.* SALIERI *sits at the fortepiano, and they show him the music alternately, as* SERVANTS *unobtrusively remove the Waldstädten table and wing chair.*]

V.1.: Six fortepiano sonatas composed in Munich.

SALIERI: Clever.

V.2.: Two in Mannheim.

SALIERI: They were all clever.

V.1.: A Parisian symphony.

SALIERI [*to Audience*]: And yet they seemed to me completely empty!

V.1.: A Divertimento in D.

SALIERI: The same.

V.2.: A Cassazione in G.

SALIERI: Conventional.

V.1.: A Grand Litany in E flat.

SALIERI: Even boring. [*To Audience.*] The productions of a precocious youngster—Leopold Mozart's swanky son—nothing more. That serenade was obviously an exception in his work: the sort of accident which might visit any composer on a lucky day!

[*The* VENTICELLI *go off with the music.*]

Had I in fact been simply taken by surprise that the filthy creature could write music at all? . . . Suddenly I felt immensely cheered! I would seek him out and welcome him myself to Vienna!

* * * *

THE ROYAL PALACE

[*Quick light change. The* EMPEROR *is revealed standing in bright light before the gilded mirrors and the fireplace, attended by* CHAMBERLAIN STRACK. *His Majesty is a dapper, cheerful figure, aged forty, largely pleased with himself and the world. Downstage, from opposite sides,* VAN SWIETEN *and* ROSENBERG *hurry on.*]

JOSEPH: Fêtes and fireworks, gentlemen! Mozart is here! He's waiting below!

[*All bow.*]

ALL: Majesty!

JOSEPH: *Je suis follement impatient!*

SALIERI [*to Audience*]: The Emperor Joseph the Second of Austria. Son of Maria Theresa. Brother of Marie Antoinette. Adorer of music—provided that it made no demands upon the royal brain. [*To the* EMPEROR, *deferentially.*] Majesty, I have written a little march in Mozart's honor. May I play it as he comes in?

JOSEPH: By all means, Court Composer. What a delightful idea! Have you met him yet?

SALIERI: Not yet, Majesty.

JOSEPH: Fêtes and fireworks, what fun! Strack, bring him up at once.

[STRACK *goes off. The* EMPEROR *comes on to the stage proper.*]

*Mon Dieu,* I wish we could have a competition! Mozart against some other virtuoso. Two keyboards in contest. Wouldn't that be fun, Baron?

VAN SWIETEN [*stiffly*]: Not to me, Majesty. In my view, musicians are not horses to be run against one another.

[*Slight pause.*]

JOSEPH: Ah. Well—there it is.

[STRACK *returns.*]

STRACK: Herr Mozart, Majesty.

JOSEPH: Ah! Splendid! . . . [*Conspiratorially he signs to* SALIERI, *who moves quickly to the fortepiano.*] Court Composer—*allons!* [*To* STRACK.] Admit him, please.

[*Instantly* SALIERI *sits at the instrument and strikes up his march on the keyboard. At the same moment* MOZART *struts in, wearing an extremely ornate surcoat, with dress sword. The* EMPEROR *stands downstage, center, his back to the Audience, and as* MOZART *approaches he signs to him to halt and listen. Bewildered,* MOZART *does so—becoming aware of* SALIERI *playing his "March of Welcome." It is an extremely banal piece, vaguely—but only vaguely— reminiscent of another march to become very famous later on. All stand frozen in attitudes of listening, until* SALIERI *comes to a finish. Applause.*]

JOSEPH [*to* SALIERI]: Charming . . . *Comme d'habitude!* [*He turns and extends his hand to be kissed.*] Mozart.

[MOZART *approaches and kneels extravagantly.*]

MOZART: Majesty! Your Majesty's humble slave! Let me kiss your royal hand a hundred thousand times!

[*He kisses it greedily, over and over, until its owner withdraws it in embarrassment.*]

JOSEPH: *Non, non, s'il vous plait!* A little less enthusiasm, I beg you. Come sir, *levez-vous!* [*He assists* MOZART *to rise.*] You will not recall it, but the last time we met you were also on the floor! My sister remembers it to this day. This young man—all of six years old, mind you—slipped on the floor at Schönbrunn—came a nasty purler on his little head. . . . Have I told you this before?

ROSENBERG [*hastily*]: No, Majesty!

STRACK [*hastily*]: No, Majesty!

SALIERI [*hastily*]: No, Majesty!

JOSEPH: Well, my sister Antoinette runs forward and picks him up herself. And do you know what he does? Jumps right into her arms—hoopla, just like that!—kisses her on both cheeks and says, "Will you marry me: yes or no?"

[*The* COURTIERS *laugh politely.* MOZART *emits his high-pitched giggle. The* EMPEROR *is clearly startled by it.*]

I do not mean to embarrass you, Herr Mozart. You know everyone here, surely?

MOZART: Yes, sire. [*Bowing elaborately to* ROSENBERG.] Herr Director! [To VAN SWIETEN.] Herr Prefect.

JOSEPH: But not, I think, our esteemed Court Composer! . . . A most serious omission! No one who cares for art can afford not to know Herr Salieri. He wrote that exquisite little "March of Welcome" for you.

SALIERI: It was a trifle, Majesty.

JOSEPH: Nevertheless . . .

MOZART [*to* SALIERI]: I'm overwhelmed, *Signore!*

JOSEPH: Ideas simply pour out of him—don't they, Strack?

STRACK: Endlessly, sire. [*As if tipping him.*] Well done, Salieri.

JOSEPH: Let it be my pleasure then to introduce you! Court Composer Salieri—Herr Mozart of Salzburg!

SALIERI [*sleekly, to* MOZART]: *Finalmente. Che gioia. Che diletto straordinario.*

[*He gives him a prim bow and presents the copy of his music to the* OTHER COMPOSER, *who accepts it with a flood of Italian.*]

MOZART: *Grazie Signore! Mille milione di benvenuti! Sono commosso! E un onore ecrezionale incontrae! Compositore brillante e famosissimo!* [*He makes an elaborate and showy bow in return.*]

SALIERI [*dryly*]: *Grazie.*

JOSEPH: Tell me, Mozart, have you received our Commission for the opera?

MOZART: Indeed I have, Majesty! I am so grateful I can hardly speak! . . . I swear to you that you will have the best—the most perfect entertainment ever offered a monarch. I've already found a libretto.

ROSENBERG [*startled*]: Have you? I didn't hear of this!

MOZART: Forgive me, Herr Director, I entirely omitted to tell you.

ROSENBERG: May I ask why?

MOZART: It didn't seem very important.

ROSENBERG: Not important?

MOZART: Not really, no.

ROSENBERG [*irritated*]: It is important to *me*, Herr Mozart.

MOZART [*embarrassed*]: Yes, I see that. Of course.

ROSENBERG: And who, pray, is it by?

MOZART: Stephanie.

ROSENBERG: A most unpleasant man.

MOZART: But a brilliant writer.

ROSENBERG: Do you think?

MOZART: The story is really amusing, Majesty. The whole plot is set in a—[*he giggles*]—in a . . . It's set in a . . .

JOSEPH [*eagerly*]: Where? Where is it set?

MOZART: It's—it's—rather saucy, Majesty!

JOSEPH: Yes, yes! Where?

MOZART: Well, it's actually set in a *seraglio*.

JOSEPH: A what?

MOZART: A pasha's harem. [*He giggles wildly.*]

ROSENBERG: And you imagine that is a suitable subject for performance at a national theater?

MOZART [*in a panic*]: Yes! No! Yes, I mean yes, yes, I do. Why not? It's very funny, it's amusing. . . . On my honor—Majesty—there's nothing offensive in it. Nothing offensive in the world. It's full of proper German virtues, I swear it! . . .

SALIERI [*blandly*]: *Scusate, Signore*, but what are those? Being a foreigner I'm not sure.

JOSEPH: You are being *cattivo*, Court Composer.

SALIERI: Not at all, Majesty.

JOSEPH: Come then, Mozart. Name us a proper German virtue!

MOZART: Love, sire. I have yet to see that expressed in any opera.

VAN SWIETEN: Well answered, Mozart.

SALIERI [*smiling*]: *Scusate*. I was under the impression one rarely saw anything *else* expressed in opera.

MOZART: I mean manly love, *Signore*. Not male sopranos screeching. Or stupid couples rolling their eyes. All that absurd Italian rubbish. [*Pause. Tension.*] I mean the real thing.

JOSEPH: And do you know the real thing yourself, Herr Mozart?

MOZART: Under your pardon, I think I do, Majesty. [*He gives a short giggle. The Courtiers look at each other.*]

JOSEPH: Bravo. When do you think it will be done?

MOZART: The first act is already finished.

JOSEPH: But it can't be more than two weeks since you started!

MOZART: Composing is not hard when you have the right audience to please, sire.

VAN SWIETEN: A charming reply, Majesty.

JOSEPH: Indeed, Baron. Fetes and fireworks! I see we are going to have fetes and fireworks! *Au revoir, Monsieur Mozart. Soyez bienvenu à la court.*

MOZART [*with expert rapidity*]: *Majesté!—je suis comblé d'honneur d'être accepté dans la maison du Père de tous les musiciens! Servir un monarque aussi plein de discernement que votre Majesté, c'est un honneur qui dépasse le sommet de mes dûs!*

[*A pause. The* EMPEROR *is taken aback by this flood of French.*]

JOSEPH: Ah. Well—there it is. I'll leave you gentlemen to get better acquainted.

SALIERI: Good day, Majesty.

MOZART: *Votre Majesté.*

[*They both bow.* JOSEPH *goes out.*]

ROSENBERG: Good day to you.

STRACK: Good day.

[*They follow the King.*]

VAN SWIETEN [*warmly shaking his hand*]: Welcome, Mozart. I shall see much more of you. Depend on it!

MOZART: Thank you.

[*He bows. The* BARON *goes.* MOZART *and* SALIERI *are left alone.*]

SALIERI: *Bene.*

MOZART: *Bene.*

SALIERI: I too wish you success with your opera.

MOZART: I'll have it. It's going to be superb. I must tell you I have already found the most excellent singer for the leading part.

SALIERI: Oh. Who is that?

MOZART: Her name is Cavalieri. Katherina Cavalieri. She's really German, but she thinks it will advance her career if she sports an Italian name.

SALIERI: She's quite right. It was my idea. She is in fact my prize pupil. Actually, she's a very innocent child. Silly in the way of young singers—but, you know, she's only twenty.

[*Without emphasis* MOZART *freezes his movements and* SALIERI *takes one easy step forward to make a fluent aside.*]

[*To Audience.*] I had kept my hands off Katherina. Yes! But, I could not bear to think of anyone else's upon her—least of all his!

MOZART [*unfreezing*]: You're a good fellow, Salieri! And that's a jolly little thing you wrote for me.

SALIERI: It was my pleasure.

MOZART: Let's see if I can remember it. May I?

SALIERI: By all means. It's yours.

MOZART: *Grazie, Signore.*

[MOZART *tosses the manuscript on to the lid of the fortepiano where he cannot see it, sits at the instrument, and plays* SALIERI*'s "March of Welcome"* *perfectly from memory—at first slowly, recalling it—but on the reprise of the tune, very much faster.*]

The rest is just the same, isn't it? [*He finishes it with insolent speed.*]

SALIERI: You have a remarkable memory.

MOZART [*delighted with himself*]: *Grazie ancora, Signore!* [*He plays the opening seven bars again, but this time stops on the interval of the fourth, and sounds it again with displeasure.*] It doesn't really *work*, that fourth—does it? . . . Let's try the third above . . . [*He does so—and smiles happily.*] Ah yes! . . . Better! . . .

[*He repeats the new interval, leading up to it smartly with the well-known military-trumpet arpeggio which characterizes the celebrated march from* The Marriage of Figaro, "*Non più andrai.*" *Then, using the interval—tentatively—delicately—one note at a time, in the treble—he steals into the famous tune itself.*

*On and on he plays, improvising happily what is virtually the March we know now, laughing gleefully each time he comes to the amended interval of a third.* SALIERI *watches him with an answering smile painted on his face.* MOZART'*s playing grows more and more exhibitionistic—revealing to the Audience the formidable virtuoso he is. The whole time he himself remains totally oblivious to the offense he is giving. Finally he finishes the march with a series of triumphant flourishes and chords!*

*An ominous pause.*]

SALIERI: *Scusate.* I must go.

MOZART: Really? [*Springing up and indicating the keyboard.*] Why don't *you* try a variation?

SALIERI: Thank you, but I must attend on the Emperor.

MOZART: Ah.

SALIERI: It has been delightful to meet you.

MOZART: For me too! . . . And thanks for the march!

[MOZART *picks up the manuscript from the top of the fortepiano and marches happily offstage. A slight pause.* SALIERI *moves toward the Audience. The lights go down around him.*]

SALIERI [*to Audience*]: Was it then—so early—that I began to have thoughts of murder? . . . Of course not: at least not in life. In art it was a different matter. I decided I would compose a huge tragic opera: something to astonish the world!—and I knew my theme. I would set the Legend of Danaius, who, for a monstrous crime, was chained to a rock for eternity—his head repeatedly struck by lightning! Wickedly I saw Mozart in that position. In reality the man was in no danger from me at all. . . . Not yet.

* * * *

THE FIRST PERFORMANCE OF THE ABDUCTION FROM THE SERAGLIO

[*The light changes, and the stage instantly turns into an Eighteenth-Century theater. The backdrop projection shows a line of softly gleaming chandeliers. The* SERVANTS *bring in chairs and benches. Upon them, facing the Audience and regarding it as if watching an opera, sit the* EMPEROR JOSEPH, STRACK, ROSENBERG, *and* VAN SWIETEN.

*Next to them:* KAPELLMEISTER BONNO *and* TERESA SALIERI. *A little behind them:* CONSTANZE. *Behind her:* CITIZENS OF VIENNA.]

SALIERI: The first performance of *The Abduction from the Seraglio.* The German expression of manly love.

[MOZART *comes on briskly, wearing a gaudy new coat and a new powdered wig. He struts quickly to the fortepiano, sits at it, and mimes conducting.* SALIERI *sits nearby, next to his wife, and watches* MOZART *intently.*]

SALIERI: He himself contrived to wear for the occasion an even more vulgar coat than usual. As for the music, it matched the coat completely. For my dear pupil Katherina Cavalieri he had written quite simply the showiest aria I'd ever heard.

[*Faintly we hear the whizzing scale passages for* SOPRANO *which end the aria "Marten Aller Arten."*]

Ten minutes of scales and ornaments, amounting in sum to a vast emptiness. So ridiculous was the piece in fact—so much what might be demanded by a foolish young soprano—that I knew precisely what Mozart must have demanded in return for it.

[*The final orchestral chords of the aria. Silence. No one moves.*]

Although engaged to be married, *he'd had her!* I knew that beyond any doubt. [*Bluntly.*] The creature had had my darling girl.

[*Loudly we hear the brilliant Turkish Finale of* Seraglio. *Great applause from those watching.* MOZART *jumps to his feet and acknowledges it. The* EMPEROR *rises—as do all—and gestures graciously to the "stage" in invitation.* KATHERINA CAVALIERI *runs on in her costume, all plumes and flounces, to renewed cheering and clapping. She curtsies to the* EMPEROR*—is kissed by* SALIERI*—presented to his wife—curtsies again to* MOZART *and, flushed with triumph, moves to one side.*

*In the ensuing brief silence* CONSTANZE *rushes down from the back, wildly excited. She flings herself on* MOZART, *not even noticing the* EMPEROR.]

CONSTANZE: Oh, well done, lovey! . . . Well done, pussy-wussy! . . .

[MOZART *indicates the proximity of His Majesty.*]

CONSTANZE: Oh! . . . 'Scuse *me!* [*She curtsies in embarrassment.*]

MOZART: Majesty, may I present my fiancée, Fräulein Weber.

JOSEPH: *Enchanté, Fräulein.*

CONSTANZE: Your Majesty!

MOZART: Constanze is a singer herself.

JOSEPH: Indeed?

CONSTANZE [*embarrassed*]: I'm not at all, Majesty. Don't be silly, Wolfgang!

JOSEPH: So, Mozart—a good effort. Decidedly that. A good effort.

MOZART: Did you really like it, sire?

JOSEPH: I thought it was most interesting. Yes, indeed. A trifle—how shall one say? [*To* ROSENBERG.] How shall one say, Director?

ROSENBERG [*subserviently*]: Too many notes, Your Majesty?

JOSEPH: Very well put. Too many notes.

MOZART: I don't understand.

JOSEPH: My dear fellow, don't take it too hard. There are in fact only so many notes the ear can hear in the course of an evening. I think I'm right in saying that, aren't I, Court Composer?

SALIERI [*uncomfortably*]: Well, yes, I would say yes, on the whole, yes, Majesty.

JOSEPH: There you are. It's clever. It's German. It's quality work. And there are simply too many notes. Do you see?

MOZART: There are just as many notes, Majesty, neither more nor less, as are required.

[*Pause.*]

JOSEPH: Ahh. . . . Well, there it is. [*He goes off abruptly, followed by* ROSENBERG *and* STRACK.]

MOZART [*nervous*]: Is he angry?

SALIERI: Not at all. He respects you for your views.

MOZART [*nervously*]: I hope so. . . . What did you think yourself, sir? Did you care for the piece at all?

SALIERI: Yes, of course, Mozart—at its best it is truly charming.

MOZART: And at other times?

SALIERI [*smoothly*]: Well, just occasionally at other times—in Katherina's aria, for example—it was a little excessive.

MOZART: Katherina is an excessive girl. In fact she's insatiable.

SALIERI: All the same, as my revered teacher the Chevalier Gluck used to say to me—one must avoid music that smells of music.

MOZART: What does that mean?

SALIERI: Music which makes one aware too much of the virtuosity of the composer.

MOZART: Gluck is absurd.

SALIERI: What do you say?

MOZART: He's talked all his life about modernizing opera, but creates people so lofty they sound as though they shit marble.

[CONSTANZE *gives a little scream of shock.*]

CONSTANZE: Oh, 'scuse me! . . .

MOZART [*breaking out*]: No, but it's too much! Gluck says! Gluck says! Chevalier Gluck! . . .What's Chevalier? I'm a Chevalier. The Pope made me a Chevalier when I was still wetting my bed.

CONSTANZE: Wolferl!

MOZART: Anyway, it's ridiculous. Only stupid farts use titles.

SALIERI [*blandly*]: Such as Court Composer?

MOZART: What? . . . (Realizing) Ah. Oh. Ha. Ha. Well! . . . My father's right again. He always tells me I should padlock my mouth. . . . Actually, I shouldn't speak at all!

SALIERI [*soothingly*]: Nonsense. I'm just being what the Emperor would call *cattivo*. Won't you introduce me to your charming fiancée?

MOZART: Oh, of course! Constanze, this is Herr *Court Composer* Salieri. Fräulein Weber.

SALIERI [*bowing*]: Delighted, *cara Fräulein.*

CONSTANZE [*bobbing*]: How do you do, Excellency?

SALIERI: You are the sister of Aloysia Weber, the soprano, are you not?

CONSTANZE: I am, Excellency.

SALIERI: A beauty herself, but you exceed her by far, if I may observe so.

CONSTANZE [*flattered*]: Oh, thank you!

SALIERI: May I ask when you marry?

MOZART [*nervously*]: We have to secure my father's consent. He's an excellent man—a wonderful man—but in some ways a little stubborn.

SALIERI: Excuse me, but how old are you?

MOZART: Twenty-six.

SALIERI: Then your father's consent is scarcely indispensable.

CONSTANZE [*to* MOZART]: You see?

MOZART [*uncomfortably*]: Well, no, it's not *indispensable*—of course not! . . .

SALIERI: My advice to you is to marry and be happy. You have found—it's quite obvious—*un tesoro raro!*

CONSTANZE: Ta very much.

SALIERI [*Kisses* CONSTANZE'*s hand. She is delighted*]: Good night to you both.

CONSTANZE: Good night, Excellency!

MOZART: Good night, sir. And thank you . . . Come, Stanzerl.

[*They depart delightedly. He watches them go.*]

SALIERI [*to Audience*]: As I watched her walk away on the arm of the Creature, I felt the lightning thought strike—"Have her! Her for Katherina!" . . . Abomination! . . . Never in my life had I entertained a notion so sinful!

[*Light change: the Eighteenth Century fades. The* VENTICELLI *come on merrily, as if from some celebration.* ONE *holds a bottle; the* OTHER *a glass.*]

V.1.: They're married.

SALIERI [*to them*]: What?

V.2.: Mozart and Weber—married!

SALIERI: Really?

V.1.: His father will be furious!

V.2.: They didn't even wait for his consent!

SALIERI: Have they set up house?

V.1.: Wipplingerstrasse.

V.2.: Number twelve.

V.1.: Not bad.

V.2.: Considering they've no money.

SALIERI: Is that really true?

V.1.: He's wildly extravagant.

V.2.: Lives way beyond his means.

SALIERI: But he has pupils.

V.1.: Only three.

SALIERI [*to them*]: Why so few?

V.1.: He's embarrassing.

V.2.: Makes scenes.

V.1.: Makes enemies.

V.2.: Even Strack, whom he cultivates.

SALIERI: Chamberlain Strack?

V.1.: Only last night.

V.2.: At Kapellmeister Bonno's.

* * * *

BONNO'S HOUSE

[*Instant light change.* MOZART *comes in with* STRACK. *He is high on wine, and holding a glass. The* VENTICELLI *join the scene, but still talk out of it to* SALIERI. *One of them fills* MOZART'*s glass.*]

MOZART: Seven months in this city and not one job! I'm not to be tried again, is that it?

STRACK: Of course not.

MOZART: I know what goes on, and so do you. Vienna is completely in the hands of foreigners. Worthless wops like *Kapellmeister Bonno!*

STRACK: Please! You're in the man's house!

MOZART: Court Composer *Salieri!*

STRACK: Hush!

MOZART: Did you see his last opera, *The Chimney Sweep?* . . . Did you?

STRACK: Of course I did.

MOZART: Dogshit. . . . *Dry* dogshit.

STRACK [*outraged*]: I beg your pardon!

[MOZART *goes to the fortepiano and thumps on it monotonously.*]

MOZART [*singing*]: Pom-pom, pom-pom, pom-pom, pom-pom! Tonic and dominant, tonic and dominant from here to resurrection! Not one interesting modulation all night. Salieri is a musical idiot!

STRACK: Please!

V.1. [*to* SALIERI]: He'd had too much to drink.

V.2.: He often has.

MOZART: Why are Italians so terrified by the slightest complexity in music? Show them one chromatic passage and they *faint!* . . . "Oh, how sick!" "How morbid!" [*Falsetto.*] *Moroso!* . . . *Nervoso!* . . . *Ohimè!* . . . No wonder the music at this Court is so dreary.

STRACK: Lower your voice.

MOZART: Lower your breeches! . . . That's just a joke—just a joke!

[*Unobserved by him* COUNT ROSENBERG *has entered upstage and is suddenly standing between the* VENTICELLI, *listening. He wears a waistcoat of bright green silk, and an expression of supercilious interest.* MOZART *sees him. A pause.*]

[*Pleasantly, to* ROSENBERG.] You look like a toad. . . . I mean you're goggling like a toad.

ROSENBERG [*blandly*]: You would do best to retire tonight, for your own sake.

MOZART: Salieri has fifty pupils. I have three. How am I to live? I'm a married man now! . . . Of course I realize you don't concern yourselves with *money* in these exalted circles. All the same, did you know behind his back His Majesty is known as Kaiser Keep It? [*He giggles wildly.*]

STRACK: *Mozart!*

[*He stops.*]

MOZART: I shouldn't have said that, should I? Forgive me. It was just a joke. Another joke! . . . I can't help myself! . . . We're all friends here, aren't we?

[STRACK *and* ROSENBERG *glare at him. Then* STRACK *leaves abruptly, much offended.*]

MOZART: What's wrong with him?

ROSENBERG: Good night.

[*He turns to go.*]

MOZART: No, no, no—please! [*He grabs the* DIRECTOR*'s arm.*] Your hand please, first!

[*Unwillingly* ROSENBERG *gives him his hand.* MOZART *kisses it.*]

[*Humbly.*] Give me a post, sir.

ROSENBERG: That is not in my power, Mozart.

MOZART: The Princess Elizabeth is looking for an instructor. One word from you could secure it for me.

ROSENBERG: I regret that is solely in the recommendation of Court Composer Salieri.

[*He disengages himself.*]

MOZART: Do you know I am better than any musician in Vienna? . . .Do you?

[ROSENBERG *follows* STRACK *out of the room. The* VENTICELLI *are left looking at* MOZART *smiling maliciously.*]

The devil take the lot of them! . . . Nothing but cabals and cliques everywhere you look! What's here for an honest German fellow?

[*He becomes aware of the* VENTICELLI *and makes an attempt at dignity. Negligently he sings to the tune of* La ci darem.]

"The girl who doesn't like me—
The girl who doesn't like me—
The girl who doesn't like me—
Can lick my arse instead!"

[*He struts offstage, holding his head high as the lights go out.* SALIERI *watches him depart.*]

SALIERI: Barely one month later, that thought of revenge became more than thought.

* * * *

THE WALDSTÄDTEN LIBRARY

[*Two simultaneous shouts bring up the lights again. Against the handsome wallpaper stand three masked figures:* CONSTANZE, *flanked on either side by the* VENTICELLI. *All three are guests at a party, and are playing a game of forfeits.* TWO SERVANTS *stand frozen, holding the large wing chair between them. Two more hold the big table of sweetmeats.*]

V.1.: Forfeit! . . . Forfeit! . . .

V.2.: Forfeit, Stanzerl! You've got to forfeit!

CONSTANZE: I won't.

V.1.: You have to.

V.2.: It's the game.

[*The* SERVANTS *unfreeze and set down the furniture.* SALIERI *moves to the wing chair and sits.*]

SALIERI [*to Audience*]: Once again—believe it or not—I was in the same concealing chair in the Baroness's library—[*taking a cup from the little table*]—and consuming the same delicious dessert.

V.1.: You lost—now there's the penalty!

SALIERI [*to Audience*]: A party celebrating the New Year's Eve. I was on my own—my dear spouse Teresa visiting her parents in Italy.

CONSTANZE: Well, *what?* . . . What is it?

[VENTICELLO ONE *snatches up an old-fashioned round ruler from off the fortepiano.*]

V.1.: I want to measure your calves.

CONSTANZE: Oooo!

V.1.: Well?

CONSTANZE: Definitely not! You cheeky bugger!

V.1.: Now come on!

V.2.: You've got to let him, Stanzerl. All's fair in love and forfeits.

CONSTANZE: No, it isn't—so you can both buzz off!

V.1.: If you don't let me, you won't be allowed to play again.

CONSTANZE: Well, choose something else.

V.1.: I've chosen that. Now get up on the table. Quick, quick! *Allez-oop!* [*Gleefully he shifts the plates of sweetmeats from the table.*]

CONSTANZE: Quick, then! . . . Before anyone sees!

[*The* TWO *masked men lift the shrieking masked girl up on to the table.*]

V.1.: Hold her, Friedrich.

CONSTANZE: I don't have to be held, thank you!

V.2.: Yes, you do: that's part of the penalty.

[*He holds her ankles firmly, while* VENTICELLO ONE *thrusts the ruler under her skirts and measures her legs. Excitedly* SALIERI *reverses his position so that he can kneel in the wing chair, and watch.* CONSTANZE *giggles delightedly, then becomes outraged—or pretends to be.*]

CONSTANZE: Stop it! . . . Stop that! That's quite enough of that! [*She bends down and tries to slap him.*]

V.1.: Seventeen inches—knee to ankle!

V.2.: Let me do it! You hold her.

CONSTANZE: That's not fair!

V.2.: Yes, it is. You lost to me too.

CONSTANZE: It's been done now! Let me *down!*

V.2.: Hold her, Karl.

CONSTANZE: No! . . .

[VENTICELLO ONE *holds her ankles.* VENTICELLO TWO *thrusts his head entirely under her skirts. She squeals.*]

No—stop it . . . *No!* . . .

[*In the middle of this undignified scene* MOZART *comes rushing on—also masked.*]

MOZART [*outraged*]: Constanze!

[*They freeze.* SALIERI *ducks back down and sits hidden in the chair.*]

Gentlemen—if you please.

CONSTANZE: It's only a game, Wolferl! . . .

V.1.: We meant no harm, 'pon my word.

MOZART [*stiffly*]: Come down off that table, please.

[*They hand her down.*]

Thank you. We'll see you later.

V.2.: Now look, Mozart, don't be pompous—

MOZART: Please excuse us now.

[*They go. The little man is very angry. He tears off his mask.*]

[*to* CONSTANZE.] Do you realize what you've done?

CONSTANZE: No, what? . . .[*Flustered, she removes her mask and busies herself restoring the plates of sweetmeats to the table.*]

MOZART: Just lost your reputation, that's all! You're now a loose girl.

CONSTANZE: Don't be so stupid.

MOZART: You are a married woman, for God's sake!

CONSTANZE: And what of it?

MOZART: A young wife does not allow her legs to be handled in public. Couldn't you at least have measured your own ugly legs?

CONSTANZE: *What?* Of course they're not as good as Aloysia's! My sister has perfect legs, we all know that!

MOZART [*raising his voice*]: Do you know what you've done?! . . . You've shamed me—that's all! *Shamed* me!

CONSTANZE: Oh, don't be so ridiculous!

MOZART: Shamed me—in front of *them!*

CONSTANZE [*suddenly furious*]: *You*—shamed *you?* . . . That's a laugh! If there's any shame around, lovey, it's *mine!*

MOZART: What do you mean?

CONSTANZE: You've only had every pupil who ever came to you.

MOZART: That's not true.

CONSTANZE: Every single female pupil!

MOZART: Name them! *Name them!*

CONSTANZE: The Aurnhammer girl! The Rumbeck girl! Katherina Cavalieri—that sly little whore! *She* wasn't even your pupil—she was Salieri's.

Which actually, my dear, may be why he has hundreds and you have none! He doesn't drag them into bed!

MOZART: Of course he doesn't! He can't get it up, that's why! . . . Have you heard his music? That's the sound of someone who *can't get it up!* At least *I* can do that!

CONSTANZE: I'm sick of you!

MOZART [*shouting*]: No one ever said I couldn't do *that!*

CONSTANZE [*bursting into tears*]: I don't give a fart! I hate you! I hate you forever and ever—I hate you!

[*A tiny pause. She weeps.*]

MOZART [*helplessly*]: Oh, Stanzerl, don't cry. Please don't cry . . . I can't bear it when you cry. I just didn't want you to look cheap in people's eyes, that's all. Here! [*He snatches up the ruler.*] Beat me. Beat me . . . I'm your slave. Stanzi marini! . . . Stanzi marini bini gini! . . . I'll just stand here like a little lamb and bear your strokes. Here. Do it. . . . *Batti.*

CONSTANZE: No.

MOZART: *Batti, batti. Mio tesoro!*

CONSTANZE: No!

MOZART: Stanzerly-wanzerly-piggly-poo!

CONSTANZE: Stop it.

MOZART: Stanzy-wanzy had a fit. Shit her stays and made them split!

[*She giggles despite herself.*]

CONSTANZE: Stop it.

MOZART: When they took away her skirt, Stanzy-wanzy ate the dirt!

CONSTANZE: Stop it now! [*She snatches the ruler and gives him a whack with it. He yowls playfully.*]

MOZART: Ooooo! Oooo! Oooo! Do it again! Do it again! I cast myself at your stinking feet, Madonna!

[*He does so. She whacks him some more as he crouches, but always lightly, scarcely looking at him, divided between tears and laughter.* MOZART *drums his feet with pleasure.*]

MOZART: Ow! Ow! Ow!

[*And then suddenly* SALIERI, *unable to bear another second, cries out involuntarily.*]

SALIERI: *Ah!!!*

[*The young couple freezes.* SALIERI*—discovered—hastily converts his noise of disgust into a yawn, and stretches as if waking up from a nap. He peers out of the wing chair.*]

Good evening.

CONSTANZE [*embarrassed*]: Excellency . . .

MOZART: How long have you been there?

SALIERI: I was asleep until a second ago. Are you two quarreling?

MOZART: No, of course not.

CONSTANZE: Yes, we are. He's been very irritating.

SALIERI [*rising*]: *Caro* Herr, tonight is the time for New Year resolutions. Irritating lovely ladies cannot surely be one of yours. May I suggest you bring us each a sorbetto from the dining room?

MOZART: But why don't we all go to the table?

CONSTANZE: Herr Salieri is quite right. Bring them here—it'll be your punishment.

MOZART: Stanzi!

SALIERI: Come now, I can keep your wife company. There cannot be a better peace offering than a sorbetto of almonds.

CONSTANZE: I prefer tangerine.

SALIERI: Very well, tangerine. [*Greedily.*] But if you could possibly manage almond for me, I'd be deeply obliged. . . . So the New Year can begin coolly for all three of us.

[*A pause.* MOZART *hesitates—and then bows.*]

MOZART: I'm honored, *Signore,* of course. And then I'll play you at billiards. What do you say?

SALIERI: I'm afraid I don't play.

MOZART [*with surprise*]: You don't?

CONSTANZE: Wolferl would rather play at billiards than anything. He's very good at it.

MOZART: I'm the best! I may nod occasionally at composing, but at billiards—never!

SALIERI: A virtuoso of the cue.

MOZART: Exactly! It's a virtuoso's game! . . . [*He snatches up the ruler and treats it as if it were a cue.*] I think I shall write a Grand Fantasia for Billiard Balls! *Trills. Accacciaturas!* Whole *arpeggios* in ivory! Then I'll play it myself in public! . . . It'll have to be me because none of those Italian charlatans like Clementi will be able to get his fingers round the cue! *Scusate, Signore!*

[*He gives a swanky flourish of the hand and struts off. A pause.*]

CONSTANZE: He's a love, really.

SALIERI: And lucky, too, in you. You are, if I may say so, an astonishing creature.

CONSTANZE: Me? . . . Ta very much.

SALIERI: On the other hand, your husband does not appear to be so thriving.

CONSTANZE [*seizing her opportunity*]: We're desperate, sir.

SALIERI: What?

CONSTANZE: We've no money and no prospects of any. That's the truth.

SALIERI: I don't understand. He gives many public concerts.

CONSTANZE: They don't pay enough. What he needs is pupils. Illustrious pupils. His father calls us spendthrifts, but that's unfair. I manage as well as anyone could. There's simply not enough. Don't tell him I talked to you, please!

SALIERI [*intimately*]: This is solely between us. How can I help?

CONSTANZE: My husband needs security, sir. If only he could find regular employment, everything would be all right. Is there nothing at Court?

SALIERI: Not at the moment.

CONSTANZE [*harder*]: The Princess Elizabeth needs a tutor.

SALIERI: Really? I hadn't heard.

CONSTANZE: One word from you and the post would be his. Other pupils would follow at once.

SALIERI [*looking off*]: He's coming back.

CONSTANZE: Please . . . please, Excellency. You can't imagine what a difference it would make.

SALIERI: We can't speak of it now.

CONSTANZE: When then? Oh, please!

SALIERI: Can you come and see me tomorrow? Alone?

CONSTANZE: I can't do that.

SALIERI: I'm a married man.

CONSTANZE: All the same.

SALIERI: When does he work?

CONSTANZE: Afternoons.

SALIERI: Then come at three.

CONSTANZE: I can't possibly!

SALIERI: Yes or no? In his interests?

[*A pause. She hesitates—opens her mouth—then smiles and abruptly runs off.*]

[*To Audience.*] So I'd done it. Spoken aloud. Invited her! What of that vow made in church? Fidelity . . . virtue . . . all of that? . . . What did she think of me—this careful Italian? Sincere friend or hopeful seducer? . . . Would she come? . . . I had no idea!

[SERVANTS *remove the Waldstädten furniture. Others replace it with two small gilded chairs, center, quite close together. Others again surreptitiously bring in the old dressing gown which* SALIERI *discarded before Scene Three, placing them on the fortepiano.*]

* * * *

SALIERI'S SALON

[*On the curtains are thrown again projections of long windows.*]

SALIERI: If she did, how would I behave? I had no idea of that either. . . . Next afternoon I waited in a fever! Was I actually going to seduce a young wife of two months' standing? . . . Part of me—much of me—wanted it, badly. Badly! yes, badly was the word! . . .

[*The clock strikes three. On the first stroke the bell sounds. He rises excitedly.*]

There she was! On the stroke! She'd come. . . . She'd *come!*

[*Enter from the right the* COOK, *still as fat, but forty years younger. He proudly carries a plate piled with brandied chestnuts.* SALIERI *takes them from him nervously, nodding with approval, and sets them on the table.*]

SALIERI [*to the* COOK]: *Grazie tanti . . . Via, via, via!*

[*The* COOK *bows as* SALIERI *dismisses him, and goes out the same way. The* VALET *comes in from the left—he is also of course forty years younger—and behind him* CONSTANZE, *wearing a pretty hat and carrying a portfolio.*]

*Signora!*

CONSTANZE [*curtsying*]: Excellency.

SALIERI: *Benvenuta.* [*To* VALET *in dismissal.*] *Grazie.*

[*The* VALET *goes.*]

Well. You have come.

CONSTANZE: I should not have done. My husband would be frantic if he knew. He's a very jealous man.

SALIERI: Are you a jealous woman?

CONSTANZE: Why do you ask?

SALIERI: It's not a passion I understand. . . . You're looking even prettier than you were last night, if I may say so.

CONSTANZE: Ta very much! . . . I brought you some manuscripts by Wolfgang. When you see them you'll understand how right he is for a royal appointment. Will you look at them, please, while I wait?

SALIERI: You mean now?

CONSTANZE: Yes, I have to take them back with me. He'll miss them otherwise. He doesn't make copies. These are all the originals.

SALIERI: Sit down. Let me offer you something special.

CONSTANZE [*sitting*]: What's that?

SALIERI [*producing the box*]: *Capezzoli di Venere.* Nipples of Venus. Roman chestnuts in brandied sugar.

CONSTANZE: No, thank you.

SALIERI: Do try. They were made especially for you.

CONSTANZE: Me?

SALIERI: Yes. They're quite rare.

CONSTANZE: Well then, I'd better, hadn't I? Just one. . . . Ta very much.

[*She takes one and puts it in her mouth. The taste amazes her.*] Oh! . . . Oh! . . . Oh! . . . They're *delish!*

SALIERI [*lustfully watching her eat*]: Aren't they?

CONSTANZE: Mmmmm!

SALIERI: Have another.

CONSTANZE [*taking two more*]: I couldn't possibly.

[*Carefully he moves round behind her, and seats himself on the chair next to her.*]

SALIERI: I think you're the most generous girl in the world.

CONSTANZE: Generous?

SALIERI: It's my word for you. I thought last night that Constanze is altogether too stiff a name for that girl. I shall rechristen her "Generosa." *La Generosa*. Then I'll write a glorious song for her under that title and she'll sing it, just for me.

CONSTANZE [*smiling*]: I am much out of practice, sir.

SALIERI: *La Generosa*. [*He leans a little toward her.*] Don't tell me it's going to prove inaccurate, my name for you.

CONSTANZE [*coolly*]: What name do you give your wife, Excellency?

SALIERI [*equally coolly*]: I'm not an Excellency, and I call my wife Signora Salieri. If I named her anything else it would be *La Statua*. She's a very upright lady.

CONSTANZE: Is she here now? I'd like to meet her.

SALIERI: Alas, no. At the moment she's visiting her mother in Verona.

[*She starts very slightly out of her chair.* SALIERI *gently restrains her.*]

SALIERI: Constanze: tomorrow evening I dine with the Emperor. One word from me recommending your husband as tutor to the Princess Elizabeth, and that invaluable post is his. Believe me, when I speak to His Majesty in matters musical, no one contradicts me.

CONSTANZE: I believe you.

SALIERI: *Bene*. [*Still sitting, he takes his* mouchoir *and delicately wipes her mouth with it.*] Surely service of that sort deserves a little recompense in return?

CONSTANZE: How little?

[*Slight pause.*]

SALIERI: The size of a kiss.

[*Slight pause.*]

CONSTANZE: Just one?

[*Slight pause.*]

SALIERI: If one seems fair to you.

[*She looks at him—then kisses him lightly on the mouth.*]

SALIERI: Does it?

[*She gives him a longer kiss. He makes to touch her with his hand. She breaks off.*]

CONSTANZE: I fancy that's fairness enough. [*Pause.*]

SALIERI [*carefully*]: A pity. . . . It's somewhat small pay, to secure a post every musician in Vienna is hoping for.

CONSTANZE: What do you mean?

SALIERI: Is it not clear?

CONSTANZE: No. Not at all.

SALIERI: Another pity. . . . A thousand pities. [*Pause.*]

CONSTANZE: I don't believe it . . . I just don't believe it!

SALIERI: What?

CONSTANZE: What you've just said.

SALIERI [*hastily*]: I said nothing! What did I say?

[CONSTANZE *gets up and* SALIERI *rises in panic.*]

CONSTANZE: Oh, I'm going! . . . I'm getting out of this!

SALIERI: Constanze . . .

CONSTANZE: Let me pass, please.

SALIERI: Constanze, listen to me! I'm a clumsy man. You think me sophisticated—I'm not at all. Take a true look. I've no cunning. I live on ink and sweetmeats. I never see women at all. . . . When I met you last night, I envied Mozart from the depths of my soul. Out of that envy came stupid thoughts. For one silly second I dared imagine that—out of the vast store you obviously possess—you might spare me one coin of tenderness your rich husband does not need—and inspire me also. [*Pause. She laughs.*] I amuse.

CONSTANZE: Mozart was right. You're wicked.

SALIERI: He said that?

CONSTANZE: "All wops are performers," he said. "Be very careful with that one." Meaning you. He was being comic, of course.

SALIERI: Yes. [*Abruptly he turns his back on her.*]

CONSTANZE: But not that comic, actually. I mean you're acting a pretty obvious role, aren't you, dear? A small-town boy, and all the time as clever as cutlets! . . . [*Mock tender.*] Ah!—you are sulking? *Are* you? . . . When Mozart sulks I smack his botty. He rather likes it. Do you want me to scold you a bit and smack your botty too? [*She hits him lightly with the portfolio. He turns in a fury.*]

SALIERI: How dare you?! . . . *You silly, common girl!*

[*A dreadful silence.*]

[*Icy.*] Forgive me. Let us confine our talk to your husband. He is a brilliant keyboard player, no question. However, the Princess Elizabeth also requires a tutor in vocal music. I am not convinced he is the man for that. I would like to look at the pieces you've brought, and decide if he is mature enough. I will study them overnight—and you will study my proposal. Not to be vague: that is the price. [*He extends his hand for the portfolio, and she surrenders it.*] Good afternoon.

[*He turns from her and places it on a chair. She lingers—tries to speak—cannot—and goes out quickly.*]

* * * *

THE SAME

[SALIERI *turns in a ferment to the Audience.*]

SALIERI: Fiasco! . . . Fiasco! . . . The sordidness of it! The sheer sweating sordidness! . . . Worse than if I'd actually done it! . . . To be that much in sin and feel so *ridiculous* as well! There was no excuse. If now my music was rejected by God forever, it was my fault, mine alone! . . . Would she return tomorrow? Never. And if she did, what then? What would I do? . . . Apologize profoundly—or try again? . . . [*Crying out.*] *Nobilè, nobilè Salieri!* . . . What had he done to me—this Mozart! Before he came did I behave like this? Did I? Toy with adultery? Blackmail women? Twist myself into cruelties? It was all going!—slipping!—growing *rotten*—because of *him!*

[*He moves upstage in a fever—reaches out to take the portfolio on the chair—but as if fearful of what he might find inside it, he withdraws his hand and sits instead. A pause. He contemplates the music lying there as if it were a great confection he is dying to eat, but dare not. Then suddenly he snatches at it—tears the ribbon—opens the case and stares greedily at the manuscripts within.*

*Music sounds instantly, faintly, in the theater, as his eye falls on the first page. It is the opening of the* Twenty-Ninth Symphony, in A Major. *Over the music, reading it.*]

SALIERI: She had said that these were his original scores. First and only drafts of the music. Yet they looked like fair copies. They showed no corrections of any kind.

[*He looks up from the manuscript at the Audience: the music abruptly stops.*]

It was puzzling—then suddenly alarming: What was evident was that Mozart was simply transcribing music—

[*He resumes looking at the music. Immediately the* Sinfonia Concertante for Violin and Viola *sounds faintly.*]

—completely finished in his head. And finished as most music is never finished.

[*He looks up again: the music breaks off.*]

Displace one note and there would be diminishment. Displace one phrase and the structure would fall.

[*He resumes reading, and the music also resumes: a ravishing phrase from the slow movement of the* Concerto for Flute and Harp.]

Here again—only now in abundance—were the same sounds I'd heard in the library. The same crushed harmonies—glancing collisions—agonizing delights.

[*And he looks up: again the music stops.*]

The truth was clear. That serenade had been no accident.

[*Very low, in the theater, a faint thundery sound is heard accumulating, like a distant sea.*]

I was staring through the cage of those meticulous ink strokes at an Absolute Beauty!

[*And out of the thundery roar writhes and rises the clear sound of a* SOPRANO, *singing the "Kyrie" from the* C Minor Mass. *The accretion of noise around her voice falls away—it is suddenly clear and bright—then clearer and brighter. The light grows bright: too bright: burning white, then scalding white!* SALIERI *rises in the downpour of it, and in the flood of the music which is growing ever louder—filling the theater—as the* SOPRANO *yields to the full* CHORUS, *fortissimo, singing its massive counterpoint. This is by far the loudest sound the Audience has yet heard.* SALIERI *staggers toward us, holding the manuscripts in his hand, like a man caught in a tumbling and violent sea.*

*Finally the drums crash in below:* SALIERI *drops the portfolio of manuscripts—and falls senseless to the ground. At the same second the music explodes into a long, echoing, distorted boom, signifying some dreadful annihilation.*

*The sound remains suspended over the prone* FIGURE *in a menacing continuum—no longer music at all. Then it dies away, and there is only silence.*

*The light fades again.*

*A long pause.*

SALIERI *quite still, his head by the pile of manuscripts.*

*Finally the clock sounds: nine times.* SALIERI *stirs as it does. Slowly he raises his head and looks up. And now—quietly at first—he addresses his God.*]

SALIERI: *Capisco*! I know my fate. Now for the first time I feel my emptiness as Adam felt his nakedness. . . . [*Slowly he rises to his feet.*] Tonight at an inn somewhere in this city stands a giggling child who can put on paper, without actually setting down his billiard cue, casual notes which turn my most considered ones into lifeless scratches. *Grazie, Signore!* You gave me the desire to serve you—which most men do not have—then saw to it the service was shameful in the ears of the server. *Grazie!* You gave me the desire to praise you—which most do not feel—then made me mute. *Grazie tanti!* You put into me perception of the Incomparable—which most men never know!—then ensured that I would know myself forever mediocre. [*His voice gains power.*] *Why? . . . What is my fault? . . .* Until this day I have pursued virtue with rigor. I have labored long hours to relieve my fellow men. I have worked and worked the talent you allowed me. [*Calling up.*] *You know how hard I've worked!* Solely that in the end, in the practice of the art which alone makes the world comprehensible to me, I might hear Your Voice! And now I do hear it—and it says only one name: MOZART! . . . Spiteful, sniggering, conceited, infantine Mozart!—who has never worked one minute to help another man!—shit-talking Mozart with his botty-smacking wife!—*him* you have chosen to be your sole conduct! And *my* only reward—my sublime privilege—is to be the sole man alive in this time who shall clearly recognize your Incarnation! [*Savagely.*] *Grazie e grazie ancora!* [*Pause.*] So be it! From this time we are enemies, You and I! I'll not accept it from You. *Do you hear? . . .* They say God is not mocked. I tell you, *Man* is not mocked! . . . *I* am not mocked! . . . They say the spirit bloweth where it listeth: I tell you NO! It must list to virtue or not blow at all! [*Yelling.*] *Dio Ingiusto!* You are the Enemy! . . . I name Thee now—*Nemico Eterno!* And this I swear. To my last breath I shall *block* you on earth, as far as I am able! [*He glares up at God. To Audience.*] What use, after all, is Man, if not to teach God His lessons?

[*Pause. Suddenly he speaks again to us in the voice of an old man.*] And now—

[*He slips off his powdered wig, crosses to the fortepiano and takes from its lid, where they lie, the old dressing gown and shawl which he discarded when he conducted us back to the Eighteenth Century. These he slips on over his Court coat. It is again 1823.*]

—before I tell you what happened next—God's answer to me—and indeed Constanze's—and all the horrors that followed—let me stop. The bladder, being a human appendage, is not something you ghosts need concern yourselves with yet. I being alive, though barely, am at its constant call. It is now one hour before dawn—when I must dismiss us both. When I return I'll tell you about the war I fought with God through his preferred Creature—Mozart, named *Amadeus*. In the waging of which, of course, the Creature had to be destroyed.

[*He bows to the Audience with malignant slyness—snatches a pastry from the stand—and leaves the stage, chewing at it voraciously. The manuscripts lie where he spilled them in his fall.*

*The lights in the theater come up as he goes.*]

END OF ACT ONE

* * * *

# ACT TWO

SALIERI'S SALON

[*The lights go down in the theatre as* SALIERI *returns.*]

SALIERI: I have been listening to the cats in the courtyard. They are all singing Rossini. It is obvious that cats have declined as badly as composers. Domenico Scarlatti owned one which would actually stroll across the keyboard and pick out passable subjects for fugue. But that was a Spanish cat of the Enlightenment. It appreciated counterpoint. Nowadays all cats appreciate is coloratura. Like the rest of the public.

[*He comes downstage and addresses the Audience directly.*]

This is now the very last hour of my life. You must understand me. Not forgive. I do not seek forgiveness. I was a good man, as the world calls good. *What use was it to me?* Goodness could not make me a good composer. Was Mozart good? . . . Goodness is nothing in the furnace of art.

[*Pause.*]

On that dreadful night of the manuscripts my life acquired a terrible and thrilling purpose. The blocking of God in one of his purest manifestations. I had the power. God needed Mozart to let himself into the world. And Mozart needed *me* to get him worldly advancement. So it would be a battle to the end—and Mozart was the battleground.

[*Pause.*]

One thing I knew of Him. God was a cunning Enemy. Witness the fact that in blocking Him in the world I was also given the satisfaction of obstructing a disliked human rival. I wonder which of you will refuse that chance if it is offered.

[*He regards the Audience maliciously, taking off his dressing gown and shawl.*]

I felt the danger at once, as soon as I'd uttered my challenge. How would He answer? Would He strike me dead for my impiety? Don't laugh. I was not a sophisticate of the salons. I was a small-town Catholic, full of dread!

[*He puts on his powdered wig, and speaks again in his younger voice. We are back in the Eighteenth Century.*]

SALIERI: The first thing that happened—suddenly Constanze was back! At ten o'clock at night!

[*The doorbell sounds.* CONSTANZE *comes in followed by his* VALET.]

[*In surprise.*] Signora!

CONSTANZE [*stiffly*]: My husband is at a soirée of Baron Van Swieten. A concert of Sebastian Bach. He didn't think I would enjoy it.

SALIERI: I see. [*Curtly, to the goggling* VALET.] I'll ring if we require anything. Thank you.

[*The* VALET *goes out. Slight pause.*]

CONSTANZE [*calmly*]: Where do we go, then?

SALIERI: What?

CONSTANZE: Do we do it in here? . . . Why not?

[*She sits, still wearing her hat, in one of the little gilded upright chairs. Deliberately she loosens the strings of her bodice, so that one can just see the tops of her breasts, hitches up her silk skirts above the knees, so that one can also just see the flesh above the tops of the stockings, spreads her legs and regards him with an open stare:*

[*Speaking softly.*] Well? . . . Let's get on with it.

[*For a second* SALIERI *returns the stare, then looks suddenly away.*]

SALIERI [*stiffly*]: Your manuscripts are there. Please take them and go. Now. At once.

[*Pause.*]

CONSTANZE: You shit. [*She jumps up and snatches the portfolio.*]

SALIERI: *Via! Don't return!*

CONSTANZE: You rotten shit!

[*Suddenly she runs at him—trying furiously to hit at his face. He grabs her arms, shakes her violently, and hurls her on the floor.*]

SALIERI: *Via!*

[*She freezes, staring up at him in hate.*]

[*Calling to the Audience*] You see how it was! I would have liked her—oh yes, just then more than ever! But now I wanted nothing petty! . . . My quarrel wasn't with Mozart—it was through him! Through him to God who loved him so. [*Scornfully*] *Amadeus! . . . Amadeus! . . .*

[CONSTANZE *picks herself up and runs from the room.*
*Pause. He calms himself, going to the table and selecting a "Nipple of Venus" to eat.*]

The next day when Katherina Cavalieri came for her lesson, I made the same halting speech about "coins of tenderness"—and I dubbed the girl *la Generosa*. I regret that my invention in love, as in art, has always been limited. Fortunately Katherina found it sufficient. She consumed twenty "Nipples of Venus"—kissed me with brandied breath—and slipped easily into my bed.

[KATHERINA *comes in languidly, half-dressed, as if from his bedroom. He embraces her, and helps slyly to adjust her peignoir.*]

She remained there as my mistress for many years behind my good wife's back—and I soon erased in sweat the sense of his little body, the Creature's, preceding me.

[*The* GIRL *gives him a radiant smile, and ambles off.*]

So much for my vow of sexual virtue. [*Slight pause.*] The same evening I went to the palace and resigned from all my committees to help the lot of poor musicians. So much for my vow of social virtue. . . . Then I went to the Emperor and recommended a man of no talent whatever to instruct the Princess Elizabeth.

* * * *

THE ROYAL PALACE

[*The* EMPEROR *stands before the vast fireplace, between the golden mirrors.*]

JOSEPH: Herr Sommer. A dull man, surely? What of Mozart?

SALIERI: Majesty, I cannot with a clear conscience recommend Mozart to teach royalty. One hears too many stories.

JOSEPH: They may just be gossip.

SALIERI: One of them I regret relates to a protégée of my own. A very young singer.

JOSEPH: *Charmant!*

SALIERI: Not pleasant, Majesty, but true.

JOSEPH: I see. . . . Let it be Herr Sommer, then. [*He walks down on to the main stage.*] I daresay he can't do much harm. To be frank, no one can do much harm musically to the Princess Elizabeth.

[MOZART *enters. He wears a more natural-looking wig from now on: one indeed intended to represent his own hair of light chestnut, full and gathered at the back with ribbon.*]

SALIERI [*to Audience*]: Mozart certainly did not suspect me. The Emperor announced the appointment in his usual way—

JOSEPH: Well, there it is. [JOSEPH *strolls offstage.*]

SALIERI: —and I commiserated with the loser.

[SALIERI *shakes his hand.*]

MOZART [*bitterly*]: It's my own fault. My father always writes, I should be more obedient. *Know my place!* . . . He'll send me sixteen lectures when he hears of this!

[*He goes wretchedly up to the fortepiano. The lights lower.*]

SALIERI [*to Audience, watching him*]: It was a most serious loss as far as Mozart was concerned.

* * * *

VIENNA, AND GLIMPSES OF OPERA HOUSES

[*The* VENTICELLI *glide on.*]

V.1.: His list of pupils hardly moves.

V.2.: Six at most.

V.1.: And now a child to keep!

V.2.: A boy.

SALIERI: Poor fellow. [*To Audience.*] I by contrast prospered. This is the extraordinary truth. If I had expected anger from God—none came. *None!* . . . Instead—incredibly—in '84 and '85 I came to be regarded as infinitely the superior composer. And this despite the fact that these were the two years in which Mozart wrote his best keyboard concerti and his string quartets.

[*The* VENTICELLI *stand on either side of* SALIERI. MOZART *sits down at the fortepiano.*]

V.1.: Haydn calls the quartets unsurpassed.

SALIERI: They were—but no one heard them.

V.2.: Van Swieten calls the concerti sublime.

SALIERI: They were, but no one noticed.

[MOZART *plays and conducts from the keyboard. Faintly we hear the "Rondo" from the* Piano Concerto in A major, K488.]

SALIERI [*over this*]: The Viennese greeted each unique concerto with the squeals of pleasure they usually reserved for a new style of bonnet. Each was played once—then totally forgotten! . . . I alone was empowered to recognize them fully for what they were: the most perfect things made by man in the whole of the Eighteenth Century. By contrast, my operas were played everywhere and saluted by everyone! I composed my *Semiramide* for Munich.

V.1.: Rapturously received!

V.2.: People *faint* with pleasure!

[*In the Light Box is seen the interior of a brilliantly colored Opera House, and an Audience standing up applauding vigorously.* SALIERI, *flanked by the* VENTICELLI, *turns upstage and bows to it. The concerto can scarcely be heard through the din.*]

SALIERI: I wrote a comic opera for Vienna. *La Grotta di Trofonio.*

V.1.: The talk of the city!

V.2.: The cafés are buzzing!

[*Another Opera House interior is lit up. Another Audience claps vigorously. Again* SALIERI *bows to it.*]

SALIERI [*to Audience*]: I finally finished my tragic opera *Danaius*, and produced it in Paris.

V.1.: Stupendous reception!

V.2.: The plaudits shake the roof!

V.1.: Your name sounds throughout the Empire!

V.2.: Throughout all Europe!

[*Yet another Opera House and another excited Audience.* SALIERI *bows a third time. Even the* VENTICELLI *now applaud him. The concerto stops.* MOZART *rises from the keyboard and, whilst* SALIERI *speaks, crosses directly through the scene and leaves the stage.*]

SALIERI [*to Audience*]: It was incomprehensible. Almost as if I were being pushed deliberately from triumph to triumph! . . . filled my head with golden opinions—yes, and this house with golden furniture!

* * * *

SALIERI'S SALON

[*The stage turns gold.* SERVANTS *come on carrying golden chairs upholstered in golden brocade. They place these all over the wooden floor.*

*The* VALET *appears—looking a little older—divests* SALIERI *of his sky-blue coat and clothes him instead in a frockcoat of gold satin.*

*The* COOK*—also of course a little older—brings in a golden cake stand piled with more elaborate cakes.*]

SALIERI: My own taste was for plain things—but I denied it! . . . I grew confident. I grew resplendent. I gave Salons and soirées, and worshiped the season round at the altar of sophistication!

[*He sits at ease in his salon. The* VENTICELLI *sit with him, one on either side.*]

V.1.: Mozart heard your comedy last night.

V.2.: He spoke of it to the Princess Lichnowsky.

V.1.: He said you should be made to clean up your own mess.

SALIERI [*taking snuff*]: Really? What charmers these Salzburgers are!

V.2.: People are outraged, by him.

V.1.: He empties drawing rooms. Now Van Swieten is angry with him.

SALIERI: Lord Fugue? I thought he was the Baron's little pet.

V.2.: Mozart has asked leave to write an Italian opera.

SALIERI [*briskly, aside to Audience*]: *Italian opera! Threat! My kingdom!*

V.1.: And the Baron is scandalized.

SALIERI: But why? What's the theme of it?

[VAN SWIETEN *comes on quickly from upstage.*]

VAN SWIETEN: Figaro! . . .*The Marriage of Figaro!* That disgraceful play of Beaumarchais!

[*At a discreet sign of dismissal from* SALIERI the VENTICELLI *slip away.* VAN SWIETEN *joins* SALIERI, *and sits on one of the gold chairs.*]

[*To* SALIERI.] That's all he can find to waste his talent on: a vulgar farce. When I reproved him, he said I reminded him of his father! Noblemen lusting after chambermaids! Their wives dressing up in stupid disguises anyone could penetrate in a second! . . . Why set such rubbish to music?

[MOZART *enters quickly from upstage, accompanied by* STRACK. *They join* SALIERI *and* VAN SWIETEN.]

MOZART: Because I want to do a piece about real people, Baron! And I want to set it in a real place! A *boudoir!*—because that to me is the most exciting place on earth! Underclothes on the floor! Sheets still warm from a woman's body! Even a pisspot brimming under the bed!

VAN SWIETEN [*outraged*]: Mozart!

MOZART: I want life, Baron. Not boring legends!

STRACK: Herr Salieri's recent *Danaius* was a legend and that did not bore the French.

MOZART: It is impossible to bore the French—except with real life!

VAN SWIETEN: I had assumed, now that you had joined our Brotherhood of Masons, you would choose more elevated themes.

MOZART [*impatiently*]: Oh, elevated! Elevated! . . . The only thing a man should elevate is his doodle.

VAN SWIETEN: You are provoking, sir! Has everything to be a joke with you?

MOZART [*desperate*]: Excuse language, Baron, but really! How can we go on forever with these gods and heroes?

VAN SWIETEN [*passionately*]: Because they *go* on forever—that's why! They represent the eternal in us. Opera is here to ennoble us, Mozart—you and me just as well as the Emperor. It is an aggrandizing art! It celebrates the eternal in Man and ignores the ephemeral. The Goddess in Woman and not the laundress.

STRACK: Well said, sir. Exactly!

MOZART [*imitating his drawl*]: Oh, well said, yes, well said! Exactly! [*To all of them.*] I don't understand you! You're all up on perches, but it doesn't hide your arsholes! You don't give a shit about gods and heroes!

If you are honest—each one of you—which of you isn't more at home with his hairdresser than Hercules? Or Horatius? [*To* SALIERI.] Or your stupid *Danaius*, come to that! Or mine—mine! *Mitridate, King of Pontus*! *Idomeneo, King of Crete*! All those anguished antiques! They're all bores! Bores, bores, bores! [*Suddenly he springs up and jumps on to a chair, like an orator. Declaring it.*] All serious operas written this century are boring!

[*They turn and look at him in shocked amazement. A pause. He gives his little giggle, and then jumps up and down on the chair. . . .*]

Look at us! Four gaping mouths. What a perfect quartet! I'd love to write it—just this second of time, this *now*, as we are! Herr Chamberlain thinking, "Impertinent Mozart: I must speak to the Emperor at once!" Herr Prefect thinking, "Ignorant Mozart: debasing opera with his vulgarity!" Herr Court Composer thinking, "German Mozart: what can he finally know about music?" And Herr Mozart himself, in the middle, thinking, "I'm just a good fellow. Why do they all disapprove of me?" [*Excitedly, to* VAN SWIETEN.] That's why opera is important, Baron. Because it's realer than any play! A dramatic poet would have to put all those thoughts down one after another to represent this second of time. The composer can put them all down at once—and still make us hear each one of them. Astonishing device: a vocal quartet! [*More and more excited.*] . . . I tell you I want to write a finale lasting half an hour! A quartet becoming a quintet becoming a sextet. On and on, wider and wider—all sounds multiplying and rising together—and the together making a sound entirely new! . . . I bet you that's how God hears the world. Millions of sounds ascending at once and mixing in His ear to become an unending music, unimaginable to us! [*To* SALIERI.] That's our job! That's our job, we composers: to combine the inner minds of him and him and him, and her and her—the thoughts of chambermaids and Court Composers—and turn the audience into God.

[*Pause.* SALIERI *stares at him fascinated. Embarrassed,* MOZART *blows a raspberry and giggles.*]

I'm sorry. I talk nonsense all day: it's incurable—ask Stanzerl. [*To* VAN SWIETEN.] My tongue is stupid. My heart isn't.

VAN SWIETEN: No. You're a good fellow under all your nonsense: I know that. He'll make a fine new Brother Mason, won't he, Salieri?

SALIERI: Better than I, Baron.

VAN SWIETEN: Just try, my friend, to be more serious with your gifts.

[*He smiles, presses* MOZART'*s hand, and goes.* SALIERI *rises.*]

SALIERI: *Buona fortuna, Mozart.*

MOZART: *Grazie, Signore.* [*Rounding on* STRACK.] Stop frowning, Herr

Chamberlain. I'm a jackass. It's easy to be friends with a jackass: just shake his "hoof."

[*He forms his hand into a "hoof." Warily* STRACK *takes it—then springs back in distaste as* MOZART *brays loudly like a donkey.*]

MOZART: *Hee-haw!* . . . Tell the Emperor the opera's finished.

STRACK: Finished?

MOZART: Right here in my noodle. The rest's just scribbling. Goodbye.

STRACK: Good day to you.

MOZART: He's going to be proud of me. You'll see. [*He gives his ornate flourish of the hand and goes out, delighted with himself.*]

STRACK: That young man really is . . .

SALIERI [*blandly*]: Very lively.

STRACK [*exploding*]: Intolerable! . . . *Intolerable!*

[STRACK *freezes in a posture of indignation.*]

SALIERI [*to Audience*]: How could I stop it? . . . How could I block this opera of Figaro? . . . Incredible to hear, within six weeks! . . .

[ROSENBERG *bustles in.*]

ROSENBERG: Figaro is complete! The first performance will be on May the first!

SALIERI: So soon?

ROSENBERG: There's no way we can stop it!

[*A slight pause.*]

SALIERI [*slyly*]: I have an idea. *Una piccola idea!*

ROSENBERG: What?

SALIERI: *Mi ha detto chec'è un balletto nel terzo atto?*

ROSENBERG [*puzzled*]: *Si.*

STRACK: What does he say?

SALIERI: *E dimmi—non è vero che l'Imperatore ha probito il balletto nelle sue opere?*

ROSENBERG [*realizing*]: *Uno balletto* . . . ah!

SALIERI: *Precisamente.*

ROSENBERG: *Oh, capisco! Ma che meraviglia! Perfetto?* [*He laughs in delight.*] *Veramente ingegnoso!*

STRACK [*irritated*]: What is it? What is he suggesting?

SALIERI: See him at the theater.

ROSENBERG: Of course. Immediately. I'd forgotten. You are brilliant, Court Composer.

SALIERI: I? . . . I have said nothing. [*He moves away upstage.*]

[*The dim light begins to change, dimming down.*]

STRACK [*very cross*]: I must tell you that I resent this extremely. Mozart is right in some things. There is far too much Italian *chittero-chattero* at this Court! Now please to inform me at once, what was just said?

ROSENBERG [*lightly*]: *Pazienza*, my dear Chamberlain. *Pazienza*. Just wait and see!

[*From upstage* SALIERI *beckons to* STRACK. *Baffled and cross, the* CHAMBERLAIN *joins him. They watch together, unseen. The light dims further.*]

* * * *

AN UNLIT THEATER

[*In the background a projection of lamps glowing faintly in the darkened auditorium.* ROSENBERG *sits on one of the gold chairs, center.*

ROSENBERG: Mozart! . . . *Mozart!*

[MOZART *comes in quickly from the left, wearing another of his bright coats, and carrying the score of* Figaro. *He crosses to the fortepiano.*]

MOZART: Yes, Herr Director.

ROSENBERG [*agreeably*]: A word with you, please. Right away.

MOZART: Certainly. What is it?

ROSENBERG: I would like to see your score of *Figaro*.

MOZART: Oh yes. Why?

ROSENBERG: Just bring it here to me. Into my hand, please.

[MOZART *crosses and hands it to him, puzzled.* ROSENBERG *turns the pages.*]

Now tell me: did you not know that His Majesty has expressly forbidden ballet in his operas?

MOZART: Ballet?

ROSENBERG: Such as occurs in your third act.

MOZART: That is not a ballet, Herr Director. That is a dance at Figaro's wedding.

ROSENBERG: Exactly. A dance.

MOZART [*trying to control himself*]: But, the Emperor doesn't mean to prohibit dancing when it's part of the story. He made that law to prevent *insertions* of stupid ballet like in French operas, and quite right too.

ROSENBERG: It is not for you, Herr Mozart, to interpret the Emperor's edicts. Merely to obey them. [*He seizes the offending pages between his fingers.*]

MOZART: What are you doing? . . . What are you doing, Excellency?

ROSENBERG: Taking out what should never have been put in.

[*In a terrible silence* ROSENBERG *tears out the pages,* MOZART *watches in disbelief. Upstage* SALIERI *and* STRACK *look on together from the dimness.*]

Now, sir, perhaps in future you will obey imperial commands. [*He tears out some more pages.*]

MOZART: But . . . but—if all that goes—there'll be a hole right at the climax of the story! . . . [*Crying out suddenly.*] *Salieri! This is Salieri's idea!*

ROSENBERG: Don't be absurd.

SALIERI [*to Audience*]: How did he think of that? Nothing I had ever done could possibly make him think of that on his own. Had God given him the idea?!

MOZART: It's a conspiracy. I can smell it. I can smell it!

ROSENBERG: Control yourself!

MOZART [*howling*]: *But what do you expect me to do?* The first performance is two days off!

ROSENBERG: Write it over. That's your forte, is it not?—writing at speed.

MOZART: Not when the music's *perfect!* Not when it's absolutely perfect as it is! . . . [*Wildly.*] I shall appeal to the Emperor! I'll go to him myself! I'll hold a rehearsal especially for him!

ROSENBERG: The Emperor does not attend rehearsals.

MOZART: He'll attend this one. Make no mistake—he'll come to this one! Then he'll deal with *you!*

ROSENBERG: This issue is simple. Write your act again today—or withdraw the opera. That's final.

[*Pause. He hands back the mutilated score to its composer.* MOZART *is shaking.*]

MOZART: You shit-pot.

[ROSENBERG *turns and walks imperturbably away from him.*]

Woppy, foppy, wet-arsed, Italian-loving, shit-pot!

[*Serenely,* ROSENBERG *leaves the stage.*]

[*Screeching after him.*] Count Orsini-Rosenbugger! . . . Rosenshit! . . . Rosenclit! . . . I'll hold a rehearsal! You'll see! The Emperor will come! You'll see! You'll see! . . . *You'll see!!* [*He throws down his score in a storm of hysterical rage.*]

[*Upstage in the dimness* STRACK *goes out, and* SALIERI *ventures down toward the shrieking little man.* MOZART *suddenly becomes aware of him. He turns, his hand shooting out in an involuntary gesture of accusation.*]

[*To* SALIERI.] I am *forbidden!* . . . I am—forbidden! . . . But of course you know already!

SALIERI [*quietly*]: Know what?

[MOZART *flings away from him.*]

MOZART [*bitterly*]: No matter!

SALIERI [*always blandly*]: Mozart, permit me. If you wish, I will speak to the Emperor myself. Ask him to attend a rehearsal.

MOZART [*amazed*]: You wouldn't.

SALIERI: I cannot promise he will come—but I can try.

MOZART: Sir!

SALIERI: Good day. [*He puts up his hands, barring further intimacy.*]

[MOZART *retreats to the fortepiano.*]

SALIERI [*to Audience*]: Needless to say I did nothing whatever in the matter. Yet—to my total stupefaction—

[STRACK *and* ROSENBERG *hurry on downstage.*]

—in the middle of the last rehearsal of *Figaro* next day . . .

[*The* EMPEROR JOSEPH *comes on from upstage.*]

JOSEPH [*cheerfully*]: Fetes and fireworks! Fetes and fireworks! Gentlemen, good afternoon!

* * * *

THE THEATER

SALIERI [*to Audience*]: Entirely against his usual practice, the Emperor appeared!

[STRACK *and* ROSENBERG *look at each other in consternation.* JOSEPH *seats himself excitedly on one of the gold chairs, facing out front. As with the premiere of* Seraglio *seen in Act I, he watches the Audience as if it were the opera.*]

JOSEPH: I can't wait for this, Mozart, I assure you! *Je prévois des merveilles!*

MOZART [*bowing fervently*]: Majesty!

[*The* COURTIERS *sit also:* STRACK *on his right-hand side,* ROSENBERG *on his left.* SALIERI *also sits, near the keyboard.*]

SALIERI [*to Audience*]: What did this mean? Was this proof God had finally decided to defend Mozart against me? Was he engaging with me at last?

[MOZART *passes behind* SALIERI.]

MOZART [*earnestly, sotto voce*]: I am so grateful to you, I cannot express it!

SALIERI [*aside, to him*]: Hush. Say nothing.

[MOZART *goes on quickly to the fortepiano and sits at it.*]

SALIERI [*to Audience*]: One thing about the event certainly seemed more than coincidence.

[*Music sounds faintly: the end of the third act of* Figaro, *just before the dance music starts.*]

Strangely, His Majesty had arrived at precisely the moment when the dancers would have begun—had not they and their music been entirely cut.

[*The music stops abruptly.*]

He and all of us watched the action proceed in total silence.

[*Flanked by his* COURTIERS, *the* EMPEROR *stares out front, following with his eyes what is obviously a silent pantomime. His face expresses bewilderment.* ROSENBERG *watches his* SOVEREIGN *anxiously. Finally the* MONARCH *speaks.*]

JOSEPH: I don't understand. Is it modern?

MOZART [*jumping up nervously from the keyboard*]: No, Majesty.

JOSEPH: Then what?

MOZART: The Herr Director has removed a dance that would have occurred at this point.

JOSEPH [*to* ROSENBERG]: Why was this done?

ROSENBERG: It's your own regulation, sire. No ballet in your opera.

MOZART: Majesty, this is not a ballet. It is part of a wedding feast: entirely necessary for the story.

JOSEPH: Well, it certainly looks very odd the way it is. I can't say I like it.

MOZART: Nor do I, Majesty.

JOSEPH: Do you like it, Rosenberg?

ROSENBERG: It's not a question of liking, Majesty. Your own law decrees it.

JOSEPH: Yes. All the same, this is nonsense. Look at them: they're like waxworks up there.

ROSENBERG: Well, not exactly, Majesty.

JOSEPH: I don't like waxworks.

MOZART: Nor do I, Majesty.

JOSEPH: Well, who would? What do you say, Salieri?

SALIERI: Italians are fond of waxworks, Majesty. [*Pause.*] Our religion is largely based upon them.

JOSEPH: You are *cattivo* again, Court Composer.

STRACK [*intervening creamily*]: Your Majesty, Count Rosenberg is very worried that if this music is put back it will create the most unfortunate precedent. One will have thereafter to endure hours of dancing in opera.

JOSEPH: I think we can guard against that, you know, Chamberlain. I really think we can guard against hours of dancing. [*To* ROSENBERG.] Please restore Herr Mozart's music.

ROSENBERG: But Majesty, I must insist—

JOSEPH [*with a touch of anger*]: You will oblige me, Rosenberg! I wish to hear Mozart's music. Do you understand me?

ROSENBERG: Yes, Majesty.

[MOZART *explodes with joy, jumps up and throws himself at* JOSEPH'*s feet.*]

MOZART: Oh, God, I thank Your Majesty! [*He kisses the* EMPEROR'*s hand extravagantly, as at their first meeting.*] Oh, thank you—thank you—thank you, sire, forever!

JOSEPH [*withdrawing hand*]: Yes, yes—very good. A little less enthusiasm, I beg you!

MOZART [*abashed*]: Excuse me.

[*The* EMPEROR *rises. All follow suit.*]

JOSEPH: Well. *There it is!*

* * * *

THE FIRST PERFORMANCE OF *FIGARO*

[*The theater glows with light for the first performance of* Figaro. COURTIERS *and* CITIZENS *come in swiftly.*

*The* EMPEROR *and his* COURT *resume their seats, and the* OTHERS *quickly take theirs. In the front row we note* KATHERINA CAVALIERI, *all plumes and sequins, and* KAPELLMEISTER BONNO—*older than ever. Behind them sit* CONSTANZE *and the* VENTICELLI. *All of them stare out at the Audience as if it were the opera they have come to see:* PEOPLE OF FASHION *down front;* POORER PEOPLE *crowded into the Light Box upstage.*

SALIERI *crosses as he speaks, to where two chairs have been placed side by side apart from the rest, on the left, to form his box. On the chair upstage sits his good wife* TERESA—*as statuesque as before.*]

SALIERI [*to Audience*]: And so *Figaro* was produced in spite of all my efforts. I sat in my box and watched it happen. A conspicuous defeat for me. And yet I was strangely excited.

[*Faintly we hear Figaro singing the tune of "Non più andrai." The stage* AUDIENCE *is obviously delighted: they smile out front as they watch the (invisible) action.*]

My march! My poor "March of Welcome"—now set to enchant the world forever!

[*It fades. Applause. The* EMPEROR *rises, and with him the Audience, to denote an Intermission.* JOSEPH *greets* KATHERINA *and* BONNO, ROSENBERG *and* STRACK *approach* SALIERI'*s box.*]

ROSENBERG [*to* SALIERI]: Almost in your style, that last bit. But more vulgar of course. Far more obvious than you would ever be.

STRACK [*drawling*]: Exactly!

[*A bell rings signaling the end of the Intermission. The* EMPEROR *returns quickly to his seat. The* AUDIENCE *sits. A pause. All look out front, unmoving.*]

SALIERI [*raptly and quietly: to Audience*]: Trembling, I heard the second act. [*Pause.*] The restored third act. [*Pause.*] The astounding fourth. What shall I say to you who will one day hear this last act for yourselves? You will—because whatever else shall pass away, this must remain.

[*Faintly we hear the solemn closing ensemble from Act Four of* Figaro, *"Ah! Tutti contenti. Saremo così."*]

[*Over this.*] The scene was night in a summer garden. Pinprick stars gleamed down on shaking summerhouses. Plotters glided behind paste-board hedges. I saw a woman, dressed in her maid's clothes, hear her husband utter the first tender words he has offered her in years only because he thinks she is someone else. Could one catch a realer moment? And how except in a net of pure artifice? The disguises of opera had been invented for Mozart. [*He can barely look out at the "stage" for emotion.*] The final reconciliation melted sight. [*Pause.*] Through my tears I saw the Emperor yawn.

[JOSEPH *yawns. The music fades. There is scant applause.* JOSEPH *rises and the* COURTIERS *follow suit.* MOZART *bows.*]

JOSEPH [*coolly*]: Most ingenious, Mozart. You are coming along nicely. . . . I do think we must omit encores in future. It really makes things far too long. Make a note, Rosenberg.

ROSENBERG: Majesty.

[MOZART *lowers his head, crushed.*]

JOSEPH: Gentlemen, good night to you. Strack, attend me.

[JOSEPH *goes out, with* STRACK. *Director* ROSENBERG *gives* MOZART *one triumphant look and follows.* SALIERI *nods to his* WIFE *who leaves with the rest of the* AUDIENCE. *Only* CONSTANZE *lingers for a second, then she too goes. A pause.* MOZART *and* SALIERI *are left alone:* SALIERI *deeply shaken by the opera.* MOZART *deeply upset by its reception. He crosses and sits next to* SALIERI.]

MOZART [*low*]: Herr Salieri.

SALIERI: Yes?

MOZART: What do you think? Do you think I am coming along nicely?

SALIERI [*moved*]: I think the piece is . . . extraordinary. I think it is . . . *marvelous*. Yes.

[*Pause.* MOZART *turns to him. He smiles with genuine pleasure.*]

MOZART: I'll tell you what it is. It's the best opera yet written. That's what it is. And only I could have done it. No one else living!

[SALIERI *turns his head swiftly, as if he has been slapped.* MOZART *rises and walks away. The light changes. The* VENTICELLI *rush on.* SALIERI *and* MOZART *both freeze.*]

V.1.: Rosenberg is furious.

V.2.: He'll never forgive Mozart.

V.1.: He'll do anything to get back at him!

SALIERI [*rising: to Audience*]: So it wasn't hard to get the piece canceled. I saw to it through the person of the resentful director that in the entire year *Figaro* was played only *nine times!* . . . My defeat finally turned into a victory. And God's response to my challenge remained as inscrutable as ever. . . . Was He taking any notice of me *at all?* . . .

[MOZART *breaks his freeze and comes downstage.*]

MOZART: *Withdrawn!* . . . Absolutely no plans for its revival!

SALIERI: I commiserate with you, my friend. But if the public does not like one's work, one has to accept the fact gracefully. [*Aside, to Audience.*] And certainly they didn't.

V.1. [*complaining*]: It's too complicated!

V.2. [*complaining*]: Too tiresome!

V.1.: All those weird harmonies!

V.2.: And never a good bang at the end of songs so you know when to clap!

[*The* VENTICELLI *go off.*]

SALIERI [*to Audience*]: Obviously I would not need to plot too hard against his operas in future. The Viennese could be relied upon to destroy those for me. I must concentrate on the man. I decided to see him as much as possible; to learn everything I could of his weaknesses.

* * * *

THE WALDSTÄDTEN LIBRARY

[SERVANTS *again bring on the wing chair.*]

MOZART: I'll go to England. England loves music. That's the answer!

SALIERI [*to Audience*]: We were yet again in the library of the Baroness Waldstädten: that room fated to be the scene of ghastly encounters between us. Again, I took the compensating *crema al mascarpone.*

[*He sits in the chair and eats greedily.*]

MOZART: I was there when I was a boy. They absolutely adored me. I had more kisses than you've had cakes! . . . When I was a child, people loved me.

SALIERI: Perhaps they will again. Why don't you go to London and try?

MOZART: Because I have a wife and child and no money. I wrote to Papa to take the boy off my hands just for a few months so I could go—and he refused! . . . In the end everyone betrays you. Even the man you think loves you best. . . . He's a bitter man, of course. After he'd finished showing me off around Europe he never went anywhere himself. He just stayed up in Salzburg year after year, kissing the ring of the Fartsbishop and lecturing me! . . . [*Confidentially.*] The real thing is, you see, he's jealous. Under everything he's jealous of me! He'll never forgive me for being cleverer than he is.

[*He leans excitedly over* SALIERI*'s chair like a naughty child.*]

I'll tell you a secret. Leopold Mozart is just a jealous, dried-up old turd . . . and I actually detest him.

[*He giggles guiltily. The* VENTICELLI *appear quickly, and address* SALIERI, *as* MOZART *freezes.*]

V.1. [*solemnly*]: Leopold Mozart—

V.2. [*solemnly*]: Leopold Mozart—

V.1. & V.2.: Leopold Mozart is dead!

[*They go off.* MOZART *recoils. A long pause.*]

SALIERI: Do not despair. Death is inevitable, my friend.

MOZART [*desperately*]: How will I go now?

SALIERI: What do you mean?

MOZART: In the world. There's no one else. No one who understands the wickedness around. *I can't see it*! . . . He watched for me all my life—and I betrayed him.

SALIERI: No!

MOZART: I talked against him.

SALIERI: No!

MOZART [*distressed*]: I married where he begged me not. I left him alone. I danced and played billiards and fooled about, and he sat by himself night after night in an empty house, and no woman to care for him. . . .

[SALIERI *rises in concern.*]

SALIERI: Wolfgang. My dear Wolfgang. Don't accuse yourself! . . . Lean upon me, if you care to . . . Lean upon me.

[SALIERI *opens his arms in a wide gesture of paternal benevolence.* MOZART *approaches, and is almost tempted to surrender to the embrace. But at the last moment he avoids it, and breaks away down front, to fall on his knees.*]

MOZART: *Papa!*

SALIERI [*to Audience*]: So rose the Ghost Father in *Don Giovanni*!

* * * *

[*The two grim chords which open the Overture to* Don Giovanni *sound through the theater.* MOZART *seems to quail under them, as he stares out front. On the backdrop in the Light Box appears the silhouette of a giant black figure, in cloak and tricorne hat. It extends its arms, menacingly and engulfingly, toward its begetter.*]

SALIERI: A father more accusing than any in opera. So rose the figure of a Guilty Libertine, cast into Hell! . . . I looked on astounded as from his ordinary life he made his art. We were both ordinary men, he and I. Yet he from the ordinary created legends—and I from legends created only the ordinary.

[*The figure fades.* SALIERI *stands over the kneeling* MOZART.]

Could I not have stopped my war? Shown him some pity? Oh yes, my friends, at any time—if He above had shown me one drop of it! Every day I set to work I prayed—I still prayed, you understand—"Make this one good in my ears! Just this one! *One!*" But would He ever? . . . I heard my music calmed in convention—not one breath of spirit to lift it off the shallows. And I heard *his*—

[*We hear the exquisite strains of the Terzetto "Soave il Vento" from* Così Fan Tutte.]

The spirit singing through it unstoppable to my ears alone! I heard his comedy of the seduction of two sisters, *Così Fan Tutte*: *Thus do all women*. Aloysia and Constanze immortalized—two average girls turned into divinities: their sounds of surrender sweeter than the psalms in Heaven. [*To God, in anguish.*] "Grant this to me! . . . *Grant this to me!* . . ." [*As "God."*] "No, no, no: I do not need you, Salieri! I have Mozart! Better for you to be silent!" *Hahahahaha!*

[*The music cuts offs.*]

The Creature's dreadful giggle was the laughter of God. I had to end it. But how? There was only one way. *Starvation*. Reduce the man to destitution. Starve out the God!

* * * *

VIENNA AND THE ROYAL PALACE

SALIERI [*to* MOZART]: How do you fare today?

MOZART: Badly. I have no money, and no prospect of any.

SALIERI: It would not be too hard, surely.

[*Lights up on the Royal Palace. The* EMPEROR *stands in the Light Box, in his golden space.*]

JOSEPH: We must find him a post.

SALIERI [*to Audience*]: One danger! The Emperor.

[SALIERI *goes upstage to* JOSEPH.]

There's nothing available, Majesty.

JOSEPH: There's Chamber Composer now that Gluck is dead.

SALIERI [*shocked*]: Mozart to follow Gluck?

JOSEPH: I won't have him say I drove him away. You know what a tongue he has.

SALIERI: Then grant him Gluck's post, Majesty, but not his salary. That would be wrong.

JOSEPH: Gluck got two thousand florins a year. What should Mozart get?

SALIERI: Two hundred. Light payment, yes, but for light duties.

JOSEPH: Perfectly fair. I'm obliged to you, Court Composer.

SALIERI [*bowing*]: Majesty.

[*Lights down a little on* JOSEPH *who still stands there.* SALIERI *returns to* MOZART.]

[*To Audience.*] Easily done. Like many men obsessed with being thought generous, the Emperor Joseph was quite essentially stingy.

[MOZART *kneels before the* EMPEROR.]

JOSEPH: Herr Mozart. *Vous nous faites honneur!* . . .

[*Lights out on the* EMPEROR. MOZART *turns and walks downstage.*]

MOZART: It's a damned insult! Not enough to keep a mouse in cheese for a week!

SALIERI: Regard it as a token, *caro* Herr.

MOZART: When I was young they gave me snuffboxes. Now it's tokens! And for what? Pom-pom, for fireworks! Twang-twang for contredanzes!

SALIERI: I'm sorry it's made you angry. I'd not have suggested it if I'd known you'd be distressed.

MOZART: You suggested it?

SALIERI: I regret I was not able to do more.

MOZART: Oh . . . forgive me! You're a good man! I see that now! You're a truly kind man—and I'm a monstrous fool!

[*He grasps* SALIERI*'s hand.*]

SALIERI: No, please . . .

MOZART: You make me ashamed . . . you excellent man!

SALIERI: No, no, no, no—*s'il vous plait.* A little less enthusiasm, I beg you!

[MOZART *laughs delightedly at this imitation of the* EMPEROR. SALIERI *joins in.* MOZART *suddenly doubles over in pain.*

*Wolfgang!* What is it?

MOZART: I get cramps sometimes in my stomach.

SALIERI: I'm sorry.

MOZART: Excuse me . . . it's nothing really.

SALIERI: I will see you soon again?

MOZART: Of course.

SALIERI: Why not visit me?

MOZART: I will . . . I promise!

SALIERI: *Bene.*

MOZART: *Bene.*

SALIERI: My friend. My new friend.

[MOZART *giggles with pleasure and goes off. A pause.*]

SALIERI [*to Audience*]: Now if ever was the moment for God to crush me. I waited—and do you know what happened? I had just ruined Mozart's career at Court. God rewarded me by granting my dearest wish!

[*The* VENTICELLI *come on.*]

V.1.: Kapellmeister Bonno.

V.2.: Kapellmeister Bonno.

V.1. & V.2.: Kapellmeister Bonno is dead!

[SALIERI *opens his mouth in surprise.*]

V.1.: You are appointed—

V.2.: By Royal Decree—

V.1.: To fill his place.

[*Lights full up on the* EMPEROR *at the back. He is flanked by* STRACK *and* ORSINI-ROSENBERG, *standing like icons as at their first appearance.*]

JOSEPH [*formally as* SALIERI *turns and bows to him.*]: First Royal and Imperial Kapellmeister to our Court!

[*The* VENTICELLI *applaud.*]

V.1.: Bravo.

V.2.: Bravo.

ROSENBERG: *Eviva,* Salieri!

STRACK: Well done, Salieri!

JOSEPH [*warmly*]: Dear Salieri—there it is!

[*The lights go down on the Palace. In the dark the* EMPEROR *and his Court leave the stage for the last time.* SALIERI *turns around.*]

SALIERI [*to Audience*]: I was now truly alarmed. How long would I go unpunished?

V.1. & V.2.: Congratulations, sir!

V.1.: Mozart looks appalling.

V.2.: It must be galling, of course.

V.1.: I hear he's dosing himself constantly with medicine.

SALIERI: For what?

V.2.: Envy, I imagine.

V.1.: I hear there's another child on the way . . .

V.2.: There is, I've seen the mother.

* * * *

THE PRATER

[*Fresh green trees appear on the backdrop. The light changes to yellow, turning the blue surround into a rich verdant green.*

MOZART *and* CONSTANZE *enter arm-in-arm. She is palpably pregnant and wears a poor coat and bonnet; his clothes are poorer too.* SALIERI *promenades with the* VENTICELLI.]

SALIERI: I met him next in the Prater.

MOZART [*to* SALIERI]: Congratulations, sir!

SALIERI: I thank you. And to you both! [*To Audience.*] Clearly there was a change for the worse. His eyes gleamed, oddly, like a dog's when the light catches. [To MOZART] I hear you are not well, my friend.

[*He acknowledges* CONSTANZE, *who curtsies to him.*]

MOZART: I'm not. My pains stay with me.

SALIERI: How wretched. What can they be?

MOZART: Also, I sleep badly . . . I have . . . bad dreams.

CONSTANZE [*warningly*]: Wolferl!

SALIERI: Dreams?

MOZART: Always the same one. . . . A figure comes to me cloaked in gray—doing this. [*He beckons slowly.*] It has no face. Just gray—like a mask. . . . [*He giggles nervously.*] What can it mean, do you think?

SALIERI: Surely you do not believe in dreams?

MOZART: No, of course not—really!

SALIERI: Surely *you* do not, madame?

CONSTANZE: I never dream, sir. Things are unpleasant enough to me, awake.

[SALIERI *bows.*]

MOZART: It's all fancy, of course!

CONSTANZE: If Wolfgang had proper work he might dream less, First Kapellmeister.

MOZART [*embarrassed, taking her arm*]: Stanzi, please! . . . Excuse us, sir. Come, dearest. We are well enough, thank you!

[*Husband and wife go off.*]

V.1.: He's growing freakish.

V.2.: No question.

V.1.: Gray figures with masked faces!

SALIERI [*looking after him.*]: He broods on his father too much, I fancy. Also his circumstances make him anxious.

V.1.: They've moved house again.

V.2.: To the Rauhensteingasse. Number 970.

V.1.: They must be desperate.

V.2.: It's a real slum.

SALIERI: Does he earn any money at all, apart from his post?

V.1.: Nothing whatever.

V.2.: I hear he's starting to beg.

V.1.: They say he's written letters to twenty Brother Masons.

SALIERI: Really?

V.2.: And they're giving him money.

SALIERI [*to Audience*]: Of course! They *would!* . . . I had *forgotten* the Masons! *Naturally* they would relieve him—*how stupid of me!* . . . There could be no finally starving him with the Masons there to help! (As long as he asked they would keep supplying his wants.) . . . How could I stop it? And quickly! . . .

V.1.: Lord Fugue is most displeased with him!

SALIERI: *Is* he?

[*The* VENTICELLI *glide off.*]

* * * *

A MASONIC LODGE

[*A huge golden emblem descends, encrusted with Masonic symbols. Enter* VAN SWIETEN. *He is wearing the ritual apron over his sober clothes. At the same time* MOZART *enters from the left. He too wears the apron. The two men clasp hands in fraternal greeting.*]

VAN SWIETEN [*gravely*]: This is not good, Brother. The Lodge was not created for you to beg from.

MOZART: What else can I do?

VAN SWIETEN: Give concerts, as you used to do.

MOZART: I have no subscribers left, Baron. I am no longer fashionable.

VAN SWIETEN: I am not surprised. You write tasteless comedies which give offense. I warned you, often enough.

MOZART [*humbly*]: You did. I admit it. [*He holds his stomach in pain.*]

VAN SWIETEN: I will send you some fugues of Bach tomorrow. You can arrange those for my Sunday concert. You shall have a small fee.

MOZART: Thank you, Baron.

[VAN SWIETEN *nods and goes out.* SALIERI *steps forward. He again wears the Masonic apron.*]

MOZART [*shouting after* VAN SWIETEN]: I cannot live by arranging Bach!

SALIERI [*sarcastically*]: A generous fellow.

MOZART: All the same, I'll have to do it. If he were to turn the Lodge against me, I'd be finished. My Brother Masons virtually keep me now.

SALIERI: That's fine.

MOZART: Never mind. I'll manage: you'll see! Things are looking up already. I've had a marvelous proposal from Schickaneder. He's a new member of this Lodge.

SALIERI: Schickaneder? The actor?

MOZART: Yes. He owns a theater in the suburbs.

SALIERI: Well, more of a music hall, surely?

MOZART: Yes . . . . He wants me to write him a vaudeville—something for ordinary German people. Isn't that a wonderful idea? . . . He's offered me half the receipts when we open.

SALIERI [*concerned*]: Nothing in advance?

MOZART: He said he couldn't afford anything. I know it's not much of an offer. But a popular piece about Brotherly Love could celebrate everything we believe as Masons!

SALIERI: It certainly could! . . . Why don't you put the Masons *into* it?

MOZART: Into an opera? . . . I couldn't!

[SALIERI *laughs, to indicate that he was simply making a joke.*]

All the same—what an idea!

SALIERI [*earnestly*]: Our rituals are secret, Wolfgang.

MOZART: I needn't copy them exactly. I could adapt them a little.

SALIERI: Well . . . it would certainly be in a great cause.

MOZART: Brotherly Love!

SALIERI: Brotherly love!

[*They both turn and look solemnly at the great golden emblem hanging at their backs.*]

SALIERI [*warmly*]: Try it and see. Take courage, Wolfgang. It's a glorious idea.

MOZART: It is, isn't it? It *really is!*

SALIERI: Of course say nothing till it's done.

MOZART: Not a word.

SALIERI [*making a sign: closed fist*]: Secret!

MOZART [*making a similar sign*]: Secret!

SALIERI: Good.

[*He steps out of the scene downstage.*]

[*To audience.*] And if that didn't finish him off with the Masons—nothing would!

[*The gold emblem withdraws. We hear the merry dance of Monastatos and the hypnotized slaves from* The Magic Flute, "*Das Klinget, so heimlich Das Klinget so schön!*" *To the tinkling of the glockenspiel,* SERVANTS *bring in a long plain table loaded with manuscripts and bottles. It also bears a plain upturned stool. They place this in the wooden area head-on to the*

*Audience. At the same time* CONSTANZE *appears wearily from the back, and enters this apartment: the Rauhensteingasse. She wears a stuffed apron, indicating the advanced state of her pregnancy. Simultaneously upstage left, two other* SERVANTS *have placed the little gilded table bearing a loaded cake stand and three of the gilded chairs from* SALIERI*'s resplendent salon. We now have in view the two contrasting apartments. As soon as the Masonic emblem withdraws, the* VENTICELLI *appear to* SALIERI.]

* * * *

MOZART'S APARTMENT: SALIERI'S APARTMENT

V.1.: Mozart is delighted with himself!

V.2.: He's writing a secret opera!

V.1. [*crossly*]: And won't tell anyone its theme.

V.2.: It's really too tiresome.

[*The* VENTICELLI *go off.*]

SALIERI: He told me. He told me everything! . . . Initiation ceremonies. Ceremonies with blindfolds. All rituals copied from the Masons! . . . He sat at home preparing his own destruction. A home where life grew daily more grim.

[*He goes upstage and sits on one of his gilded chairs, nibbling a cake.* MOZART *also sits at his table, wrapped in a blanket, and starts to write music. Opposite him* CONSTANZE *sits on a stool, wrapped in a shawl.*]

CONSTANZE: I'm cold . . . I'm cold all day . . . hardly surprising since we have no firewood.

MOZART: Papa was right. We end exactly as he said. Beggars.

CONSTANZE: It's all his fault.

MOZART: Papa's?

CONSTANZE: He kept you a baby all your life.

MOZART: I don't understand. You always loved Papa.

CONSTANZE: Did I?

MOZART: You adored him. You told me so often.

[*Slight pause.*]

CONSTANZE [*flatly*]: I hated him.

MOZART: What?

CONSTANZE: And he hated me.

MOZART: That's absurd. He loved us both very much. You're being extremely silly now.

CONSTANZE: Am I?

MOZART [*airily*]: Yes, you are, little-wife-of-my-heart!

CONSTANZE: Do you remember the fire we had last night, because it was so cold you couldn't even get the ink wet? You said, "What a blaze"—remember? "What a blaze! All those old papers going up!" [*Maliciously.*] Well, my dear, those old papers were just all your father's letters, that's all—every one he wrote since the day we married.

MOZART: *What?*

CONSTANZE: Every one! All the letters about what a ninny I am—what a bad housekeeper I am! Every one!

MOZART [*springing up*]: Stanzi!

CONSTANZE: *Shit on him! . . . Shit on him!*

MOZART: *You bitch!*

CONSTANZE [*savagely*]: At least it kept us warm! What else will do that? Perhaps we should dance! You love to dance, Wolferl—let's dance! Dance to keep warm! [*Grandly.*] Write me a contredanze, Mozart! It's your job to write dances, isn't it?

[*Hysterical, she snatches up his manuscripts from the table and scatters them over the floor—pulling up her skirts and dancing roughly round the room like a demented peasant to the tune of "Non più andrai." Mozart pursues her desperately.*]

[*singing wildly.*] *Non più andrai, farfallone amoroso—*
*Notte e giorno d' intorno girando!*

MOZART [*shrieking*]: *Stop it! Stop it!* [*He seizes her.*] Stanzi-marini! Marini-bini! Don't please. Please, please, please, I beg you. . . . Look, there's a kiss! Where's it coming from? Right out of that corner! There's another one—all wet, all sloppy wet coming straight to *you!* Kiss—kiss—kiss!

[*She pushes him roughly away from her.*]

CONSTANZE: Get off!

[*A long pause.*]

MOZART: I'm frightened, Stanzi. Something awful's happening to me. . . .

CONSTANZE: I can't bear it. I can't bear much more of this. . . .

MOZART [*absorbed in himself.*]: And the figure's like this now—[*Beckoning faster.*]—"Here! Come here! Here!" Its face still masked—invisible! It becomes realer and realer to me!

CONSTANZE: Stop it, for God's sake! . . . Stop! . . . It's me who's frightened . . . *Me!* . . . You frighten me. . . . If you go on like this I'll leave you. I swear it.

MOZART [*shocked*]: Stanzi!

CONSTANZE: I mean it . . . I do . . .

[*She puts her hand to her stomach, as if in pain.*]

MOZART: I'm sorry . . . Oh, God, I'm sorry . . . I'm sorry, I'm sorry,

I'm sorry! . . . Come here to me, little wife of my heart! Come . . . Come . . .

*[He kneels and coaxes her to him. She comes half reluctantly, half willingly.]*

Who am I? . . . Quick: tell me. Hold me and tell who I am.

CONSTANZE: Pussy-wussy.

MOZART: Who else?

CONSTANZE: Miaowy-powy.

MOZART: And you're Squeeky-peeky. And Stanzi-manzi. And Bini-gini!

*[She surrenders.]*

CONSTANZE: Wolfi-polfi!

MOZART: Poopy-peepee!

*[They giggle.]*

CONSTANZE: Now don't be stupid.

MOZART *[insistent: like a child]*: Come on—do it. Do it—let's do it. "Poppy!"

*[They play a private game, gradually doing it faster, on their knees.]*

CONSTANZE: Poppy.

MOZART *[changing it]*: Pappy.

CONSTANZE *[copying]*: Pappy.

MOZART: Pappa.

CONSTANZE: Pappa.

MOZART: Pappa-pappa!

CONSTANZE: Pappa-pappa!

MOZART: Pappa-pappa-pappa-pappa!

CONSTANZE: Pappa-pappa-pappa-pappa!

*[They rub noses.]*

TOGETHER: Pappa-pappa-pappa-pappa! Pappa-pappa-pappa-pappa!

CONSTANZE: *Ah!*

*[She suddenly cries out in distress, and clutches her stomach.]*

MOZART: Stanzi! . . . Stanzi, what is it?

*[The* VENTICELLI *hurry in.]*

V.1.: News!

V.2.: Suddenly!

V.1.: She's been delivered.

V.2.: Unexpectedly.

V.1.: Of a boy!

V.2.: Poor little imp.

V.1.: To be born to that couple.

V.2.: In that room.

V.1.: With that money.

V.2.: And the father a baby himself.

[*During the above* CONSTANZE *has slowly risen, and divested herself of her stuffed apron—thereby ceasing to be pregnant. Now she turns sorrowfully and walks slowly upstage and off it.*

MOZART *follows her for a few steps, alarmed. He halts.*]

V.1.: And now I hear—

V.2.: Now I hear—

V.1.: Something more has happened.

V.2.: Even stranger.

[MOZART *picks up a bottle—then moves swiftly into* SALIERI*'s room.*]

MOZART [*wildly*]: *She's gone!*

SALIERI: What do you mean?

[*The* VENTICELLI *go off.* MOZART *moves up to* SALIERI*'s apartment, holding his bottle, and sits on one of the gilded chairs.*]

MOZART: Stanzerl's gone away! Just for a while, she says. She's taken the baby and gone to Baden. To the spa. . . . It will cost us the last money we have!

SALIERI: But *why?*

MOZART: She's right to go. . . . It's my fault. . . . She thinks I'm mad.

SALIERI: Surely not?

MOZART: Perhaps I am . . . I think I am. . . . Yes . . .

SALIERI: Wolfgang . . .

MOZART [*very disturbed*]: Let me tell you! Last night I saw the figure again—the figure in my dreams. Only this time I was *awake!* It stood before my table, all in gray, its face still gray, still masked. And this time it spoke to me! "Wolfgang Mozart—you must write now a Requiem Mass. Take up your pen and begin!"

SALIERI: A Requiem?

MOZART: I asked, "Who is this requiem for, who has died?" It said, "The work must be finished when you see me next!" Then it turned and left the room!

SALIERI: Oh, this is morbid fancy, my friend!

MOZART: It had the force of real things! . . . To tell the truth—I do not know whether it happened in my head or out of it. . . . No wonder Stanzi has gone. I frightened her away. . . . And now she'll miss the Vaudeville.

SALIERI: You mean it's finished? So soon?

MOZART: Oh yes—music is easy: it's marriage that's hard!

SALIERI: I long to see it!

MOZART: Would you come, truly? The theater isn't grand. It's just a popular music hall. No one from Court will be there.

SALIERI: Do you think that matters to me? I would travel anywhere for a work by you! . . . I am no substitute for your little wife—but I know someone who could be!

[*He gets up.* MOZART *rises also.*]

MOZART: Who?

SALIERI: I'll tell you what—I'll bring Katherina! She'll cheer you up!

MOZART: Katherina!

SALIERI: As I remember it, you quite enjoyed her company!

[MOZART *laughs heartily.* CAVALIERI *enters, now fatter and wearing an elaborate plumed hat. She curtsies to* MOZART *and takes his arm.*]

MOZART [*bowing*]: *Signora!*

SALIERI [*to Audience*]: And so to the opera we went—a strange band of three!

[*The other two freeze.*]

The First Kapellmeister—sleek as a cat. His mistress—now fat and feathered like a great songbird she'd become. And Mozart, demented and drunk on the cheap wine which was now his constant habit.

[*They unfreeze.*]

We went out into the suburbs—to a crowded music hall—in a tenement. . . .

* * * *

THE THEATER BY THE WEIDEN

[*Two benches are brought in and placed down front. Sudden noise. A crowd of working-class Germans swarm in from the back: a chattering mass of humanity through which the three have to push their way to the front. The long table is pushed horizontally, and the rowdy audience piles on top of it, smoking pipes and chewing sausages.*

*Unobserved,* BARON VAN SWIETEN *comes in also and stands at the back.*]

MOZART: You must be indulgent now! It's my first piece of this kind!

[*The three sit on the front bench:* MOZART *sick and emaciated;* CAVALIERI *blowsy and bedizened;* SALIERI *as elegant as ever.*]

SALIERI: We sat as he wished us to, among ordinary Germans! The smell of sweat and sausage was almost annihilating!

[CAVALIERI *presses a* mouchoir *to her sensitive nose.*]

[*To* MOZART] This is so exciting!

MOZART [*happily*]: Do you think so?

SALIERI [*looking about him*]: Oh yes! This is exactly the audience we should be writing for: not the dreary Court!. . . . As always—*you* show the way!

[*The* AUDIENCE *freezes.*]

[*To us*] As always, he did. My pungent neighbors rolled on their benches at the jokes—

[*They unfreeze—briefly—to demonstrate this mirth.*]

And I alone in their midst heard—*The Magic Flute.*

[*They freeze again. The great hymn at the end of Act 2 is heard: "Heil sei euch Geweihten."*]

He had put the Masons into it right enough. Oh, yes, but how? He had turned them into an Order of Eternal Priests. I heard voices calling out of ancient temples. I saw a vast sun rise on a timeless land, where animals danced and children floated, and by its rays all the poisons we feed each other drawn up and burnt away!

[*A great sun does indeed rise inside the Light Box, and standing in it the gigantic silhouette of a priestly figure extending its arms to the world in universal greeting.*]

And in this sun—behold—I saw his father. No more an accusing figure, but forgiving! The Highest Priest of the Order—his hand extended to the world in love! Wolfgang feared Leopold no longer: a final legend has been made! . . . Oh, the sound, the sound of that newfound peace in him—mocking my undiminishing pain! *There* was the Magic Flute—*there beside me!*

[*He points to* MOZART. *Applause from all.* MOZART *jumps up excitedly onto the bench and acknowledges the clapping with his arms flung out. He turns to us, a bottle in his hand—his eyes staring: all freeze again.*]

Mozart the flute, and God the relentless player. How long could the Creature stand it—so frail, so palpably mortal? . . . And what was this I was tasting suddenly? Could it be pity? . . . *Never!*

VAN SWIETEN [*calling out*]: *Mozart!*

[VAN SWIETEN *pushes his way to the front through the crowd of dispersing citizens. He is outraged.*]

MOZART [*turning joyfully to greet him*]: Baron! You here! How wonderful of you to come!

SALIERI [*to Audience*]: I had of course suggested it.

VAN SWIETEN [*with cold fury*]: What have you done?

MOZART: Excellency?

VAN SWIETEN: You have put our rituals into a vulgar show!

MOZART: No, sir—

VAN SWIETEN: They are plain for all to see! And to laugh at! You have betrayed the Order.

MOZART [*in horror*]: No!

SALIERI: Baron, a word with you—

VAN SWIETEN: Don't speak for him, Salieri! [*To* MOZART, *with frozen contempt.*] You were ever a cruel vulgarian we hoped to mend. Stupid, hopeless task! Now you are a betrayer as well. I shall never forgive you. And depend upon it—I shall ensure that no Freemason or person of distinction will do so in Vienna so long as I have life!

SALIERI: Baron, please, I must speak!

VAN SWIETEN: No, sir! Leave alone. [*To* MOZART.] I did not look for this reward, Mozart. Never speak to me.

[*He goes out. The crowd disperses. The lights change. The benches are taken off.* SALIERI, *watching* MOZART *narrowly, dismisses* KATHERINA. MOZART *stands as one dead.*]

SALIERI: Wolfgang? . . .

[MOZART *shakes his head sharply—and walks away from him, upstage, desolate and stunned.*]

Wolfgang—all is not lost.

[MOZART *enters his apartment and freezes.*]

[*To Audience.*] But of course it was! Now he was ruined. Broken and shunned by all men of influence. And for good measure, he did not even get his half receipts from the opera.

* * * *

[*The* VENTICELLI *come in.*]

V.1.: Schickaneder pays him nothing.

V.2.: Schickaneder cheats him.

V.1.: Gives him enough for liquor.

V.2.: And keeps all the rest.

SALIERI: I couldn't have managed it better myself.

[MOZART *takes up a blanket and muffles himself in it. Then he sits at his worktable, down front, staring out at the audience, quiet still, the blanket almost over his face.*]

And then silence. No word came from him at all. Why? . . . I waited each day. Nothing. Why? . . . [*to the* VENTICELLI, *brusquely*] *What does he do?*

[MOZART *writes.*]

V.1: He sits at his window

V.2: All day and all night.

V.1: Writing—

V.2: Writing—like a man possessed.

[MOZART *springs to his feet, and freezes.*]

V.1: Springs up every moment!

V.2: Stares wildly at the street!

V.1: Expecting something—

V.2: Someone—

V.1 & V.2: *We can't imagine what!*

SALIERI: [*to Audience*] *I* could!

[*He also springs up excitedly, dismissing the* VENTICELLI. MOZART *and* SALIERI *now both stand staring out front.*]

Who did he look for? A figure in gray, masked and sorrowing, come to take him away. I knew what he was doing, alone in that slum! He was writing his Requiem Mass—*for himself!* [*Pause.*] . . . And now I confess the wickedest thing I did to him.

[*His* VALET *brings him the clothes which he describes, and he puts them on, turning his back to us to don the hat—to which is attached a mask.*]

My friends—there is no blasphemy a man will not commit, compelled to such a war as mine! . . . Yes. I got me a hat of gray. Yes. And a mask of gray—Yes!

[*He turns round: he is masked.*]

And appeared myself to the demented Creature as—the *Messenger of God!* . . . I confess that in November 1791, I, Antonio Salieri, then as now First Royal Kapellmeister to the Empire, walked empty Vienna in the freezing moonlight for seven nights on end! That precisely as the clocks of the city struck one I would halt beneath Mozart's window—and become his more terrible clock.

[*The clock strikes one.* SALIERI *without moving from the left side of the stage, raises his arms: his fingers show seven days.* MOZART *rises—fascinated and appalled—and stands equally rigidly on the right side, looking out in horror.*]

Every night I showed him one day less—then stalked away. Every night the face he showed me at the glass was more crazed. Finally—with no days left to him—*horror!* I arrived as usual. Halted. And instead of fingers, reached up beseechingly as the figure of his dreams! "Come!—Come!—Come! . . ."

[*He beckons to* MOZART, *insidiously.*]

He stood swaying, as if he would faint off into death. But suddenly—incredibly—he realized all his little strength, and in a clear voice called down to me the words out of his opera *Don Giovanni,* inviting the statue to dinner.

MOZART [*pushing open the "window"*]: *O statua gentilissima—venite a cena!*

[*He beckons in his turn.*]

SALIERI: For a long moment one terrified man looked at another. Then—

unbelievably—I found myself nodding, just as in the opera. Starting to move across the street!

[*The rising and falling scale passage from the Overture to Don Giovanni sounds darkly, looped in sinister repetition. To this hollow music* SALIERI *marches slowly upstage.*]

Pushing down the latch of his door—tramping up the stairs with stone feet. There was no stopping it. *I was in his dream!*

[MOZART *stands terrified by his table.* SALIERI *throws open the door. An instant light change.*

SALIERI *stands still, staring impassively downstage.* MOZART *addresses him urgently, and in awe.*]

MOZART: It's not finished! . . . Not nearly! . . . Forgive me. Time was I could write a mass in a week! . . . Give me one month more and it'll be done: I swear it! . . . He'll grant me that, surely? You can't want it unfinished! . . . Look—look, see what I've done.

[*He snatches up the pages from the table and brings them eagerly to the* FIGURE.]

Here's the Kyrie—that's finished! Take that to Him—He'll see it's not unworthy! . . . Kyrie the first theme, Eleison the second. Both together make a double fugue.

[*Unwillingly* SALIERI *moves across the room—takes the pages, and sits behind the table in* MOZART*'s chair, staring out front.*]

Grant me time, I beg you! If you do, I swear I'll write a real piece of music. I know I've boasted I've written hundreds, but it's not true. I've written nothing finally good!

[SALIERI *looks at the pages. Immediately we hear the somber opening of the* Requiem Mass. *Over this* MOZART *speaks.*]

Oh, it began so well! . . . Once the world was so full, so happy! . . . All the journeys—all the carriages—all the rooms of smiles! Everyone smiled at me once—the King at Schönbrunn; the Princess at Versailles—they lit my way with candles to the clavier!—my father bowing, bowing, bowing with such joy! . . . "Chevalier Mozart, my miraculous son!" . . . Why has it all gone? . . . Why? . . . Was I so bad? So wicked? . . . [*Desperately.*] Answer for Him and tell me!

[*Deliberately* SALIERI *tears the paper into halves. The music stops instantly. Silence.*]

[*Fearfully.*] Why? . . . Is it not good?

SALIERI [*stiffly*]: It is good. Yes. It is good.

[*He tears off a corner of the music paper, elevates it in the manner of the Communion Service, places it on his tongue and chews it.*]

[*In pain.*] I eat what God gives me. Dose after dose. For all my life. His poison. We are both poisoned, Amadeus. I with you: you with me.

[*In horror* MOZART *moves slowly behind him, placing his hand over* SALIERI*'s mouth—then, still from behind, slowly removes the mask and hat.* SALIERI *stares ahead, and speaks numbly.*]

[*Ecco mi.*] Antonio Salieri. Ten years of my hate have poisoned you to death.

[MOZART *falls to his knees, by the table.*]

MOZART: Oh, God!

SALIERI [*contemptuously*]: God?! . . . God will not help you! God *does* not help!

MOZART: Oh, God! . . . Oh, God! . . . Oh, God!

SALIERI: God does not love you, Amadeus! God does not love! He can only *use!* . . . He cares nothing for who He uses: nothing for who He denies! . . . You are no use to Him any more. You're too weak, too sick! He has finished with you! All you can do now is *die!* He'll find another instrument! He won't even remember you!

MOZART: *Ah!*

[*With a groan* MOZART *crawls quickly through the trestle of the table, like an animal finding a burrow—or a child a safe place of concealment.* SALIERI *kneels by the table, calling in at his victim in desperation.*]

SALIERI: . . . Die, Amadeus! Die, I beg you, die! . . . Leave me alone, *ti imploro!* Leave me alone at last! Leave me alone!

[*He beats on the table in his despair.*]

*Alone! Alone! Alone! Alone! Alone!*

MOZART [*crying out at the top of his lungs*]: PAPA—AAA!

[*He freezes—his mouth open in the act of screaming—his head staring out from under the table.*

SALIERI *rises in horror. Silence. Then very slowly,* MOZART *crawls out from under the table. He sits. He sees* SALIERI. *He smiles at him.*]

MOZART [*in a childish voice*]: Papa!

[*Silence.*]

Papa . . . Papa . . .

[*He extends his arms upward, imploringly to* SALIERI. *He speaks now as a very young boy.*]

Take me, Papa. Take me. Put down your arms and I'll hop into them. Just as we used to do it! . . . Hop-hop-hop-hop-UP!

[*He jumps up on to the table, and embraces* SALIERI, *who stands horrified and unmoving.*]

Hold me close to you, Papa. Let's sing our little Kissing Song together. Do you remember? . . .

[*He sings in an infantine voice.*]

*Oragna figata fa! Marina gamina fa!*

[*Gently* SALIERI *disengages himself.*]

SALIERI: Reduce the man: reduce the God. Behold my vow fulfilled. The profoundest voice in the world reduced to a nursery tune.

[*He leaves the room, slowly, as* MOZART *resumes his singing.*]

MOZART: *Oragna figata fa! Marina gamina fa!*

[*As* SALIERI *withdraws,* CONSTANZE *appears from the back of the stage, her bonnet in her hand. She has returned from Baden. She comes downstage toward her husband, and finds him there on the table, singing in an obviously childish treble.*]

*Oragna figata fa! Marina gamina fa. Fa! Fa!*

[*He kisses the air, several times. Finally he becomes aware of his wife standing beside him.*]

[*Uncertainly.*] Stanzi?

CONSTANZE: Wolfi? . . .

MOZART [*in relief*]: Stanzi!

CONSTANZE [*with great tenderness*]: Wolfi—my love! Little husband of my heart!

[*He virtually falls off the table into her arms.*]

MOZART: *Oh!*

[*He clings to her in overwhelming pleasure. She helps him gently to move around the table to the chair behind it, facing out front.*]

CONSTANZE: Oh, my dear one—come with me. . . . Come on . . . come on now. There . . . there . . .

[MOZART *sits weakly.*]

MOZART [*like a child still, and most earnestly*]: Salieri . . . Salieri has killed me.

CONSTANZE: Yes, my dear.

[*Practically she busies herself clearing the table of its candle, its bottle, and its inkwell.*]

MOZART: He has. He told me so.

CONSTANZE: Yes, yes: I'm sure.

[*She finds two pillows and places them at the left-hand head of the table.*]

MOZART [*petulantly*]: He did . . . he did!

CONSTANZE: Hush now, lovey.

[*She helps her dying husband on to the table, now his bed. He lies down, and she covers him with her shawl.*]

I'm back to take care of you. I'm sorry I went away. I'm here now, for always!

MOZART: Salieri . . . Salieri . . . Salieri . . . Salieri!

[*He starts to weep.*]

CONSTANZE: Oh, lovey, be silent now. No one has hurt you. You'll get better soon, I promise. Can you hear me? Try to, Wolferl . . . Wolfi-polfi, please! . . .

[*Faintly the Lacrimosa of the* Requiem Mass *begins to sound.* MOZART *rises to hear it—leaning against his wife's shoulder. His hand begins feebly to beat out drum measures from the music. During the whole of the following it is evident that he is composing the Mass in his head, and does not hear his wife at all.*]

If I've been a bore—if I've nagged a bit about money, it didn't mean anything. It's only because I'm spoiled. You spoiled me, lovey. You've got to get well, Wolfi—because we need you. Karl and Baby Franz as well. There's only the three of us, lovey: we don't cost much. Just don't leave us—we wouldn't know what to do without you. And you wouldn't know much either, up in heaven, without us. You soppy thing. You can't even cut up your own meat without help! . . . I'm not clever, lovey. It can't have been easy living with a goose. But I've looked after you, you must admit that. And I've given you fun too—quite a lot really! . . . Are you listening?

[*The drum strokes get slower, and stop.*]

Know one thing. It was the best day of my life when you married me. And as long as I live I'll be the most honored woman in the world. . . . Can you hear me?

[*She becomes aware that* MOZART *is dead. She opens her mouth in a silent scream, raising her arm in a rigid gesture of grief.*

*The great chord of the "Amen" does not resolve itself, but lingers on in intense reverberation.*]

* * * *

[CITIZENS OF VIENNA *come in, dressed in black, from the right.* CONSTANZE *kneels and freezes in grief, as* SERVANTS *come in and stand at each of the four corners of the table on which the dead body lies.* VAN SWIETEN *also comes in.*]

SALIERI [*hard*]: The Death Certificate said kidney failure, hastened by exposure to cold. Generous Lord Fugue paid for a pauper's funeral. Twenty other corpses. An unmarked limepit.

[VAN SWIETEN *approaches* CONSTANZE.]

VAN SWIETEN: What little I can spare, you shall have for the children. There's no need to waste it on vain show.

[*The* SERVANTS *lift the table and bear it, with its burden, upstage, center, to the Light Box. The* CITIZENS *follow it.*]

SALIERI: What did I feel? Relief, of course! I confess it. And pity too, for the man I helped to destroy. I felt the pity God can never feel. I weakened God's flute to thinness. God blew—as He must—without cease. The flute split in the mouth of His insatiable *need!*

[*The* CITIZENS *kneel. In dead silence the* SERVANTS *throw* MOZART*'s body off the table into the space at the back of the stage.*

*All depart save* SALIERI *and* CONSTANZE. *She unfreezes and starts assiduously collecting the manuscripts scattered over the floor.*

SALIERI *now speaks with an increasingly aging voice: a voice poisoned more and more by his own bitterness.*]

As for Constanze, in the fullness of time she married again—a Danish diplomat as dull as a clock—and retired to Salzburg, birthplace of the composer, to become the Final Authority in all matters Mozartian!

[CONSTANZE *rises, wrapping her shawl about her, and clasping manuscripts to her bosom.*]

CONSTANZE [*reverentially*]: A sweeter-tongued man never lived! In ten years of blissful marriage I never heard him utter a single coarse or conceited word. The purity of his life is reflected absolutely in the purity of his music! . . . [*More briskly.*] In selling his manuscripts I charge by the ink. So many notes, so many schillings. That seems to me the simplest way.

[*She leaves the stage, a pillar of rectitude.*]

SALIERI: One amazing fact emerged. Mozart did not *imagine* that masked figure in gray who said, "Take up your pen and write a requiem." It was *real!* . . . A certain bizarre nobleman called Count Walsegg had a longing to be thought a composer. He actually sent his steward in disguise to Mozart to commission the piece—secretly, so that he could pass it off as his own work. And this he even did! After Mozart's death it was actually performed as Count Walsegg's Requiem . . . and I conducted it.

[*He smiles at the Audience.*]

Naturally I did. In those days I presided over all great musical occasions in Vienna.

[*He divests himself of his cloak.*]

I even conducted the salvos of cannon in Beethoven's dreadful *Battle Symphony.* An experience which made me almost as deaf as he was!

[*The* CITIZENS *turn round and bow to him, kissing their hands extravagantly.*] And so I stayed on in the City of Musicians, reverenced by all! *On* and *on* and *on! . . . For thirty-two years! . . .* And slowly I understood the nature of God's punishment. [*Directly, to the Audience.*] What had I asked for in that church as a boy? Was it not Fame? Well, now I had it! I was to become quite simply the most famous musician in Europe! . . . I was to be bricked up in Fame! Buried in Fame! Embalmed in Fame! But for work I knew to be absolutely worthless! . . . This was my sentence! I must endure thirty years of being called "distinguished" by people incapable of distinguishing!

[*The* CITIZENS *have fallen on their knees to him during the preceding, and are all clapping their hands at him silently in an adoring mime, relentlessly extending their arms upward and upward until they seem almost to obliterate him.*]

I must smell as I wrote it the deadness of my music, while their eyes brimmed with tears and their throats brayed with cheering! . . . And finally—when my nose had been rubbed in Fame to vomiting—Receptions, Awards, Civic Medals, and Chains— Suddenly His Masterstroke!—*Silence!*

[*The* CITIZENS *freeze.*]

It would all be taken away from me—every scrap.

[*The* CITIZENS *rise, turn away from him, and walk indifferently offstage.*] Mozart's music would sound everywhere—and mine in no place on earth. I must survive to see myself become *extinct!* . . . When they trundled me out in a carriage to get my last honor a man on the curb said, "Isn't that one of the Generals from Waterloo?" [*Calling up savagely.*] *Nemico dei Nemici! Dio implacabile!*

[*The curtains close. The wheelchair is brought on by a* SERVANT. *Another hands* SALIERI *his old dressing gown and cap, as he divests himself of his wig and becomes once more the old man.*

*The lights change. Six o'clock strikes. We are back in—*]

* * * *

SALIERI'S APARTMENT

[*The* SERVANTS *leave.*]

SALIERI: Dawn has come. I must release you. One moment's violence and it is over. You see, I cannot accept this. To be sucked into oblivion—not even my name remembered. Oh no. I did not live on earth to be His joke for eternity. I have one trick left me: see how He deals with this! [*Confidentially, to the Audience.*] All this week I have been shouting out about murder. You heard me yourselves—do you remember? "Mozart—pietà! Pardon your Assassin! Mozart!"

[*Whispers of* SALIERI *begin: at first faintly, as at the start of the play. During the following they grow in volume, in strict and operatic counterpoint to* SALIERI*'s speeches.*]

WHISPERERS [*faintly*]: *Salieri!*

SALIERI [*triumphantly*]: I did this deliberately! . . . My servants carried the news into the streets!

WHISPERERS [*louder*]: *Salieri!*

SALIERI: The streets repeated it to one another!

WHISPERERS [*louder*]: *Salieri! . . . Salieri!*

SALIERI: Now my name is on every tongue! Vienna, City of Scandals, has a scandal worthy of it at last!

WHISPERERS: SALIERI! . . . ASSASSIN! . . . ASSASSIN! . . . SALIERI!

SALIERI [*falsetto: enjoying it*]: "Can it be true? . . . Is it possible? . . . Did he do it after all?" . . .

WHISPERERS [*fortissimo*]: SALIERI!!!

SALIERI: Well, my friends, now they all will know for sure! They will learn of my dreadful death—and they will believe the lie forever! After today, whenever men speak Mozart's name with love, they will speak mine with loathing! As his name grows in the world so will mine—if not in fame, then in infamy. *I'm going to be immortal after all!* And He is powerless to prevent it! . . . [*He laughs harshly.*] So, *Signore*—see now if Man is mocked!

[*He produces a razor from his pocket. Then he rises, opens it, and addresses the Audience most simply, gently, and directly.*]

*Amici cari.* I was born a pair of ears, and nothing else. It is only through hearing music that I know God exists. Only through writing music that I could worship. . . . All around me men hunger for general rights. I hungered only for particular notes. They seek liberty for mankind. I sought only slavery for myself. To be owned—ordered—exhausted by an Absolute. This was denied me, and with it all meaning. Now I go to become a Ghost myself. I will stand in the shadows when you come here to this earth in your turns. And when you feel the dreadful bite of your failures—and hear the taunting of unachievable, uncaring God—I will whisper my name to you: "Antonio Salieri: Patron Saint of Mediocrities!" And in the depth of your downcastness you can pray to me. And I will forgive you. *Vi saluto.*

[*He cuts his throat, and falls backward into the wheelchair.*

*The* COOK *who has just entered carrying a plate of buns for breakfast, screams in horror. The* VALET *rushes in at the same time from the other side. Together they pull the wheelchair, with its slumped body, backward upstage, and anchor it in the center.*

*The* VENTICELLI *appear again, in the costume of 1823.*]

V.1.: Beethoven's Conversation Book, November, 1823. Visitors write the news for the deaf man.

[*He hands a book to* VENTICELLO TWO.]

V.2. [*reading*]: "Salieri has cut his throat—but is still alive!"

[SALIERI *stirs and comes to life, looking about him bewilderedly. The* VALET *and the* COOK *depart. He stares out front like an astounded gargoyle.*]

V.1.: Beethoven's Conversation Book, 1824. Visitors write the news for the deaf man.

[*He hands another book to* VENTICELLO TWO.]

V.2. [*reading*]: "Salieri is quite deranged. He keeps claiming that he is guilty of Mozart's death, and made away with him by poison."

[*The light narrows into a bright cone, beating on* SALIERI.]

V.1.: The German *Musical Times,* May 25, 1825.

[*He hands a newspaper to* VENTICELLO TWO.]

V.2. [*reading*]: "Our worthy Salieri just cannot die. In the frenzy of his imagination he is even said to accuse himself of complicity in Mozart's early death. A rambling of the mind believed in truth by no one but the deluded old man himself."

[*The music stops.*

SALIERI *lowers his head, conceding defeat.*]

V.1.: I don't believe it.

V.2.: I don't believe it.

V.1.: I don't believe it.

V.2.: I don't believe it.

V.1. & V.2.: No one believes it in the world!

[*They go off. The light dims a little.* SALIERI *stirs—raises his head—and looks out far into the darkness of the theater. With difficulty he rises.*]

SALIERI: Mediocrities everywhere—now and to come—I absolve you all. Amen!

[*He extends his arms upward and outward to embrace the assembled Audience in a wide gesture of benediction—finally folding his arms high across his own breast in a gesture of self-sanctification. The light fades completely. The last four chords of the Masonic Funeral Music of* AMADEUS MOZART *sound throughout the theater.*]

END OF PLAY